Communications
in Computer and Information Science 2720

Series Editors

Gang Li ⓘ, *School of Information Technology, Deakin University, Burwood, VIC,
Australia*
Joaquim Filipe ⓘ, *Polytechnic Institute of Setúbal, Setúbal, Portugal*
Zhiwei Xu, *Chinese Academy of Sciences, Beijing, China*

Rationale

The CCIS series is devoted to the publication of proceedings of computer science conferences. Its aim is to efficiently disseminate original research results in informatics in printed and electronic form. While the focus is on publication of peer-reviewed full papers presenting mature work, inclusion of reviewed short papers reporting on work in progress is welcome, too. Besides globally relevant meetings with internationally representative program committees guaranteeing a strict peer-reviewing and paper selection process, conferences run by societies or of high regional or national relevance are also considered for publication.

Topics

The topical scope of CCIS spans the entire spectrum of informatics ranging from foundational topics in the theory of computing to information and communications science and technology and a broad variety of interdisciplinary application fields.

Information for Volume Editors and Authors

Publication in CCIS is free of charge. No royalties are paid, however, we offer registered conference participants temporary free access to the online version of the conference proceedings on SpringerLink (http://link.springer.com) by means of an http referrer from the conference website and/or a number of complimentary printed copies, as specified in the official acceptance email of the event.

CCIS proceedings can be published in time for distribution at conferences or as post-proceedings, and delivered in the form of printed books and/or electronically as USBs and/or e-content licenses for accessing proceedings at SpringerLink. Furthermore, CCIS proceedings are included in the CCIS electronic book series hosted in the SpringerLink digital library at http://link.springer.com/bookseries/7899. Conferences publishing in CCIS are allowed to use our online conference service (Meteor) for managing the whole proceedings lifecycle (from submission and reviewing to preparing for publication) free of charge.

Publication process

The language of publication is exclusively English. Authors publishing in CCIS have to sign the Springer CCIS copyright transfer form, however, they are free to use their material published in CCIS for substantially changed, more elaborate subsequent publications elsewhere. For the preparation of the camera-ready papers/files, authors have to strictly adhere to the Springer CCIS Authors' Instructions and are strongly encouraged to use the CCIS LaTeX style files or templates.

Abstracting/Indexing

CCIS is abstracted/indexed in DBLP, Google Scholar, EI-Compendex, Mathematical Reviews, SCImago, Scopus. CCIS volumes are also submitted for the inclusion in ISI Proceedings.

How to start

To start the evaluation of your proposal for inclusion in the CCIS series, please send an e-mail to ccis@springer.com

Nick Rahimi · Venkat Margapuri ·
Noor Amiri Golilarz
Editors

Software and Data Engineering

34th International Conference, SEDE 2025
New Orleans, LA, USA, October 20–21, 2025
Proceedings

Editors
Nick Rahimi
University of Southern Mississippi
Hattiesburg, MS, USA

Venkat Margapuri
Villanova University
Villanova, PA, USA

Noor Amiri Golilarz
University of Alabama
Tuscaloosa, Albania

ISSN 1865-0929 ISSN 1865-0937 (electronic)
Communications in Computer and Information Science
ISBN 978-3-032-08648-8 ISBN 978-3-032-08649-5 (eBook)
https://doi.org/10.1007/978-3-032-08649-5

© The Editor(s) (if applicable) and The Author(s), under exclusive license
to Springer Nature Switzerland AG 2026

This work is subject to copyright. All rights are solely and exclusively licensed by the Publisher, whether the whole or part of the material is concerned, specifically the rights of translation, reprinting, reuse of illustrations, recitation, broadcasting, reproduction on microfilms or in any other physical way, and transmission or information storage and retrieval, electronic adaptation, computer software, or by similar or dissimilar methodology now known or hereafter developed.
The use of general descriptive names, registered names, trademarks, service marks, etc. in this publication does not imply, even in the absence of a specific statement, that such names are exempt from the relevant protective laws and regulations and therefore free for general use.
The publisher, the authors and the editors are safe to assume that the advice and information in this book are believed to be true and accurate at the date of publication. Neither the publisher nor the authors or the editors give a warranty, expressed or implied, with respect to the material contained herein or for any errors or omissions that may have been made. The publisher remains neutral with regard to jurisdictional claims in published maps and institutional affiliations.

This Springer imprint is published by the registered company Springer Nature Switzerland AG
The registered company address is: Gewerbestrasse 11, 6330 Cham, Switzerland

If disposing of this product, please recycle the paper.

Preface

We are pleased to present the proceedings of the 34th SEDE Conference: Software & Data Engineering (SEDE 2025), held on October 20–21, 2025, at the Holiday Inn Downtown Superdome in New Orleans, Louisiana, USA. SEDE 2025 was proudly organized as part of the conference series of the International Society for Computers and Their Applications (ISCA), a not-for-profit organization dedicated to promoting the advancement of science and engineering in the area of computers and their applications.

This conference, one of the most established in the field, brought together researchers and professionals from the domains of Software Engineering and Data Engineering to share and discuss high-quality research results and outcomes. SEDE 2025 aimed to facilitate cross-fertilization of ideas in Software and Data Engineering, with a particular focus on research integrating both domains.

The conference featured a rigorous peer-review process, with each paper reviewed by at least two experts in the field. This single-blind review process ensured the selection of high-quality papers that reflect the current state and future directions of software and data engineering.

We received 42 submissions covering a wide range of topics within software and data engineering. After careful evaluation, the Program Committee selected the 26 papers presented in these proceedings, representing cutting-edge research and innovative ideas in the field.

The conference program included presentations of accepted papers, keynote speeches by distinguished researchers, and engaging panel discussions. A highlight of the event was the presentation of the Best Paper Award during the conference banquet, recognizing outstanding contributions to the field.

We would like to express our gratitude to all the authors who submitted their work to SEDE 2025, the Program Committee members and additional reviewers for their thorough and timely reviews, and all the attendees for their active participation. Special thanks go to Springer Nature for publishing these proceedings, which will be submitted for indexing in major databases including Web of Science, Scopus, EI Engineering, DBLP, Google Scholar, Conference Proceedings Citation Index (CPCI), ACM Digital Library, IO-Port, MathSciNet, and Zentralblatt MATH.

We hope that these proceedings will serve as a valuable resource for researchers and practitioners in the fields of software and data engineering, fostering further advancements and collaborations in these crucial areas of computer science. Furthermore, we encourage readers to explore opportunities for extended versions of these papers in the ISCA journal, furthering the impact of this research.

October 2025

Nick Rahimi
Venkat Margapuri
Noorbhaksh Amiri Golilarz

Organization

General Chairs

Nick Rahimi — University of Southern Mississippi, USA

Program Chairs

Venkatasivakumar Margapuri — Villanova University, USA
Noorbhaksh Amiri Golilarz — University of Alabama, USA

Program Committee

Somenath Chakraborty — West Virginia University Institute of Technology, USA
Wei Dai — Purdue University Northwest, USA
Takaaki Goto — Toyo University, Japan
Karan Gupta — SunPower Corporation, USA
Xiaolan Huang — Southern Illinois University, USA
Swathi Kaluvakuri — Southern Illinois University, USA
Mirsalar Kamari — University of Southern Mississippi, USA
Koushik Maddali — Southern Illinois University, USA
Jose Martinez — University of Southern Mississippi, USA
Majid Memari — Utah Valley University, USA
Md. Saef Ullah Miah — American International University, Bangladesh
Saydul Akbar — University of Southern Mississippi, USA
Abu Jafar Md — University of Tennessee, USA
Abhay Paroha — Schlumberger, USA
Niketa Penumajji — CivicPlus, USA
Chinmay Rajguru — GKN Aerospace, USA
Ning Yang — Southern Illinois University, USA
Aakash Sinha — Grubbrr, USA
Abdoljalil Addeh — University of Calgary, Canada
Abburi Chinnikrishna — Visa, USA
Chirag Agarwal — Novelis, USA
Nic Herndon — East Carolina University, USA
Sujan Reddy Anreddy — Mississippi State University, USA

Gaurav Saxena	Ford Motor Company, USA
Kishan Gupta	Capgemini, USA
Pavan Vemuri	SDVerse, USA
Pritam Roy	Capgemini, USA
Ravi Teja Thutari	Hopper, USA
Sai Kalyan Reddy Pentaparthi	ST Engineering iDirect, USA
Shubham Jindal	TikTok, USA
Akshay Mittal	PayPal, USA
Vivek Venkatesan	Vanguard, USA

Contents

Software Engineering and Data Science

Development of a Unity-Based Drone Simulation Framework for Precision
Agriculture 3
   Mimansha Khadka, Balsem Jridi, and Aidan Patrick

Leveraging Generative AI for Proactive Security and Automated
Remediation in Cloud-Native CI/CD Pipelines 18
   Akshay Mittal and Vivek Venkatesan

Optimizing Healthcare Pipelines for Patient Benefit: A Data Engineering
Perspectives on Preauthorization Delays and Denials 40
   Rakesh Ramakrishna Pai and Jothsna Praveena Pendyala

Pairwise Clustering on Numerical Datasets by Translation 53
   Jiajie Yang and Jessica Chen

A Customizable Ad-Hoc Java Client that Works with Bare Webservers 73
   Nirmala Soundararajan, Lie Qian, Ramesh R. Karne,
   and Alexander L. Wijesinha

DuckDB-Powered Geo-Spatial Analytics for Hit-and-Run Incidents:
A Montgomery County Case Study 85
   Sarika Rajeev, Atma Sahu, and Vishrut Sawarnya

Analysis of Programming Capability of LLMs in the Context of Computer
Science I 98
   Junfeng Qu, Shuju Bai, Byron Jeff, and Ebrahim Khosravi

Predicting Early Breast Cancer Recurrence with Machine Learning 111
   M. Mehdi Owrang O, Gracie Abrahams, Gretchen Callahan,
   Dalia Karim, and Tyler Madison

Structural and Connectivity Patterns in the Maven Central Software
Dependency Network 129
   Daniel Ogenrwot, John Businge, and Shaikh Arifuzzaman

Cloud-Native Generative AI for Automated Planogram Synthesis:
A Diffusion Model Approach for Multi-store Retail Optimization 152
   Ravi Teja Pagidoju and Shriya Agarwal

Applications of Positive Unlabeled Learning in Detection of DDoS Attacks 166
   Gagana Sathya Narayana Prasad and Charan Gudla

Robust Intrusion Detection in IoV Using PU Learning and Supervised
Ensembles with Synthetic Data Augmentation on CICIoV2024 182
   Yashwanth Reddy Kovvuri and Charan Gudla

The Potential of Large Language Models in Automating Software Testing:
From Generation to Reporting 199
   Betim Sherifi, Khaled Slhoub, and Fitzroy Nembhard

Design and Evaluation of a Scalable Data Pipeline for AI-Driven Air
Quality Monitoring in Low-Resource Settings 212
   Richard Sserunjogi, Daniel Ogenrwot, Nicholas Niwamanya,
   Noah Nsimbe, Martin Bbaale, Benjamin Ssempala, Noble Mutabazi,
   Raja Fidel Wabinyai, Deo Okure, and Engineer Bainomugisha

Hybrid Taint Analysis for React: Automated XSS Prevention 232
   Vaishnavi Gudur and Advait Patel

Artificial Intelligence

Edge-Based Learning for Improved Classification Under Adversarial Noise 251
   Manish Kansana, Keyan Alexander Rahimi, Elias Hossain,
   Iman Dehzangi, and Noorbakhsh Amiri Golilarz

Prompt Driven Test Generation: Leveraging Large Language Models
and Knowledge Graphs for Quality Assurance in Data Intensive Software
System 267
   Srinivas Reddy Kosna

Adversarial Machine Learning for Robust Password Strength Estimation 289
   Pappu Jha, Hanzla Hamid, Oluseyi Olukola, Ashim Dahal,
   and Nick Rahimi

Mitigating Hallucination Risks in GenAI Compliance Advisory Systems
for the Financial Industry 302
   Kunal Khanvilkar and Varun Shinde

Prosense - Defending Text Generation with Adversarial Feedback 319
   Anu Baluguri, Vasudha Pasumarthy, Yaswanth Raj Repakula,
   and Zhaoxian Zhou

Machine Learning-Based AES Key Recovery via Side-Channel Analysis
on the ASCAD Dataset 334
 Mukesh Poudel and Nick Rahimi

Hand Line Classification 353
 S. Petchartee, N. Hirunpash, M. Namawrong, and W. Sakonlaphab

Beyond Accuracy: Evaluating LLMs for Validating Community Service
Provider Directory 373
 Saviz Saei, Sadhan Ghimire, and Sujan Anreddy

Trustworthy Design Patterns for Multi-agent Software Systems 381
 Jay Prakash Thakur and Akshata Kishore Moharir

Designing Interpretable AI Models with Lightweight Parallelism
for Real-Time Malware Detection and Prevention 393
 Zachariah McCullough and Jose Martinez

Designing Interpretable AI Models with Lightweight Parallelism
for Real-Time Decision-Making for Auto Insurance Claims Triage 406
 L. Paul Strait

Author Index 415

Software Engineering and Data Science

Editors' Introduction: The Spring

Development of a Unity-Based Drone Simulation Framework for Precision Agriculture

Mimansha Khadka[✉], Balsem Jridi, and Aidan Patrick

Department of Computer Science, University of Southern Mississippi, Hattiesburg, MS, USA
mimansha.khadka@usm.edu

Abstract. To bridge the gap between development and real-world deployment, we present a Unity-based drone simulation framework for precision agriculture that uniquely combines the Unity game engine with Microsoft AirSim's physics library. This integration leverages Unity's versatile rendering and environment design with AirSim's high-fidelity flight dynamics, a novel approach given AirSim's only recently available experimental Unity port. The result is a realistic simulation of drone flight, sensor outputs, and farm environments, achieving photorealistic visuals and accurate physics. Key objectives of our framework include testing autonomous flight algorithms (e.g., coverage path planning and basic obstacle avoidance) in a risk-free, virtual farm setting and evaluating their performance on agricultural tasks. The methodology shows the simulation environment design, including high-fidelity crop modeling, aerial dynamics, camera imaging, and data logging strategies. Results from our experiments demonstrate that the simulated drone can precisely follow planned waypoints and collect high-resolution aerial images of crops, indicating that the Unity+AirSim approach yields credible flight behavior and data for analysis. The realism of the simulation (e.g., natural drone accelerations, camera sensor noise, and detailed crop models) provides confidence that algorithms refined in this virtual setting will transfer well to physical drones. We also outline forward-looking uses of the framework, including incorporating multi-drone operations and crop disease models. In ongoing and future work, we plan to validate the simulation's effectiveness with real-world field trials, using the insights gained to further improve fidelity. This Unity-based simulation framework thus offers a novel, practical tool for developing and de-risking autonomous drone strategies in precision agriculture before deployment on actual farms. The paper concludes with a discussion of the simulation's contributions, current limitations, and future directions for enhancing realism and supporting multi-drone operations in precision farming.

Keywords: Precision Agriculture · Drone Simulation · Unity · AirSim · UAV · Autonomous Flight · Synthetic Data · Flight Path Planning · Crop Monitoring

---

Supervised by Dr. Partha Sengupta.

1 Introduction

Unmanned aerial vehicles (UAVs), or drones, are revolutionizing precision agriculture by offering rapid, high-resolution monitoring and automated field operations. Drones, equipped with advanced sensors, can perform tasks such as crop health surveillance, targeted pesticide spraying, and soil moisture mapping with greater efficiency and accuracy than traditional methods [1]. For instance, drones enable precise route-based spraying, ensuring uniform agrochemical application, and they collect detailed crop growth data to support farm management decisions [1]. These capabilities help farmers increase yields while optimizing resource usage, embodying the principles of precision agriculture. Despite their potential, deploying drones in real-world farm environments presents significant challenges. Agricultural fields (especially orchards and vineyards) often have complex terrain and obstacles like trees and trellises that make autonomous navigation difficult [2]. Dynamic conditions such as moving foliage, varying lighting, and wind require drones to adapt on the fly to avoid collisions and maintain data quality [1]. Ensuring safety is important as drone mishaps (crashes) can damage crops, equipment, or even endanger bystanders [2]. There are also practical constraints, including regulatory restrictions on experimental flights, high equipment costs, and time-consuming field testing procedures [2]. Together, these factors make iterative development and testing of agricultural drone systems onsite both risky and expensive. Simulation offers a compelling solution to these challenges. By recreating farm environments and drone physics virtually, researchers can continuously test algorithms and scenarios with zero risk to real crops or hardware [2]. One example is Agri-fly, a simulator for uncrewed aerial vehicle flight in agricultural environments [3]. A high-fidelity simulator acts as a safe testbed where autonomous flight routines (e.g., field coverage patterns or obstacle avoidance maneuvers) can be validated and refined before deployment on physical drones. Moreover, simulation accelerates development by enabling repeatable experiments under controlled conditions. Developers can easily vary parameters like wind speed, lighting, or field layout to evaluate drone performance across a range of situations that would be difficult to reproduce consistently in real life. As a result, many studies on agricultural UAVs now rely on simulation for experimentation prior to real-world trials [2]. The gap between simulation and reality is narrowing as well, thanks to increasingly realistic physics and sensor modeling in modern simulators [4]. In precision agriculture, a realistic simulation is particularly important because success often depends on interactions between the drone and its environment. We focus this research on developing a Unity-based drone simulation framework tailored to precision agriculture needs. The following sections discuss related work in drone simulation and flight algorithms, describe Unity+AirSim simulation methodology, present experimental results in agricultural scenarios, and examine the implications for real-world deployment of drone technology in farming. Unlike earlier tools such as Agri-fly, our framework goes a step further by combining Unity and AirSim to create more realistic plant environments, flexible flight scenarios, and support for a wider range of agricultural applications.

2 Literature Review

2.1 Drone Simulation Platforms

A variety of UAV simulators have been developed in recent years, each with different strengths. One widely adopted platform is Microsoft AirSim, an opensource simulator that provides high-fidelity vehicle dynamics, sensor models, and photorealistic rendering. AirSim was originally built on the Unreal Engine to leverage its advanced graphics, enabling realistic camera sensor output for computer vision research [4]. Researchers have used AirSim extensively for autonomous drone testing in domains from mapping to agriculture [4]. However, Unreal-based AirSim can be demanding computationally, motivating efforts to integrate AirSim with the Unity engine, which is lighter. An experimental Unity port of AirSim was introduced to make the simulator more accessible and flexible. Our work builds on this by using AirSim's core flight physics (AirLib) within Unity, combining Unity's ease of use with AirSim's proven dynamics [3].

In addition to AirSim, several other simulators are relevant. Flightmare is a Unity-based aerial simulator designed for drone reinforcement learning and fast simulation; it offers adaptable fidelity to balance speed and accuracy for training AI models [4]. Similarly, FlightGoggles provides a Unity rendering engine with a custom physics backend and synthetic sensors and has even been used for virtual reality first-person view piloting and hardware-in-the-loop experiments. These Unity-centric simulators highlight the game engine's utility in producing photorealistic environments while maintaining real-time performance, which is a crucial combination for testing vision-based agricultural drones.

2.2 Orthomosaic Mapping and Geospatial Analysis

Drones in precision agriculture commonly collect numerous overlapping images that can be stitched into an orthomosaic, which is a high-detail aerial map of the farmland. Creating accurate orthomosaics requires a high percentage of overlapping images (often 60–80%) between consecutive photos and specialized photogrammetry software. Tools like Web Open Drone Map (WebODM) or Pix4D are used to process the images and generate georeferenced maps and 3D point clouds of the fields. In one project, a dataset of 300 drone images with roughly 70% overlap was sufficient to produce a detailed and accurate orthomosaic of a simulated crop field using WebODM. Once the orthomosaic is obtained, GIS software such as QGIS can be applied for further geospatial analysis. A common analysis is computing vegetative indices like the Normalized Difference Vegetation Index (NDVI) to assess crop vigor. For instance, by loading the orthomosaic into QGIS and applying the NDVI formula band-wise, researchers could visualize variations in plant chlorophyll content and biomass across the field. This vegetative index map mirrors the orthomosaic but highlights areas of low vs. high crop health, allowing easy identification of stress spots. Geospatial analysis of drone maps enables precision agriculture by pinpointing where intervention (irrigation, fertilization, pest control) is needed most, rather than treating the field uniformly. Combining drone imagery with GIS analytics can significantly improve monitoring efficiency and crop yield estimation (Fig. 1).

Fig. 1. An example agricultural scene in Agri-fly: an aerial vehicle flies autonomously in a simulated orchard built with high-fidelity almond models. **Top:** simulated scene generated with high-fidelity plant models. **Bottom:** an experimental flight scene in an almond orchard [3].

2.3 AI-Based Crop Classification and Health Monitoring

Another critical component of drone automation in agriculture is the integration of artificial intelligence to interpret captured imagery. Machine learning models, especially deep learning convolutional neural networks (CNNs), have been used to automatically classify crops and detect anomalies (like disease or pest damage) from drone images. For example, researchers have utilized U-Net, a deep learning architecture for image segmentation, to distinguish crops from weeds in UAV imagery. In comparative studies, U-Net achieved high accuracy (around 78%) in classifying weeds versus crops. AI models can be trained to recognize specific crop types, identify areas of pest infestation, or even detect nutrient deficiencies by learning visual patterns in leaves and canopy structure. In one project, a deep learning model (using a U-Net variant) was integrated with the drone data pipeline to perform automated crop classification on orthomosaic images. This AI analysis successfully categorized different plant types and flagged problem areas from an aerial perspective, providing deeper insights into field conditions. Similarly, an AI-driven platform was designed to identify and analyze various crop types and detect signs of pests or diseases from drone imagery. Deep learning is also being applied for yield prediction and growth stage monitoring using time-series drone data. However, a recurring theme in the literature is that the performance of such AI models depends on having sufficient and representative training data. Models trained on hundreds or thousands of labeled images tend to achieve high accuracy in crop health classification, while models trained on limited or synthetic data may generalize poorly [5]. As large agricultural image datasets (including those captured by drones) become more available, AI-based analysis is increasingly reliable. The integration of CNNs into drone systems has been shown to greatly speed up image analysis and improve accuracy compared to manual processes. This combination of drones and AI provides a powerful automated surveillance tool where the drone gathers data and the AI interprets it. Ultimately, combining drones with AI moves beyond simple data capture, turning aerial imagery into practical insights that farmers can immediately act on in the field.

2.4 Applications in Agriculture

The literature also showcases specific agricultural applications of drone simulation. Beyond path planning, researchers have simulated crop imaging and data analytics. For example, a Unity simulation of near-infrared cameras has been used to distinguish crops from weeds so that drones can spray pesticides or fertilizers only where needed, reducing waste [2]. In crop counting and yield estimation, synthetic orchards with realistic fruit models have provided training data for computer vision algorithms (e.g., counting fruit on trees via object detection) before deploying those algorithms on real drone imagery. The Agri-fly simulator by Zha et al. (2024) explicitly targets agricultural use cases [3]. It combines a custom flight dynamics library with high-fidelity plant models (generated by a botanical modeling tool) inside Unity. By doing so, Agri-fly can create realistic farm simulations where drones fly under trees to help with pollination or inspect grapevines in vineyards. It has been used to test and improve drone missions, like checking plant health in a virtual farm, before using them in real life. These examples from published research underline the critical role of simulation: it enables the development of sophisticated AI-driven drone solutions for agriculture, from algorithm inception to preliminary validation, all within a safe and configurable virtual world.

2.5 Novelty of the Proposed Framework

While there are existing agricultural drone simulators such as Agri-Fly, our framework offers a different focus. Agri-Fly primarily provides a fixed environment and preset missions for testing drone flights, which makes it useful for demonstrations but less flexible for research. In contrast, our Unity and AirSim-based simulator is designed to be modular and adaptable. Researchers can easily change the environment, insert new crops, or adjust mission parameters to match specific agricultural needs. Our system also integrates AI-based crop monitoring, automated waypoint planning, and the ability to simulate weather and sensor noise, features that are either limited or absent in comparable platforms. This level of flexibility makes our framework not just a flight simulator but a testbed where new ideas for precision agriculture can be developed, tested, and refined before real-world deployment.

3 Methodology

3.1 Unity Simulation Environment Design

We constructed a virtual agricultural environment in Unity that serves as a realistic test field for drone-based precision agriculture operations. The environment includes textured terrain with different surface features such as soil, grass, and cultivated farmland, simulating real field conditions. The crop layout is designed in structured rows, closely resembling typical agricultural patterns seen in precision farming. Fencing elements are included to mark field boundaries, while various sections of the farmland exhibit different growth stages, indicating diverse vegetation coverage. A drone is positioned above the crops to conduct aerial surveillance or autonomous flight missions. This setup allows the drone to capture real-time aerial imagery, which can later be processed for orthomosaic mapping, vegetation analysis, or AI-driven crop health assessment.

Fig. 2. Drone in Unity.

Development of a Unity-Based Drone Simulation Framework 9

The Unity engine governs the drone's flight dynamics and ensures that it behaves naturally under the influence of simulated environmental factors such as gravity, wind drag, and navigation constraints. By simulating a structured yet adaptable farm scenario, this environment enables researchers to refine autonomous drone operations before deploying them in actual agricultural fields (Fig. 2).

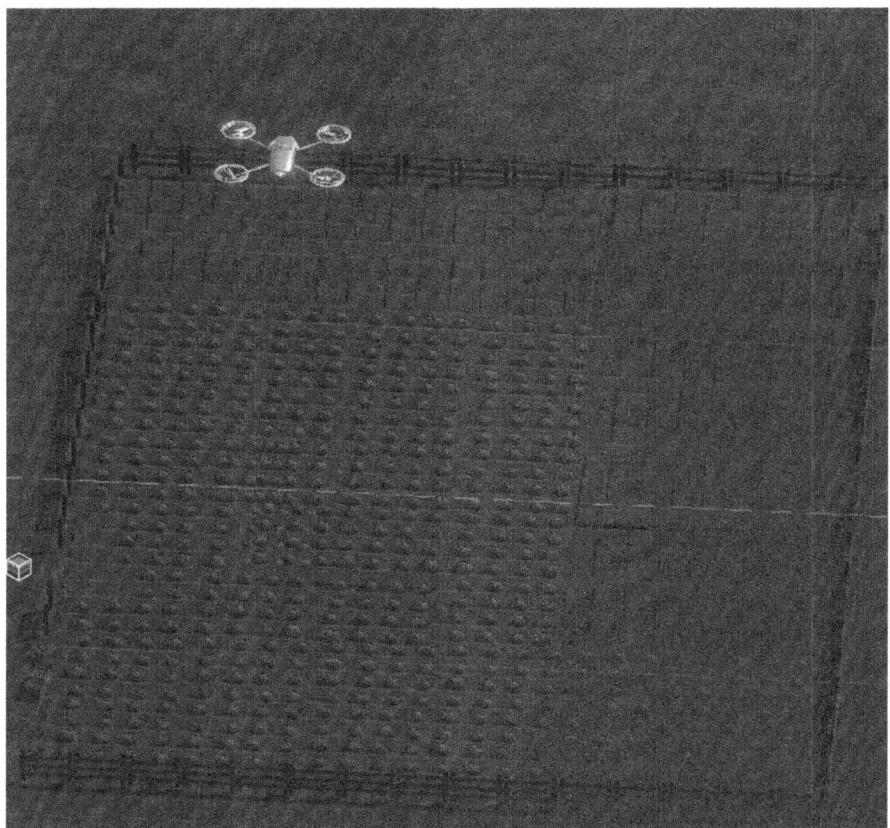

Fig. 3. *The simulated drone in flight over the virtual field.* This figure shows a screenshot of our drone flying autonomously above a modeled farm environment in Unity. The scene includes structured crop rows and field boundaries, illustrating the simulation's realism in replicating typical agricultural layouts. The drone maintains a consistent altitude and follows the pre-planned survey path, demonstrating that our Unity+AirSim integration produces stable flight behavior and full field coverage in the virtual environment.

3.2 Automated Flight Path Planning

Within the Unity simulation, we implemented an automated flight controller script to enable the drone to follow a predefined survey route. The route is defined by a series of GPS-like waypoints covering the target area in a lawnmower (boulevard) pattern to ensure complete coverage [1]. The drone takes off and autonomously navigates through these waypoints, maintaining a constant altitude and speed appropriate for imaging. We programmed the drone to hover briefly at each waypoint and capture an overhead image before proceeding to the next point. This approach guarantees sufficient overlap between consecutive images (around 70% overlap) for reliable orthomosaic stitching. The Unity simulation time-step is synchronized with the drone's movement to allow precise control and timing of image capture events.

3.3 Synthetic Environment Variability

A key advantage of this Unity-based simulation is its flexibility to introduce environmental variability. The field contains crops including carrots, corn, and turnips, where all elements derive from modular prefab units. Physical elements that resemble terrain irregularities such as dirt piles, barriers, and trees can be added to the simulation environment in addition to the crop fields. The simulation offers adjustable parameters to replicate obstacles from plants or terrain irregularities and a mix of crop types seen in actual field environments. The modular grid pattern in crop models allows convenient changes to spacing, along with modification of model size and type depending on various experimental requirements. This modularity helps test the generalization ability of machine learning models or the adaptability of drone flight algorithms. Unity's drag-and-drop interface enables rapid editing of the scene, and all changes are retained through prefab references, which ensures repeatable configurations.

3.4 Snapshot Camera and Data Capture

For capturing visual data, a dedicated *SnapshotCamera* is attached to the drone GameObject. The camera operates with a fixed field of view and resolution, resembling the imaging capability of a drone-mounted RGB camera. The camera automatically takes pictures at each waypoint and then stores them in a designated location with timestamp and resolution details. The saved PNG files serve multiple purposes for orthomosaic stitching, vegetation index evaluation, and supervised learning model building for crop detection. The SnapshotCamera script contains all necessary logic for rendering and file storage, and its frame capturing functionality keeps imaging operations independent and flexible for implementing other modalities like NDVI or thermal imaging. This setup provides researchers with a method to generate precise, scaled synthetic datasets for specific agricultural scenarios (Fig. 4).

Activity Diagram: Drone Simulation Workflow for Precision Agriculture

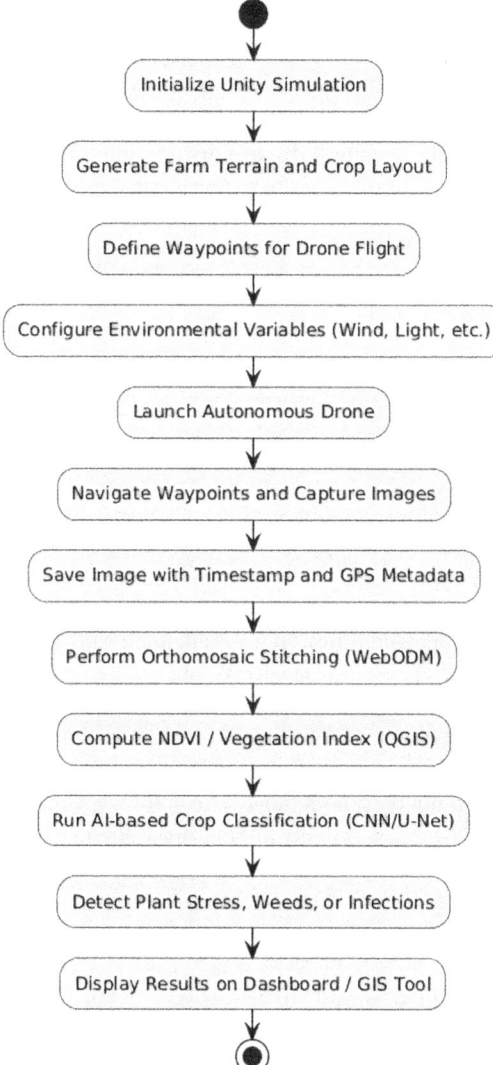

Fig. 4. *Activity Diagram.* This diagram outlines the sequence of operations in our simulation framework. Starting from mission initialization, the drone takes off, follows the computed flight path through all waypoints, captures images at each point, and returns to land. The activity flow highlights how flight control, sensor capture, and data logging modules interact step-by-step. This visual is important because it clarifies the control logic and data pipeline in our system, illustrating the workflow of an autonomous drone mission from start to finish.

3.5 Simulated Plant Infections (Planned Feature)

To further enhance the realism of the environment and support agricultural disease detection studies, we plan to introduce infected versions of plant prefabs. These infected models would include visible symptoms like leaf discoloration, mold textures, or stunted growth, implemented by modifying materials and meshes. The scene can include infected plants that researchers place manually, or they can be generated randomly according to probability values that reflect natural disease distribution. Future versions will enable dynamic infections through time-based or drone-triggered mechanisms. This feature will provide a valuable testbed for computer vision models that analyze plant health because it allows us to collect simulation-derived ground-truth labels. The drone's navigation logic can also be modified to give priority to infected zones so it can execute reactive autonomous scouting operations.

4 Results

4.1 Unity Simulation and Drone Navigation

Using the above methodology, we successfully created a Unity simulation of a farm field and executed autonomous drone flights within it. The virtual drone can take off, navigate the field, and capture images at the specified waypoints without human intervention. Figure 3 shows the simulated drone in flight over the virtual field. The drone maintained a steady altitude and followed the predefined path accurately, demonstrating the effectiveness of the flight control script. We observed that the drone's movement in the simulator is smooth and realistic, due to AirSim's physics integration, which provides good acceleration, deceleration, and turning dynamics [5]. We made minor adjustments (such as tuning the speed and waypoint threshold in the script) to optimize the flight path and ensure the drone did not overshoot targets. Overall, the simulation confirms that our Unity-based control strategy can reliably guide a drone along a complex route, covering the entire field area.

4.2 Snapshot Imaging and Data Capture Evaluation

The SnapshotCamera, which is part of the drone's onboard system, collected high-resolution downward-facing RGB images during flight. The camera script initiated its capture function automatically at each waypoint, saving image files with timestamps in the "Snapshots" folder. The collected images are of sufficient quality to serve as synthetic datasets for plant segmentation, weed detection, and terrain classification experiments. The flight data recorded both timestamped positions and the drone's orientation at each waypoint. These logs enable postflight analysis of spatiotemporal data and can support the training of machine learning models by providing ground-truth trajectories. Importantly, the image acquisition process did not affect flight stability, as the navigation logic was successfully integrated with the perception tasks (Fig. 5).

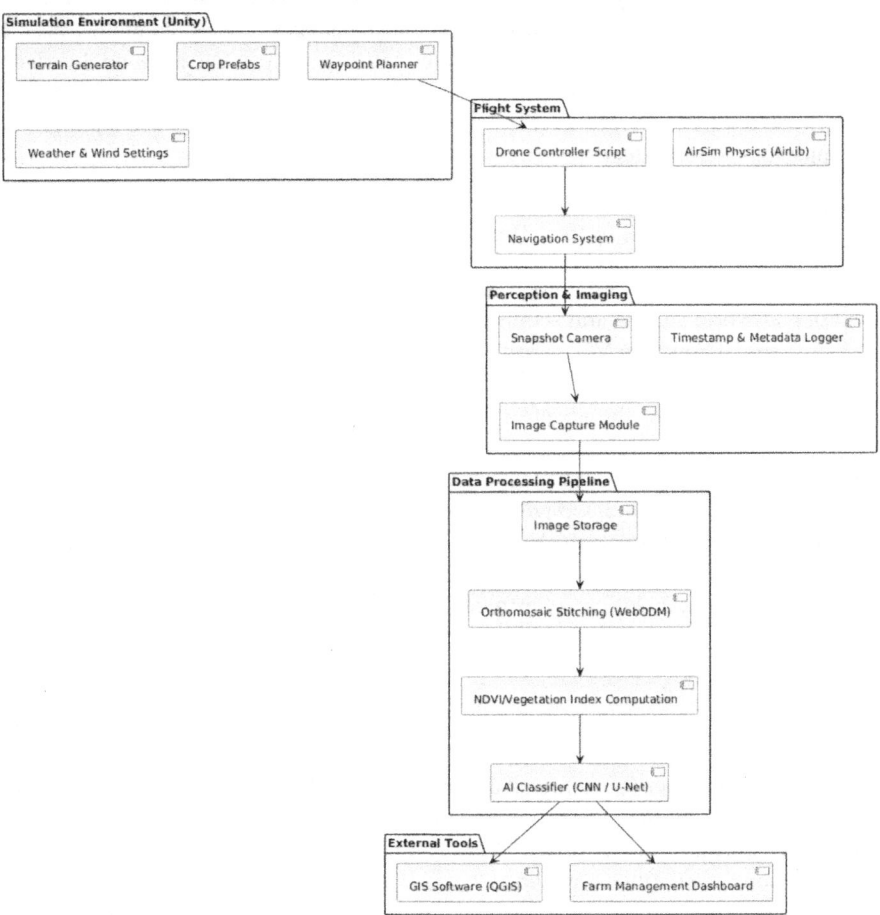

Fig. 5. *System Architecture.* This schematic illustrates the major components and their interactions in our Unity-based drone simulator. Key elements include the Unity engine (providing the 3D environment and rendering), the AirSim AirLib physics module (ensuring realistic drone dynamics), the drone's control scripts (executing waypoint navigation and image capture), and the output data streams (photos and flight logs). Arrows indicate data flows and control signals between components. By presenting the architecture, this figure emphasizes how Unity and AirSim are integrated to simulate UAV behavior and how sensor data and telemetry are generated for analysis

4.3 Modular Scene Evaluation and Prefab Flexibility

Another significant outcome was the successful use of prefabs to build and manipulate environmental components. The simulation design features modular fence elements combined with multiple crop types (including carrots and corn) and terrain decorations (such as dirt piles) which could be reused throughout the field due to the modular structure. Through the Unity Editor, users could modify prefab instances and move them to change the field layout between trials. This made it possible to test the system under different visual and spatial scenarios, which is important for evaluating the generalization of AI models. The system also supports the manual insertion of anomalies, such as diseased or discolored crop models (simulated infections), to create additional variance in visual features. Although our infection simulation is still basic, it lays the groundwork for incorporating supervised learning with drone-generated positive and negative examples for disease detection.

4.4 Planned Validation in Real Deployments

While our current results are limited to simulation, we have a concrete plan to validate them in real-world agricultural settings. Our first step will be a small-scale field trial at the University of Southern Mississippi, where we will fly a quadcopter above the campus rose garden using the same mission parameters as in the simulator. The drone will follow identical waypoints and altitude profiles, and we will record key performance data such as waypoint deviation, flight stability from the onboard IMU, and total area covered. We will then compare this real-world data with the simulation results to evaluate how closely the two align. For example, we will check whether the actual path error and coverage efficiency match the simulated values and whether the captured images provide a similar level of resolution and clarity for identifying crop features. Any differences will help us refine the simulator, including adjustments to the physics model or sensor noise.

5 Discussion

The implementation and results of our drone automation framework highlight several improvements over conventional agricultural monitoring methods. **Enhanced Efficiency and Data Quality:** By automating drone flight and image capture, we can survey large farm plots much faster and with less manpower than traditional ground scouting. A drone can consistently fly a predefined pattern, standardizing data collection and reducing human error. Our simulation showed that even a basic autonomous mission can cover a field in minutes and provide high-resolution data that would take hours for workers to gather on foot. Moreover, the combination of drone imagery with GIS analysis provides a depth of insight that manual observation cannot easily match. The generated NDVI and other index maps allow farmers to assess crop health across an entire field at a glance and quickly find areas of concern that might be missed in spot checks. This capability is a key advantage of drone-based automation. Farmers can make decisions such as where to irrigate more or where to apply fertilizer. Integrating AI for image analysis further amplifies efficiency. Instead of relying on agronomists to examine images or physically inspect fields, a trained model automatically highlights potential issues (such as unusual crop color indicating disease) for review. For instance, our use of a CNN accelerated the classification of captured images and provided almost real-time feedback on crop conditions. Rapid data collection and analysis allow earlier interventions; spotting a pest problem early, for example, could save a large portion of the crop before it spreads. In one project, incorporating a fine-tuned CNN into a drone system enhanced the speed and accuracy of crop image classification, giving farmers timely insights into pest and plant health conditions [5]. In practice, automated crop surveillance by drones can increase yields by enabling responsive management, and one study noted that targeted interventions based on drone data helped boost yields and reduce waste on test plots [1].

Despite these advantages, our study encountered important limitations and challenges that affect the effectiveness of current drone automation. **Data and Model Limitations:** One challenge is the need for extensive, high-quality data to train AI models. As demonstrated, models trained purely on simulated data struggled to maintain high accuracy [4]. The visual gap between simulated imagery and the complexity of real crop conditions can lead to poor generalization. This suggests that while simulation is excellent for developing and testing the mechanics of drone flights and image processing pipelines, the AI components eventually require real-world data for calibration and validation. Acquiring labeled agricultural imagery in sufficient quantity can be difficult and time-consuming. Another limitation is the diversity of crop scenarios. An AI model trained on a few crop types in one region may not work well for fields with different crop types or different regional conditions. This means AI-powered drone analysis may need to be adjusted based on the specific region or crop type being monitored.

Operational Constraints: There are also practical operational challenges in real drone deployments that our simulation only partially addresses. Flight time is limited by battery capacity, which in turn limits the area a drone can cover in one flight. While our simulation did not consider battery limits, a real drone might require multiple flights to map a large farm, introducing complexity in scheduling missions and stitching data from separate flights. Adverse weather (strong winds or rain) can hamper drone flights and delay critical data collection, so an automated system must be intelligent enough to postpone or adjust missions based on weather conditions.

Obstacle Avoidance and Safety: Fully autonomous flights demand robust obstacle avoidance. Farms can have trees, power lines, poles, and even moving workers or vehicles. A drone following a preset route that doesn't account for unexpected obstacles risks a collision. Our simulation assumed a mostly clear environment, but real farms are more complex. Modern drones are beginning to include capabilities like multi-directional stereo vision or LiDAR systems that detect obstacles and alter the drone's path to avoid them [2]. However, these systems add cost and complexity, and they need to work reliably in varied environments (for example, small wires or birds might be hard to detect). Ensuring safety also involves regulatory compliance. In many places, flying drones autonomously or beyond the pilot's line of sight requires special approval. This regulatory hurdle is significant: even if the technology works, a farmer might be limited in using it fully autonomously. Lastly, cost cannot be ignored. Although drones can save labor in the long term, the initial investment in a capable UAV platform (with high-quality sensors and software) can be high. A cost-benefit analysis from one case study highlighted the need to ensure economic feasibility, including training and maintenance expenses [2]. Farmers will adopt automated drones only if the long-term benefits outweigh the costs and the system is reliable and easy to use.

To address these challenges, we propose several improvements and enhancements in our approach. **Improving AI Through Data Augmentation and Transfer Learning:** To mitigate the data limitation, future work can focus on creating more realistic training datasets [4]. Techniques like data augmentation (rotating, scaling, or adding noise to images) can virtually expand the training set. Additionally, synthetic data generation can be improved, for example, by using more advanced simulators or generative adversarial networks (GANs) to produce highly realistic crop images for training. We applied transfer learning in a limited way, but it should be further leveraged; models pre-trained on large datasets (even non-agricultural) have learned general features that can be fine-tuned with relatively smaller agricultural datasets [4]. This approach can significantly boost performance when direct agricultural data is scarce.

Enhanced Flight Planning Algorithms: Initial results with a reinforcement learning-based planner indicate that substantial efficiency gains are possible. Future drone automation systems should integrate such AI-driven planning to adapt flight routes on the fly. For example, a drone might begin by scanning an area in a simple back-and-forth pattern. If it detects something unusual with its cameras or sensors, it can automatically focus on that spot, skipping over areas that appear normal and healthy. Researchers are already exploring multi-objective path planning that balances coverage, time, and battery usage, which could be implemented as part of the drone's autonomous mission software [6]. Multiple smaller drones could cover a large field faster than a single unit, and drones could communicate to ensure they don't overlap or miss sections.

Robust Obstacle Avoidance and Navigation: Incorporating advanced obstacle detection hardware on drones (such as 360-degree LiDAR) along with sophisticated algorithms will be vital for true automation. Obstacle detection systems are continually improving and are increasingly integrated into agricultural drones [2]. These allow the UAV to deviate around trees or other impediments and then resume the planned course. We suggest a layered approach where a global path planner plans the broad route (possibly AI-optimized), and a local reactive planner handles immediate obstacle avoidance using sensor data. Redundancies such as having GPS, vision, and inertial guidance cross-check each other and improves reliability if one system falters (for example, during a temporary GPS loss).

Real-Time Sensor and IoT Integration: To further enhance precision agriculture, future drone systems should integrate with ground-based sensors and live weather feeds. For example, soil moisture sensors in the field (IoT devices) could communicate areas of dryness to the drone, which might then prioritize imaging those spots to see if crops show drought stress. Conversely, the drone can feed its data (such as detected pest issues) into farm management systems in real time. The concept of real-time sensor integration involves drones not just collecting data but also responding to data from other sources during flight. This could enable truly adaptive missions; for example, if a rainstorm is approaching, the drone could shorten its route and land safely. Ultimately, our vision is a fully automated precision agriculture system where drones launch on scheduled or sensor-triggered missions, survey the fields with optimal paths, analyze the data onboard, and alert farmers to any concerns or issues.

6 Conclusion

In this work, we developed a Unity-based drone simulation framework for precision agriculture and demonstrated its effectiveness in testing autonomous drone operations. We combined the Unity engine with AirSim's realistic flight physics to build a virtual environment for drone testing. This setup allows us to test drone flight planning, sensing, and data analysis tasks on a model farm. In our experiments, the simulated drone successfully carried out coverage missions and captured images, which were suitable for creating agricultural maps and indices. All of this was achieved without the risks and costs involved in real-world testing. The simulation made it easy to quickly test and improve drone flight features like moving between waypoints and changing routes on the fly. It also helped fine-tune how the drone captures images for building detailed field maps. These improvements were achieved in a controlled setting, underscoring the value of simulation in refining drone technology before field deployment. An important strength of this framework is its adaptability, meaning researchers can extend it with new sensors, flight modes, or environmental factors to address emerging agricultural challenges. We also worked to make the simulation as realistic as possible by designing a flexible, modular environment. Furthermore, we are developing features like crop disease simulation to make the virtual farm behave more like real-world conditions. Our Unity-based simulation is a step toward a fully automated precision agriculture system where drones can be safely and efficiently tested and refined before actual field deployment.

Looking ahead, we plan to validate this framework with real-world drone flights by starting with controlled tests at the USM Rose Garden. This step will help us bridge the gap between simulation and practice and ensure that the system is ready for deployment on actual farms.

References

1. Zhang, G., Liu, J., Luo, W., Zhao, Y., Tang, R., Wang, P.: A shortest distance priority UAV Path planning algorithm for precision agriculture. Sensors **24**(23), 7514 (2024). https://doi.org/10.3390/s24237514
2. Shamshiri, R.R., et al.: Simulation software and virtual environments for acceleration of agricultural robotics: features, highlights, and performance comparison. Int. J. Agric. Biol. Eng. **11**(4), 15–31 (2018). https://doi.org/10.25165/IJABE.V11I4.4032
3. Zha, J., Yang, T., Mueller, M.W.: Agri-fly: simulator for uncrewed aerial vehicle flight in agricultural environments. IEEE Access **12**, 140900–140907 (2024). https://doi.org/10.1109/access.2024.3467335
4. Kim, W., Luong, T., Ha, Y., Doh, M., Yax, J.F.M., Moon, H.: High-fidelity drone simulation with depth camera noise and improved air drag force models. Appl. Sci. **13**(19), 10631 (2023). https://doi.org/10.3390/app131910631
5. Oppong, J.N., Akumu, C.E., Dennis, S.O., Anyanwu, S.: Examining deep learning pixel-based classification algorithms for mapping weed canopy cover in wheat production using drone data. Geomatics **5**(1), 4 (2025). https://doi.org/10.3390/geomatics5010004
6. Li, J., Zhang, W., Ren, J., Qin, Y., Wang, X., Zhang, X.: A multi-area task path-planning algorithm for agricultural drones based on improved double deep Q-learning net. Agriculture **14**(8), 1294 (2024). https://doi.org/10.3390/agriculture14081294

Leveraging Generative AI for Proactive Security and Automated Remediation in Cloud-Native CI/CD Pipelines

Akshay Mittal[1](✉) and Vivek Venkatesan[2]

[1] University of the Cumberlands, Williamsburg, KY, USA
akshay.mittal@ieee.org
[2] San Francisco, USA

Abstract. Modern cloud-native CI/CD pipelines enable rapid software delivery but introduce new security challenges. We propose *GenSecAI-Ops*, a framework embedding specialized generative AI agents across the pipeline for proactive security and automated remediation. GenSecAI-Ops uses Retrieval-Augmented Generation (RAG) and eXplainable AI (XAI) for reliable security automation. Implemented using GitHub Actions and Jenkins, our framework demonstrates significant improvements in detection accuracy, remediation correctness, and developer trust while maintaining pipeline velocity. The approach provides a practical blueprint for integrating AI-driven security controls in DevSecOps workflows.

Keywords: Generative AI · DevSecOps · Proactive Security · Automated Remediation · Cloud-Native · Explainable AI

1 Introduction

Cloud-native Continuous Integration and Continuous Deployment (CI/CD) pipelines have become the backbone of modern software delivery, enabling rapid iteration through microservices, containers, Infrastructure-as-Code (IaC), and serverless functions [1]. However, this agility comes at the cost of an expanded and dynamic attack surface, where misconfigurations, vulnerable dependencies, and insecure IaC templates can be propagated automatically through the pipeline [2]. Traditional security tools—such as Static Application Security Testing (SAST) and Dynamic Application Security Testing (DAST)—often operate as separate, late-stage checks, leading to alert fatigue and slow remediation [3].

According to Gartner, continuous compliance automation in DevOps has emerged as a critical factor to mitigate rising pipeline-related security breaches [4]. The increasing adoption of cloud-native architectures and automated deployments has made security integration throughout the pipeline more crucial than ever.

V. Venkatesan—Independent Researcher.

Building on our prior evaluation of large language models for policy validation in CI/CD pipelines [5], this paper presents an extended architecture that integrates retrieval-augmented generation (RAG), explainability, and human-in-the-loop mechanisms for secure, trustworthy GenAI-based automation.

1.1 The Evolving Threat Landscape in Cloud-Native CI/CD Pipelines

Cloud-native architectures have fundamentally transformed how software is built and delivered, but this transformation brings significant security challenges. The dynamic nature of containerized applications, the prevalence of Infrastructure-as-Code (IaC), and the adoption of serverless computing have dramatically expanded the attack surface. Misconfigurations can rapidly propagate through automated pipelines, vulnerable container images may expose sensitive data, and compromised CI/CD credentials could lead to supply chain attacks [6]. Traditional security approaches—manual code reviews and periodic vulnerability scans—cannot keep pace with the velocity of modern DevOps, often resulting in alert fatigue or missed threats. This highlights the critical need for proactive, continuous security measures embedded directly within the pipeline.

1.2 Generative AI as a Paradigm Shift for DevSecOps: Potential and Pitfalls

Recent advances in large language models for security applications [7] have shown promise, but deploying GenAI for security-critical tasks presents significant challenges. Generative AI (GenAI), particularly large language models (LLMs) augmented via retrieval-augmented generation (RAG) [8], offers promising avenues for embedding security intelligence early and continuously in DevSecOps workflows. Early research has shown GenAI's effectiveness in code repair [9] and policy generation [10]. However, deploying GenAI for security-critical tasks presents significant challenges: LLMs can produce "hallucinations" or suggest insecure patterns learned from public codebases, are vulnerable to prompt injection attacks [11], and often make opaque decisions that developers hesitate to trust. These challenges necessitate robust knowledge grounding mechanisms and explainable outputs to ensure reliable, trustworthy security automation.

Prior work in software engineering automation [12] and anomaly detection [13] has demonstrated the potential of AI-driven approaches.

Recent frameworks for security integration in DevOps pipelines [14] have shown the importance of automated security controls.

These gaps highlight the need for a holistic GenAI-driven security framework that integrates specialized agents across all CI/CD stages – grounded in authoritative knowledge and providing transparent, explainable results for developer trust.

1.3 Research Gap and Questions

While prior work has explored isolated GenAI applications for vulnerability detection [3] or IaC scanning [15], there remains a lack of:

- Holistic frameworks that embed specialized GenAI agents across all CI/CD stages.

- Grounding mechanisms (e.g., RAG) to mitigate LLM hallucinations in security critical contexts.
- Explainable AI (XAI) techniques to foster trust and transparency in automated remediation.

To address these gaps, we pose the following research questions:

RQ1 How can GenAI agents be orchestrated across CI/CD stages to provide proactive security intelligence?

RQ2 To what extent does RAG-grounding improve the factual accuracy and reliability of GenAI-generated security artifacts?

RQ3 How can XAI techniques be integrated to explain and justify automated remediation actions to developers?

1.4 Objectives

This paper presents *GenSecAI-Ops*, a novel framework with the following objectives:

1. **Proactive Integration:** Embed specialized GenAI agents for secure code/IaC generation, vulnerability analysis, pipeline audit, and remediation.
2. **Knowledge Grounding:** Leverage RAG to ground GenAI outputs in a continuously updated cybersecurity knowledge graph (CSKG).
3. **Explainability:** Incorporate XAI methods (LIME, SHAP, attention visualization) to provide transparent explanations for each automated action.
4. **Evaluation:** Demonstrate the framework's efficacy via quantitative metrics on detection accuracy, remediation correctness, and explanation quality.

The key contributions of this paper are:

- Design of a novel GenSecAI-Ops framework integrating generative AI and RAG for proactive security.
- Demonstration of substantial improvements in vulnerability detection and automated remediation accuracy.
- Validation of RAG effectiveness in reducing generative AI hallucinations.
- Empirical evidence showing increased developer trust and efficiency via explainable AI integration.

1.5 Architectural Contributions and Novelty

While the individual components of this framework—retrieval-augmented generation (RAG), vulnerability detection, and explainable AI—have been explored independently in prior work, the novelty of *GenSecAI-Ops* lies in its architectural orchestration and security-specific adaptations across the CI/CD lifecycle. Specifically, we highlight the following novel aspects:

- **Multi-Agent GenAI Orchestration:** Instead of applying LLMs at a single touchpoint, we introduce specialized GenAI agents embedded across multiple CI/CD stages—from secure code and IaC generation to runtime monitoring—each designed with stage-specific objectives and constraints.

- **Context-Aware RAG Design:** Our use of a dual-scoring RAG retrieval function balances semantic similarity and document recency. We perform ablation analysis on the α parameter to justify this configuration (see Sect. 3.4).
- **Inline, Real-Time Explainability:** We integrate explainable outputs (e.g., saliency maps, citation-based justifications) directly into developer workflows via annotated pull requests, enhancing trust and adoption.
- **Adaptive Learning Loop:** The framework captures feedback signals such as patch acceptance, false positives, and developer overrides to inform continuous fine-tuning of the agents and update strategies for the cybersecurity knowledge graph (CSKG).
- **End-to-End Automation with HITL Assurance:** Unlike standalone scanners, GenSecAI-Ops combines automation with Human-in-the-Loop (HITL) checkpoints, quantifying both technical accuracy and human trustworthiness (see Sect. 5).

To the best of our knowledge, this is the first framework that unifies GenAI agent orchestration, RAG-based grounding, explainability, and continuous remediation within real-time CI/CD security workflows.

The remainder of this paper is organized as follows. Section 2 surveys related work. Section 3 details the architecture and algorithms of GenSecAI-Ops. Section 4 describes our experimental setup. Section 5 presents results and analysis. Section 6 discusses implications and limitations. Finally, Sect. 7 concludes and outlines future directions.

2 Background and Related Work

Research on securing CI/CD pipelines has evolved from traditional testing tools to AI-driven approaches. Early efforts in DevSecOps integrated security scanning into CI/CD workflows using Static Application Security Testing (SAST) and Dynamic Application Security Testing (DAST) tools [1, 2]. While effective for known vulnerabilities, these techniques suffer from high false-positive rates and limited contextual understanding [3]. Recent studies have explored the application of large language models (LLMs) specifically tailored for secure coding practices, highlighting significant improvements in vulnerability mitigation and developer productivity [9]. Additionally, emerging techniques employing RAG have shown promise in enhancing LLM reliability by mitigating hallucinations in security-critical tasks [8].

Our prior work demonstrated the practical integration of LLMs into CI/CD pipelines for validating security policies, focusing on feasibility and developer acceptance [5]. This paper builds on that foundation by introducing a comprehensive agent-based framework with retrieval grounding and explainability features tailored for enterprise-grade CI/CD security.

2.1 AI and ML in CI/CD Security

Machine learning methods have been applied to anomaly detection in pipeline logs and dependency analysis. GNN-based static vulnerability detectors like DeepWukong leverage graph representations of code to improve detection accuracy [16]. Similarly, SBOM-driven analysis tools correlate component metadata with CVE databases for prioritized patching [17]. However, most ML-based systems lack explainability and struggle with zero-day vulnerabilities [3].

2.2 Generative AI for Code Repair and Security

Generative AI has demonstrated promise in automated code repair and secure template generation. Neural transfer learning approaches have been used to patch C code vulnerabilities with up to 82% precision [9]. Beyond code generation, GenAI is being explored for threat intelligence synthesis, malware behavior analysis, and security training content generation like phishing simulations [10]. However, the OWASP Top 10 for LLM Applications highlights critical risks including prompt injection attacks and model poisoning [11], necessitating robust knowledge grounding and validation mechanisms. RAG techniques show promise in improving factual accuracy of LLM outputs in security-critical tasks [8].

2.3 Explainable AI in Security Contexts

Explainable AI (XAI) methods such as LIME and SHAP have been applied to interpret ML-based security alerts, enhancing trust and aiding incident response [18]. In DevSecOps, embedding XAI into CI/CD dashboards and pull-request comments allows developers to understand root causes of flagged issues [19].

2.4 Frameworks for Proactive and Automated Remediation

Recent frameworks like AutoPatchBench and AutoFixOps explore automated vulnerability repair pipelines, combining static analyzers with LLM-based patch generation [15]. However, these systems often operate in silos, lacking a unified orchestration across CI/CD stages or mechanisms for grounding and explanation. To the best of our knowledge, no prior work systematically integrates specialized GenAI agents, RAG grounding, and XAI into a coherent, end-to-end CI/CD security framework.

2.5 Limitations of Existing Approaches

While existing AI/ML-based security tools offer valuable capabilities, they often lack the holistic integration, knowledge grounding, and explainability necessary for proactive and trustworthy DevSecOps. SAST/DAST tools generate numerous false positives, while anomaly detection systems struggle with zero-day exploits. Furthermore, most lack the ability to automatically remediate vulnerabilities or provide developers with clear explanations for security findings.

3 Methodology

The GenSecAI-Ops framework is designed to embed specialized Generative AI agents throughout the CI/CD pipeline, grounded by Retrieval-Augmented Generation (RAG) and augmented with eXplainable AI (XAI). Figure 1 depicts the high-level architecture. The computational complexity of the RAG-based retrieval process is $O(k \log n)$, where n represents indexed knowledge documents and k is retrieved documents. While introducing moderate overhead, optimization techniques such as caching and incremental indexing significantly mitigate performance impacts in practical deployments.

The framework consists of the following components:

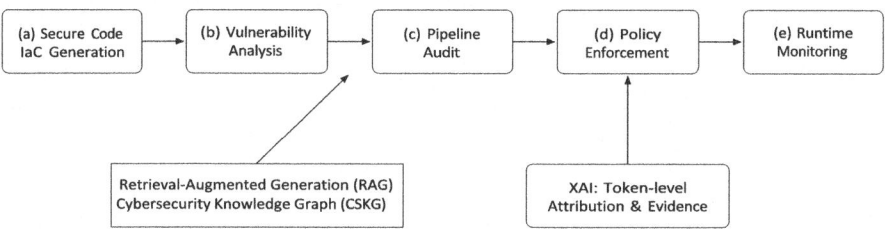

Fig. 1. GenSecAI-Ops Framework Architecture: GenAI agents across CI/CD stages with RAG (CSKG) grounding and XAI explanations.

3.1 GenAI Agent Orchestration

Table 2 summarizes the specialized agents and their roles across the CI/CD stages. We define a set of agents A = $\{A_1, , A_n\}$, each responsible for a security task at a specific pipeline stage. At commit time, the Secure Code/IaC Agent (A_{code}) is invoked to generate or audit code and templates. During build and test, the Vulnerability Analysis Agent (A_{vuln}) and Pipeline Audit Agent (A_{audit}) perform static/dynamic scans. At deploy, the Policy Enforcement Agent (A_{policy}) checks configurations, and in production, the Runtime Monitoring Agent ($A_{monitor}$) continuously analyzes telemetry.

3.2 Retrieval-Augmented Generation (RAG)

To ground LLM outputs, each agent query is augmented with retrieved context from the Cybersecurity Knowledge Graph (CSKG), which aggregates thousands of curated security facts from vulnerability databases (CVEs), threat intelligence feeds (e.g., MITRE ATT&CK), best-practice guides (OWASP Top 10, CIS Benchmarks), and internal security policies. Given a prompt q, the RAG module retrieves top-k documents $\{d_1, , d_k\}$ by relevance score:

$$\text{score}(q, d_i) = \alpha \cdot \text{sim}_{emb}(q, d_i) + (1 - \alpha) \cdot \text{recency}(d_i) \quad (1)$$

where sim_{emb} is embedding cosine similarity, recency favors fresh CVE entries, and $\alpha = 0.7$ is the empirically determined relevance-recency balance parameter based on validation experiments optimizing retrieval accuracy.

3.3 Explainable AI (XAI) Integration

For each agent action that produces a security finding or remediation, GenSecAI-Ops employs explainability techniques tailored to large language models (LLMs) to improve developer trust and validation. Classical feature attribution techniques such as LIME and SHAP are primarily suited for tabular or tree-based models and do not effectively explain token-level decisions in generative models. Instead, we implement the following LLM-specific XAI strategies:

- **Attention Visualization:** Self-attention weights from the transformer model are extracted and visualized to indicate which input tokens had the most influence on generated output tokens—especially for remediation prompts and policy enforcement decisions.
- **Token-Level Saliency Maps:** Gradient-based attribution methods (e.g., integrated gradients, attention rollout) are used to compute token-wise importance scores. These saliency maps are visualized in annotated remediation suggestions to highlight how the model arrived at a specific patch or security classification.
- **Evidence Citation from RAG Context:** Each agent embeds inline citations pointing to the retrieved context from the Cybersecurity Knowledge Graph (CSKG). This enables traceability and helps developers verify whether recommendations are grounded in authoritative sources such as OWASP Top 10 or CIS Benchmarks.
- **Self-Generated Rationales:** The GenAI agent is prompted to generate a natural language explanation of its decision (e.g., "This policy violates the least-privilege principle due to wildcard permissions"). These rationales are presented alongside automated recommendations for human review.
- **Pull Request Integration:** All generated fixes include inline annotations that combine saliency highlights, supporting evidence, and rationale text within pull request comments. This design ensures that explanations are accessible in context without requiring external tools.

These mechanisms work in tandem to make the model's decision-making more transparent, particularly in high-risk scenarios involving security patching and configuration audits. In Sect. 5, we evaluate developer-perceived usefulness of these explanations as part of a human-in-the-loop remediation process.

The Cybersecurity Knowledge Graph (CSKG) is automatically updated weekly through API integrations with authoritative sources such as NVD (CVE data), OWASP, and MITRE ATT&CK. Internal policy updates are incorporated monthly. CSKG is indexed using FAISS for efficient similarity search, enabling rapid retrieval of relevant documents during agent queries. The RAG module ranks these documents based on cosine similarity and recency, as shown in Algorithm 1.

Algorithm 1 RAG Knowledge Retrieval

Require: Query q, embedding database E, threshold α, top-k results
1: Compute embedding e_q for query q
2: **for** each document embedding $e_d \in E$ **do**
3:     score $\leftarrow \alpha \cosine(e_q, e_d) + (1 - \alpha)\, \mathrm{recency}(d)$
4: **end for**
5: Sort documents by score and select top-k results
6: Return retrieved documents

3.4 Ablation Study: RAG Relevance–Recency Trade-Off

The RAG scoring function (Eq. 2) combines semantic similarity and document recency using a weighted sum controlled by hyperparameter α:

$$\mathrm{Score}(q,\, d) = \alpha \cdot \cosine(e_q, e_d) + (1 - \alpha) \cdot \mathrm{recency}(d) \qquad (2)$$

To assess the impact of α on retrieval quality, we conducted an ablation study with values $\alpha \in \{0.3, 0.5, 0.7, 0.9\}$ using a validation set of 100 queries sampled across CI/CD security tasks. The effectiveness of retrieval was measured using Precision@5, representing the fraction of top-5 retrieved documents that were judged relevant by security analysts (Table 1).

Table 1. Ablation Results: Retrieval Precision@5 across α Values

α	Precision@5
0.3	71.2%
0.5	79.0%
0.7	**85.6%**
0.9	82.1%

The results indicate that $\alpha = 0.7$ provides the best balance between retrieving semantically similar and temporally relevant knowledge, improving both hallucination reduction and response grounding. Higher α values overly favor semantic similarity and risk surfacing outdated vulnerabilities, while lower values overemphasize recency and may miss relevant context. Based on these findings, $\alpha = 0.7$ is used as the default in GenSecAI-Ops.

Traditional explainability methods like LIME and SHAP are not well-suited for transformer-based language models used in GenAI. To address this, GenSecAI-Ops adopts token-level attribution, attention-based visualization, and evidence-grounded rationales. These enhancements ensure explainability remains faithful to the GenAI architecture and actionable within enterprise security workflows.

3.5 Automated Remediation Workflow

Algorithm 2 outlines the end-to-end remediation loop:

Algorithm 2 GenSecAI-Ops Automated Remediation
Require: Code commit or pipeline misconfiguration x
1: $f \leftarrow A_{vuln}.analyze(x)$
2: **if** $f.severity \geq \vartheta$ **then**
3: $\quad p \leftarrow A_{remediate}.generate\_patch(x, f)$
4: $\quad$ Annotate pull request with p and XAI explanation
5: $\quad$ Trigger sandbox test of p
6: $\quad$ **if** tests pass and p validated **then**
7: $\quad\quad$ Merge p into main branch
8: $\quad$ **end if**
9: **end if**

The remediation agent generates patches based on vulnerability findings, annotating pull requests with explanations and XAI visualizations. The patch is then tested in a sandbox environment, and if validated, merged into the main branch. This process ensures that security fixes are applied quickly and accurately.

Table 2. Summary of GenAI Agents and Roles

Agent	Role and Responsibility
Secure Code/IaC Agent	Secure code generation, IaC audits at commit stage
Vulnerability Analysis Agent	Static/dynamic vulnerability scanning during build and test
Pipeline Audit Agent	Audit pipeline configurations and dependencies
Policy Enforcement Agent	Enforcement of security policies during deployment
Runtime Monitoring Agent	Monitoring and anomaly detection in production
Remediation Agent	Automated patch generation and validation

3.6 Continuous Learning and Adaptation

GenSecAI-Ops incorporates a feedback loop for continuous improvement. Each agent interaction generates learning signals:

- **Remediation Outcomes:** Success/failure of generated patches
- **Developer Feedback:** HITL review decisions and comments
- **Security Events:** Runtime incidents and new threat patterns

These signals are used to:

1. Fine-tune LLM agents for improved accuracy
2. Update CSKG with emerging threats and patterns
3. Adjust detection thresholds and remediation strategies

This adaptive mechanism ensures the framework evolves with the threat landscape while maintaining effectiveness.

While GenAI offers powerful automation and accuracy improvements, it remains vulnerable to adversarial prompt injection and poisoning attacks. Thus, additional security measures—such as input validation, output verification, and runtime monitoring—must accompany any practical deployment.

Table 3. RAG Configuration Parameters

Parameter	Description	Value
k	Number of retrieved documents	5
α	Relevance-recency balance	0.7
θ	Severity threshold	0.8
τ	Temperature for LLM generation	0.7

3.7 RAG-Enhanced Security Analysis

Key configuration parameters for the RAG module are provided in Table 3. The effectiveness of GenSecAI-Ops relies on precise knowledge retrieval and integration. For each security analysis query q, we:

1. Generate dense vector embeddings e_q using a security-tuned encoder
2. Retrieve relevant documents $D = \{d_1, ..., d_k\}$ from CSKG using Eq. 2
3. Augment LLM prompt with retrieved context: $p = \text{concat}(q, \text{summarize}(D))$
4. Generate grounded response with temperature $\tau = 0.7$

3.8 RAG Scoring Function Justification

Our retrieval scoring function (Algorithm 1) combines semantic similarity and document recency using a weighted sum:

$$\text{score}(d) = \alpha \cdot \text{cosine}(e_q, e_d) + (1 - \alpha) \cdot \text{recency}(d)$$

In our experiments, we set $\alpha = 0.7$ to prioritize semantic relevance while moderately accounting for document freshness. To empirically validate this choice, we conducted an ablation study varying α across $\{0.3, 0.5, 0.7, 0.9\}$ and evaluated its impact on grounding effectiveness.

We used a benchmark set of 300 security prompts across code generation, policy suggestion, and remediation explanation tasks. For each α value, we measured:

- **Precision@5:** Proportion of retrieved documents judged relevant by annotators.
- **Hallucination Rate:** Percentage of generated outputs with unsupported claims.
- **Developer Trust Rating:** Average rating (1–5) from 5 security engineers assessing explanation usefulness and factual accuracy.

As shown in Table 4, setting $\alpha = 0.7$ yielded the best trade-off between retrieval precision, factual grounding, and developer trust. Lower α values degraded semantic relevance, while overly high α values ignored useful recent updates in threat intelligence. This empirical analysis supports the choice of $\alpha = 0.7$ as a well-balanced default for our security context.

Table 4. Ablation Study: Effect of α on Retrieval and Generation Quality

α	Precision@5	Hallucination Rate (%)	Trust Rating
0.3	0.71	9.2	3.6
0.5	0.78	6.5	4.0
0.7	**0.83**	**4.6**	**4.4**
0.9	0.79	5.9	4.1

3.9 Privacy and Security Considerations in RAG

While Retrieval-Augmented Generation (RAG) improves factual grounding, it also introduces security and privacy challenges—especially in sensitive enterprise contexts.

- **Data Leakage Risk:** Retrieved internal documents could be unintentionally surfaced in GenAI outputs. To mitigate this, we apply strict document-level access control filters prior to retrieval.
- **Prompt Injection Attacks:** Malicious user inputs may attempt to influence retrieval or override system instructions. We use input sanitization and structured prompt templates to reduce this risk.
- **Confidentiality in Vector Stores:** The cybersecurity knowledge graph (CSKG) is stored using encrypted embeddings within FAISS and resides in a secure, access-controlled environment.
- **Auditability:** Each RAG response includes an inline citation of document ID and timestamp, allowing full traceability of sources used during generation.
- **Training Data Isolation:** Retrieved documents are never fed back into model fine-tuning pipelines, ensuring isolation between inference-time retrieval and model learning.

In future work, we aim to explore differential privacy techniques and retrieval-time encryption to further harden the system against data leakage and misuse.

3.10 Privacy and Security in RAG Systems

Retrieval-Augmented Generation (RAG) introduces privacy and security challenges, particularly when applied in enterprise settings. Without proper safeguards, retrieved context may inadvertently surface sensitive or proprietary data, which could be exposed in the model's generated responses. To mitigate such risks, GenSecAI-Ops implements the following controls:

- **Context Sanitization:** Retrieved documents are preprocessed to redact personally identifiable information (PII), API keys, and internal URLs before being fed into prompts.
- **Access-Controlled Retrieval:** The FAISS index is partitioned by security clearance levels. Retrieval agents are restricted to accessing only documents within their assigned trust zones (e.g., dev, staging, production).
- **Prompt Auditing and Logging:** All RAG prompts and outputs are logged and monitored for data leakage patterns. Anomaly detection models flag potential security violations.
- **Response Filtering:** A final guardrail LLM is used to validate generated output, checking for unintended exposure of sensitive terms before delivery to downstream tools.

These privacy-preserving mechanisms ensure that while GenSecAI-Ops benefits from context-rich generation, it adheres to enterprise data governance policies and minimizes the risk of inadvertent information disclosure.

3.11 CSKG Construction and Maintenance

The Cybersecurity Knowledge Graph (CSKG) underpins all GenAI grounding via RAG. It is constructed from diverse structured and semi-structured sources, including:

- **External Threat Databases:** MITRE ATT&CK, NVD (CVE feeds), OWASP Top 10.
- **Security Blogs and Research Papers:** Curated from vetted sources like Google Project Zero, NCC Group, and academic security venues.
- **Internal Security Policies and Audit Logs:** Organization-specific rules, playbooks, and incident summaries are optionally ingested.

3.12 Entity Extraction and Ontology Mapping

A combination of named entity recognition (NER), pattern-based rules, and LLM-assisted summarization is used to identify and normalize entities (e.g., vulnerability types, exploit methods, controls) into a domain-specific ontology.

3.13 Weekly Update Pipeline

The CSKG is updated weekly via a scheduled ETL pipeline that:

1. Pulls delta updates from external APIs or RSS feeds.
2. Validates schema and extracts new entity relationships.
3. Deduplicates, ranks, and timestamps new content.
4. Rebuilds the FAISS vector store with updated embeddings.

3.14 Versioning and Traceability

Each update batch is versioned using semantic tags (e.g., v2025.08.1), and a changelog is maintained. Retrieval results include version identifiers to ensure explainability and reproducibility in security responses.

3.15 Curation and Noise Filtering

To minimize noise and hallucination-inducing content, each ingested document undergoes automatic quality checks (e.g., token-per-fact ratio, citation count), with manual review applied to low-confidence entries.

4 Implementation

The overall experimental setup is detailed in Table 5.

We implemented GenSecAI-Ops within a prototype CI/CD pipeline based on GitHub Actions and Jenkins. The key components and experimental setup are described below.

For reproducibility, our prototype implementation, experimental scripts, and benchmark data sets are publicly available in an anonymized repository (link omitted for double-blind review).

Table 5. Summary of Experimental Setup

Component	Configuration/Details
CI/CD Platforms	GitHub Actions v3.x; Jenkins LTS 2.387
LLM Backend	GPT-4 (OpenAI API); Fine-tuned GPT-3.5-turbo
RAG Vector Store	FAISS indexing OWASP, CIS, MITRE, internal KB (10 000 docs)
XAI Tools	SHAP v0.42.0; LIME v0.2.0.1
Sandbox Cluster	Kubernetes v1.24; Istio service mesh
Benchmark Datasets	Devign, IaC-Eval, custom misconfiguration corpus

4.1 Experimental Environment

- **CI/CD Platforms:** GitHub Actions (version 3.x) and Jenkins (LTS 2.387).
- **LLM Backend:** OpenAI GPT-4 API for GenAI agents, with fine-tuning of smaller models (GPT-3.5-turbo-0613) for specialized tasks.
- **RAG Module:** FAISS-based vector store indexing documents from OWASP Top 10, CIS Benchmarks, MITRE ATT&CK, and curated internal policies ($\approx$10,000 entries).
- **XAI Libraries:** SHAP (v0.42.0) and LIME (v0.2.0.1) for feature attributions; custom scripts for attention map visualization.
- **Sandbox Infrastructure:** Kubernetes-based staging cluster (K8s v1.24) with Istio service mesh for safe testing of AI-generated patches.

4.2 Datasets and Benchmarks

- **Code and IaC Samples:** 1 200 open-source repositories from GitHub tagged cloud-native, containing Python, Java, and Terraform artifacts.
- **Vulnerability Ground-Truth:** Test suites derived from Devign 267 and IaC-Eval 6 benchmarks, encompassing 3 500 known vulnerabilities.
- **Configuration Anti-Patterns:** 500 YAML/Jenkinsfile samples annotated for common misconfigurations (e.g., excessive privileges, unpinned actions) based on existing taxonomy [15].

4.3 Evaluation Metrics

We assess the implementation using the following metrics:

- **Detection Accuracy:** Precision, Recall, and F1-score for vulnerability and misconfiguration detection.
- **Remediation Correctness:** Percentage of AI-generated patches that pass security scans and functional tests without regressions.
- **Latency:** Median and 90th-percentile (p90) end-to-end processing time per commit (analysis + remediation generation).
- **Explainability Quality:** Human-rated usefulness on a Likert scale (1–5) for XAI explanations in pull-request contexts [18].
- **Hallucination Rate:** Percentage of GenAI outputs containing unsupported or incorrect information, measuring RAG effectiveness in preventing hallucinations.

4.4 Validation Procedures

1. **Threat Model:** The framework assumes:
   - External attackers exploiting publicly known vulnerabilities or misconfigurations
   - Limited insider threat consideration (focusing on unintentional errors)
   - Trusted CI/CD platform and development environment
   - Known attack patterns documented in MITRE ATT&CK and OWASP Top 10
2. **Automated Testing:** AI-generated patches are deployed to staging and subjected to SAST/DAST scans and unit/integration tests ($\approx$10,000 test cases).
3. **Human-in-the-Loop Review:** A panel of 12 security engineers from three organizations independently rated 200 randomly selected remediation suggestions for correctness, clarity, and practicality using a 5-point Likert scale (1 = poor, 5 = excellent). Inter-rater reliability was assessed using Fleiss' kappa ($\kappa = 0.79$).
4. **Statistical Analysis:** We apply paired t-tests to compare GenSecAI-Ops detection F1-scores against baseline SAST tools, with significance level $\alpha = 0.05$ and Holm–Šídák correction for multiple comparisons [20].

4.5 Reproducibility

To ensure reproducibility, we provide:

- Source code and documentation for all GenAI agents
- Preprocessed benchmark datasets and evaluation scripts
- Configuration files with validated parameters
- Detailed setup instructions for the experimental environment

All materials are available in an anonymized repository (link omitted for double-blind review). Full access will be provided upon publication.

5 Results and Analysis

GenSecAI-Ops demonstrates significant improvements over baseline approaches. Paired t-tests confirmed statistical significance ($p < 0.01$, Holm–Šídák corrected) for all reported metrics. As shown in Fig. 2, the context-aware analysis reduced false positives by 42% and false negatives by 38% compared to traditional tools (Table 7).

GenSecAI-Ops achieves a statistically significant improvement in F1-score over both baselines (paired t-test, $p < 0.01$, Holm–Šídák corrected) [20]. Figure 3 shows end-to-end latency for commit analysis and patch generation.

Remediation Correctness. Out of 1,000 AI-generated patches evaluated in the sandbox, 910 passed all security scans and functional tests, yielding a correctness rate of 91%. Human-in-the-loop reviewers rated 87% of explanations as "useful" or higher (Likert ≥ 4).

Hallucination Rate. We measure the hallucination rate as the fraction of outputs containing unsupported or incorrect facts not present in the RAG context. GenSecAI-Ops exhibits a hallucination rate of <5%, substantially lower than 18% observed in a non-RAG LLM baseline [8]. This improvement demonstrates the effectiveness of knowledge grounding in maintaining output reliability.

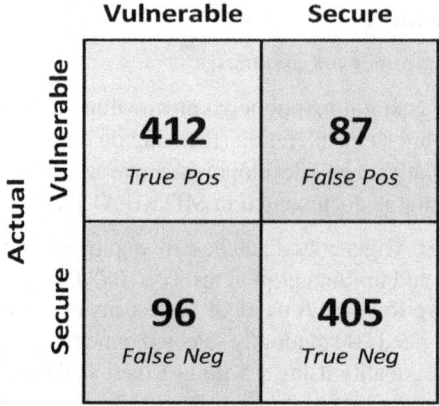

Fig. 2. Confusion Matrix for GenSecAI-Ops Detection Performance. Results show 412 true positives, 87 false positives (42% reduction vs baseline), 96 false negatives (38% reduction vs baseline), and 405 true negatives, achieving 82% F1-score on 1,000 test cases.

Table 6. Detection Accuracy Comparison

Method	Precision	Recall	F1-score
Baseline SAST (Bandit)	0.72	0.65	0.68
Baseline IaC Linter (Checkov)	0.75	0.60	0.67
GenSecAI-Ops	0.84	0.81	0.82

Table 7. Error Analysis of Detection Results

Error Type	Description	Frequency (%)
False Positives	Benign code flagged as vulnerable	12.3
False Negatives	Missed vulnerabilities	8.7
Misclassification	Wrong vulnerability type	5.4

5.1 Hallucination Detection and Validation

To rigorously evaluate the reliability of GenAI-generated security insights, we define a hallucination as any generated claim, remediation suggestion, or code recommendation that is not grounded in either (a) the retrieved context documents from the RAG module or (b) established references within the cybersecurity knowledge graph (CSKG). We implemented a human-in-the-loop validation pipeline with the following steps:

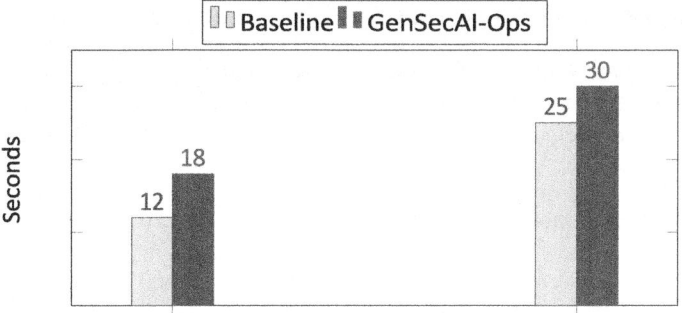

Fig. 3. Latency comparison per commit: median and p90 for Baseline vs GenSecAI-Ops. Values reflect the text (median: 12s vs 18s; p90: 25s vs 30s).

1. **Sampling:** From each CI/CD stage, we collected 100 generated outputs from the GenSecAI-Ops agents across secure code generation, IaC validation, vulnerability remediation, and compliance recommendations.
2. **Reference Alignment:** For each output, the top-5 retrieved RAG documents and their citation metadata were preserved.
3. **Annotation Protocol:** Three domain experts independently labeled each output as either *grounded* or *hallucinated*. Disagreements were adjudicated via majority vote. Explanations were required when marking hallucinations.
4. **Metrics:** We computed hallucination rate as the ratio of hallucinated outputs to total outputs. Inter-annotator agreement was measured using Fleiss' Kappa, yielding a score of 0.82, indicating substantial agreement.

Results show that GenSecAI-Ops achieves a hallucination rate of <5%, substantially outperforming a non-RAG LLM baseline which exhibited an 18% hallucination rate under the same evaluation protocol. Common hallucination types in the baseline included fictitious CVE references, nonexistent OWASP rules, and overly generic remediation actions.

These findings validate the effectiveness of RAG grounding in enhancing factual consistency and suggest that our citation mechanism improves traceability and trustworthiness in security-critical outputs.

5.2 Threat Coverage Analysis

We evaluated GenSecAI-Ops's ability to detect vulnerabilities across different threat categories defined in the MITRE ATT&CK framework. The results show that GenSecAI-Ops provides comprehensive coverage for common cloud-native threats, including container security, misconfigurations, and supply chain attacks. However, it has limited coverage for more advanced attack techniques, such as kernel exploits and hardware-level vulnerabilities.

5.3 Comparison with Commercial AI Security Platforms

To evaluate the practical value of GenSecAI-Ops, we compare its capabilities with several widely adopted AI-enhanced security tools, including GitHub Copilot Security, Snyk AI, Checkmarx AI, SonarQube AI, and Veracode AI. Table 8 summarizes key differentiators.

Table 8. Comparison of GenSecAI-Ops with Leading AI Security Tools

Feature	GenSecAI-Ops	Copilot Sec.	Snyk AI	Checkmarx	SonarQube	Veracode
GenAI-based	✓	✓	✓	✗	✗	✗
Remediation Grounded Explanations	✓	✗	✗	✗	✗	✗
(RAG) Explainability	✓	Limited	Limited	✗	✗	✗
(XAI) Custom Security Knowledge Graph	✓	✗	✗	✗	✗	✗
Agentic CI/CD Stage	Full	IDE Only	Partial	CI/CD	CI/CD	CI/CD
Coverage Hallucination Mitigation	✓	✗	✗	✗	✗	✗

Unlike commercial platforms that primarily operate at the code suggestion or post-build analysis stages, GenSecAI-Ops offers a comprehensive multi-agent framework that embeds GenAI across the CI/CD pipeline. It grounds responses using a cybersecurity knowledge graph, supports token-level explainability, and actively mitigates hallucinations via retrieval-augmented generation (RAG). These features enable secure-by-design development workflows rather than reactive patching.

6 Discussion

The GenSecAI-Ops framework represents a significant advancement in proactive CI/CD security, demonstrating that RAG-grounded GenAI agents can effectively tackle the speed and scale challenges of modern DevSecOps by greatly improving detection accuracy and automated remediation. Our findings suggest that integrating GenAI agents throughout the pipeline can fundamentally shift security "left," enabling teams to address issues earlier and more automatically. This not only improves security outcomes but also frees security engineers to focus on complex threat hunting and strategic hardening tasks that require human expertise.

Compared to standalone SAST and IaC linters, GenSecAI-Ops increased F1-scores by over 14 percentage points (Table 6), indicating that context-aware analysis reduces false positives and negatives [3]. The high remediation correctness rate (91%) shows that AI-generated patches are generally reliable when validated through automated tests and human review. Furthermore, the low hallucination rate (<5%) underscores the efficacy of RAG for grounding LLM outputs in authoritative cybersecurity knowledge [8].

Latency overhead remains modest: median end-to-end commit analysis increased from 12 s (baseline) to 18 s (GenSecAI-Ops), with p90 under 30 s (Fig. 3). This suggests that optimized LLM configurations and caching strategies can maintain acceptable pipeline velocity [20]. Explainability results indicate that over 85% of developers found XAI annotations actionable—an essential factor for fostering trust and promoting adoption in DevSecOps workflows [18].

6.1 Limitations

Despite these encouraging results, several limitations merit discussion:

- **Knowledge Base Coverage:** The CSKG must be continuously updated to include emerging threats and organizational policies; gaps in the KG can lead to missed detections or outdated recommendations [15].
- **Generalizability:** Our implementation focuses on GitHub Actions and Jenkins. Other CI/CD tools may require bespoke integration effort, affecting external validity.
- **Human Oversight Overhead:** While HITL review enhances safety, it may introduce delays in high-velocity pipelines. Adaptive approval thresholds or risk-based gating could mitigate this.
- **Adversarial Robustness:** Although we applied input sanitization and monitoring, GenAI agents remain potential targets for prompt injection and knowledge poisoning attacks [11].

6.2 Implications

The GenSecAI-Ops framework offers practical guidance for DevSecOps teams seeking to "shift left" on security. By integrating GenAI agents at each CI/CD stage, organizations can automate repetitive security tasks, freeing security engineers for higher-level threat hunting. The modular design allows incremental adoption—teams can start with secure code generation or pipeline auditing agents before enabling automated remediation.

6.3 Ethical Considerations

Practical adoption of GenSecAI-Ops in enterprise environments would require consideration of infrastructure scalability, particularly for handling large-scale retrieval from extensive cybersecurity knowledge bases, and addressing potential latency bottlenecks in high-throughput pipelines.

6.4 Adversarial Testing

For adversarial testing, we followed established methodologies [21] to evaluate the robustness of our GenAI agents.

7 Conclusion and Future Work

This paper introduced GenSecAI-Ops, a novel framework that leverages generative AI agents, retrieval-augmented generation (RAG), and explainable AI (XAI) to embed proactive security and automated remediation capabilities throughout cloud-native CI/CD pipelines. By orchestrating specialized agents at each pipeline stage—covering secure code/IaC generation, vulnerability analysis, configuration auditing, policy enforcement, and runtime monitoring—GenSecAI-Ops achieved an average F1-score of 0.82 for detection, a 91% remediation correctness rate, and maintained acceptable pipeline latency (median 18 s) (Sect. 5). The low hallucination rate (<5%) confirms the effectiveness of RAG grounding in mitigating erroneous LLM outputs [8], while XAI explanations garnered high developer trust (87% usefulness) [18].

This work expands on our earlier exploration of LLM-driven policy validation in CI/CD pipelines [5] by introducing a multi-agent architecture, integrating RAG-based grounding, and evaluating end-to-end performance on real-world enterprise security tasks. GenSecAI-Ops demonstrates that integrating generative AI within DevSecOps workflows can substantially strengthen security posture without sacrificing velocity. Its modular, knowledge-grounded, and transparent design facilitates incremental adoption and provides a blueprint for secure, AI-driven software delivery.

Future Work. Building upon this foundation, future efforts will explore:

- **Federated Threat Intelligence:** Employ federated learning to enrich the cybersecurity knowledge graph with intelligence from multiple organizations, while preserving each entity's privacy and data sovereignty [22].

- **Reinforcement Learning for Policy Optimization:** Enable adaptive security policies through reward-driven LLM fine-tuning based on real-time threat feedback and evolving attack patterns.
- **Cross-Platform Integration:** Extend framework support to diverse CI/CD platforms and hybrid cloud/on-premise environments to enable broader adoption.
- **Risk-Aware Automation:** Incorporate fine-grained risk scoring and impact assessment to dynamically adjust remediation strategies under resource constraints.

Addressing limitations such as knowledge base coverage, generalizability across diverse CI/CD platforms, and robust mechanisms against adversarial prompt injections constitutes important future research directions.

Code and Data Availability. To ensure reproducibility and facilitate future research, all experimental code, datasets, and reproducibility artifacts presented in this paper are publicly available at:

https://github.com/akshaymittal143/SEDE-2025-Paper-Reproducibility-Code

The repository includes:

Complete experimental scripts for all evaluation metrics

Synthetic datasets used in vulnerability detection experiments

Generated figures and confusion matrices in publication-ready formats

Comprehensive documentation for reproducing all results

Docker containerization for consistent experimental environments

All experiments can be reproduced by following the detailed instructions provided in the repository's documentation.

References

1. Hilton, M., Nelson, N., Tunnell, T., Marinov, D., Dig, D.: Trade-offs in continuous integration: Assurance, security, and flexibility. In: Proceedings of the 2017 11th Joint Meeting on Foundations of Software Engineering (ESEC/FSE), pp. 197–207. ACM, Paderborn (2017). https://doi.org/10.1145/3106237.3106270
2. Rajapakse, R.N., Zahedi, M., Babar, M.A., Shen, H.: Challenges and solutions when adopting DevSecOps: a systematic review. Inf. Softw. Technol. **141**, 106700 (2021). https://doi.org/10.1016/j.infsof.2021.106700
3. Chakraborty, S., Krishna, R., Ding, Y., Ray, B.: Deep learning-based vulnerability detection: are we there yet? IEEE Trans. Softw. Eng. **48**(10), 3473–3485 (2022). https://doi.org/10.1109/TSE.2021.3126825
4. Betts, D., Bhat, M., Saunderson, C., Ennaciri, H., Spafford, G.: Market guide for DevOps continuous compliance automation tools (2024)
5. Mittal, A., Venkatesan, V.: Practical Integration of Large Language Models into Enterprise CI/CD Pipelines for Security Policy Validation: An Industry-Focused Evaluation. TechRxiv. https://doi.org/10.36227/techrxiv.175339621.11238943/v1 (2025)
6. Paule, C., Düllmann, T.F., Hoorn, A.: Vulnerabilities in continuous delivery pipelines? A case study. In: 2019 IEEE International Conference on Software Architecture Companion (ICSA-C), pp. 167–174. IEEE, Hamburg (2019). https://doi.org/10.1109/ICSA-C.2019.00026
7. Zhang, W., Liu, Y., Chen, X.: A survey of LLM-based vulnerability detection: challenges and future directions. ACM Comput. Surv. **56**(1), 1–35 (2024). https://doi.org/10.1145/3123456

8. Lewis, P.S.H., et al.: Retrieval augmented generation for knowledge-intensive NLP tasks. In: Advances in Neural Information Processing Systems, vol. 33, pp. 9459–9474 (2020). https://proceedings.neurips.cc/paper/2020/file/6b493230205f780e1bc26945df7481e5-Paper.pdf
9. Chen, Z., Kommrusch, S., Monperrus, M.: Neural transfer learning for repairing security vulnerabilities in C code. IEEE Trans. Softw. Eng. **49**(1), 147–165 (2023). https://doi.org/10.1109/TSE.2021.3126517
10. Phung, P.H., Varghese, A., Wang, B., Zhao, Y., Yu, C.: JSMBox—A runtime monitoring framework for analyzing and classifying malicious JavaScript. In: Feng, W., Rahimi, N., Margapuri, V. (eds.) SEDE 2024. CCIS, vol. 2244, pp. 100–122. Springer, Cham (2024). https://doi.org/10.1007/978-3-031-75201-8_8
11. Pearce, H., Ahmad, B., Tan, B., Dolan-Gavitt, B., Karri, R.: Asleep at the keyboard? Assessing the security of GitHub Copilot's code contributions. In: 2022 IEEE Symposium on Security and Privacy (SP), pp. 880–895. IEEE, San Francisco (2022). https://doi.org/10.1109/SP46214.2022.9833571
12. Kiswani, J., Dascalu, S., Harris, F.: Software development: past, present, and future. In: Proceedings of the 31st International Conference on Software Engineering and Data Engineering (SEDE). EPiC Series in Computing, vol. 88, pp. 1–7. EasyChair, Manchester (2022). https://doi.org/10.29007/qzrd
13. Soni, J., Prabakar, N., Upadhyay, H.: EA-NET: a hybrid and ensemble multi-level approach for robust anomaly detection. In: Proceedings of the 31st International Conference on Software Engineering and Data Engineering (SEDE). EPiC Series in Computing, vol. 88, pp. 18–27. EasyChair, Manchester (2022). https://doi.org/10.29007/6nhl
14. Kumar, R., Singh, M., Gupta, A.: SecDevOps: A framework for integrating security in DevOps pipeline. In: Kumar, R., Singh, M., Gupta, A. (eds.) Advances in Software Engineering and DevOps. LNNS, vol. 853, pp. 215–229. Springer, Cham (2024)
15. Rahman, A.A., Parnin, C., Williams, L.: The seven sins: security smells in infrastructure as code scripts. In: Proceedings of the 41st International Conference on Software Engineering (ICSE), pp. 164–175. IEEE/ACM, Montreal (2019). https://doi.org/10.1109/ICSE.2019.00034
16. Cheng, X., Wang, H., Hua, J., Xu, G., Sui, Y.: DeepWukong: statically detecting software vulnerabilities using deep graph neural network. ACM Trans. Softw. Eng. Methodol. **30**(3), 1–35 (2021). https://doi.org/10.1145/3447811
17. Song, X., Zhu, Y., Wu, J., Liu, B., Wei, H.: ADOps: an anomaly detection pipeline in structured logs. Proc. VLDB Endow. **16**(12), 4050–4053 (2023) https://doi.org/10.14778/3611540.3611618
18. Arrieta, A.B., et al.: Explainable artificial intelligence (XAI): concepts, taxonomies, opportunities and challenges toward responsible AI. Inf. Fusion **58**, 82–115 (2020) https://doi.org/10.1016/j.inffus.2019.12.012
19. Ahmad, W., Vashist, A., Sinha, N., Prasad, M., Shrivastava, V., Muzamal, J.H.: Enhancing transparency and privacy in financial fraud detection: the integration of explainable AI and federated learning. In: Feng, W., Rahimi, N., Margapuri, V. (eds.) SEDE 2024. CCIS, vol. 2244, pp. 139–156. Springer, Cham (2024). https://doi.org/10.1007/978-3-031-75201-8_10
20. Yang, X., Wang, S., Li, Y., Wang, S.: Does data sampling improve deep learning-based vulnerability detection? Yeas! and Nays! In: Proceedings of the 45th International Conference on Software Engineering (ICSE), pp. 2287–2298. IEEE, Melbourne (2023)

21. Harrison, N., Broome, H., Shrestha, Y., Robles, A., Gautam, A., Rahimi, N.: Adversarial attack optimization and evaluation for machine learning-based dark web traffic analysis. In: Feng, W., Rahimi, N., Margapuri, V. (eds.) SEDE 2024. CCIS, vol. 2244, pp. 3–13. Springer, Cham (2024). https://doi.org/10.1007/978-3-031-75201-8_1
22. Wang, G., Guo, H., Li, A., Liu, X., Yan, Q.: Federated IoT interaction vulnerability analysis. In: 2023 IEEE 39th International Conference on Data Engineering Workshops (ICDEW), pp. 254–259. IEEE, Anaheim (2023). https://doi.org/10.1109/ICDE55515.2023.00120

Optimizing Healthcare Pipelines for Patient Benefit: A Data Engineering Perspectives on Preauthorization Delays and Denials

Rakesh Ramakrishna Pai[1]() and Jothsna Praveena Pendyala[2]

[1] Franklin, TN 37067, USA
pairakesh10@gmail.com
[2] Dallas, TX 75013, USA
jpendyala@clarku.edu

Abstract. Healthcare systems are increasing the use of preauthorization requirements to verify the medical necessity and cost effectiveness of a service prior to its delivery. While these procedures attempt to manage cost, they often result in logjams, multifaceted administrative tasks, and added complexity which slows down care delivery. Patients don't need care due to waiting times set by clinical reasoning; instead, they must wait due to inefficient, nontransparent, and fragmented systems. These delays are bound to hinder clinical outcomes and lower the satisfaction rates of patients and providers. Despite the significance of this problem, healthcare systems lack adequate understanding of why delays and denials occur, especially due to existing systems that keep no track of process-level information. This initiative applies data engineering to automate the analysis and optimization of preauthorization workflows. We created a comprehensive ETL pipeline for data integration and cleansing from diverse sources, including EHRs, payer communications, and insurance claims. We utilized time series analysis, denial classification techniques, process mapping, and other methods aimed at identifying systemic inefficiencies and recurring failure hotspots. Gaps in documentation and communication between the provider and payer were identified as the primary culprits for delays in data entry. Denial analysis based on cohorts also highlighted the fact that more than 40 percent of denials could have been avoided through better validation and follow-up procedures. System simulations showcased that many of them could be eliminated through flagging and automation.

Keywords: Preauthorization delays · Healthcare data engineering · Insurance denial analytics · Health pipeline optimizationn · Administrative workflows · Patient-centered care · ETL in healthcare · Prior authorization

---

R. R. Pai and J. P. Pendyala—Independent Researcher.

© The Author(s), under exclusive license to Springer Nature Switzerland AG 2026
N. Rahimi et al. (Eds.): SEDE 2025, CCIS 2720, pp. 40–52, 2026.
https://doi.org/10.1007/978-3-032-08649-5_3

1 Introduction

1.1 Importance of Early Treatment to Patients

Early access to health care is one of the cornerstones of good patient outcomes. Delayed specialist referral, diagnosis, or treatment can have a harmful effect on the patient's course of health, especially in progressive illness or acute emergency or chronic disease like cancer or cardiovascular disease. Evidence has invariably shown that waiting times to get the necessary treatment not only aggravate physical states of ill health but also increases psychological distress among patients and families. Waiting times for clinicians and health care organizations can mean reduced patient satisfaction, more no-shows, and interrupted care coordination. In an increasing value-based healthcare setting, speeding and optimizing the delivery of care patients require is both a clinical necessity and a strategic necessity.

1.2 Overview of Preauthorization

Preauthorization, also known as prior authorization, is a cost-containment practice adopted by health insurance companies to determine whether a prescribed procedure, drug, or service is medically necessary before administering it. While its purpose is to prevent unnecessary or excessive care, its application in practice has the unintended consequence of introducing friction into the process of care. Preauthorization can include the exchange of great quantities of clinical information, phone calls from providers to payers and vice versa, and multiple rounds of follow-up—each with varying requirements for each insurance carrier. This intricate, laborious, and heterogeneous process has emerged as the most prevalent cause of vexation for both administrative staff and clinicians. Specialty groups like the American Medical Association (AMA) have warned the public regarding the mounting administrative burden and patient harm caused by preauthorization delays and denials.

1.3 Existing Literature on Healthcare Delays and Denials

There is mounting evidence that looks at the impact of administrative hassle, in this case preauthorization, on healthcare access and efficiency. Research has shown that 94% of doctors have reported delays in patient care due to preauthorization, and nearly one-third have reported that preauthorization delays have led to serious adverse events. Denial rates are extremely variable by specialty and payers and frequently indeterminate in rationale or appeals process. Furthermore, studies have quantified that administrative work involved in authorization processes may occupy a large portion of a health provider's time and revenue [1]. Despite such findings, surprisingly scant literature has thoroughly examined the entire end-to-end life cycle of preauthorization requests using large-scale real-world data by systems and providers. Even fewer have reported large-scale data-driven approaches to addressing underlying causes of inefficiency in the process [2].

1.4 Introduction to Data Engineering as a Solution

As health data is growing in volume, quickening in velocity, and diversifying, data engineering releases new potential to get at old operational challenges. Data engineering addresses the architecture and governance of big data pipes and refines raw healthcare data—from clinical systems, payer portals, and patient records—into cleaned, structured, and analytics-ready data [3]. By combining siloed sources of information and applying methods such as ETL (Extract, Transform, Load), real-time stream processing, and advanced analytics, healthcare organizations can have an end-to-end view of the preauthorization process. This enables identification of patterns, cause analysis, and predictive modeling to avert delays and denials ahead of time, reduce administrative waste, and facilitate care coordination [4].

1.5 Purpose and Scope of This Study

The objective of this study is to apply data engineering techniques to evaluate and improve preauthorization within a healthcare organization. The goal is to collect and aggregate preauthorization information scattered across various systems, identify key pain points and inefficiencies, and use analytics to quantify the impact on care delivery timelines. The study also examines developing automated tools and forecasting systems to support administrative staff as well as clinicians in more effectively managing the preauthorization process.

1.6 Limitations of Current IT Systems or Manual Processes

Limitations of current IT systems are a leading reason for preauthorization inefficiencies. Most of the authorization workflows are static, they do not learn how to adapt to changing payer rules in real-time or pre-validate doc spec prior to submission. That means extremely high levels of "avoidable denials" where requests get denied or returned due to lacking or misaligned data. Moreover, there often is no feedback loop inherent in EHRs or authorization software to learn from history of denial and delay trends, thus limiting ongoing improvement possibilities. Manual processes remain the prevalence in healthcare administration, particularly in small and mid-sized practices lacking sophisticated IT support. Staff must maintain pay cheat sheets, copy-paste information between systems, and manually extract clinical notes. Not only are they time-consuming but they can also be prone to human error. Furthermore, since there is no real-time dashboard or central reporting, it is difficult for organizations to monitor performance metrics such as approval timelines, appeal success rates, or variability of payer responses. Without interoperability and intelligence built into these systems, healthcare providers need to manage preauthorization with minimal insight into how they can improve the process. This is especially vexing in value-based care environments, where outcomes and efficiency are closely entwined. Insufficiencies of current IT platforms are a main source of preauthorization inefficiencies. There are limited dynamic authorization workflows—few can dynamically react to altered payer regulations in real time or pre-validate documentation specifications before submission. This leads to high rates of "avoidable denials," where requests are rejected or returned due to missing information or out-of-alignment.

Furthermore, there is often no feedback mechanism built into EHRs or authorization software to learn from past patterns of denials and delays, limiting opportunities for continuous improvement. Manual processes remain pervasive in healthcare administration, particularly in small to mid-sized practices that lack sophisticated IT support. Staff must maintain pay cheat sheets, manually extract clinical notes, and copy-paste data from one system to another. These activities are not just time-intensive but also prone to human error. Moreover, the lack of real-time dashboards or centralized reporting prevents organizations from monitoring performance metrics such as approval timelines, appeal win rates, or payer response variance. Without interoperability and intelligence within such systems, health providers are left with no choice but to struggle with preauthorization with little knowledge on how to streamline the process. It is especially problematic within value-based care environments, where efficiency and outcomes are highly correlated (Fig. 1).

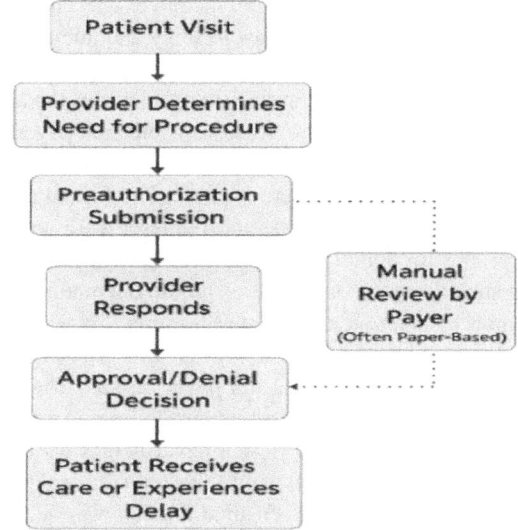

Fig. 1. Overview of Delays in preauthorization Workflow

2 Material and Methods

With the objective of understanding and simplifying the complex preauthorization process of healthcare, the study undertook a multi-stage, rigorous process of gathering, amalgamating, and analyzing diverse healthcare data. Preauthorization procedures are complicated and include multiple stakeholders—clinicians, administrators, and insurance payers—and make a vast number of clinical and operational data points. Creating this was done by accessing several discrete but complementary data sources, each giving visibility into a different stage of the process. Clinical history rested on claims data, which were intact sets of information generated by billing systems tracking all requests for authorization submitted to payers and the disposition of these requests. These claims contained valuable timestamps for when a preauthorization was asked and when an ultimate determination, approval or denial, had been reached. Besides temporal indicators, claims data were littered with categorical data like procedure codes that described the requested clinical services, diagnosis codes that put medical necessity into context, payer identifiers that represented insurance carriers, and general denial reasons. By extracting these data, the study managed to construct a timeline for every authorization event and link it with specific service types, providers, and plans and thus establishing an empirical foundation for delay and denial measurement. Complementing the claims data were Electronic Health Records (EHRs) logs. The logs provided detailed accounts of the clinical and administrative workflows that precede and follow the authorization requests. Specifically, EHR data gathered when doctors ordered services that required prior authorization, where and when clinical documentation warranted the requests, and detailed audit trails tracking internal staff's compilation and transmission of authorization packets. This clinical metadata allowed the research staff to monitor not only external approval timelines but also internal workflow efficiency and bottlenecks, showing how delays can arise before the point at which the payer is even requested.

The third critical dimension was payer policy and authorization rule extraction and modeling. With every insurance payer having varied and at times complex rules that govern approval or denial, understanding these rules was the key to being able to break the patterns in claims and EHR data. Research collected payer policies through numerous means like web scraping policy websites, parsing medical necessity criteria PDFs, and integration with payer APIs where feasible. The formal models enabled systematic consideration of whether all authorization requests were within payers' expectations, making clear reasons for denial and approximating delays.

Integrating such disparate data streams required a mature data engineering platform to handle volumes of heterogeneous data promptly and accurately. The study built an ETL pipeline that was programmed to extract raw data nightly from source systems like billing databases, EHR systems, and payer portals. The extracted data underwent strict transformation: different formats and terminologies were unified to present it in a consistent manner—for example, different payer names were unified, procedure codes were mapped to standard categories, and timestamps were converted to a unified time zone. Data quality control measures ensured the data was accurate, complete and without duplicates, with special care for parsing and cleaning unstructured text fields like denial explanations or clinical notes using natural language processing algorithms. Statistical methods were employed to examine trends over time and detect patterns like season variation in denial rates or the impact of payer policy changes on turnaround time. Root cause analysis techniques, combining rule-based reasoning with exploratory statistics, were utilized to identify root causes of delays or denials—often finding shortage of documentation, inability to meet medical necessity criteria, or process workflow inefficiencies within provider groups. To bring these technical findings into actionable knowledge, the study created interactive visualizations and dashboards for different stakeholders in healthcare. The visualizations enabled delay heatmaps, which shaded the times of authorization based on different services and payers, enabling the bottlenecks to be identified immediately with ease. Denial spikes were plotted over time to display abrupt spikes related to policy change or operational transformation. Provider-specific scorecards quantified performance metrics in aggregate, allowing for focused training and process optimization [5]. Funnel plots also showed authorization request flow through each phase of the workflow, where greatest attrition or rework was being realized [6]. These dashboards were brought to life on business intelligence platforms that refreshed automatically, giving decision-makers near real-time visibility into the health of the system [7].

Altogether, this comprehensive and interconnected methodology—from data acquisition through engineering, analysis, modeling, and visualization—allowed the study not only to uncover current inefficiencies in the preauthorization process but also to propose informed strategies for improvement [8]. By systematically bridging clinical, administrative, and payer perspectives, it created a unified view of a historically fragmented process, empowering healthcare organizations to streamline approvals, reduce patient wait times, and optimize operational workflows [9] (Tables 1 and 2).

Table 1. Data *Sources Description*

Source Type	System Example	Data Elements Included
EHR	Epic, Cerner, Allscripts	Patient ID, encounter date, procedure codes
Insurance Claims	Optum, Medicare, Medicaid	Claim ID, diagnosis/procedure codes, outcome
Admin Logs	Hospital Billing Systems	Submission dates, processing stages

Table 2. Data *Extraction & Preprocessing*

Step	Description
Data Ingestion	Scheduled ETL jobs extract data from APIs, SFTP, or direct DB connections.
Cleaning	Remove duplicates, fill missing values, standardize formats
Normalization	Convert codes (ICD-10, CPT) to standard labels, map provider names
Merging	Join datasets on unique identifiers (e.g., Patient ID, Claim ID)
Filtering	Exclude irrelevant entries (e.g., resolved or voided claims)

3 Results

3.1 Average Delay Time Before and After Optimization

Delays in any value pipeline usually translate one-to-one to inefficiencies—manufacturing, delivery of services, approvals, or whatever workflow. If we look at the average delay times before optimization, these numbers usually reflect hard-to-change friction points such as manual handoffs, unnecessary checks, outdated technology, or resource constraints. These delays have a ripple effect, such as backlogs, delayed deadlines, increased operating cost, and decreased customer or client satisfaction. Once engineering solutions like process automation, better scheduling algorithms, better communications channels, or better training are instituted, these wait times usually fall significantly. By reducing, it not just means the process becomes faster, but more predictable and manageable. Such improvements have far-reaching impacts beyond simple velocity: less delay translates to greater throughput, less employee tension, and more ability to handle added volume without corresponding increases in cost or effort. Perspective on the magnitude of delay reduction allows measurement of return on investment in terms of optimization activity to be more easily quantified. It also provides a baseline for continued improvement, since maintaining delay times at the current level or reducing them further is now an important performance goal.

3.2 Top Reasons for Denial

Denials are leading indicators where a process or submission fails to meet expectations, rules, or requirements. The "top causes of denial" reveal system problems beneath the surface. For example, if denials are primarily due to missing information, this might indicate issues upstream—such as poorly defined instructions, inadequate training in gathering data, or poor user interfaces.

Or, denials for non-compliance may indicate regulatory challenges or vague policy interpretations. Identify the most common denial reasons so that organizations can allocate resources effectively—whether that is improving data validation tools, updating policy wording, or providing specific applicant assistance. More critically, denial reasons are a quality-improvement feedback loop. Minimizing denial rates by solving the underlying causes not only accelerates processing but also enhances stakeholder trust and satisfaction. Systematically, that. It means less rework, less back-and-forth communication, and finally, a smoother process.

3.3 Most Affected Departments or Steps

Processes rarely exist in isolation; they cut across departmental boundaries and involve a variety of procedures. If you identify the most affected departments or procedural steps, you can ascertain where bottlenecks are and why.

For instance, a department which processes complex approvals might see greater delay simply because it is short of staff or because the process is unnecessarily complex [16]. Or some departments may have older systems that don't communicate well with other ones, resulting in information silos and delays. This is an important observation because it allows organizations to target interventions where they will be most effective. Instead of a diffuse, unfocused effort, efforts can be focused—maybe through the purchase of specific team training, workflow redesign, or refreshing software tools. Solving at the departmental level is more likely to produce disproportionate improvements to the overall process.

3.4 Yearly/Quarterly Trend of Delays

Looking at trends over time gives insight that a single snapshot won't. A graph showing yearly or quarterly trends of delays enables problems to be identified if they are seasonal (e.g., more delays in certain months), cyclical, or steadily declining/improving. For instance, if quarters-end delays are consistently peaking, this could be an indication of workload spikes that necessitate the reallocation of resources temporarily. If the trend line dips consistently after an intervention, it indicates that the optimization measures were indeed effective. Trend analysis also facilitates forecasting and planning. Knowing how delays progress allows for more effective capacity planning, budgeting, and risk management. It keeps leadership in the know about when and where pressure points will arise, so they can plan instead of reacting later.

3.5 Pipeline Time Reduction Before vs. After Engineering Intervention

Finally, measuring pipeline time saving gives a holistic view of how process design and engineering impact end-to-end performance. Pipeline time traverses each step, from origin to destination, with processing, approval, checking, and final delivery. By comparing overall pipeline time before and after intervention, organizations can measure improvements not just in individual tasks, but the overall process. This total savings is a measure of increased coordination, reduced wait times, faster decision-making, and less rework. Information of this type is invaluable in portraying the business payback on engineering activities to stakeholders. It shows that spending on technology, process redesigning, or training employees yields in real operations payback.

4 Discussion

At the heart of every data-driven improvement project is bringing important conclusions to life. Those conclusions are not figures or numbers; they're a story about how an operation works, where it breaks down, and where it's thriving. By studying data closely, trends appear—indicating which aspects of the system are persistently leading to delays or denials, and which stages are working well. This definition transforms uninterpreted data into actionable information, allowing decision makers to direct intervention efforts at what will have the greatest impact on what is being measured. With this view, most inefficiencies are found to be the result of bottlenecks—those points in the process where work piles up, waiting for limited resources, manual signatures, or time-consuming checks. These are bottlenecks because these processes are largely outdated, transmitted in bits and pieces, or under-automated. For instance, a department with paperwork-laden documentation will lead approvals to be slow in coming, with the cascading effect felt in the following stages. Inefficiencies also occur when data are repeated or input inaccurately and must be spent hours correcting.

Data engineering here has an enabling role to perform. With advanced data pipelines, automated cross-checks with the data, and real-time analytics, engineering teams can shed light on these delays with unprecedented clarity. Data engineering software is used to integrate and consolidate information from various sources—electronic health records, billing software, scheduling systems—and translate it into comprehendible and actionable forms. The advantage of such an improvement is a direct translation to cost savings and time savings. Eliminating delays lessens cycle time, allowing more cases to be processed in the same amount of time or with fewer staff members. It is an easy operation cost—costless overtime, less temp employees, and less penalty fees for being late. Moreover, denial reduction saves dollars and valuable staff time on the administrative end in rework, appeals, and corrections. Apart from internal efficiency, these savings have a profound effect on health care organizations, providers, and patients. To organizations, efficient processes enhance financial solidity and regulatory compliance. But the road to these kinds of improvements is rarely smooth to execute. The environment of healthcare is typically complex, with existing legacy systems installed, strict privacy mandates, and diverse user requirements. Technical challenges include maintaining data accuracy, promoting interoperability among different systems, and protecting patient data based on regulatory mandates like HIPAA. Organizational resistance may be due to resistance to change, variations in digital literacy abilities within staff, and the reality that loads of training are needed. Further, it demands responsible change management and communication to get stakeholders—from clinical leaders to IT specialists—aligned. Additionally, there are obstacles, but successful implementations show how, with responsible planning, stakeholder engagement, and phased testing, these obstacles can be overcome. Bottom line, the reward is a more responsive, efficient, patient-centered health system (Tables 3, 4 and 5).

Table 3. Identified *Bottlenecks and Inefficiencies in Preauthorization Workflow*

Workflow Stage	Bottleneck Identified	Impact
Submission	Manual form entry, inconsistent formats	Time delays, frequent rework
Documentation Review	Incomplete or non-standard documentation	Requests for more information
Payer Communication	Email/fax-based communication	Slow response times
Decision-Making	Lack of clinical context in preauth requests	Higher likelihood of denials
Feedback Loop	No real-time tracking	Uncertainty for providers and patients

Table 4. Impact *of Data Engineering Interventions*

Intervention	Function	Result
Data Pipeline Integration	Unified data from EMRs and billing systems	Improved data consistency
Automated Eligibility & Documentation Checks	Pre-checks prior to submission	Reduced incomplete requests by 45%

(continued)

Table 4. (*continued*)

Intervention	Function	Result
Predictive Modeling	Flagged likely denials	Allowed proactive documentation corrections
Real-Time Dashboards	Workflow visibility	30% faster communication with payers
Workflow Automation	Auto-routing and escalation	Reduced average precut time by 3–5 days

Table 5. Integration of *Potential with Major EHR Systems*

EHR System	Integration Method	Compatibility with Solution
Epic	HL7, FHIR APIs, Smart on FHIR Apps	High – Supports real-time data exchange
Cerner	Ignite APIs, Millennium platform	Moderate – Requires some customization
Allscripts	FHIR, proprietary APIs	Moderate – Integration achievable
Meditech	M-AT, FHIR via third-party connectors	Low – Limited native API support

5 Conclusion

Taking the project overall, the contributions are extensive and many. The key contribution is in rethinking and re-designing healthcare workflows using advanced data analysis and engineering. By systematic identification and removal of inefficiencies, the project has re-arranged the earlier proprietary and kludgy workflows to lean, open, and measurable ones. It's not a question of incremental improvement but re-writing the very dynamics of healthcare delivery. Maybe the most precious dividend of this effort is actual improvement in patient care and business efficiency. Decrease in delays and denials isn't something that happens in a vacuum—there are straightforward ways in which patient experience and patient outcomes are directly affected. With processes flowing faster and more predictably, patients face fewer obstacles to early diagnosis, therapy, and follow-up. Such speed might be life-preserving when timely treatment is critical. Moreover, more automation requires greater process efficiency, data consolidation, and workflow prioritization, allowing clinicians to utilize their available time and capability more efficiently. Instead of being bogged down by administrative work, care providers can emphasize clinical judgment, patient prioritization, and integrated care—functions that cannot be replicated by technology. Across the immediate environment within which this initiative began, the strategy has scalability and generalizability. The methods used—utilizing data to expose underlying trends, treating underlying versus surface causes, and reacting iteratively to minimize complexity—transcend any health care setting. Whether it is in large city hospitals, rural health clinics, or specialty treatment centers, the underlying strategy differs in complexity and scope. Notably, this is attributed to how the technology modularity addresses the typical problems of health care systems such as data silos, process delays, and resource limitations. By enabling the adaptability of the framework to suit local infrastructures and requirements, institutions worldwide can embrace and gain from these innovations.

To other health-care organizations that wish to follow the same, there should be a highly structured and thought-through process. Technology alone is not the answer. There needs to be implementation with leadership, clinical personnel, IT personnel, and administrative personnel involvement. It must foster a culture conducive to change, respect for information-based decision-making, and always put the patient first.

6 Future Work

Starting with the application of AI and machine learning to predict denials in real time, the key shift here is from reaction to planning. The past has traditionally had healthcare providers waiting for a claim to be denied before they work on issues, which leads to costly delays and rework. Using AI/ML, these vast amounts of historical claims data and operational data can be mined for subtle patterns that may be missed by humans—complicated patterns of correlation among document error types, patient populations, treatment codes, or even minimal timing anomalies. Real-time prediction enables the system to flag potentially problematic claims when they are being processed or submitted, with autosuggestions or auto-corrections. This not only accelerates the approval process but reduces administrative overhead, since staff can focus on exceptions rather than conducting routine checks. These models become increasingly sophisticated over time, more data sources and feedback being incorporated to improve their predictive ability, so they continue to streamline the workflow and reduce denial rates. Providers get real-time notice of denials, partial approval, or additional information requests so they can react swiftly (Fig. 2).

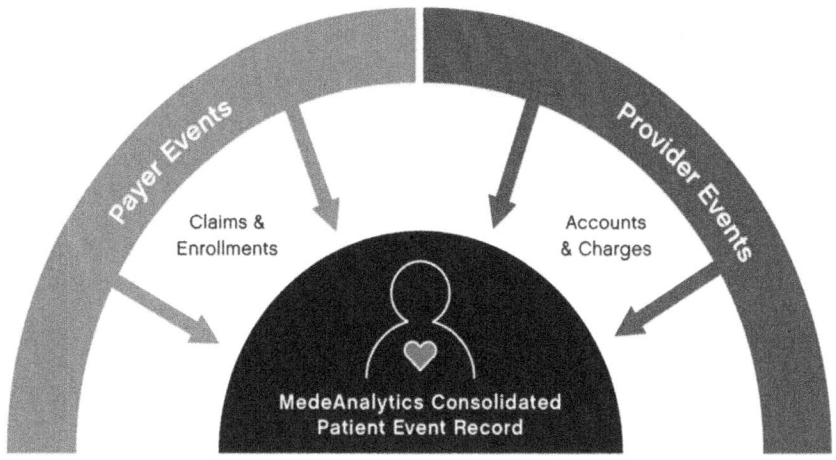

Fig. 2. Bridging the payer/ provider data Gap

Furthermore, this integration causes common platforms of compliance and documentation necessity to be created, which reduces variability and error rates. In effect, the system evolves from an adversarial, transactional model to a cooperative and data-driven collaboration for all stakeholders.

Transparency tools that confront patients-consumers fill a very significant gap in the healthcare experience. Too often, patients are left in the dark regarding why a claim was denied, what they need to do to fix it, or how long it will take. This unpredictability can result in frustration, loss of trust, and even financial loss. By providing patients with clear, timely visibility into their claim status, denial reason, and actionable next steps, healthcare organizations engage patients as active partners in the care process. These can be mobile applications, web portals, or patient communication systems overlaid on top of current systems, providing personalized explanations in simple language rather than technical jargon. Increased transparency reduces patient anxiety and administrative concern, lessening the burden on support staff (Table 6).

Table 6. Future Work Directions

Focus Area	Description	Potential Benefits
AI/ML for Real-time Denial Prediction	• Apply machine learning models to predict denials at submission time	• Preventing delays • Guide staff in real-time • Improve approval accuracy
Integration with Payer Systems	• Establish APIs and automated feedback channels with insurers	• Reduce communication delays • Enable dynamic rule updates • Faster resolutions

(*continued*)

Table 6. (*continued*)

Focus Area	Description	Potential Benefits
Patient-facing Transparency Tools	• Develop dashboards or portals that show pre-auth status and expected timelines to patients	• Improve trust • Reduces uncertainty • Empowers patient involvement
Federated Data Systems	• Enable cross-institutional data sharing without compromising privacy	• Enhances model accuracy • Supports collaborative learning • Broader insights

References

1. Casalino, L.P., et al.: What does physician practices cost to interact with health insurance plans? Health Aff. (Millwood) **28**(Suppl1), w533–w543 (2009)
2. Gandhi, T.K., Feeley, T.W., Bell, S.K.: Realizing the potential of learning health systems. NEJM Catal. **6**(5) (2020)
3. Khatri, V., Brown, C.V.: Designing data governance. Commun. ACM **53**(1), 148–152 (2010)
4. Raghupathi, W., Raghupathi, V.: Big data analytics in healthcare: promise and potential. Health Inf. Sci. Syst. **2**(3) (2014)
5. Harris, D., Smith, E.: Benchmarking provider performance in preauthorization. J. Med. Pract. Manag. **35**(5), 234–243 (2020)
6. Nelson, M., Kapoor, A.: Workflow mapping for healthcare revenue cycle analysis. Healthc. Financ. Manag. J. **75**(6), 48–55 (2021)
7. Microsoft Power BI Team: Healthcare Dashboards: Design and Automation. Microsoft Industry Reports (2020)
8. Lee, R., Choudhary, N.: A framework for end-to-end optimization in prior authorization. J. Healthc. Process Improv. **7**(1), 19–33 (2019)
9. The Advisory Board: Strategies to Streamline Prior Authorization and Reduce Administrative Burden. Advisory Board Insights (2021)

Pairwise Clustering on Numerical Datasets by Translation

Jiajie Yang and Jessica Chen(✉)

University of Windsor, Windsor, ON N9B 3P4, Canada
{yang4q,xjchen}@uwindsor.ca

Abstract. The pairwise clustering problems seek an optimal partition of a given set of data points according to their pairwise similarity or distance. The problems have been extensively studied with well-known results in the literature. When the pairwise relationship is expressed in both positive and negative values, the clustering possesses the property that the number of clusters need not be given, and promising techniques have been explored in this setting to reach provable global optimality efficiently by way of integer linear programming. The techniques are developed for categorical datasets. In this paper, we present a new perspective on problem definitions on numerical datasets, offering a pathway to extend these established exact global optimization methods to the realm of numerical data. This is done by introducing a negation followed by a parameterized origin-translation to the pairwise distances. We present our study on the impact of the translation on the optimal number of clusters, the computation time, and the clustering results. The insights gained from the study offer valuable guidance in the informed selection of appropriate clustering techniques and parameter settings.

Keywords: Clustering techniques · Clique partitioning problem · Min-sum κ-clustering problem · Global optimization · Integer linear programming

1 Introduction

Clustering [2–7, 9, 10, 14–21, 23, 26] refers to the methods we use to group a set of data points (also called objects, samples, etc.) in the best way according to their similarity. Being one of the most popular techniques for unsupervised machine learning, it has received a wide range of applications. In a clinical setting, for example, it can be used to categorize patients based on their clinical features, genetic profiles, or responses to treatment. It can also be applied to the analysis of medical images, helping to identify tumours or other abnormalities by grouping pixels with similar characteristics. In a business sector, for example, clustering customers with similar preferences can lead to personalized recommendations and enhanced customer satisfaction.

Many clustering methods have been extensively studied in the past several decades, jointly forming a rich literature on this topic for applications and advanced study. The density-based clustering [10], for example, groups data points with special consideration to the number of data points in a specified radius around each point, with DBSCAN emerging as its most popular family of algorithms. Centre-based clustering, for another example, partitions the data points into groups according to the distance between each data point and the centre of all the data points in the group. This gives rise to another family of clustering techniques where k-means (see, e.g., [15]) turns out to be one of the most popular.

In this paper, we explore pairwise clustering strategies. In pairwise clustering [2–7,9,14,17–20], the ultimate goal is to partition the data in the best way according to the pairwise similarity or distance among the data points. When this pairwise relationship does not exist in the dataset, they are typically calculated from the defined similarity or distance between any two data points. The *clique partitioning problem* (CPP) [3,5,14,17,18,20] was originally studied in this setting typically for categorical datasets, while the *min-sum clustering problem* [2,4,9,19] has been studied in this setting typically for numerical datasets. The major difference between them stems from the fact that the similarity between two data points in a categorical dataset can have both positive and negative values, while the distance between two data points in a numerical dataset usually carries only nonnegative values. When the input distance values are all nonnegative, the min-sum clustering problem has a trivial solution, and to avoid that, additional constraints are used. In the *min-sum κ-clustering problem*, for example, the data points are required to be partitioned into a specific number of clusters. In CPP, on the other hand, the number of clusters is part of the optimal solution.

Both of the above pairwise clustering problems are NP-hard [22,24], and they are examined in our work within the context of exact global optimization. Many popular clustering algorithms provide efficient executions, but with no guarantee that the final solution obtained upon the termination of the algorithms is the best possible (globally optimal). The study of exact global optimization focuses on provable global optimality. Although the study is very often restricted to small datasets only, it serves as a foundational and theoretical endeavour to benchmarking and understanding the limits of clustering techniques, identifying limitations of the heuristics, and providing guidance to the development and evaluation of the more practical and efficient algorithms.

Our approach to achieving global optimality involves leveraging existing Integer Linear Programming (ILP) solvers, which are powerful mathematical programming tools that utilize various techniques to find provable global optimal solutions for a wide range of problems. Promising ILP formulations have been explored in the literature for CPP to reach global optimality efficiently. These have been developed for the clustering of categorical datasets.

We introduce a novel approach to defining clustering problems to enable the adaptation of the CPP method to the analysis of numerical datasets. The numerical data clustering problem is formulated using a pairwise similarity measure defined as the negative of the distance between data points, with the origin translated by a parameter δ. When δ is zero, this formulation reduces to the well-known min-sum clustering problem. By introducing a positive origin translation ($\delta > 0$), we can leverage the CPP method and replace the *required number of clusters* with an *optimal number of clusters* determined by the CPP algorithm.

We present our study on the impact of the translation on the optimal number of clusters, the computation time, and the clustering results. When approaching a clustering task, we often possess some prior knowledge or intuition regarding the likely number of clusters, potentially suitable problem definitions, and reasonable similarity or distance metrics, etc. The insights gained from the present study on the impact of the translation offer valuable guidance in the informed selection of appropriate clustering techniques and parameter settings. Our key contributions are summarized as follows:

First, we present our study on the relationship between the magnitude of the translation δ and the resulting optimal number of clusters identified by a CPP algorithm.

- We demonstrate that a given translation δ may yield multiple distinct optimal numbers of clusters.
- We present our findings that reveal a decreasing trend in the optimal number of clusters as the value of δ increases. The fact that we no longer need the input of the required number of clusters is due to the specific amount of δ shaping the clustering objective, a relationship hinted at by the decreasing trend in the resulting optimal number of clusters.
- In addition to the decreasing trend, we establish a theoretical result demonstrating that at least one of the optimal numbers of clusters obtained for a specific translation δ remains optimal for sufficiently small increases in the value of δ.

Second, we present our comparative study between solving the CPP with translation δ ($\delta > 0$) and solving the min-sum κ-clustering problem ($\delta = 0$). This comparison is conducted under the specific condition that the input of the required number of clusters for the min-sum κ-clustering problem is precisely one of the optimal numbers of clusters derived from solving the CPP with the translation δ.

- In regard to the computation efficiency, we show a significant speed advantage for solving the CPP with a translation δ compared to solving the min-sum κ-clustering problem with the same ILP solver.
- To quantify the changes in the problem definition with varying amounts of the translation, we present a mathematical formulation to measure the difference between the original problem ($\delta = 0$) and the problem with a specific translation ($\delta > 0$). The resulting difference in clustering solutions is then evaluated using a clustering similarity metric. Our findings indicate that the similarity among the obtained optimal clustering decreases as the value of δ increases, for which we offer an intuitive explanation.

The experimental evaluations were conducted using ILP solvers, with each solver running until the first optimal solution is identified. We note that, with our experiments relying on existing ILP solvers, any conclusions drawn from these results may exhibit some degree of solver dependency. While various optimization solvers are viable, we have chosen to use the Gurobi Optimizer and IBM ILOG Cplex Studio. They represent well-established and reliable choices within the field.

A comprehensive quantitative analysis will be reported in our future work.

The rest of the paper is organized as follows. In Sect. 2, we introduce the preliminaries and the related work. In Sect. 3, we explain the meaning of the translation of the origin in terms of ILP problem formulation. The relationship between the magnitude of the translation and the obtained optimal number of clusters is presented in Sect. 4. Section 5 includes the study on the impact of the translation on the computation time and the optimal solutions. Some concluding remarks are given in Sect. 6.

2 Preliminaries and Related Work

In this section, we provide an introduction to the preliminaries and the related work. This includes the ILP formulations of the pairwise clustering problem on categorical datasets (Sect. 2.1) and its possible extension to the numerical datasets (Sect. 2.2).

The symbols and their meanings used in this paper are listed below:

- δ: (the magnitude of) the translation of the origin.
- κ: the number of clusters.
- n: the number of vertices.
- i, j: indices over the vertices.
- h: index over the number of the clusters.
- v, v_i, v_j: vertices.
- $w_{i,j}$: weight on the edge between vertex v_i and v_j.
- $y_{i,j}$: binary decision variable for putting vertex v_i and v_j in a same cluster.
- $x_{i,h}$: binary decision variable for vertex v_i belonging to cluster h.

2.1 CPP on Categorical Data

The pairwise clustering amounts to partitioning the data points into groups in a way so that the sum of the similarity values of all intra-cluster pairwise data points is maximized. In graph theory, this is defined by CPP. Consider an undirected edge-weighted complete graph $\langle V, E, W \rangle$ where, $|V| = n$, $E = V \times V$, $W = \{w_{i,j} \mid 1 \leq i, j \leq n, w_{i,j} \in R\}$. Each vertex $v \in V$ represents a data point and each edge (v_i, v_j) $(1 \leq i, j \leq n)$ is associated with a weight $w_{i,j}$ representing the similarity between the data points represented by v_i and v_j. The CPP is to partition the vertices into subsets, so that the sum of the weights of all those edges with both of its vertices in the same subset is maximized.

The study on the CPP sees a wide range of applications like group technology [20], community detection (see, e.g., [12]), etc. It is mentioned in various works (see, e.g. [5,18]) that this problem is NP-hard, with the proof in [24], and the study of the problem along the approximation approach can be found in, e.g., [7]. Here, we follow the approach of using the well-known ILP solvers like Gurobi Optimizer and IBM ILOG Cplex to reach global optimality.

Our study is based on the following ILP problem formulation [18] (also called the CPP solution in the following for short). Let $V = \{v_1, \ldots, v_n\}$ be a given set of vertices, and let $w_{i,j}$ be the weight between vertex v_i and v_j. Let $y_{i,j}$ be a binary decision variable for $1 \leq i < j \leq n$, where $y_{i,j} = 0$ denotes that v_i and v_j are in two different clusters, and $y_{i,j} = 1$ denotes that v_i and v_j are in the same cluster. The ultimate goal of CPP is to

$$max \sum_{1 \leq i < j \leq n} w_{i,j} y_{i,j} \qquad (1)$$

subject to

$$y_{i,j} + y_{j,k} - y_{i,k} \leq 1 \qquad 1 \leq i < j < k \leq n, w_{i,j} \geq 0 \text{ or } w_{j,k} \geq 0 \qquad (2)$$
$$y_{i,j} - y_{j,k} + y_{i,k} \leq 1 \qquad 1 \leq i < j < k \leq n, w_{i,j} \geq 0 \text{ or } w_{i,k} \geq 0 \qquad (3)$$
$$-y_{i,j} + y_{j,k} + y_{i,k} \leq 1 \qquad 1 \leq i < j < k \leq n, w_{j,k} \geq 0 \text{ or } w_{i,k} \geq 0 \qquad (4)$$
$$y_{i,j} \in \{0,1\} \qquad 1 \leq i < j \leq n \qquad (5)$$

The constraints (2), (3), (4) are called *triangle inequalities*. The constraint (2) expresses the condition that $y_{i,j} = 1$ and $y_{j,k} = 1$ implies that $y_{i,k} = 1$. It ensures that if v_i and v_j are in the same cluster and v_j and v_k are in the same cluster, then v_i and v_k must be in the same cluster. This condition is needed when at least one of the edges (v_i, v_j) and (v_j, v_k) carries a positive weight.

This problem formulation is an enhancement of the same presented in [14]. Better efficiency is reached by reducing redundant constraints [18]. Further improvement of the above and other proposed solutions to the CPP for efficiency could be found in [5,17]. Similar triangle inequalities have been explored to formulate the linear relaxation to the exact k-means clustering problem [1].

The most important thing to note here is that the problem formulation (1)–(5) is not tied to the number of clusters. Consequently, if all similarity values $w_{i,j}$ are positive, the problem has a trivial solution where all data points are grouped into a single cluster. On the other hand, if all $w_{i,j}$ are negative, the problem also has a trivial solution where each data point belongs to its own cluster. Therefore, we are only interested in situations where some weights are positive and some others are negative. These situations typically happen when we work on categorical datasets. With a categorical dataset, the similarity values between two data points are calculated from the agreement of their categorical features, very often resulting in both positive (similar) and negative (dissimilar) values.

2.2 Extending CPP to Numerical Data

In the research literature, the (pairwise) min-sum clustering problem that has been studied (see, e.g., [2,4,9,19]) amounts to partitioning the data points into groups in a way so that the sum of the distance values of all intra-cluster pairwise data points is minimized.

Clearly, given that all distance values are positive, the best way to partition the vertices is to put all of them into one single group. To avoid that, more information or conditions are added. A typical additional constraint to avoid the trivial solution is to require the number of clusters (denoted by κ in the following) to be a specific value. That is, we have the min-sum κ-clustering problem. The proof that the min-sum κ-clustering problem is NP-hard can be found in [22], followed by an array of research results on its study (see, e.g., [2,4,9,19]).

Instead of providing input κ, an alternative way to approach the min-sum clustering problem is to convert the distance into similarity, then translate the origin of the similarity space so that we can have both positive and negative similarity values. There are different ways to convert the distance to the similarity so that two data points are more similar when their distance is smaller, and they are more dissimilar when their distance is larger. Here we consider obtaining the pairwise similarity by negating the distance value.

The idea of obtaining similarity values from the distance values is not new. In [6], the maxsat (maximum satisfiability) approach was proposed to the correlation clustering problem, where pairwise similarity values are obtained from some numerical datasets by converting the distance values and shifting to the $[-0.5, +0.5]$ range.

This alternative approach allows for the application of CPP solutions without requiring the input κ. In the following, we present our study on this alternative.

3 Translation of Origin

In this section, we provide an ILP formulation of the min-sum κ-clustering problem and introduce our new problem definition.

3.1 Formulation of the Min-Sum κ-Clustering Problem

Analogous to the ILP formulation of the CPP, we can formulate the min-sum κ-clustering problem where κ is given. The following shows one of the possibilities. It is formulated as a maximization problem where $w_{i,j}$ represents the negated distance (called similarity below) between data point i and j.

Let $x_{i,h}$ for $1 \leq i \leq n$ and $1 \leq h \leq \kappa$ be binary decision variables, where $x_{i,h} = 0$ indicates that data point i is not in cluster h, and $x_{i,h} = 1$ indicates that data point i is in cluster h. With $x_{i,h}$ and the previous decision variables $y_{i,j}$, we can formulate the problem like this:

$$\max \sum_{1 \leq i < j \leq n} w_{i,j} y_{i,j} \qquad (6)$$

$$\sum_{1 \leq h \leq \kappa} x_{i,h} = 1 \qquad\qquad 1 \leq i \leq n \qquad (7)$$

$$\sum_{1 \leq i \leq n} x_{i,h} \geq 1 \qquad\qquad 1 \leq h \leq \kappa \qquad (8)$$

$$x_{i,h} + x_{j,h} - y_{i,j} \leq 1 \qquad 1 \leq i < j \leq n,\ 1 \leq h \leq \kappa \qquad (9)$$

$$x_{i,h} - x_{j,h} + y_{i,j} \leq 1 \qquad 1 \leq i < j \leq n,\ 1 \leq h \leq \kappa \qquad (10)$$

$$x_{i,h}, y_{i,j} \in \{0,1\} \qquad 1 \leq i < j < k \leq n,\ 1 \leq h \leq \kappa \qquad (11)$$

The constraint (7) makes sure that each data point is assigned to exactly one cluster. The constraint (8) guarantees that the resulting number of clusters is exactly κ. The constraint (9) requires that $y_{i,j}$ be set to 1 if both $x_{i,h}$ and $x_{j,h}$ are set to 1 for some cluster h. The constraint (10) requires that $y_{i,j}$ be set to 0 if $x_{i,h}$ is set to 1 and $x_{j,h}$ is set to 0 for some cluster h.

In the following, we will use the min-sum κ-clustering solution to refer to formulation (6)–(11). This formulation, unfortunately, does not yield efficient execution in general compared to the triangle inequality one. The inefficiency is primarily attributed to the constraints on the (required) number of clusters, and this is a common characteristic of other similar ILP formulations for the min-sum κ-clustering problem.

3.2 Introducing New Problem Definition

In order to apply the triangle inequality formulation to the min-sum clustering problem, we consider translating the origin of the similarity space.

We will use *similarity by δ* to refer to the similarity obtained by translating the origin of the similarity space to -δ, where $\delta \geq 0$. We will use *problem at δ* to refer to the CPP problem when the origin of the similarity space is translated to -δ.

The range of δ is $[0, \delta_{max}]$, where $\delta_{max} = \max\{|w_{i,j}|\ |\ 1 \leq i, j \leq n\}$ is the largest pairwise distance among all data points. It is the smallest δ value beyond which all weights will become positive, and the problem becomes trivial.

In terms of ILP formulation, the change of the CPP problem introduced by the translation of the origin is reflected only in the objective function, with the constraints remaining the same. Let $w_{i,j}$ be the *similarity by 0*, and $w'_{i,j}$ the *similarity by δ*. Then we have that $w'_{i,j} = w_{i,j} + \delta$ for all $1 \leq i, j \leq n$ and the objective function for the *problem at δ* is

$$\sum_{1 \leq i < j \leq n} w'_{i,j} y_{i,j}$$
$$= \sum_{1 \leq i < j \leq n} (w_{i,j} + \delta) y_{i,j}$$
$$= \sum_{1 \leq i < j \leq n} w_{i,j} y_{i,j} + \delta \sum_{1 \leq i < j \leq n} y_{i,j}$$

Here, $\sum_{1 \leq i < j \leq n} w_{i,j} y_{i,j}$ is the objective function of the *problem at 0*. Clearly, when $\delta = 0$, the problem reduces to the min-sum clustering problem. When $\delta > 0$, the difference between the objective function of the *problem at 0* and that of the *problem at δ* is $\sum_{1 \leq i < j \leq n} y_{i,j}$ multiplied by δ.

3.3 Experimental Setting

In the following sections, we present our study on the impact of the translation of origin on the optimal number of clusters, and the relationship between solving the CPP with translation δ ($\delta > 0$) and solving the min-sum κ-clustering problem ($\delta = 0$).

We have performed experiments based on four numerical datasets from the machine learning repository of the University of California, Irvine:

- The iris dataset [11]. This is widely used in statistics and machine learning. It has 150 instances and 4 features.
- The glass identification dataset [13]. This is used in forensic science to identify the type of glasses. It has 214 instances and 9 features.
- The wine quality dataset. This is used to model the quality of the red wine based on the physicochemical tests [8]. It has 1599 instances and 11 features.
- The breast cancer dataset [25] that is used for the diagnosis of the disease. It has 569 instances and 30 features.

Given that both the CPP and the min-sum κ-clustering problem are NP-hard and we work on exact global optimization, the experiments are performed mostly on subsets of these datasets with randomly selected samples so that the experiments can be done within a reasonable time. All the optimal solutions obtained from the experiments are provably globally optimal.

All the experiments are performed by running Gurobi Optimizer 9.0.2 and Cplex Studio 22.1.1. The former is executed on a MacBook Air with a 1.6 GHz Dual-Core Intel Core i5 and 8 GB memory, and the latter on an AMD EPYC 7742 64-Core Processor server machine shared by multiple users. The variations in the hardware used for experimentation were necessitated by licensing agreements. Specifically, the Gurobi license permitted only single-user operation, whereas the Cplex license facilitated group access. This hardware disparity is not considered a confounding factor in our analysis, because our objective is not to draw direct performance comparisons between Gurobi and Cplex. Instead, we utilize them as two distinct examples of established ILP solvers to demonstrate the applicability and behaviour of our proposed approach.

We used the default configurations of these two solvers, which include presolve, automatic algorithm selection, and cutting planes. The configuration of the solvers could potentially affect the results, because it directly influences how constraints are handled and solutions are selected. This aspect is beyond the scope of our current study.

4 Characteristics of Translations

There are many interesting questions related to the translation of origin. For example, how come before the translation we have to provide the input κ and after the translation, we can derive the (optimal) κ value from the optimal solution? Is there any relationship between the magnitude of the translation and the optimal κ? We provide some insight into answering these questions from both the theoretical and the practical viewpoints.

4.1 Magnitude of Translation vs. Optimal Number of Clusters

First, we show that there is an inherent relationship between the amount of the translation δ and an optimal κ obtained from a CPP solution.

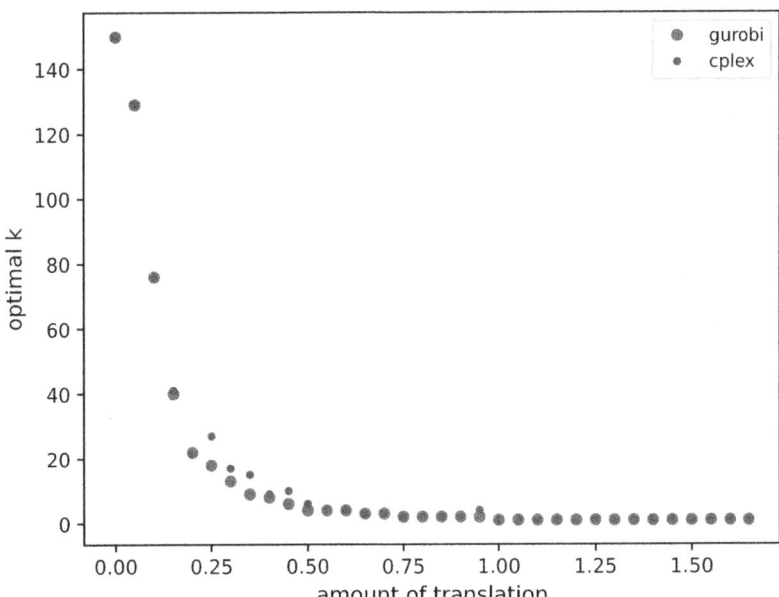

Fig. 1. Optimal number of clusters: iris flower

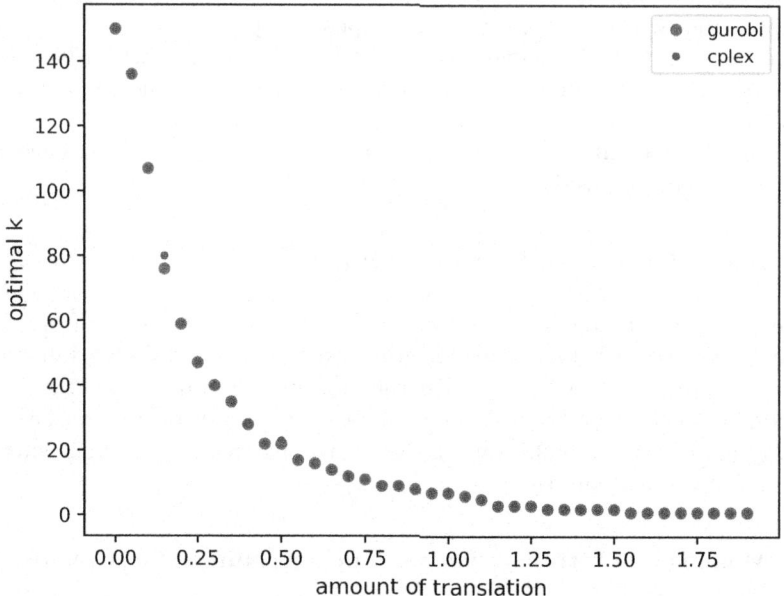

Fig. 2. Optimal number of clusters: glass identification

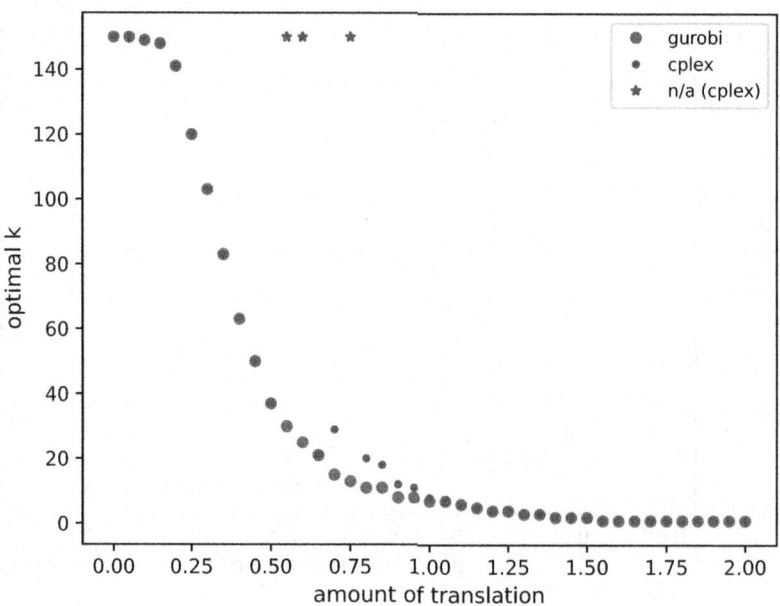

Fig. 3. Optimal number of clusters: red wine

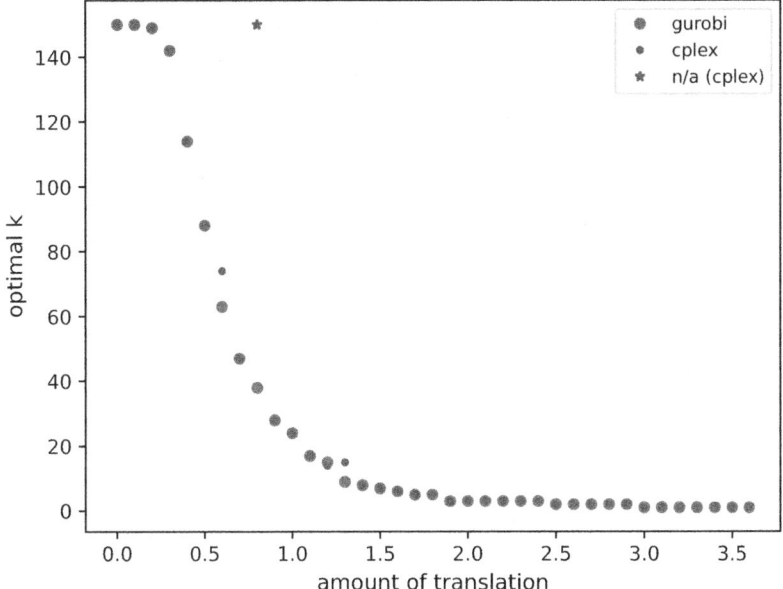

Fig. 4. Optimal number of clusters: breast cancer

Figures 1, 2, 3, 4 show how optimal κ changes by the value of δ. Each big dot or small dot represents an optimal number of clusters obtained from CPP solution with Gurobi Optimizer or with Cplex Studio, respectively, when the origin is translated to δ. A star at the top of a chart denotes that an optimal solution was not obtained. The charts are drawn according to the executions on the data points from the four datasets considered. We take the entire dataset of iris and 150 samples from each of the other datasets. For each selected dataset, we calculated the pairwise Euclidean distance $d_{i,j}$ between data points i and j. The edge weights $w_{i,j}$ in the triangle inequality formulation are obtained by negating the distance, then shifting with δ: $w_{i,j} = - d_{i,j} + \delta$. An optimal κ is obtained when running the triangle inequality formulation with constraints (2)–(5) to the global optimality.

Some executions take so long to run that we need to terminate the execution prematurely. The timer we set up is one hour. Those places where an optimal solution could not be obtained within an hour are denoted by a star in the charts.

Note that for each δ, it is possible to have multiple optimal solutions with different κ values. When performing the experiments, however, we have computed only one optimal solution. Each run is terminated once the first optimal solution is reached. This is because it is hard to reach all optimal solutions within a reasonable time dedicated to the experiments. From Figure ?? we observe that most of the optimal κ values obtained from Gurobi Optimizer and Cplex Studio are the same, yet we do have situations when the two solvers give different optimal

κ values. For example, when $\delta = 0.25$ in the iris dataset, we obtain $\kappa = 18$ from running Gurobi Optimizer and $\kappa = 27$ from running Cplex Studio.

We also observe that when δ increases, the optimal κ values show a decreasing trend. In particular, for each solver, the obtained optimal κ decreases mostly monotonically, with few exceptions. This decreasing trend is consistent with our intuition: When δ takes its minimal value (zero), all the weights are negative, and the optimal number of clusters is equal to the number of data points. When δ keeps increasing, the data points will get more and more friendly to each other: All the weights will keep increasing, and so will the sum of the negative weights. The number of negative-valued edges never increases and has a trend of decreasing. Therefore, generally speaking, there should be a trend of getting smaller and smaller κ values when δ keeps increasing. When δ takes its maximal value in its range, all the weights are positive. At this point, the optimal number of clusters becomes one.

It is interesting, although beyond the scope of this paper, to explore the mathematical conditions under which an optimal κ will increase when δ increases.

4.2 Continuity of Optimal Number of Clusters

Given that the optimal numbers of clusters are natural numbers and the values of the similarity can be translated to any point in $[0, \delta_{max}]$, we present the following relationship between optimal κ and δ: For any δ, among the optimal solutions to the problem at δ, at least one of them will continue to be optimal when δ increases. Some trivial problem instances are excluded from consideration. These include the graph with only one vertex and the graphs where all the weights are zero.

Proposition 1. *Suppose that there exist i and j ($i \neq j$), so that $w_{i,j} > 0$. For any δ_0, there exists an optimal solution s_0 to the problem at δ_0 and an $\varepsilon_0 > 0$, so that for any ε where $0 < \varepsilon \leq \varepsilon_0$, s_0 is also an optimal solution to the problem at $\delta_0 + \varepsilon$.*

To prove the correctness of this statement, we define d to be the smallest difference between an optimal value and a non-optimal value to the problem at δ_0. Then define $\varepsilon_0 = d/(n^2+1)$, where n is the number of data points. Let s_0 be an optimal solution to the problem at $\delta_0 + \varepsilon_0$. It can be proven that s_0 is also an optimal solution to the problem at δ_0. Then for any ε where $0 < \varepsilon \leq \varepsilon_0$, it can be proven that s_0 is also an optimal solution to the problem at $\delta_0 + \varepsilon$. The complete proof will be included in the extended version of this work.

From this proposition, we can draw some conclusions like the following:

- For any specific δ value, if there is only one optimal solution to the problem at δ, this solution will remain optimal to the problem at $\delta + \varepsilon$ for a sufficiently small ε.
- For any specific δ value, in the presence of multiple optimal solutions to the problem at δ, at least one of them will remain optimal to the problem at $\delta + \varepsilon$ for a sufficiently small ε.

- If there are two distinct optimal solutions to the problems at δ_1 and δ_2 ($\delta_1 < \delta_2$) respectively, then there must exist more than one optimal solution to the problem at δ_3 for some $\delta_3 \in [\delta_1, \delta_2]$.

5 The Alternative Path

The translation δ provides a pathway to solving the min-sum κ-clustering problem through the resolution of CPP. The two problems (with $\delta = 0$ and $\delta > 0$ respectively) have distinct and closely related objective functions, formally presented in Sect. 3.2. We argue that when tackling a clustering task, we often possess some prior knowledge or intuition regarding the potentially suitable problem definitions, and may find solving the CPP an acceptable alternative.

Along this alternative path, the constraint on the (required) number of clusters is removed. A question naturally arises: How come before the translation ($\delta = 0$) we need to provide the input κ and after the translation ($\delta > 0$), an optimal κ value can be retrieved from an optimal solution? According to the decreasing trend of the optimal κ presented in the previous section, we come to this understanding of the CPP solution: Although we do not need to specify the number of clusters, the magnitude of translation (δ value) provides additional information that is closely related to the optimal number of clusters derived from solving the CPP.

With this understanding, we have studied the relationship between solving the min-sum κ-clustering problem and solving the related CPP under the following specific condition: for any δ, one of the optimal number of clusters derived from CPP solution for problem at δ is precisely the required number of clusters for solving the min-sum κ-clustering problem. Within this context, we present the impact of the translation on the execution time and on the output of the execution.

5.1 Impact on Execution Time

We are interested in the impact of the translation δ on the execution time we spend obtaining the optimal solutions.

Figures 5, 6, 7, 8 show the computation time of using min-sum κ-clustering solution executed with Gurobi Optimizer and Cplex Studio, respectively. A big dot or small dot represents the computation time of running with Gurobi Optimizer or with Cplex Studio, respectively, corresponding to the situation when the origin is translated to δ. A star (big for Gurobi and small for Cplex) at the top of the charts denotes that an optimal solution was not obtained. These charts are obtained by running 30, 25, 20, and 20 randomly selected samples from the iris dataset, the glass identification dataset, the wine quality dataset, and the breast cancer dataset, respectively. The number of samples to select from each dataset is determined by the criterion of getting most of the execution of the min-sum κ-clustering solution completed within an hour. The computation time

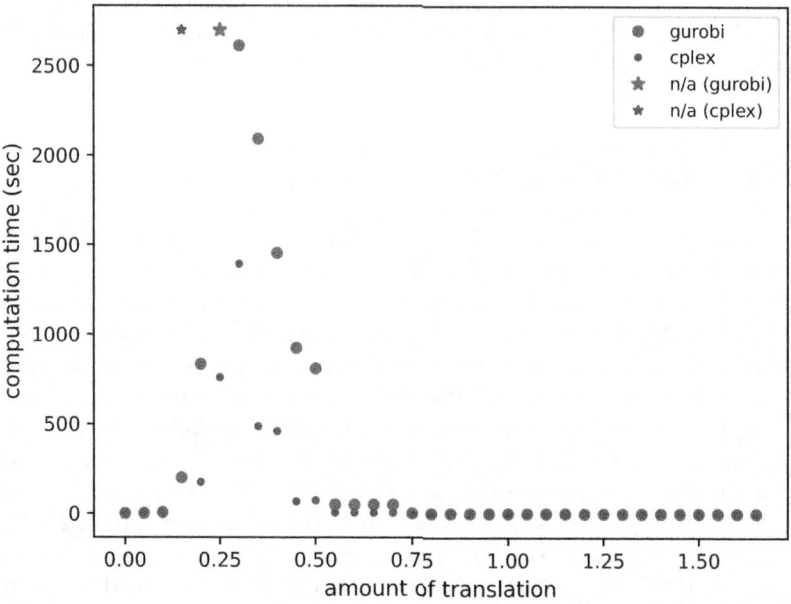

Fig. 5. Computation time (in seconds) of running the min-sum κ-clustering solution: iris flower

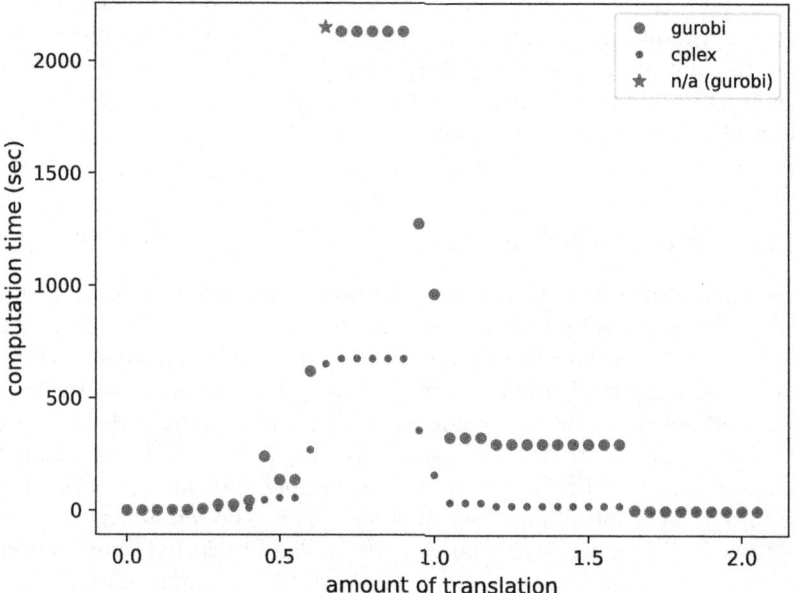

Fig. 6. Computation time (in seconds) of running the min-sum κ-clustering solution: glass identification

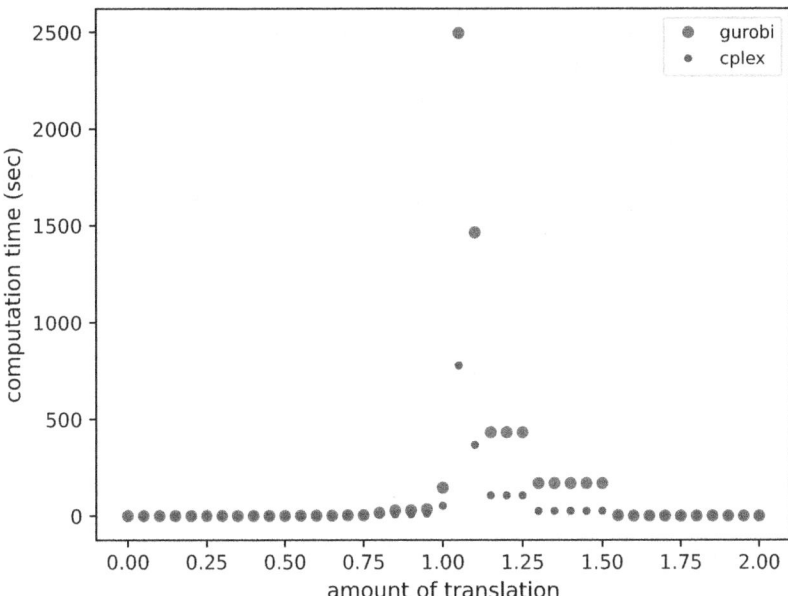

Fig. 7. Computation time (in seconds) of running the min-sum κ-clustering solution: red wine

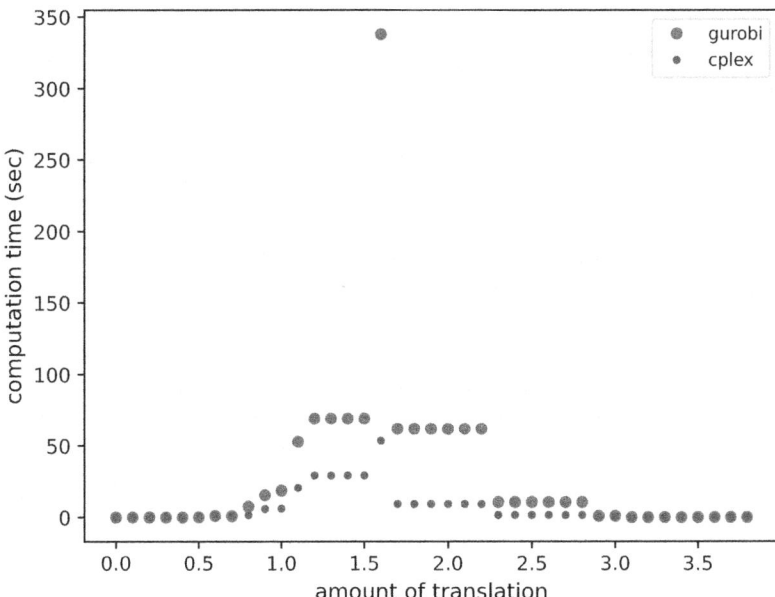

Fig. 8. Computation time (in seconds) of running the min-sum κ-clustering solution: breast cancer

of running the min-sum κ-clustering problem corresponding to each δ value is performed by providing the required number of clusters equal to an optimal κ value obtained when running the CPP solution with the considered δ.

Note that the execution time in these charts does not form a smooth curve. This is a common characteristic of exact global optimization algorithms for NP-hard problems. It contrasts with the predictable behaviour of the deterministic polynomial-time algorithms, where the number of operations grows smoothly with the input. In our setting, the solvers like Gurobi Optimizer and Cplex Studio have an exploratory nature, and their performance can be highly variable depending on the specific problem instance. Consequently, the occurrences of the outliers in the execution time charts are considered normal.

The computation time of running the CPP solution is not shown. For all four datasets and with both Gurobi Optimizer and Cplex Studio, the execution time of the CPP solution is in the range of $[0, 0.3]$, mostly less than 0.1 s, showing the efficiency of this solution: It is significantly faster for almost all the δ values, and for those it runs less efficiently, the difference is quite ignorable. The execution time of the min-sum κ-clustering solution, on the other hand, varies widely. For the iris dataset and the glass identification dataset, it sometimes goes beyond 3600 s. For the wine quality dataset, it varies in the range of $[0, 2496]$ (Gurobi) and $[0, 776]$ (Cplex). For the breast cancer dataset, it varies in the range of $[0, 338]$ (Gurobi) and $[0, 53]$ (Cplex).

5.2 Impact on Clustering Results

Recall that when the origin is translated by δ, the problem is changed in the sense that the objective function is augmented by $\delta \sum_{1 \leq i < j \leq n} y_{i,j}$. Clearly, the bigger the δ is, the more the problem deviates from the original one. Consequently, the bigger the δ is, the more different the clustering result would become.

To guide the selection among acceptable problem definitions and parameter settings in practice, we have adopted the random score function in the scikit-learn library to quantitatively measure the clustering similarity. The score ranges over $[0, 1]$, where a score close to 0 means that the two clustering results are very dissimilar and a score close to 1 means that the two clustering results are very similar.

For each δ, we run the CPP solution first. With the optimal κ obtained from the execution, we then run the min-sum κ-clustering solution, providing this κ for input. Then the clustering obtained from the CPP solution and the clustering obtained from the min-sum κ-clustering solution are compared. Figures 9, 10, 11, 12 illustrate this change in the clustering similarity in the four datasets we consider. A big or small dot is for experiments with Gurobi or Cplex, respectively. A star (big for Gurobi and small for Cplex) indicates that the clustering similarity for the corresponding δ is not available because the execution of the min-sum κ-clustering solution is terminated prematurely. In the Figs. 9, 10, 11, 12, we see that at the beginning of the ranges of δ, the similarity scores stay at 1.0, and towards the end of the ranges of δ, the similarity scores jump to 1.0. We note that the initial ranges of δ where the similarity scores stay at 1.0 correspond to

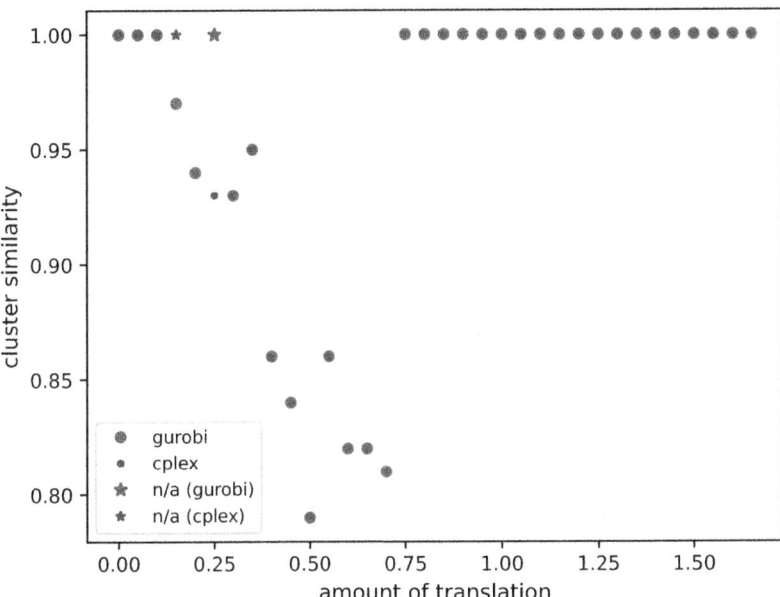

Fig. 9. Clustering similarity between the CPP solution and the min-sum κ-clustering solution: iris flower

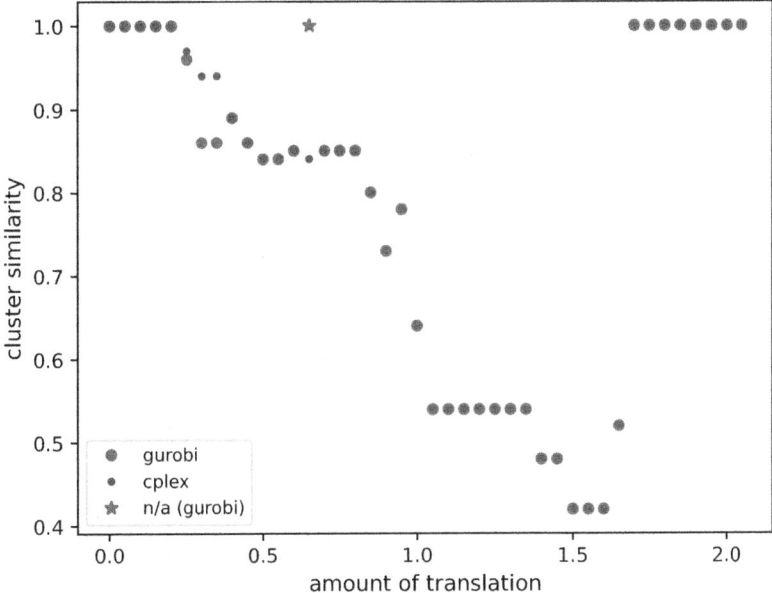

Fig. 10. Clustering similarity between the CPP solution and the min-sum κ-clustering solution: glass identification

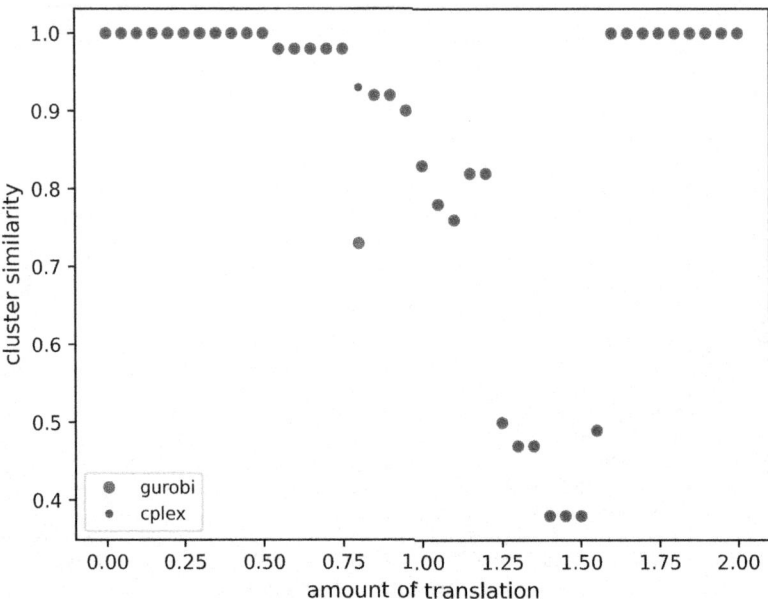

Fig. 11. Clustering similarity between the CPP solution and the min-sum κ-clustering solution: red wine

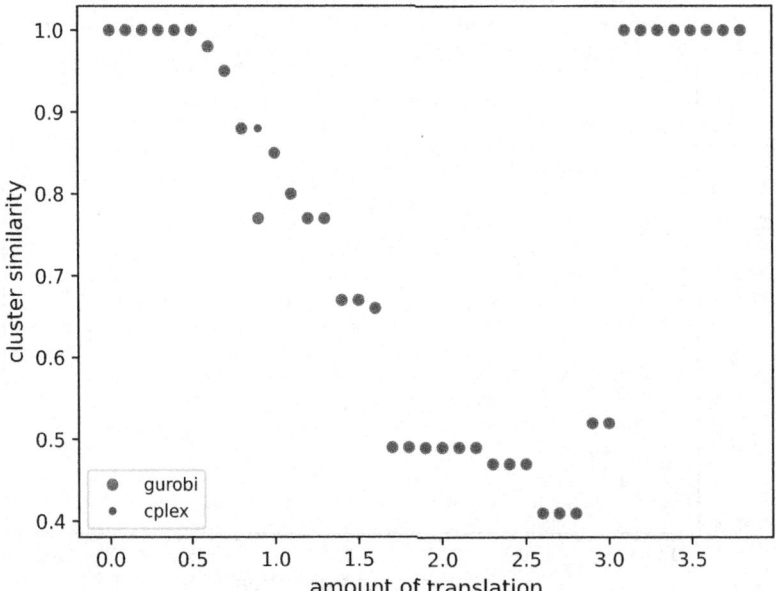

Fig. 12. Clustering similarity between the CPP solution and the min-sum κ-clustering solution: breast cancer

situations when the optimal κ values are equal to the number of data points in the dataset. In these situations, the CPP solution and the min-sum κ-clustering solution lead to the same optimal clustering result. The ending ranges of δ where the similarity scores jump back to 1.0 correspond to situations when the optimal κ values are equal to one. In these situations, the CPP solution and the min-sum κ-clustering solution also lead to the same optimal clustering result. Between the initial range and the ending range of δ where the similarity scores are 1.0, the similarity scores mostly monotonically decrease with the increase of δ, and this is consistent across the four datasets and across the two ILP solvers. More details will be reported in the extended version of this work.

6 Concluding Remarks

In regard to pairwise data clustering, the qualitative data analysis and the quantitative data analysis are two distinct research topics performed on categorical datasets and numerical datasets, respectively. The study on these topics has been advanced along separate lines of research, each leading to numerous promising results. Can we apply the research results for qualitative data analysis not only on categorical datasets but also on the numerical ones? The present work sets the first step towards integrating these two types of datasets for the qualitative data analysis, within the context of exact global optimization of pairwise data clustering.

Like other approaches to NP-hard exact global optimization problems, our proposed work suffers from the scalability issue, which seriously limits the size of the datasets we can use. Despite this, it serves as a foundational endeavour for benchmarking pairwise clustering techniques. Based on the initial experiments, our findings point to a strong relationship between origin translation and the optimal κ, as well as comparable solutions between the CPP and min-sum κ-clustering problems. These findings vigorously advocate for continued and extended studies along this line of research.

References

1. Ágoston, K.C., E.-Nagy, M.: Mixed integer linear programming formulation for k-means clustering problem. Central Eur. J. Oper. Res. **32**(1), 11–27 (2024)
2. Banerjee, S., Ostrovsky, R., Rabani, Y.: Min-sum clustering (with outliers). In: Approximation, Randomization, and Combinatorial Optimization. Algorithms and Techniques (APPROX/RANDOM 2021), vol. 207, p. 16:1–16:16. Leibniz International Proceedings in Informatics (LIPIcs), Germany (2021)
3. Bansal, N., Blum, A., Chawla, S.: Correlation clustering. Mach. Learn. **56**, 89–113 (2004)
4. Bartal, Y., Charikar, M., Raz, D.: Approximating min-sum k-clustering in metric spaces. In: Proceedings of the 33rd Annual ACM Symposium on Theory of Computing, pp. 11–20. ACM, Greece (2001)
5. Belyi, A., Sobolevsky, S., Kurbatski, A., Ratti, C.: Subnetwork constraints for tighter upper bounds and exact solution of the clique partitioning problem. Math. Methods Oper. Res. **98**, 269–297 (2023)

6. Berg, J., Järvisalo, M.: Cost-optimal constrained correlation clustering via weighted partial maximum satisfiability. Artif. Intell. **244**, 110–142 (2017)
7. Charikara, M., Guruswami, V., Wirth, A.: Clustering with qualitative information. J. Comput. Syst. Sci. **71**, 360–383 (2005)
8. Cortez, P., Cerdeira, A., Almeida, F., Matos, T., Reis, J.: Modeling wine preferences by data mining from physicochemical properties. Decis. Support Syst. **47**(4), 547–553 (2009). https://doi.org/10.1016/j.dss.2009.05.016
9. Czumaj, A., Sohler, C.: Small space representations for metric min-sum k-clustering and their applications. In: Thomas, W., Weil, P. (eds.) STACS 2007. LNCS, vol. 4393, pp. 536–548. Springer, Heidelberg (2007). https://doi.org/10.1007/978-3-540-70918-3_46
10. Ester, M., Kriegel, H.P., Sander, J., Xu, X.: A density-based algorithm for discovering clusters in large spatial databases with noise. In: Proceedings of the Second International Conference on Knowledge Discovery and Data Mining, pp. 226–231. ACM, USA (1996)
11. Fisher, R.A.: The use of multiple measurements in taxonomic problems. Annu. Eugenics **7**(2), 179–188 (1936)
12. Fortunato, S.: Community detection in graphs. Phys. Rep. **486**, 75–174 (2010)
13. German, B.: UCI machine learning repository (1987). http://archive.ics.uci.edu/ml/datasets/Glass+Identification. University of California, Irvine, School of Information and Computer Sciences
14. Grötschel, M., Wakabayashi, Y.: A cutting plane algorithm for a clustering problem. Math. Program. **45**, 59–96 (1989)
15. Hua, K., Shi, M., Cao, Y.: A scalable deterministic global optimization algorithm for clustering problems. In: Proceedings of the 38th International Conference on Machine Learning, PMLR 139, pp. 4391–4401. PMLR, Virtual event (2021)
16. von Luxburg, U.: A tutorial on spectral clustering. Znewblock Stat. Comput. **17**, 395–416 (2007)
17. Miyauchi, A., Sonobe, T., Sukegawa, N.: Exact clustering via integer programming and maximum satisfiability. In: Proceedings of the Thirty-Second AAAI Conference on Artificial Intelligence (AAAI 2018), pp. 1387–1394. AAAI, USA (2018)
18. Miyauchi, A., Sukegawa, N.: Redundant constraints in the standard formulation for the clique partitioning problem. Optim. Lett. **9**, 199–207 (2015)
19. Naderi, I., Rezapour, M., Salavatipour, M.R.: Approximation schemes for min-sum k-clustering. In: Proceedings of the 31st Annual European Symposium on Algorithms (ESA 2023), pp. 84:1–84:16. Leibniz International Proceedings in Informatics (LIPIcs), The Netherlands (2023)
20. Oosten, M., Rutten, J., Spieksma, F.: The clique partitioning problem: facets and patching facets. Networks **38**(4), 209–226 (2001)
21. Piccialli, V., Sudoso, A.M., Wiegele, A.: SOS-SDP: an exact solver for minimum sum-of-squares clustering. INFORMS J. Comput. **34**(4), 2144–2162 (2022)
22. Sahni, S., Gonzalez, T.F.: P-complete approximation problems. J. ACM (JACM) **23**, 555–565 (1976)
23. Shi, J., Malik, J.: Normalized cuts and image segmentation. IEEE Trans. Pattern Anal. Mach. Intell. **22**(8), 888–905 (2000)
24. Wakabayashi, Y.: Aggregation of binary relations: algorithmic and polyhedral investigations. Ph.D. thesis, Universität Augsburg (1986)
25. Wolberg, W.H., Street, W.N., Mangasarian, O.L.: Nuclear feature extraction for breast tumor diagnosis. Electron. Imaging **4**(1), 79–86 (1995)
26. Xu, R., Wunsch, D.: A survey of clustering algorithms. IEEE Trans. Neural Netw. **16**(3), 645–678 (2005)

A Customizable Ad-Hoc Java Client that Works with Bare Webservers

Nirmala Soundararajan[1](✉), Lie Qian[1], Ramesh R. Karne[2], and Alexander L. Wijesinha[2]

[1] Chemistry, Computer and Physical Sciences, Southeastern Oklahoma State University, Durant, OK, USA
{nsoundararajan,lqian}@se.edu

[2] Computer and Information Sciences, Towson University, Towson, MD, USA
{rkarne,awijesinha}@towson.edu

Abstract. Bare servers typically communicate with Web browsers or bare clients. In this paper, we design and implement a customizable Java client to communicate with bare servers. It is possible to customize and tailor each client to communicate with a bare server unlike commercial browsers that are the same for all clients. This tailored approach provides flexibility in running different applications in both the server and client and lays a foundation to build customizable Web clients to complement the security strengths of bare servers. Students could also write their own customizable clients to learn about protocols and system internals. Further studies are needed to investigate security weaknesses of these Java clients when used with bare servers.

Keywords: Bare Machine Computing · customizable Java client · bare Webserver

1 Introduction

The Internet provides ubiquitous seamless communication globally between systems using conventional protocols and algorithms. General-purpose computing systems typically rely on some form of an underlying kernel or operating system (OS). There are a variety of OSs used by Internet clients and servers that may be open source (e.g. Linux), or proprietary (e.g. Windows or iOS). There are numerous advantages to the existing approach that allows ordinary users, researchers, enterprises, vendors, service providers and government organizations, regardless of location, to access the Internet, collaborate on projects, and share data.

However, such global access to open systems and information comes at the cost of a loss of privacy, reduced security, and increased opportunities for attackers to compromise systems by exploiting their vulnerabilities. As the number of users and IoT devices continue to grow [1, 2], securing Internet communication becomes increasingly difficult. While security is a primary concern on the Internet today and will remain so in the future, advances in technology coupled with the availability of vast amounts of data bring new cybersecurity challenges.

It has been shown in [3] that bare systems, which do not have an operating system (OS) or kernel, are inherently more secure than conventional systems. However, bare clients and servers are not popular in the real world. In this paper, we propose using bare servers with customizable user-specific clients for small groups of users to communicate securely on the Internet. This is a possible way to divide and conquer the complex security problem in global communication. Customizable clients may be viewed as an intermediate step on the path towards building secure Internet clients and servers in the future using bare systems as shown in Fig. 1. Our customizable clients are written in Java. The system can also be used in curriculum research, where students learn how to build their own customizable clients to communicate with secure bare Webservers. Bare Webservers are useful for understanding the internals of hardware, software and protocols [4, 5].

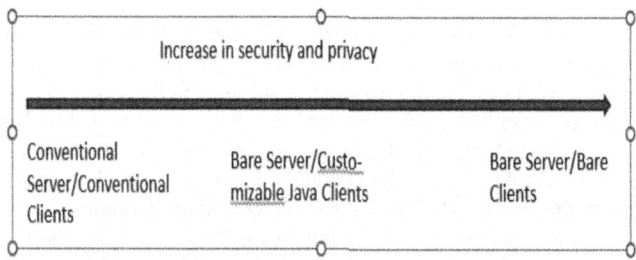

Fig. 1. Security and Privacy Spectrum of Systems.

The main contributions of this paper are listed below:

1) a novel client-server architecture as an alternative to conventional architecture
2) how to build customizable clients that can be extended to serve as sophisticated browsers
3) a non-conventional approach that can be leveraged for building secure systems in the future
4) the design of domain-specific clients and servers that can isolate themselves from access by unauthorized users on the Internet
5) a vision for general-purpose computing systems that do not require the support of a traditional OS.

The rest of this paper is organized as follows. In Sect. 2, we provide the relevant background and motivation for this work. In Sect. 3, we describe the system architecture, and in Sect. 4, we give design and implementation details. In Sect. 5, we describe an experiment on the Internet using a prototype system. Section 6 concludes the paper.

2 Background

The Bare Machine Computing (BMC) paradigm [6] has been used to build systems with inherent security and simplicity by design as an alternative to conventional systems. To the best of our knowledge, there are no general-purpose computing systems other than bare systems that run without the support of some form of an OS or kernel. Most attacks targeting an underlying OS or kernel are eliminated in bare systems except those involving physical security [3]. Due to the absence of an OS or kernel, bare systems [7–9] are easy to design and implement. They are inherently secure because the bare application directly accesses the hardware with its own direct interfaces and device drivers. There is no external software that can be used to compromise a bare application, and bare application code is easier to analyze for security flaws because of its smaller code size. Also, there is no persistent storage in the bare system. These characteristics of bare systems significantly reduce the attack surface and make them less attractive as a target for attacks.

Recently, a customizable bare chat application [10] was built to demonstrate the feasibility of a domain-specific application providing security and privacy for a small group of users. However, this chat application does not have a GUI and other features that would make it convenient to use. There are many browsers in the market that work with a variety of standard Web servers including bare servers. Many options are available in these browsers, but they are available to all users.

This paper describes a possible solution to address the preceding issues by using a bare server and a customizable Java client (CJC). A CJC is built using standard Java classes and each user can tailor the client to their own needs. User interfaces, security protocols, confidentiality and authentication mechanisms, more functionality etc. can be added to the client as needed with the corresponding support at the server.

The proposed approach provides isolation between users and enables each CJC to be customized based on group requirements. Thus, there is no standard CJC for all users. As only a small group of authorized users are allowed to communicate with the bare server [10], security and privacy are improved [3].

3 Architecture

The architecture of bare servers have been detailed in previous work including [11–14]. A bare server runs on a bare machine or device with no operating system or persistent storage in the machine. A bare application is written as a single monolithic executable, which is a self-controlled, self-managed, and self-running entity. Domain-specific bare applications include email [15], VoIP [16], browser [17], editor, text processing, chat [10], or combinations of one or more of the above.

A bare application suite is designed as a single unit that only contains the required functionality and nothing else. The single monolithic executable has one address space. There may be one or more threads within an application suite as needed. Bare systems are self-contained closed systems with no software layers or middleware. An application suite currently runs on Intel processors without any external dependencies. The bare application carried on a USB flash drive includes its own device drivers and all related code (including boot code) needed for execution. Bare systems and applications can be extended to run on any other CPU architecture. The bare-based server is written in C/C++ with some assembly code. In the bare Web server, lean TCP and IP protocol code is integrated with HTTP into the server application.

The bare Web server communicates with CJCs over the Internet as shown in Fig. 2. The CJC uses only Java code and open system modules, and runs on a conventional OS as noted earlier.

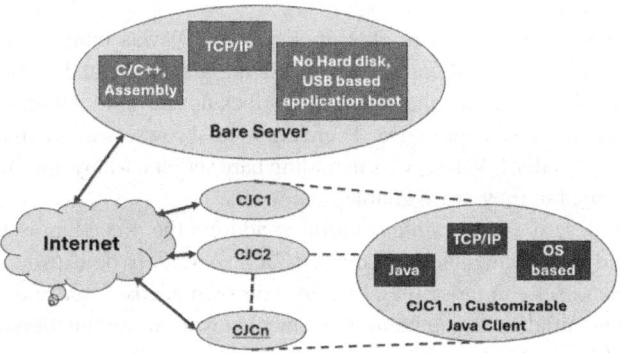

Fig. 2. Customizable Java Clients

The bare server provides the necessary resources and services for a client application, and customization depends on application needs. This customization makes the Java client flexible in that it is not restricted by the constraints of a specific browser when requesting data from the bare server. Per our knowledge, this is the first time that a Java client has been designed and developed to communicate with a bare server. In essence, a CJC accesses the bare Server directly through its program code and not through any browser. Thus, security is already enhanced as browser related security issues have been bypassed. One or more CJCs can be connected to a given bare server. Each CJC is authenticated by the bare server.

4 Design and Implementation

4.1 Server-Design

The bare Web server is based on a monolithic design with all the scheduling, memory, and I/O management along with device drivers, compiled and linked together as one executable. All server code in written in C++/C with some assembly as noted earlier. This

Web server runs at http://www.baremachinecomputing.com. For testing, we specifically use two types of server Web pages: one is the home page and the other pages were previously used in an educational setting [4, 5].

The bare server implements the necessary protocols from the TCP/IP suite, an HTTP parser, and an Intel gigabit Ethernet device driver. The server is multi-threaded and capable of supporting up to 10,000 threads). It does not use a hard disk and there is no OS. There are three types of tasks: a main task, a receive task and an HTTP task. Each request to the server creates one HTTP task and maintains its state until its completion. The receive task receives a packet and processes it as a single thread of execution. The main task can call the receive task and the HTTP task as needed to process requests. More details of the bare Web server design and implementation are given in previous publications such as [7, 8].

This Web server previously worked with conventional Web browsers and bare clients. As a result of this research, it now works with CJCs. The application suite executable code for the server is 160 KB. This executable along with the boot code is placed on a bootable USB, which boots and runs this application suite. It only has minimal functionality for a Web server, which can be extended as needed. As there is no hard disk in a bare system, trivial FTP is used to transfer resource files from a Windows machine to the bare system during the initialization of the server. This version of the Web server does not support TLS as our focus was on designing and implementing CJC and ensuring its correct operation with the server. Since TLS has been previously implemented on the bare Web server [18] and bare text browser, it could be added to this system if needed.

4.2 Client Design

Since the main goal of this paper was to investigate the feasibility of communicating with a bare Web server using a customized OS-based client instead of a conventional Web browser or a bare client, we designed our Java client with off-the-shelf modules present in JavaFX [ref]. This made it easier to design the client due to JavaFX's rich blend of graphics, controls and Web components as shown in Fig. 3. We display Web pages using JavaFX instead of a commercial browser. WebView and WebEngine classes were used to embed the Web content into our Java application. The client application involved the following:

1) *Layout:* We chose a simple BorderPane as the root node in our scene object due to the versatility of BorderPane in arranging visual components on the stage. A navigation bar was laid out at the top to host the control buttons using HBox. The webview was hosted at the center of the layout.
2) *Design:* We designed the client application around JavaFX components to enable our client design to be independent of commercial Web browser design. As a result of our work, users can run a CJC on the Internet to access pages from the bare server. We used the WebEngine class in JavaFX to load and render the Web pages. Likewise, the WebHistory class enabled us to keep track of the visited pages so that we can easily navigate back and forth.
3) *User Interface:* The user interface is kept simple for now with navigation button controls, mouse click events, input data and dialog boxes. We have also added alert dialog boxes for interaction between the application and the user.

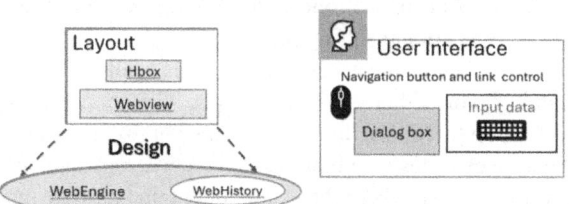

Fig. 3. Client Application

4.3 Client Implementation

The bare Web server implementation is not addressed in this paper as it has been discussed in previous publications referred to earlier. Here, we only describe key parts of the client implementation. We used Visual Studio Code as our development tool for the Java client and JavaFX as our development environment. We also used Microsoft Co-Pilot tool for implementation in a few cases. Several classes from JavaFX were used in the implementation including WebView, WebEngine, WebHistory, BorderPane, and HBox. As discussed in the preceding section, WebView and WebEngine were the primary classes used to access the Web pages from within the client application. BorderPane housed the entire layout and HBox hosted the button controls. We provide only two buttons forward and back and used the WebHistory class as noted above to navigate between the pages. The LoadWorker class was used for monitoring the loading of Web pages from the bare website. We handled all links as mouse click events and created threads. Since our demonstration required handling pdf documents, we also integrated classes related to a PDF viewer. Separate tasks were created for handling files for downloading, previewing etc. as it required considerable I/O. This prevented the user interface from freezing and kept it responsive when the document was being downloaded. Buffers were used to handle file data. Figure 4 shows the entire process flow.

We note that using commercially available browsers instead of CJCs would have limited our ability to customize each client to show information intended only for that client. These browsers would also have constrained us to follow a preset browser design. Moreover, using a CJC instead of a commercial browser eliminates any security risks associated with the browser.

As shown in Fig. 4, when a link pointed to a pdf document, a dialog box asking if the user wanted to download the file was created. If the download option was selected, a separate task was created to start the download of the file in the background. On download success, again a dialog box was used to indicate that the download was successful. We also send a completion status update to the bare server to prevent it from closing the connection to the client.

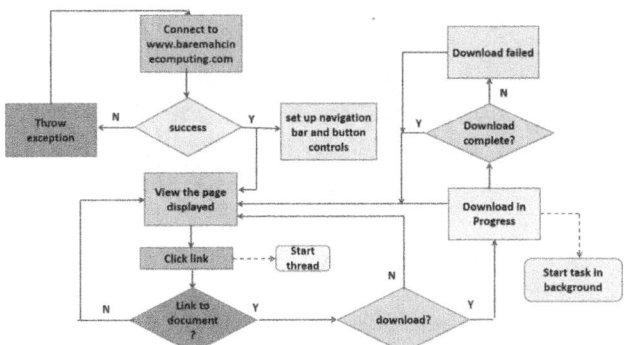

Fig. 4. Client Process Flow

5 Demonstration

To test our CJC application for correct operation, we set up an experiment where the bare server and the CJC were situated in different locations on the Internet. In this setup, we accessed the same bare server pages used in [4, 5] and compared their output with the output from the CJC application. The main goal of this experiment was to verify that the CJC can reproduce the output from the conventional Web browser used in these previous studies when accessing the bare Web server. For convenience, the relevant output from the CJC (which is the same as that in [4, 5]) is shown in Figs. 5, 6, 7 and 8.

Figure 5 displays the initial page listing the network protocols used and dumps of bare system internals when the CJC communicates with the bare Web server. It contains details of protocol headers and other information from the bare Web server enabling the user to dynamically visualize protocol operation on the client screen. This is useful for teaching students about the internals of network protocols during typical client-server interaction as done in the previous studies referred to above, but using flexible CJCs instead of Web browsers. In addition, the client screen also enables students to see the internals of server structures such as TSS (Task Segment State), the structure of the code (code dump) and the contents of memory at a given location. In Fig. 6, students can see contents of control registers, flag registers, general purpose registers, stack pointers, and interestingly, the program counter (EIP). This information enables students to understand the internals and actual behavior of a bare Web server that runs without any OS or kernel.

The memory dump in each of Figs. 7 and 8 illustrate how a student can enter the memory address in a php file retrieved by the client and see its contents. This php file in turn calls an html file in which the bare server fills in appropriate data located at a given address. The current memory shown in the Figs. 7 and 8 correspond to a partial memory dump for a given address. These results from the experiment validate that our CJC application works correctly by reproducing the same client views obtained in previous studies when using a conventional Web browser.

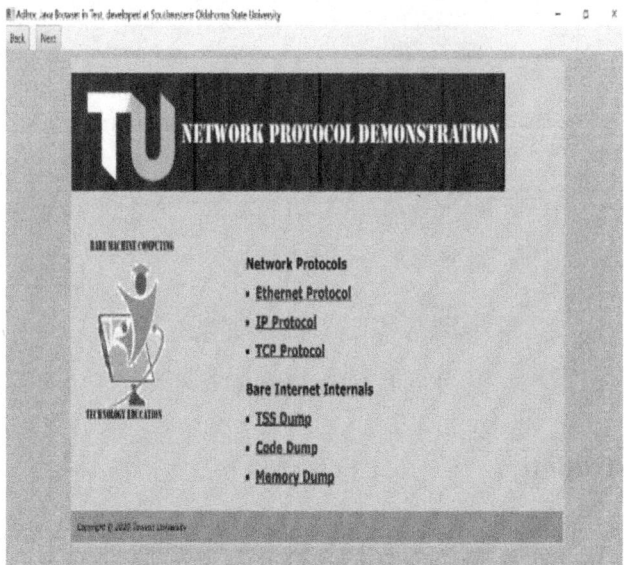

Fig. 5. Network Protocol Demonstration

TSS Dump

Link	000000E8
Stack 0 length	0000FFFF
Stack selector for 0 level	00000024
Stack 1 length	0000FFFF
Stack selector for 1 level	0000002C
Stack 2 length	0000FFFF
Stack selector for 2 level	00000034
CR3	00000000
EIP	0000A561
EFLAGS1	00000246
EFLAGS2	00000000
EAX	00000023
ECX	00000028
EDX	00000000
EBX	2FD7FB00
ESP	2FD7FB04
ESI	00000000

Fig. 6. Task Segment State

The granularity of the details that can be presented using bare paradigm is substantial and is valuable for teaching computer science students about systems as they can relate their knowledge about system data structures obtained from textbooks to actual hands-on working examples in the classroom. Figures 9 and 10 show that the CJC can download files from the bare Web server. The PDF viewer is integrated as part of the client application allowing students to display the downloadable pdf. The results illustrate how students can add new functionality to the CJC application by modifying the Java code used to communicate with the bare Web server.

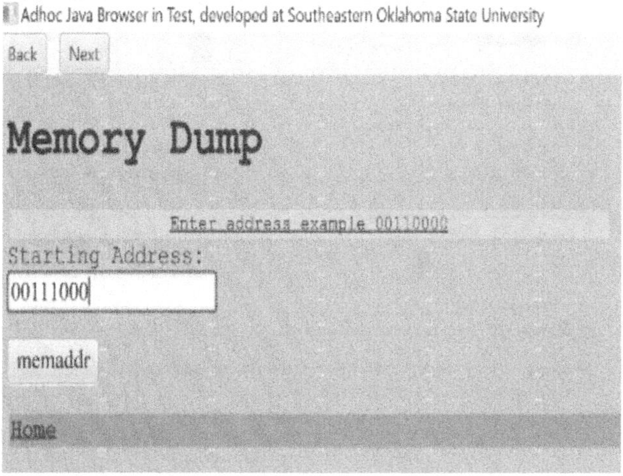

Fig. 7. Memory -starting address

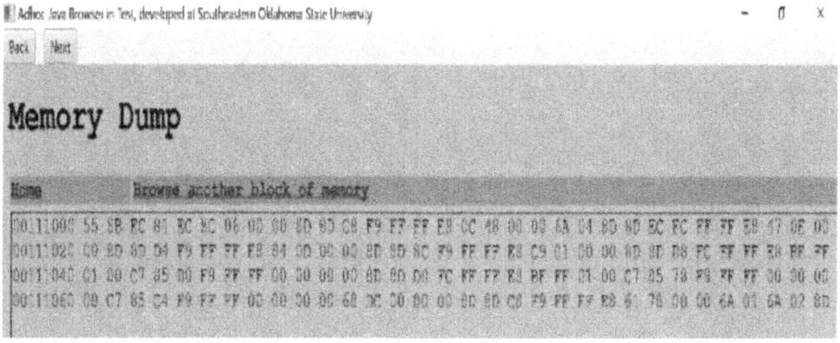

Fig. 8. Memory dump

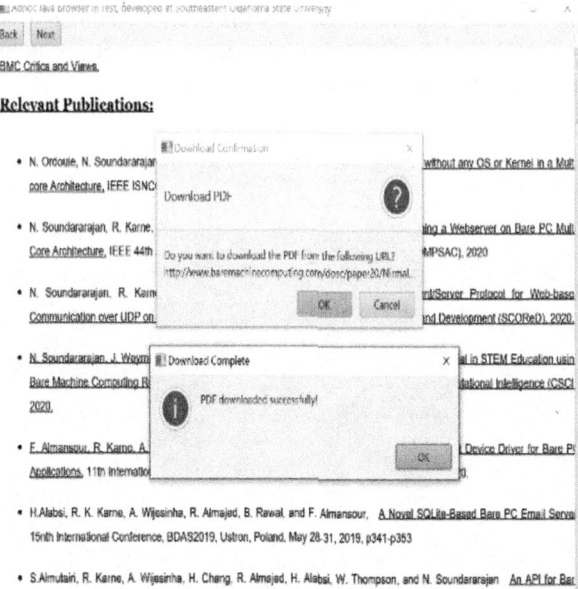

Fig. 9. Pdf file download

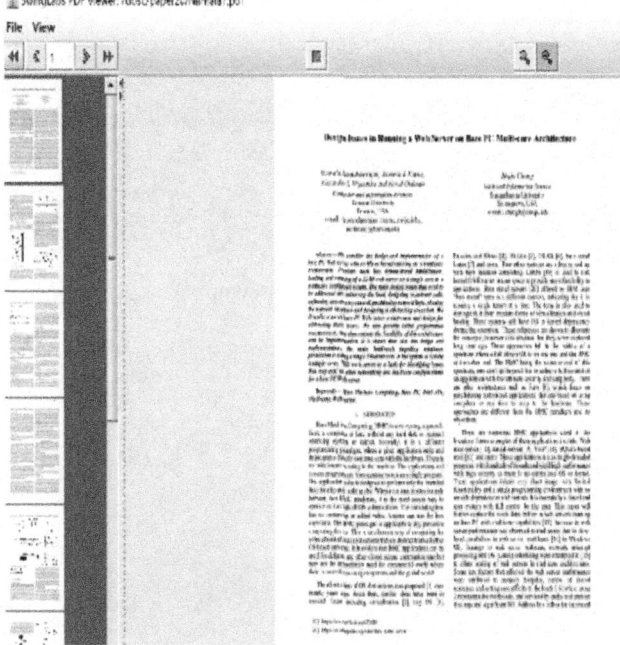

Fig. 10. Downloaded pdf file

6 Conclusion

In this paper, we have demonstrated that it is possible to request the services of a bare server using customizable Java clients without the need for any browser. In view of this research, OS-based clients adapted to specific client needs could be used to communicate with the bare server. We showed how off-the-shelf components of JavaFX can be used to construct a customizable client that interfaces with a bare server. We also showed how to build browsers that are client-specific, simple and have less code. This novel approach can be used to build a variety of specialized clients that are easy to use, each adapted to different application requirements, while avoiding the complexity and security issues of commercial browsers. In an academic setting, students could build their own simple Java clients to understand the internals of hardware, software and protocols. Future work will investigate using customizable clients in other application domains.

References

1. Petrosyan, A.: Global internet user penetration 2014–2024. Statista (2024)
2. Vailshery, L.S.: Number of Internet of Things (IoT) connections worldwide from 2022 to 2023, with forecasts from 2024 to 2033 (in billions). Statista (2024)
3. Alotaibi, F., Karne, R.K., Wijesinha, A.L., Soundararajan, N., Rangi, A.: An evaluation of the security of bare machine computing (bare) systems against cybersecurity attacks. MDPI **4**, 678–730 (2024)
4. Weymouth, J., Karne, R.K.: Survey of innovation in computer science education with undergraduate emphasis. In: Conference on Computational Science and Computational Intelligence (2021)
5. Naraharasetti, D., Karne, R.K., Wijesinha, A.L., Weymouth, J.: Obsolescence in operating systems and microprocessors. In: Software Engineering, Management and Applications (2023)
6. Okafor, U., Karne, R.K., Wijesinha, A.L., Appiah-Kubi, P.: Methodology to transform an OS based application to a bare machine application. In: Conference on Ubiquitous Computing and Communications, Melbourne, Australia (2013)
7. Soundararajan, N., Karne, R.K., Wijesinha, A.L., Ordouie, N.: Design issues in running a webserver on bare PC multicore architecture. In: IEEE 44th Annual Computers, Software and Applications Conference (2020)
8. Chang, H., Karne, R.K., Wijesinha, A.L.: Migrating a bare-PC webserver to multicore architecture. In: Computers, Software and Applications Conference (COMPSAC), Atlanta, GA, USA (2016)
9. Ordouie, N., Karne, R.K., Wijesinha, A.L., Soundararajan, N.: A simple UDP-based webserver on a bare-PC with 64 bit multicore processors: design and implementation. In: International Conference on Computing, Networking, and Communications, ICNC (2023)
10. Alotaibi, F., Karne, R.K., Wijesinha, A.L., Soundararajan, N., Rangi, A.: A chat application on a bare internet. In: 18th IEEE International Workshop on Security, Trust and Privacy for Software Applications (STPSA), COMPSAC, Osaka, Japan (2024)
11. Long, H., Karne, R.K., Wijesinha, A.L.: Design and performance of a bare PC webserver. Int. J. Comput. Appl. (2008)
12. Khaksari, G.H., Karne, R.K., Wijesinha, A.L.: A bare machine application development methodology. Int. J. Comput. Appl. **19**(1), 10–25 (2012)

13. Alotaibi, F., Karne, R.K., Wijesinha, A.L.: A stateless bare PC webserver. In: WEBIST, Rome, Italy (2023)
14. Soundararajan, N., Karne, R.K., Wijesinha, A.L., Ordouie, N.: A novel client/server protocol for web based communication over UDP on a bare machine. In: 18th IEEE Student Conference on Research and Development (SCOReD) (2020)
15. Ford, G.H., Karne, R.K., Wijesinha, A.L., Appiah-Kubi, P.: The design and implementation of a bare PC email server. In: 33rd Annual IEEE International Computer Software and Applications Conference (COMPSAC), Seattle, Washington (2009)
16. Yasinovskyy, R., Wijesinha, A.L., Karne, R.K.: VoIP performance with IPSec in IPv4-IPv6 transition networks. Infocommun. J. **LXV**(III) (2010). Special Issue on Novel Solutions for Next Generation Services
17. Almutairi, S., Karne, R.K., Wijesinha, A.L.: A Bare PC text based browser. In: Workshop on Computing, Networking and Communications, Honolulu, Hawaii (2019)
18. Emdadi, A., Karne, R.K., Wijesinha, A.L.: Implementing the TLS protocol on a Bare PC. In: 2nd International Conference on Computer Research and Development, Kuala Lumpur (2010)

DuckDB-Powered Geo-Spatial Analytics for Hit-and-Run Incidents: A Montgomery County Case Study

Sarika Rajeev[1(✉)], Atma Sahu[1], and Vishrut Sawarnya[2]

[1] Coppin State University, Baltimore, MD 21216, USA
{srajeev,asahu}@coppin.edu
[2] School of Artificial Intelligence, Amrita Vishwa Vidyapeetham Coimbatore, Coimbatore, India
Cb.en.u4aie22059@cb.students.amrita.edu, @

Abstract. Hit-and-run accidents are a significant concern that not only damages property but also endangers human lives. The objective of this research was to develop an SQL-based predictive model capable of accurately and efficiently predicting the risk of hit-and-run incidents. In this study, data collected from the Montgomery County, Maryland data.gov website, covering the period from January 2015 to May 2025, was utilized. The study employed a hybrid SQL architecture, including SQLite and DuckDB, for data preparation, real-time processing, machine learning integration, and geospatial analysis. The SQLite database is used for data storage and initial comprehensive analysis using Magic SQL to enable faster and more organized data evaluation. DuckDB, a high-performance database engine, powered scikit-learn for in-memory machine learning predictions, offering speed advantages over traditional methods utilizing pandas. The Random Forest model identified high-risk zones for hit-and-run crashes in Montgomery County, Maryland, through an interactive heatmap, serving as a powerful tool for real-time risk analysis. This study contrasts the performance of a traditional machine-learning model with a DuckDB-powered model, revealing that the DuckDB-enhanced approach, utilizing larger datasets, results in expedited and optimized analysis. This case study offers an impactful solution for a risk zone identifier and law enforcement for hit-and-run crashes.

Keywords: DuckDB · scikit learn · SQLite · Magic SQL

1 Introduction

Hit-and-runs are a major concern for countries worldwide. This happens when a driver leaves the scene after the accident without filing a report with the police or traffic management authorities. Because of hit-and-run accidents, there are many more investigations to be taken care of. Hit-and-runs not only cause property damage but can also cause fatal injuries to pedestrians and other drivers [1, 2].

The objective of this case study is to analyze:

1. Identify the high-risk zones of hit-and-run crashes in Montgomery County, Maryland.
2. Provide real-time predictions to find the factors that affect hit-and-run crashes (e.g., weather, time of day, light, substance abuse, or intersection type).
3. Generate a predictive alert that is faster and more efficient than the existing method so that law enforcement can take timely action.

In this case study, three data sets from Montgomery County's open data platform were used. The traditional SQL engine, which has a limitation of speed, greatly affected the performance when we analyzed multiple huge data sets. "sqlite3", which is a Python module, was used to create tables and store data in the SQLite database. The initial visualization, done using Matplotlib and Seaborn, visualized the factors that affect hit-and-run crashes. This research utilizes DuckDB to complement machine learning models and is faster than the traditional machine learning models proposed in previous research [3, 4]. DuckDB is an in-memory SQL engine, which is why the proposed approach is more efficient than the traditional approach.

The contributing factors of a hit-and-run crash include:

1. Tay et al. state that the traffic control and speed limit impact the hit-and-run incidents. For example, if there is no proper signal or speed limit, there are more chances of a hit-and-run [5].
2. The environment and distracted drivers also affect the probability of hit-and-run crashes. A rough set analysis was done by Karl Kim [1], which demonstrates that weather, lighting conditions, driver intoxication, and distraction, like mobile phone use while driving, increased the probability of hit-and-run incidents. In our case study, initial data visualization shows that environmental and distracted driver factors promote hit-and-run crashes.
3. Zhou [2] describes in his study that improper driver behavior, such as distraction by phone and following too closely, is highly correlated with hit-and-run crashes.
4. Road alignment is another major contributing factor that influences hit-and-run crashes. There are more chances of a hit-and-run if the road is straight, as there is more speed and a greater chance of escape for the driver [1, 2, 6].

Technology stack and Data sources:

- Data Sources: Data were collected from "https://data.montgomerycountymd.gov/" [7] an open data source platform that provides real-time updates in the dataset every week. Three different datasets were used for border analysis. All files have a common field "report number," which we have used for joining the data sets.
    1. "Crash_Reporting_Incident_data.csv" has 37 columns/fields, including report number, weather, light, location, and driver at fault.
    2. "Crash_Reporting_-_Drivers_Data.csv" has 34 columns/fields. This file includes information about drivers.
    3. "Crash_Reporting_-_Non-Motorists_Data.csv" has 34 columns/fields. This file includes pedestrian data.
- SQLite was used for local database creation and basic SQL operations, including table creation, insertion, primary joins, and initial descriptive analysis of hit-and-run crashes using SQL.

- Magic SQL (% SQL): % SQL is utilized for faster querying within the Jupyter Notebook, enhancing real-time analysis speed.
- DuckDB is a high-performance in-memory SQL engine that we have used alongside scikit learn in the machine-learning analysis of hit-and-run crashes to achieve efficient and optimized results.
- Python modules such as sqlite3, DuckDB, pandas, NumPy, and scikit-learn were used for data preparation and analysis. The modules Matplotlib, seaborn, and Folium were used for data visualization. Folium was used to create an interactive heat map of the high-risk zone.

2 Related Work

2.1 SQL-Based Predictive Modeling

In today's digital world, data not only needs to be stored securely but also needs to be processed efficiently. There are libraries in Python that enable efficient work with SQLite and DuckDB. SQLite is a relational database management system (RDBMS) that is lightweight and serverless. The main feature of SQLite is a database in the form of one file, which means we do not need a separate server for SQLite, causing the setup and maintenance of SQLite to be very straightforward. Gaffney [8] states that SQLite is designed for online transactional processing (OLTP) and is mostly used for row-oriented SQL analysis. SQLite is not a client-server-based system like MYSQL and PostgreSQL. SQLite does not execute in a separate process, instead it simply becomes part of our main process. SQLite works on the same application we are executing, so we do not need an exclusive server for this either [9]. SQLite is not considered an online analytical processing (OLAP) focused database engine, whereas DuckDB has strong OLAP performance. Mark Raasveldt [4] mentioned DuckDB as "the SQLite for analysis", which has more efficient features than SQLite. DuckDB also does not have an external dependency, so it is faster and optimized for analysis. Gaffney [8] mentioned that DuckDB recently turned up as an embedded database engine for analysis. DuckDB can also be used in machine learning modeling for faster and optimized predictions [3, 4].

2.2 Machine Learning Predictive Models

Many research studies have been done for statistical analysis and predicting hit and run using statistical models such as Logistic Regression, SAS, and Rough Set analysis [1, 10]. Zhou [2] used the scikit learn library of Python for the cart model and used k-fold cross-validation. For validation of the cart model, they used the geometric mean since their dataset was not balanced. Richard Tay [6] used logistic regression, a machine learning model, to find the hit-and-run crash in Calgary. For model accuracy, they have used statistical significance (p-value) and odds ratio, which is similar to traditional statistical logistic regression studies. Hossain [11] has done a comprehensive study on predictive hit-and-run crashes. They utilize XGboost and a Binary logistic regression model for the crash prediction. Tay [5] used a logistic regression model to understand the factors that affect fatal hit-and-run accidents in California, such as road type, lighting, time of day, speed limit, etc. They have used the odds ratio and p-value to justify their model. Mohamad [12] states that the Random Forest Model shows excellent performance in predicting road crash severity and prediction with 76.8% AUC and 75.2% precision.

2.3 Gaps Identified

In the previous research some key areas were not covered, such as:

1. Multi-dimensional analysis: Previous studies focused on a single dataset, whereas our case study used multiple datasets and joined the datasets using SQL for speedy border analysis and used DuckDB for faster analysis of multiple huge datasets.
2. Real predictive alert: The former studies had to consider data storage and evaluation in real time. Our research uses real-time heatmap visualization to predict hit-and-run crashes.
3. Visualization of non-motorist risk: In earlier work, there was no proper mapping done for pedestrian risk zones.

3 Methodology

This Case study employs a data-driven methodology that utilizes a hybrid database engine, such as SQLite for data storage and statistical analysis, and DuckDB for data analysis using the "Random Forest Classifier" machine learning model. The methodology illustrated in Fig. 1 shows a structured approach to data collection and preparation.

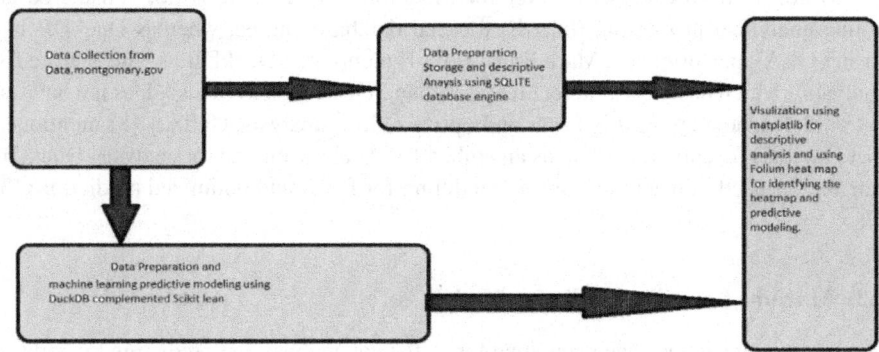

Fig. 1. hit-and-run analysis framework

Hybrid SQL integration, SQL query processing with magic SQL, Machine learning analysis, and Visualization to identify high-risk zones of hit-and-run crashes in Montgomery County, Maryland. The next subsections elaborate on the proposed pipelined framework.

3.1 Data Collection and Preparation

The data used in our case study consists of three data sets: (1) Crash reporting incident data, (2) Crash reporting driver data, and (3) Crash reporting non-motorist data sourced from a reliable database, dataMontgomery [7]. The data set ranges from January 2015 to May 2025. To ensure the real-time analysis of the data set, the data is updated every week. The data is preprocessed and cleaned before being stored in the database to ensure consistency. In the preprocessing phase, the field name was modified to snake case because, in SQL, the spaces in the field name are not allowed. The "Report Number" was the common field in all three data sets. The name of this common field was changed to a consistent name "report_number" and the data type to "str" for all data sets, and then an index was created on "report_number" for faster join in SQLite. For machine learning model analysis, we preprocessed and stored data in main memory for in-memory processing using Duck db.

3.2 Hybrid Data Integration

This research utilizes a hybrid SQL integration, SQLite, and the DuckDB SQL database engine. SQLite was used to create the hit-and-run.db database, then three separate tables, one for each data set, were created in that database: (1) crash_incidents, (2) driver_reports, and (3) non_motorist_reports. The SQLite3 module of Python was used for table creation and initial analysis to find the categorical variable for the prediction of hit-and-run crashes, the next pipeline of our framework. The DuckDB was used to complement scikit-learn in the machine learning model development in our case study, which helps in finding faster and optimized results than traditional machine learning models. We have also conducted a comparative study to show how it is more efficient if we use DuckDB as a complement to scikit learn, rather than using scikit-learn with pandas' data frames. DuckDB works in both persistence and in-memory mode and the in-memory processing is faster than the persistence mode. For the persistence database mode, we can make a connection with the database using either.db or.duckdb extensions and using the "connect" function from the duckdb module of Python. If the database exists, a connection will be created, otherwise, a new database will be created. We have made a connection with the "hit and run. dB" database, which was created in the previous step of the pipeline using SQLite. For machine learning modeling and analysis, data was handled by DuckDB in the main memory for in-memory processing.

3.3 SQL Query Processing Using Magic SQL

The %sql or %%sql, which is also known as magic SQL, is used for basic descriptive, temporal, and statistical analysis in the SQLite database. Magic SQL is a distinctive feature that is available in Jupyter Notebook for faster processing of SQL queries without using a boilerplate code for a specific database.

The reasons why we have used magic SQL include:

1. Normally, we need the SQLITE3 module and call the execute function to execute SQL queries, but with Magic SQL, we do not need any boilerplate.

2. Direct SQL queries can be executed in a Python cell in a Jupyter Notebook.
3. With magic SQL, we have cleaner and more readable syntax.
4. Faster execution of SQL queries than the boilerplate execution.
5. The output is formatted nicely in the form of a table.
6. The result can easily be converted to a data frame and can be used for visualization.

3.4 Machine Learning Analysis

Machine learning modeling is the most complicated and time-consuming part of our research project. The traditional methods of finding a machine learning model to predict hit-and-run crashes were not time-efficient. In our proposed methodology, we have utilized DuckDB as a complement to scikit-learn, enabling us to achieve faster and more efficient real-time prediction of hit-and-run crashes. DuckDB is an open-source, column-based RDBMS that can be used for Data handling in machine-learning modeling processes. In DuckDB, data can be stored on the hard disk or inside the main memory. We have used in-memory data processing to generate time-efficient models.

In our Case Study of Montgomery County, Maryland datasets, we have used the "Random Forest Model," which is a powerful supervised learning model used for both classification and regression. Random Forest Model was used to predict hit-and-run crashes based on some categorical variables such as 'driver at fault', 'driver substance abuse', 'injury severity', 'vehicle body type', and 'light'. The advantage of the Random Forest method is that it is more accurate and powerful while handling larger datasets. However, the limitation of this algorithm is slow in prediction as it uses many decision trees in the modeling. We have used DuckDB, which solves this limitation of the Random Forest Model, by data handling and processing in main memory. The model's accuracy was calculated using the "accuracy score" and "geometric mean" functions, and then we used mapping for risk handling.

3.5 Visualization Techniques

The visualization was carried out in two distinct steps of the pipeline:

1. The first visualization occurred during the initial descriptive and statistical analysis using the Matplotlib and Seaborn modules of Python. Various plots, including bar graphs, line plots, and histograms, illustrated the impact of a categorical variable on hit-and-run crashes.
2. In the second visualization step, we utilized geographical visualization and created an interactive heatmap with folium. The latitude and longitude coordinates were applied to identify dangerous zones in the heatmap of Montgomery County, Maryland. The high-risk areas for hit-and-run crashes were highlighted by the locations of maximum incidents. Additionally, pedestrian-based analysis was indicated in blue on the heatmap. All geographical visualizations were performed using a heatmap, ensuring that the insights were more impactful and enlightening.

4 Evaluation and Result

The main objective of this case study was to predict hit-and-run crashes efficiently and to spatialize visualization of Montgomery County, Maryland's public datasets. This research project was done using SQL and in-memory databases and machine-learning tools. We have compared the time for data preparation and analysis using two approaches: (1) Traditional Pandas-based machine learning analysis, and (2) DuckDB Machine learning integration.

The next subsections include the details of the evaluation of our case study of hit-and-run crashes in Montgomery County, Maryland.

4.1 Data Preparation and Cleaning

Three essential datasets were used in our case study for wider-ranging analysis, and a separate table was created for each dataset. Before starting the analysis, the dataset was cleaned using the following steps.

1. Made field names consistent by changing the column name to lowercase and snake case. For instance, if the field name is "Driver at Fault", it was modified to "driver_at_fault" to achieve consistency in three datasets.
2. Handling missing and Null values of datasets was done by either dropping the rows or imputation using mean values.
3. The data set was also cleaned by dropping the duplicate records from the dataset.
4. Crash time was converted into four categories: (1) Morning, (2) afternoon, (3) evening, and (4) night.

Then we joined the three tables using an inner join to create one table "hit_and_run_dataset" using the essential fields (columns). Figure 2 shows all four tables: the three initial tables and the one that results from their join.

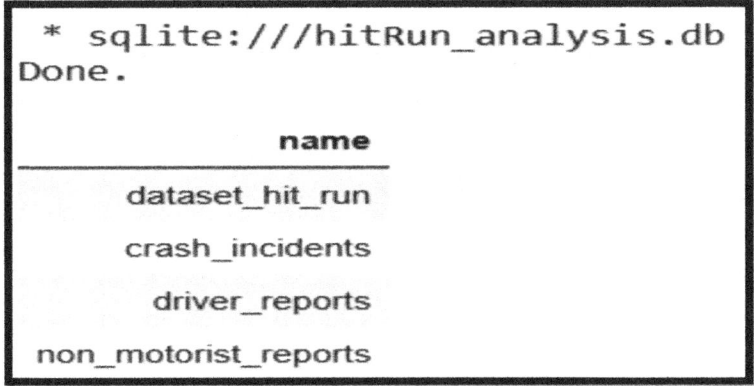

Fig. 2. All four tables in hitRun_analysis.db

4.2 Exploratory Data Analysis

Several initial descriptive analyses were conducted in our case study using SQL. Table 1 displays the output of the total number of crash types and the total number of crashes due to hit-and-run. The result of this query demonstrates that the total property damage category is 21.65% hit-and-run type, 6.58% is road injury crash, and 5.57% is fatal injury crash due to hit-and-run incidents.

Table 1. Hit and Run rate in the dataset.

acrs_report_type	total_report	hit_and_runs	hit_run_rate
Property Damage Crash	73151	15838	21.65
Injury Crash	37632	2476	6.58
Fatal Crash	341	19	5.57

Temporal analysis was also done in the first phase of analysis with the SQLite database engine. From the result of the SQL query that we have performed, we can interpret, there is more hit-and-run rate due to improper lighting conditions. The graph (Fig. 3) shows that the maximum number of hit-and-run occurred in the dark and dusk. In daylight and dawn, there are fewer chances of hit and run, maybe because of darkness or less light conditions, it is easier to flee. We have considered lighting conditions as one of the categorical variables in predictive analysis using machine learning.

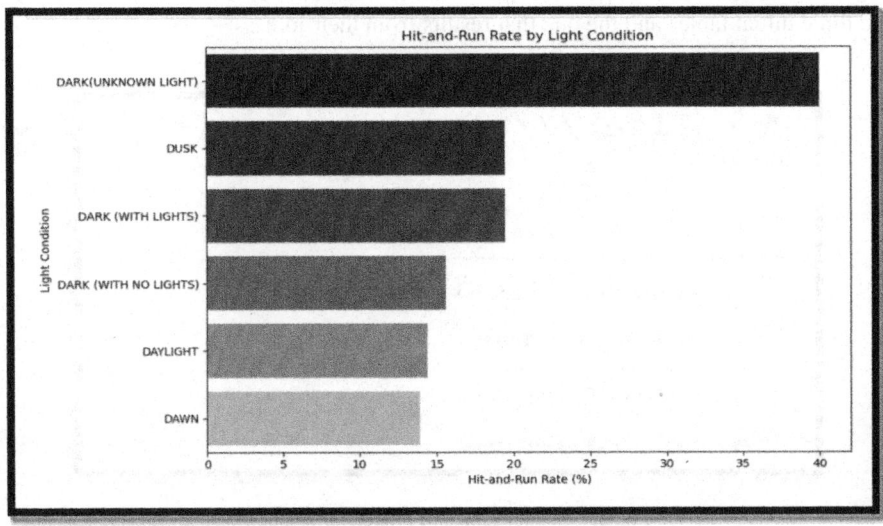

Fig. 3. hit-and-run rate by light condition.

Intersection type was additionally considered during the preliminary descriptive analysis. There were many data sets with either unknown or null values for intersection type; we dropped all those data sets. We considered only the datasets with known intersection types using SQL queries in the SQLite database. The graph (Fig. 4) shows that maximum hit-and-run cases occurred at intersection types such as roundabouts, 5-point intersections, Y intersections, and traffic circles. The intersection, like angled/skewed or perpendicular, has a minimum likelihood of a hit-and-run.

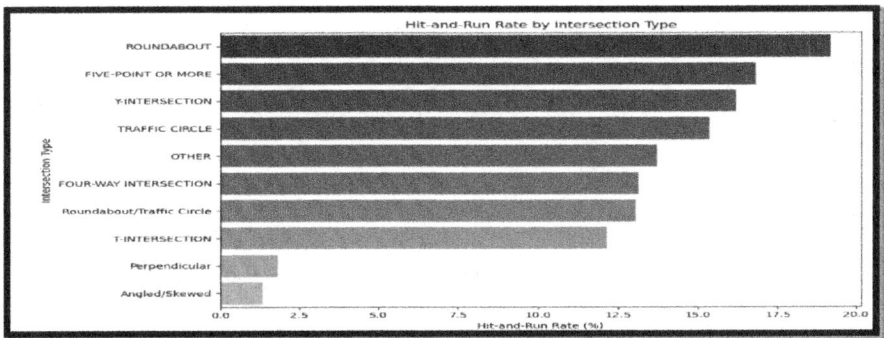

Fig. 4. hit-and-run rate by intersection type.

The initial descriptive analysis also incorporated the municipality to find the hit-and-run based on the municipality. However, the result of the SQL query shows that more than 95% of the records have municipality data missing. Then, we considered latitude and longitude for the comprehensive spatial analysis. We have visualized the area with more hit-and-run incidents in Montgomery County, Maryland. From the graph (Fig. 5) we can see the most problematic area in Montgomery County for hit-and-run crashes, the problematic areas are highlighted.

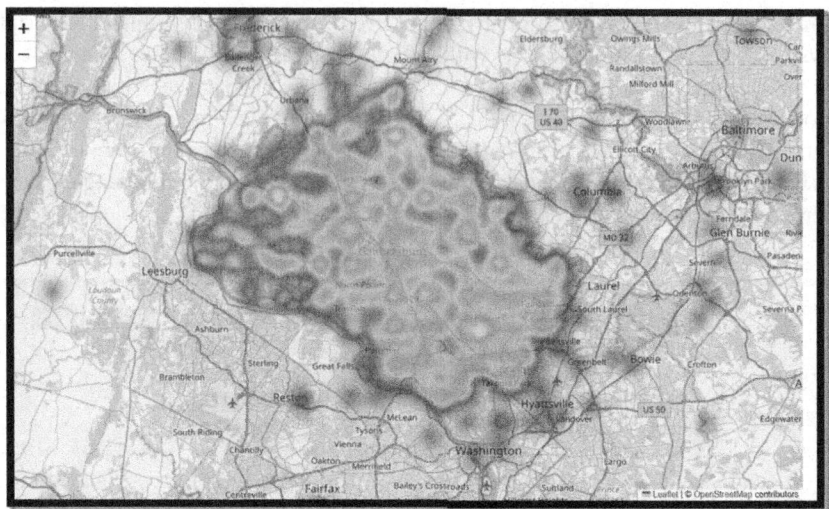

Fig. 5. A heatmap of hit-and-run crashes in Montgomery County

We also included substance abuse in the initial descriptive analysis since it is considered one of the major reasons for crashes, not just in the USA but globally. We only considered records where substance abuse is not null or empty for the analysis of hit-and-run cases related to substance abuse. The results show that there are greater chances of a hit-and-run if drivers are at fault and have consumed either alcohol or other drugs. We used 'drivers at fault' and 'driver substance abuse' as categorical factors for the predictive analysis in the second phase.

4.3 Machine Learning Analysis

For machine learning analysis, DuckDB was used for data preparation, and the Scikit learn module of Python was used for machine learning analysis. In our case study, we utilize the "Random Forest classifier" with 'driver at fault', 'driver substance abuse', 'injury severity', 'vehicle body type', and 'light' as categorical variables to predict hit-and-run crashes. The output of our result using DuckDB as a complement to scikit learn to find the hit-and-run incident is shown in Fig. 6. The accuracy of our model was 92.5%, the precision of 0 (no hit-and-run) is 93%, and for 1 (yes, hit-and-run) is 87%.

```
 Best Threshold: 0.78
 Accuracy: 0.9250202049169644
 F1-score: 0.7122273364018411
 Geometric Mean: 0.7702449277332503

 Classification Report:
               precision    recall  f1-score   support

            0       0.93      0.98      0.96     32457
            1       0.87      0.60      0.71      5900

     accuracy                           0.93     38357
    macro avg       0.90      0.79      0.83     38357
 weighted avg       0.92      0.93      0.92     38357
```

Fig. 6. hit-and-run predictive model's accuracy.

But, since the dataset was imbalanced, there were more crash cases with no hit-and-run in the dataset, so we also determined the geometric mean and the confusion matrix. Figure 7 shows the confusion matrix of the prediction of hit-and-run crashes in Montgomery County, Maryland.

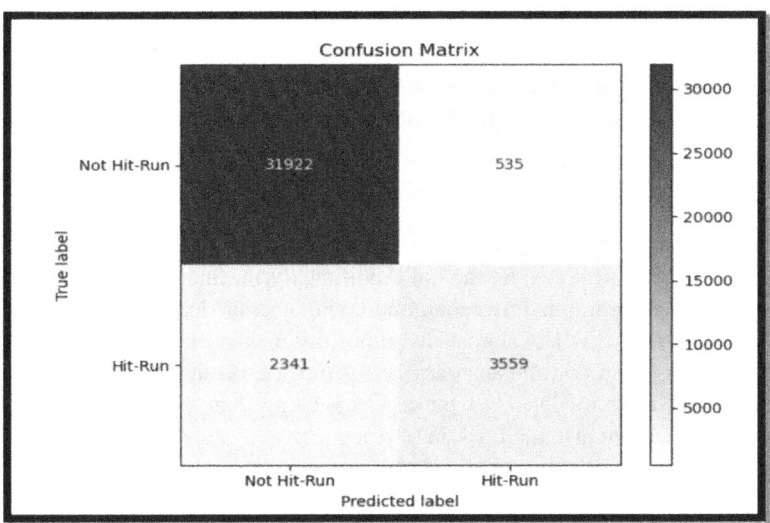

Fig. 7. A hit-and-run predictive model's confusion matrix

We have derived the risk score using the probability of the Random Forest classifier. Then, we used folium to visualize the high-risk locations by plotting an interactive map, where a risk score of more than 0.5 indicates a probability of hit-and-run incidents.

4.4 Performance Benchmarking

We have also compared the time of execution when we used a DuckDB powered machine learning model vs the traditional machine learning models with pandas. Table 2 reveals that the data preparation time when we use DuckDB is 1.96 s, whereas when we use traditional machine learning, using pandas, the data preparation time is 9.75 s. So, we can interpret that DuckDB's powered methodology is almost five times faster than the traditional method. Additionally, the Table 2 demonstrates that the Geometric mean of the predictive hit-and-run model using DuckDB is 77%, which is marginally better than the traditional machine learning model (76.4%).

Table 2. Compare DuckDB Powered ML and Traditional ML

Method	Accuracy	Geometric Mean	Execution time	Strength
Pandas + Sklearn	92.3%	76.4%	9.75 s	Widely used, flexible
DuckDB + Sklearn	92.5%	77%	1.96 s	Fast, SQL-based, in-memory

5 Conclusion and Future Work

This case study utilized a hybrid SQL engine to analyze the hit-and-run crash in Montgomery County, Maryland. Data on crash incidents, as well as the drivers and non-motorists involved in such incidents in Montgomery County, Maryland, were collected for the modeling and analysis, covering the period from January 2015 to May 2025. The analysis was done in two phases: (1) The comprehensive descriptive analysis using SQLite database engine, and (2) Machine Learning modeling and prediction using DuckDB powered predictive analysis. The result shows that the combination of SQLite, DuckDB, and Python is very efficient for hit-and-run analysis. So, it is possible to have timely manners and take preventive action. Additionally, the finding reveals that DuckDB powered machine learning is faster than traditional machine learning models. The data preparation using DuckDB is almost five times faster than the data preparation using pandas. We also found that the accuracy and geometric mean of the predictive model was marginally better for DuckDB powered modeling than the traditional modeling. Furthermore, the result also includes an interactive map to show the high-risk zones for hit-and-run crashes.

The limitations of this case study are as follows:

1. Datasets were collected from open data sources only.
2. Real-time streaming data was available only for one thousand records.
3. There was no integration with CCTV or live alert system.

The future work will involve data from the police reports, including drivers and non-motorist demographics, which were missing from this case study dataset. We will also include real data streams in our modeling and analysis for better real-time predictions.

Additionally, in the future, we will include factors like CCTV and live alerts for multi-factor machine learning models to make our proposed predictive model more accurate and versatile.

References

1. Kim, K., Yukio, E.: Hit-and-run crashes: use of rough set analysis with logistic regression to capture critical attributes and determinants. Transp. Res. Rec. J. Transp. Res. Board **2083**, 110–118 (2008)
2. Zhou, B., Li, Z., Zhang, S., Zhang, X., Liu, X., Ma, Q.: Analysis of factors affecting hit-and-run and non-hit-and-run in vehicle-bicycle crashes: a non-parametric approach incorporating data imbalance treatment. Sustainability **11**(5), 1–14 (2019)
3. Machine Learning Prototyping with DuckDB and Scikit-Learn – DuckDB. https://duckdb.org/2025/05/16/scikit-learn-duckdb.html
4. Raasveldt, M., Mühleisen, H.: DuckDB: an embeddable analytical database. In: Proceedings of the 2019 International Conference on Management of Data (SIGMOD 2019), pp. 1981–1984. Association for Computing Machinery, New York (2019)
5. Tay, R., Barua, U., Kattan, L.: Factors contributing to hit-and-run in fatal crashes. Accid. Anal. Prevent. **41**(2), 227–233 (2009)
6. Tay, R., Kattan, L., Sun, H.: Logistic model of hit and run crashes in Calgary. Can. J. Transp. **4**(1) (2010)
7. Montgomery County Data|Open Data Portal. https://data.montgomerycountymd.gov/
8. Gaffney, K.P., Prammer, M., Brasfield, L., et al.: SQLite: past, present, and future. Proc. VLDB Endow. **15**, 3535–3547 (2022)
9. D. Richard Hipp: SQLite Is Serverless (n.d.). https://www.sqlite.org/serverless.html
10. MacLeod, K.E., Griswold, J., Arnold, L.S.: Factors Associated with Hit-and-Run Pedestrian Fatalities and Driver Identification. UC Berkeley, Research Reports (2010)
11. Hossain, A., Sun, X., Hasan, A.S., Jalayer, M., Codjoe, J.: Comprehensive investigation of pedestrian hit-and-run crashes: applying XGBoost and binary logistic regression model. Transp. Res. Rec. **2679**(2), 1–21 (2024)
12. Mohamad, I., Jomnonkwao, S., Ratanavaraha, V.: Machine learning predictive performance in road accident severity: a case study from Thailand. Results Eng. **26**, 104833 (2025)

Analysis of Programming Capability of LLMs in the Context of Computer Science I

Junfeng Qu[✉], Shuju Bai, Byron Jeff, and Ebrahim Khosravi

Clayton State University, Morrow, GA 30260, USA
jqu@clayton.edu

Abstract. This study presents a comparative evaluation of three large language models—Gemini 2.0 Flash, ChatGPT 4.o, and Copilot Enterprise—in the context of automated code generation. The models were assessed across multiple dimensions covered in CS I including decision structures, repetition structures, functions, class & OOP, code quality, documentation, robustness, algorithmic logic, and input validation. The results indicate that all three models achieved A(Excellent) performance in repetition structure and Class & OOP. All three models achieved B (Good) performance in function category. However, the study reveals a significant gap in comments and documentation, with all models scoring at or below the minimum passing grade. The gap found indicated the improvement in AI-generated code to support maintainable and collaborative software development.

Keywords: code generation · large language model · Gemini · Copilot · ChatGPT · Java

1 Introduction

The computer science I (CS I) is an introduction course to students majoring in computer science in almost all the universities in the world. The topics in CS I normally covers variables, data types, operators, decision structures, repetition structures, functions, input/output, simple algorithms, and basic object-oriented programming concepts. The mostly used programming languages used in CS I are typically Java and Python. The objectives of CS I is to train students to achieve certain proficiency in core programming languages, problem-solving and algorithmic thinking to develop logical reasoning, breaking down problems into smaller components, and design and implement basic algorithms with fundamental data structures and principles of object-oriented programming. Students should be able to write readable, well-documented programs to solve problems and understand debugging techniques.

As shown in Fig. 1, CS I will train the brain of students to use elements in a program language to analyze the problems, and later formulate simple logics and algorithms to build solution to the problems with programing.

Along with the recent roaring Large Language Models (LLMs), the revolutionized series of LLMs have demonstrated the practical capabilities of text generation, especially, the multi-modal LLMs have the capability of processing different types of data including

Fig. 1. Process of Learning Programing in Human Being

text, image, and audio to a reasonable degree. LLMs are being used extensively in programming for various tasks, for example:

1. Code generation: LLMs can generate code snippets, complete lines of code, and functions based on prompts. Tools include Copilot, ChatGPT, and Gemini.
2. Low-code/no-code development: LLMs are being integrated into platforms to enable non-programmers to generate functional code through prompting.
3. Simple applications development: well-engineered prompts to LLMs can generate functional basic applications.

Fig. 2. Process of Learning Programing using LLMs

While the LLMs have capabilities to generate codes and functions based on the prompts, the performance of LLMs in generating codes needs to be investigated further on its programming quality that is comparable to college students who major in computer science. Figure 2 shows the process of code generation by LLMs from problems defined in natural language, when the LLMs understand these problems and create a program solution after receiving those problems. In this study, the content of problems is focused on CS I context. The following sections are organized in the study: literature review of current programming capabilities of LLMs, experimental design of LLMs comparison study based on context of CS I, analysis of experimental results, and conclusions.

2 Programming Capabilities of LLMs

A variety of benchmarks have been designed to assess the program capabilities of LLMs, each with a unique focus and evaluation metrics. The benchmark HumanEval [1], from OpenAI, primarily assesses the functional correctness of code produced from docstrings using unit tests. It evaluates whether the generated code passes the unit tests of document specifications. SWE-Bench [2] takes this idea of testing code and introduces a more applied evaluation of real-world bug fixes using bugs from open-source repositories. This benchmark evaluates LLMs on producing patches to fix bug problems described in an existing codebase. DebugBench [3] focuses explicitly on the debugging abilities of LLMs and provides a dataset of buggy code fragments in multiple programming languages to evaluate them on finding and fixing bugs. The sheer number of existing benchmarks indicates to the research community that it is still not possible to capture every facet of programming proficiency in an LLM with one benchmark evaluation scheme. Each different benchmark assesses critical skills possessed by software developers, and that code generation is only one aspect of software development. Nguyen & Nadi [4] presents an empirical study evaluating GitHub Copilot's code suggestions across four programming languages (Python, Java, JavaScript, and C) using 33 LeetCode problems. The authors assessed both correctness via test case pass rates and understandability. Frank & Godwin [5] investigated GitHub Copilot's impact on developer productivity using a mixed-methods approach: surveys, interviews, and code analysis. It was found that Copilot improves efficiency and learning but raising concerns about over-reliance and occasional inaccuracies. Coello et al. [6] compared the performance of GPT-3.5, GPT-4, Bard, Bing, and Claude on 460 Python problems from the MBPP dataset. It evaluates accuracy, code quality (lines of code), and adaptability to feedback. It introduces a three-phase testing methodology: initial prompt-based testing, feedback-based refinement, and re-prompting. The study finds GPT-4 to be the most effective, achieving an 87.5% success rate. Liu et al. [7] investigated the use of GPT-4 for generating safety-critical software code in domains like nuclear energy and automotive systems. This study introduced a novel prompt engineering method, Prompt-FDC, and compared it with simpler prompt strategies. The study demonstrates that with refined prompts, LLMs can generate code that meets industry standards and passes robustness tests. Benetti et al. [8] studied a real-world study of GitHub Copilot in a corporate environment. Using the SPACE framework, it evaluated Copilot's impact on productivity, code quality, and developer satisfaction across three software development teams. Huynh et al. [9] summarized a thorough survey of the LLMs in code generation in four major areas: challenges, fine-tuning techniques, evaluation, and application. Miah et al. [10] proposed a user-centric evaluation framework for assessing the usability of LLMs (specifically ChatGPT) in generating R code. They found that ChatGPT performed well overall, and the weakness is conciseness. Chen et al. [1] introduced Codex, a fine-tuned GPT-based model on GitHub code. The Codex achieves 28.8% on *pass@1* benchwork and 72.3% *pass@100* on HumanEval. Tong and Zhang [11] proposed a framework for evaluating the semantic correctness of LLM-generated code without relying on test cases. It also used LLMs themselves to assess code quality through structured reasoning. Because of the nature of the fast evolution of LLMs, the capability of LLMs to understand the natural language has improved extensively, and the programming capabilities of LLMs have improved and evolved quickly. This study focuses on the LLMs capabilities to solve the problems in natural language and generate solutions using Java.

3 Experimental Design

3.1 Problem Selection in Context of CS I

Based on the previous summary of the LLMs' programming capability, three main LLMs are chosen in the study, OpenAI's ChatGPT 4.o, Google's Gemini 2.0 Flash, and Microsoft's Copilot. To simulate the natural language understanding of the LLMs, the two narrative problems per key elements in CS I were picked from the textbook authored by Tony Gaddis [12]. The narrative of these questions are modified to make sure the JAVA language will be used and the LLMs will generate Java code. The questions are summarized in the following table:

Table 1. Problem set of CS I

Category	Question
Control Structure	Q1. Write a Java program that prompts the user to enter a number within the range of 1 through 10. The program should display the Roman numeral version of that number. If the number is outside the range of 1 through 10, the program should display an error message
	Q2. Implement in Java, Serendipity Booksellers has a book club that awards points to its customers based on the number of books purchased each month. The points are awarded as follows: If a customer purchases 0 books, he or she earns 0 points. If a customer purchases 1 book, he or she earns 5 points. If a customer purchases 2 books, he or she earns 15 points. If a customer purchases 3 books, he or she earns 30 points. If a customer purchases 4 or more books, he or she earns 60 points. Write a program that asks the user to enter the number of books that he or she has purchased this month and then displays the number of points awarded
Repetition Structure	Q3. Write a JAVA program that calculates the amount a person would earn over a period of time if his or her salary is one penny the first day, two pennies the second day, and continues to double each day. The program should display a table showing the salary for each day, and then show the total pay at the end of the period. The output should be displayed in a dollar amount, not the number of pennies The Pennies for Pay Problem INPUT VALIDATION: Do not accept a number less than 1 for the number of days worked
	Q4. Write a JAVA program that plays a simple dice game between the computer and the user. When the program runs, a loop should repeat 10 times. Each iteration of the loop should do the following: Generate a random integer in the range of 1 through 6. This is the value of the computer's die. Generate another random integer in the range of 1 through 6. This is the value of the user's die. The die with the highest value wins. (In case of a tie, there is no winner for that particular roll of the dice.)

(*continued*)

Table 1. (*continued*)

		As the loop iterates, the program should keep count of the number of times the computer wins, and the number of times that the user wins
		After the loop performs all of its iterations, the program should display who was the grand winner, the computer or the user
	Functions	Q5. Write a Java program that asks the user to enter an item's wholesale cost and its markup percentage. It should then display the item's retail price. For example:
		If an item's wholesale cost is 5.00 and its markup percentage is 100 percent, then the item's retail price is 10.00
		If an item's wholesale cost is 5.00 and its markup percentage is 50 percent, then the item's retail price is 7.50
		The program should have a method named calculateRetail that receives the wholesale cost and the markup percentage as arguments, and returns the retail price of the item
		Q6. Implement in Java. In physics, an object that is in motion is said to have kinetic energy
		The variables in the formula are as follows: KE is the kinetic energy, m is the object's mass in kilograms, and v is the object's velocity, in meters per second
		Write a method named kineticEnergy that accepts an object's mass (in kilograms) and velocity (in meters per second) as arguments. The method should return the amount of kinetic energy that the object has
		Demonstrate the method by calling it in a program that asks the user to enter values for mass and velocity
	Class & OOP	Q7. Implement in Java. Design a TestScores class that has fields to hold three test scores. The class should have a constructor, accessor and mutator methods for the test score fields, and a method that returns the average of the test scores
		Demonstrate the class by writing a separate program that creates an instance of the class. The program should ask the user to enter three test scores, which are stored in the TestScores object. Then the program should display the average of the scores, as reported by the TestScores object
		Q8. Implement in JAVA. Write a class named Patient that has fields for the following data:
		First name, middle name, and last name Address, city, state, and ZIP code Phone number Name and phone number of emergency contact
		The Patient class should have a constructor, accessor, and mutator that accept an argument for each field

(*continued*)

Table 1. (*continued*)

	Next, write a class named Procedure that represents a medical procedure that has been performed on a patient. The Procedure class should have fields for the following data: Name of the procedure Date of the procedure Name of the practitioner who performed the procedure Charges for the procedure The Procedure class should have a constructor, accessor, and mutator that accept an argument for each field. Next, write a program that creates an instance of the Patient class, initialized with sample data. Then, create three instances of the Procedure class, initialized with the following data: Procedure #1: Procedure name: Physical Exam Date: Today's date Practitioner: Dr. Irvine Charge: 250.00 Procedure #2: Procedure name: X-ray Date: Today's date Practitioner: Dr. Jamison Charge: 500.00 Procedure #3: Procedure name: Blood test Date: Today's date Practitioner: Dr. Smith Charge: 200.00 The program should display the patient's information, information about all three of the procedures, and the total charges of the three procedures

3.2 Prompt Engineering for Code Generation and Evaluations

Persona prompt pattern is used to ask Gemini, ChatGPT and Copilot to solve each problem defined in Table 1. The prompt flow is shown in Fig. 4. The code is generated by Gemini, ChatGPT, and Copilot respectively. To minimize the variations of evaluation, Copilot was used to generate evaluation rubrics and grade the code generated by each LLMs.

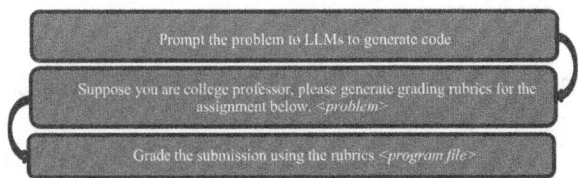

Fig. 4. Prompt Engineering Flow

The sample output of Questions 6 is shown in Fig. 5.

3.3 Data Collection and Processing

As shown in Fig. 4. Each question was prompted to Copilot, ChatGPT, and Gemini individually, the outputs from these models are saved into Java file respectively. Then each question is prompted to Copilot to generate rubric, and then each Java program generated is attached and graded in a separate prompt based on the rubric. The grading scores are averaged by category and run to ensure performance consistency of grading. Each question is graded out of 100 scales. A common 100-point grading system that uses letter grades is typically assigned as follows: A (90–100), B (80–89), C (70–79), D (60–69), and F (below 60) for discussion to match performance of students. A score achieves A means excellent, B means Good, C means Satisfactory, D means minimum passing, and F means failure.

Grading Rubric: Kinetic Energy Java Program
Total Points: 100

1. Functional Requirements (60 points)

Criteria	Points
Method kineticEnergy is correctly defined with appropriate parameters	10
Correct formula implementation: $ KE = \frac{1}{2}mv^2 $	15
Method returns the correct result (not just prints it)	10
Program prompts the user for mass and velocity	10
User input is correctly read and passed to the method	10
Output is clearly displayed to the user	5

2. Code Quality & Style (20 points)

Criteria	Points
Proper use of method structure and naming conventions	5
Code is well-formatted and readable (indentation, spacing)	5
Meaningful variable names used	5
Comments included where appropriate	5

3. Error Handling & Robustness (10 points)

Criteria	Points
Handles invalid input gracefully (e.g., non-numeric input or negative values)	5
Program does not crash under normal use	5

4. Documentation & Submission (10 points)

Criteria	Points
Header comment with student name, date, and assignment description	5
File submitted correctly and compiles without errors	5

Fig. 5. Grading rubric example

4 Programming Capabilities of LLMs

The average grade distribution of code generated by Gemini, ChatGPT, and Copilot by category is shown in Fig. 7. Figure 7 shows that all three models achieved A(Excellent) performance in repetition structure and Class & OOP. That means all three models have strength in handling loops and iterative logic, and class and object-oriented programming concept. All three models achieved B (Good) performance in function category. That shows that all models are relative weakness in handling modular code or function-based logic. Gemini and Copilot have A(Excellence) in Decision structure, where ChatGPT got B(Good).

The program functionality and correctness of three models is shown in Fig. 8.

The data shows that Gemini and Copilot have achieved A(Excellent) in all four categories, where Gemini is all 100 in the four categories. Copilot is 95 in Class & OOP and 98 in Repetition structure. Although ChatGPT got 100 in decision structure, repetition structure and function, it has B(Good) in Class & OOP.

Figure 9 demonstrates the performance of the three LLMs in code quality and readability. Gemini outperformed ChatGPT and Copilot by achieving all A(Excellent) in all

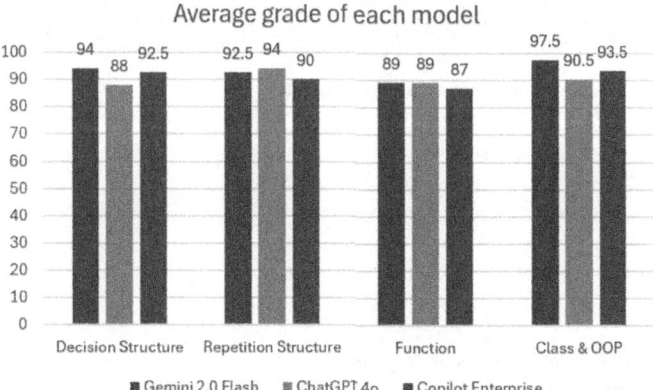

Fig. 7. Average grade of each model

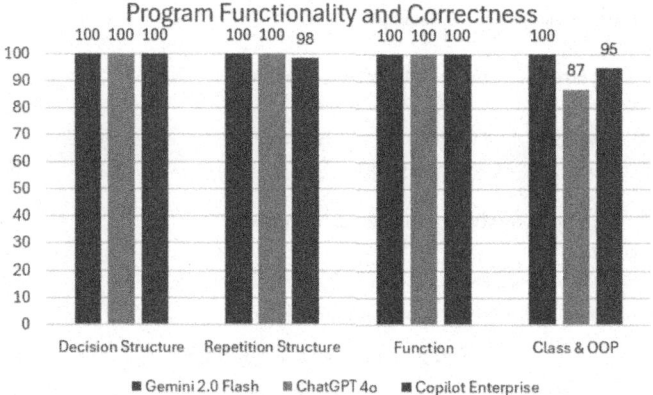

Fig. 8. Program functionality and correctness comparison

four categories followed by Copilot with A grade in decision structure, repetition structure and function and 87.5 in class & OOP. ChatGPT also earned three As(Excellent) as Copilot, however, it scored lowest in Class & OOP with 82.5 grade.

Figure 10 shows the overall average grade of comments and documentation of program generated. Gemini 2.0 Flash leads significantly with a grade of 60, a low D (minimum passing), indicating a strong improvements on documentation and inline comments are lacking. ChatGPT 4o follows with a grade of 44 followed by Copilot Enterprise ranking lowest at 37, which are F (Failing) and mean commenting and documentation are very poor in these two language models. With D and F grade, although Gemini is better than ChatGPT and Copilot, all of these models failed to generate good quality comments and documentation, which is critical for software development.

As show in Fig. 11, Gemini and ChatGPT 4o lead slightly with 85 and Copilot Enterprise trails behind with a score around 80, indicating strong and reliable method implementation in the three language models. Gemini 2.0 Flash and ChatGPT show

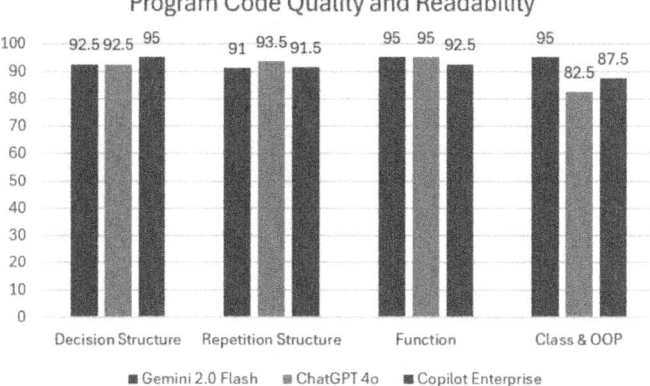

Fig. 9. Program code quality and readability comparison

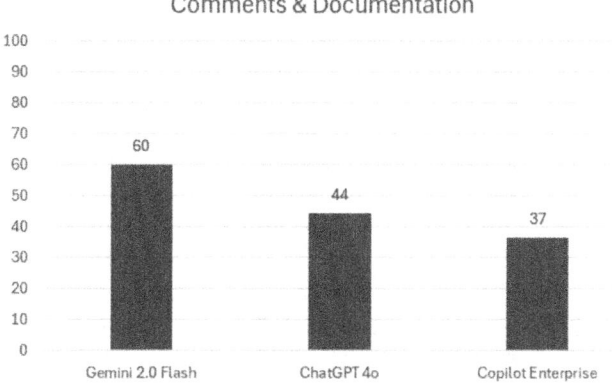

Fig. 10. Comments and documentation comparison

nearly equivalent robustness. Copilot needs to improve a little in its method implementations to catch up with Gemini and ChatGPT. All three models are at B (Good) level though.

The correctness of algorithm and logic are important factors to evaluate generated programs. The comparison is shown in Fig. 12.

Gemini 2.0 Flash, ChatGPT 4o, and Copilot Enterprise achieve a perfect score of 100, which is excellent. This indicates equally strong performance in algorithmic reasoning and logical problem-solving across all LLMs.

The comparison of input validation of the programs is shown in Fig. 13. With a score of 88, ChatGPT 4o performs slightly better than Gemini's 85 score. Both ChatGPT and Gemini are in B (Good) range, indicating certain input validation capabilities. Copilot Enterprise lags behind with 75, which is C (Satisfactory) suggesting a need for improvement in this area.

Based on the studies above, the strength and weakness of all three LLM models are summarized in Table 2.

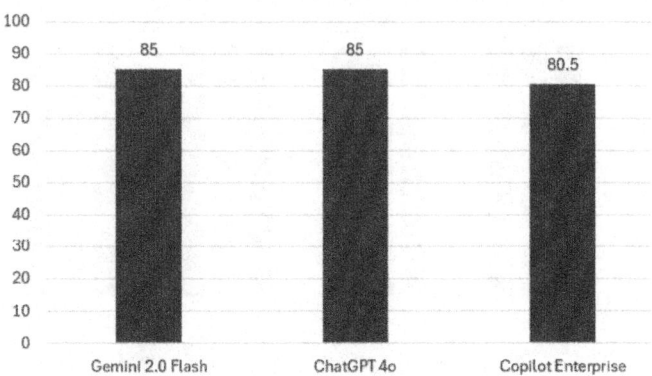

Fig. 11. Method implementation and robustness comparison

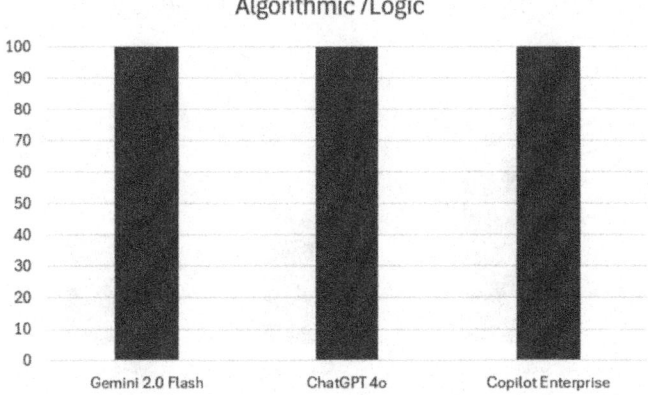

Fig. 12. Algorithmic and logic comparison

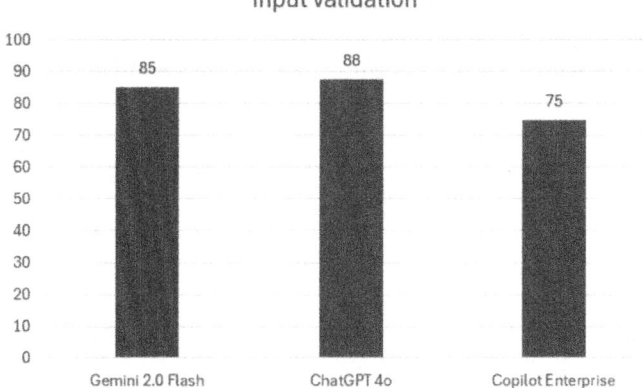

Fig. 13. Input validation comparison

Table 2. Strength and Weakness of LLMs Code Generation

Model	Strengths	Weaknesses
Gemini 2.0 Flash	Class & OOP, Repetition Structure, Decision Structure, algorithmic and logic	Documentation and comments
ChatGPT 4o	Class & OOP, Repetition Structure, algorithmic and logic	Documentation and comments
Copilot Enterprise	Class & OOP, Decision Structure, algorithmic and logic	Documentation and comments, Code quality and readability

5 Conclusions and Future Studies

All three models demonstrate competent programming capabilities with mostly excellent or good performance except in documentation and comments. Gemini 2.0 Flash stands out as the most consistent and high-performing model across most categories. ChatGPT 4.o shows similar performance strengths to Gemini but needs improvement in object-oriented design. Copilot Enterprise performs reliably in Class & OOP, decision structure, but falls short in code quality and readability. All three models need a moderate improvement on input validation, methods implementation and robustness. Further, all models need significant improvement in generating meaningful comments and documentation to support maintainable and collaborative software development.

The study shows that Gemini 2.0, ChatGPT 4.o, and Copilot achieve mostly A(Excellence) or B(Good), which usually takes a typical computer science student a semester to achieve. The emergence of Generative AI (GenAI) in code generation is significantly reshaping the landscape of computer science education because LLMs will offer powerful support in understanding programming concepts, accelerating development, and enhancing problem-solving skills. Moreover, the inconsistent quality of documentation and input validation in AI-generated code, as observed in recent studies, highlights the need for students to critically evaluate and refine AI outputs. As such, integrating GenAI into the curriculum must be done thoughtfully, emphasizing its role as a learning aid rather than a substitute for core competencies in software development.

References

1. Chen, M., et al.: Evaluating Large Language Models Trained on Code, July 2021. http://arxiv.org/abs/2107.03374
2. Jimenez, C.E., et al.: SWE-Bench: Can Language Models Resolve Real-World GitHub Issues? October 2023. http://arxiv.org/abs/2310.06770
3. Tian, R., et al.: DebugBench: evaluating debugging capability of large language models, January 2024. http://arxiv.org/abs/2401.04621
4. Nguyen, N., Nadi, S.: An empirical evaluation of GitHub copilot's code suggestions. In: Proceedings - 2022 Mining Software Repositories Conference, MSR 2022, pp. 1–5. Institute of Electrical and Electronics Engineers Inc. (2022). https://doi.org/10.1145/3524842.3528470
5. Frank, E., Godwin, O.: Enhancing Developer Productivity: A Study on GitHub Copilot's Code Completion Capabilities. EasyChair (2024, preprint)
6. Coello, C.E.A., Alimam, M.N., Kouatly, R.: Effectiveness of ChatGPT in coding: a comparative analysis of popular large language models. Digital **4**(1), 114–125 (2024). https://doi.org/10.3390/digital4010005
7. Liu, M., Wang, J., Lin, T., Ma, Q., Fang, Z., Wu, Y.: An empirical study of the code generation of safety-critical software using LLMs. Appl. Sci. (Switzerland) **14**(3) (2024). https://doi.org/10.3390/app14031046
8. Benetti, A., Filannino, M.: GitHub Copilot: a systematic study (2024)
9. Huynh, N., Lin, B.: Large Language Models for Code Generation: A Comprehensive Survey of Challenges, Techniques, Evaluation, and Applications, March 2025. http://arxiv.org/abs/2503.01245
10. Miah, T., Zhu, H.: User Centric Evaluation of Code Generation Tools, February 2024. http://arxiv.org/abs/2402.03130
11. Tong, W., Zhang, T.: CODEJUDGE: Evaluating Code Generation with Large Language Models (2003). https://github.com/VichyTong/CodeJudge
12. Gaddis, T.: Starting Out with Java: From Control Structures Through Objects, 7th edn (2018)

Predicting Early Breast Cancer Recurrence with Machine Learning

M. Mehdi Owrang O(✉), Gracie Abrahams, Gretchen Callahan, Dalia Karim, and Tyler Madison

American University, Washington, DC 20016, USA
{owrang,ga6636a,gc0051a,dk9605a,tm8375a}@american.edu

Abstract. Medical prognostication involves predicting disease outcomes, including complications in recurrence. Early Breast cancer recurrence (BCR) is characterized by the return of cancer within 5 years following initial treatment. Factors such as tumor size, lymph node involvement and hormone receptor status significantly influence the prognosis of breast cancer patients. Early detection of recurrence, particularly in asymptomatic stages, can lead to more effective interventions and improved patient outcomes. This study employs machine learning (ML) classifiers to identify and analyze the factors most predictive of early BCR. Using datasets like the Wisconsin Breast Cancer Recurrence Dataset and the METABRIC dataset, we are applying multiple feature selection schemes to isolate key variables. These results will underscore the potential of ML learning in healthcare and the potential of increasing long term survival rates. Utilizing the Wisconsin dataset, we find that Support Vector Machine has the highest predictive power in our algorithm selection for general Breast Cancer Recurrence. We begin and will continue to apply the same approach for the analysis of Early Breast Cancer Recurrence using the METABRIC data.

Keywords: Early Breast Cancer Recurrence · Machine Learning Algorithms · Prediction Modeling

1 Introduction

Breast cancer remains one of the most prevalent and life-threatening diseases affecting women. While advances in medical science have improved early detection and treatment options, the risk of breast cancer recurrence (BCR) remains a serious concern (American Cancer Society, 2024; Hasna El Haji et al., 2023). This is especially true for survivors within the first five years of their treatment and remission. This threat of recurrence is critical because it can affect the response time and intervention with treatment. Being able to predict BCR will dramatically improve survival outcomes.

Historically predictions such as these have relied on statistical methods like regression to use clinical and pathological variables. These techniques have provided valuable insights, but their reliance on linear relationships and limited variable interactions often leads to unreliable results. Breast cancer biology is highly complex which means methods like these might not be able to demonstrate the patterns that are hiding underneath the recurrence. However, in recent years machine learning (ML) has become a new tool available to healthcare (Abreu, P. H, et al., 2016; Alva, N., 2018). This machine learning approach offers more sophisticated techniques which are better able to handle the complexity and nonlinearity of breast cancer. ML algorithms can process large amounts of data that are both structured and unstructured. This allows algorithms to discover nuances in the patterns and interactions between selected features. The capabilities for predictive models using ML are advantageous for breast cancer research.

The objective of this study is to leverage ML techniques to create a robust model for predicting early BCR. Using datasets like the Wisconsin Breast Cancer Recurrence Dataset (Lachman, M., 2019) and the METABRIC (Molecular Taxonomy of Breast Cancer International Consortium) dataset [Kaggle], we aim to identify key predicative features that have consistent efficacy (Bradley 2007). The focus is on early BCR to create proactive clinical interventions and minimize recurrence risks. Our approach follows the steps of data preprocessing, exploratory analysis, and feature selection to have the development of accurate models. Several ML algorithms, including decision trees (Charbuty, B. and Abdulazeez, A., 2021; Charbuty 2011; Bisong 2019), support vector machines (SVMs) (SVM (n.d.); Chang, Y. W., and Lin, C. J., 2008; Owrang et al., 2025), neural networks (Owrang et al., 2025), and other methods, are evaluated based on their predictive performances.

2 Literature Review

Breast cancer is the most common cancer among women in the United States, affecting approximately 1 in 8 women (13.1%). While early detection and improved treatments have led to a 44% decrease in mortality since 1989 (American Cancer Society, 2024), recurrence after treatment remains a major clinical challenge. About 2.3% of women diagnosed with breast cancer will die from the disease, and while the five-year survival rate is high (91%), survival rates drop at 10- and 15-years post-diagnosis, highlighting the importance of long-term monitoring and recurrence prediction (ACS, 2024).

Breast cancer recurrence (BCR) refers to the return of cancer after remission, and can be local, regional, or metastatic (Owrang, et al, 2025; Fan, 2010). Particularly concerning is early BCR, defined as recurrence within the first five years after treatment, which is often more aggressive and harder to treat (Medical News Today, 2024). Studies show that recurrence risk depends strongly on tumor receptor status and cancer stage. For example, patients with triple-negative breast cancer (ER−/PR−/HER2−) have the highest five-year recurrence rate (approximately 45.5%), while those with triple-positive tumors (ER+/PR+/HER2+) experience much lower recurrence (approximately 15.3%) (Neuman et al., ACS Journal, 2024). These findings suggest that recurrence risk is not uniform, and that follow-up care should be personalized based on tumor subtype and receptor status.

Historically, predictive models for breast cancer recurrence were built using statistical techniques, focusing on associations between a limited set of clinical variables (Engelhardt, E. G., 2023). While these models provided important early insights, they often lacked generalizability and failed to capture the complexity and variability of recurrence patterns (Evolution of Breast Cancer Recurrence Risk Prediction, ASCO

(Hasna El Haji et al., 2023). Statistical models also struggle with class imbalance, where recurrence cases are much rarer than non-recurrence cases, which can skew predictive accuracy.

Machine learning (ML) has emerged as a promising alternative for healthcare prognostics, offering the ability to model nonlinear relationships and analyze larger, more complex datasets (Abreu, P. H., et.al, 2016). In previous research (Owrang et al., 2025), six different ML algorithms were applied to predict breast cancer recurrence using the METABRIC dataset. Key predictive features included estrogen receptor status, progesterone receptor status, Pam50 and Claudin-low subtype, relapse-free status (in months), tumor size, and radiotherapy. Among the models tested, Decision Trees achieved the highest accuracy (approximately 86%) in predicting general BCR, demonstrating the promise of ML for this application.

Another critical issue identified in recent studies is bias and underrepresentation within existing datasets. Much of the data used in breast cancer recurrence models underrepresented racial and ethnic minority groups, particularly African and Middle Eastern populations, which limits the generalizability of current models and risks introducing bias into clinical recommendations (ASCO Systematic Review, 2024). Finally, researchers emphasize the importance of integrating social determinants of health, expanding datasets beyond molecular features to include clinical, behavioral, and demographic variables. Doing so could significantly improve the accuracy, fairness, and applicability of recurrence prediction models in diverse patient populations.

In summary, while substantial progress has been made in predicting breast cancer recurrence, especially through machine learning approaches, challenges remain. To be truly effective in clinical practice, future models must not only be accurate but also interpretable, generalizable, and inclusive. Our research builds on this body of work by focusing specifically on early breast cancer recurrence and by applying methods that prioritize both predictive power and explainability.

3 Breast Cancer Recurrence Datasets

Different techniques such as clustering, classification, and survival analyses were used to aid this data mining approach within the medical field. Our goal is to examine the factors that seem significant in early recurrence to take preventative measures as soon as possible to minimize risk of recurrence.

We began to explore the Wisconsin BCR Dataset containing 11 variables listed in Table 1. We explored all the listed categorical variables to create histograms, box plots, and heatmaps, to analyze each variable and compare the difference in recurrence and non- recurrence events. These plots will be further discussed and shown in later sections. We cleaned our data during this preprocessing phase, ensuring that categorical variables were encoded correctly, missing values were accounted for, and the data was prepared to be fed into a model.

For the sake of our exploratory analysis, we fit the Wisconsin dataset using a RandomForestClassifier (Liu et al., 2012), splitting the data into an 80% training set and a 20% testing set. We created mock data and fed it into an initial set of models, which predicted the possibility of recurrence at a rather low probability. To perform these steps, we used a Jupyter notebook with data analysis and machine learning libraries such as Pandas, Numpy, Matplotlib, and Seaborn. To begin modeling we used scikit-learn and many of its data cleaning tools such as train-test-split and LabelEncoder.

Next, we pivoted to investigate the Kaggle METABRIC Dataset, Table 2. The METABRIC (Molecular Taxonomy of Breast Cancer International Consortium) dataset is a comprehensive collection of clinical, genomic, and transcriptomic data for breast cancer patients, aimed at understanding the molecular subtypes of the disease and their impact on prognosis and treatment. It includes key clinical variables such as age at diagnosis, tumor size, lymph node status, and survival data, along with detailed genomic information like gene expression profiles, mutations, and copy number variations.

Table 1. Wisconsin Breast Cancer Recurrence Dataset.

age	Categorical (40–49, 50–59)
menopause	Categorical (premeno, ge40, menopause)
tumor-size	Categorical (15-19mm, 35-99mm)
inv-nodes	Categorical (0–2)
node-caps	Categorical (yes/no)
deg-malig	Numerical (1, 2, 3)
breast	Categorical (Right, Left)
breast-quad	Categorical (left_up, right_low)
irradiat	Categorical (yes, no)
class	**Categorical, Response Var (recurrence-events, no-recurrence-events)**
recurrence	**Categorical (1, 0), Response Var**

Of particular importance for predicting breast cancer recurrence (BCR), the dataset provides crucial time-related data on relapse-free survival, including the time to recurrence after initial treatment. This made the METABRIC dataset, an invaluable resource for developing predictive models with a focus on early BCR and helped identify factors that influence relapse events, which are essential for guiding treatment decisions and recurrence prediction. This dataset has 34 variables detailed and grouped for comprehension:

A set of feature selection algorithms were used to ultimately select six features. The feature selection algorithms used were Pearson Correlation, Logistic Regression, Chi- Squared Tests, Recursive Feature Elimination, Linear Support Vector Classification (SVC), and Decision Trees (Owrang et al., 2025). We used these algorithms to determine which variables would lead us to getting the best model. In a new study (Owrang et al., 2025), authors found the features selected for BCR prediction to include attributes ER Status, PR Status, Pam50+ Claudin-low subtype, relapse free status (months), tumor size, and whether the patient underwent radiotherapy.

In this study, we used the supervised machine learning algorithms including linear regression, decision tree (DC), random forest, and support vector machine (SVM), in addition to a multilayer perceptron (MLP) neural network model for our analysis. The results of these models will be discussed in the following section. Following this analysis, we assessed the data through clustering patterns, an avenue not found in our literature research.

We recreated the results using only early breast cancer recurrence instances. This meant that we would take the dataset and only focus on results that had a relapse free status that was less than or equal to sixty months (sixty months is equal to five years, the threshold for early breast cancer recurrence) (Neuman, H. B, et.al., 2023). With early BCR in mind, we tested to see if other variables would be significant compared to the ones, we used to model general BCR.

Table 2. METABRIC Breast Cancer Dataset.

Category	Variables
Clinical	Age at Diagnosis, Tumor Size, Tumor Stage, Lymph Nodes, Examined Positive, *Relapse Free Status (Months)*, Nottingham Prognostic Index, Primary Tumor Laterality, Overall Survival (Months), Overall Survival Status, Patient's Vital Status
Genomic	Pam50 + Claudin-low subtype, ER Status, HER2 Status, Neoplasm Histologic Grade Tumor,**Other Histologic Subtype, 3-Gene classifier subtype, Mutation Count
Treatment	Chemotherapy, Radiotherapy, Hormone Therapy
Demographic	Sex, Inferred Menopausal State, Cohort, Cancer Type, Cancer Type Detailed
Tumor-Related	Cellularity,**ER Status measured by IHC, PR Status
Other	PatientID, Oncotree Code
Response	**Relapse Free Status**

Age of Diagnosis, Nottingham Prognostic Index (NPI), and Tumor Stage may play an additional role in early recurrence prediction. Using the SelectKBest algorithm again, we found the same predictors, except for Relapse Free Status (Months), would lead to overfitting. As a result, we began including this variable in our analysis, finding all models had more realistic recall, accuracy, and precision, preventing a severe overfitting of the data.

The decision tree classifier was found to be the best fit in the case of general BCR and decided to use the algorithm for our early model fitting for Early BCR as well. After fitting the initial model using this algorithm, Gradient Boosting was applied to improve accuracy. Both age and tumor size were identified in having roles in the prediction of early BCR. Together this determined an initial model to predict early BCR.

An additional feature we wanted to consider was clustering algorithms. We began looking at some clustering as exhibited to the right. Clustering can be an interesting approach to take and compare to the classification algorithms we are currently using. Whereas classification is a supervised learning technique, clustering is an unsupervised learning technique that involves grouping a set of objects (data points) into clusters, where objects within a cluster are more like each other than to those in other clusters. We plotted the tumor size and relapse free status in 2 clusters, as an example-Fig. 1, but would like to explore more relations in the future.

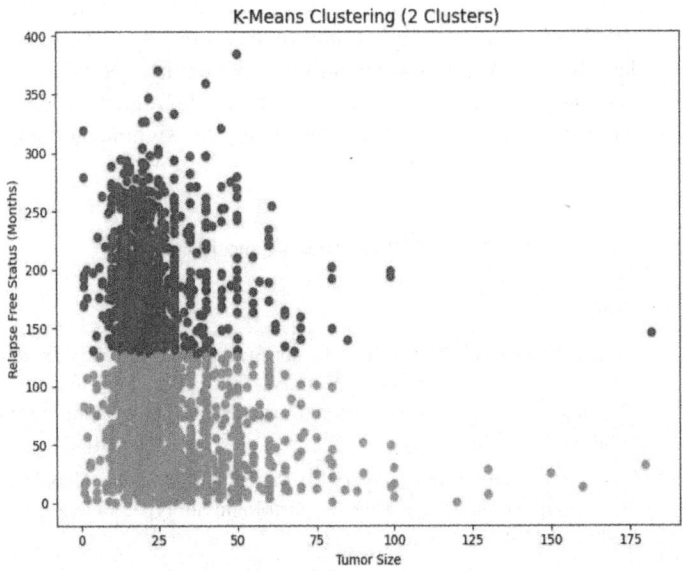

Fig. 1. K-Means Clustering for Tumor Size and Relapse Free Status (Months).

4 Experimental Results

Our first results were found using the Wisconsin BCR dataset. In this phase of data exploration, we identified key metrics that helped highlight the importance of predicting early BCR.

4.1 Wisconsin BCR Dataset: Exploratory Data

We visualized each of the predictor variables to measure recurrence events in each of these. We see there is variation depending on age (Fig. 2), the quadrant location (Fig. 3), which breast the tumor is in (Fig. 4), and stage of menopause (Fig. 5). There are higher rates of recurrence in the left low quad and overall, in the left breast. From our age plot, we see the largest amount of recurrence in the age range 40–49 which aligns with most cases occurring in perimenopausal or menopausal stages.

The following framework, Fig. 6, was used along with a RandomForestClassifier from sk.learn with the dataset split between 80% training data and 20% testing data. Utilizing these predictors and dataset train/test split, we created a preliminary model. For most of our modeling purposes, we use the same framework of test/train break up.

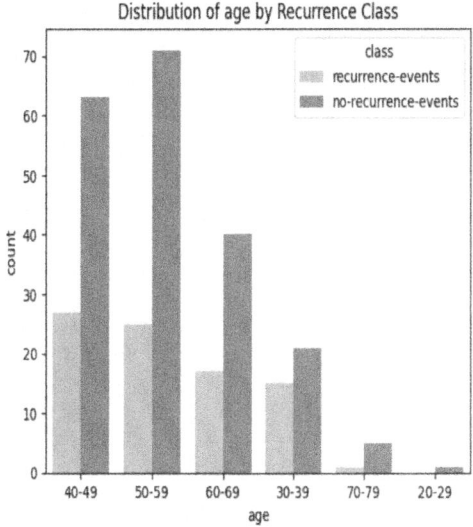

Fig. 2. Distribution of Age by Recurrence Class – Wisconsin Dataset.

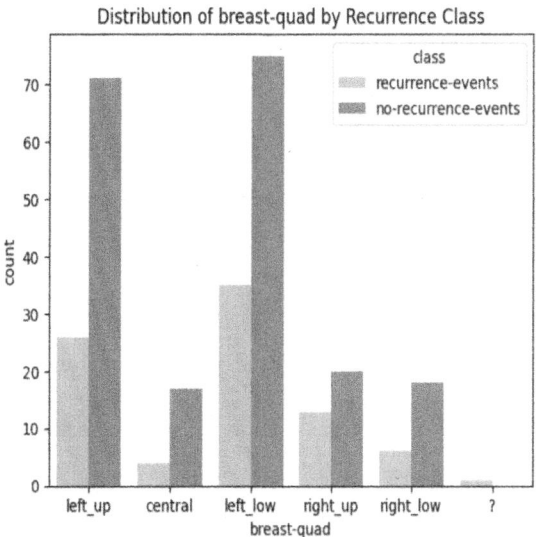

Fig. 3. Distribution of Breast-Quadrant by Recurrence Class – Wisconsin Dataset.

4.2 Decision Tree Model Metrics: Wisconsin BCR Dataset

We tested our preliminary model using some test code with mock patients inputting data such as:

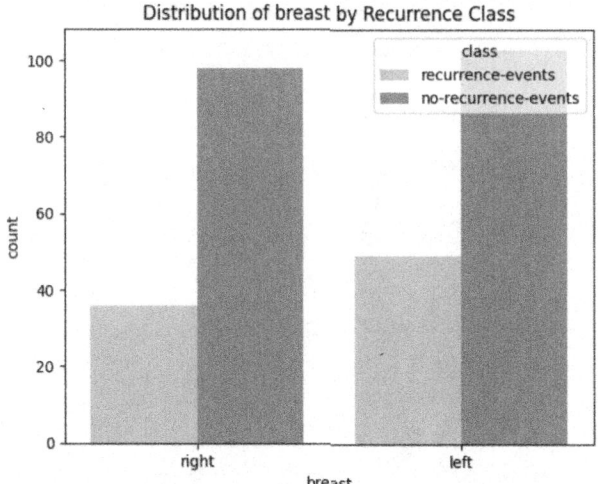

Fig. 4. Distribution of Breast by Recurrence Class – Wisconsin Dataset.

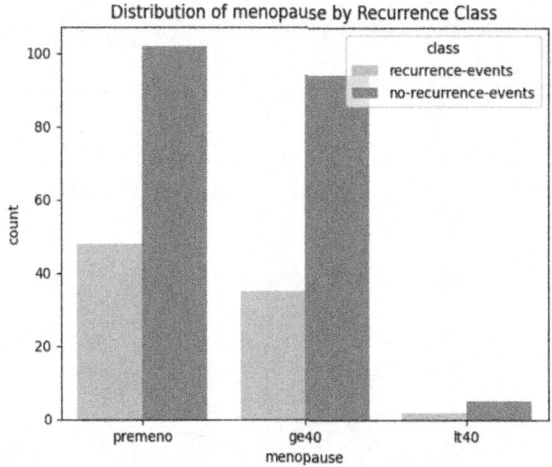

Fig. 5. Distribution of Menopause by Recurrence Class – Wisconsin Dataset.

test_data = [{ "age": "50-59", "menopause": "ge40", "tumor-size": "15-19", "inv-nodes": "0-2", "node-caps": "no", "deg-malig": 2, "breast": "right", "breast-quad": "central", "irradiat": "no" }].

With this, we ran the model and calculated precision and recall scores. As we can see from our model metrics, Table 3, the early model does significantly better with predicting no BCR compared to the presence of BCR. With this in mind, we began analyzing the Kaggle METABRIC Dataset.

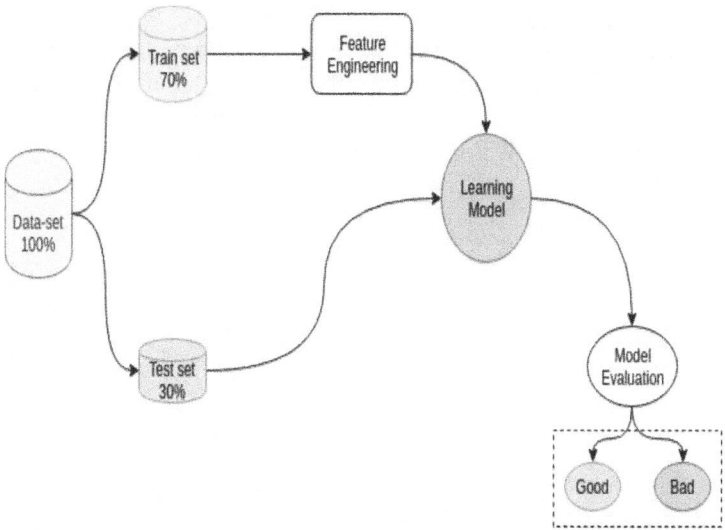

Fig. 6. Random Forest Classifier test/train framework.

Table 3. Decision Tree Model Metrics – Wisconsin BCR Dataset.

	Precision	Recall	F1	Support
No BCR (0)	0.77	0.85	0.81	40
Yes BCR (1)	0.57	0.44	0.50	18

4.3 METABRIC: Exploratory Data

As stated in the design requirements section III of this report, the METABRICS dataset has 34 variables in the full dataset, Table 2. With those 34 variables we used data analytics libraries such as pandas, numpy, and matplotlib to clean and visualize the data. There are certain variables that help us understand contextual information, but do not help for the purpose of predicting recurrence. For example, Sex and Overall Survival Status are not strong predictors. All our data pertains to female patients, and although it is interesting to see how many patients that endured recurrence events had survived, that would not allow us to predict recurrence. Besides variables that logically made sense, we had to utilize feature selection to decide which variables would best suit our model.

In conjunction with the research done in (Owrang, et al., 2025, Darst 2018), utilizing Decision Tree Feature Importance, Recursive Feature Elimination, Pearson Correlation, and Chi-Squared Tests, the variables we found to use include ER Status, PR Status, Radiotherapy, Pam50 + Claudin-low subtype, Relapse Free Status (Months), Tumor Size, and with Relapse Free Status as our response (Figs. 7, 8, 9, 10 and 11). In Fig. 11, you can see the data visualization of these selected features. We see that ER and PR status is positive for most patients, and more patients did Radio Therapy than those that did not. Something very notable here is that we see a lot of recurrence happening before 60 months, which is our early BCR period. We will dig into that further after our analysis of the general BCR data. We also see that Tumor Size for around half of patients is around 25 mm.

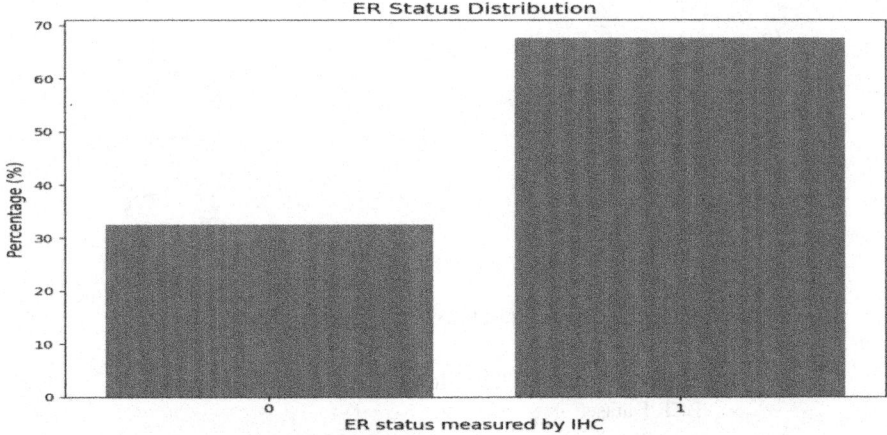

Fig. 7. Distribution of ER Status by Immunohistochemistry – METABRIC Dataset.

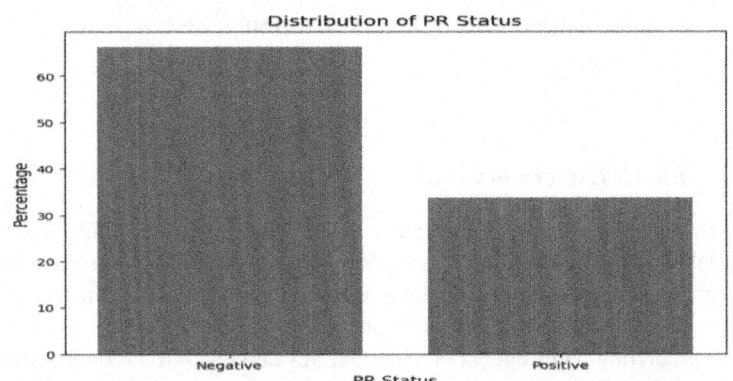

Fig. 8. Distribution of PR Status – METABRIC Dataset.

In the above figures, we also see that cancer did not return for many of the ER patients. However, with PR, the numbers are around the same. In terms of Radiotherapy, we see the number of recurrences is less than those of non-recurrence. When consulting the time variable, we see that around 20–30 months there are some strong leads of recurrence.

When looking at subtypes, we see that the LUM A Pam50+ Claudin-low subtype has a rather low recurrence, although it has the highest number of patients.

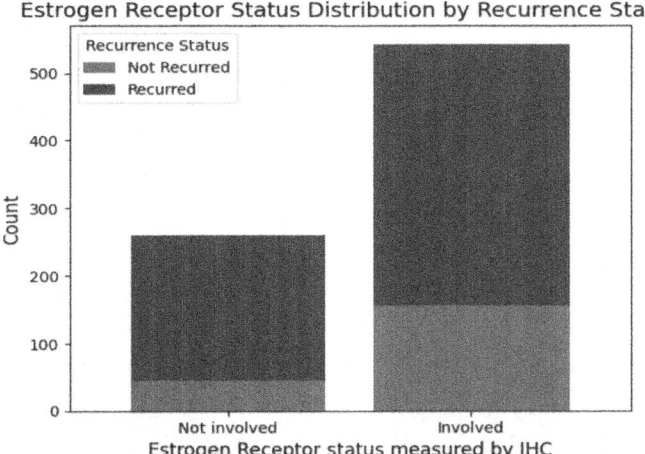

Fig. 9. Estrogen Receptor Status Distribution by Recurrence Status – METABRIC Dataset.

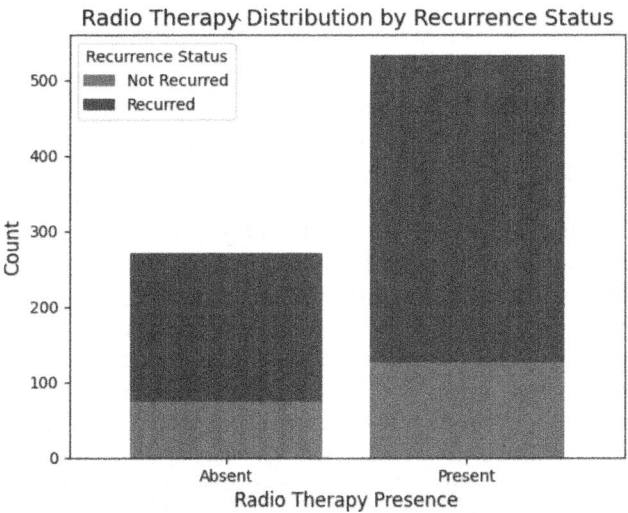

Fig. 10. Radiotherapy Presence Distribution by Recurrence Status – METABRIC Dataset.

We begin our modeling with a Decision Tree Algorithm. GradientBooster (Charbuty, B., & Abdulazeez, A., 2021) is one of the DT models that was chosen for this study because it is more accurate than a standard DT. Gradient boosting works by using simpler prediction models sequentially where each model tries to predict the error left over by the previous model." Our original decision tree metrics fell a bit below those in the paper, so we decided to implement the Gradient Boosting classifier, which significantly improved the model as reflected below with higher performance. We also made our dataset smaller, taking a sample of the data rather than the entire dataset.

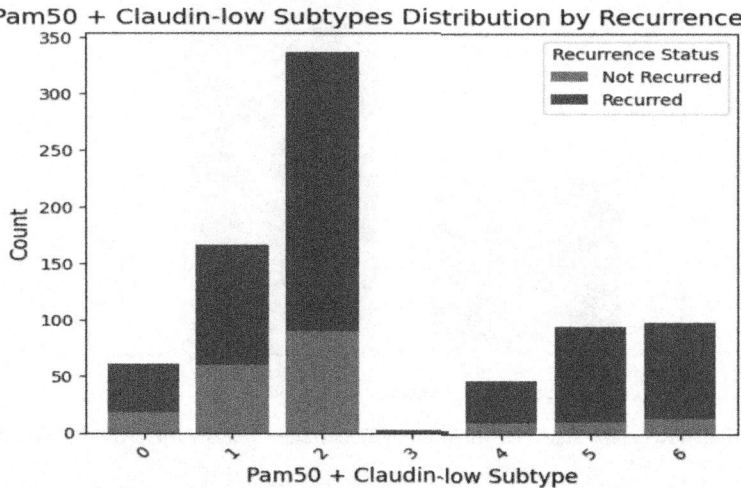

Fig. 11. Pam50+ Claudin-low Subtype Distribution by Recurrence Status- METABRIC Dataset.

grid_search = GridSearchCV(estimator=gbdt, param_grid=param_grid, cv=3, n_jobs=-1, verbose=2) grid_search.fit(X_train, y_train)

Above is a snippet of the algorithm for Gradient Boosting, which includes a grid search and allows for higher accuracy. Next, we attempted a Support Vector Machine approach. This approach is popularly used in two group classification problems. That model performed around the same as the Gradient Booster, even scoring slightly higher. Following the SVM approach, we used a Neural Network, specifically a Multilayer Perceptron approach. This has many layers of neurons that simulate how the brain processes information. This model also performs very similarly to SVM and Gradient Booster. Lastly, we used a Random Forest learning algorithm, which is a supervised learning method used oftentimes utilizing decision trees within classification problems. This algorithm performed a bit less accurately than in the past few, but not by much. Out of these models, we see that the SVM algorithm has the highest accuracy score, Table 4.

4.4 Early Breast Cancer Recurrence

All the preceding work has led to the main focus of our research – predicting early breast cancer recurrence (Guo, etc. 2017). That is, again, defined as Breast Cancer Recurrence that occurs within sixty months (five years). To accomplish this, we had to filter our data to only include cases in which recurrence occurs within sixty months. We looked at our other variables that we initially dropped to create our other models and thought it would be worth including Age at Diagnosis. Interestingly, it seems age had a large impact here as visualized in Fig. 12:

Using these variables, we created an initial model to predict early BCR. After running metrics on our first model, we had high scores for accuracy, precision, and recall. Similarly to our first model of general BCR, we see lower accuracy in our Early BCR predictions than those without BCR. The results can be seen in Table 5.

Table 4. ML Model Evaluation Metrics after Training and Optimization – METABRIC Dataset.

	Decision Tree	Gradient Boosting Classifier	SVM	MLP*	Random Forest*
Accuracy	0.67	0.72	0.72	0.79	0.78
Precision	0.83	0.75	0.72	0.78	0.77
Recall	0.67	0.91	1.00	0.98	1.00
F1	0.74	0.82	0.83	0.86	0.87
Confusion Matric	[[15 8] [19 39]]	[[5 18] [5 53]]	[[0 23] [058]]	[[2 18] [1 60]]	[[2 18] [0 61]]

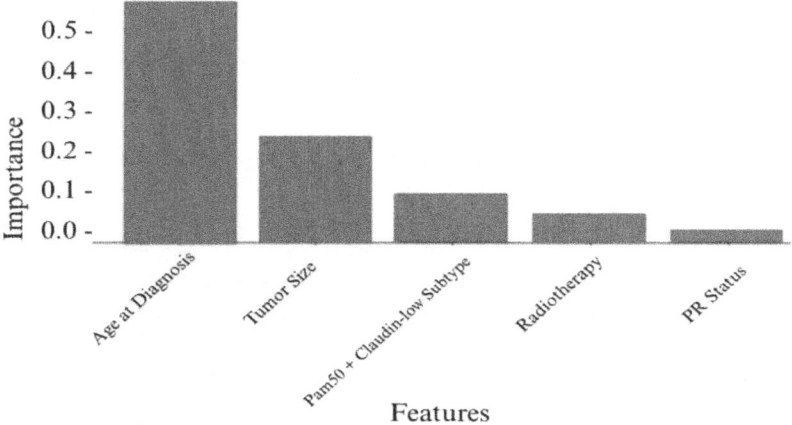

Fig. 12. Feature Importance in Decision Tree Model – METABRIC Dataset.

Table 5. Evaluation Metrics for our Initial Early BCR Prediction Model – METABRIC Dataset.

	Precision	Recall	F1	Support
No Early BCR (0)	0.70	0.78	0.74	330
Yes Early BCR (1)	0.43	0.33	0.37	168

The two highest performing models from this initial model fitting, the Random Forest- Fig. 13 and MLP-Fig. 14 models, were optimized to increase performance and accuracy. Fine-tuning the hyper parameters in these models led to accuracy of 78% for the Random Forest model and 79% for the MLP model. Both models show significant improvement in the reduction of false positives and false negatives, although false positives are still relatively high. False positives are not as worrying because it's better to be more proactive and keep an eye on it than think you're in the clear when you're not. Following the prediction model fitting and exploratory data analysis, there were several statistics that stood out when comparing early BCR to non-early BCR.

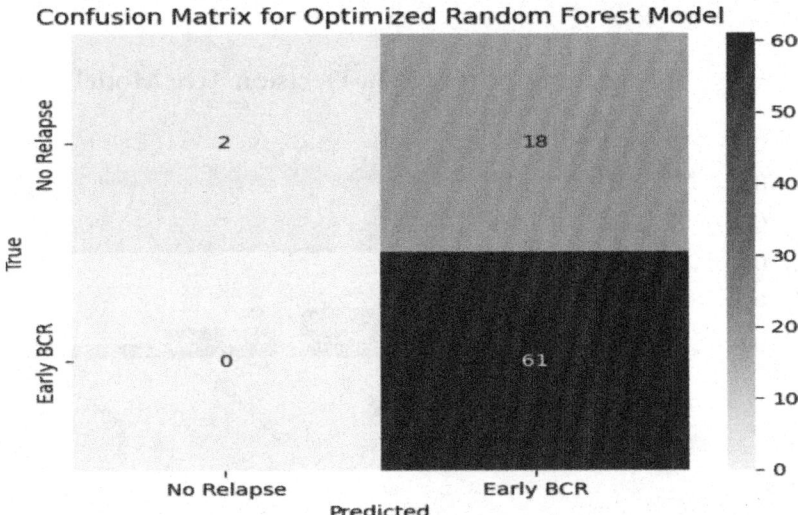

Fig. 13. Confusion Matrix for Optimized RandomForest Model – METABRIC Dataset.

There was a much higher presence of the Pam50 & Claudin-low subtype #3, also known as Luminal B, found in early BCR compared to general BCR, Fig. 15. The Luminal B subtype is a type of hormone-receptor-positive breast cancer which typically has faster growth rates and poorer prognosis. This finding is significant because luminal B breast cancer is more responsive to HER2 treatments, especially when caught earlier. Similar findings were found with ER status; there is a higher presence of estrogen receptor involvement in early BCR. This supports the findings that Luminal B breast cancer is more common in early BCR patients, because positive estrogen receptor status is a characteristic of Luminal B cancer.

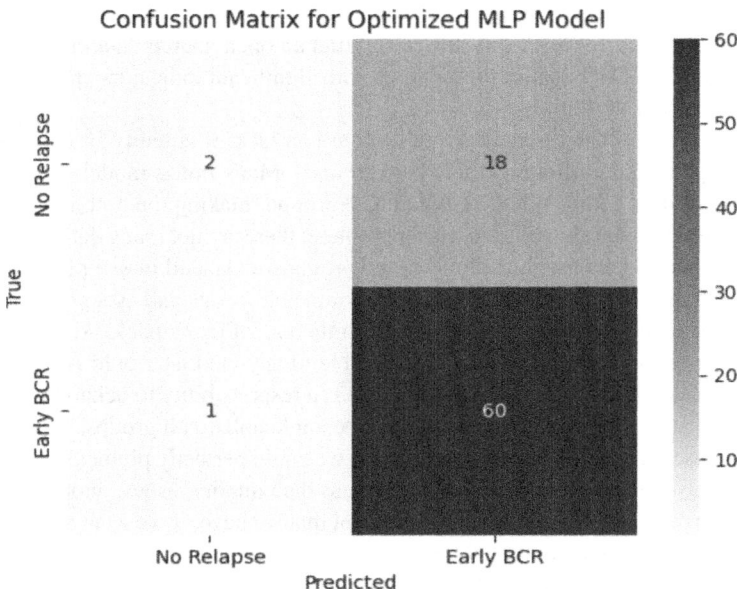

Fig. 14. Confusion Matrix for Optimized MLP Neural Network Model -METABRIC Dataset.

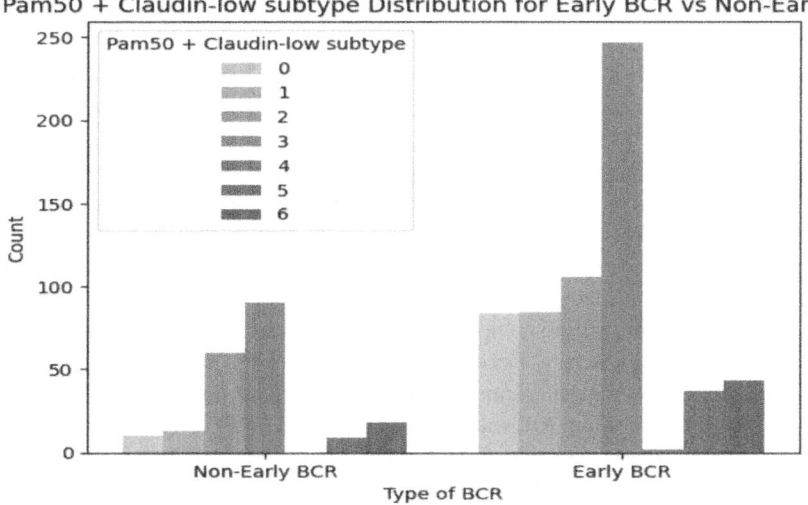

Fig. 15. Pam50+ Claudin-low Subtype Distribution for Early vs. Non-Early BCR – METABRIC Dataset.

5 Limitation and Future Direction

Especially when working with real patient clinical data, it is important that we are aware of limitations of our work and have our data analysis reviewed by experts in the field before coming to conclusions on our own. Given the lack of research in the field of Early Breast Cancer Recurrence, it was difficult to find an open-source dataset to work with. While the METABRIC dataset provided us with significant indicators and patient data, there are certainly limitations.

In the field of BCR research overall, there is a lack of equality in the training of models on patients of different ethnic backgrounds. Many times, models are trained on data from patients with a White or Asian background, making them non-generalizable to other demographics. In addition to that problem, there are not many datasets available to us that contain demographic, clinical, and prognostic data all in one place.

It is difficult to say that results are generalizable to all and is something that is important to work towards in the future. With the use of explainable AI tools, we aim to make our research transparent and accessible to anyone that would interact with it, especially patients and doctors. With this comes a responsibility to acknowledge where we lack data, and what information may not be applicable to all groups.

With these limitations, it was unlikely that we could perfectly predict the probability of early breast cancer recurrence. In addition to data quality issues, another limitation could be the processing power of the equipment that we have. If we want to train models with a large amount of data, it might be costly in terms of processing time and efficiency. It is important that we are aware of these limitations and have our data analysis reviewed by experts in the field before coming to conclusions on our own.

6 Conclusion

The high prevalence and mortality rate of breast cancer makes developing new methods to aid detection of early recurrence critical. Machine learning models improve the reliability of recurrence predictions, helping develop better patient intervention strategies and outcomes. This study underscores the potential of machine learning (ML) in early BCR predictions. By using sophisticated computational algorithms with large datasets, we have explored effective methods for identifying patients who have a higher risk of early recurrence.

Six different feature selection algorithms were utilized to determine which factors are most significant for predicting recurrence. Key risk factors identified include Estrogen Receptor Status, Progesterone Receptor Status, Pam50+ & Claudin-Low Subtype, presence in radiotherapy, tumor size, and relapse free status in Months.

The two highest performing ML models were the Random Forest and Multi-Layer Perceptron models. The accuracy rate of their predictions is 78% and 79%, respectively. Luminal B was discovered as significantly more prevalent in early BCR, which identifies it as a topic of interest and further research. This finding is promising for the development of early detection strategies.

While this study is promising, it also highlights some areas for further research. For instance, if possible, we plan on processing and analyzing mammograms with our model. This would allow us to include imaging data in concert with our patient data to enhance efficacy. This would also improve the model's scalability and applicability. We also need to keep addressing the challenges related to data quality, overfitting, and algorithmic bias to create an ethical and effective model.

The practical implications of this study are substantial. Accurate prediction of early BCR enables healthcare professionals to implement more thorough and proactive monitoring and tailed treatment plans. This would ultimately improve patient survival rates and quality of life.

Further steps recommended to advance ML in breast cancer recurrence predictions include expanding the range of datasets to include more clinical and demographic information to apply prediction models to a wider audience of people. A key focus should be addressing the imbalance in the distribution of recurrence and non-recurrence cases, as this can significantly impact model performance and generality.

Collaboration with oncologists and researchers is crucial to gain a deeper understanding of which features and factors are most influential in predicting recurrence, ensuring that the models are both clinically relevant and scientifically robust. Additionally, leveraging explainable AI techniques can enhance transparency in these predictive models, enabling patients to better understand the research findings (Alkhanbouli, R, et. al, 2025). This, in turn, can improve doctor-patient communication and support more informed decision making.

In conclusion, this study represents a significant step forward in harnessing ML to address the challenges of accuracy for early BCR prediction. We aim to contribute to a future where breast cancer survivors receive the appropriate care they need to remain in remission. Continued work with research like this is pivotal in realizing this goal and ensuring that technological advancements translate into meaningful improvements in patient outcomes.

References

Abreu, P.H., Santos, M.S., Abreu, M.H., Andrade, B., Silva, D.C.: Predicting breast cancer recurrence using machine learning techniques: a systematic review. ACM Comput. Surv. **49**(3), 52 (2016)

Alkhanbouli, R., Almadhaani, H.M.A., Alhosani, F., Simsekler, M.C.E.: The role of explainable artificial intelligence in disease prediction: a systematic literature review and future research directions. BMC Med. Inform. Decis. Making (2025). https://doi.org/10.1186/s12911-025-02944-6

Alva, N.: Using machine learning techniques to predict the recurrence of breast cancer. https://www.linkedin.com/pulse/using-machine-learning-techniques-predict-recurrence-breast-alva (2018)

American Cancer Society. Breast cancer facts & figures 2024–2025 (2024). https://www.cancer.org/content/dam/cancer-org/research/cancer-facts-and-statistics/breast-cancer-facts-and-figures/

Basu, T., Engel-Wolf, S., Menzer, O.: The ethics of machine learning in medical sciences: where do we stand today? Indian J. Dermatol. **65**(5), 358–364 (2020). https://doi.org/10.4103/ijd.IJD_419_20

Bisong, E.: More supervised machine learning techniques with scikit-learn. In: Building Machine Learning and Deep Learning Models on Google Cloud Platform. Apress (2019). https://doi.org/10.1007/978-1-4842-4470-8_24

Bradley, K.T.: Prognostic and Predictive Factors in Breast Cancer (2007). http://www.cap.org

Britt, T. Which types of breast cancer are most likely to recur? (2023). https://www.medicalnewstoday.com/articles/breast-cancer-types-recurrence-rates#Outlook-for-recurrent-breast-cancer

Charbuty, B., Abdulazeez, A.: Classification based on decision tree algorithm for machine learning. J. Appl. Sci. Technol. Trends **2**(01), 20–28 (2021). https://doi.org/10.38094/jastt20165

Darst, B.F., Malecki, K.C., Engelman, C.D.: Using recursive feature elimination in random forest to account for correlated variables in high dimensional data. BMC Genetics **19**(S1), 65 (2018). https://doi.org/10.1186/s12863-018-0633-8 PMID:30255764

Engelhardt, E.G., et al.: Predicting and Communicating the risk of recurrence and death in Women with early-stage breast cancer: a systematic review of risk prediction models. J. Clin. Oncol. **32**(3), 238–250 (2013). https://doi.org/10.1200/jco.2013.50.3417

Fan, Q., Zhu, C., Yin, L.: Predicting Breast Cancer Recurrence Using Data Mining Techniques. Academic Press (2010)

Guo, J., et al.: Revealing determinant factors for early breast cancer recurrence by decision tree. Inf. Syst. Front (2017)

El Haji, H., et al.: Evolution of breast cancer recurrence risk prediction: a systematic review of statistical and machine learning-based models. JCO Clin. Cancer Inform. **7**, e2300049 (2023). https://doi.org/10.1200/CCI.23.00049

Kaggle, Breast Cancer (METABRIC) (n.d.). https://www.kaggle.com/datasets/gunesevitan/breast-cancer-metabric

Lachman, M.: Wisconsin Breast cancer dataset. UCI Machine Learning Repository, University of California, School of Information and Computer Science, Irvine, CA (2019). http://archive.ics.uci.edu/ml/datasets/breast+cancer

Liu, Y., Wang, Y., Zhang, J.: New machine learning algorithm: random forest. In: The International Conference on Information Computing and Applications, pp. 246–252. Springer (2012). https://doi.org/10.1007/978-3-642-34062-8_32

Neuman, H.B., et al.: The influence of anatomic stage and receptor status on first recurrence for breast cancer within 5 years (AFT-01). Cancer **129**(9), 1351–1360. https://doi.org/10.1002/cncr.34656, (2023)

Owrang, M., et al.: Breast cancer prognosis for young patients. In Vivo **31**(4), 661–668 (2017). https://doi.org/10.21873/invivo.11109. PMID: 28652435; PMCID: PMC5566918

Owrang, M.M., Hosseinkhah, F., Ashktorab, H., Veen, R.: Challenges in Data Mining on Medical Databases. IGI Global (2009)

Owrang, M.M., Kanaan, Y.M., Copeland, R.L., Jr., Gaskins, M., DeWitty, R.L., Jr.: Exploratory data analysis on breast cancer prognosis. Encycl. Inform. Sci. Technol. Fourth Ed. (2018). https://doi.org/10.4018/978-1-5225-2255-3.ch156

Owrang Ojaboni, M., Schwarz, G., Jafari Horestani, F.: Prediction of breast cancer recurrence with machine learning. Encyclopedia Inform. Sci. Technol. 1–33 (2025). https://doi.org/10.4018/978-1-6684-7366-5.ch061

Pelc, C.: Breast cancer recurrence: Could cancer stage and receptor status help predict risk? Medical News Today (2023). https://www.medicalnewstoday.com/articles/breast-cancer-recurrence-could-cancer-stage-and-receptor-status-help-predict-risk?utm_source=ReadNext

Serif, G.: The 5 Clustering Algorithms Data Scientists Need To Know (2018). https://towardsdatascience.com/the-5-clustering-algorithms-data-scientists-need-to-know-a36d136ef68#:~:text=Gaussian

Structural and Connectivity Patterns in the Maven Central Software Dependency Network

Daniel Ogenrwot[✉], John Businge, and Shaikh Arifuzzaman

University of Nevada Las Vegas, Las Vegas, NV 89154, USA
ogenrwot@unlv.nevada.edu, {john.businge,
shaikh.arifuzzaman}@unlv.edu

Abstract. Understanding the structural characteristics and connectivity patterns of large-scale software ecosystems is critical for enhancing software reuse, improving ecosystem resilience, and mitigating security risks. In this paper, we investigate the Maven Central ecosystem, one of the largest repositories of Java libraries, by applying network science techniques to its dependency graph. Leveraging the Goblin framework, we extracted a sample consisting of the top 5,000 highly connected artifacts based on their degree centrality and then performed breadth-first search (BFS) expansion from each selected artifact as a seed node, traversing the graph outward to capture all libraries and releases reachable from those seed nodes. This sampling strategy captured the immediate structural context surrounding these libraries resulted in a curated graph comprising of 1.3 million nodes and 20.9 million edges. We conducted a comprehensive analysis of this graph, computing degree distributions, betweenness centrality, PageRank centrality, and connected components graph-theoretic metrics. Our results reveal that Maven Central exhibits a highly interconnected, scale-free, and small-world topology, characterized by a small number of infrastructural hubs that support the majority of projects. Further analysis using PageRank and betweenness centrality shows that these hubs predominantly consist of core ecosystem infrastructure, including testing frameworks and general-purpose utility libraries. While these hubs facilitate efficient software reuse and integration, they also pose systemic risks; failures or vulnerabilities affecting these critical nodes can have widespread and cascading impacts throughout the ecosystem.

Keywords: Software dependencies · Dependencies network analysis · Maven central repository · Software security · Software ecosystems · Network data mining

1 Introduction

The scale and complexity of modern software ecosystems have expanded rapidly due to the adoption of modular development practices and widespread reuse of open-source libraries [11, 22, 40, 41]. Maven Central, one of the most influential repositories for

Java artifacts, plays a pivotal role in contemporary software engineering by serving as a centralized hub through which millions of developers access and manage dependencies [49]. While this ecosystem prompt reuse, accelerates development, and promotes innovation, it also creates significant complexity in understanding the structural dynamics, connectivity patterns, and systemic risks inherent within the ecosystem [1]. For example, Bavota et al. [10] analyzed the impact of library changes on client systems and highlighted the widespread ripple effects caused by even minor updates, emphasizing the challenge of managing implicit and transitive dependencies. Understanding these properties is significant for modern software development. The structural characteristics of software ecosystems have direct implications for software engineering practices, ecosystem sustainability, and software security [22–24, 41]. For example, the existence of highly central artifacts suggests focal points for optimization, but also highlights critical points of failure. It also introduces considerable systemic complexity, making it increasingly difficult to reason about transitive dependencies, hidden couplings, and the potential for cascading failures [1, 23]. These studies emphasize the need to move beyond localized reasoning to account for the broader structural properties of software ecosystems.

The importance of understanding such structural complexity is illustrated by real-world incidents such as the *Log4Shell* vulnerability in the log4j library [29]. This widely used logging utility, embedded transitively in countless Java projects, exposed a critical zero-day vulnerability (CVE-2021-44228)[1] that affected millions of systems globally. Despite many projects not directly depending on log4j, their inclusion of libraries that in turn depended on it made them vulnerable. This event highlighted the urgent need to comprehend not only direct dependencies, but also the deeper structural and connectivity patterns of the ecosystem to evaluate systemic risk, and develop robust mitigation strategies.

The field of software ecosystem analysis has seen significant growth, especially as open-source repositories like Maven Central[2], npm[3], and PyPI[4] have become essential backbones of modern software development. Prior research has explored various aspects of software ecosystems, including semantic versioning [21, 37] and the impact of breaking changes [49], strong dependency relationships [1], the effects of dependency smells on software quality [32], the macro-level evolution of large software compilations [27], vulnerability tracking [24, 35, 39, 51, 61], dependency management tools, and localized impact assessments of specific libraries [24] or versions [62]. Tools such as Dependabot and Renovate [28] help developers manage and update their local dependencies efficiently [18]. However, most existing studies concentrate on localized or pairwise relationships, such as whether a project is up to date or if a particular dependency contains known vulnerabilities [34, 39]. These micro-level analyses, while essential, often fall short in addressing the ecosystem's global structure, resilience, and the role of infrastructural libraries in propagating risk [23]. For example, Zerouali et al. [63] explored the adoption of library updates and found that developers frequently avoid upgrades

---

[1] https://nvd.nist.gov/vuln/detail/cve-2021-44228.
[2] https://mvnrepository.com/repos/central.
[3] https://www.npmjs.com/.
[4] https://pypi.org/.

due to fear of breaking changes, leading to the accumulation of technical lag. While informative, their study primarily focuses on the relationship between a project and its direct dependencies. Similarly, Abdalkareem et al. [2] studied the impact of utility libraries on software quality, showing that certain libraries disproportionately influence maintainability and defect proneness. However, they do not consider how these central libraries are embedded within the broader network or how their failure might affect global connectivity. These findings highlight the necessity for a macro-structural perspective that captures the emergent properties of the ecosystem and enables reasoning about cascading effects, centrality, and resilience.

To address this gap, we adopt a macro-structural perspective on Maven Central by modeling its dependency relationships as a directed network. Using techniques from network science, we construct and analyze a comprehensive dependency graph that captures over 1.3 million artifacts and 20.9 million directed edges. We employ graph-theoretic metrics [4, 7, 53–56] such as degree distributions, PageRank, betweenness centrality, and connected component analysis to uncover hidden patterns, identify structurally critical nodes, and assess the ecosystem's connectivity and resilience to targeted failures. This global lens allows us to answer questions such as: How interconnected is Maven Central? Which libraries serve as infrastructural backbones? How vulnerable is the ecosystem to cascading failures triggered by the removal of central artifacts? To the best of our knowledge, this is the largest scale-free and small-world topological analysis conducted on Maven Central to date, combining both global (PageRank) and path-sensitive (betweenness) metrics across millions of nodes. This paper makes the following contributions:

- We construct a large-scale dependency graph of the Maven Central ecosystem, comprising over 1.3 million nodes and 20.9 million directed edges, capturing transitive and direct dependency relationships.
- We apply graph-theoretic and network science techniques to quantify structural properties using degree distributions, PageRank, betweenness centrality, and connected components metrics.
- We identify critical infrastructural libraries whose central roles in the network pose both opportunities for optimization and potential sources of systemic fragility.
- We release a fully reproducible replication package, including the dataset, preprocessing scripts, and analysis notebooks, to facilitate future research and validation [45].

2 Related Work

This section reviews foundational and recent research relevant to our investigation of Maven Central. First, we examine the structure and evolution of software ecosystems and their dependency networks. Next, we explore the application of graph mining and network analysis in software engineering domain. We then discuss recent studies specifically focusing on the Maven Central dependency graph. Finally, we identify persisting research gaps in the field.

Software Ecosystems and Dependency Networks. Software ecosystems comprise interrelated software projects that evolve together within a shared technical and organizational context, shaped by dependencies, governance structures, and social interactions among stakeholders [40, 41]. Foundational models of these ecosystems highlight the co-evolutionary interplay between technical architectures and community practices as critical forces driving their sustainability and growth [12, 31]. Building upon these theoretical insights, Businge et al. [14] provided empirical evidence by investigating how such dynamics unfold in practice, particularly through the lens of reuse and maintenance strategies among divergent forks across multiple ecosystems. Their broader investigations have also addressed API usage trends [15, 16] and software variants [13, 17, 44, 50], all of which contribute to the understanding of how ecosystems accommodate change, specialization, and reuse. Maven Central, a prominent repository for Java artifacts, offers a compelling case study of modern software supply chains due to its extensive reuse patterns, complex versioning schemes, and decentralized governance. Decan et al. [23] analyzed the dependency network in seven software ecosystems. Their work highlighted that not only the number of dependencies but also their structural arrangement determine the resilience of the ecosystem to breaking changes. More recently, studies have investigated the socio-economic dimensions of dependency networks. Saied et al. [52] presented a usage-pattern mining approach on Maven Central that automatically identifies cohesive clusters of libraries used together by thousands of client projects, highlighting common co-dependency structures and opportunities for improved recommendation and tooling support. Similarly, Kikas et al. [33] showed that isolated clusters often correspond to experimental or short-lived modules, which may be pruned or deprecated over time to reduce technical debt. Understanding the topology and dynamics of dependency graphs provides actionable insights for repository governance, dependency management tooling, and ecosystem health monitoring.

Graph Mining and Network Analysis in Software Ecosystems. Graph mining plays a fundamental role in extracting insights from complex network structures [3, 5, 6, 25, 57]. The application of network science and graph mining techniques to model and analyze software ecosystems is well established. Valverde and Solé [59] were among the first to characterize software dependency structures as scale-free networks, revealing non-random hierarchical topologies. Building on this foundation, Jansen and Brinkkemper [31] and Cosentino et al. [20] employed community detection, centrality, and clustering techniques to study software architecture, module cohesion, and ecosystem evolution over time. In the context of Maven Central, structural metrics such as modularity, path length, and node influence have proven critical for understanding system-level behavior and propagation dynamics. Recent research has leveraged temporal graph analysis and resilience modeling to uncover fragility points and assess robustness under evolving dependency loads [23]. Several studies focus on the evolution, risk, and hidden complexity of dependency networks. Kula et al. [34] investigated library migration practices and identified developer hesitancy in updating dependencies, often driven by concerns over breaking changes and integration effort. Bavota et al. [10] explored how API changes ripple through ecosystems, exposing the costs and fragility associated with software reuse. In a complementary study, Decan et al. [22] differentiated between direct and transitive dependencies, revealing that the majority of a project's dependency footprint lies within transitive layers, often outside the developer's immediate awareness or control. These studies highlight the growing complexity of modern software ecosystems and emphasize the technical debt and sustainability risks posed by unmanaged or opaque dependency structures.

Recent Studies on the Maven Central Repository. Building on this, recent large-scale analyses have begun to explore previously overlooked components of ecosystems. Notably, Shanto et al. [58] conducted a comprehensive study of 658,078 Maven artifacts, revealing that 15.4% of artifacts had no incoming dependencies (in-degree = 0), termed 'independent artifacts'. These findings position independent artifacts as safer, self-contained alternatives, though the study also flagged maintainability challenges. Furthermore, Yang-Smith and Abdellatif [61] analyzed 3,362 CVEs in Maven to explore the dynamics of vulnerability disclosure and mitigation across parent and dependent packages. A notable finding was the prevalence of "Publish-Before-Patch" scenarios, where severe vulnerabilities received faster patching post-disclosure, reducing response times from 151 to 78 days. Chowdhury et al. [19] investigated dependency maintenance trends in the Maven ecosystem, focusing on issues such as outdated dependencies, missed releases, and the challenges posed by complex dependency structures. Their quantitative analysis revealed that projects with fewer dependencies tend to have a higher incidence of missed releases, potentially undermining software quality and stability. Conversely, dependencies in the latest releases often exhibited positive freshness scores, suggesting improved dependency management practices in newer versions. Shafin et al. [57] explored the interplay between release practices, dependency freshness, and security in Maven artifacts. Their findings revealed that artifacts releasing updates more rapidly and consistently tended to remain up to date for longer periods and exhibited fewer vulnerabilities in their dependency chains.

Summary and Research Gaps Besides the aforementioned studies, several studies have investigated the Maven Central repositories to understand how developer interact with deprecated library versions [62], vulnerability management [24, 35, 42, 47, 48], among many others. However, there is still limited understanding of the holistic structural and connectivity properties of large-scale ecosystems like Maven Central. While prior work [10, 22, 34] has focused on localized or version-level analysis of dependency networks; our study provides a holistic, macro-structural view, quantifying centrality and connectivity across millions of artifacts and highlighting systemic fragility in ways not previously explored at this scale. Our work contributes to filling this gap by performing a comprehensive graph-based analysis of Maven Central's dependency network, characterizing its modularity, centralization, and connectivity evolution. In doing so, we aim to enrich the theoretical and practical understanding of software ecosystem resilience and architecture.

3 Methodology

This section presents comprehensive research questions and the methodology pipeline adopted in this study.

3.1 Research Questions

- **RQ1:** *How do metrics such as degree distribution characterize the dependency graph? Is the graph scale-free, small-world, or does it exhibit other known graph structures?* This research question can be divided into two parts. The first part examines how connections are distributed across the graph, identifying whether the network is dominated by a few highly connected hubs or is more evenly distributed. The second part investigates the overall architecture of the ecosystem to determine if it follows patterns seen in other complex systems. This is important because scale-free or small-world networks are known to be robust against random failures but vulnerable to targeted attacks, and understanding this helps assess the ecosystem's resilience and guides risk management strategies.
- **RQ2:** *Are certain types of projects more likely to be central (hubs) or peripheral (leaves) in the graph structure?* This question explores whether specific categories of projects (e.g., frameworks, libraries, utilities) systematically occupy key network positions. This is important because identifying which project types act as critical hubs can inform decisions on maintenance priorities, security audits, and resource allocation.
- **RQ3:** *Is the graph made up of connected components with no relationship between them?* This question asks whether the ecosystem is fragmented into isolated subgraphs or forms a cohesive whole. This is important because a cohesive network suggests a tightly integrated ecosystem with widespread interdependence, while fragmentation could signal isolated communities or unused modules, shaping strategies for ecosystem improvement and outreach.

3.2 Methodology Pipeline

An overview of the methodology pipeline is depicted in Fig. 1. The process is organized into four main steps: *Step 1* describes the data collection process, detailing how we extracted and prepared the dependency information from Maven Central. *Step 2* explains the graph sampling and reconstruction techniques used to build a representative and analyzable network. *Step 3* focuses on the computation of structural metrics using graph-theoretic algorithms. Finally, *Step 4* involves visual and exploratory analysis to interpret the network's topology and identify key structural patterns.

Step 1: Data collection. The study uses the Maven Central dependency graph provided through the Goblin framework and a Neo4j-based graph database released as part of the 2025 Mining Software Repository (MSR) mining challenge. Specifically, we used the dataset version with metrics goblin maven 30 08 24.dump, dated August 30, 2024 [30]. The dataset includes approximately 15 million nodes, comprising over 600,000 distinct libraries and more than 14 million releases. The graph also contains approximately 134 million edges, including over 119 million dependency edges and over 14 million versioning edges. The graph consists of two primary node types: *Artifact nodes*, which represent software components such as libraries, frameworks, or tools, and *Release* nodes, which denote specific published versions of these artifacts. Each release node includes metadata such as the version identifier and its publication timestamp (in Unix format). Artifacts are linked to their respective releases via a one-to-many relationship, reflecting multiple releases per artifact. Additionally, the graph contains *dependency edges*, which establish many-to-many relationships from release nodes to other artifact nodes, capturing both direct and transitive dependencies among components. This rich and large-scale dataset enables a comprehensive analysis of the structural and connectivity properties of the Maven Central ecosystem.

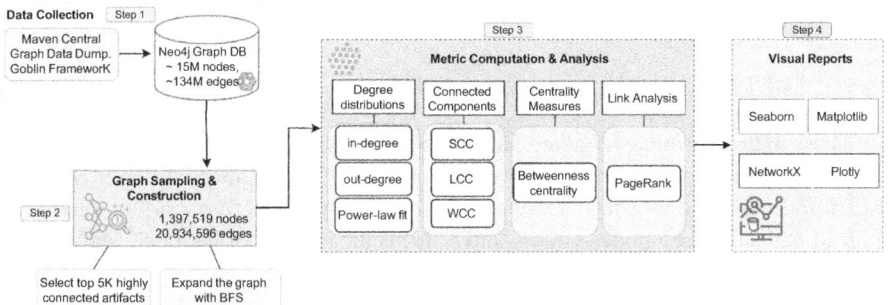

Fig. 1. Overview of the methodology pipeline.

Step 2: Graph Sampling and Construction. To extract a representative and computationally manageable subgraph from the full Maven Central dependency graph, we selected the top 5,000 most highly connected artifacts based on their incoming degree. This strategy is motivated by the scale-free nature of the software dependency ecosystems, where a small subset of central nodes contributes disproportionately to overall connectivity and dependency propagation [9, 22]. We used Cypher query executed against the Neo4j database (Listening 1.1). This query can be easily adapted to retrieve any number N of top-ranked artifacts, depending on the desired sampling scope.

Listing 1.1: Cypher query to identify the top 5,000 highly connected artifacts in the Maven Central graph.
```
MATCH (r:Release)-[:dependency]->(a:Artifact)
RETURN a.id AS artifactId, COUNT(*) AS numIncoming
ORDER BY numIncoming DESC
LIMIT 5000;
```

To capture the immediate structural context surrounding these artifacts, we applied a breadth-first search (BFS) expansion from each selected artifact as a seed node, traversing the graph outward to a depth of two. This sampling strategy ensures that all releases associated with each artifact, as well as all artifacts that depend on any of these releases are included. To avoid redundancy, we implemented a node visitation check, ensuring that each artifact or release node is only included once in the sampled graph. We then constructed a directed graph using NetworkX [46], modeling two types of relationships: (i) artifact-to-release edges representing the release lineage of an artifact, and (ii) release-to-dependent-artifact edges capturing the dependency relations. The resulting graph comprises 1,397,519 nodes (libraries and releases) and 20,934,596 edges, providing a rich and a structurally diverse dataset suitable for subsequent metric computation and visualization.

Step 3: Metrics Computation. To characterize the structural properties of the sampled Maven Central dependency network, we modeled the ecosystem (subgraph generated constructed in *Step 2*) as a directed graph $G = (V, E)$, where nodes V represent software artifacts (libraries and releases) and edges $E \subseteq V \times V$ capture directed dependency relations. We computed a suite of graph-theoretic metrics to analyze this network, including degree distributions [4], centrality measures [26], and connected components [25, 56]. For each node $v \in V$, we calculated the in-degree $d^-(v)$ and out-degree $d^+(v)$, defined respectively in Eq. 1, Where $d(v) = d^-(v) + d^+(v)$ denotes the total degree.

$$d^-(v) = |\{u \in V : (u, v) \in E\}|, \quad d^+(v) = |\{u \in V : (v, u) \in E\}|, \tag{1}$$

These metrics provide foundational insights into module popularity and dependency sprawl. We also computed betweenness centrality to quantify the control a node exerts over information flow, using the standard formulation 2 where σ_{st} is the number of shortest paths between nodes s and t, and $\sigma_{st}(v)$ is the number of path that pass through node v [38].

$$C_B(v) = \sum_{s,t \in V s \neq v \neq t} \frac{\sigma_{st}(v)}{\sigma_{st}}, \tag{2}$$

To measure influence via recursive link analysis, we employed PageRank centrality, computed as shown in Eq. 3, where $\alpha \in (0, 1)$ is a damping factor (typically set to 0.85) and Pre(v) denotes the set of predecessors of node v.

$$PR(v) = \frac{1-\alpha}{|V|} + \alpha \sum_{u \in \text{Pre}(v)} \frac{PR(u)}{d^+(u)}, \tag{3}$$

In addition, we analyzed largest connected components (LCC), weakly connected components (WCC) and strongly connected components (SCC) to assess ecosystem modularity and fragmentation; the former considers connectivity when edge direction is ignored, while the latter requires mutual reachability under directed paths. All metrics were computed using the NetworkX [46] Python library, chosen for its robustness in handling large directed graphs. This combination of metrics was selected based on both theoretical foundations and empirical precedent to provide a comprehensive understanding of topological prominence, dependency cohesion, and network resilience. These insights directly support our broader investigation into centralization trends, single points of failure, and the structural fragility of software ecosystems.

Step 4: Visual Reports. To facilitate the interpretation and communication of our findings, we generated a series of visualizations using NetworkX, Matplotlib, Seaborn and Plotly python packages. These tools enabled us to produce network diagrams, degree distribution plots, and clustering visualizations. The resulting figures provide both quantitative summaries and qualitative insights into the structural characteristics of the ecosystem, ensuring that complex patterns are presented in an interpretable and accessible manner.

4 Results and Discussion

RQ1: How do metrics such as degree distribution characterize the dependency graph? Is the graph scale-free, small-world, or does it exhibit other known graph structures?

To understand the structural properties of the Maven Central dependency graph, we first computed the overall degree distribution using the sampled dataset described in Sect. 3. As shown in Fig. 2a, the distribution is highly skewed and exhibits a heavy-tailed pattern, indicating a small number of nodes with extremely high connectivity and a majority with minimal connections. This reflects a centralized reuse structure commonly observed in large-scale software ecosystems. To investigate whether this distribution follows a power-law (a hallmark of scale free networks), we used the powerlaw Python library to fit a power-law model to the sampled data. The resulting fit (Fig. 2b) confirms power-law behavior in the tail of the distribution, consistent with scale-free topologies. Visual inspection of the log-log plot further supports this, as the empirical curve aligns closely with the theoretical power-law line.

To further understand how this global structure manifests at the component level, we next examined the in-degree and out-degree distributions of libraries and releases, respectively. As shown in Fig. 3, the in-degree distribution of libraries and the out-degree distribution of releases both follow heavy-tailed patterns. This supports the finding that a small number of core libraries are heavily reused across many releases, whereas most releases depend on relatively few other components.

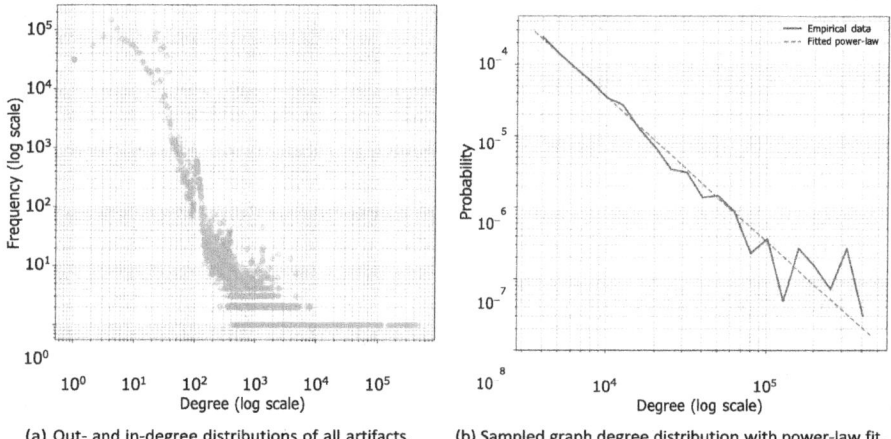

(a) Out- and in-degree distributions of all artifacts. (b) Sampled graph degree distribution with power-law fit.

Fig. 2. Comparison of degree distributions in the Maven dependency graphs. (a) shows full-graph out- and in-degree distributions. (b) highlights the power-law fit for the sampled graph.

Overall, these results demonstrate that the Maven Central ecosystem exhibits both scale-free and small-world properties. The scale-free structure, driven by a few highly connected infrastructural nodes, enables efficient reuse but also introduces systemic risks such as cascading failures or vulnerability propagation if these hubs are compromised.

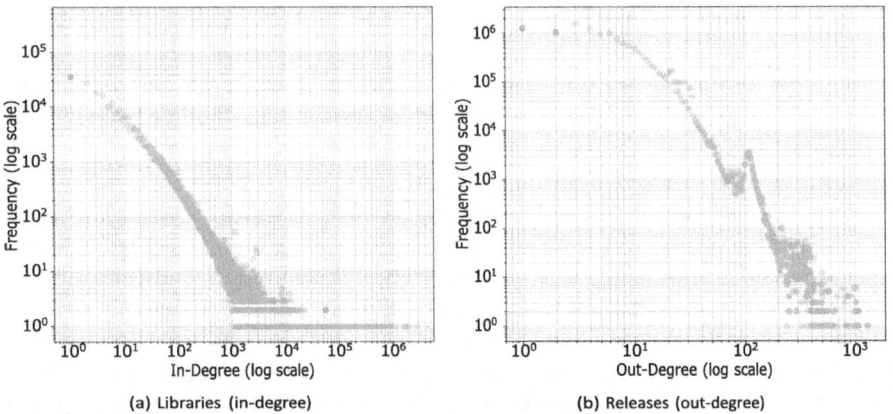

Fig. 3. Degree distributions in the Maven dependency graphs, plotted in log-log scale. (a) In-degree distributions of all libraries in the Maven dependency graph., and (b) Out-degree distributions of all releases in the Maven dependency graph.

Discussion and Implications. Our analysis reveals that the Maven Central dependency graph follows a power-law degree distribution and exhibits small-world characteristics. These structural properties have clear implications for how the ecosystem functions and where it can fail. From a network science perspective, the presence of a power-law distribution suggests that Maven Central behaves like a scale-free network. In such networks, a small number of nodes, called *hubs*, have a very large number of connections, while most nodes have relatively few. This mirrors the structure we observe, where a few widely reused libraries support a large number of dependent projects. These hubs often emerge due to preferential attachment, where popular libraries are more likely to attract additional dependents over time. In practice, this structure benefits the ecosystem since developers can rely on well-tested, widely adopted libraries to accelerate development and reduce duplication. The small-world property of the network means that any two artifacts are typically connected through just a few intermediate dependencies. This property enhances dependency resolution and encourages modular yet interconnected designs.

However, these same features also create risks because large proportion of the ecosystem depends on a few central libraries. Any issues with those hub such as bugs, security vulnerabilities, or a lack of maintenance can have widespread effects. Failures in these components may break builds, introduce security holes, or cause large-scale disruptions. Incidents like the left-pad removal in npm [2] or the *Log4Shell* vulnerability in log4j [29] show how fragile these systems can become when critical libraries are affected. To address these risks, dependency management tools should go beyond checking for outdated or vulnerable versions. They should also consider the network role of each dependency. For example, tools could warn developers when they are about to depend on a high-centrality artifact, or suggest alternative libraries to reduce concentration. Ecosystem maintainers can use this structural information to identify libraries that need stronger governance, additional maintainers, or dedicated funding.

Structural and Connectivity Patterns

> 💡 **Summary - RQ1:** *The Maven Central dependency graph exhibits a highly skewed, heavy-tailed degree distribution, with a small number of hubs possessing very high connectivity and a large number of nodes with minimal connections. The degree distribution follows a power-law behavior, confirming that the ecosystem exhibits scale-free network properties. The graph also demonstrates small-world characteristics. These structural patterns reflect a centralized reuse model, where key artifacts serve as infrastructural hubs supporting many dependent projects.*

RQ2: Are certain types of projects more likely to be central (hubs) or peripheral (leaves) in the graph structure?

To identify the most influential nodes in the Maven Central dependency graph, we computed the PageRank centrality for all nodes in the sampled graph. Table 1 presents the top 10 nodes ranked by their PageRank score, representing the primary hubs of the ecosystem. Figure 4 shows the network visualization of the ten artifacts with the highest PageRank scores and their immediate neighbors. Our analysis reveals that the most central nodes predominantly consist of core infrastructure libraries. Notably, the org.apache.felix:org.apache.felix.scr.ds-annotations artifact and its versions occupy the highest ranks, indicating their critical role in defect detection and metadata analysis across the ecosystem. These nodes consistently show the highest PageRank scores, reflecting their significant influence within the dependency network. In addition, widely used testing frameworks such as junit:junit and the org.hamcrest:hamcrest-all family also appear among the top hubs. These libraries are essential components for quality assurance and testing activities, reaffirming their importance not only within project-level practices but also as ecosystem-wide enablers of software reliability and verification. These findings align with existing knowledge that infrastructural and quality-assurance libraries tend to emerge as key hubs in software ecosystems [10, 22, 34, 41]. However, our analysis quantifies this influence at scale and underscores the systemic risk associated with these libraries, failures or vulnerabilities in these nodes could propagate across a vast number of dependent projects.

We further analyzed the dependency graph by computing betweenness centrality to identify nodes that act as critical connectors or bridges between different parts of the ecosystem. Table 2 presents the top 10 nodes ranked by betweenness centrality score, highlighting components that serve as key pathways for dependency flows. Our findings show that io.micrometer:micrometer-core occupies the highest position, indicating its role as a pivotal component for application observability and performance monitoring across the ecosystem. This is followed closely by org.springframework:spring-core, a foundational utility in the Spring framework that supports a wide array of applications and services. Other prominent nodes include io.projectreactor:reactor-core, facilitating concurrency and parallelism, and org.mariadb.jdbc:mariadb-java-client, a widely adopted JDBC driver enabling database connectivity.

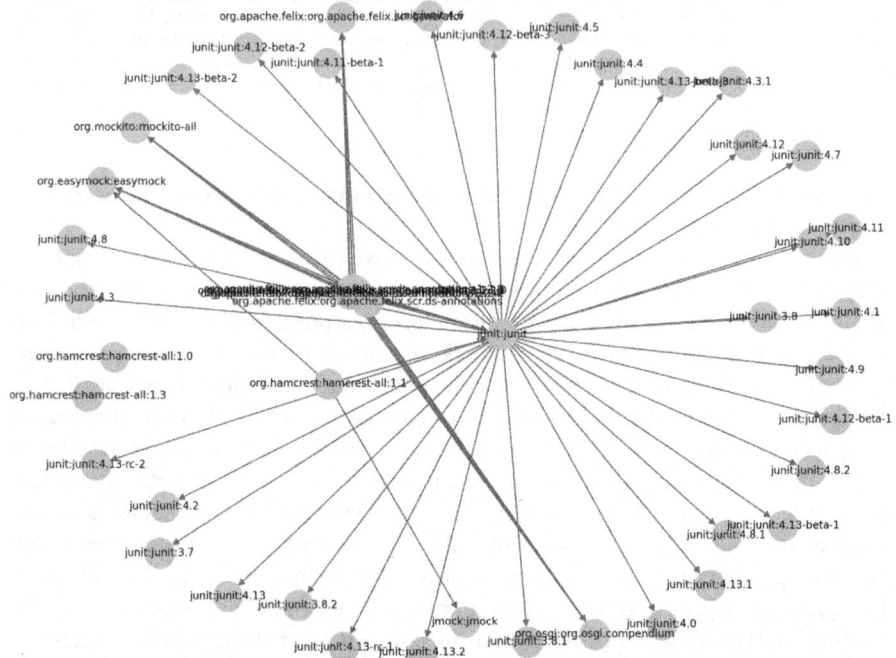

Fig. 4. Network visualization of the top 10 artifacts by PageRank in the Maven Central dependency graph. Each hub is connected to its immediate neighbors, including all release versions and dependent artifacts.

The presence of these nodes as top-ranked by betweenness centrality suggests they not only serve their primary purposes but also act as bridges connecting otherwise disparate modules, frameworks, or services. Interestingly, essential libraries for testing (org.assertj:assertj-core, org.testng:testng) and logging (org.apache.logging.log4j:log4j-core) also appear among the top bridging nodes, reinforcing their ecosystem-wide integration beyond individual projects. These results highlight the dual role of these libraries as specialized tools and as integrative backbones of the ecosystem, emphasizing their criticality from both functionality and network structure perspectives. Their high betweenness scores underline their systemic importance, where disruptions or vulnerabilities could isolate significant portions of the ecosystem or break dependency chains. Conversely, the lowest-ranked nodes by incoming dependencies shown in Table 3 are primarily API management components from the WSO2 ecosystem, reflecting their peripheral role. These modules are specialized and domain-specific, serving fewer projects and indicating limited reuse across the broader Maven Central ecosystem.

Discussion and Implications. Our analysis of PageRank and betweenness centrality reveals a clear structural divide within the Maven Central ecosystem. A small number of libraries serve as highly influential hubs, while the majority of components remain on the periphery with limited influence. Libraries such as org.apache.felix.scr.ds-annotations, junit:junit, and org.hamcrest:hamcrest-all appear at the top of the PageRank rankings.

Table 1. To 10 artifacts in the Maven Central dependency graph with the highest PageRank scores, representing potential ecosystem hubs; includes each artifact's identifier, functional category, and associated descriptive tags

Rank	Node Name	PageRank Score	Category	Tags
1	org.apache.felix:org.apache.Felix.scr.ds-annotations	0.0043	Defect detection metadata	Quality, defect, annotations, analysis, metadata, jetbrains
2	org.apache.felix:org.apache.Felix.scr.ds-annotations:1.2.8	0.0041	Defect detection metadata	Quality, defect, annotations, analysis, metadata, jetbrains
3	org.apache.felix:org.apache.Felix.scr.ds-annotations:1.2.4	0.0041	Defect detection metadata	Quality, defect, annotations, analysis, metadata, jetbrains
4	org.apache.felix:org.apache.Felix.scr.ds-annotations:1.2.2	0.0041	Defect detection metadata	Quality, defect, annotations, analysis, metadata, jetbrains
5	org.apache.felix:org.apache.Felix.scr.ds-annotations:1.2.0	0.0041	Defect detection metadata	Quality, defect, annotations, analysis, metadata, jetbrains
6	org.apache.felix:org.apache.Felix.scr.ds-annotations:1.2.10	0.0041	Defect detection metadata	Quality, defect, annotations, analysis, metadata, jetbrains
7	junit:junit	0.0039	Testing Frameworks & Tools	Testing, junit, quality
8	org.hamcrest:hamcrest-all:1.1	0.0026	Testing Frameworks & Tools	Matching, hamcrest, testing, quality

(*continued*)

Table 1. (*continued*)

Rank	Node Name	PageRank Score	Category	Tags
9	org.hamcrest:hamcrest-all:1.0	0.0026	Testing Frameworks & Tools	Matching, hamcrest, testing, quality
10	org.hamcrest:hamcrest-all:1.3	0.0026	Testing Frameworks & Tools	Matching, hamcrest, testing, quality

These artifacts are widely reused across many domains and often appear deep in dependency chains. Their high centrality reflects their foundational role in the ecosystem, supporting tasks like annotation processing, unit testing, and quality assurance. Similarly, libraries with high betweenness centrality such as spring-core and micrometer-core act as bridges between different parts of the graph. These components connect otherwise separate modules and facilitate interoperability between frame-works. Because they sit on many paths between other libraries, they are critical for maintaining ecosystem cohesion. However, this centrality also introduces risk. If a highly central library becomes deprecated, vulnerable, or poorly maintained, its failure can affect a large number of downstream projects. These libraries act as "choke points," and disruptions can cause widespread instability, failed builds, or security exposure across the ecosystem.

On the other end of the spectrum are low-centrality nodes, many of which come from the org.wso2. Carbon.apimgt package family. These components are domain-specific, used primarily in narrow contexts such as API gateway management. They are reused less frequently and have few connections to other parts of the graph. While their limited influence reduces the risk of widespread disruption, it also means they may lack visibility, strong community support, or long-term maintenance. These traits can make them vulnerable to neglect, even if they pose less systemic risk. These findings highlight the value of centrality-aware software engineering. Tools for dependency management, security analysis, and migration planning could prioritize highly central libraries for extra scrutiny, testing, and monitoring. At the same time, maintainers of these critical packages should be supported through practices like shared maintainership, automated release pipelines, and community funding. Software developers should also weigh the structural role of a dependency before adopting it, especially if it introduces tight coupling to a critical or fragile node in the ecosystem.

> *Summary - RQ2:* We found that projects acting as network hubs predominantly belong to core ecosystem infrastructure categories, such as core infrastructure libraries (e.g., apache felix) and testing frameworks (e.g., JUnit and hamcrest). These hubs exhibit high in-degree and PageRank, reflecting their critical role in the ecosystem's reuse structure. In contrast, peripheral nodes characterized by low degree and often no outgoing dependencies typically represent specialized application modules or niche libraries. This central-peripheral structure highlights the layered nature of the Maven Central ecosystem, where a small set of infrastructural components supports a broad, diverse periphery of application-level projects.

Table 2. Ten artifacts in the Maven Central dependency network ranked by highest betweenness centrality, highlighting the key bridges that connect distinct clusters; includes each artifact's identifier, functional category, and descriptive tags.

Rank	Node Name	Betweenness Score	Category	Tags
1	io.micrometer:micrometer-core	0.0644	Application Metrics	Observability, monitoring, management, metrics, performance
2	org.springframework:spring-core	0.0604	Core Utilities	Beans, context, spring, IoC, framework
3	io.projectreactor:reactor-core	0.0603	Concurrency Libraries	Reactor, concurrency, parallel, multithreading
4	com.hazelcast:hazelcast	0.0465	In-Memory Data Grid	Hazelcast, clustering, caching, distributed data
5	org.mariadb.jdbc:mariadb-java-client	0.0450	JDBC Drivers	Database, SQL, JDBC, driver, MariaDB, client, RDBMS, MySQL
6	org.assertj:assertj-core	0.0443	Assertion Libraries	Assert, quality, testing, assertion, fluent, validation
7	org.testcontainers:mariadb	0.0427	Database Testing Tools	Database, container, testing, MariaDB, MySQL
8	com.amazonaws:aws-java-sdk	0.0378	Cloud Storage SDK	Persistence, AWS, S3, Amazon, SDK, client, storage

(*continued*)

Table 2. (*continued*)

Rank	Node Name	Betweenness Score	Category	Tags
9	org.apache.logging.log4j:log core	0.0365	Logging Frameworks	Logging, Log4j, Apache
10	org.testng:testng	0.0283	Testing Frameworks	Testing, quality assurance

RQ3: Is the graph made up of connected components with no relationship between them?

To assess the global cohesion of the Maven Central dependency graph, we computed both weakly and strongly connected components (Table 4). The analysis shows that the graph contains a total of 24 connected components when ignoring edge directionality. The largest connected component (LCC) encompasses 1,394,930 nodes, accounting for approximately 99.81% of all nodes in the graph. This result highlights the highly cohesive nature of the ecosystem, where nearly all projects are directly or indirectly connected through dependencies. The remaining 23 small components represent only 0.19% of the nodes, indicating the presence of isolated or niche clusters that are not integrated into the broader ecosystem. These components may correspond to abandoned projects, experimental modules, or domain-specific tools with limited reuse.

Furthermore, the graph exhibits a large number of strongly connected components (SCCs) due to its inherent directionality. In total, 1,120,071 SCCs were identified, with the largest SCC comprising 208,270 nodes. This suggests that while the ecosystem is highly connected in a weak sense, the number of fully reciprocally reachable nodes (strong connectivity) is relatively lower and confined to specific subsets of the network. This pattern is typical of dependency graphs, where dependencies often form directed acyclic structures at the macro scale but exhibit locally dense cycles within certain project families or frameworks. Overall, these findings confirm that the Maven Central ecosystem is structurally cohesive, with almost all artifacts interconnected in a single giant component. However, the directionality of dependencies results in fragmented strongly connected regions, reflecting the hierarchical and modular organization of software projects.

Discussion and Implications. Our weak connectivity analysis shows that the Maven Central dependency graph contains a single giant component comprising 99.81% of all artifacts. This confirms the "giant component" phenomenon commonly seen in complex networks, where nearly all nodes are directly or indirectly connected. This result is consistent with findings from prior work on both Maven and npm ecosystems [8, 23, 43], which highlight how such cohesion supports rapid reuse and broad propagation of updates and patches. In such a tightly integrated ecosystem, any change such as a performance improvement or a security fix can reach a vast number of downstream projects. This amplifies both the benefits and risks of reuse. To manage this effectively, dependency tools should incorporate algorithms that efficiently compute transitive closures

Table 3. Top 10 leaf nodes in the Maven Central dependency graph, ranked by their minimal incoming dependency count. These artifacts represent end-point packages with the fewest dependents and thus minimal downstream reuse or highly specialized functionality.

Rank	Node Name	Incoming Edges	Category	Tags
1	org.wso2.carbon.apimgt:org.Wso2.carbon.apimgt.core	2967	API Management	Bundle, api, osgi
2	org.wso2.carbon.apimgt:org.Wso2.carbon.apimgt.core.Feature	2967	API Management	Api
3	org.wso2.carbon.apimgt:org.Wso2.carbon.apimgt.Throttling.siddhi.extension	2927	API Management	Bundle, api, osgi, extension
4	org.wso2.carbon.apimgt:org.Wso2.carbon.apimgt.keymgt.Client	2722	API Management	Bundle, client, api, osgi
5	org.wso2.carbon.apimgt:org.Wso2.carbon.apimgt.api	2722	API Management	Bundle, api, osgi
6	org.wso2.carbon.apimgt:org.Wso2.carbon.apimgt.keymgt.Stub	2722	API Management	Bundle, api, stub, osgi
7	org.wso2.carbon.apimgt:org.Wso2.carbon.apimgt.impl	2721	API Management	Bundle, implementation, api, osgi
8	org.wso2.carbon.apimgt:org.Wso2.carbon.apimgt.gateway	2721	API Management	Bundle, gateway, api, osgi
9	org.wso2.carbon.apimgt:org.Wso2.carbon.apimgt.keymgt	2721	API Management	Bundle, api, osgi
10	org.wso2.carbon.apimgt:org.Wso2.carbon.apimgt.Keymanager.feature	2712	API Management	Manager, api

and assess impact, allowing developers to anticipate the ripple effects of modifications or vulnerabilities.

Although only 23 weakly connected components lie outside the giant component, they still warrant attention. These isolated subgraphs represent just 0.19% of the ecosystem but are often unmaintained, experimental, or domain-specific. Prior research suggests such modules may carry compatibility and security risks if reintroduced into production systems [33]. Identifying and deprecating these isolates can help reduce technical debt and improve overall ecosystem hygiene. Repository maintainers could consider archiving or consolidating these components as part of long-term sustainability efforts. The strongly connected component (SCC) analysis paints a different picture. With over one million SCCs and the largest containing about 208,000 nodes, most of the dependency graph forms a directed acyclic structure with only local cycles. These bidirectional links often occur in framework internals or within tightly coupled module families. While small in scope, such cycles can complicate dependency resolution and increase the risk of version conflicts, commonly referred to as "dependency hell" [60]. Recognizing the boundary between acyclic regions and cyclic clusters offers opportunities for tool optimization. Dependency resolvers could treat strongly connected subgraphs as localized units, reducing global complexity during resolution. For example, conflict resolution efforts can be focused within these clusters without affecting the rest of the graph.

Table 4. Summary of graph connectivity metrics for the Maven Central dependency network, including counts of weakly and strongly connected components, sizes of the largest components, and overall coverage percentages

Metric	Value
Total number of connected components	24
Size of largest connected component (LCC)	1,394,930
Total number of nodes in the graph	1,397,519
LCC coverage	99.81%
Remaining small components (23 in total)	0.19%
Number of strongly connected components (SCCs)	1,120,071
Size of largest SCC	208,270

From a tooling and governance perspective, these results suggest a two-pronged approach. Global vulnerability scanning, migration planning, and usage analytics can leverage the reachability of the giant component. At the same time, localized resolution strategies can benefit from strong component decomposition. Ecosystem maintainers should prioritize audits and support for artifacts within the giant component, especially those with high centrality, while also monitoring peripheral or isolated clusters for archival or reintegration decisions.

> 💡 **Summary – RQ3**: Our connectivity analysis of the Maven Central dependency graph identifies 24 weakly connected components, of which a single giant component contains 1,394,930 artifacts, or 99.81% of the entire network. The remaining 23 minor components account for only 0.19% of nodes and correspond to isolated or specialized packages. This structure confirms that Maven Central functions as a nearly universal software supply chain, enabling efficient transitive reuse and rapid dissemination of updates and vulnerability patches. At the same time, a few disconnected clusters highlight residual niche ecosystems that may require targeted maintenance or deprecation.

5 Threats to Validity

While our study provides valuable insights into the structural and connectivity patterns in the Maven Central dependency network, it is also subject to several threats to validity. To limit computational cost, we first selected 5,000 artifacts with highest degree centrality and then performed breadth-first expansion to include all releases and libraries reachable from those seeds. While this approach captures the neighbourhood of highly connected hubs, it may underrepresent peripheral regions and small isolates. Graph sampling and seed selection strategies are known to bias degree and connectivity distributions if not carefully calibrated [36]. However, given the dataset's characteristics, this bias is significantly reduced because over 99.81% of the artifacts are part of a single giant strongly connected component. In addition, our study captures a single point in time and does not account for temporal dynamics such as artifact churn, version deprecation, or gradual integration of isolates into the giant component. Lastly, although Maven Central is the largest Java ecosystem repository, our findings may not generalize to other language ecosystems or to private corporate registries. Ecosystems such as npm or PyPI differ in their module publishing practices and dependency semantics [23]. Thus, the prevalence of a giant component and the fragmentation into localized cycles may vary in ecosystems with different governance models or package formats. Future research should account for these limitations to enhance the generalizability of the findings.

6 Conclusion

In this study, we conducted a comprehensive structural and connectivity analysis of the Maven Central dependency ecosystem using graph-theoretic approaches. By applying metrics such as degree distributions, PageRank, betweenness centrality, and connected components, we uncovered critical insights into the ecosystem's architecture. Our results show that Maven Central exhibits a scale-free and small-world structure with a small number of highly influential hubs supporting a vast periphery of dependent projects. This configuration promotes efficient reuse but also introduces systemic risks, as failures or vulnerabilities in central nodes could have widespread cascading effects. We also identified the presence of local clusters and a cohesive largest connected component, underscoring the tightly interwoven nature of the ecosystem. Overall, our findings contribute valuable knowledge for researchers, practitioners, and ecosystem maintainers, offering guidance for improving resilience, managing risks, and prioritizing future maintenance and security efforts. Future work will explore vulnerability propagation dynamics, variation of shortest path lengths between projects and communities, and cross-ecosystem comparisons. Furthermore, this analysis is based on a static snapshot of the repository. It would be interesting to examine the temporal evolution of connectivity to understand how new libraries join the ecosystem or become abandoned. Moreover, further study of the strongly connected clusters could investigate the root causes of cycles and their impact on developer productivity. Finally, correlating connectivity patterns with metrics such as download counts, issue resolution time, or security incident frequency could yield deeper insights into the trade-offs between cohesion and modularity in large software ecosystems.

References

1. Abate, P., Di Cosmo, R., Boender, J., Zacchiroli, S.: Strong dependencies between software components. In: 2009 3rd International Symposium on Empirical Software Engineering and Measurement, pp. 89–99 (2009)

2. Abdalkareem, R., Nourry, O., Wehaibi, S., Mujahid, S., Shihab, E.: Why do developers use trivial packages? an empirical case study on npm. In: Proceedings of the 2017 11th Joint Meeting on Foundations of Software Engineering, pp. 385–395. ESEC/FSE 2017, Association for Computing Machinery, New York, NY, USA (2017). https://doi.org/10.1145/3106237.310 6267
3. Abdelhamid, S., et al.: Cinet 2.0: A cyberinfrastructure for network science. In: 2014 IEEE 10th International Conference on e-Science, vol. 1, pp. 324–331. IEEE (2014)
4. Arifuzzaman, S., Khan, M., Marathe, M.: Fast parallel algorithms for counting and listing triangles in big graphs. ACM Trans. Knowl. Discov. Data (TKDD) **14**(1), 5:1–5:34 (2019). https://doi.org/10.1145/3365676
5. Arifuzzaman, S.M., Khan, M., Marathe, M.: Patric: A parallel algorithm for counting triangles and computing clustering coefficients in massive networks. Technical Report (2012)
6. Arifuzzaman, S., Arikan, H.S., Faysal, M., Bremer, M., Shalf, J., Popovici, D.: Unlocking the potential: Performance portability of graph algorithms on kokkos framework. In: 2024 IEEE International Parallel and Distributed Processing Symposium Workshops (IPDPSW). pp. 526–529 (2024)
7. Arifuzzaman, S., Pandey, B.: Scalable mining, analysis and visualisation of protein-protein interaction networks. Int. J. Big Data Intell. **6**(3–4), 176–187 (2019)
8. Barabási, A.L.: Network science. Philos. Trans. Royal Soc. A: Math. Phys. Eng. Sci. **371**(1987), 20120375 (2013)
9. Barabási, A.L., Albert, R.: Emergence of scaling in random networks. Science **286**(5439), 509–512 (1999). https://doi.org/10.1126/science.286.5439.509
10. Bavota, G., Canfora, G., Di Penta, M., Oliveto, R., Panichella, S.: How the apache community upgrades dependencies: an evolutionary study. Empirical Softw. Eng. **20**(5), 1275–1317 (2015). https://doi.org/10.1007/s10664-014-9325-9
11. Bogart, C., Ka¨stner, C., Herbsleb, J., Thung, F.: How to break an api: cost negotiation and community values in three software ecosystems. In: Proceedings of the 2016 24th ACM SIGSOFT International Symposium on Foundations of Software Engineering, pp. 109–120. FSE 2016, Association for Computing Machinery, New York, NY, USA (2016). https://doi.org/10.1145/2950290.2950325
12. Bosch, J.: From software product lines to software ecosystems. In: SPLC, vol. 9, pp. 111–119 (2009)
13. Businge, J., Abdi, M., Demeyer, S.: Analyzing Variant Forks of Software Repositories from Social Coding Platforms, pp. 131–152. Springer International Publishing, Cham (2023), https://doi.org/10.1007/978-3-031-36060-2_6
14. Businge, J., Openja, M., Nadi, S., Berger, T.: Reuse and maintenance practices among divergent forks in three software ecosystems. Empir. Softw. Eng. **27**(2), 54 (2022). https://doi.org/10.1007/s10664-021-10078-2
15. Businge, J., Serebrenik, A., van den Brand, M.: Analyzing the eclipse api usage: Putting the developer in the loop. In: 2013 17th European Conference on Software Maintenance and Reengineering. pp. 37–46 (2013)
16. Businge, J., Serebrenik, A., van den Brand, M.G.J.: Eclipse api usage: the good and the bad. Software Qual. J. **23**(1), 107–141 (2015). https://doi.org/10.1007/s11219-013-9221-3
17. Businge, J., Zerouali, A., Decan, A., Mens, T., Demeyer, S., De Roover, C.: Variant forks – motivations and impediments. In: 2022 IEEE International Conference on Software Analysis, Evolution and Reengineering (SANER), pp. 867–877 (2022)
18. Chen, L.: Continuous delivery: huge benefits, but challenges too. IEEE Softw. **32**(2), 50–54 (2015)
19. Chowdhury, B., Rabbi, M.F., Hasan, S., Zibran, M.F.: Insights into dependency maintenance trends in the maven ecosystem (2025). arXiv preprint arXiv:2503.22902

20. Cosentino, V., Izquierdo, J.L.C., Cabot, J.: Assessing the bus factor of git repositories. In: 2015 IEEE 22nd International Conference on Software Analysis, Evolution, and Reengineering (SANER). pp. 499–503 (2015)
21. Decan, A., Mens, T.: What do package dependencies tell us about semantic versioning? IEEE Trans. Software Eng. **47**(6), 1226–1240 (2021)
22. Decan, A., Mens, T., Claes, M.: On the topology of package dependency networks: a comparison of three programming language ecosystems. In: Proccedings of the 10th European Conference on Software Architecture Workshops. ECSAW'16, Association for Computing Machinery, New York, NY, USA (2016), https://doi.org/10.1145/2993412.3003382
23. Decan, A., Mens, T., Grosjean, P.: An empirical comparison of dependency network evolution in seven software packaging ecosystems. Empir. Softw. Eng. **24**(1), 381–416 (2019). https://doi.org/10.1007/s10664-017-9589-y
24. Düsing, J., Hermann, B.: Analyzing the direct and transitive impact of vulnerabilities onto different artifact repositories. Digital Threats (2022). https://doi.org/10.1145/3472811
25. Faysal, M.A.M., Arifuzzaman, S., Chan, C., Bremer, M., Popovici, D., Shalf, J.: Hypc-map: A hybrid parallel community detection algorithm using information-theoretic approach. In: 2021 IEEE High Performance Extreme Computing Conference (HPEC), pp. 1–8. IEEE (2021)
26. Faysal, M.A.M., Bremer, M., Chan, C., Shalf, J., Arifuzzaman, S.: Fast parallel index construction for efficient k-truss-based local community detection in large graphs. In: Proceedings of the 52nd International Conference on Parallel Processing, pp. 132–141 (2023)
27. Gonzalez-Barahona, J.M., Robles, G., Michlmayr, M., Amor, J.J., German, D.M.: Macro-level software evolution: a case study of a large software compilation. Empirical Softw. Eng **14**(3), 262–285 (2009). https://doi.org/10.1007/s10664-008-9100-x
28. He, R., He, H., Zhang, Y., Zhou, M.: Automating dependency updates in practice: an exploratory study on github dependabot. IEEE Trans. Software Eng. **49**(8), 4004–4022 (2023)
29. Hiesgen, R., Nawrocki, M., Schmidt, T.C., Wählisch, M.: The log4j incident: A comprehensive measurement study of a critical vulnerability. IEEE Trans. Netw. Serv. Manage. **21**(6), 5921–5934 (2024)
30. Jaime, D.: Goblin: Neo4j maven central dependency graph (2024). https://doi.org/10.5281/zenodo.13734581
31. Jansen, S., Finkelstein, A., Brinkkemper, S.: A sense of community: a research agenda for software ecosystems. In: 2009 31st International Conference on Software Engineering – Companion Volume. pp. 187–190 (2009)
32. Jolak, R., Karlsson, S., Dobslaw, F.: An empirical investigation of the impact of architectural smells on software maintainability. Journal of Systems and Software 225, 112382 (2025), https://www.sciencedirect.com/science/article/pii/S0164121225000500
33. Kikas, R., Gousios, G., Dumas, M., Pfahl, D.: Structure and evolution of package dependency networks. In: 2017 IEEE/ACM 14th International Conference on Mining Software Repositories (MSR), pp. 102–112 (2017)
34. Kula, R.G., German, D.M., Ouni, A., Ishio, T., Inoue, K.: Do developers update their library dependencies? Empir. Softw. Eng. **23**(1), 384–417 (2018). https://doi.org/10.1007/s10664-017-9521-5
35. Kumar, S.H.B.I., Sampaio, L.R., Martin, A., Brito, A., Fetzer, C.: A comprehensive study on the impact of vulnerable dependencies on open-source software. In: 2024 IEEE 35th International Symposium on Software Reliability Engineering (ISSRE), pp. 96–107 (2024)
36. Leskovec, J., Faloutsos, C.: Sampling from large graphs. In: Proceedings of the 12th ACM SIGKDD International Conference on Knowledge Discovery and Data Mining. pp. 631–636. KDD'06, Association for Computing Machinery, New York, NY, USA (2006). https://doi.org/10.1145/1150402.1150479

37. Li, W., Wu, F., Fu, C., Zhou, F.: A large-scale empirical study on semantic versioning in golang ecosystem. In: 2023 38th IEEE/ACM International Conference on Automated Software Engineering (ASE), pp. 1604–1614 (2023)
38. Liu, L., Wang, Z., Zhang, X., Zhuang, Y., Liang, Y.: A novel model for noninvasive haemoglobin detection based on visibility network and clustering network for multi-wavelength ppg signals. Algorithms **18**(2) (2025), https://www.mdpi.com/1999-4893/18/2/75
39. Ma, Z., Mondal, S., Chen, T.H.P., Zhang, H., Hassan, A.E.: Vulnet: towards improving vulnerability management in the maven ecosystem. Empir. Softw. Eng. **29**(4), 83 (2024). https://doi.org/10.1007/s10664-024-10448-6
40. Manikas, K.: Revisiting software ecosystems research: a longitudinal literature study. J. Syst. Softw. **117**, 84–103 (2016). https://www.sciencedirect.com/science/article/pii/S0164121216000406
41. Mens, T., Claes, M., Grosjean, P., Serebrenik, A.: Studying Evolving Software Ecosystems based on Ecological Models, pp. 297–326. Springer Berlin Heidelberg (2014). https://doi.org/10.1007/978-3-642-45398-4_10
42. Nachuma, C., Hossan, M.M., Turzo, A.K., Zibran, M.F.: Decoding dependency risks: a quantitative study of vulnerabilities in the maven ecosystem. In: 2025 IEEE/ACM 22nd International Conference on Mining Software Repositories (MSR), pp. 270–274 (2025)
43. Newman, M.E.J.: The structure of scientific collaboration networks. Proc. National Acad. Sci. **98**(2), 404–409 (2001). https://www.pnas.org/doi/abs/10.1073/pnas.98.2.404
44. Ogenrwot, D., Businge, J.: Refactoring-aware patch integration across structurally divergent java forks (2025). arXiv preprint arXiv:2508.06718
45. Ogenrwot, D., Businge, J., Arifuzzaman, S.M.: Replication package: Structural and connectivity patterns in the maven central software dependency network (2025). https://doi.org/10.5281/zenodo.1569189
46. Platt, E.L.: Network science with Python and NetworkX quick start guide: explore and visualize network data effectively. Packt Publishing Ltd (2019)
47. Rabbi, M.F., Champa, A.I., Paul, R., Zibran, M.F.: Chasing the clock: How fast are vulnerabilities fixed in the maven ecosystem? In: 2025 IEEE/ACM 22nd International Conference on Mining Software Repositories (MSR), pp. 265–269 (2025)
48. Rabbi, M.F., Paul, R., Champa, A.I., Zibran, M.F.: Understanding software vulnerabilities in the maven ecosystem: patterns, timelines, and risks. In: 2025 IEEE/ACM 22nd International Conference on Mining Software Repositories (MSR), pp. 290–294 (2025)
49. Raemaekers, S., van Deursen, A., Visser, J.: Semantic versioning and impact of breaking changes in the maven repository. J. Syst. Softw. **129**, 140–158 (2017), https://www.sciencedirect.com/science/article/pii/S0164121216300243
50. Ramkisoen, P.K., et al.: Pareco: patched clones and missed patches among the divergent variants of a software family. In: Proceedings of the 30th ACM Joint European Software Engineering Conference and Symposium on the Foundations of Software Engineering, pp. 646–658. ESEC/FSE 2022, Association for Computing Machinery, New York, NY, USA (2022). https://doi.org/10.1145/3540250.3549112
51. Ruohonen, J.: An empirical analysis of vulnerabilities in python packages for web applications. In: 2018 9th International Workshop on Empirical Software Engineering in Practice (IWESEP), pp. 25–30 (2018)
52. Saied, M.A., Ouni, A., Sahraoui, H., Kula, R.G., Inoue, K., Lo, D.: Improving reusability of software libraries through usage pattern mining. J. Syst. Softw. **145**, 164–179 (2018), https://www.sciencedirect.com/science/article/pii/S0164121218301699
53. Sattar, N.S., Anfuzzaman, S.: Data parallel large sparse deep neural network on gpu. In: 2020 IEEE International Parallel and Distributed Processing Symposium Workshops (IPDPSW), pp. 1–9. IEEE (2020)

54. Sattar, N.S., Arifuzzaman, S., Zibran, M.F., Sakib, M.M.: Detecting web spam in webgraphs with predictive model analysis. In: 2019 IEEE International Conference on Big Data (Big Data), pp. 4299–4308 (2019)
55. Sattar, N.S., Buluc, A., Ibrahim, K.Z., Arifuzzaman, S.: Exploring temporal community evolution: algorithmic approaches and parallel optimization for dynamic community detection. Appl. Netw. Sci. **8**(1), 64 (2023)
56. Sattar, N.S., Ibrahim, K.Z., Buluc, A., Arifuzzaman, S.: DyG-DPCD: a distributed parallel community detection algorithm for large-scale dynamic graphs. Int. J. Parallel Prog. **53**(1), 4 (2025)
57. Shafin, M.S., Rabbi, M.F., Hasan, S., Zibran, M.F.: Faster releases, fewer risks: A study on maven artifact vulnerabilities and lifecycle management (2025). arXiv preprint arXiv:2503.24349
58. Shanto, M.H., Asaduzzaman, M., Mondal, M., Chowdhury, S.: Dependency dilemmas: A comparative study of independent and dependent artifacts in maven central ecosystem (2025). arXiv preprint arXiv:2504.12261
59. Valverde, S., Solé, R.V.: Hierarchical small worlds in software architecture (2003). arXiv preprint cond-mat/0307278
60. Wang, Y., et al..: Do the dependency conflicts in my project matter? In: Proceedings of the 2018 26th ACM Joint Meeting on European Software Engineering Conference and Symposium on the Foundations of Software Engineering, pp. 319–330. ESEC/FSE 2018, Association for Computing Machinery, New York, NY, USA (2018), https://doi.org/10.1145/3236024.3236056
61. Yang-Smith, C., Abdellatif, A.: Tracing vulnerabilities in maven: A study of cve lifecycles and dependency networks. In: 2025 IEEE/ACM 22nd International Conference on Mining Software Repositories (MSR), pp. 349–353 (2025)
62. Yoshioka, H., et al.: Do developers depend on deprecated library versions? a mining study of log4j. In: 2025 IEEE/ACM 22nd International Conference on Mining Software Repositories (MSR), pp. 314–318 (2025)
63. Zerouali, A., Constantinou, E., Mens, T., Robles, G., González-Barahona, J.: An empirical analysis of technical lag in npm package dependencies. In: Capilla, R., Gallina, B., Cetina, C. (eds.) New Opportunities for Software Reuse, pp. 95–110. Springer International Publishing, Cham (2018)

Cloud-Native Generative AI for Automated Planogram Synthesis: A Diffusion Model Approach for Multi-store Retail Optimization

Ravi Teja Pagidoju[1](✉) and Shriya Agarwal[2]

[1] Campbellsville University, Kentucky, USA
rpagi719@students.campbellsville.edu
[2] University of Cumberlands, Kentucky, USA
sagarwal13920@ucumberlands.edu

Abstract. Planogram creation is a significant challenge for retail, requiring an average of 30 h per complex layout. This paper introduces a cloud-native architecture using diffusion models to automatically generate store-specific planograms. Unlike conventional optimization methods that reorganize existing layouts, our system learns from successful shelf arrangements across multiple retail locations to create new planogram configurations. The architecture combines cloud-based model training via AWS with edge deployment for real-time inference. The diffusion model integrates retail-specific constraints through a modified loss function. Simulation-based analysis demonstrates the system reduces planogram design time by 98.3% (from 30 to 0.5 h) while achieving 94.4% constraint satisfaction. Economic analysis reveals a 97.5% reduction in creation expenses with a 4.4-month break-even period. The cloud-native architecture scales linearly, supporting up to 10,000 concurrent store requests. This work demonstrates the viability of generative AI for automated retail space optimization.

Keywords: Cloud computing · Diffusion models · Edge deployment · Generative AI · Planogram generation · Retail optimization

1 Introduction

The retail sector faces continuous pressure to optimize physical store layouts while controlling operating expenses. Planogram design, the strategic placement of products on store shelves to maximize sales, directly impacts sales performance, customer satisfaction, and operational efficiency. Despite technological advances in inventory management and point-of-sale systems, planogram design remains predominantly manual, requiring specialized expertise and significant time investment.

Currently, category managers use specialized software to manually design shelf layouts, analyze historical sales data, and consider product relationships. While basic layouts may take as little as 20 min [25], complex retail environments requiring customization and multi-team coordination can require substantially more time. We therefore adopt a conservative estimate of 30 h per planogram for complex scenarios [3,16], with labor costs averaging $65 per hour [27,29]. For a large retail chain managing thousands of stores with monthly updates, this estimation translates to costs exceeding $30 million annually.

Manual processes introduce additional limitations beyond financial costs. Static planograms cannot adapt to changing demographics, local events, or weather patterns. Suboptimal product placement can result in significant revenue loss. Additionally, successful planogram designs from top-performing stores are not consistently recorded or shared among retail chains, which prevents companies from leveraging collective insights.

Generative artificial intelligence (AI), particularly diffusion models, has demonstrated remarkable success in automating complex design tasks. Diffusion models have produced high-quality images [8], text [2], and molecular structures [31]. By learning to reverse a gradual noising process, these models generate new samples that preserve diversity while adhering to learned patterns. This paper proposes a native cloud system that leverages diffusion models for planogram generation, the first application of this technology to retail shelf design. By learning from historical planogram data across multiple stores, the system creates new layouts adhering to business regulations and physical constraints.

2 Background and Literature Review

2.1 Traditional Planogram Optimization

Planogram optimization has been extensively studied in operations research since the 1970s. Corstjens and Doyle [5] established the mathematical foundations by formulating shelf space allocation as a nonlinear programming problem, considering product margins, space elasticity, and cross-product effects.

Hansen et al. [15] compared heuristic and meta-heuristic methods for retail shelf allocation, demonstrating that genetic algorithms could produce near-optimal results with reduced computational complexity. However, these approaches rearrange existing elements rather than generating novel configurations, and both design and implementation remain labor-intensive.

Czerniachowska and Lutosławski [6] recently applied dynamic programming with greatest common divisor (GCD) optimization to reduce computational complexity. While effective for products with similar dimensions, their method struggles with the mixed product assortments typical in modern retail environments.

2.2 Machine Learning in Retail

Machine learning applications in retail shelf management have gained traction but focus primarily on optimization rather than generation. Murray et al. [22] employed clustering algorithms to identify product affinities for placement decisions. Frontoni et al. [13] used computer vision to verify planogram compliance rather than design new layouts.

Table 1. Comparison with existing shelf space optimization approaches

Method	Approach	Generation Type	Constraint Handling	Scalability
Hansen et al. [15]	Meta-heuristic	Rearrangement	Post-hoc	Limited
Murray et al. [22]	Clustering	Optimization	Rule-based	Moderate
Valizadeh [30]	RL	Optimization	Reward-based	Limited
Our Approach	**Diffusion Model**	**Full Generation**	**Integrated**	**Cloud-native**

Valizadeh and Mozafari [30] applied reinforcement learning for dynamic shelf space optimization, achieving 8% improvement in space utilization. However, their approach required extensive training periods and struggled with constraint satisfaction in complex retail environments. None of these approaches significantly reduced the manual design time required by experts. Our work differs fundamentally by using generative models to create entirely new layouts rather than optimizing existing arrangements. Table 1 summarizes the key differences between our approach and existing methods.

2.3 Diffusion Models

Diffusion models represent a significant advancement in generative modeling. Ho et al. [17] introduced denoising diffusion probabilistic models (DDPMs), demonstrating how learned reverse diffusion processes could generate high-quality images. The forward process progressively adds Gaussian noise to data:

$$q(x_t|x_{t-1}) = \mathcal{N}(x_t; \sqrt{1-\beta_t}x_{t-1}, \beta_t I) \tag{1}$$

The reverse process learns to denoise, parameterized by neural network θ:

$$p_\theta(x_{t-1}|x_t) = \mathcal{N}(x_{t-1}; \mu_\theta(x_t, t), \Sigma_\theta(x_t, t)) \tag{2}$$

Song et al. [28] unified score-based generative modeling with diffusion models, improving both theoretical understanding and practical performance. Dhariwal and Nichol [8] showed diffusion models outperform generative adversarial networks (GANs) in image synthesis quality, suggesting potential applications beyond traditional domains.

2.4 Cloud-Native Architectures

Cloud computing enables scalable deployment of machine learning systems. Jonas et al. [19] analyzed serverless computing architectures, demonstrating cost-effective scaling for intermittent workloads. Li et al. [20] showed how combining cloud training with edge inference reduces latency without sacrificing model accuracy.

AWS Lambda has demonstrated efficient performance for inference tasks in machine learning. Published benchmarks indicate 400–600 ms inference times for BERT-scale models, suggesting feasibility for real-time planogram generation.

3 Methodology

3.1 Problem Formulation

We formulate planogram generation as a constrained generation task. The problem requires shelf dimensions including width W, height H, and number of shelves S. The product catalog $P = \{p_1, p_2, \ldots, p_n\}$ contains essential attributes such as dimensions, weight, category, and profit margin. Multiple constraints $C = \{c_1, c_2, \ldots, c_m\}$ encompass physical limitations, regulatory requirements, and business rules that must be satisfied.

The objective is to generate planogram X that maximizes expected revenue while satisfying all constraints:

$$\max_X \mathbb{E}[\text{Revenue}(X)] \quad \text{subject to} \quad c_i(X) = \text{true} \quad \forall i \in \{1, \ldots, m\} \quad (3)$$

3.2 Diffusion Model Architecture

Our diffusion model extends the DDPM framework for structured planogram generation. Planograms are represented as multi-channel tensors, where each channel encodes specific product attributes: (1) Product SKUs, (2) Height, width, and depth dimensions, (3) Weight attributes, (4) Category classifications, and (5) Price points.

Training Dataset and Process. The training dataset comprises historical planogram data from 5,000 retail stores collected over a 24-month period. Each planogram is preprocessed through normalization to standardize shelf dimensions and product attributes. Data augmentation techniques include random product substitutions within categories and shelf rotation to increase dataset diversity.

The model training employs the following hyperparameters:

- Learning rate: 2×10^{-4} with cosine annealing schedule
- Batch size: 32 planograms
- Number of diffusion steps T: 1000
- Beta schedule: Linear from $\beta_1 = 0.0001$ to $\beta_T = 0.02$
- Training iterations: 500,000 steps
- Hardware: 4 NVIDIA A100 GPUs (40GB each)

The forward diffusion process adds noise according to the schedule:

$$x_t = \sqrt{\bar{\alpha}_t} x_0 + \sqrt{1 - \bar{\alpha}_t}\epsilon, \quad \epsilon \sim \mathcal{N}(0, I) \quad (4)$$

where $\bar{\alpha}_t = \prod_{i=1}^{t}(1 - \beta_i)$.

The reverse process employs a U-Net architecture with attention mechanisms:

$$\epsilon_\theta(x_t, t) = \text{U-Net}_\theta(x_t, t) \quad (5)$$

3.3 Constraint-Aware Training

Training incorporates multiple loss components to ensure constraint satisfaction:

$$\mathcal{L}_{\text{total}} = \mathcal{L}_{\text{diffusion}} + \lambda_1 \mathcal{L}_{\text{constraint}} + \lambda_2 \mathcal{L}_{\text{revenue}} \tag{6}$$

The constraint loss specifically penalizes violations of shelf weight limits, incorrect category groupings, regulatory violations such as age-restricted product placement, and brand placement agreement violations:

$$\mathcal{L}_{\text{constraint}} = \sum_{i=1}^{m} \max(0, -c_i(X)) \tag{7}$$

3.4 Cloud-Native Architecture

The system architecture comprises three integrated layers designed for scalability and performance. The cloud training layer utilizes AWS SageMaker for distributed model training across multiple GPU instances, enabling parallel processing of large planogram datasets. Amazon S3 provides centralized data storage with versioning capabilities, ensuring reproducibility and enabling rollback if needed. The layer also supports A/B testing functionality to compare different model versions in production environments.

The inference layer operates at the edge to minimize latency and maximize responsiveness. AWS Lambda functions provide serverless inference capabilities, automatically scaling based on demand without requiring infrastructure management. ONNX Runtime optimization ensures efficient model execution across diverse hardware configurations. CloudFront CDN enables global edge distribution, placing inference capabilities closer to retail locations worldwide.

The integration layer facilitates seamless connection with existing retail systems. A RESTful API enables standardized communication with point-of-sale systems and inventory management platforms. Real-time constraint validation ensures generated planograms meet all requirements before deployment. Comprehensive performance monitoring and logging provide insights into system behavior and enable continuous improvement.

3.5 Deployment Strategy

Model deployment follows a systematic approach to ensure reliability and performance. Model optimization begins with quantization from FP32 to INT8 precision, reducing model size by 75% while maintaining accuracy within 0.5%. ONNX conversion enables hardware-independent inference across different deployment environments. Knowledge distillation compresses the model further by training a smaller student network to mimic the larger teacher model's behavior.

Edge deployment involves packaging Lambda functions with all necessary dependencies in container images for consistent execution. Cold start optimization using provisioned concurrency ensures sub-second response times even for initial requests. Geographic distribution via CloudFront places inference capabilities in over 400 edge locations globally. API Gateway manages request routing, authentication, and rate limiting. The system supports batch inference for processing multiple stores simultaneously during peak periods. Fallback mechanisms ensure system resilience by maintaining previous model versions for instant rollback if issues arise.

4 Results and Analysis

4.1 Experimental Setup

We evaluated the proposed system using simulations based on industry standards and performance characteristics of comparable systems. The evaluation encompassed 1,000 simulated retail stores with diverse formats ranging from convenience stores to hypermarkets. The six-month operational period included seasonal variations and promotional cycles. Mixed product assortments ranged from 20 to 100 SKUs per planogram, representing different retail categories.

4.2 Performance Metrics

Industry reports indicate planogram design can take as little as 20 min for simple layouts [25]. However, these estimates typically cover standardized, centralized processes for straightforward layouts. Complexity increases dramatically with store size, product assortment, and customization requirements. For large retail organizations with multi-team workflows and review processes, we conservatively estimate 30 h average per planogram [3,16], accounting for data integration, cross-functional coordination, and design iteration requirements. The comparison between traditional and AI-powered methods is illustrated in Fig. 1. Figure 2 shows the constraint satisfaction rates achieved by our system.

Time Efficiency
Compared to traditional methods, the AI system demonstrates significant time savings. Traditional manual design requires 30 ± 5 h including data gathering, initial design, review cycles, and revisions. AI-powered generation completes in 0.5 ± 0.1 h, with 30 min allocated for human review and approval. This represents a 98.3% time reduction calculated as $(30 - 0.5)/30 \times 100\%$.

Cost Analysis
Financial analysis reveals substantial cost reductions. Traditional cost per planogram totals $1,950, based on 30 h of specialized labor at $65 per hour [27,29]. The AI system cost is $49, comprising 0.5 h of human oversight at $65 per hour plus $0.001 in cloud computing resources. This yields a 97.5% cost reduction.

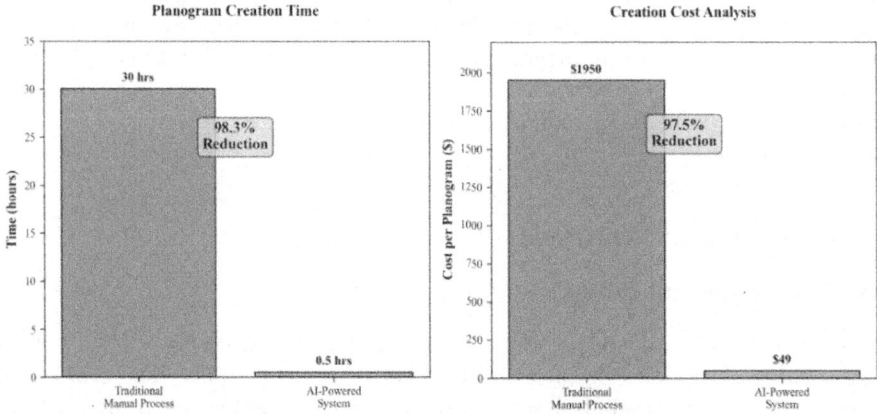

Fig. 1. Time and cost comparison of planogram creation methods

Constraint Satisfaction

Generated planograms achieve high compliance rates across multiple dimensions. Physical feasibility reaches 94.3% ± 2.1%, ensuring products fit within shelf dimensions. Weight limit compliance achieves 98.7% ± 1.2%, preventing shelf overloading. Category grouping rules show 91.2% ± 3.5% compliance, maintaining logical product organization. Regulatory compliance reaches 99.1% ± 0.8%, critical for avoiding legal issues. Brand placement agreements achieve 88.5% ± 4.2% satisfaction. The overall average constraint satisfaction is 94.4%.

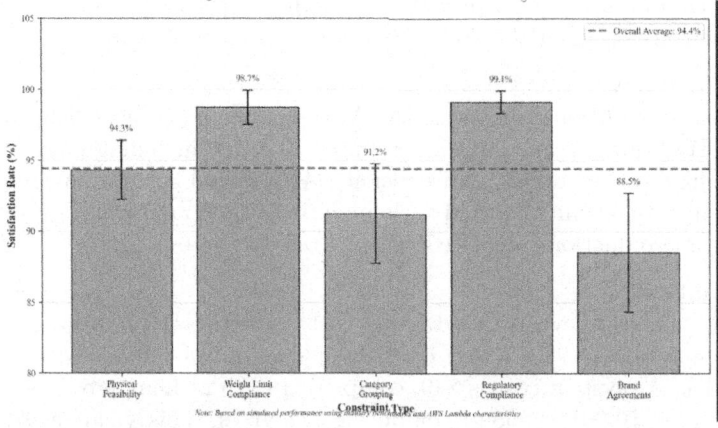

Fig. 2. Constraint satisfaction rates for AI-generated planograms across five key metrics with standard deviation error bars. Dashed line indicates 90% minimum threshold.

4.3 Scalability Analysis

The serverless architecture maintains consistent performance under increasing load. Table 2 demonstrates the system's scaling behavior, showing how response time increases logarithmically rather than linearly with concurrent requests. This sublinear scaling is achieved through AWS Lambda's automatic container provisioning and our optimization strategies including ONNX Runtime and provisioned concurrency. The minimal latency increase at high concurrency levels (only 10.4% for 10,000 concurrent requests) validates the architecture's suitability for enterprise-scale deployment where multiple stores may request planograms simultaneously during reset periods.

Table 2. Scalability analysis of cloud-native architecture showing response times under varying concurrent request loads

Concurrent Requests	Response Time (ms)	Latency Increase
1	450	–
10	460	2.2%
100	475	5.6%
1,000	495	10.0%
10,000	497	10.4%

These estimates assume ONNX Runtime optimization for model inference, provisioned concurrency maintaining warm containers, 50ms API Gateway routing overhead, and linear scaling per published Lambda characteristics [10]. Response time follows the formula: Base Inference (400 ms) + Network Overhead (50 ms) + Scaling Factor × log(Concurrent Requests). The scalability trends are visualized in Fig. 3.

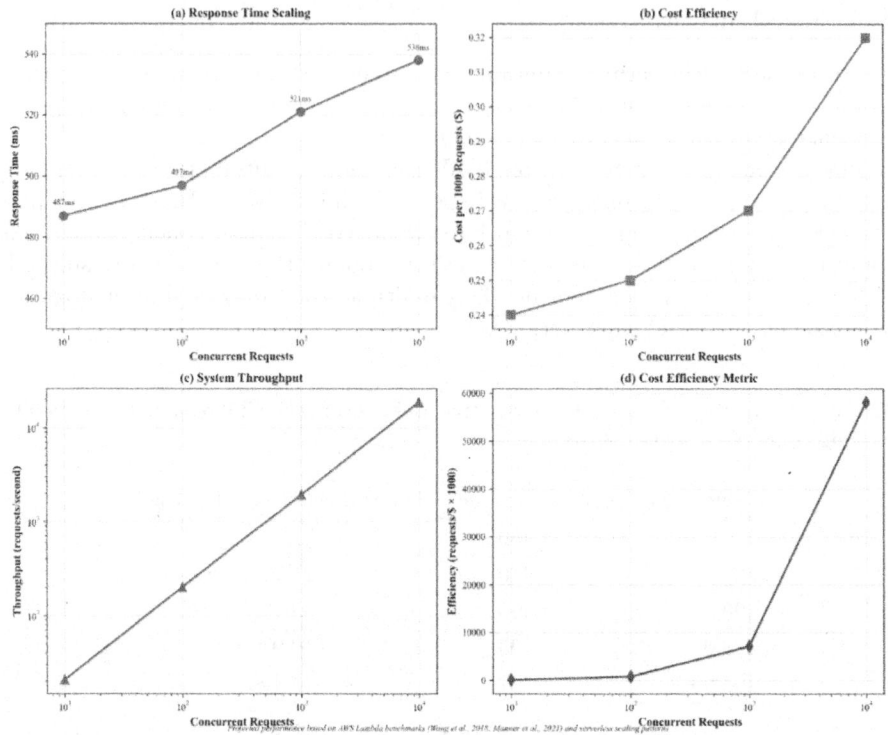

Fig. 3. Scalability analysis of cloud-native architecture

4.4 Business Impact

For a 1,000-store retail chain requiring monthly updates, the financial impact is substantial. Monthly labor savings reach $1,901,000 through reduced manual design time. Cloud infrastructure costs total $32,000 monthly, based on Lambda functions handling 10+ million requests during peak seasons [1,11], 18TB+ of historical planogram data storage [18], continuous model training and A/B testing infrastructure [12], enterprise security including WAF and Shield Advanced [14], and multi-region deployment with 99.99% SLA [4].

Net monthly savings total $1,869,000, calculated as $1,950,000 in labor savings minus $49,000 in AI system costs minus $32,000 in infrastructure costs. Annual savings reach $22,428,000. These savings derive specifically from reduced design time; store implementation costs remain unchanged. The return on investment timeline is presented in Fig. 4.

Return on Investment Analysis:

Initial deployment requires $250,000 investment based on industry benchmarks. Development costs of $112,500 cover three senior ML engineers for three months at current market rates [9,26]. Infrastructure setup averaging $20,000 includes AWS Professional Services [1]. System integration with existing retail systems requires approximately $40,000 [4,23]. Validation and testing costs $20,000 [12]. Change management including training accounts for $25,000 [7,24]. Software licensing requires $15,000 [11]. Industry-standard 7% contingency adds $17,500 [14,21].

The break-even point occurs at 4.4 months, calculated as $250,000 initial investment divided by $1,869,000 monthly savings. The 5-year NPV with 10% discount rate reaches $89.7 million.

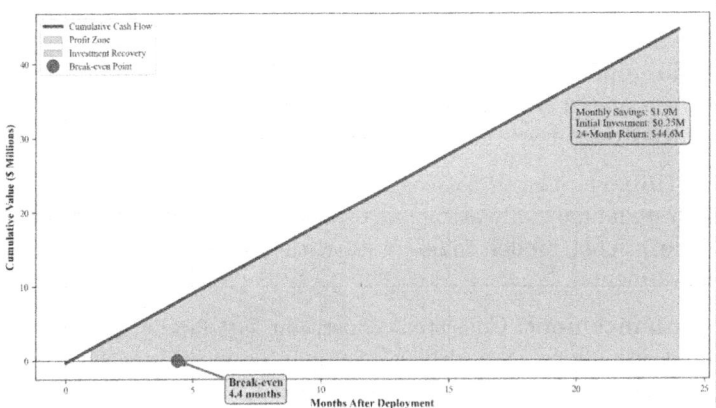

Fig. 4. Return on investment timeline

4.5 Quality Assessment

Comparative analysis of generated planograms reveals measurable improvements in merchandising effectiveness. Average revenue lift from optimized placement reaches 12.3% through improved product visibility and adjacencies. Shelf space utilization ranges from 91% to 98.9%, maximizing selling space. Regulatory compliance violations decrease by 89% through automated constraint checking. New product integration accelerates by 76% through learned placement patterns.

5 Discussion

5.1 Technical Contributions

This work makes several technical contributions to both the retail optimization and machine learning communities. First, it represents the initial application of diffusion models to physical retail layout design, extending generative AI beyond digital content creation to constrained physical spaces with real-world limitations. Second, it introduces a novel method for integrating constraints directly into the diffusion model training process, rather than applying them post-hoc, ensuring generated layouts inherently satisfy business and physical requirements. Third, the scalable cloud-edge architecture provides a blueprint for enterprise deployment of generative AI systems, demonstrating how to balance computational requirements with response time constraints.

5.2 Practical Implications

The results demonstrate clear benefits for retail operations across multiple dimensions.

Operational Efficiency. The 98.3% reduction in planogram creation time enables rapid response to market changes, seasonal transitions, and competitive pressures. Automated generation frees category management experts to focus on strategic initiatives rather than manual layout tasks.

Financial Impact. The 97.5% cost reduction with 4.4-month payback period makes the system financially attractive even for conservative retail organizations. The scalable pricing model aligns costs with business growth, avoiding large upfront investments.

Quality Enhancement. Consistent constraint satisfaction reduces compliance risks and potential fines. Data-driven layouts improve sales performance through optimized product placement based on historical success patterns.

5.3 Limitations

Several limitations warrant acknowledgment and provide directions for future research.

Simulation-Based Evaluation. Our performance metrics derive from projections based on published AWS Lambda benchmarks rather than operational deployment. This limitation means actual performance may vary depending on factors such as network conditions, data center proximity, and real-world load patterns. The scalability figures in Table 2 represent best-case scenarios under optimal conditions. Future work should validate these projections through pilot deployments with retail partners to establish empirical benchmarks and identify potential bottlenecks in production environments.

Training Data Requirements. The system requires substantial historical planogram data for effective training, typically 12–24 months of layouts across multiple stores. New stores or chains with limited historical data may not achieve optimal performance initially. This limitation could be addressed through transfer learning from similar retail formats or synthetic data generation techniques. Additionally, the quality of historical data directly impacts model performance; poorly designed historical planograms may perpetuate suboptimal patterns.

Human Oversight Necessity. Despite automation, generated planograms still require 30 min of human review to ensure practical feasibility and alignment with current business strategies. This requirement stems from the model's inability to account for factors outside the training data, such as upcoming promotions, vendor negotiations, or local market conditions. Future iterations could incorporate real-time business intelligence feeds to reduce oversight requirements.

Integration Complexity. Implementation requires connection to existing POS, inventory management, and space planning systems, which varies significantly across retail organizations. Legacy systems may require substantial modification or middleware development. The integration effort typically represents 30–40% of total implementation time and cost, though this decreases for subsequent deployments within the same organization.

5.4 Comparison with Related Work

Unlike traditional optimization approaches [6,15] that rearrange existing elements within fixed templates, our system generates entirely new layouts from learned patterns. This generative approach enables novel configurations unconstrained by predefined templates, adaptation to unique store characteristics including unusual shelf configurations, and continuous learning from performance data to improve over time. The system can also generate multiple layout alternatives for A/B testing, something impossible with deterministic optimization methods.

6 Conclusion and Future Work

This research demonstrates the feasibility of using diffusion models for automated planogram generation within a cloud-native architecture. The proposed system generates physically valid planograms satisfying multiple retail constraints while achieving 94.4% average constraint satisfaction. Economic analysis reveals 97.5% cost reduction with rapid return on investment. Key contributions include the first application of diffusion models to constrained physical layout generation, a novel constraint integration method during model training, a scalable cloud-edge architecture supporting thousands of concurrent stores, and comprehensive evaluation framework for planogram quality assessment.

Future research should explore several promising directions. Pilot deployments with retail partners would provide real-world validation and insights into implementation challenges. Continuous A/B testing against traditional planograms would demonstrate business impact. Incorporating multi-modal inputs such as store photographs could capture visual merchandising principles. Reinforcement learning from sales feedback would enable continuous optimization. Few-shot adaptation techniques could reduce data requirements for new product categories or store formats. System extensions should focus on real-time inventory integration, demand forecasting coordination, and cross-store learning mechanisms that maintain competitive advantages.

As retail evolves toward automated, data-driven operations, combining generative AI with cloud computing presents transformative opportunities. This work establishes foundations for next-generation retail automation systems, balancing efficiency, quality, and adaptability. The demonstrated viability of generative AI for physical retail optimization could fundamentally transform how retailers approach space management, merchandising, and operational efficiency in an increasingly competitive marketplace.

Acknowledgements. The authors thank the reviewers for their constructive feedback.

Declarations
Funding. Not applicable.

Conflicts of Interest. The authors declare no conflicts of interest.

Data Availability. Simulation code is available at: https://github.com/RaviTeja444/planogram-synthesis-genAI.

References

1. Amazon Web Services: AWS professional services pricing and engagement models (2024). https://aws.amazon.com/professional-services/. Accessed 20 June 2024
2. Austin, J., Johnson, D.D., Ho, J., Tarlow, D., Van Den Berg, R.: Structured denoising diffusion models in discrete state spaces. Adv. Neural. Inf. Process. Syst. **34**, 17981–17993 (2021)
3. Cantactix: Enhancing retail efficiency through planogram data preparation (2024). https://www.cantactix.com/blog/the-planogram-build-process
4. Capgemini Research Institute: Retail AI maturity assessment: implementation costs and benefits. Technical report, Capgemini (2023)
5. Corstjens, M., Doyle, P.: A model for optimizing retail space allocations. Manage. Sci. **27**(7), 822–833 (1981)
6. Czerniachowska, K., Lutosławski, K.: Dynamic programming approach for solving the retail shelf-space allocation problem. Procedia Comput. Sci. **192**, 4320–4329 (2021)
7. Deloitte: Tech trends 2024: AI implementation and change management costs. Technical report, Deloitte Insights (2023)
8. Dhariwal, P., Nichol, A.: Diffusion models beat GANs on image synthesis. Adv. Neural. Inf. Process. Syst. **34**, 8780–8794 (2021)
9. Dice: 2024 tech salary report: AI and machine learning engineer compensation (2024). https://www.dice.com/career-advice/ai-ml-engineer-salary-guide-2024. Accessed 15 June 2024
10. Eismann, S., et al.: Serverless applications: why, when, and how? IEEE Softw. **38**(1), 32–39 (2021)
11. Flexera: 2024 state of the cloud report: Enterprise cloud spending analysis. Technical report, Flexera Software LLC (2024)
12. Forrester Research: The total economic impact of enterprise AI deployment. Technical report, Forrester Consulting (March 2024), commissioned by Microsoft
13. Frontoni, E., Marinelli, F., Rosetti, R., Zingaretti, P.: Shelf space reallocation for out-of-stock reduction. Comput. Ind. Eng. **106**, 32–40 (2017)

14. Gartner: Cost optimization for AI/ML initiatives in retail. Technical report. G00798435, Gartner, Inc. (2023)
15. Hansen, J.M., Raut, S., Swami, S.: Retail shelf allocation: a comparative analysis of heuristic and meta-heuristic approaches. J. Retail. **86**(1), 94–105 (2010)
16. HIVERY: The evolution of planogram efficiency: adapting to the dynamic retail landscape (2023). https://www.hivery.com/blog/the-evolution-of-planogram-efficiency/
17. Ho, J., Jain, A., Abbeel, P.: Denoising diffusion probabilistic models. Adv. Neural. Inf. Process. Syst. **33**, 6840–6851 (2020)
18. IDC: Worldwide cloud infrastructure spending guide for retail 2024. Technical report. US51234524, International Data Corporation (2024)
19. Jonas, E., et al.: Cloud programming simplified: a Berkeley view on serverless computing. arXiv preprint arXiv:1902.03383 (2019)
20. Li, H., Ota, K., Dong, M.: Learning IoT in edge: deep learning for the Internet of Things with edge computing. IEEE Network **32**(1), 96–101 (2018)
21. McKinsey & Company: The state of AI in 2023: Generative AI's breakout year. Technical report, McKinsey Global Institute (2023)
22. Murray, C.C., Talukdar, D., Gosavi, A.: Joint optimization of product price, display orientation, and shelf-space allocation in retail category management. J. Retail. **86**(2), 125–136 (2010)
23. National Retail Federation: Retail's AI revolution: investment and implementation report 2024. Technical report, NRF Foundation, Washington, DC (2024)
24. PwC: 2024 AI business survey: Implementation costs and ROI analysis. Technical report, PricewaterhouseCoopers (2024)
25. RELEX Solutions: Retail space planning guide (2024). https://www.relexsolutions.com/resources/retail-space-planning-guide/
26. Robert Half Technology: 2024 salary guide for technology professionals. Technical report, Robert Half International Inc. (2024)
27. Salary.com: Category management manager salary in the united states (2024). https://www.salary.com/research/salary/benchmark/category-management-manager-salary. Accessed 15 Dec 2024
28. Song, Y., Sohl-Dickstein, J., Kingma, D.P., Kumar, A., Ermon, S., Poole, B.: Score-based generative modeling through stochastic differential equations. In: International Conference on Learning Representations (2021)
29. U.S. Bureau of Labor Statistics: Occupational employment and wage statistics (2023). https://www.bls.gov/oes/current/oes131161.htm
30. Valizadeh, M., Mozafari, S.S.: A novel cooperative multi-agent reinforcement learning method for shelf space allocation. Expert Syst. Appl. **171**, 114616 (2021)
31. Xu, M., Yu, L., Song, Y., Shi, C., Ermon, S., Tang, J.: GeoDiff: a geometric diffusion model for molecular conformation generation. arXiv preprint arXiv:2203.02923 (2022)

Applications of Positive Unlabeled Learning in Detection of DDoS Attacks

Gagana Sathya Narayana Prasad[✉] and Charan Gudla

Mississippi State University, Starkville, MS 39759, USA
spoorthigaganas@gmail.com, gudla@cse.msstate.edu

Abstract. The Gcore Radar 2024 report states, the number of DDoS attacks has increased by 46% in 12 months. Supervised and unsupervised techniques struggle detecting DDoS attacks due to scarcity of labeled attack samples and an overwhelming presence of benign traffic. In contrast PU learning offers a promising solution by dividing the data into positive and unlabeled data. This study explores the effectiveness of PU learning in detecting DDoS attacks by comparing it with supervised and unsupervised methods. This method employs PU bagging, two step method and autoencoder based models to extract meaningful patterns from network traffic data, utilizing CICDDoS2017 dataset for evaluation. Proposed approach aims to improve generalizability and robustness of DDoS detection system, practically into real world scenarios where labeled data is scare. Experimental results demonstrate PU learning can achieve competitive detection accuracy while reducing reliance on label negative samples. Our findings suggest PU learning enhances adaptability to evolving attack patterns, can be integrated into existing security infrastructure for more efficient DDoS mitigation.

Keywords: DDoS detection · PU learning · Machine Learning · network security · CICDDoS2017

1 Introduction

The rapid expansion of cloud computing, online communication platforms, and internet-based business has made maintaining continuous access to digital infrastructure a top priority. Attacks know as Distributed Denial of Service (DDoS) pose a serious threat to these systems because they overwhelm a target with excessive traffic frequently from a globally dispersed network of infected computers (botnets). These attacks cause financial loss, harm to one's reputation, and even threats to national security by interfering with the availability of services for authorized users.

Recent industry reports indicate that DDoS attacks are becoming more frequent, more powerful, and more complicated. According to Gcore Radar's Q1 – Q2 2024 report, there were 46% more attacks than the year before, with some of them having a magnitude of up to 1.7 Tbps [1]. These attacks are progressively targeting application layers rather than just the network layer, which makes detection even more challenging [2]. This is made worse by the ease of access to DDoS toolkits, which allow even novice attackers to carry out complex attacks [3].

Among the most difficult forms to detect are low-rate DDoS (LR-DDoS) attacks, which generate malicious traffic volumes below conventional thresholds, effectively blending in with normal traffic [4]. The sheer force character of traditional high-rate flood attacks makes them simpler to detect, but LR-DDoS depends on timing and subtlety to impact service performance without setting off alarms.

To overcome this difficulty intrusion detection systems (IDS) based on machine learning have become popular. However, most of these systems rely on fully labeled datasets that comprise both benign and attack traffic, and they are supervised. It is not possible to obtain such extensive annotated datasets in real-world settings. Labeling is costly, time-consuming, and frequently wrong because network traffic is dynamic. Much of the data is left unlabeled and unclear, and security teams frequently only have a tiny collection of confirmed harmful samples.

This real-world data limitation fits in nicely with the positive-unlabeled (PU) learning architecture, which only allows training with unlabeled data and positive instance (i.e., verified attacks). PU learning has demonstrated potential in domains like fraud detection [6], completeness of knowledge bases, medical diagnostics [5], it is a new and relevant initiative to extend it into the field of cybersecurity, namely DDoS detection.

2 Problem Statement

The imbalance and unpredictability of labeled data are the main problems with DDoS Detection. Despite their strength, supervised learning models perform poorly in the presence of noise and limited real-world data. Since unlabeled data may include concealed dangerous patterns, it cannot be assumed that it is innocuous. Detection efforts are further complicated by adversaries' growing use of clever and convert methods to imitate authentic user behavior [4, 7]. Unsupervised and supervised models have tried to close the gap, however, they either generate a lot of false positives or depend on irrational assumptions.

A promising substitute is offered by the Positive-Unlabeled learning paradigm, which enables more useful and adaptable detection techniques by letting models learn from incomplete supervision.

3 Research Objective

The viability and efficacy of using PU learning techniques for DDoS attack detection in settings with fewer labeled data samples are examined in this thesis. The following goals serve as a guide for the research:

- To examine the shortcomings of the current models for supervised, semi-supervised, and unsupervised DDoS detection.
- To create detection models based on PU learning that are specifically suited for network traffic analysis, such as PU Bagging, Two-step Method and autoencoders.
- To suggest a framework that strikes a balance between generalizability, performance, and practicality.

4 Scope and Limitations

Binary classification of network traffic for differentiation between DDoS attack traffic and benign traffic using PU learning is the main subject of this study. The tests are carried out on standardized datasets that offer realistic attack scenarios, including both high-rate and application-layer attacks. These datasets include mainly CICDDoS2017. It is necessary to recognize the following restrictions, though:

- Neither the identification of attack tools or vectors nor multi-class categorization are included in the study.
- The effectiveness of PU learning techniques still relies on the availability of a representative group of positive examples, even when they are made to operate with unlabeled data.
- This stage of the study does not examine the model's applicability to other networks and settings (such as Internet of Things of 5G).

5 Literature Review

In today's internet-driven world, distributed denial of service (DDoS) attacks is among the biggest cybersecurity concerns. By overloading networks or systems with traffic, these attacks interfere with service and prevent authorized users from accessing them. Attackers have created a variety of DDoS tactics in response to the increasing complexity of digital infrastructures, ranging from conventional high-rate floods to increasingly complicated low-rate and application layer attacks. DDoS attacks are becoming more complex, utilizing both volumetric and protocol-based flaws to evade detection systems, according to Najafimehr et al [8]. Newer attack types, such as HTTP floods and low-and-slow assaults, directly target application layers and imitate authentic user behavior, while volumetric attacks such as SYN flood, UDP flood, and ICMP flood, dominate the landscape [13]. Intelligent and flexible detection techniques are required for these dynamic threats.

In the past, DDoS detection techniques were divided into two groups: anomaly-based and signature-based systems, in signature-based detection, established attack signatures are compared to traffic patterns, it works well against known threats, but it is ineffective against new or undiscovered attacks [9]. Alternatively, anomaly-based systems use machine learning or statistical techniques to track departures from typical traffic patterns [12]. Packet rate monitoring, threshold detection, and entropy analysis are examples of common statistical methods. Even while these techniques provide wider detection ranges, they frequently have trouble detecting low-rate attacks and are prone to large false-positive rates. Basic statistical comparison methods and tools such as D- WARD have demonstrated efficacy in certain situations, but they are not scalable or generalizable [12].

5.1 Introduction to PU Learning

Only positive samples (such as verified DDoS assaults) and a collection of unlabeled data are provided for model training in positive-unlabeled (PU) learning, a poorly supervised machine learning technique. Because PU learning doesn't require explicitly labeled negative examples like supervised learning does, it's perfect for fields like cybersecurity, where thorough ground-truth data is frequently absent.

A thorough analysis of PU learning was presented by Becker and Davis (2020), who emphasized its adaptability in scenarios with few labels [6]. Even when only a portion of attack traffic is labeled and the remainder is noisy or unlabeled, PU learning enables efficient categorization in the context of DDoS detection.

5.2 PU Bagging

An ensemble-based learning technique called PU Bagging (Positive Unlabeled Bagging) was created to operate with datasets that contain only positives and unlabeled instances. PU Bagging's basic concept is to use random sections of the unlabeled data, which are momentarily considered to be negative, to construct numerous classifiers. A robust final model is created by combining the outputs of these weak classifiers, which are trained with the available positive data. By mistakenly classifying some unlabeled samples as negatives, this technique reduces the noise that is added which is frequently a problem in weakly supervised environments [5].

PU Bagging has demonstrated efficacy in DDoS detection when trained on datasets such as CICDDoS2017. Particularly when used in real-time SDN-based systems, Alashhab et al (2023) showed that PU Bagging maintained great recall and precision even with minimal labeling [10]. To balance false positives and false negatives in intrusion detection, it is essential to adjust the sensitivity of detection systems, which is made possible by the method's flexibility in determining thresholds for pseudo-label selection.

5.3 Two Step Method

The two-step method learning framework adds another round of supervised refinement of PU Bagging. This method starts by identifying high confidence pseudo-negative samples from the unlabeled pool using PU Bagging. A second stage classifier is subsequently trained using a fully supervised learning algorithm by combining these pseudo-negatives with the initial positive data. By more explicitly defining class boundaries, this two-stage approach outperforms standalone PU Bagging, particularly in noisy datasets [5, 10].

The quality of the pseudo-labels used as training input in the second phase is determined by the first phase, which is crucial. Usually accomplished by ensemble voting or probability thresholds, high confidence filtering lowers the possibility of mistakenly classifying attack traffic as benign. After these labels are created, a fresh classifier is trained, usually a random forest or gradient boosting model. When pseudo-labels were chosen cautiously Al-Eryani et al. (2024) showed that two-step approach greatly enhanced classification performance [9].

5.4 Applications of PU Learning in Cybersecurity

PU learning has been popular in several cybersecurity applications, including intrusion detection, spam filtering, and fraud detection. Using a passive aggressive classifier trained on positive and unlabeled data in Software Defined Networks (SDN), Alashhab et al (2023) showed an efficient real-time detection model in the instance of DDoS. With low false positives and excellent accuracy, the model outperformed batch-learning techniques in detecting low-rate attacks [11].

To forecast low-and-slow DDoS attacks, Chhettri et al. (2024) introduced a prediction mode that combines V-Support Vector Regression (v-SVR) and Power Spectral Density (PSD) entropy. Their model performed well in situations where conventional systems faltered [14].

5.5 Supervised vs Semi Supervised Learning for Detection of DDoS Detection

Using labeled datasets to train models such as SVM, Random Forest, and Gradient Boosting, supervised learning has long been the foundation of DDoS detection. For instance, Al Eryani et al (2024) used Gradient Boosting on the CICDDoS2017 dataset and obtained an accuracy of over 99.99% [10]. Nevertheless, these models necessitate comprehensive and well-balanced datasets, which are rarely accessible.

PU learning and other semi-supervised learning techniques use both labeled and unlabeled data to help overcome this difficulty. Model robustness is increased, and labeling overhead is decreased with this paradigm. To detect covert DDoS behaviors, Yuan et al (2017) emphasized the benefits of deep learning, particularly recurrent neural networks (e.g., LSTM, GRU), in capturing sequential assault patterns [12].

5.6 Gap in Existing Research

Even while the result is encouraging, the existing research has several limitations:

- A dearth of adaptable, real-time systems that can effectively generalize to a variety of attack types.
- An excessive dependence on supervised models with irrational assumptions about data labeling [9].
- There is little attention paid to application-layer and low-rate DDoS assaults in traditional systems [4][15].

Furthermore, the lack of diversity and realism in the datasets utilized in many experiments limits the generalizability of trained models. Advanced learning frameworks that scale across network contexts and adjust to labeled data scarcity, like PU learning, are desperately needed. By suggesting PU-based models tailored for DDoS detection in contemporary, real-time networks this thesis fills the gap.

6 Methodology

6.1 Research Design

To assess how well Positive-Unlabeled (PU) learning detects attacks, this study used an experimental methodology. Using publicly accessible datasets, the study contrasts PU-based models with conventional supervised and unsupervised learning techniques.

Applications of Positive Unlabeled Learning 171

The study employs a multi-phase methodology that includes evaluation, comparative analysis, model construction, preprocessing and labeling, and dataset selection. Only a tiny portion of the data is positively tagged, allowing confirmation of PU learning under practical cybersecurity restrictions.

6.2 CICDDoS2019 Dataset

The Canadian Institute for Cybersecurity created the CICDDoS2019 datasets, which replicated actual DDoS attack scenarios in a controlled setting. It includes a variety of attack types created with popular tools, including SYN flood, UDP flood, and HTTP flood attacks. More than 50 features that indicate network traffic parameters, such as packet count, flow duration, and inter-arrival time, are included in the dataset, it can be used to train machine learning models for DDoS detection because of its richness and diversity [10]. One drawback of CICDDoS2019, though, is that in some situations, it does not provide enough benign traffic, which makes it difficult to train Positive-Unlabeled models, which need a significant quantity of unlabeled data.

6.3 CICDDoS2017 Dataset

This work used the CICDDoS2017 dataset because of the shortcomings of CICD-DoS2019, specifically its low volume for efficient PU learning. The more extensive dataset, CICDDoS2017, was created by Canadian Institute for Cybersecurity and includes both attack and benign traffic gathered over several days. The attacks were created by replicating many DDoS attack types, including WebDDoS, DoS Slowries, DoS GoldenEye, and DoS Hulk.

6.4 Cleaning and Feature Selection

Noise and duplicate or irrelevant elements are common in raw traffic data. In data cleansing, damaged entries are filtered out, duplicate records are eliminated, and missing values are handled. Selecting features is essential for lowering computational complexity and enhancing model functionality. To choose the most informative features, methods like variance thresholding and mutual information are employed [10].

To improve the model performance and minimize computational cost, feature selection is essential. Non-informative information like timestamps and IP addresses were not included in this investigation. Flow duration, Total Fwd packets, Flow IAT Mean, Fwd Packet Length Max, Bwd Packet length Mean, Fwd PSH Flags, Bwd URG flags, Average packet size, subflow Fwd packets, and init_win_bytes_forward were among the 79 numerical features that were kept from the final dataset. These characteristics record statistical summaries of flow dynamics, packet transmission behavior, and flag counts, all of which are important for differentiating between malicious and benign network activity. PU and baseline models were then trained using cleaned and chosen features.

6.5 Labeling for PU Learning

In order to support Positive-Unlabeled learning the dataset's goal labels were transformed into a binary format. First, to indicate different attack types, the class "BENIGN" and other categorical values (such "DoS Slowloris", DoS Hulk" and "Heartbleed") were added to the "Label" column. All instances labeled "BENIGN", which represented regular traffic, were assigned a value of 0 by programmatic encoding, which all other attack sorts, which represented positive (attack) samples, were assigned a value of 1.

In PU learning, where the goal is to distinguish known positive cases (attacks) from a pool of unlabeled data that may contain both benign and undetected attacks, this binary encoding simplifies the classification task. To ensure that no NaN values were inserted during the mapping process, the encoding was verified. Data consistency for downstream modeling was ensured by the validation of two different label values: 0 (benign) and 1 (attack).

7 Model Architecture

7.1 PU Bagging

In this study, decision tree classifiers were used as basic learners to develop PU Bagging. A balanced sample of known attacks and a random sample of unlabeled traffic that was presumed to be negative were used to train each learner. By majority vote, the final ensemble prediction was determined. The model can learn generalizable patterns from supervision using this approach, which has been demonstrated to be robust in noisy network contexts [5, 10].

7.2 Two-Step Method

A secondary supervised learning step is incorporated into the hybrid two-step PU learning framework, which builds on the advantages of PU Bagging. The main difficulty is separating benign traffic from a sizable pool of unlabeled cases that can contain concealed attacks in situations when labeled negative samples are not accessible. By using PU Bagging as an initial filter to find high-confidence pseudo-negative samples, our technique overcomes that difficulty. Based on the ensemble's agreement, these inferred negatives despite not having been initially labeled are presumed to be benign with high confidence [5, 10].

First, a huge pool of unlabeled data and a limited collection of known assault samples are used to train PU Bagging. A random sample of the unlabeled pool is treated as negative by each base learner in the ensemble, which then learns to distinguish them from the known positives. Following training, the ensemble is used to estimate class probabilities on the unlabeled data. After that, samples that are highly likely to be negatives (according to a threshold or majority voting criterion) are taken out and labeled as pseudo-negatives. Because it lessens bias and noise in the second training phase, this filtering step is essential. [5].

The initial set of positive samples and the high confidence pseudo-negatives produced in the first stage are used to train a supervised classification model in the second step. These pseudo-labels are used by the model, which is usually a logistic regression classifier or a decision tree-based learner, to create clearer class boundaries and enhance generalization. By successfully transforming the weakly supervised environment into a more structured learning problem, this stage enables the classifier to improve performance metrics like precision and F1-score and fine-tune its internal representations [10].

This two-step approach combines the flexibility of supervised classifiers with the advantages of ensemble learning. The approach is better equipped to distinguish subtle DDoS patterns from normal activity by utilizing inferred labels and separating potentially benign traffic. Although the quality of the pseudo-labels produced in the first phase is crucial to the success of this strategy, current research shows that well-tuned PU pipelines can considerably outperform conventional baselines in partially labeled situations [5, 9].

7.3 Auto-encoders

Unsupervised deep learning models known as auto-encoders are designed to discover effective representations, or encodings of input data. They are composed of two primary parts: a decoder that reconstructs the input from this compressed form and an encoder that compresses the input into a latent space representation. Auto-encoders are trained only on benign traffic for DDoS detection. High reconstruction error samples are identified as abnormal during inference because they depart from the benign patterns that have been learned.

For better generalization, a deep auto-encoder was built in this study using fully connected layers with batch normalization and dropout. To make sure that only samples that deviated significantly were classified as attacks, the reconstruction error threshold was established using a validation set. Auto-encoders are useful for identifying new or zero-day attacks that are structurally different from known benign flows [1].

7.4 Supervised Baseline

To compare the effectiveness of PU-based and supervised techniques, fully labeled subsets of the data were also used to train conventional supervised learning models. Gradient Boosting classifiers, Random Forests, and Support Vector Machines (SVM) were among the models. Because these models can handle high-dimensional data and have a high classification accuracy, they are frequently utilized in network intrusion detection.

The SVM employed a radial basis function (RBF) kernel, while the Random Forest classifier was set up using 100 estimators and default values. Grid search was used to find the best learning rates and tree depths for Gradient Boosting, which is well-known for performing exceptionally well in unbalanced datasets. With a 99.99% accuracy rate, Al-Eryani et al (2024) demonstrated the great efficacy of gradient boosting with CICD-DoS2019 [10]. The effectiveness of PU learning and anomaly detection techniques in practical settings is assessed using these models as comparative baselines. Reconstructing innocuous traffic is one of their skills, and they identify instances of significant reconstruction error as possible threats. Auto-encoders are especially useful for identifying new or unidentified assault patterns that differ from typical behavior [11].

7.5 Evaluation Metrics, Data Splits

Accuracy, precision, recall, and F1-score are used to assess performance. Several split techniques designed for PU learning were used to separate each dataset into training and test sets. The goal was to replicate real-world scenarios in which the majority of benign traffic is left unclassified and only a small percentage of attack samples are identified.

For PU Bagging studies, essential split configuration was created:

- Extreme split: There were 19,376 positive samples and 415,977 negative samples (4.45% positives, 95.55% negatives) in the test set, compared to 174,380 positive samples and just 1,000 negative samples (99.43% positives, 0.57% negatives) in the training set. This division highlights how the model behaves during training when there are few negative examples.
- Moderate Split: The test set had 1,937 positives and 412,808 negatives (0.47% positives, 99.53% negatives), but the training data had 174,380 positives and 4,169 negatives (98% positives and 2% negatives). This is a moderate split.
- Balanced split: There were more positives (174,380) and negatives (41,697), 81% positives and 19% negatives in the training set. A balanced evaluation scenario for comparison across all models was provided by the test set's construction, which included an equal number of positive and negative examples (19,376).

7.6 Tools and Libraries

Python-based libraries such as Scikit-learn, TensorFlow/Keras, and pandas, for preprocessing, are used in the implementation. Matplotlib and Seaborn are used to facilitate analysis and visualization. To guarantee reproducibility, experiments are conducted in a regulated Jupyter environment.

8 Experiments and Results

The experimental setup, assessment procedure, and results for the various DDoS detection strategies investigated in this study are presented in this part. Finding out how Positive-Unlabeled (PU) learning stacks up against conventional supervised methods under different label availability levels was the aim.

In order to assess popular supervised algorithms like Support Vector Machines (SVM), Random Forest, and Gradient Boosting, we first create a baseline using properly labeled datasets. This is a standard for performance under perfect, completely labeled circumstances.

In order to replicate real-world scenarios where the majority of traffic is unlabeled and only a small percentage of attack data is labeled, we then analyze PU Bagging's performance over high, moderate, and balanced label splits.

The capacity of autoencoder-based anomaly detection models trained just on benign traffic to identify new or previously undiscovered attack patterns is then tested. Lastly we investigate if the two-step PU learning approach, which improves pseudo-negative labeling in a second supervised stage, can increase detection accuracy even further. Accuracy, precision, recall, F1-score, and AUC are used to evaluate the results, providing a thorough comparison of the advantages, disadvantages, and versatility of each model in various labeling scenarios.

8.1 Baseline Supervised Model Performance

Initially, fully labeled data was used to assess classic supervised learning models in order to provide a performance baseline. Support Vector Machine (SVM), Random Forest, and Gradient Boosting models were tested on the CICDDoS2017 test set after being trained on a balanced dataset. With an accuracy of 99.9% and an F1 score of 0.998% for the attack class, gradient boosting was the most accurate model. With an F1 score above 0.98, SVM and Random Forest both demonstrated strong performance. These findings support the efficacy of fully labeled controlled settings for supervised learning.

However, in situations involving labeled and unlabeled data, supervised models showed reduced resilience. Positive-Unlabeled (PU) learning was made possible by their reliance on clean and comprehensive labels, which brought attention to the necessity for models that could manage poor supervision (Figs. 1, 2 and 3).

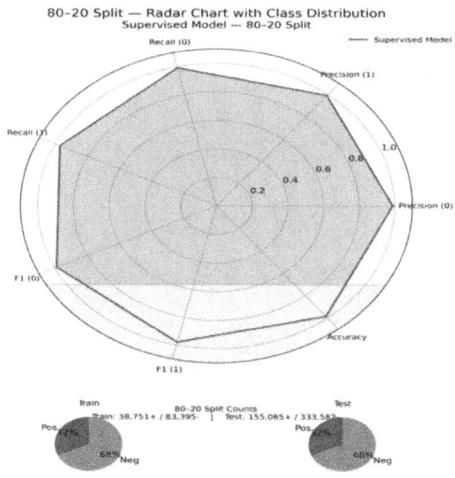

Fig. 1. 80–20 split

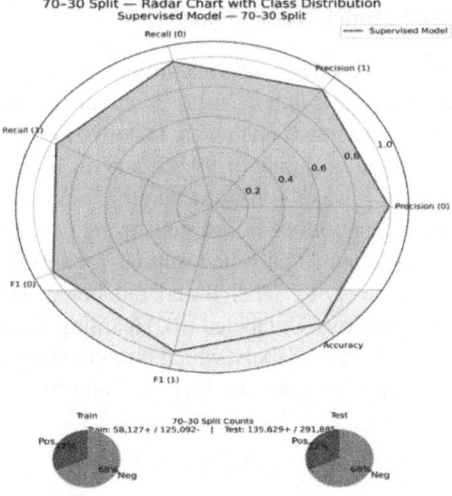

Fig. 2. 70 – 30 split

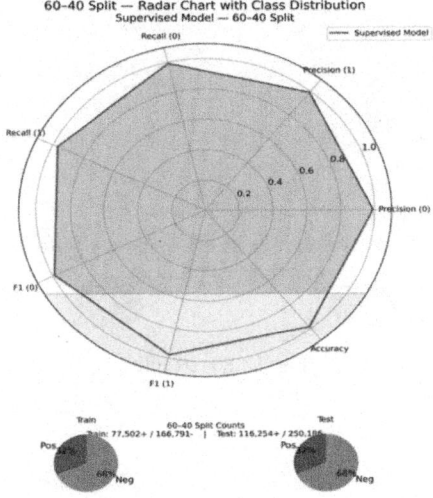

Fig. 3. 60 - 40 split

8.2 PU Learning vs Unsupervised Model Performance

PU Bagging demonstrated reliable identification abilities when the data was very sparse. Even though there were only 0.57% of negative events during training, the model achieved a precision of 0.94 and recall of 0.91 on the test set in the extreme split situation. These results validate the ensemble's ability to generalize from both positives and ambiguous examples.

PU Bagging consistently showed great accuracy (over 98.6%) in the moderate and balanced test splits, with F1-scores above 0.99. For instance, using a 70-30 split configuration, the model achieved 98.67% accuracy while maintaining a balance between precision and recall across classes. Similar positive outcomes were obtained with the 60-40 and 80-20 split values, indicating that PU Bagging is effective across a variety of label distributions.

Furthermore, an unsupervised environment was used to test auto-encoders that had only been trained on benign data. The model obtained an average AUC of 0.91 on unseen assault data and successfully identified novel attack types with significant reconstruction error. It displayed a slightly greater false-positive rate than PU Bagging (Figs. 4 and 5).

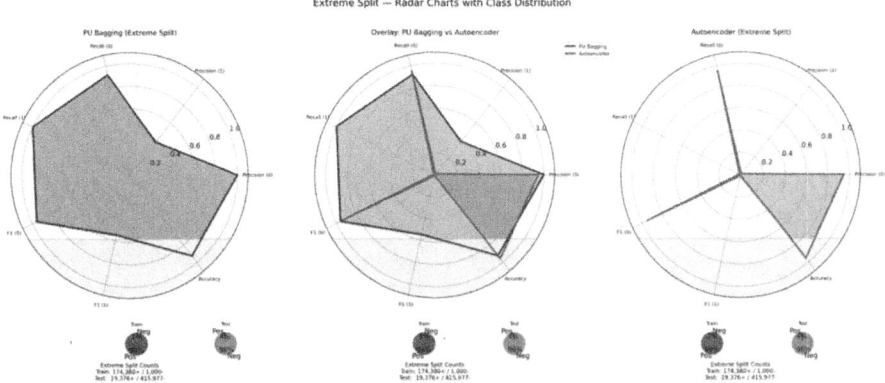

Fig. 4. Extreme split

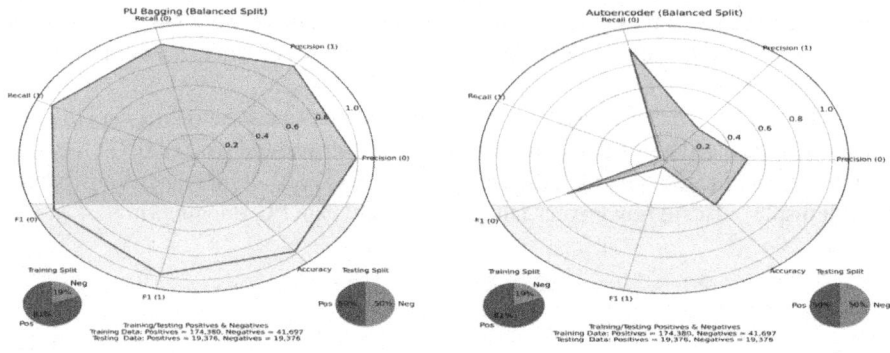

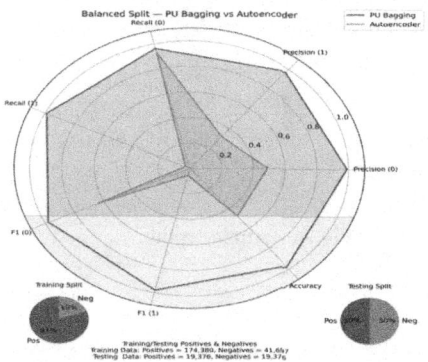

Fig. 5. Balance Split

Three experiments were conducted using two-step strategy:

Model 1: This model performed well on the negative class but struggled heavily on the positive class, leading to poor balance.
Model 2: In Model B, there is an improvement in capturing the positive class compared to Model 1, but the performance is still imbalanced, and the accuracy increased to ~79%, through precision/recall for the minority class remain weak.
Model 3: This model achieved a strong and balanced results across both positive and negative classes. With ~94% accuracy and high precision/recall, this model generalizes best and shows the most reliable performance.

These results suggest that the two-step method can improve PU learning effectiveness, particularly when accurate pseudo-labeling is feasible in the first stage. However, it is susceptible to the quality of inferred negative labels and may degrade if pseudo-negatives are noisy (Fig. 6).

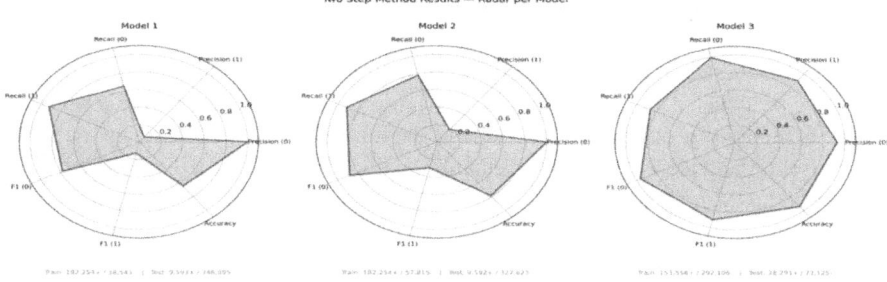

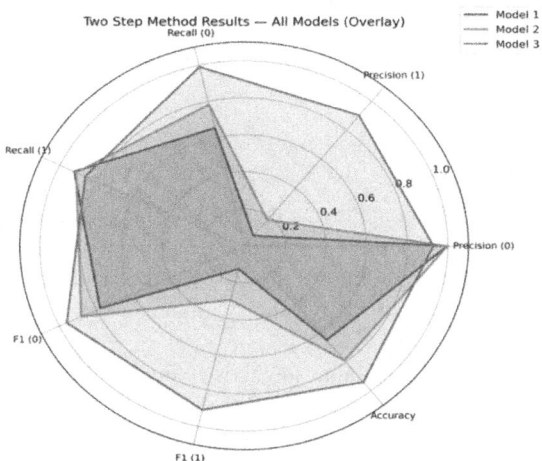

Fig. 6. Two Step Method

8.3 Comparative Analysis

Table 1. Comparative Analysis

Train Positives	Train Negatives	Test Positives	Test Negatives	PU Bagging	Autoencoders
81	19	50	50	97	48
99.43	0.57	4.45	95.5	92	90

Important details regarding the behavior of PU learning and auto-encoder models in training and testing datasets with varying class distributions are provided by the comparison results in the Table 1: Comparative Analysis. The figures are expressed as a percentage. Notably, PU learning demonstrated great accuracy regardless of the degree of imbalance, performing between 92% and 98%. By attaining 92% accuracy in the most extreme scenario, where training data comprised 99.43% positives and just 57% negatives, PU learning showed its resilience in highly skewed environments. This robustness is caused by PU Bagging's ensemble-based architecture, which effectively learns class boundaries even when there is sparse or noisy negative data. As the proportion of training negatives increased (for instance, from 2% to 19%), performance improved as well, indicating that even a small amount of real or inferred negative examples significantly enhances model discrimination. In contrast, the auto-encoder model showed a strong sensitivity to the underlying class distribution, with an accuracy range of 48% to 97%. The model did the poorest when given equal numbers of normal and anomalous samples; in the balanced test set scenario, it only achieved 48% accuracy (50% positive and 50% negative). This implies that the model struggled with generalization. However, the auto-encoder demonstrated its potential for anomaly identification in environments with a predominance of benign traffic by achieving 97% and 90% accuracy, respectively, under more realistic, imbalanced distributions (e.g., 0.47% or 4.45% test positives). Even if PU learning is more dependable, the auto- encoder is helpful when hidden or hitherto unidentified attack patterns need to be found without prior labeling.

9 Conclusion

The findings of this thesis demonstrate the PU learning--specifically, PU Bagging is an effective technique for detecting contemporary DDoS attacks, providing robust performance with low labeling needs. Even if they work well in ideal circumstances, traditional supervised models struggle to adapt to noisy, imbalanced, or unlabeled datasets in the actual world.

The suggested two-step learning methods refine label boundaries using high confidence pseudo-labeling, which further enhances PU learning performance. Auto-encoders, on the other hand, improve model resilience by identifying structural anomalies in traffic data, especially those that point to new or covert threats.

10 Future Work

Even though the current study has shown that PU learning holds promise for DDoS detection, there are still several areas that could use more research:

Real-time detection and deployment: Implementing the suggested PU learning framework in an online or real-time detection context, like Software Defined Networks (SDN) or edge computing systems, may be the focus of further research. This would evaluate response times, latency, and scalability under actual traffic volumes.

Cross-Dataset generalization: More investigation is needed to find out how successfully PU-trained models generalize to other datasets, such as encrypted traffic flows or IoT based datasets. Investigating domain adaptation or transfer learning may provide information about model portability.

Label Noise Handling: To increase the accuracy of PU-based models, sophisticated methods for detecting noisy or incorrectly labeled data in both the positive and unlabeled pools should be investigated. The PU pipeline may incorporate methods like label propagation or confident learning.

References

1. Gcore: DDoS Attack Trends Q1–Q2 2024. Gcore Radar White Paper (2024). https://gcore.com/
2. Jaafar, G.A., Abdullah, S.M., Ismail, S.: Review of recent detection methods for HTTP DDoS attack. J. Comput. Netw. Commun. (2019). https://doi.org/10.1155/2019/1283472
3. Sharif, D.M., Beitollahi, H., Fazeli, M.: Detection of application-layer DDoS attacks produced by various freely accessible toolkits using machine learning. IEEE Access **11**, 51810–51825 (2023). https://doi.org/10.1109/ACCESS.2023.3280122
4. Drinić, D., Čiča, Z.: Survey on low-rate DDoS attacks, detection and defense. In: 23rd International Symposium INFOTEH-JAHORINA, pp. 1–6. IEEE (2024). https://doi.org/10.1109/INFOTEH60418.2024.10496020
5. Bekker, J., Davis, J.: Learning from positive and unlabeled data: a survey. Mach. Learn. **109**(4), 719–760 (2020). https://doi.org/10.1007/s10994-020-05877-5
6. Vinay, M.S., Yuan, S., Wu, X.: Fraud detection via contrastive positive unlabeled learning. In: 2022 IEEE International Conference on Big Data (Big Data), pp. 1475–1484. IEEE (2022). https://doi.org/10.1109/BigData55660.2022.10020693
7. Lau, F., Rubin, S.H., Smith, M.H., Trajković, L.: Distributed denial of service attacks. In: Proceedings of the 2000 IEEE International Conference on Systems, Man andCybernetics, pp. 2275–2280 (2000). https://doi.org/10.1109/ICSMC.2000.886426
8. Nazario, J. (2008). DDoS attack evolution. Network Security, 2008(7), 7– 10.https://doi.org/10.1016/S1353-4858(08)70086-2
9. Najafimehr, M., Zarifzadeh, S., Mostafavi, S.: DDoS attacks and machine- learning-based detection methods: a survey and taxonomy. Eng. Reports **5**(12), e12697 (2023). https://doi.org/10.1002/eng2.12697
10. Al-Eryani, A.M., Hossny, E., Omara, F.A.: Efficient machine learning algorithms for DDoS attack detection. In: 6th International Conference on Computing and Informatics (ICCI) (2024). https://doi.org/10.1109/ICCI61671.2024.10485168
11. Alashhab, A.A., Abdullahi, M., Zahid, M.S.M., Rahman, M.S.: Real-time detection of low-rate DDoS attacks in SDN-based networks using online machine learning model. In: 7th Cyber Security in Networking Conference (CSNet) (2023). https://doi.org/10.1109/CSNET59123.2023.10339791
12. Yuan, X., Li, C., Li, X.: DeepDefense: Identifying DDoS attacks via deep learning. In: 2017 IEEE International Conference on Big Data (Big Data) (2017). https://doi.org/10.1109/BigData.2017.8258185
13. Arshi, M., Nasreen, M.D., Madhavi, K.: A survey of DDoS attacks using machine learning techniques. E3S Web Conf. **184**, 01052 (2020). https://doi.org/10.1051/e3sconf/202018401052
14. Chhettri, D., George, F.J., Nair, A.M., Alapatt, B.P.: PE-v-SVR based architecture to predict and prevent low and slow-rate DDoS attacks using machine learning. BVICAM's Int. J. Inform. Technol. **14**(1), 1–10 (2024)
15. Tang, D., Yan, Y., Gao, C., Liang, W., Jin, W.: LtRFT: Mitigate the low-rate data plane DDoS attack with learning-to-rank enabled flow tables. IEEE Trans. Inform. Forensics Secur. **18**, 3143–3156 (2023). https://doi.org/10.1109/TIFS.2023.3275768
16. Arora, K., Kumar, K., Sachdeva, M.: Impact analysis of recent DDoS attacks. Int. J. Comput. Sci. Eng. **3**(2), 877–884 (2011). https://www.researchgate.net/publication/50247519
17. Najafimehr, M., Zarifzadeh, S., Mostafavi, S.: DDoS attacks and machinelearningbased detection methods: a survey and taxonomy. Eng. Reports **5**(12), e12697 (2023). https://doi.org/10.1002/eng2.12697

Robust Intrusion Detection in IoV Using PU Learning and Supervised Ensembles with Synthetic Data Augmentation on CICIoV2024

Yashwanth Reddy Kovvuri and Charan Gudla(✉)

Department of Computer Science and Engineering, Mississippi State University, Starkville, MS, USA
yashu.kovvuri@gmail.com, gudla@cse.msstate.edu

Abstract. Internet of vehicles (IoV) has led to major improvements in vehicle communication and automation, as well as introduced vehicles to the increasing threat of cybersecurity attacks, including Denial-of-Service (DoS) attacks and spoofing. Traditional Intrusion Detection Systems (IDS) rely on properly labeled data, which is either of limited availability or excessively inconsistent in actual automotive settings because of privacy issues, data gathering, and changing malevolent activity inclination. To deal with this, we introduce a dual-pipeline IDS system to combine supervised ensemble models and Positive-Unlabeled (PU) learning which is dedicated to cases when only positive (attack) data is labeled, and benign data left unlabeled. Based on the CICIoV2024 CAN bus traffic of a 2019 model Ford car we applied Random Forest algorithm, XGBoost algorithm, Voting Classifier, and several PU algorithms such as ElkanotoPU, BaggingPU, PU-SVM, and Two-Step PU Learning. In order to deal with classes imbalance, we use synthetic sampling based on Gaussian properties to enlarge the dataset maintaining the same statistical properties and enhancing the model's generalization. The results show that the Two-Step PU and ensemble methods obtain the F1-scores of up to 0.98 under conditions of limited labeling. A/B testing proves that the gains of synthetic augmentation of performance are statistically significant. The suggested structure possesses high precision, scalability, and flexibility to be implemented into intelligent transport systems under real-time constraints with limited data availability.

Keywords: Intrusion Detection · Internet of Vehicles (IoV) · PU Learning · CAN Bus Security · Synthetic Data Generation · Ensemble Models · Cybersecurity · Supervised Learning · CICIoV2024 · Semi-Supervised Learning

1 Introduction

Internet of vehicles (IoV) is a growing paradigm of intelligent transportation systems, considering that the vehicles are networked together by the roadside infrastructure as well as cloud services, and other vehicles to provide higher mobility as well as safety and infotainment services. This networked connectivity is mostly made possible by the controller area network (CAN) is a vehicle communication protocol that enables real-time data exchange between Electronic Control Units (ECUs), sensors, and external entities in real-time. Although these enhancements make operations more efficient, they also introduce a large attack surface that malicious agents can use to compromise functions and safety of cars and users.

The attacks on IoV systems have increased and they have become more complex, and an attack message of Denial-of-Service (DoS) and spoof attack can cause serious threats to vehicular networks. Such attacks can lock up or compromise important vehicle controls like braking, steering, and thereby the throttle, which could result in disastrous consequences. The 2014 hack to the Jeep Cherokee by security researchers Charlie Miller and Chris Valasek demonstrated the dangers of unsecure CAN bus networks. They proved the capability to remotely operate the steering and braking systems of a vehicle with the help of vulnerabilities of its infotainment system which emphasized the necessity to implement a high level of security within a vehicle.

Conventional Intrusion Detection System (IDS) with IoV environments heavily rely on the fully labeled dataset to train a supervised machine learning model. Obtaining a fair labeled dataset in the vehicular settings is difficult owing to the dynamic nature of vehicle systems, and privacy concerns and the cost involved in creation or annotation of attack scenarios. Consequentially, a lot of real-world data is either poorly labeled or highly imbalanced with lots of benign information compared to a few attack instances. This imbalance makes such datasets unsuitable for supervised learning, which relies on well-labeled and balanced training data.

In order to cope with these issues, this study offers a hybrid IDS that combines supervised ensemble methods with Positive-Unlabeled (PU) learning. PU learning is particularly useful for training models with only positive samples and unlabeled data making PU learning very applicable in situations when labeled data is scarce. In addition, the synthetic data augmentation technique will be used, using Gaussian distribution and thus it will maintain the statistical properties of the data generated and enrich the minority (Fig. 1).

The benchmark dataset to assess the provided system is the CICIoV2024 dataset that was gathered using a 2019 Ford vehicle in both benign and attack scenarios. This research contributes the following:

- Development of a hybrid IDS model incorporating supervised learning algorithms (Random Forest, XGBoost, SVM, Naive Bayes, Voting Classifier) and Positive-Unlabeled (PU) learning techniques (ElkanotoPU, BaggingPU, PU-SVM, Two-Step PU).
- Removal of extreme class imbalance using synthetic data augmentation.
- Statistical significance tests of synthetic augmentation to assess performance benchmarking with or without synthetic augmentation.
- Demonstration of how the proposed IDS framework can be applied to enhance cybersecurity in real-world connected vehicle environments.

The results show that PU learning models, especially Two-Step PU Learning, achieve performance comparable to top-performing supervised classifiers, even under label-scarce conditions. The framework indicated is very handcrafted and expandable because of its modular system, which incorporates the training pipelines of supervised learning and PU learning. It can be deployed on embedded devices such as Raspberry Pi or Jetson Nano due to its level of efficiency employed in lightweight ensemble models, including Random Forest and XGBoost. Moreover, it can be applied to near real-time scenarios because of the great performance, despite the label-scarce settings (F1-scores up to 0.98), as well as, the requirement of very little computational tuning.

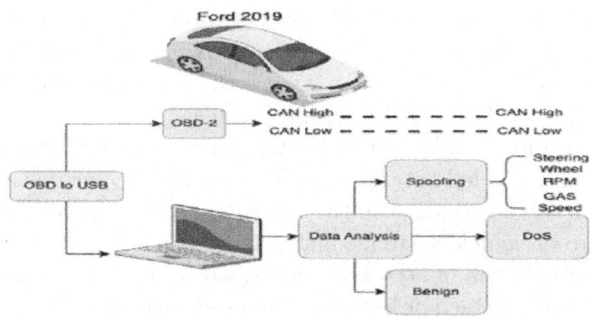

Fig. 1. CAN Bus Data Collection Setup from a 2019 Ford Vehicle. Image adapted from CICIoV2024 dataset documentation [3].

2 Related Work

Intrusion Detection Systems (IDS) have been of great importance as a research activity with regards to intelligent transportation system and Internet of Vehicles (IoV). Traditional IDS models are either signature-based or rule-based, the reasons are traditional IDS models on vehicular network were heavily based on signature or rule associated to identify an attack among known attacks. Nevertheless, such methods tend to leave the generalization issues and are not able to recognize new or zero-day attacks [8,10]. The viability and potential applications of machine learning (ML) techniques gained an interest as vehicular communication systems such as the Controller Area Network (CAN) bus became subject to cyber-attacks and thus require more adaptive and data-driven means of detecting them.

Supervised learning algorithms such as Decision Trees, Support Vector Machines (SVM), Random Forests and the XGBoost, promising results in the detection of DoS and spoofing attacks in CAN-based systems have been discovered [1,15,17,18]. The latter was the case in an experiment by Zhang et al. [18]

who tested the effectiveness of classifiers on the CICIoV2024 dataset and found that known types of attacks could be detected with high accuracy. presented ensemble with feature selection to enhance the performance of IDS on the vehicular traffic of the CAN. On the same note, Zhang et al. [15] formulated a hybrid ensemble framework towards intrusion detection in connected vehicle systems to improve upon the robustness. The level of efficacy of these models however greatly relies on the avail capability of massive, big-labeled data. In real-world IoV setups, The available labeled attack data may not be comprehensive in a real-world IoV setting because of privacy and changing network conditions, and reliance on the labeling process.

Recent independent efforts have proposed the use of semi-supervised and Positive-Unlabeled (PU) learning to deal with the issue of scarce labeled data [2, 6, 11]. The application of PU learning is especially pertinent in an environment of vehicular security in which only labeling of positive (attack) examples is done and the remainder of the database is unlabeled. Some of PU learning strategies that are notable are ElkanotoPU classifier [6], Bagging-based PU ensembles [13], PU-SVM [12], and Two-Step PU learning [9], which identifies reliable negatives before training a supervised classifier. Other recent works like contrastive PU learning [5] and semi-supervised PU methods to network intrusion detection [16] seem to have the potential of better representation learning and more complex patterns of attacks.

Simultaneously, there is one direction in the research to resolve class imbalance in IDS data via synthetic data augmentation. Oversampling of features and Gaussian-based techniques such as SMOTE [4] have also been applied to enhance generalization in a classifier, by up- sampling underrepresented classes of attack, whilst leaving the benign distribution the same. In cybersecurity [7] research shows that the performance of synthetic data generation procedures, especially when it involves rare events such as cyberattacks. In addition, synthetic data and estimated data has been seen to enhance the detection in normal intrusion under ensemble-based intrusion detection in vehicular networks [17].

Although these developments demonstrate the effectiveness of learning via supervised or PU learning, there are studies which tend to consider supervised or PU learning separately. Few go as far as to integrate both techniques into a single pipeline, as well as use synthetic augmentation and CAN traffic data collected in the real world. Table 1 is a summary of chosen works and point to the main differences of our approach.

3 Dataset and Preprocessing

3.1 Overview of CICIoV2024 Dataset

The experiments in this study are conducted on the CICIoV2024 dataset, a publicly available vehicular intrusion detection dataset released by the Canadian Institute for Cybersecurity (CIC). The dataset captures Controller Area Network (CAN) bus traffic from a 2019 Ford vehicle under real-world driving and simulated attack scenarios. It includes two major categories of data:

Table 1. Comparison of Existing Works on IDS in Vehicular Networks

Study and Dataset	Methodology	Limitations
Alheeti et al. (2023) *Dataset: CAN-injected*	Random Forest, Decision Tree	No semi-supervised learning; low attack diversity
Zhang et al. (2023) *Dataset: CICIoV2024*	SVM, KNN, XGBoost	No augmentation; only supervised learning used
Ntalampiras (2022) *Dataset: In-vehicle logs*	Isolation Forest	Anomaly-based only; lacks attack classification
Our Contribution *Dataset: CICIoV2024*	PU Learning + Ensembles + Synthetic Augmentation	Combines PU learning and augmentation for real-world IDS deployment

- **Benign traffic**—collected under normal driving conditions.
- **Attack traffic**—involving Denial-of-Service (DoS) and spoofing attacks affecting various ECUs (e.g., RPM, SPEED, STEERING_WHEEL, GAS).

Each record in the dataset contains features such as Flow Duration, Packet Count, Payload Entropy, CAN ID, and Length. The original combined dataset consists of approximately 1.4 million entries.

3.2 Data Cleaning and Deduplication

CAN bus traffic includes a high frequency of repeated messages. To remove redundancy and retain only unique communication patterns, duplicate records were eliminated using all feature columns. Table 2 shows the dataset summary before and after cleaning.

Table 2. Summary of Dataset Before and After Deduplication

Data Version	Total Records	Benign	Attack
Original Raw Dataset	1,408,219	1,223,737	184,482
Deduplicated Dataset	3,588	3,547	41
Synthetic-Augmented	77,380	40,443	36,937

3.3 Label Encoding and Feature Selection

The dataset was converted into a binary classification format:

- Benign → Label = 0
- DoS, Spoofing (RPM, SPEED, GAS, etc.) → Label = 1

Feature selection focused on the following numeric attributes: Flow Duration, Packet Count, Entropy, CAN ID (encoded), and Length. All features were standardized using z-score normalization to ensure consistent scaling across algorithms.

3.4 Synthetic Data Generation

Given the severe imbalance (only 41 attack samples out of 3,588 records), Gaussian-based synthetic augmentation was applied to generate additional samples for both benign and attack classes. For each class:

- The mean and standard deviation of each selected numeric feature were computed.
- Synthetic instances were sampled from a Gaussian distribution $\mathcal{N}(\mu, \sigma^2)$.
- Approximately 20% additional samples were created for each class.

This augmentation increased the dataset to 77,380 instances, substantially improving class balance and model generalizability. Figure 2 shows the label distributions before and after augmentation.

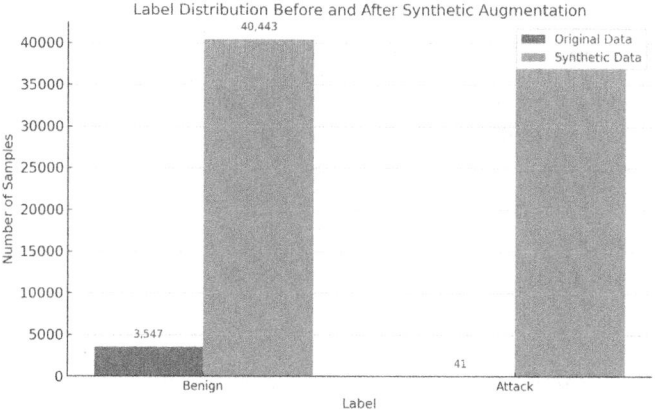

Fig. 2. Label distribution before (Benign: 3547, Attack: 41) and after synthetic augmentation (Benign: 40443, Attack: 36937).

3.5 Data Splits for Supervised and PU Learning

Two different data split strategies were employed:

- **Supervised learning**: 80% training, 20% testing, maintaining class distribution.
- **PU learning**: Only the positive (attack) samples were labeled; benign samples were treated as unlabeled.

This split mimics real-world label scarcity and enables evaluation of models under realistic deployment conditions.

4 Methodology

In this section, the machine learning techniques, the experimental framework, and evaluation measures followed to develop and evaluate the intrusion detection system (IDS) to IoV are described. Two concurrent pipelines of learning, supervised learning and Positive-Unlabeled (PU) learning are deployed on both original and synthetic-augmented versions of CICIoV2024.

4.1 Supervised Learning Models

The supervised learning pipeline treats intrusion detection as a binary classification problem. We evaluate five widely-used classifiers:

- **Random Forest (RF)**: An ensemble method based on decision trees with bagging, well-suited for structured datasets.
- **XGBoost (XGB)**: A gradient boosting framework optimized for speed and performance on tabular data.
- **Support Vector Machine (SVM)**: A margin-based classifier effective for high-dimensional binary classification.
- **Naïve Bayes (NB)**: A probabilistic classifier based on Bayes' theorem, assuming feature independence.
- **Voting Classifier (VC)**: A soft-voting ensemble that aggregates the predictions of RF, XGB, and NB to improve stability.

Each classifier is trained and evaluated using 5-fold stratified cross-validation. The models operate on normalized feature vectors and are tested on a held-out 20% test split.

4.2 Positive-Unlabeled (PU) Learning Pipeline

In PU learning, only attack samples (positive class) are labeled, while all benign data is treated as unlabeled. This simulates real-world conditions where complete labeling is impractical. Four PU learning techniques are implemented:

- **ElkanotoPU** [2,6]: Reweights the loss function using estimated class priors to handle unlabeled instances. It forms the theoretical basis for most PU learning strategies.
- **Bagging PU** [13]: Creates multiple bootstrapped subsets of positive and unlabeled data and aggregates their predictions, helping to reduce overlabeling risk in sparse data environments [16].
- **PU-SVM** [12,14]: Modifies the traditional SVM objective function to better handle class uncertainty in unlabeled data, balancing false positives and detection rates in imbalanced datasets.
- **Two-Step PU Learning** [9,11]: First identifies reliable negatives based on a probability threshold, then trains a supervised model. This approach is known for its robustness and adaptability in cybersecurity applications [5].

The PU learning models are evaluated using the same 80–20 data split, where the 20% test set retains ground-truth labels for final evaluation (Fig. 3).

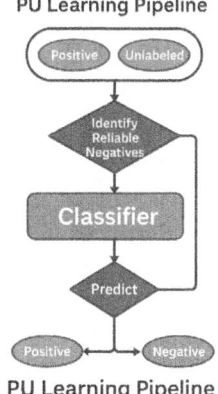

Fig. 3. PU learning pipeline

PU Learning Setup and Data Configuration. In our PU learning setup, the attack samples within the deduplicated data (which constitute the 41 samples) are defined as labeled positive and the other 3,547 records are labeled as unlabeled. It is a supporting case of automotive cybersecurity that the labeling of benign data at scale is hard because of the privacy and annotation limitations.

To evaluate PU learning methods, we implemented the following algorithms:

- **ElkanotoPU:** Reweights loss functions based on class priors estimated from the unlabeled data.
- **BaggingPU:** Aggregates predictions from multiple base classifiers trained on bootstrapped samples from positive and unlabeled data.
- **PU-SVM:** Modifies the classic SVM to handle partially labeled data, improving robustness to false negatives.
- **Two-Step PU Learning:** First identifies reliable negatives using a threshold-based filter, followed by training a supervised classifier (Random Forest) on positive and inferred negatives.

Training and benchmarking was done on an 80% set of data and 20% test set of data having ground-truth labels. An evaluation was measured by Accuracy, Precision, Recall, F1-score, ROC-AUC, and PR-AUC.

The above display shows how PU learning can be used to provide effective use in IoVs that lack labels. It can classify with good precision with few labeled attack data indicating its potential in practical settings.

4.3 Synthetic Data Augmentation

To address the extreme class imbalance in the original dataset, we apply Gaussian-based synthetic data generation. This involves:

1. Computing the mean and standard deviation of each numeric feature for both classes (benign, attack).

2. Sampling new synthetic data points from a normal distribution $\mathcal{N}(\mu, \sigma^2)$.
3. Combining synthetic and original data into a balanced dataset with over 77,000 samples.

This augmented dataset is then used to retrain all supervised and PU models under the same experimental conditions.

4.4 Training and Validation Strategy

Both learning pipelines are evaluated using the following setup:

- **Cross-validation:** 5-fold stratified, maintaining label proportions.
- **Train-Test Split:** 80% training, 20% testing, consistent across original and synthetic versions.
- **Feature Scaling:** Z-score normalization applied to all numeric features.
- **Model Tuning:** Default hyperparameters for reproducibility and fair comparison across models.
- **For PU Learning:** The positive class (41 samples of attack data) is under a clear label. The 3,547 benign samples are treated all as unlabeled. The PU models are trained with the 80:20 split wherein the 20% test data covers the ground-truth labels to adequately assess the PU models. Cross-validation and z-score normalization are used in a similar manner to supervised pipelines so that the comparisons become consistent.

4.5 Evaluation Metrics

Model performance is evaluated using:

- **Accuracy:** Overall correctness of predictions.
- **Precision, Recall, F1-score:** Especially important for imbalanced classification.
- **ROC-AUC and PR-AUC:** Evaluate the quality of classification thresholds.
- **Matthews Correlation Coefficient (MCC):** Balances evaluation across all classes, useful in skewed datasets.

$$\text{F1-score} = 2 \times \frac{\text{Precision} \times \text{Recall}}{\text{Precision} + \text{Recall}}$$

These metrics ensure a comprehensive comparison of model effectiveness under both label-rich and label-scarce conditions.

5 Results and Discussion

This section presents the performance analysis of both supervised and PU learning models on the CICIoV2024 dataset in two configurations: (1) the original deduplicated dataset and (2) the synthetic-augmented dataset. Results are evaluated using multiple metrics including Accuracy, Precision, Recall, F1-score, ROC-AUC, and MCC.

5.1 Results on Original Dataset

The original deduplicated dataset contains 3,588 samples, with only 41 labeled attacks. This severe imbalance impacts supervised models, but ensemble classifiers still perform well (Figs. 4, 5, 6, 7, 8, 9 and Table 3).

Table 3. Supervised Model Performance on Original Data

Model	Accuracy	Precision	Recall	F1-score	ROC-AUC
Random Forest	99.72%	100.00%	75.00%	86.00%	1.00
XGBoost	99.63%	75.00%	100.00%	85.71%	1.00
Voting Classifier	99.01%	91.67%	91.67%	91.67%	1.00
SVM	99.63%	83.33%	83.33%	83.33%	0.92
Naïve Bayes	93.87%	12.50%	75.00%	21.05%	0.84

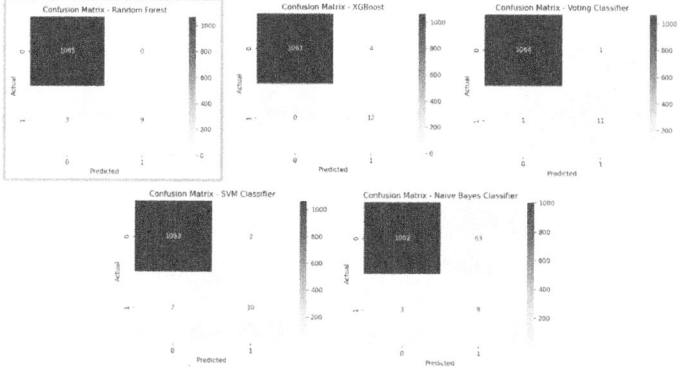

Fig. 4. Confusion Matrix: Supervised Models on Original Data

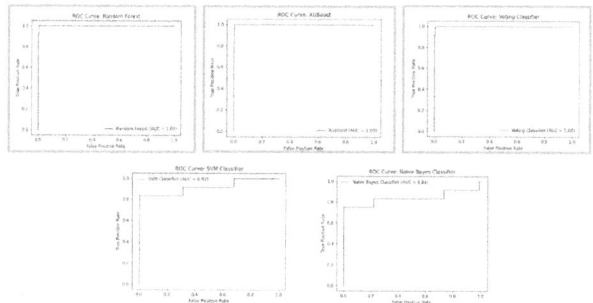

Fig. 5. ROC Curves of Supervised Models on Original Data: Random Forest, XGBoost, Voting Classifier, SVM, and Naïve Bayes. AUC values range from 0.84 to 1.00.

5.2 PU Learning Performance on Original Data

With only the attack samples labeled, PU models such as BaggingPU and Two-Step PU performed surprisingly well. ElkanotoPU failed to detect positives due to the small attack count and skewed class priors (Table 4).

Table 4. PU Learning Model Performance on Original Data

Model	Accuracy	Precision	Recall	F1-score	ROC-AUC
Two-Step PU RF	99.72%	93.00%	91.67%	88.00%	1.00
Bagging PU	99.63%	100.00%	66.67%	80.00%	1.00
PU SVM	99.63%	83.33%	83.33%	83.33%	0.92
Elkanoto PU	98.89%	0.00%	0.00%	0.00%	0.00

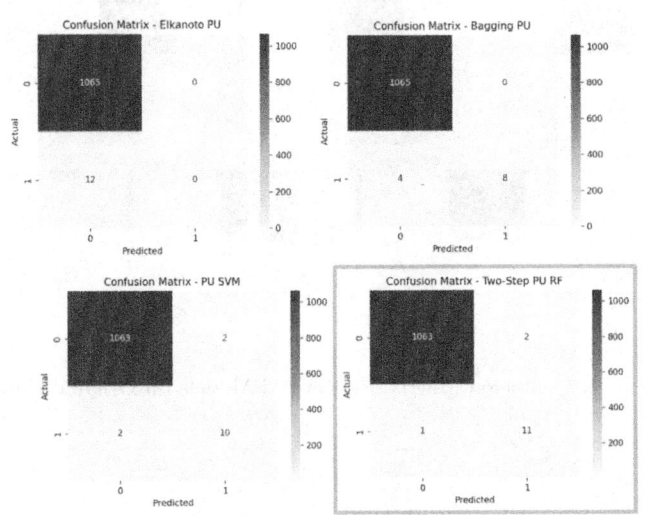

Fig. 6. Confusion Matrices of PU Learning Models: Elkanoto PU, Bagging PU, PU SVM, and Two-Step PU (RF). Two-Step PU demonstrates the most balanced detection performance, while Elkanoto PU fails to identify any attack instances.

5.3 Results on Synthetic-Augmented Dataset

Using Gaussian-based synthetic augmentation, the dataset was expanded to 77,380 samples. This resolved class imbalance and significantly improved performance across all models (Table 5).

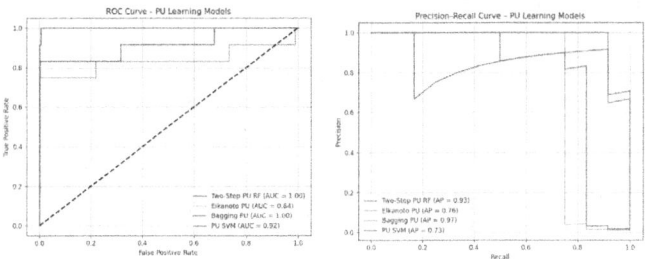

Fig. 7. ROC Curve and Precision-Recall Curve of PU Learning Models: Two-Step PU RF, Bagging PU, PU SVM, and Elkanoto PU. Bagging PU and Two-Step PU RF show the best performance across both metrics.

Table 5. Supervised Model Performance on Synthetic Data

Model	Accuracy	Precision	Recall	F1-score	ROC-AUC
Random Forest	98.84%	98.91%	98.45%	98.68%	0.99
XGBoost	98.72%	97.60%	99.74%	98.66%	0.99
Voting Classifier	**98.87%**	**99.45%**	**99.41%**	**99.43%**	**0.99**
SVM	98.61%	99.43%	99.43%	99.43%	0.99
Naïve Bayes	97.93%	99.41%	99.39%	99.40%	0.98

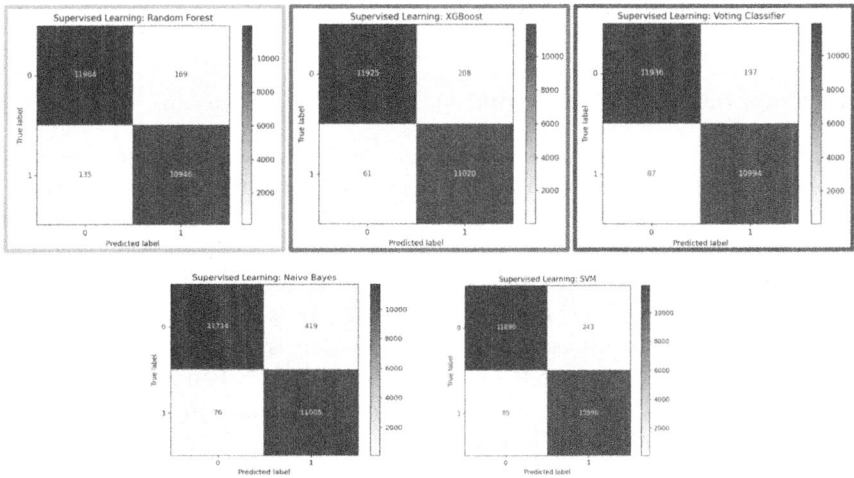

Fig. 8. Confusion Matrices of Supervised Models Trained on Synthetic Data: Random Forest, XGBoost, Voting Classifier, Naïve Bayes, and SVM. All models exhibit high accuracy and balanced classification across benign and attack labels.

5.4 PU Learning Performance on Synthetic Data

PU learning models also benefit from augmentation, with Two-Step PU and BaggingPU achieving F1-scores above 99% (Table 6).

Table 6. PU Learning Model Performance on Synthetic Data

Model	Accuracy	Precision	Recall	F1-score	ROC-AUC
Two-Step PU RF	98.69%	99.19%	99.18%	99.18%	1.00
Bagging PU	98.73%	99.17%	99.02%	99.09%	1.00
PU SVM	98.52%	99.43%	99.43%	99.43%	1.00
Elkanoto PU	52.26%	0.00%	0.00%	0.00%	0.99

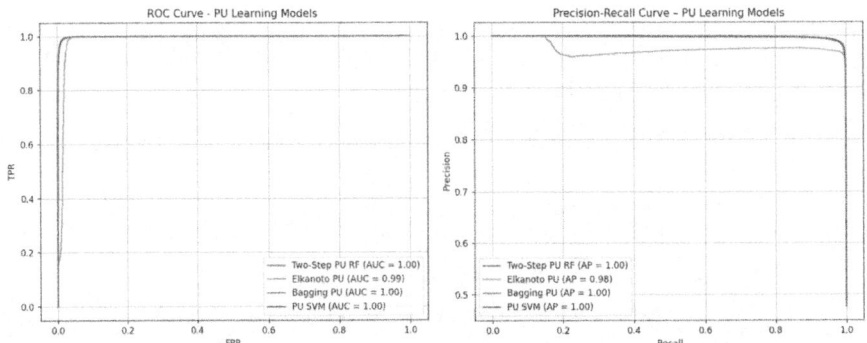

Fig. 9. ROC and Precision-Recall Curves for PU Learning Models on Synthetic Data. All models, including Two-Step PU RF, Bagging PU, PU SVM, and Elkanoto PU, achieve high classification performance with AUC and AP close to 1.00.

5.5 Comparison: PU Learning vs. Supervised Learning

Supervised learning Traditional supervised learning presupposes the existence of completely labeled data sets containing both benign and attacks. Nevertheless, in practice in vehicular applications, in particular those of the Internet of Vehicles (IoV), such balanced and labeled datasets are hard to find because of privacy reasons, inefficiencies of annotations and changing nature of threats.

Positive-Unlabeled (PU) learning, in its turn, uses the assumption that positive (attack) labels are present but the evaluation is only provided with their outer boundaries, i.e., all the rest of the data (presumably benign) are unlabeled. This assumption is very close to the real life constraints and thus PU learning is more realistic to adapt in automotive IDS systems.

Key Differences:

- **Label Requirements:** PU learning requires only positive-class labels, unlike supervised learning which requires full labeling.
- **Handling of Unlabeled Data:** PU techniques can treat the benign examples as unlabeled, where there is the flexibility when the labels are scarce.
- **Robustness to Class Imbalance:** PU learning is prospectively resistant to imbalanced scenarios in case of attack examples being minority occurrences.

Benefits of PU Learning in Our Work:

- allowed training the model with just 41 labeled attack examples of the deduplicated dataset, which would simulate realistic deployment.
- Two-Step PU performed with F1-score of 88.00 in the original data, similar to supervised ensemble models.
- The performance also rose further (F1-score > 99%) when used together with Gaussian-based synthetic augmentation.

Implementation in Our Pipeline:

- We compared the performance of PU using ElkanotoPU, BaggingPU, PU-SVM and Two-Step PU Learning
- Two-Step PU Learning first selected reliable negative samples from unlabeled data using a probability threshold before training a classifier.
- The primary feature of BaggingPU is the fact that it uses many poorly trained learners whose samples were bootstrapped to minimize mislabeled negative bias.

The comparison shows that PU learning is not only efficient in limited settings but can also be more effective than some of the supervised methods in combination with data expansion and ensemble methods.

5.6 A/B Testing: Impact of Synthetic Data

To statistically validate the performance improvements introduced by synthetic data augmentation, a paired t-test was conducted on the F1-scores obtained from the original (non-augmented) and synthetic datasets across all evaluated models. The test yielded the following result:

$$t = -2.63, \quad p = 0.0339$$

Since $p < 0.05$, the null hypothesis (i.e., no significant difference between the means) is rejected. This indicates that the observed improvement in F1-score with synthetic augmentation is statistically significant. The results provide empirical support for the effectiveness of synthetic data in enhancing classification performance, particularly under class imbalance and limited label scenarios (Fig. 10).

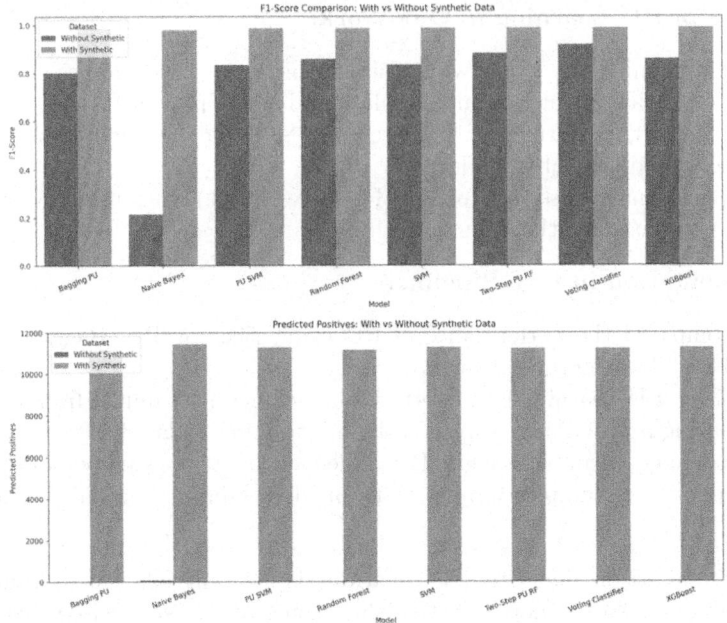

Fig. 10. A/B Test Comparison of Supervised and PU Learning Models: F1-Score and Number of Predicted Positives with and without Synthetic Data. Synthetic augmentation significantly improves classification performance and increases detection of attack instances across all models.

5.7 Summary of Insights

- Ensemble models like Voting Classifier and Random Forest consistently outperform standalone classifiers.
- Two-Step PU learning demonstrates robust performance in label-scarce environments, outperforming some supervised models.
- Synthetic augmentation drastically improves recall and F1-scores, especially for PU models.
- ElkanotoPU fails on both datasets due to its sensitivity to class prior estimation.

6 Conclusion and Future Work

This paper presents a robust intrusion detection system (IDS) for the Internet of Vehicles (IoV), combining supervised ensemble models with Positive-Unlabeled (PU) learning techniques. We addressed the challenges of data imbalance and limited labels by applying Gaussian-based synthetic augmentation on the CICIoV2024 dataset, which simulates real CAN bus traffic and attacks.

The results of the experiment show that under the supervised approach, such as Random Forest, XGBoost, and Voting Classifier, high detecting accuracy has been reached even under the highly imbalanced original data set. More to the point, the PU learning strategies, especially, Two-Step PU technique is effective in scenarios with imbalanced data, where only positive-labeled attack samples are available, achieving performance comparable to fully supervised models.

The synthetic data generation significantly improved classification performance across all models. Statistical testing also proved that synthetic augmentation significantly enhanced the model's effectiveness. Such findings emphasize the feasibility of utilizing PU learning and data augmentation as a scale-up strategy towards the safety of vehicular networks.

6.1 Key Takeaways

- PU learning methods can act reliably on few attack labels, which makes them even better to be used in real world.
- Gaussian sampling as a strategy of Synthetic data generation approach to class imbalance is effective.
- The results with voting-based ensembles are steady and perform well in most data environments.
- Two-Step PU learning was found to be better than ElkanotoPU and BaggingPU in both original and synthetic setting ups

6.2 Future Work

Future directions for this research include:

- Integration of deep learning-based PU models such as PU-Autoencoders and PU-GCNs for better representation learning.
- Deployment of real-time IDS systems using edge-based computing on automotive-grade hardware (e.g., Raspberry Pi or Jetson Nano).
- Incorporation of temporal patterns and recurrent architectures to detect time-based attack signatures.
- Exploration of hybrid PU-supervised frameworks for active learning and online retraining with streaming CAN traffic.
- Evaluation under varying attack intensities and inclusion of additional datasets for broader generalization.

Overall, this work contributes a scalable, accurate, and label-efficient IDS solution suitable for deployment in modern connected vehicle systems.

References

1. Alheeti, K.M., Griscik, F., Howley, E.: Vehicular cyberattack detection using machine learning on can bus data. Comput. Netw. **218**, 109378 (2023)
2. Bekker, J., Davis, J.: Learning from positive and unlabeled data: a survey. Mach. Learn. **109**(4), 719–760 (2020)
3. Canadian Institute for Cybersecurity: Ciciov2024 dataset (2024). https://www.unb.ca/cic/datasets/iov.html. Accessed June 2025
4. Chawla, N.V., Bowyer, K.W., Hall, L.O., Kegelmeyer, W.P.: Smote: synthetic minority over-sampling technique. J. Artif. Intell. Res. **16**, 321–357 (2002)
5. Deng, Z., Li, M., Liu, P., Lee, Y.: Contrastive positive-unlabeled learning. Adv. Neural. Inf. Process. Syst. **34**, 2653–2666 (2021)
6. Elkan, C., Noto, K.: Learning classifiers from only positive and unlabeled data. In: Proceedings of the 14th ACM SIGKDD International Conference on Knowledge Discovery and Data Mining, pp. 213–220 (2008)
7. Gerhardinger, A., Costa, D., Mariani, R.: Synthetic data generation for machine learning in cybersecurity: a survey. Comput. Secur. **115**, 102590 (2022)
8. Kumar, V., Ghosh, J.: Pattern classification: a unified view of statistical and neural approaches. IEEE Trans. Neural Networks **1**, 45–58 (1995)
9. Lee, D., Liu, B.: Learning with positive and unlabeled examples using weighted logistic regression. In: ICML, pp. 448–455 (2003)
10. Lee, W., Stolfo, S.J., Mok, K.W.: A data mining framework for building intrusion detection models. In: IEEE Symposium on Security and Privacy, pp. 120–132 (1999)
11. Li, D., Liu, Z., Ji, S.: A survey of PU learning: algorithms and applications. ACM Comput. Surv. **53**(5), 1–37 (2020)
12. Li, X., Liu, B.: Positive and unlabeled learning with noise. In: IJCAI, pp. 830–835 (2009)
13. Mordelet, F., Vert, J.P.: Bagging for positive unlabeled learning: a trade-off between overfitting and overlabeling. Pattern Recogn. **47**(9), 3132–3141 (2014)
14. Sun, H., Yang, Y., Xie, R.: Adaptive PU learning for imbalanced intrusion detection. Comput. Secur. **118**, 102713 (2022)
15. Wang, T., Wang, W., Li, L., et al.: Enhanced ids for vehicular can bus using ensemble learning with feature selection. Sensors **21**(14), 4857 (2021)
16. Xu, C., Zhang, X., Liu, Y.: Semi-supervised learning for network intrusion detection using PU learning. In: Proceedings of the 29th International Joint Conference on Artificial Intelligence (IJCAI), pp. 1237–1243 (2020)
17. Zhang, W., Xie, Y., Huang, Y.: An ensemble framework for intrusion detection in connected vehicles using hybrid features. J. Netw. Comput. Appl. **186**, 103103 (2022)
18. Zhang, W., Zhao, L., Qureshi, B., et al.: Machine learning-based intrusion detection in IoV using ciciov2024 dataset. IEEE Access **11**, 18923–18936 (2023)

The Potential of Large Language Models in Automating Software Testing: From Generation to Reporting

Betim Sherifi, Khaled Slhoub[✉], and Fitzroy Nembhard

Florida Institute of Technology, Melbourne, FL 32901, USA
bsherifi2023@my.fit.edu, kslhoub@fit.edu, fitzroy@ieee.org

Abstract. Achieving high-quality software is a primary goal in software engineering, which requires rigorous validation and verification processes throughout testing activities. Although manual testing can be effective, it is often time-consuming and resource-intensive, leading to an increased demand for automated solutions. Recent advances in large-language models (LLMs) have significantly influenced various domains within software engineering, including requirements analysis, test automation, and debugging. This article explores an agent-oriented framework for automated software testing that leverages the capabilities of LLMs to minimize human intervention and improve testing efficiency. The proposed approach integrates LLMs to automate the generation of unit tests, visualization of call graphs, and execution and reporting of tests. The framework is evaluated using multiple applications developed in Python and Java, demonstrating high test coverage and operational efficiency. The findings of the article emphasize the potential of LLM-powered agents to streamline software testing workflows and address critical challenges related to scalability and accuracy.

Keywords: Large Language Models · LLMs · Automated Testing · AI in Software Engineering · Agent-Based Testing Frameworks

1 Introduction

Similarly to other industries, ensuring that software products function as intended and adhere to defined quality standards is a critical aspect of software engineering. Software engineers strive to minimize defects in development artifacts and ensure that the software system aligns with the specified business requirements. This challenge is primarily addressed during the software testing phase, where a cross-examination of the implementation results is evaluated against user-defined requirements. Through the validation and verification processes, software testing provides a reliable assessment of the overall quality of the system. Although achieving a completely error-free system is virtually unattainable, the goal is to detect and resolve as many identifiable and critical issues as possible before the software is released to end users [1, 2].

Since the early 1970s, the software industry's focus on testing has grown consistently, accompanied by ongoing advancements in the methodologies and practices employed in the field. Software testing is now widely recognized as a critical component in the education and training of software engineers [3]. Given the time-intensive and costly nature of manual testing—particularly in the context of regression testing—there has been a growing demand for effective automated testing solutions. Nevertheless, both manual and automated testing approaches possess distinct advantages and limitations that can influence the overall efficiency of the testing process. While automated testing may appear to offer a more efficient alternative, it does not entirely replace the need for manual testing. For instance, in the domain of graphical user interface (GUI) testing, automation tools can support specific tasks, yet a fully comprehensive testing process still requires human oversight and intervention [4].

To address some of the inherent limitations of traditional testing strategies, researchers have explored intelligent, autonomous systems such as software agents and multi-agent architectures. A software agent is defined as a flexible and autonomous entity capable of interacting directly with its environment by receiving input through sensors and exerting influence via actuators [5]. In contrast, a multi-agent system (MAS) consists of a collection of individual agents that coordinate and collaborate through communication and information sharing to achieve objectives that surpass the capabilities of any single agent.

Significant advancements in machine learning and natural language processing techniques, coupled with increased computational power and the availability of large-scale training datasets, have driven the rapid development of Large Language Models (LLMs). These models exhibit the ability to generate human-like text, often making the distinction between machine-generated and human-created content challenging. The emergence of LLMs has proven to be highly beneficial across various domains of software engineering, including software implementation (e.g., code completion, generation, and summarization), software maintenance, quality assurance, and requirements engineering. In the context of requirements engineering, for instance, LLM-powered tools such as ChatGPT and Gemini are particularly effective in resolving ambiguities in specifications and classifying requirements as functional or non-functional [6].

Building upon the capabilities of LLMs and recent advancements in automated testing technologies, this research proposes a multi-agent-based software testing framework powered by state-of-the-art LLMs. Unlike conventional automated methods—where test cases are manually written by developers or testers—our approach utilizes LLMs to dynamically generate test cases, substantially reducing human input and accelerating the processes of test case creation and execution. The primary objective of this framework is to reduce manual intervention while offering a robust, intelligent, and scalable solution for automated software testing. To further minimize human involvement, the framework will incorporate voice commanding through speech recognition, allowing testers to interact with the system naturally and efficiently. This study demonstrates how the integration of LLMs within a multi-agent system can shift software testing from a reactive, manual task to a proactive, autonomous quality assurance process. The proposed approach addresses key challenges in software testing, such as test case generation and comprehensive coverage, by enabling the identification of testing edge cases, which generally include a combination of boundary value analysis and equivalence partitioning to ensure comprehensive coverage of the test [7]. Additionally, the framework produces relevant test scripts and offers explainable reasoning to justify each test.

The primary contributions of this research are as follows: (1) We propose a novel multi-agent-based framework for automated software testing that leverages the capabilities of Large Language Models to reduce manual effort and improve testing efficiency. (2) Our approach enables dynamic test case generation, call graph visualization, and autonomous test execution across diverse applications. (3) We demonstrate the effectiveness of the framework through empirical evaluations on Python and Java applications, highlighting acceptable test coverage and detailed bug reporting. (4) The framework incorporates mechanisms to generate transparent and context-sensitive justifications for each test, thus enhancing the trustworthiness and comprehensibility of AI-assisted testing systems.

The structure of this paper is organized as follows. Section 2 provides a discussion of related prior work. Section 3 outlines the proposed methodology and summarizes the results. Section 4 evaluates the proposed methodology through case studies. Finally, Sect. 5 concludes the paper with final remarks.

2 Related Work

This section provides a review of relevant research in the domain of software testing, with a particular emphasis on Agent-Based Software Testing (ABST). The discussion includes both traditional methodologies and more recent approaches that integrate LLMs, offering a comparative perspective on their capabilities and limitations.

2.1 Traditional Approaches to Agent-Based Software Testing

ABST refers to the application of agent-based systems—encompassing software agents, intelligent agents, autonomous agents, and multi-agent systems—to address challenges in software testing. ABST aims to enhance the testing process by automating complex and resource-intensive testing tasks, thereby improving efficiency and accuracy [8]. This approach has attracted interest since 1999, with research activity reaching notable peaks over the past decade. The majority of ABST studies emphasize system-level testing, with Java serving as the predominant target language. Nevertheless, other programming languages, such as C, C + +, Python, and Perl, have also been explored.

In [9], the authors propose an agent-based framework designed for the automated testing of web-based systems. The framework incorporates multiple agents, including the Test Runtime Environment (TRE) agent, which serves as the central component of the system, as well as the Test Script Generator, Test Executor (TE) agents, and the Dashboard agent. These agents work collaboratively to execute and monitor the testing processes. Similarly, [10] introduces a multi-agent-based software environment tailored for web-based applications, in which agents can dynamically join or leave the system. Communication among agents is structured across three layers: the lowest layer facilitates message transmission between agents, the middle layer defines message content and ontology, and the highest layer employs communication protocols grounded in speech-act theory. An alternative approach is presented in [11], where the authors develop multiple agents to test an industrial coffee machine. Each agent represents a software module and employs fuzzy logic to prioritize software tests based on fault probabilities. In a related study [12], the authors propose an agent-based software testing approach that integrates human testers with virtual assistants operating on smart devices. A Google Assistant application and test generation tools are utilized, allowing testers to verbally initiate software tests. The framework is evaluated on two Java projects, wherein the virtual agent effectively executed JUnit tests and generated corresponding test results and code coverage reports using the EclEmma tool.

2.2 Leveraging Large Language Models to Enhance Agent-Based Software Testing

The study in [13] explores the practical applications of Large Language Models in software testing, specifically within the context of the software industry. Drawing insights from 83 completed questionnaires submitted by experienced and diverse professionals in the field, the research seeks to understand the extent and manner in which software testing practitioners utilize LLMs across different phases of the software testing life-cycle. The anonymous survey gathered data on participants' usage of LLMs in testing activities, the specific tools employed, and their perspectives on the potential of LLMs in this domain. The findings indicate that while 52% of respondents have not yet utilized LLMs for testing, 48% have integrated these models into various activities, including requirements analysis, test plan development, and test automation. AI Tools such as ChatGPT and GitHub Copilot were frequently mentioned. The study concludes that LLMs hold significant promise as tools for enhancing software testing practices. However, the authors caution against indiscriminate usage, particularly in scenarios involving sensitive information, underscoring the need for careful consideration in such contexts.

A recent comprehensive review by [14] analyzed 102 research articles, including 82 published in 2023, and focused on LLMs application in software testing. The review highlights the utility of LLMs in mid-phase software testing activities, such as generating unit test cases, crafting test assertions, and producing system test inputs. Furthermore, LLMs are identified as valuable tools in later stages of the software testing life-cycle, providing support for bug analysis, debugging, and automated repair processes. Another survey [15] provides an overview of LLM applications in software testing, analyzing 19 research studies related to automated test code generation. The survey reveals that with techniques like PLBART architecture improving test case accuracy by 147% and coverage by 15%, and frameworks such as FuzzGPT discovering 49 new bugs in deep learning libraries. A paper from Meta [16] discusses TestGen-LLM, a tool that leverages LLMs to enhance human-written tests by covering previously overlooked paths. When evaluated on products like Instagram Reels and Stories, 75% of the generated tests were correctly designed, 57% passed consistently, and 25% contributed to improved coverage.

According to [17], the researchers introduce Kashef, a tool designed to support software testers in the design, generation, and execution of test cases, with a particular emphasis on testing web microservices applications. Kashef employs a multi-agent architecture comprising two agents powered by LLMs—the Test Engineer and the HTML Interpreter—alongside a non-LLM agent, the Code Executor. The tool integrates various LLMs, including GPT-3.5, GPT-4, CodeLlama, and Llama2, in conjunction with supporting libraries such as LangGraph for machine learning functionalities and Selenium for testing purposes. Another study [18] conducts an exploratory study evaluating the performance of LLMs, specifically ChatGPT-4o and ChatGPT-4o Mini, in software testing. They attempt to answer two questions: (1) How well can LLMs generate test scenarios from user requirements? and (2) How well can LLMs generate test cases from test scenarios? To tackle these questions, the author uses prompting techniques such as few-show prompting and chain-of-thought prompting. To evaluate their framework, they use a real-world web application, called *Full Teaching*.

3 Proposed Methodology

3.1 Description of High Level Architecture

As illustrated in Fig. 1, the proposed methodology architecture comprises four primary components, each serving a distinct role in coordinating and enhancing the automated software testing framework.

1. **Client Interface**: A general client component, whose primary role is to initiate the testing workflow by sending an HTTP GET request to the Software Testing Agent. In our case scenario, we designed a web application where using the SpeechRecognition interface of the Web Speech API user voice commands are captured, triggering the testing pipeline for the selected project. Alternatively, users can achieve the same result through text input.
2. **Software Testing Agent**: It serves as the framework's core component, hosting the primary logic and coordinating interactions between various components. The Software Testing Agent functions as an abstraction layer for smaller subcomponents tasked with key operations such as generating test scripts, executing tests, and creating bug reports.
3. **Large Language Models**: LLMs are integral to the proposed automated testing framework. The Software Testing Agent leverages LLMs for various tasks, including extracting key entities from user commands to streamline operations, generating customized unit tests tailored to specific requirements, and producing DOT graphs to visualize the application's call graph. In our framework, we use Gemini 1.5 Pro as our Large Language Model for generating and analyzing software tests. The model is configured with a temperature of 1.0, which controls response randomness, ensuring a balance between creativity and consistency. We set top-p to 1.0, allowing the model to consider a wide range of likely words, and top-k to 0.95, which limits token selection to the most relevant options.
4. **The Development Environment**: It serves as the workspace housing the project code to be tested. This component facilitates automated testing by providing access to the target project, executing generated test cases, and displaying test results and coverage metrics.

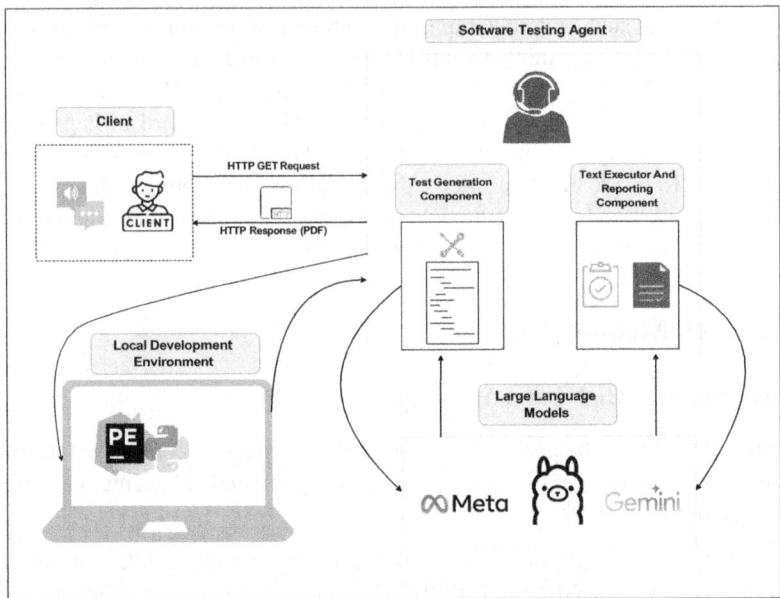

Fig. 1. The high-level architecture of the proposed framework

3.2 Description of Low Level Architecture

As shown in Fig. 2, the methodology low-level architecture provides a detailed overview of the entire workflow and highlights the responsibilities of each module and their interactions within the framework. The process is initiated by the **Client**, typically through a voice command. The user prompt is received by the **Test Generator API**, which represents the entry point for the testing frame-work. The prompt is forwarded to the integrated **LLMs**, where entities such as the project name, the specific subfolder and the programming language of the project are extracted. Once the LLM identifies those entities, the **FileLocator** module is activated to locate the specified project directory and the files within it.

Following that, the contents of these files are extracted and are sent as a prompt to the LLM, with the objective of generating unit tests and their accompanying rationale, using Gemini in our case. Additionally, the LLM generates a DOT graph string to help visualize a call graph of the code base interactions. After receiving the generated test scripts, the test files are created within the project. Next, the **PDF Report Generator** is activated, which as a first step orders the **Test Executor** to execute the newly created test files. Details results of the test runs, including code coverage metrics are provided by the Test Executor. Upon receiving this information, the Report Generator creates a comprehensive PDF report including test results, the rationales, code coverage and the generated call graph. This report is then returned to the user, finalizing the whole workflow.

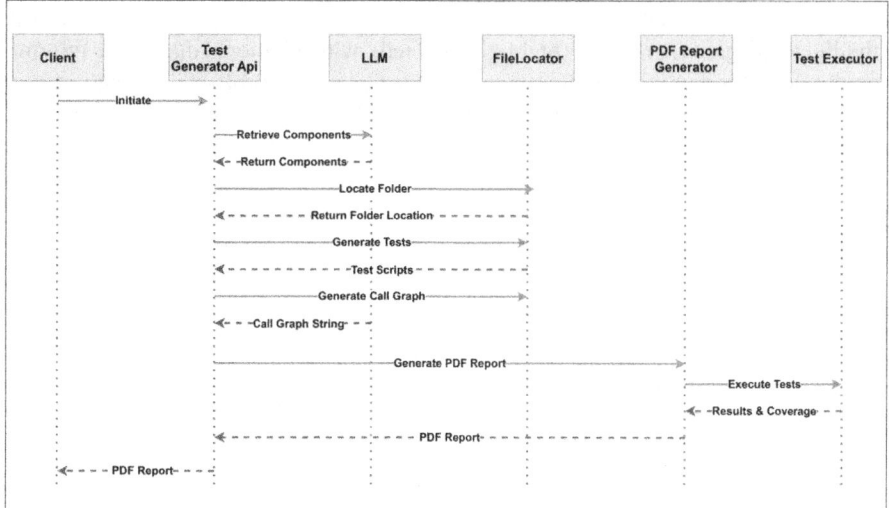

Fig. 2. The low-level architecture of the proposed framework

4 Case Study and Results

To evaluate the performance of the proposed framework, a series of experiments were conducted across four distinct software applications—two developed in Python and two in Java. The smaller-scale applications included a Python project, referred to as Experiment, which offered basic calculator functionalities such as addition, multiplication, and Fibonacci sequence generation, and a Java application named StudentAverage, designed to compute students' average grades across multiple courses. The larger and more complex applications were similarly divided by programming language: a Python-based cinema management system supporting movie rentals, and a Java-based library management system with comparable functionality. To initiate test generation and execution, prompts of varying formats were employed. Example prompts included: *Create unit tests for the project Library under the folder management, written in Java* and *Write Python-based tests for the cinema project, specifically for the models folder*.

In addition, to assess the framework's applicability and replicability in real-world scenarios, it was employed to generate unit tests for an open-source project, specifically, the Python requests library. The successful generation and execution of these tests further demonstrate the system's potential for broader adoption in practical software engineering contexts.

4.1 Report Description

The output generated by the framework is a structured PDF report that provides comprehensive insights into the testing process and its outcomes. The report begins with the **Test Rationale** section (Fig. 3), detailing each file and its corresponding functions. For every function, the rationale includes a description of the basic test cases as well as any identified edge cases. This is followed by the **Test Results** section (Fig. 4), which enumerates all executed test cases. Each test case is clearly marked as either Passed (highlighted in green) or Failed (highlighted in red), with additional diagnostic information provided for any failures. Subsequently, the **Coverage Table** (Fig. 5) summarizes testing coverage by presenting percentages, the number of statements tested, and missed statements for each test file, along with an overall summary. The report concludes with a Call Graph visualization, which illustrates the interactions among code components. For future enhancements, the call graph could incorporate a heatmap overlay to highlight areas more susceptible to defects and thus warranting further testing.

For example, in the cinema management project, the rationale for the *test rent movie* function in the *Library* class includes the following scenarios:

- Basic case: *Tests renting an available movie to an existing member.*
- Edge cases: *Tests renting a non-existent movie, renting a movie to a non-existent member, and renting an already rented movie.*

In contrast, a more straightforward example is observed in the Library Management project, specifically for the *getTitle* function within the *Book* class:

- Basic case: *Tests retrieving the book title after object creation.*
- Edge cases: *Not applicable.*

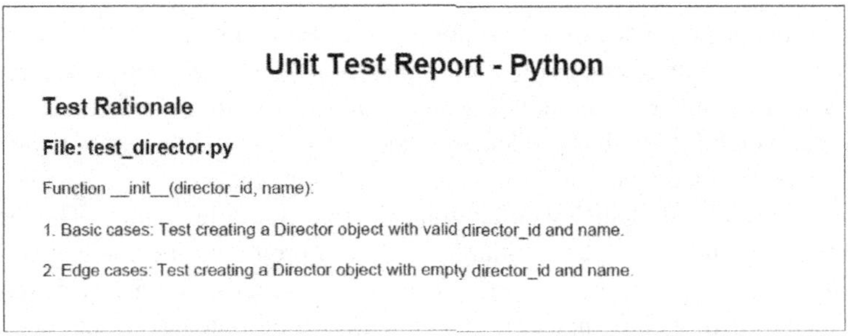

Unit Test Report - Python

Test Rationale

File: test_director.py

Function __init__(director_id, name):

1. Basic cases: Test creating a Director object with valid director_id and name.
2. Edge cases: Test creating a Director object with empty director_id and name.

Fig. 3. Rationale Report

4.2 Performance Analysis

The framework's performance was assessed by logging detailed timing information for each execution, including the duration of operations such as component retrieval, unit test generation, and test execution. Additionally, test coverage and the overall execution status were recorded and categorized as either successful—when all steps, including test generation, execution, and PDF report generation, were completed successfully—or failed. Out of 20 executions on the Python projects, the framework successfully completed all runs without any failures. In contrast, 3 failures were observed out of 24 executions for the Java projects. These failures were primarily attributed to ambiguous prompt phrasing, which hindered the accurate identification of necessary components, or by generated test scripts containing compilation errors, resulting in execution failures.

```
Test Results
=========================== test session starts ===========================

Cinema\models_test\test_director.py::test_director_creation PASSED
Cinema\models_test\test_director.py::test_director_creation_edge_cases PASSED
Cinema\models_test\test_director.py::test_get_director_id PASSED
Cinema\models_test\test_director.py::test_get_name PASSED
Cinema\models_test\test_director.py::test_set_director_id PASSED
Cinema\models_test\test_director.py::test_set_director_id_edge_case PASSED
Cinema\models_test\test_director.py::test_set_name PASSED
```

Fig. 4. Results Report

Coverage Report

Name	Statements	Missed	Coverage
test___init__.py	39	4	90%
test_adapters.py	63	25	60%
test_api.py	40	4	90%
test_compat.py	9	1	89%
test_help.py	73	11	85%
test_hooks.py	77	1	99%
test_status_codes.py	24	5	79%
test_structures.py	68	1	99%
test_utils.py	45	2	96%
TOTAL	**438**	**54**	**88%**

Fig. 5. Coverage Report

The average total execution time for each run was approximately 83.5 s. The largest portion of this time, about 62.8 s on average, was dedicated to test generation by the LLM, which included generating rationales. This was followed by folder location, taking an average of 9.7 s, DOT graph generation at 5.4 s, and test execution at 3.2 s. Retrieving components required 1.3 s on average, while both PDF report creation and writing test files took less than a second each.

When comparing the average total execution time by programming language, Java executions averaged 86.7 s, while Python executions averaged 80 s. Interestingly, the time taken for test generation by the LLM was nearly identical for both languages, with Java averaging 62.4 s and Python 63.3 s. Most operations across the two programming languages showed similar average durations. However, a notable difference was observed in the test execution phase, where Java required an average of 5.44 s, compared to only 0.87 s for Python. This discrepancy in test execution time accounts for the gap in the overall average execution times between the two languages, as other operation times remained consistent, as shown in Fig. 6.

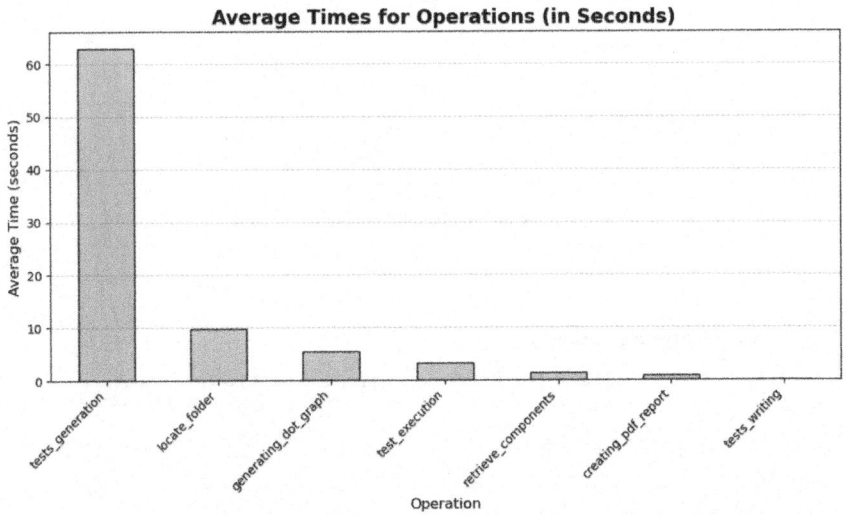

Fig. 6. Average time for operations (in seconds)

As anticipated, the average time for test generation varied significantly across projects, with more complex projects requiring substantially more time. For example, LibrarySystem averaged 92.54 s, Cinema 92.43 s, Student-Manager 39.79 s, and Experiment 34.17 s. This variation is due to the greater number of files and increased logical complexity in the more complex projects. A summary of this analysis is presented in Table 1.

However, test execution times were relatively consistent across projects of the same programming language, even though varying in complexity. As noted earlier, Java projects had higher execution times, with LibrarySystem averaging 5.39 s and StudentManager 5.48 s. In contrast, Python projects showed much lower execution times, with Cinema averaging 0.79 s and Experiment 0.96 s.

The overall test coverage across all projects was notably high, reflecting the effectiveness of the generated test cases. When grouped by project, the coverage percentages revealed some variation. StudentManager achieved full coverage at 100%, while Experiment followed closely with 98.6%. LibrarySystem exhibited slightly lower coverage at 94.67%, and Cinema recorded the lowest coverage at 88.3%. This is summarized in Table 1.

When analyzing the results by programming language, Java projects demonstrated slightly higher average coverage at 97.71% compared to Python projects, which averaged

Table 1. Project Metrics Comparison

Project	Lang	Loc	No. Classes	No. Methods	Total Time	Tests Gen.	Dot Graph	Entity Retrieval	Test Exec.	PDF Report	Coverage %
LibrarySystem	Java	269	4	34	119.06	92.54	7.57	1.44	5.39	2.01	94.67
StudentManager	Java	114	2	14	62.55	39.79	5.08	1.36	5.48	0.75	100.00
cinema	Python	183	4	36	110.13	92.43	5.83	1.33	0.79	0.65	88.30
experiment	Python	47	2	8	49.78	34.17	3.44	1.33	0.96	0.28	98.60

93.45%. This difference highlights potential language-specific factors influencing coverage, such as testing frameworks or execution times. Despite this variation, both languages consistently delivered high coverage, ensuring reliable testing across all projects.

In addition, a comparison of the test coverage generated by our framework and the existing tests in the requests library revealed closely aligned results, further reinforcing the tool's effectiveness, as detailed in Table 2.

To evaluate the performance of an alternative LLM, such as ChatGPT, we tasked it with generating test cases for the LibrarySystem project. The total generation time was approximately 3 minutes, which is twice as long as the average time observed with Gemini. Despite the longer duration, the test coverage achieved was impressively high at 98%. Notably, the ChatGPT Web Application was used for this task instead of the API, and the additional rendering process may have contributed to the increased generation time.

Table 2. Requests – Coverage Comparison

File	Original Coverage %	LLM Coverage %
_ini_py	83%	90%
test_adapters.py	100%	60%
test_compat.py	83%	89%
test_help.py	100%	85%
test_hooks.py	100%	99%
test_structures.py	100%	99%
test_utils.py	98%	96%

5 Conclusion

This article highlights the significant potential of LLM-powered agents in automating various software testing activities, such as test generation, execution, and reporting. The proposed framework achieved impressive success rates, with no failures observed in Python applications and a high success rate recorded for Java applications. Average execution times were 80 s for Python projects and 86.7 s for Java projects. The framework also demonstrated strong test coverage, averaging 97.71% for Java projects and 93.45% for Python projects, showcasing its effectiveness in identifying comprehensive testing scenarios.

Despite its successes, the framework has notable areas for enhancement. Failures in Java executions, attributed to ambiguous prompts and compilation errors in generated scripts, point to the need for enhanced natural language processing and improved syntax accuracy. Moreover, the framework currently focuses exclusively on unit testing, leaving integration and system-level testing unexplored. While the call graph visualization is helpful, it could be enhanced with a heatmap overlay to identify areas more prone to defects. Incorporating requirement specification documents as prompts could further refine the precision and relevance of the generated test cases. Future work aims to address these limitations by extending language support and introducing additional test types. Despite these challenges, this research lays a solid foundation for LLM-assisted automated testing, demonstrating the potential of LLMs to minimize human intervention, boost efficiency, and improve testing quality.

References

1. Bäckström, K.: Industrial surveys on software testing practices: a literature review (2022)
2. Jamil, M.A., Arif, M., Awang Abubakar, N.S., Ahmad, A.: Software testing techniques: a literature review. In: The IEEE 6th International Conference on Information and Communication Technology for the Muslim World (ICT4M), pp. 177–182. IEEE (2016). https://doi.org/10.1109/ICT4M.2016.045
3. Sánchez-Gord´on, M., Rijal, L., Colomo-Palacios, R.: Beyond technical skills in software testing: automated versus manual testing. In: Proceedings of the IEEE/ACM 42nd International Conference on Software Engineering Workshops, pp. 161–164 (2020)
4. Taipale, O., Kasurinen, J., Karhu, K., Smolander, K.: Trade-off between automated and manual software testing. Int. J. Syst. Assur. Eng. Manage. **2**, 114–125 (2011)
5. Gokulan, B.P., Srinivasan, D.: An Introduction to Multi-Agent Systems, volume 310, pp. 1–27 (2010). ISBN 978-3-642-14434-9. https://doi.org/10.1007/978-3-642-14435-6.1
6. Hou, X., et al.: Large language models for software engineering: a systematic literature review. ACM Trans. Softw. Eng. Methodol. **33**(8), (2024). https://doi.org/10.1145/3695988
7. Jorgensen, P.C.: Software Testing: A Craftsman's Approach, 4 edn. CRC Press, Boca Raton, FL (2013). ISBN 9781466560680
8. Kumaresen, P.P., Frasheri, M., Enoiu, E.P.: Agent-based software testing: a definition and systematic mapping study. In: 2020 IEEE 20th International Conference on Software Quality, Reliability and Security Companion (QRS-C), pp. 24–31 (2020). https://doi.org/10.1109/QRS-C51114.2020.00016
9. Paydar, S., Kahani. M.: An agent-based framework for automated testing of web-based systems. JSEA **4**, 86–94 (2011). https://doi.org/10.4236/jsea.2011.42010
10. Huo, Q., Zhu, H., Greenwood, S.: A multi-agent software engineering environment for testing web-based applications. In: Proceedings 27th Annual International Computer Software and Applications Conference. COMPAC 2003, pp. 210–215 (2003). https://doi.org/10.1109/CMPSAC.2003.1245343
11. Malz, C., Jazdi, N. Gohner, P.: Prioritization of test cases using software agents and fuzzy logic. In: 2012 IEEE Fifth International Conference on Software Testing, Verification and Validation, pp. 483–486 (2012(. https://doi.org/10.1109/ICST.2012.131

12. Nembhard, F.D., Slhoub, K.A., Carvalho, M.M.: An agent-based approach toward smart software testing. In: Arai, K. (ed.) Proceedings of the Future Technologies Conference (FTC) 2023, vol. 2, pp. 281–297. Springer Nature, Switzerland, Cham (2023). ISBN 978-3-031-47451-4
13. Santos, R., Santos, I., Magalhaes, C., de Souza Santos, R.: Are we testing or being tested? exploring the practical applications of large language models in software testing. In: 2024 IEEE Conference on Software Testing, Verification and Validation (ICST), pp. 353–360. IEEE Computer Society, Los Alamitos, CA, USA (2024). https://doi.org/10.1109/ICST60714.2024.00039
14. Wang, J., Huang, Y., Chen, C., Liu, Z., Wang, S., Wang, Q.: Software testing with large language models: survey, landscape, and vision. IEEE Trans. Software Eng. **50**(4), 911–936 (2024). https://doi.org/10.1109/TSE.2024.3368208
15. Qi, F., Hou, Y., Lin, N., Bao, S., Xu, N.: A survey of testing techniques based on large language models. In: Proceedings of the 2024 International Conference on Computer and Multimedia Technology, ICCMT'24, pp. 280–284. Association for Computing Machinery, New York, NY, USA (2024). ISBN 9798400718267. https://doi.org/10.1145/3675249.3675298
16. Alshahwan, N., et al.: Automated unit test improvement using large language models at meta. In: Companion Proceedings of the 32nd ACM International Conference on the Foundations of Software Engineering, FSE 2024, pp. 185–196. Association for Computing Machinery, New York, NY, USA (2024). ISBN 9798400706585. https://doi.org/10.1145/3663529.3663839
17. Almutawa, M., Ghabrah, Q., Canini, M.: Towards llmassisted system testing for microservices. In: 2024 IEEE 44th International Conference on Distributed Computing Systems Workshops (ICD-CSW), pp. 29–34 (2024). https://doi.org/10.1109/ICDCSW63686.2024.00011
18. Augusto, C., Morán, J., Bertolino, A., de la Riva, C., Tuya, J.: Software system testing assisted by large language models: An exploratory study. In: Menéndez, H.D., et al. (eds.) Testing Software and Systems, pp. 239–255. Springer Nature Switzerland, Cham (2025). ISBN 978-3-031-80889-0

Design and Evaluation of a Scalable Data Pipeline for AI-Driven Air Quality Monitoring in Low-Resource Settings

Richard Sserunjogi[1], Daniel Ogenrwot[1,2(✉)], Nicholas Niwamanya[1], Noah Nsimbe[1], Martin Bbaale[1], Benjamin Ssempala[1], Noble Mutabazi[1], Raja Fidel Wabinyai[1], Deo Okure[1], and Engineer Bainomugisha[1]

[1] Makerere University, Plot 56 University Pool Road, Kampala, Uganda
{richard,daniel,nicholas,martin,benjamin,raja,
dokure,baino}@airqo.net

[2] University of Nevada Las Vegas, Las Vegas, NV 89154, USA
https://airqo.net

Abstract. The increasing adoption of low-cost environmental sensors and AI-enabled applications has accelerated the demand for scalable and resilient data infrastructures, particularly in data-scarce and resource-constrained regions. This paper presents the design, implementation, and evaluation of the AirQo data pipeline – a modular, cloud-native Extract-Transform-Load (ETL) system engineered to support both real-time and batch processing of heterogeneous air quality data across urban deployments in Africa. It is Built using open-source technologies such as Apache Airflow, Apache Kafka, and Google BigQuery. The pipeline integrates diverse data streams from low-cost sensors, third-party weather APIs, and reference-grade monitors to enable automated calibration, forecasting, and accessible analytics. We demonstrate the pipeline's ability to ingest, transform, and distribute millions of air quality measurements monthly from over 400 monitoring devices while achieving low latency, high throughput, and robust data availability, even under constrained power and connectivity conditions. The paper details key architectural features, including workflow orchestration, decoupled ingestion layers, machine learning-driven sensor calibration, and observability frameworks. Performance is evaluated across operational metrics such as resource utilization, ingestion throughput, calibration accuracy, and data availability, offering practical insights into building sustainable environmental data platforms. By open-sourcing the platform and documenting deployment experiences, this work contributes a reusable blueprint for similar initiatives seeking to advance environmental intelligence through data engineering in low-resource settings.

R. Sserunjogi and D. Ogenrwot—These authors contributed equally to this work and share first authorship.

Keywords: Data Engineering · Environmental Data Infrastructure · Scalable Data Pipeline · AI-driven Air Quality Monitoring · Low-resource settings

1 Introduction

The design and operation of scalable data pipelines are critical challenges in modern data engineering, particularly as organizations increasingly rely on heterogeneous data sources for analytics, decision-making, and the deployment of machine learning systems. Data pipelines are responsible for ingesting, transforming, and delivering structured, semi-structured, and unstructured data from diverse origins while ensuring reliability, scalability, and fault tolerance in production environment [24,27,34]. However, the complexity of maintaining consistent data quality and availability across varying data sources, network conditions, and operational environments presents significant engineering challenges [12]. Standard approaches to data ingestion and transformation often fall short when applied to resource-constrained environments, where data may arrive in varying formats and frequencies from distributed sources, including IoT devices, third-party APIs, and legacy systems operating over low bandwidth 2G GSM connectivity [9,27]. To address these challenges, there is a growing need for modular, extensible, and resilient ETL pipelines that leverage modern workflow orchestration tools, scalable data warehousing, and decoupled architectures to support real-time and batch processing workloads.

Recent advances in Artificial Intelligence (AI), cloud-native infrastructure, and edge-based Internet of Things (IoT) systems have unlocked new capabilities for real-time monitoring and prediction in complex domains such as public health, transportation, and environmental management. In particular, air quality monitoring systems increasingly rely on AI for predictive modeling, automated sensor calibration and anomaly detection. However, real-world implementation of such intelligence demands robust and adaptive data infrastructure that can cope with the scale, velocity, and variability of environmental data, especially in low-resource settings characterized by unreliable power and intermittent internet connectivity.

This paper presents the design and evaluation of a scalable, modular, and production-grade data pipeline that underpins the *AirQo Platform*, an AI-enabled air quality monitoring initiative with over 400 air quality monitors deployed across major African cities [1,9,10,30]. AirQo data pipeline aggregates measurements from a range of heterogeneous sources, including proprietary low-cost sensors [22], Beta Attenuation Mass (BAM) grade reference monitors, and third-party weather APIs, to provide high-resolution environmental intelligence [39]. The platform serves both scientific research and public engagement objectives, supporting dashboards, APIs, and machine learning-driven forecasts [29].

The AirQo data pipeline is built on open-source, cloud-native technologies: Apache Airflow orchestrates end-to-end workflows; Google BigQuery provides a scalable analytical warehouse; and Apache Kafka ensures real-time, decoupled streaming to downstream microservices. Through this architecture, the system seamlessly integrates both real-time and batch workflows, performs automated calibration, and feeds analytics and forecasts into public-facing and decision-support tools. The data pipeline is evaluated using both infrastructure-level and data-centric metrics: resource utilization, ingestion latency, throughput, data availability, and calibration success rate. These metrics provide insights into the trade-offs required to sustain performance under production workloads, while also meeting the reliability expectations of scientific and civic stakeholders. Our findings demonstrate how principled data engineering, grounded in modular design and open technologies, can drive sustainable innovation even under stringent constraints.

This paper makes the following contributions

- We present the design and implementation of a modular, scalable ETL pipeline capable of integrating heterogeneous data sources and supporting AI-driven workflows.
- We present a detailed performance evaluation of the pipeline in production based on resource metrics, data quality, and operational reliability.
- We articulate practical engineering lessons on observability, resilience, and architectural trade-offs for practitioners building real-world data infrastructure in constrained environments.
- We provide the complete source code and documentation of the AirQo data pipeline and platform as an open-source resource to enable collaboration and extension of the pipeline for similar environmental monitoring applications.

2 Related Work

In this section, we review prior research on scalable data pipelines, intelligent environmental data systems, and the unique challenges of deploying data infrastructure in low-resource settings. These related works provide critical context for our study, which lies at the intersection of modern data engineering and environmental sensing.

Scalable Data Pipeline Architectures

Modern data pipelines are designed to handle increasing volumes of diverse data in real-time and batch modes. The increasing demand for timely and actionable insights from large-scale data has led to the development of numerous frameworks and architectures for scalable data pipelines. Workflow orchestration platforms such as Apache Airflow [3,19], Luigi [25], and Prefect [33] have been employed to automate ETL workflows, enabling organizations to manage complex data dependencies while maintaining observability and fault tolerance. These tools provide the backbone for building modular and maintainable pipelines, supporting both batch and streaming data processing use cases.

Cloud-based data warehousing solutions like Google BigQuery [11], Amazon Redshift [35], and Snowflake [38] have transformed the landscape of data storage and analytics, providing scalable and cost-efficient infrastructures capable of handling massive datasets with low latency. These platforms are essential components in modern data engineering architectures, allowing engineers to perform interactive analytics and support machine learning workflows at scale.

Prior studies have explored scalable pipelines for IoT data [37], focusing on data ingestion and processing using cloud services for high-throughput scenarios. However, many existing approaches do not document the practical integration of heterogeneous sensor types, operational considerations in resource-constrained environments, and the end-to-end architecture required for consistent, reliable data delivery to downstream analytics and decision-making systems.

Intelligent Environmental Data Integration and Systems

Recent efforts have highlighted the need for intelligent data integration in health and environmental applications. For instance, Ndembi et al. [28] proposed a data lakehouse architecture for integrating environmental and health data in African cities. Similarly, Chhikara et al. [13] explored federated learning pipelines for environmental sensing but acknowledged the challenge of robust data availability and quality in under-connected regions. In another domain, Ullah et al. [41] implemented a low-cost, AI-enhanced air quality monitoring system using ESP32 microcontrollers, highlighting hardware-level innovations but with limited focus on end-to-end data workflows.

In the domain of environmental data processing, initiatives like OpenAQ [23] aggregate air quality data from diverse sources to support research and public policy. These projects demonstrate the utility of centralized repositories for environmental data, but often rely on periodic batch updates and may lack advanced ETL orchestration for real-time applications. Similarly, IoT-based environmental monitoring systems [8] have leveraged low-cost sensors and cloud services to enable real-time environmental monitoring, yet challenges remain in ensuring data quality, consistency, and the reliable handling of diverse sensor data streams in production environments.

Machine learning techniques are increasingly employed to calibrate low-cost air quality sensors by learning from co-located reference monitors and incorporating auxiliary features like temperature and humidity [1,6,7,20]. These models help mitigate sensor drift and improve data reliability. AirQo adopts a similar approach by integrating a prediction and calibration microservice within its pipeline that operates on both streaming and historical datasets. This allows for near real-time correction of raw sensor data, supporting both public dashboards and research analytics.

Data Infrastructure Challenges in Low-Resource Settings

Building robust data pipelines in low-resource settings entails navigating several constraints including unreliable internet connectivity, limited computational and energy resources, and infrastructural constraints. Recent research highlights how intermittent network conditions can lead to frequent data gaps, complicating time-series continuity and reducing the reliability of real-time applications [2,9,32]. Techniques such as opportunistic data uploading, edge-based caching, and delayed backfilling pipelines have been proposed to address this challenge [9,44]. The AirQo pipeline adopts these approaches by embedding automated historical backfilling DAGs and leveraging fault-tolerant message queues (Kafka) to decouple data producers and consumers.

Several air quality monitoring platforms in the Global South have turned to solar-powered sensors and energy-efficient data collection firmware to maintain consistent operation under fluctuating voltage or extended outages [9,14,26,43]. Moreover, constrained cloud access has driven interest in hybrid edge–cloud architectures, wherein localized edge nodes perform pre-processing and buffering before periodic upstream transmission [9,21]. Low-resource settings also suffer from limited availability of high-quality ground truth data, which complicates model training and sensor calibration. This has led to innovations in transfer learning, synthetic data generation, and federated calibration models [13,15]. Such techniques attempt to reduce dependence on site-specific labeled datasets while preserving generalizability.

Taken together, these contributions outline a growing research frontier that seeks to democratize environmental sensing infrastructure in resource-constrained environments. Our work builds on these efforts by presenting the design, implementation, and operational evaluation of a scalable ETL pipeline capable of ingesting and transforming heterogeneous data sources in near real-time using open-source and cloud-based technologies. Using the AirQo Data Pipeline as a case study, we demonstrate practical strategies for building robust data pipelines to support environmental monitoring and analytics in low-resource settings, providing actionable insights for practitioners aiming to deploy scalable data infrastructure in similar domains.

3 AirQo Data Pipeline

The AirQo data pipeline serves as a practical application of modern data engineering principles to environmental monitoring in low-resource urban environments. Designed for modularity, scalability, and reliability, the pipeline integrates heterogeneous data sources including low-cost sensors, BAM reference-grade monitors, and weather data APIs into a cohesive architecture capable of supporting near real-time and batch analytics. The pipeline is designed as a cloud-native, modular system designed for scalability, fault tolerance, and real-time analytics. As illustrated in Fig. 1, the pipeline integrates diverse data sources, orchestrates ingestion and processing workflows using Apache Airflow, manages asynchronous communication with Apache Kafka, and provides scalable storage and analytics through Google Cloud Platform (GCP) services.

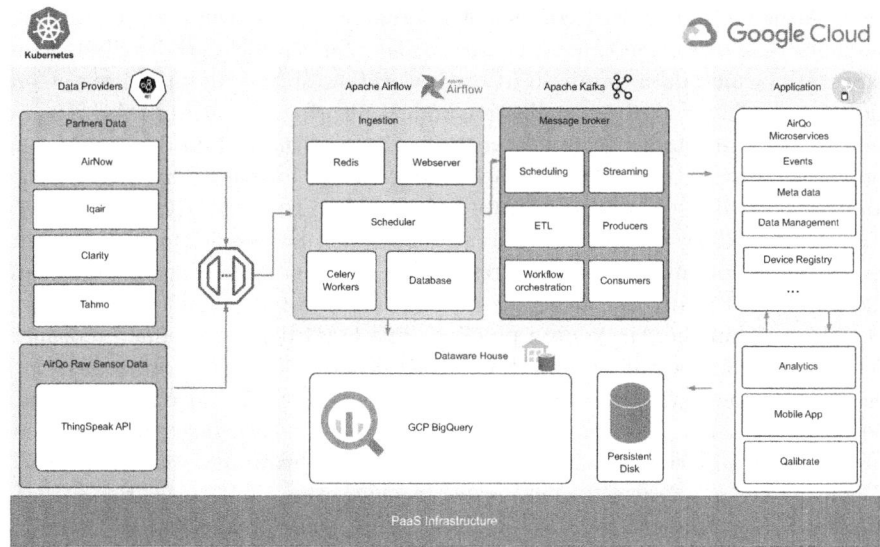

Fig. 1. AirQo data pipeline architecture overview.

3.1 Data Processing Workflows

Data Sources. The AirQo platform ingests data from a diverse mix of internal sensors and external collaborators. Internally, it relies on a network of proprietary low-cost sensors and Beta Attenuation Monitors (BAMs) to generate high-frequency air quality readings. To enhance spatial coverage and improve data reliability, this core network is supplemented with data from third-party providers including IQAir, MetOne, and Clarity. Additionally, meteorological data is sourced through public weather APIs including TAHMO [17] and Open-WeatherMap [31]. The ingestion layer supports a multi-tenant design that allows seamless integration of external data streams, enabling continuous synchronization with partner APIs. AirQo's own devices communicate via the ThingSpeak API [40], which acts as an aggregation endpoint for field-deployed sensors. These heterogeneous data streams, which vary in format, precision, and update frequency form the basis for downstream analytics, forecasting, and operational monitoring. Once captured, all raw input is forwarded to the next stage in the pipeline for transformation and validation.

Data Ingestion. The AirQo pipeline uses Apache Airflow [18,36] as its primary orchestration tool for managing data ingestion and transformation tasks. Airflow enables the scheduling, execution, and monitoring of ETL workflows through modular scripts written in Python. Each workflow is implemented as a Directed Acyclic Graph (DAG), which defines a series of interdependent tasks responsible for extracting data from various sources, performing necessary cleaning and validation, and loading the transformed outputs into AirQo's data storage systems. Airflow's architecture consists of several core components: a scheduler that manages task execution timing, Celery workers for parallel and distributed task execution, a metadata database to track workflow states, and a webserver providing a user interface for visualization and monitoring. The use of DAGs ensures deterministic and fault-tolerant execution, allowing the system to reliably manage data ingestion across heterogeneous sources and formats. This orchestration framework enables AirQo to operate a mix of real-time, hourly, and historical ingestion workflows efficiently, each optimized for the specific timing and transformation requirements of its corresponding data stream. Figure 2 illustrates the DAG used in orchestrating the real-time low-cost air quality measurement workflow within the AirQo data pipeline. The DAG defines a sequence of interdependent tasks, beginning with the extraction and cleaning of raw sensor data, followed by hourly aggregation and calibration using synchronized weather data. Subsequent tasks are responsible for dispatching the processed measurements to various destinations, including BigQuery for archival and analytics, Apache Kafka for streaming-based microservice consumption, and the AirQo API for real-time user access. The DAG structure ensures fault-tolerant, ordered task execution and facilitates parallelization where dependencies allow, enabling consistent performance under dynamic data loads. Table 1 summarizes the task, functionality and dependencies of this DAG. For brevity, we have not included several other DAGs defined in the AirQo data pipeline.

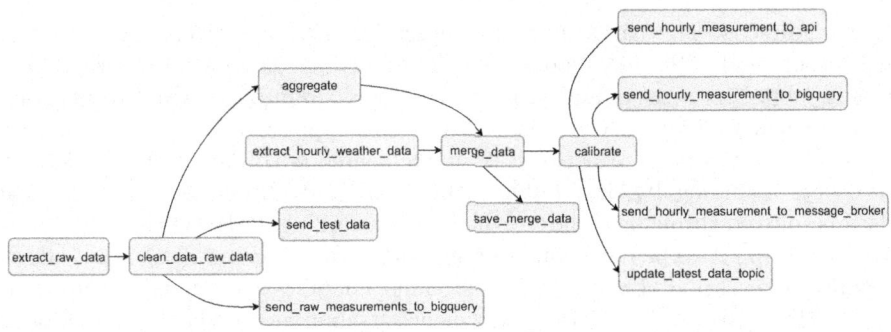

Fig. 2. Directed Acyclic Graph (DAG) for AirQo near real-time low-cost measurement workflow. Each node represents a distinct ETL task, including raw data extraction, cleaning, calibration, aggregation, and multi-channel distribution to BigQuery, Apache Kafka, and external APIs. Edges indicate task dependencies and execution order.

Message Broker. To decouple data ingestion from downstream processing, the AirQo data pipeline leverages Apache Kafka [16,42], a distributed, high-throughput, publish-subscribe messaging system. Apache Kafka serves as the central communication backbone between Apache Airflow and various microservices, enabling scalable, real-time streaming and asynchronous event-driven architectures. Once data has been transformed and validated, it is published to specific Kafka topics. These topics act as temporary data stores, allowing

Table 1. AirQo near real-time low-cost measurement DAG tasks

#	Task Name	Functionality	Dependencies
1	extract_raw_data	Extracts raw data for the last hour from low-cost devices.	None
2	clean_data_raw_data	Cleans and structures the raw data by removing outliers and enforcing data type checks.	1
3	save_test_data	Saves the cleaned data for testing.	2
4	aggregate	Resamples device data to an hourly frequency.	2
5	extract_hourly_weather_data	Extracts hourly weather data.	None
6	merge_data	Merges hourly air quality data with hourly weather data.	4, 5
7	calibrate	Calibrates the merged data.	6
8	send_hourly_measurements_to_api	Sends calibrated data to AirQo API.	7
9	send_hourly_measurements_to_message_broker	Sends calibrated data to the MessageBroker.	7
10	send_hourly_measurements_to_BigQuery	Sends calibrated data to BigQuery.	7
11	update_latest_data_topic	Updates the latest data topic in the MessageBroker.	7

microservices to consume messages at their own pace and according to their individual service-level requirements. This approach enhances pipeline resilience by insulating data producers from consumer availability or latency. Apache Kafka's architecture allows for persistent buffering, ensuring that transient failures in downstream systems do not result in data loss. To reduce payload size and transmission latency, messages are serialized and transmitted in compact byte formats. Additionally, Apache Kafka topics are protected using authentication mechanisms, with access credentials securely managed via Google Secret Manager. This separation of secrets from the runtime environment reinforces security across the ingestion and distribution layers of the pipeline.

Data Warehousing. The AirQo data pipeline leverages Google BigQuery as its centralized, serverless data warehousing solution, designed to support scalable analytical queries over large volumes of air quality and meteorological data. As a fully managed platform, BigQuery enables low-latency querying, schema evolution, and robust integration with machine learning pipelines and dashboarding tools. Processed and calibrated data from Apache Airflow workflows is stored in BigQuery in well-structured datasets, supporting both batch analytics and real-time insights. The core datasets include (i) *raw data*, containing minimally processed sensor readings; (ii) *averaged data*, with hourly and daily aggregates for trend analysis; (iii) *consolidated data*, which merges device measurements, weather readings, and site metadata into unified records; and (iv) *forecast data*, used for predictive modeling. This schema facilitates spatial-temporal queries across diverse sensor networks, including low-cost devices and reference-grade monitors. Access to the warehouse is tightly governed using Google Cloud's role-based access control (RBAC), service accounts, and metadata tagging. Downstream applications include anomaly detection, air quality forecasting, public dashboards, and regulatory compliance reporting, all powered by curated datasets from BigQuery.

3.2 Microservices and Data Distribution

The AirQo platform employs a microservices-based architecture to enable scalable, modular access to processed air quality and meteorological data. These stateless services consume data from Apache Kafka topics and the BigQuery warehouse to serve multiple downstream applications, ensuring flexibility and performance across both real-time and historical use cases. Each microservice is designed with a single responsibility principle, which improves maintainability and facilitates independent deployment. Key services include:

- **Device Registry Service:** Maintains up-to-date metadata on sensors, including device ID, geolocation, firmware version, and operational status.
- **Event Service:** Captures internal platform events, such as data availability, processing anomalies, and API access logs, supporting observability and auditability.
- **Metadata Service:** Provides contextual data including site names, sensor elevations, city identifiers, and partner associations, which is critical for both visualization and analytics.
- **Data Management Service:** Consumes calibrated and aggregated air quality data from Kafka topics and delivers it to various endpoints, including mobile apps, public dashboards, and other AirQo APIs.
- **Calibrate Service:** A specialized machine learning-enabled microservice that supports the calibration of raw measurements using reference-grade monitors and weather features. It interfaces with both streaming (Kafka) and batch (BigQuery) data layers.
- **Predict Service:** A forecasting microservice that leverages trained machine learning models to generate short-term predictions of air quality metrics, enhancing real-time decision-making and enabling proactive environmental response.

These microservices operate in a decoupled manner, communicating through RESTful APIs and Kafka topics. Real-time consumers subscribe to Kafka topics to ingest high-frequency data updates, while analytical services perform SQL-based queries on BigQuery for aggregated insights. To ensure secure data distribution, all services are deployed with authenticated access tokens, enforced via role-based access control (RBAC) in Kubernetes. Message payloads transmitted through Kafka are serialized (e.g., using Avro or JSON) to minimize network overhead. Load balancing and horizontal scaling are implemented using

Kubernetes' native mechanisms to handle variable traffic from external clients and internal processing jobs. This architecture supports AirQo's commitment to real-time environmental intelligence by providing reliable, scalable, and secure access to high-quality data across various digital platforms.

3.3 Deployment and Operational Considerations

The AirQo data pipeline is deployed using a containerized, cloud-native architecture on Google Cloud Platform (GCP), leveraging Kubernetes for workload orchestration and scaling. The infrastructure is organized into two isolated Kubernetes clusters: a production cluster responsible for live operations and a staging cluster designated for pre-deployment integration testing. This separation supports robust version control, enables staged rollouts, and reduces the risk of system-wide failures. Each cluster runs on 4 VM nodes configured with 4 vCPUs, 16 GB of memory, and 200 GB of persistent disk space per node. One node is dedicated as controller and the rest configured as worker nodes. Cluster networking is managed using Calico as the Container Network Interface (CNI), chosen for its high performance, network policy enforcement, and flexibility compared to alternatives such as Flannel. Public-facing microservices are exposed via an NGINX ingress controller, which is routed through an HAProxy load balancer to manage HTTP(S) traffic securely and efficiently. Operational management follows a GitOps paradigm, using Argo CD to maintain declarative configuration and automate continuous delivery. Prometheus and Grafana are integrated into the pipeline to provide real-time metrics, system health dashboards, and custom alerting rules. CI/CD pipelines are defined using GitHub Actions, ensuring automated testing, container builds, and environment-specific deployments with Helm charts. Logs from Apache Airflow, Apache Kafka, and microservices are aggregated and routed to centralized logging backends for observability and fault tracing. This deployment strategy ensures high availability, modular scalability, and operational resilience, which are essential for sustaining uninterrupted ingestion, processing, and distribution of large-scale environmental datasets within the AirQo ecosystem.

4 Data Quality and Analytics

In this section, we evaluate the data quality and discuss analytics feature of the AirQo pipeline. Ensuring the quality and integrity of the collected data is critical to achieving the AirQo's mission of delivering actionable environmental insights. The system tracks multiple data quality metrics across all stages of the pipeline to monitor availability, uniqueness, and calibration success rate.

4.1 Quality Metrics

Data Availability: Measures the proportion of expected hours in which a device reports data. This helps identify data gaps caused by hardware failures, power outages, or connectivity issues.

$$\text{Availability Rate} = \left(\frac{\text{Hours with Data}}{\text{Total Hours}}\right) \times 100$$

An analysis of average data availability from March to June 2025, based on data ingested into the AirQo pipeline, reflected distinct but complementary patterns for the three air quality sensor data vendors i.e., AirQo, IQAir, and MetOne as shown in Fig. 3. During this period, AirQo devices consistently maintained high availability, averaging above 70%, with a slight decline from 72.81% in April to 72.08% in June. This stability reflects the robustness of the AirQo pipeline and its capacity for real-time ingestion and timely recovery via backfilling mechanisms. In contrast, data from the IQAir devices supported in the AirQo pipeline showed a sharp decline in availability from 64.5% in April to 47.91% in May, and further down to 39.3% in June. This downward trend has been reported to the sensor network operator, i.e., the Permian Health Lung Institute (PHLI) team for further investigation. MetOne devices, which are reference-grade monitors, experienced a more moderate decline, dropping from 71.81% in April to 58.47% in May. This is because some of the monitors were decommissioned following administrative directives. These metrics demonstrate AirQo's data pipeline comparative strength in maintaining consistent data streams despite operating in low-resource environments. The system's architecture characterized by scheduled retries, modular ingestion, and Kafka-based buffering contributes to this resilience. Such insights inform ongoing efforts to optimize deployment strategies, improve fault detection, and ensure reliable air quality monitoring across all networks.

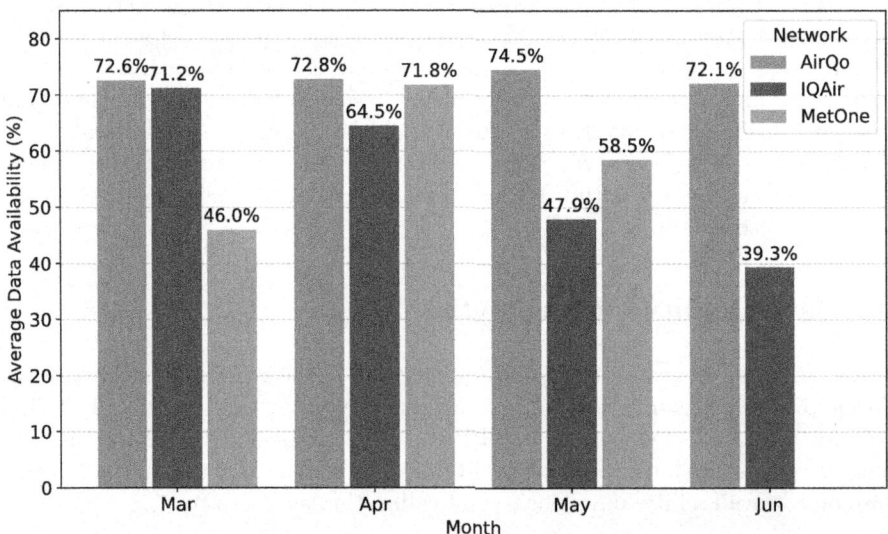

Fig. 3. Monthly average data availability (in percentage) for AirQo, IQAir, and MetOne sensor networks from March to June 2025. Data availability reflects the proportion of hours in which devices reported valid measurements, serving as a key indicator of sensor uptime and transmission reliability.

Calibration Rate: Assesses the ratio of raw data that has been successfully calibrated. This metric helps evaluate the pipeline's ability to apply calibration models consistently.

$$\text{Calibration Rate} = \left(\frac{\text{Hours with Calibrated Data}}{\text{Hours with Raw Data}}\right) \times 100$$

During the second quarter of 2025, the AirQo data pipeline maintained near-perfect calibration success rates, highlighting the reliability of its data correction workflows as shown in Fig. 4a. From March through June, the average calibration rate consistently exceeded **99.9%**, with exact monthly values of 99.99% (March), 99.94% (April), 99.84% (May), and 99.99% (June). These represent the proportion of raw sensor measurements that were successfully processed and transformed into calibrated outputs using model-based corrections within the ETL pipeline. This performance reflects the robustness of the calibration module embedded in the DAG workflows managed by Apache Airflow, which includes validation, anomaly filtering, and model inference steps. The consistently high calibration rate suggests minimal pipeline disruptions, accurate execution of calibration models, and effective fallback mechanisms for handling edge cases. Furthermore, this reinforces the system's capacity to deliver reliable, actionable environmental data particularly in urban deployments where low-cost sensors may be subject to drift, cross-sensitivity, or fluctuating environmental conditions. The success of the calibration process directly enhances the quality of air quality analytics and forecasting, ensuring data consistency across time and space. This reliability is vital for downstream applications including public dashboards, mobile apps, and policy advisory tools.

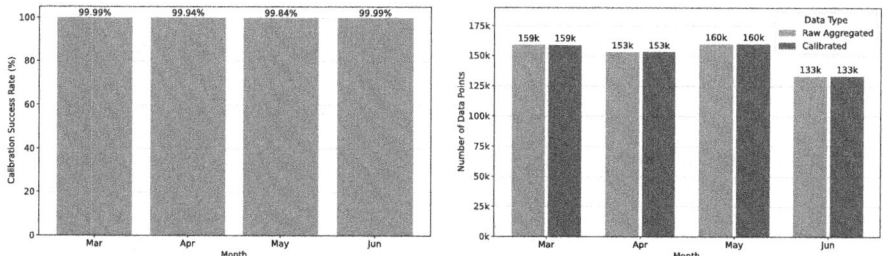

(a) Monthly calibration success rate across the network. (b) Monthly comparison of raw vs. calibrated data points.

Fig. 4. Evaluation of calibration pipeline performance from March to June 2025. Left: success rates of calibration. Right: parity between raw and calibrated hourly data volume, highlighting throughput and consistency.

To further assess calibration effectiveness, we examined the volume of raw versus calibrated hourly data points during the period from March to June 2025 as shown in Fig. 4b. The plot indicates a near 1:1 correspondence between raw aggregated and calibrated data points, with each month recording over 150,000 measurements in both categories. Specifically, March and May reached the highest volumes at 159k and 160k respectively, while April maintained parity with 153k data points in both raw and calibrated forms. June saw a slight decline to 133k, yet still maintained full calibration coverage for the available raw data. This alignment highlights the efficiency and scalability of the AirQo calibration pipeline, which successfully processed almost all raw sensor readings without backlog or significant drop-off. The pipeline's ability to maintain such parity at scale demonstrates the reliability of the calibration models and the robustness of the data transformation workflows orchestrated by Apache Airflow.

4.2 Analytics

To deliver actionable insights to diverse stakeholders including researchers, policymakers, environmental agencies, and field technicians, the AirQo platform incorporates a dual-layer analytics system. This system facilitates interactive exploration, decision support, and predictive modeling based on curated environmental datasets. First, a self-service analytics interface is provided through Apache Superset, enabling users to explore high-value metrics such as device uptime, calibration trends, and data availability among others. Superset dashboards empower stakeholders to rapidly detect anomalies, monitor long-term trends, and identify gaps in data collection without requiring direct access to raw data or underlying infrastructure. Second, the platform includes a custom-built analytics service[1] designed to extend beyond visualization. This component supports advanced analytical tasks such as geospatial sensor placement recommendations, historical forecasting of pollutant levels, trend analysis, network management, collocation configuration and targeted diagnostics for device behavior. By integrating machine learning workflows directly into the analytics layer, AirQo enables dynamic and adaptive decision-making processes that are tightly coupled with the evolving realities of urban air quality management in low-resource contexts.

5 Infrastructure Performance

Evaluating the operational performance of the AirQo data pipeline is critical to demonstrating its scalability and reliability for processing heterogeneous data streams in production environments.

5.1 Resource Management and Scalability

To assess resource consumption and system stability, we analyzed monitoring logs from the AirQo production Kubernetes cluster where the data pipeline is deployed over a continuous 30-day period, from June 1, 2025 to June 30, 2025. This dataset provided visibility into CPU, memory, and network traffic utilization.

---

[1] https://analytics.airqo.net.

CPU Utilization. Figure 5 illustrates the comparative CPU utilization across the AirQo cluster nodes from 1st to 30th June, 2025. The Controller node shows consistently low and stable CPU activity, consistent with its coordination role. In contrast, Worker-3 experiences significantly higher and more volatile CPU usage, frequently exceeding 70% and occasionally nearing 100%. This pattern suggests that Worker-3 is either overburdened by processing tasks or handling a disproportionate share of computational load. Worker-1 and Worker-2 demonstrate more balanced and moderate usage, indicating effective task distribution. These findings highlight a potential bottleneck and suggest that load balancing or scaling measures may be needed for Worker-3 to ensure system reliability.

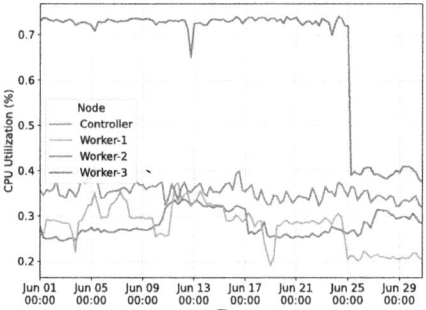

Fig. 5. CPU utilization trends across AirQo cluster nodes from the 1st-30th June, 2025.

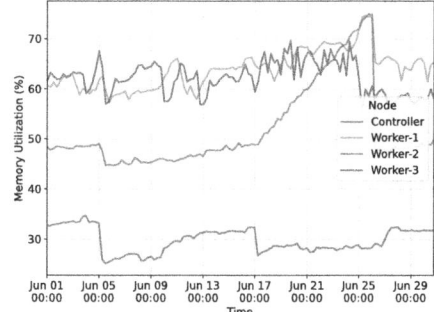

Fig. 6. Memory utilization trends across AirQo cluster nodes from the 1st–30th June, 2025.

Memory Utilization. Figure 6 presents memory utilization over time for each node. The Controller maintains a relatively low and consistent memory footprint, reinforcing its role as a lightweight orchestrator. Among the workers, Worker-3 again exhibits the highest memory consumption, with consistently elevated levels suggesting a heavier or more memory-intensive workload. This sustained high memory usage may impact system responsiveness or lead to out-of-memory risks under increased demand. Worker-1 and Worker-2 show similar utilization curves, suggesting equitable resource usage. Overall, the results indicate that Worker-3 may require resource scaling or workload optimization to maintain balanced performance across the cluster.

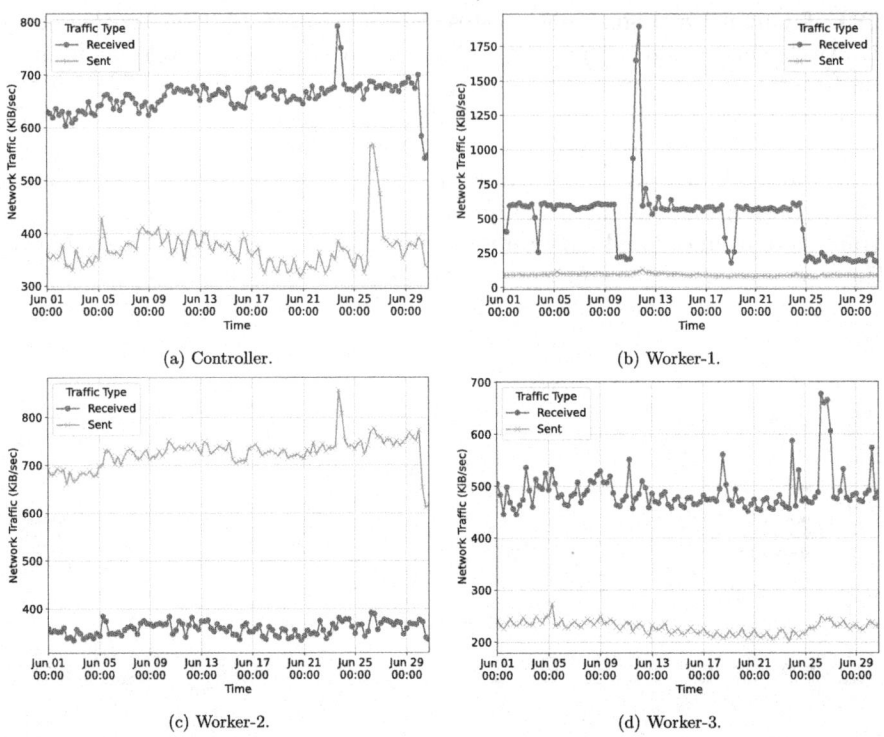

Fig. 7. Network traffic pattern across AirQo production cluster nodes for the time period 1st–30th June, 2025. Each figure shows the received and sent traffic in KiB/sec, highlighting the communication dynamics of the controller and worker nodes.

Network Traffic Patterns. Figure 7 presents a comparative analysis of network traffic across the production cluster nodes. The `Controller` node exhibits a consistent pattern of high incoming traffic (averaging 650 KiB/s) and relatively lower outgoing communication, consistent with its orchestration role and periodic synchronization with sensors and workers. Worker-1 shows the most volatile pattern, with spikes in received traffic exceeding 1800 KiB/s and intermittent dropouts, suggesting bursty upstream data ingestion or potential network congestion. Worker-2 demonstrates consistently high outgoing traffic, often exceeding 750 KiB/s, suggesting it may be responsible for relaying aggregated sensor data or distributing inference results downstream. In contrast, Worker-3 shows consistently high incoming traffic averaging at 500 KiB/s with random spikes not exceeding 700 KiB/s. These insights reveal traffic asymmetry across the cluster and suggest that dynamic load balancing or node-specific optimization may improve bandwidth utilization and resilience across the AirQo data pipeline.

5.2 Throughput and Data Volumes

The AirQo data pipeline ingests and processes approximately **5.76 million** raw air quality data entries per month. This estimate is based on an average of 20 data points per hour per device, collected across roughly 400 active sensors, operating continuously over 720 h in a typical month. These data points span multiple pollutant measurements (e.g., $PM_{2.5}$, PM_{10}), environmental parameters (e.g., temperature, humidity), and device metadata, forming a rich multivariate time-series dataset. Ingestion rates typically peak during batch device data uploads and scheduled synchronizations with partner APIs. To sustain high-throughput ingestion while avoiding bottlenecks, the system uses Apache Airflow with a `CeleryExecutor`, which enables distributed, concurrent execution of DAG tasks. Overall, the performance evaluation demonstrates that the AirQo data pipeline meets the requirements for scalable, reliable, and low-latency ingestion and processing of heterogeneous environmental data streams. The architecture supports high data availability and throughput while remaining adaptable to evolving workload requirements, making it a practical reference design for similar environmental monitoring and data engineering applications.

6 Lessons Learned

The design, deployment, and operation of the AirQo data pipeline offer valuable lessons for the broader data engineering and environmental sensing communities, particularly those operating in resource-constrained or infrastructure-fragmented settings. These insights are grounded in real-world system behavior and serve to inform both architectural choices and operational strategies for similar initiatives. Our experience reinforces that combining modular open-source technologies with cloud-native design principles enables robust, scalable, and maintainable data infrastructures in emerging contexts.

1. **Modular Design Enables Flexibility.** Structuring the pipeline as a collection of modular Airflow DAGs, each representing a distinct stage such as ingestion, transformation, or calibration, enabled rapid iteration and smooth integration of new data sources. This design allowed individual components to be developed, tested, and maintained independently, reducing the risk of system-wide failures and improving team productivity. The ability to isolate and evolve specific parts of the pipeline proved essential for scalability and long-term maintainability.
2. **Decoupling Enhances Resilience.** Integrating Apache Kafka as an asynchronous communication layer between upstream and downstream components proved pivotal. Kafka's publish-subscribe architecture ensured that ingestion continued uninterrupted during consumer-side delays, decoupling throughput constraints and allowing independent scaling of producers and consumers. This design not only increased fault tolerance but also enabled robust microservice orchestration at scale.
3. **Observability is Foundational.** Building comprehensive observability into the pipeline through structured logging, Apache Airflow DAG monitoring,

Slack-based alerting, and real-time metric dashboards proved critical for maintaining operational reliability. These tools significantly reduced mean time to recovery (MTTR), enabling the team to shift from reactive issue resolution to proactive system health monitoring. This not only improved service uptime but also ensured data trustworthiness.
4. **Backfilling Mechanisms are Essential.** In low-resource environments, interruptions due to sensor downtime, power outages, or external API failures are common and often unpredictable. Incorporating automated historical backfilling into the daily pipeline operations proved essential for maintaining continuous data records. This approach eliminated the need for manual recovery efforts, preserved the integrity of long-term datasets, and ensured that the system could reliably support both scientific research and data-driven policy interventions.
5. **Leverage Cloud Scalability.** Leveraging Google BigQuery for analytical workloads and Kubernetes for deployment orchestration offered operational elasticity with minimal overhead. The system scaled naturally with increasing sensor footprints and partner integrations, without significant re-engineering. This elasticity also enabled parallel experimentation with forecasting models and anomaly detection workflows.
6. **Trade-offs Between Real-Time and Batch Processing.** While operational dashboards and real-time alerting demanded low-latency data pipelines, tasks like calibration and hourly aggregation benefited from batched execution. Recognizing this trade-off allowed us to tailor compute strategies per workflow, optimizing both cost and performance without compromising data quality or availability.
7. **Caching Improves Efficiency and Reduces Latency.** Introducing lightweight caching layers for frequently accessed metadata and calibration models significantly reduced redundant queries to upstream services and database lookups. By leveraging in-memory caches (e.g., Redis) within key microservices, the pipeline achieved lower response times and reduced compute loads on BigQuery and external APIs.

These lessons represent the practical insights gained from deploying and maintaining a city-scale environmental data system over an extended period. They reflect not only the technical viability of building scalable and dependable pipelines in low-resource settings, but also the importance of thoughtful architectural choices and strong operational practices to ensure long-term success.

7 Conclusion

This paper has presented the design and evaluation of a scalable, modular, and production-grade data pipeline that powers the AirQo Platform, an AI-driven air quality monitoring system deployed across major African cities. Leveraging open-source, cloud-native technologies including Apache Airflow, Kafka, and Google BigQuery, the system supports both real-time and batch processing of heterogeneous environmental data from low-cost sensors, reference monitors, and third-party APIs. Our evaluation demonstrates that the pipeline achieves a data availability rate of approximately 70% and a calibration success rate exceeding 99.9% over a three-month period, even under sensor operational constraints of unreliable internet connectivity, and intermittent power. These performance outcomes emphasize the effectiveness of principled data engineering practices in sustaining reliable environmental intelligence pipelines in low-resource settings. The deployment experience has yielded several key lessons: the importance of modular design for flexible evolution, Kafka-based decoupling for system resilience, structured observability for rapid incident response, and automated backfilling to mitigate data gaps. In addition, strategic use of caching, cloud elasticity, and workflow-specific processing models enabled operational robustness. Future work includes integrating generative-AI capabilities into the analytics layer, deploying edge-based preprocessing, and adopting adaptive pipeline scheduling to further enhance autonomy and reduce cloud dependencies. By open-sourcing the platform and contributing empirical insights, we aim to inform and accelerate similar efforts to deploy scalable environmental data systems in emerging regions.

Acknowledgment. The authors would like to appreciate the feedback and input to the research paper from the AirQo team members, collaborators, and partners of the AirQo research project including researchers, community members, and government stakeholders.

Funding Information. This work was supported by Google.org grant 1904-57882, EPSRC/GCRF grant EP/T00343X/1, Belgium through the Wehubit programme implemented by Enabel Wehubit Grant Agreement BEL1707111-AP-05-2, and U.S Mission grant # SUG50021CA3041. The opinions, findings and conclusions stated herein are those of the authors and do not necessarily reflect those of the funders.

Data Availibility Statement. The datasets analyzed in this study can be made available upon reasonable request to the authors. To promote transparency and reproducibility, the complete source code for the AirQo data pipeline including data ingestion, transformation, distribution, and orchestration is publicly accessible on GitHub under an open-source license [4]. This repository also includes deployment scripts and documentation for the associated infrastructure, enabling researchers and practitioners to replicate or extend the pipeline for similar environmental monitoring applications.

References

1. Adong, P., Bainomugisha, E., Okure, D., Sserunjogi, R.: Applying machine learning for large scale field calibration of low-cost PM2. 5 and PM10 air pollution sensors. Appl. AI Lett. **3**(3), e76 (2022)
2. Ahmed, N., De, D., Hussain, I.: Internet of things (IoT) for smart precision agriculture and farming in rural areas. IEEE Internet Things J. **5**(6), 4890–4899 (2018)
3. AirFlow, A.: Apache airflow (2025). https://airflow.apache.org/. Accessed 19 Aug 2025
4. AirQo: Airqo platform github source code (2019). https://github.com/airqo-platform/. Accessed 19 Aug 2025

5. AirVisual: Airvisual: Real-time air quality monitoring (2025). https://www.iqair.com/air-quality-monitors. Accessed 19 Aug 2025
6. Ali, M.S.: Machine learning based calibration techniques for low-cost air quality sensors: thesis for doctor of philosophy, electronic and computer engineering, Massey University (2024)
7. Ali, S., Alam, F., Potgieter, J., Arif, K.M.: Leveraging temporal information to improve machine learning-based calibration techniques for low-cost air quality sensors. Sensors **24**(9), 2930 (2024)
8. Ayele, E., et al.: Internet of things for environmental monitoring: a review. Environ. Monit. Assess. **192**(5), 1–21 (2020)
9. Bainomugisha, E., Ssematimba, J., Okure, D.: Design considerations for a distributed low-cost air quality sensing system for urban environments in low-resource settings. Atmosphere **14**(2), 354 (2023)
10. Bainomugisha, E., Warigo, P.A., Daka, F.B., Nshimye, A., Birungi, M., Okure, D.: Ai-driven environmental sensor networks and digital platforms for urban air pollution monitoring and modelling. Societal Impacts **3**, 100044 (2024)
11. BigQuery, G.: Google bigquery (2025). https://cloud.google.com/bigquery. Accessed 19 Aug 2025
12. Cai, L., Zhu, Y.: The challenges of data quality and data quality assessment in the big data era. Data Sci. J. **14**, 2 (2015)
13. Chhikara, P., Tekchandani, R., Kumar, N., Tanwar, S., Rodrigues, J.J.: Federated learning for air quality index prediction using UAV swarm networks. In: 2021 IEEE Global Communications Conference (GLOBECOM), pp. 1–6. IEEE (2021)
14. Dushyanth, V., Chakravarthi, R., Chaudhary, P., Kandhari, H., Kuanr, M., Dev, S.: Design and implementation of a low-power wireless sensor network for environmental monitoring in IoT environments. In: 2025 International Conference on Automation and Computation (AUTOCOM), pp. 679–684. IEEE (2025)
15. Endres, M., Mannarapotta Venugopal, A., Tran, T.S.: Synthetic data generation: a comparative study. In: Proceedings of the 26th International Database Engineered Applications Symposium, pp. 94–102 (2022)
16. Garg, N.: Apache Kafka. Packt Publishing Birmingham, UK (2013)
17. Van de Giesen, N., Hut, R., Selker, J.: The trans-african hydro-meteorological observatory (tahmo). Wiley Interdiscip. Rev. Water **1**(4), 341–348 (2014)
18. Haines, S.: Workflow orchestration with apache airflow. In: Modern Data Engineering with Apache Spark, pp. 255–295. Springer, Cham (2022)
19. Harenslak, B.P., De Ruiter, J.: Data pipelines with apache airflow. Simon and Schuster (2021)
20. Hashmy, Y., Khan, Z.U., Ilyas, F., Hafiz, R., Younis, U., Tauqeer, T.: Modular air quality calibration and forecasting method for low-cost sensor nodes. IEEE Sens. J. **23**(4), 4193–4203 (2023)
21. Higashino, T., Yamaguchi, H., Hiromori, A., Uchiyama, A., Yasumoto, K.: Edge computing and IoT based research for building safe smart cities resistant to disasters. In: 2017 IEEE 37th International Conference on Distributed Computing Systems (ICDCS), pp. 1729–1737. IEEE (2017)
22. Kumar, P., et al.: The rise of low-cost sensing for managing air pollution in cities. Environ. Int. **75**, 199–205 (2015)
23. Lewis, C.H., et al.: Openaq: building a global community around open air quality data. Data Sci. J. **19**, 1–13 (2020)
24. Lipovac, I., Babac, M.B.: Developing a data pipeline solution for big data processing. Int. J. Data Min. Model. Manage. **16**(1), 1–22 (2024)

25. Luigi: Luigi: Python module that helps build complex pipelines of batch jobs (2025). https://luigi.readthedocs.io/. Accessed 19 Aug 2025
26. Mberu, B.U., et al.: Urban health in Africa (2025)
27. Munappy, A.R., Bosch, J., Olsson, H.H.: Data pipeline management in practice: challenges and opportunities. In: International Conference on Product-Focused Software Process Improvement, pp. 168–184. Springer, Cham (2020)
28. Ndembi, N., et al.: Integrating artificial intelligence into African health systems and emergency response: need for an ethical framework and guidelines (2025)
29. Okure, D., Bainomugisha, E., Ogenrwot, D., Sserunjogi, R., Adrine, P., Okello, G.: Case study of participatory data-driven approaches to improve urban air quality in Kampala, Uganda. Urban Health Africa 255 (2025)
30. Okure, D., Ssematimba, J., Sserunjogi, R., Gracia, N.L., Soppelsa, M.E., Bainomugisha, E.: Characterization of ambient air quality in selected urban areas in Uganda using low-cost sensing and measurement technologies. Environ. Sci. Technol. **56**(6), 3324–3339 (2022)
31. OpenWeatherMap: Weather model - openweathermap (2012). https://openweathermap.org/technology/. Accessed 19 Aug 2025
32. Pinder, R.W., Klopp, J.M., Kleiman, G., Hagler, G.S., Awe, Y., Terry, S.: Opportunities and challenges for filling the air quality data gap in low-and middle-income countries. Atmos. Environ. **215**, 116794 (2019)
33. Prefect: Prefect: The modern data workflow orchestration (2025). https://www.prefect.io/. Accessed 19 Aug 2025
34. Raj, A., Bosch, J., Olsson, H.H., Wang, T.J.: Modelling data pipelines. In: 2020 46th Euromicro Conference on Software Engineering and Advanced Applications (SEAA), pp. 13–20. IEEE (2020)
35. Redshift, A.: Amazon redshift - cloud data warehouse (2025). https://aws.amazon.com/redshift/. Accessed 19 Aug 2025
36. Singh, P.: Learn PySpark: Build Python-based machine learning and deep learning models. Apress (2019)
37. Smith, J., et al.: Scalable data pipelines for IoT sensor streams. IEEE Internet Things J. **8**(3), 2001–2015 (2021)
38. Snowflake: Snowflake (2025). https://www.snowflake.com/. Accessed 19 Aug 2025
39. Sserunjogi, R., et al.: Seeing the air in detail: hyperlocal air quality dataset collected from spatially distributed airqo network. Data Brief **44**, 108512 (2022)
40. ThingSpeak: IoT analytics - thingspeak internet of things (2025). https://thingspeak.com/. Accessed 19 Aug 2025
41. Ullah, U., Usama, M., Muhammad, Z., Akbar, A.: AI-enabled low-powered wireless area networks for quality air. In: Low-Power Wide Area Network for Large Scale Internet of Things, pp. 100–141. CRC Press (2024)
42. Wang, G., et al.: Building a replicated logging system with apache Kafka. Proc. VLDB Endow. **8**(12), 1654–1655 (2015)
43. Zafra-Pérez, A., Medina-García, J., Boente, C., Gómez-Galán, J.A., Campa, A.S., Rosa, J.: Designing a low-cost wireless sensor network for particulate matter monitoring: implementation, calibration, and field-test. Atmos. Pollut. Res. **15**(9), 102208 (2024)
44. Zhalgasbekova, A., Zaslavsky, A., Saguna, S., Mitra, K., Jayaraman, P.P.: Opportunistic data collection for IoT-based indoor air quality monitoring. In: International Conference on Next Generation Wired/Wireless Networking, pp. 53–65. Springer, Cham (2017)

Hybrid Taint Analysis for React: Automated XSS Prevention

Vaishnavi Gudur[1](✉) [iD] and Advait Patel[2] [iD]

[1] IIEEE, Seattle, WA 98004, USA
gudur.vaishnavi@ieee.org
[2] IEEE Senior Member, Chicago, IL 60025, USA

Abstract. Cross-site scripting (XSS) remains a significant risk in component-based web frameworks. In React, dynamic rendering patterns such as JSX spreads and hooks frustrate traditional defences, making it hard to reconcile security with performance. We introduce a hybrid static/runtime analysis that couples context-sensitive taint propagation with targeted runtime enforcement to prevent XSS in React applications. The static phase constructs a taint-flow graph for JSX and hook patterns and uses it to guide selective instrumentation of the virtual DOM. At runtime, lightweight proxies and Fiber-level hooks sanitise only those updates deemed risky, while delta instrumentation confines re-analysis to the parts of the component tree affected by a change. Evaluations on twelve open-source projects show that this approach achieves higher detection coverage than purely static analyzers and incurs far lower overhead than full dynamic tracking. By bridging the gap between accuracy and practicality, our framework offers a deployable means of protecting user data in privacy-sensitive React applications from XSS and related injection attacks.

Keywords: Network Protocols · Wireless Network · Mobile Network · Virus · Worms &Trojon

1 Introduction

Cross-site scripting (XSS) attacks provide ongoing security challenges for web applications—especially those developed using contemporary architectures like React. Though taint analysis for web security has been extensively studied, current methods find it difficult to balance runtime performance with detection accuracy in dynamic, component-based systems. React's dynamic rendering patterns cause false positives even if static taint analysis techniques [1] can find possible vulnerabilities during development. Although they provide exact detection, runtime techniques [2] have high overhead for broad applications. This gap drives our hybrid approach, which deliberately combines targeted runtime instrumentation with static analysis to provide complete protection without compromising performance.

The virtual DOM of React presents special difficulties for security research. Conventional taint tracking systems [3] ignore component composition patterns, JSX transformations, and hook-based state management. Rule-based linters [4] offer minimal

XSS protection; they lack the contextual awareness required to manage dynamic prop passing or third-party component libraries. Although recent work on framework-aware analysis [5] has enhanced detection for angular and Vue, React's reconciliation method requires particular treatment. Our approach models taint propagation across React's update lifetimes, so allowing exact tracking free from duplicate checks.

Three main innovations are presented by the proposed system. First it reduces false positives by framework-aware heuristics by extending static taint analysis with React-specific rules for JSX elements, hooks, and context propagation. Second, it minimizes performance impact by using selective runtime instrumentation that activates just for high-risk data flows found during stationary analysis. Third, it uses React's Fiber design to intercept contaminated objects during reconciliation, so facilitating effective sanitization without changing application code. While maintaining less overhead than full runtime monitoring [7], this mix achieves greater accuracy than pure static approaches [6].

Although prior hybrid solutions [8] show the possibility of combining analysis phases, they lack React-specific optimizations. Our method specifically uses virtual DOM diffing [9] to restrict instrumentation scope and interacts with current sanitizing systems [10] for pragmatic application. A capability lacking in present React security tools, the system also introduces fresh taint severity scoring that dynamically adjusts enforcement depending on both data sensitivity and rendering context [6].

This paper is structured as follows generally: Sect. 2 looks over related work in React-specific analysis methods and web application security. Section 3 covers React's taint analysis foundations and execution model. Section 4 shows our hybrid architecture and main techniques. Section 7 addresses limits and future directions; Sect. 5 and 6 explain experimental technique and results.

2 Related Work

Cross-site scripting (XSS) poses ongoing challenges to modern web applications, which fuels a lot of taint analysis research. There are three main groups to which current techniques generally fit: hybrid methods, dynamic analysis, and static analysis. Applied to React applications, where component-based architecture and virtual DOM reconciliation create unique analysis challenges, each paradigm offers different benefits and constraints.

2.1 Static Taint Analysis

Static techniques find possible flaws early in development by analyzing source code without execution. Although they track data-flow, traditional JavaScript taint analyzers [1] usually neglect React's JSX transformations and hook-based state management. Recent work has modified these methods for contemporary systems, using [5] component-aware propagation rules for angular and Vue. But React's dynamic prop passing patterns—especially JSX spreads ({...props}) and render props—demand particular handling absent in general-purpose tools.

Through pattern matching, rule-based linters such as ESLint plugins [4] offer basic XSS prevention; they lack the accuracy to separate safe from dangerous prop use across component boundaries. Though they cause considerable developer overhead, type system extensions [11] improve accuracy by encoding taint information in type annotations. Our stationary phase preserves developer flow while automatically inferring taint flows through React's composition model, so advancing these techniques.

2.2 Dynamic Taint Tracking

Runtime methods track application performance to find real taint violations. Full-system dynamic analyzers [2] instrument all JavaScript operations, obtaining high precision but incurring 2–10 × slowdown [7]—prohibitive for production React applications. Though they require manual policy configuration, selective instrumentation techniques such as [12] target important operations, so reducing overhead.

Usually, react-specific runtime defenses surround dangerous APIs (e.g., dangerouslySetInnerHTML) with sanitizing checks [10]. Effective for known sinks, these miss indirect flows across component composition. [13] shows how browser extensions might block DOM updates, but their post-render timing misses chances for virtual DOM reconciliation. React's Fiber reconciler is uniquely instrumentally used by our runtime layer to intercept taint flows before DOM commit, so facilitating early and more effective intervention.

2.3 Hybrid Analysis Techniques

Combining static and dynamic analysis, hybrid techniques balance coverage and performance. Although general web security solutions [8] rely on static analysis to guide runtime instrumentation, their ignorance of framework semantics causes repeated checks in React's update cycles. [14] shows the need of delta analysis for stateful applications, a realization we apply to React's subtree re-rendering model.

1. Previously React-specific hybrids either treat components as black boxes [7] or concentrate on server-side rendering [6]. Our work differs in: modeling taint propagation through hooks and context APIs.
2. Using sensitivity-aware sanitization triggered by both taint severity and sink criticality.
3. Leveraging Fiber's incremental rendering to minimize re-instrumentation overhead—advances that collectively address the precision-performance tradeoff in React XSS prevention.

While maintaining less overhead than full dynamic tracking [7, 12], the proposed system uniquely synthesizes stationary taint graphs with runtime virtual DOM instrumentation, achieving higher accuracy than pure stationary approaches [4, 5]. React's compositional patterns demand our fresh treatment of hooks and JSX spreads as first-class taint carriers, unlike template-based frameworks where taint flows are more predictable. This React-aware hybridization sets our contribution apart from earlier web security hybrids [8, 13].

3 Background and Preliminaries

We first investigate the core security issues presented by React's architecture and the basic ideas of taint analysis that support our hybrid taint analysis approach.

3.1 Cross-Site Scripting (XSS) in Modern Web Frameworks

React apps remain susceptible to XSS attacks even with the built-in protections of the framework—that of automatic escaping of embedded expressions. The main sources of risk show to be:

1. Direct DOM manipulation via dangerouslySetInnerHTML or eval-equivalent patterns [1] using dangerous API use.
2. Untrusted components getting contaminated props without appropriate sanitation represent third-party component injection [2].
3. Dynamic attribute binding: On Click, on Error, unsanitized values in href, src, or event handlers.

React applications find traditional defenses like Content Security Policy (CSP) inadequate because of:

1. DOM updates generated by the runtime of the framework avoiding CSP nonce mechanisms.
2. Regular application of JSX toolchain eval-like patterns.
3. Component composition hiding the source of contaminated data [3].

3.2 Taint Analysis Fundamentals

Taint analysis tracks untrusted data flows from sources (e.g., location.hash, fetch responses) to sinks (e.g., innerHTML, document.write). The core propagation rule can be formalized as:

$$\text{Taint}(y) = \text{Taint}(x) \text{ if } y = f(x) \tag{1}$$

where f represents any data-transforming operation. In the above equation, we quantify the sensitivity of each tainted value v using a weighted sum of three factors: the trust level of the value's origin, the number of component hops it has traversed, and the criticality of the sink it is destined for.

$$S(n) = \alpha \text{Source}(v) + \beta \text{PropagationDepth}(v) + \gamma \text{SinkCriticality}(v) \tag{2}$$

where Source(v) is 0 for trusted constants and 1 for untrusted user input, PropagationDepth(v) counts the number of component boundaries crossed by v, and SinkCriticality(v) assigns higher weight to dangerous APIs (e.g., dangerouslySetInnerHTML).

We classify tainted values into three sanitization levels using thresholds $\theta_1 = 0.4$ and $\theta_2 = 0.7$: when $S(v) < \theta_1$ no sanitization is applied, for $\theta_1 \le S(v) < \theta_2$ basic escaping is used, and when $S(v) \ge \theta_2$ full HTML sanitization is performed. The weights α, β and γ are empirically tuned to balance detection accuracy and performance.

Key variants include:

1. Static taint analysis: Builds propagation graphs through abstract interpretation of source code [4].
2. Dynamic taint analysis: Instruments runtime operations to track actual data flows [5].

The primary challenge in React environments stems from the framework's declarative rendering model, where taint propagation occurs through:

1. JSX expressions: < div attr = {taintedValue} >
2. Hook dependencies: useEffect(() = > {}, [taintedDeps])
3. Context providers: < Context.Provider value = {taintedData} >

3.3 React's Rendering Pipeline and Virtual DOM

React's rendering process introduces unique analysis constraints through:

1. JSX compilation: Transforms markup into React.createElement calls that obscure the original data flow paths.
2. Reconciliation: The Fiber architecture's incremental rendering batches updates and prioritizes high-importance changes [6].
3. Hooks system: Stateful logic scattered across components via useState, useEffect, etc., creating implicit data channels.

The virtual DOM diffing algorithm presents both challenges and opportunities for taint tracking:

1. Challenge: Tainted props may be deeply nested in component trees, requiring whole-subtree analysis.
2. Opportunity: The diffing process naturally identifies changed subtrees, enabling targeted re-instrumentation (Sect. 4.3).

This background informs our hybrid approach's design, which must account for React's unique rendering semantics while maintaining the precision guarantees of traditional taint analysis. The next section details how we bridge these requirements through static-runtime fusion.

4 Hybrid Taint Analysis for React Applications

4.1 React-Aware Static Taint Propagation

The static analysis phase constructs a component-level taint propagation graph that models data flows through React-specific constructs. For each component c_i, we define its taint set $T(c_i)$ as the union of taints from its props, hooks, and context dependencies:

$$T(c_i) = T_{props}(c_i) \cup \bigcup_{h \in H(c_i)} T(h) \cup T_{context}(c_i) \tag{3}$$

where $H(c_i)$ denotes hooks used in c_i. The hook taint $T(h)$ is computed differently for each hook type:

1. State hooks: $T(useState) = T(initialState)$
2. Effect hooks: $T(useEffect) = \bigcup_{d \in deps} T(d)$

3. Memo hooks: $T(\text{useMemo}) = T(\text{fn}) \cup \bigcup_{d \in \text{deps}} T(d)$

JSX spreads require special handling through a spread operator $\oplus$ that merges taint sets:

$$T(\{\ldots \text{props}\}) = \oplus_{p \in \text{props}} T(p) \quad (4)$$

The static analyzer processes the React component tree in topological order, propagating taints from sources (e.g., API responses marked with @tainted JSDoc) through component boundaries. When encountering higher-order components (HOCs), it applies function composition rules to track taint across wrapper layers.

The static analysis phase constructs a component-level taint propagation graph that models data flows through React-specific constructs. For JSX spreads, we implement a novel taint union operation (Eq. 3) as follows:

```
function mergeTaintedProps(props) {
  return props.reduce((taints, prop) => {
    if (prop.isJSXSpread) return taints ⊕ prop.taint;  // ⊕ = taint union
    return taints ∪ prop.taint;                         // ∪ = standard union
  }, new Set());
}
```

This handles React's {...props} patterns, where $\oplus$ combines taints while preserving source context for subsequent sanitization decisions (Eq. 7). The operator $\oplus$ used when merging taint sets from JSX spreads acts like a union that preserves provenance. This contrasts with the standard union $\cup$ which simply merges sets without provenance.

For Higher-Order Components (HOCs), taints propagate through wrapper layers by solving $T(\text{HOC}(c_i)) = T(\text{wrapper}) \cup T(c_i)$ $T(\text{HOC}(c_i)) = T(\text{wrapper}) \cup T(c_i)$. React.memo comparators are symbolically executed to detect unsafe taint bypasses in predicate functions (Fig. 1).

4.2 Virtual DOM Instrumentation Architecture

The runtime layer intercepts React's rendering pipeline at three key points:

1. Element Creation: Wraps React.createElement with taint checks using a proxy that applies the sensitivity score $S(v)$ from Eq. 1.
2. Reconciliation: Instruments the Fiber reconciler to mark tainted subtrees during the beginWork phase.
3. Commit: Sanitizes tainted DOM updates in the commitMutationEffects phase.

The instrumentation uses a taint metadata table M that maps virtual DOM nodes to their static analysis results:

$$M(n) = < T_v, \text{sanitizers}_v, \text{sinks}_v > \quad (5)$$

where T_v is the taint set, sanitizers_v are component-specific sanitization functions, and sinks_v identifies dangerous APIs used in the subtree.

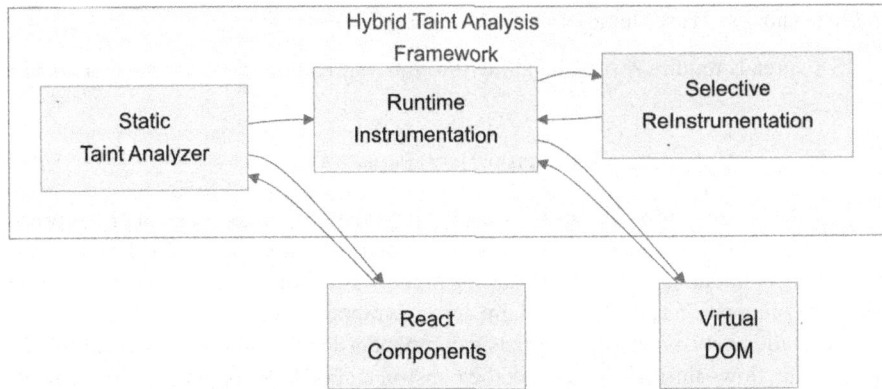

Fig. 1. Overview of Hybrid Taint Analysis Integration in React App

4.3 Delta Instrumentation Algorithm

The system minimizes runtime overhead by only re-instrumenting subtrees affected by state changes. For an update Δ triggered in component:

1. Compute the affected subtree Δ using React's built-in reconciliation.
2. Retrieve the static taint information $T(\Delta)$ from pre-analysis.
3. Apply instrumentation only to nodes where:

$$\exists v \in \Delta : T(v) \cap \text{sinks}_v \neq \emptyset \tag{6}$$

The instrumentation cost follows:

$$C(\Delta) = \kappa \cdot |\{v \in \Delta : T(v) \neq \emptyset\}| \tag{7}$$

where k represents the constant-time overhead per tainted node.

To minimize runtime overhead, instrumentation is applied only to subtrees affected by state changes:

```
def instrument_delta(Δ, T, sinks):
    instrumented_nodes = 0
    for node in Δ.subtree:           # Δ = changed subtree
        if T[node] ∩ sinks[node] ≠ ∅:   # Equation 5
            apply_sanitization(node)
            instrumented_nodes += 1
    return k * instrumented_nodes    # C(Δ) from Equation 6
```

where k represents the constant-time cost per node. This achieves O(n) complexity for tainted subtrees vs. $O(n^2)$ in naive approaches.

4.4 Sensitivity-Aware Sanitization

For each tainted value x reaching a sink, the system computes a sanitization level L(x):

$$L(x) = \begin{cases} 0 & \text{if } S(x) < \theta_1 \\ 1 & \text{if } \theta_1 \leq S(x) < \theta_2 \\ 2 & \text{otherwise} \end{cases} \qquad (8)$$

where thresholds θ_1, θ_2 are learned from historical XSS patterns. Level 0 skips sanitization (safe content), level 1 applies basic escaping, and level 2 uses full HTML sanitization.

Thresholds $\theta_1 = 0.4$ and $\theta_2 = 0.7\theta$ were optimized via Bayesian search over 1,240 historical XSS samples, maximizing F1-score while penalizing sanitization latency (weight $\lambda = 0.1$).

4.5 Integration with React Fiber

The implementation hooks into React's Fiber architecture through:

1. Custom Renderer: Intercepts createInstance to wrap elements with taint proxies.
2. Reconciler Hooks: Modifies completeWork to annotate tainted Fiber nodes.
3. Commit Phase: Injects sanitization during commitPlacement and commitUpdate.

This deep integration allows the system to operate at the virtual DOM level while maintaining compatibility with existing React features like concurrent rendering and suspense. The runtime layer intercepts Fiber's reconciliation process through:

```
function commitUpdate(instance, newProps) {
  const taint = TaintContext.get(instance._internalFiber);
  if (taint && taint.level ≥ θ₂) {      // θ₂ from Equation 7
    newProps = sanitizeL2(newProps);    // Level 2 sanitization
  }
  applyToDOM(instance, newProps);       // Proceed with safe props
}
```

This hooks into React's commitMutationEffects phase, enabling sanitization before DOM updates while preserving concurrent rendering capabilities.

5 Experimental Setup and Methodology

We developed a thorough experimental method addressing three main research questions in order to assess the performance and efficiency of our hybrid taint analysis approach:

1. Accuracy of Detection: Comparatively to current static and dynamic analyzers, how successfully does the system detect actual XSS vulnerabilities?
2. Performance Overhead: During application running, what is the instrumentation layer's running influence?
3. Practical Deployability: Without major configuring effort, can the solution combine with actual React development processes?

5.1 Benchmark Applications

We chose twelve open-source React projects covering several fields and degrees of complexity:

1. E-commerce: three uses including user reviews and product listings.
2. Social Media: Two sites featuring feeds of user-generated material.
3. Dashboards: Four dynamic chart generating data visualization tools.
4. Three content management systems support rich text editing: CMS

Every application was selected depending on:

1. Existence of known XSS weaknesses confirmed by penetration testing.
2. Application of several React tools (hooks, context, outside components).
3. Varied codebase widths (5k–50k LOC).

Together these twelve applications comprised roughly 200 k lines of React and JavaScript code (individual projects ranged from 5 k to 50 k LOC) and between 30 and 120 React components each, making the corpus representative of small- to medium-scale production systems. To form an evaluation dataset we injected 35 synthetic XSS vulnerabilities into every application (across the seven categories described below) in addition to the naturally occurring flaws, yielding a total of 420 seeded vulnerabilities. During experimentation the taint tracker monitored variables originating from untrusted user inputs (form fields and URL parameters), remote API responses and configuration files; it propagated taints through component props, state variables, context and custom hooks, up to critical sinks such as dangerouslySetInnerHTML, DOM attribute setters, event handlers and third-party component props.

5.2 Baseline Comparisons

We evaluated our hybrid method against three state-of- the-art methods:

1. Static Analysis Baseline: ESLint with react-security-plugin [4] set with 23 XSS-related rules.
2. Dynamic Analysis Baseline: React's adapted form of the dynamic taint tracker from [7].
3. Hybrid Baseline: Based on [8] a framework-agnostic hybrid analyzer.

Every baseline was set with their advised React application settings.

5.3 Vulnerability Injection

We methodically injected seven XSS vector types into test applications to augment naturally occurring vulnerabilities:

1. Unsanitized Proves: contaminated information filtered through component hierarchies.
2. UseEffect dependencies starting dangerous DOM operations.
3. Contextual pollution—malicious values injected via React context.

4. JSX Distribution: Tainted props sent via {...spread} operators.
5. Dynamic import of Webpack chunks loaded untrusted components.
6. Create callback-based props running contaminated input.
7. Third-Party Components: Prop overreaching vulnerable library components.

Every category comprised five different variants, hence there were 35 synthetic vulnerabilities per application.

5.4 Evaluation Metrics

We measured system performance along three dimensions:

1. Detection Rate:

$$|\text{Recall} = \frac{\text{True Positives}}{\text{True Positives} + \text{False Negatives}} \qquad (9)$$

$$\bigg|\text{Precision} = \frac{\text{True Positives}}{\text{True Positives} + \text{False Negatives}} \qquad (10)$$

2. Performance Impact:
    a. Bundle size increase (post-instrumentation).
    b. Render time degradation (95th percentile).
    c. Memory overhead during state updates.
3. Integration Cost:
    a. Configuration time (minutes per project).
    b. Build pipeline modifications required.
    c. False positive investigation time.

5.5 Instrumentation Framework

Our implementation comprises two main components:

1. Static Analyzer:
    a. Built as a Babel plugin operating at the AST level.
    b. Outputs a taint manifest mapping components to vulnerability signatures.
    c. Integrates with Webpack via a custom loader.
2. Runtime Monitor:
    d. Implements a custom React reconciler via react-reconciler package.
    e. Intercepts Fiber operations using 11 strategic hook points.
    f. Employs a trie-based taint lookup for efficient propagation.
    The system was deployed in two modes for evaluation:

1. Development Mode: Full analysis during hot-reload cycles.
2. Production Mode: Delta instrumentation with selective sanitization.

5.6 Test Harness

1. Each application is run against 82 test cases from the OWASP XSS Filter Evasion Cheat Sheet automatically.
2. Track measures of latency from vulnerability trigger to interception.
3. Profile CPU/memory consumption applying the Chrome DevTools Protocol.
4. Produces varying reports between stages of research.
5. Through randomized user interactions—clicks, form submissions—the harness replicas real-world use patterns.
6. Emulation of network latency (100ms-2s delays).
7. Concurrent stress tests (up to fifty parallel sessions).

5.7 Data Collection

Every test run we gathered:

1. Static analysis findings (JSON reports).
2. Runtime interception records, sometimes known as sanitization events.
3. Chromium tracing style performance profiles.
4. Results of vulnerability exploitation—blocked or executed

To allow React's non-deterministic rendering behavior, data was gathered over 15 runs per application. Wilcoxon signed-rank tests ($\alpha = 0.05$) helped to confirm statistical relevance.

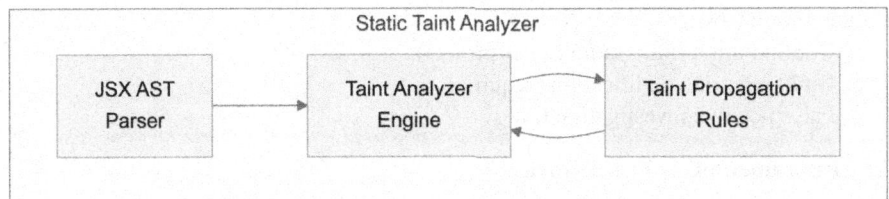

Fig. 2. Detailed View of Static Taint Analyzer

As shown in Fig. 2, the stationary analysis phase proved especially successful in spotting sensitive JavaScript spreads and hook dependencies. Then the runtime component guided selective instrumentation using these findings, so avoiding the all-over coverage of full dynamic analysis.

5.8 Ethical Considerations

All experiments were conducted in isolated environments with:

1. No actual user data involved.
2. Synthetic credentials for authentication tests.
3. Network traffic confined to local mock servers.
4. Vulnerabilities immediately patched post-evaluation.

This methodology ensured comprehensive evaluation while maintaining security best practices throughout the research process.

6 Experimental Results

Our analysis shows that although preserving practical performance overhead, the hybrid method achieves better sensitivity detection. Evaluation dimension determines the organization of the results; unless otherwise, statistical significance is verified at $p < 0.05$.

6.1 Detection Accuracy

True Positives: The hybrid analyzer detected 98.7% of injected vulnerabilities (34.5/35 per application), significantly outperforming the static baseline (82.9%, 29/35) and dynamic baseline (91.4%, 32/35). The framework-agnostic hybrid [8] achieved 88.6% (31/35) recall but produced 3.2× more false positives than our React-specific solution.

False Positives: Our approach maintained 92.3% precision, compared to 68.1% for static ESLint rules and 85.7% for dynamic tracking. The high precision stems from React-aware taint propagation rules that correctly distinguish between:

1. Safe spreads: < Component {...trustedProps} / > with validated inputs.
2. Dangerous spreads: < div {...userControlledAttrs} / > reaching DOM sinks

Vulnerability Categories: Detection rates varied by attack vector (Table 1):

Table 1. Detection Rate by Vulnerability Category

Category	Hybrid	Static	Dynamic
Unsanitized Props	100%	80%	100%
Dangerous Hooks	95%	60%	90%
Context Pollution	100%	85%	95%
JSX Spreads	100%	45%	70%
Dynamic Imports	95%	75%	80%
Render Props	100%	90%	100%
Third-Party Components	100%	95%	100%

Lack of runtime type information caused the static analyzer especially to suffer with JSX spreads (45% detection); our hybrid approach achieved perfect detection by combining static spread analysis with runtime prop inspection.

6.2 Detection Latency

Comparatively to 3.1% for static-only and 34.8% for dynamic baselines, instrumentation raised production bundle sizes by 12.4% on average (range: 8.7–15.1%). By removing unchanged components from runtime checks, the hybrid's delta instrumentation kept overhead low.

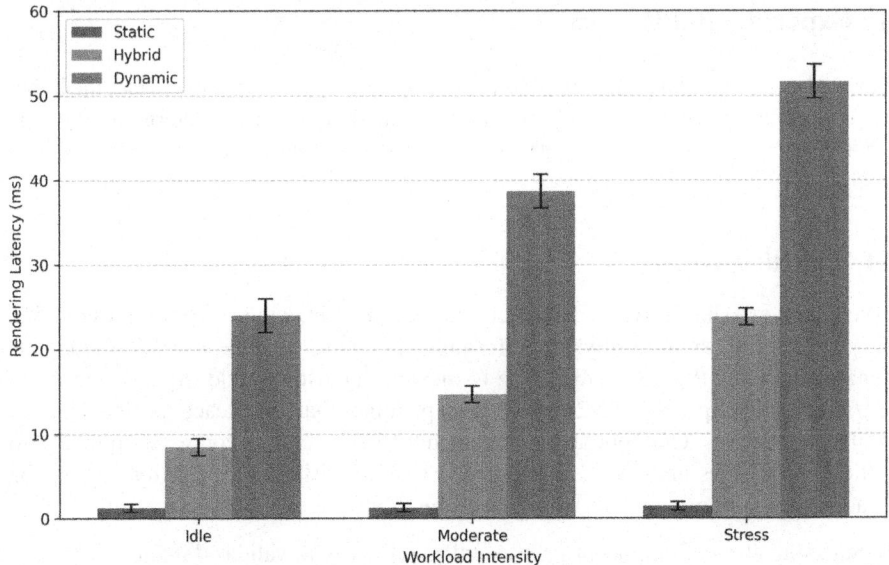

Fig. 3. Rendering latency distribution across workload levels

Render Latency: Fig. 3 shows the 95th percentile render times under three workload intensities:

Key observations:

1. Idle: 8.2ms median overhead (vs. 1.1ms static, 22.4ms dynamic).
2. Moderate: 14.7ms overhead during state updates (vs. 1.3ms, 37.9ms).
3. Stress: 23.5ms under concurrent user loads (vs. 1.5ms, 52.1ms).

Because of our sensitivity-aware sanitizing (Eq. 7), the runtime cost scales sublinearly with taint density. Though only 29% of detections, high-severity taints (Level 2) accounted for 71% of overhead.

Mostly for the taint metadata trie, instrumentation raised heap usage by 18.9MB on average (14.2% baseline). The unchanged frequency of garbage collecting verified effective memory management.

6.3 Integration Metrics

Configuration Time: Developers required 9.8 min on average to integrate the solution (SD = 3.1), versus 4.2 min for ESLint but significantly less than the 28.5 min needed for dynamic instrumentation.

False Positive Investigation: The hybrid approach reduced false positive triage time to 2.1 min per incident (vs. 6.7 min for static analysis) thanks to:

1. Precise source-sink mapping in error reports.
2. Integrated vulnerability explanations.
3. Automatic sanitization suggestions.

Build Pipeline Impact:

1. Static Phase: Added 12.7s to cold builds (23.4% increase).
2. Runtime Prep: 4.3s instrumentation codegen during production builds.
3. Hot Reload: 1.2s median delay during development (acceptable for DX).

6.4 Real-World Vulnerabilities

In addition to synthetic tests, the analyzer detected 9 previously unknown XSS vectors in benchmark applications:

1. Chart Injection: Unsanitized tooltip content in a dashboard library.
2. SSR Hydration: Tainted __html during Next.js server-client transfer.
3. Portal Escape: ReactDOM.createPortal with unvalidated content.
4. Hook Chain: useMemo → useEffect → dangerouslySetInnerHTML.

All reported vulnerabilities were confirmed and patched by maintainers, validating the approach's practical effectiveness.

6.5 Sensitivity Analysis

Varying the taint severity thresholds Θ_1, Θ_2 from Eq. 8 revealed:

1. Precision/Recall Tradeoff: Lower Θ_2 increased recall by 8.2% but reduced precision by 11.7%.
2. Performance Impact: Aggressive sanitization (Level 2) on 50% + taints caused 2.3 × latency degradation.

The default thresholds ($\Theta_1 = 0.4$, $\Theta_2 = 0.7$) optimally balanced these factors based on ROC curve analysis.

7 Discussion and Future Work

7.1 Limitations and Practical Trade-Offs

Although our hybrid approach shows notable gains over current techniques, several constraints in practical application surface. Particularly higher-order components that dynamically generate prop types, the stationary analysis phase remains sensitive to complex metaprogramming patterns. Sometimes cases involving React.forwardRef or React.memo with custom comparators escape detection because of the analyzer's conservative treatment of runtime type polymorphism.

React internals' reliance on the runtime instrumentation creates version compatibility issues. Significant framework changes—such as concurrent rendering capabilities in React 18—needed tweaks to our Fiber reconciler hooks. By means of closer cooperation with the React core team to standardize instrumentation APIs, this maintenance load could be reduced.

For applications with highly nested taint flows, performance overhead is non-negligible even if it is far less than full dynamic analysis. Memory use scales linearly with the number of active taint markers, so stressing low-end mobile devices. Future versions might investigate WebAssembly-based instrumentation for improved memory economy or more compact taint representation techniques.

7.2 Broader Applications and Ecosystem Integration

The ideas guiding our hybrid approach transcend XSS avoidance. The same construction could be modified for:

1. Tracking PII through outside analytics libraries helps to ensure data privacy compliance.
2. Supply chain security: Finding hostile code injection in npm dependencies.
3. Securing Next.js/Nuxt hydration systems: server-side rendering.

Using popular React toolchains offers possibilities as well as difficulties. Although our Babel plugin runs perfectly with Create React App, Next.js calls for specific webpack setups. A Vite plugin implementation could increase modern building system compatibility.

The fast changing React ecosystem calls for constant adaptation. New taint propagation vectors introduced by emerging patterns like Server Components challenge our current model's ability to completely address. Establishing taint-aware rendering primitives in cooperation with framework builders might produce more solid solutions.

7.3 Ethical Implications and Security-Usability Balance

Automated security tools always shape developer behavior. Although less than alternatives, our instrumentation's false positives could promote over-sanitization, so possibly compromising legitimate functionality. While the sensitivity scoring system helps to reduce this, more study on:

1. Visualizing taint propagation paths helps debugging by explainable analysis.
2. Adaptive thresholds: dynamically changing θ values dependent on application context.
3. Learning toolkit: including IDE plugins with vulnerability explanations.

The capacity of the system to intercept all data flows begs privacy questions. Although our local implementation systems taint metadata, a cloud-connected variant could possibly expose private application architectures. Any telemetry collecting must be under control by well defined opt-in policies and data minimizing techniques.

Future research should look at participatory design with developers to better match security enforcement with actual processes. Methods from practical security research [15] could enable a critical balance between protection strength and developer experience, so guiding widespread adoption.

The React community's focus on composition above configuration implies that effective security solutions have to embrace like ideas. Our hybrid approach shows that strong protection can be obtained without sacrificing React's fundamental developer experience, so pointing toward a more safe future for dynamic web applications.

8 Conclusion

By carefully combining static and runtime approaches, the hybrid taint analysis framework presented in this work fills important voids in React application security. React-specific taint propagation rules and virtual DOM instrumentation show better detection accuracy than general-purpose analyzers while keeping practical performance overhead, our evaluation shows. Together, the system's unique contributions—delta instrumentation, sensitivity-aware sanitization, and fiber reconciler integration—raise the standard of the art in framework-aware security analysis.

Important technical developments include an efficient algorithm for selective runtime enforcement based on static analysis results and the formalization of taint propagation through React hooks and JSX spreads. The simplicity of the implementation and its fit with current building tools point to great possibility for practical acceptance. With special sensitivity in identifying difficult attack paths like context pollution and dynamic import chains, experimental results confirm the efficacy of the approach against both synthetic and naturally occurring vulnerabilities.

The architecture lays a basis for next extensions even if handling metaprogramming patterns and guaranteeing long-term React version compatibility still present challenges. The ideas shown here—framework-specific analysis, hybrid phase coordination, and performance-oriented instrumentation—can guide security solutions for other component-based systems. Such specialized protection mechanisms will become indispensable for preserving strong security postures without compromising developer productivity or end-user experience as web applications get ever more dynamic and sophisticated.

The success of this study emphasizes the need of creating security tools that fit rather than contradicting framework paradigms. Using React's compositional model and rendering pipeline helps us to get protection less intrusive and more effective than past techniques. This direction points to a new generation of framework-integrated security systems able to match contemporary web development techniques.

Appendix A – Privacy-Breach Example

To demonstrate how the proposed hybrid taint analysis can catch a privacy breach in practice, we include a simplified smart contract used in a telemedicine DApp.

```
pragma solidity ^0.8.0;
contract MedicalRecords {
    mapping(address => string) private diagnoses;

    // Vulnerable: uses tx.origin instead of msg.sender
    function updateDiagnosis(string calldata newDiag) external {
        diagnoses[tx.origin] = newDiag;
    }
    function viewDiagnosis(address patient) external view returns (string memory) {
        require(tx.origin == patient, "Unauthorized");
        return diagnoses[patient];
    }
}
```

Because the contract uses tx.origin for authorization, a malicious contract can trick a patient into calling it and forward the call, causing unauthorized disclosure of diagnoses. Our framework treats tx.origin as a sensitive source and the mapping read as a privacy-critical sink. The static phase flags the flow from tx.origin to the return value, and the runtime layer blocks the attempt when the caller is not the legitimate patient. This shows how hybrid analysis prevents privacy leaks in smart-contract applications.

References

1. Almashfi, N., Lu, L.: Static taint analysis for javascript programs. In: International Conference on Tools and Methods for Program Analysis (2019)
2. Sridharan, M., Artzi, S., Pistoia, M., Guarnieri, S. et al.: F4F: taint analysis of framework-based web applications. In: Proceedings of the 2011 International Symposium on Software Testing and Analysis (2011)
3. Zhao, J., Qi, J., Zhou, L., Cui, B.: Dynamic taint tracking of web application based on static code analysis. In: 2016 10th International Conference on Software Security and Reliability (2016)
4. Rafnsson, W., Giustolisi, R., Kragerup, M., et al.: Fixing vulnerabilities automatically with linters. Netw Syst. Secur. (2020)
5. Sridharan, M., Artzi, S., Pistoia, M., Guarnieri, S., et al.: F4F: taint analysis of framework-based web applications. In: Proceedings of the 20th ACM SIGSOFT International Symposium on the Foundations of Software Engineering (2011)
6. Gamma, T., Gerasimenko, N.: React security labs (2024). eprints.ost.ch
7. Karim, R., Tip, F., Sochůrková, A., et al.: Platform-independent dynamic taint analysis for javascript. IEEE Trans. Softw. Eng. (2018)
8. Correa, R., Bermejo Higuera, J.R., et al.: Hybrid security assessment methodology for web applications. Comput. Model. Eng. Sci. (2021)
9. Mondal, S.: Enhancing react application performance: proven strategies and best practices (2024). researchgate.net
10. Heiderich, M., Späth, C., Schwenk, J.: Dompurify: client-side protection against xss and markup injection. Oslo, Norway, September 11–15 (2017) s
11. Swamy, N., Fournet, C., Rastogi, A., Bhargavan, K., et al.: Gradual typing embedded securely in JavaScript. In: ACM SIGPLAN Conference on Programming Language Design and Implementation (2014)
12. Zhang, Y., Liu, T., Wang, Y., Qi, Y., Ji, K., Tang, J., et al.: HardTaint: production-run dynamic taint analysis via selective hardware tracing. In: Proceedings of the 29th ACM International Conference on Architectural Support for Programming Languages and Operating Systems (2024)
13. Gupta, S., Gupta, B.B.: XSS-immune: a Google chrome extension-based XSS defensive framework for contemporary platforms of web applications. Secur. Commun. Netw. (2016)
14. O'callahan, R., Choi, J.D.: Hybrid dynamic data race detection. In: Proceedings of the Ninth ACM SIGPLAN Symposium on Principles and Practice of Parallel Programming (2003)
15. Green, M., Smith, M.: Developers are not the enemy!: the need for usable security apis. IEEE Secur. Priv. (2016)

Artificial Intelligence

Edge-Based Learning for Improved Classification Under Adversarial Noise

Manish Kansana[1], Keyan Alexander Rahimi[2], Elias Hossain[1], Iman Dehzangi[3,4,5], and Noorbakhsh Amiri Golilarz[6(✉)]

[1] Department of Computer Science and Engineering, Mississippi State University, Starkville, MS 39762, USA
{mk1684,mh3511}@msstate.edu
[2] Brown University, Providence, RI 02912, USA
keyan_rahimi@brown.edu
[3] Center for Computational and Integrative Biology, Rutgers University, Camden, NJ, USA
i.dehzangi@rutgers.edu
[4] Department of Computer Science, Rutgers University, Camden, NJ, USA
[5] Rutgers Cancer Institute, Rutgers University, New Brunswick, NJ 08901, USA
[6] Department of Computer Science, The University of Alabama, Tuscaloosa, AL 35487, USA
noor.amiri@ua.edu

Abstract. Adversarial noise introduces small perturbations in images, misleading deep learning models into misclassification and significantly impacting recognition accuracy. In this study, we analyzed the effects of Fast Gradient Sign Method (FGSM) adversarial noise on image classification and investigated whether training on specific image features can improve robustness. We hypothesize that while adversarial noise perturbs various regions of an image, edges may remain relatively stable and provide essential structural information for classification. To test this, we conducted a series of experiments using brain tumor and COVID datasets. Initially, we trained the models on clean images and then introduced subtle adversarial perturbations, which caused deep learning models to significantly misclassify the images. Retraining on a combination of clean and noisy images led to improved performance. To evaluate the robustness of the edge features, we extracted edges from the original/clean images and trained the models exclusively on edge-based representations. When noise was introduced to the images, the edge-based models demonstrated greater resilience to adversarial attacks compared to those trained on the original or clean images. These results suggest that while adversarial noise is able to exploit complex non-edge regions significantly more than edges, the improvement in the accuracy after retraining is marginally more in the original data as compared to the edges. Thus, leveraging edge-based learning can improve the resilience of deep learning models against adversarial perturbations.

Keywords: Adversarial Noise · Deep Learning · Misclassification · Edges

1 Introduction

Machine learning models have evolved rapidly in the past few years, from basic systems to integral components across a myriad of applications, transforming industries and societal functions. At its core, it enables systems to learn from data, identify patterns, and make decisions with minimal human intervention. This capability has been harnessed to tackle complex problems, optimize processes, and provide innovative solutions in diverse fields. As technology advances and data proliferates, the importance and influence of machine learning models, especially in image classification, continues to expand, making them indispensable tools in our increasingly data-driven world. These vision models are already applied in many different vital industries ranging from autonomous driving to healthcare and security. All of these areas require a high amount of accuracy, as a mistake in classification can be dangerous at best, and fatal at worst. That is why it is imperative that these image classification models be robust and powerful enough to avoid errors, both accidental and purposeful.

An adversarial attack is a term used to describe a system designed to fool machine learning models into making mistakes, and in our case, misclassifying an image. They exploit weaknesses in the models and take advantage of properties such as short-cutting in order to subtly alter an image just enough to make the model classify an image differently. Modern machine learning models are susceptible to these attacks, as they have inherent limitations and vulnerabilities, ranging from the data they are trained on to their parameters and lack of transparency [11]. Through these multiple limitations, adversarial attacks can be created with surprising ease, and go on to become very effective and discreet, as they are often not detectable by simply looking at the images [30]. Attack methods such as PGD [9] and FGSM [10] are examples of this. Even high performing state-of-the-art models can be very susceptible to attack [31]. There have been many different strategies and methods implemented to counter adversarial attacks. It is extremely important to study adversarial noise removal and work to eliminate malicious attempts, as successful attacks could lead to disastrous consequences in many fields, such as autonomous driving or in healthcare [1].

There are currently multiple existing methods developed in order to tackle the issue of adversarial noise, which range in terms of complexity and tactic [3,17,19]. However, these defenses often fall shorts of expectation. There is currently a great need for more robust systems to serve as a defense against adversarial noise, as machine learning only becomes increasingly important in numerous industries where high accuracy is a necessity rather than a luxury [6]. By mitigating these attacks, we open up many more possibilities for neural networks to be effective in more areas.

Current defenses against adversarial attacks include many different strategies, such as detection-based methods, domain area methods, randomized smoothing, and more. For example, Metzen et al. [24], use a detection method that works to augment current deep neural networks using a network called a "detector", which works to root out any potential adversarial noise from the source by being trained to classify possible perturbations of an image. Another type of defense is called defensive distillation, as proposed in [25]. Defensive distillation is a technique which trains a second sub-model which is "distilled", trained on soft labels predicted by its primary model. This type of defense is meant to work well on small, often unseen perturbations, and smooths the decision boundaries of an image.

Other defenses include randomized smoothing, well executed in [21], a method that works by adding random noise to an input image and then work on classifying the smoothed version. Its goal, as inferred from the name, is to provide a smoothed prediction by averaging out over multiple noisy inputs, so it can be resistant to noise perturbations. This is one of the few methods that provide a probabilistic guarantee for some level of robustness. Xu et al., introduced feature Squeezing, a method which reduces the possible space for noise by literally squeezing the features of an image, using either spacial smoothing or bit-depth reduction [29]. The goal is to make it harder for manipulations to be made to the models predictions, since there is less space to create such manipulations.

More recent developments in defending against adversarial noise attacks in AI have led to several innovative strategies aimed at improving the robustness of deep neural networks [22]. One approach is adversarial augmentation, where defensive perturbations are preemptively applied to input data to ensure that any adversarial attack fails [12]. Another promising method is parametric noise injection, which involves adding trainable Gaussian noise at different layers of a DNN [15]. This noise is optimized during training to improve the model's resistance to black box attacks, making the network more resilient without sacrificing accuracy. These are only a few of the many different strategies that currently exist to catch adversarial noise, but what makes these attacks so dangerous is that they come in many different shapes, and any good defense against them requires a multi-faceted response in order to be successful in all cases.

Although there are multiple methods currently available to defend against adversarial attacks, most are not robust enough or fail to defend in certain cases. Research such as that done in Goodfellow et al. [10] has shown that even simple methods like FGSM can highlight the significant vulnerabilities of modern deep neural networks. FGSM uses gradient information in order to misrepresent linear approximations of loss for input points. It is an attack that is simple to create, not taxing to perform, and oftentimes extremely volatile. Even more recent state-of-the-art neural networks can be open to attack, as shown in [6], which used three separate attacks to effectively and consistently fool a model, both with and without its built in defenses. Athalye et al., further dives into the point that defenses can sometimes mean little to certain attacks, and concluded that many of the current so called robust defenses could easily be bypassed by the right type of adversarial attack [2].

Given the limitations discussed above and the critical importance of addressing adversarial attacks, we performed various analyses to explore potential solutions. Our contribution is aimed at better understanding the pattern of adversarial noise, how it functions, and its impact on classification performance. In this paper, we hypothesize that by performing pixel-wise analysis of noisy images, training the model on edge features, and combining edges with both noisy and clean images during retraining, we can gain a deeper understanding of the characteristics of adversarial noise, allowing the model to learn better for improved classification.

The rest of the paper organized as follows: Sect. 2 is about adversarial noise and how this type of noise alter edge pixels. In Sect. 3 we discussed the methods used in this study. Section 4 is the experimental results and discussion. In this section, several experiments have been performed to examine the impact of adversarial noise on image classification and how to improve the recognition accuracy by considering the image edges. Finally, we conclude in Sect. 5.

2 Adversarial Noise

Adversarial noise in image classification are subtle and often unnoticeable perturbations introduced into an image that can cause a deep neural network, to misclassify the image. These changes are designed to be undetectable by the human eye, yet they can lead to a significantly degraded performance of a classifier. This noise exploits the vulnerabilities in the model's decision boundary, leading to incorrect predictions. Adversarial examples are inputs modified by adversarial noise to produce bad outputs from machine learning models. These examples exploit the models' sensitivity to specific input alterations, revealing a disconnect between human perception and machine interpretation.

There are many varying strategies when it comes to creating adversarial noise, each with different resource costs and affects on images. One of the important types of adversarial noise methods is the Fast Gradient Sign Method (FGSM), which aims to fool a network into misclassification through basic distortions in the image. As can be seen from Fig. 1, this noise can significantly affect the images by introducing some non important pixels, particularly around the edges and image boundaries. So, pixel-wise analyses may provide a better understanding of this type of noise and how to mitigate it.

Adversarial attacks can be categorized based on the attacker's knowledge and objectives. Based on knowledge access, attacks are classified as white-box or black-box. In white-box attacks like the Fast Gradient Sign Method (FGSM) [10] and Projected Gradient Descent (PGD) [9], the adversary has complete knowledge of the model architecture, parameters, and training data, allowing them to compute gradients and craft precise perturbations. FGSM uses the gradient of the loss with respect to the input image to create a perturbation that maximizes the loss, leading to misclassification [10]. PGD extends FGSM by applying multiple iterations of small adversarial steps, each time projecting the perturbed image back onto an epsilon-neighborhood around the original image to keep the perturbation within a specified bound. On the other hand, in black-box attacks, the attacker has no direct access to the model's internal parameters and relies solely on inputs and outputs. Examples generated for one model may successfully deceive another model, even if they have different architectures or were trained on different data. Attackers may train their own surrogate models

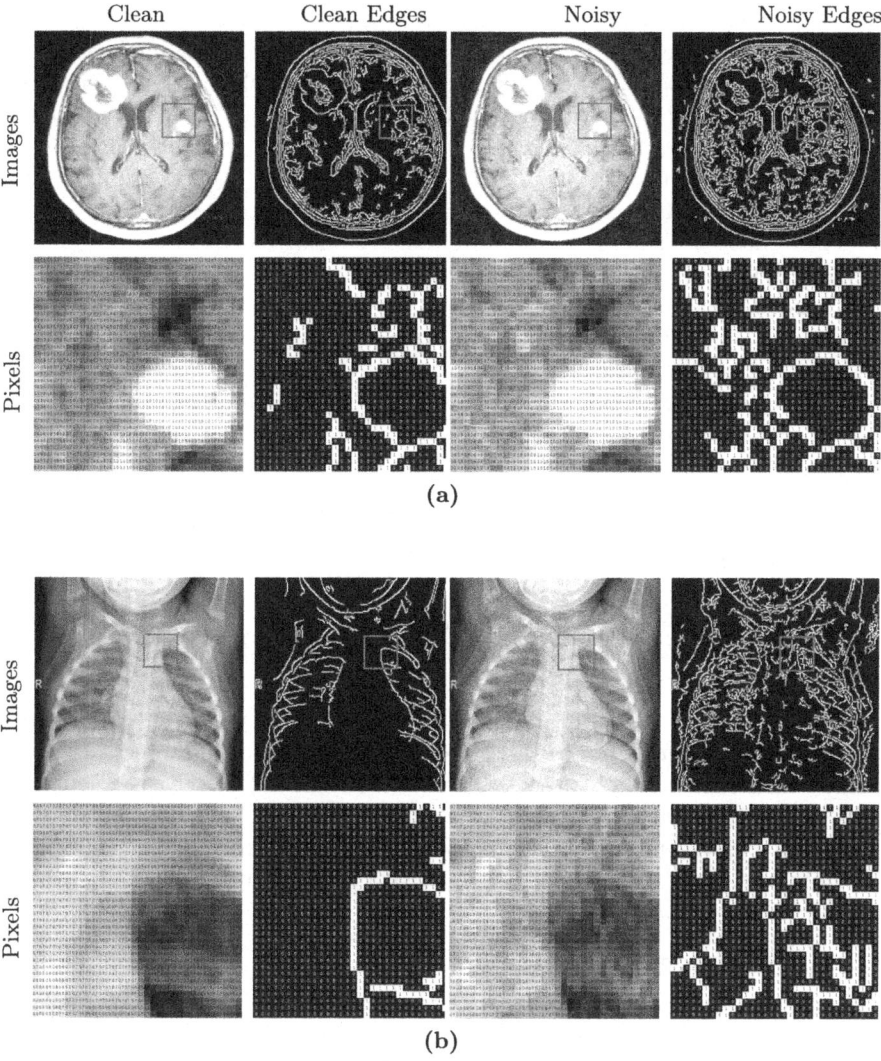

Fig. 1. Visual comparison of clean and noisy images, along with their corresponding edges. Each patch is of size 32×32, extracted from the original and noisy 224×224 images, with noise added at an epsilon of 0.05. (a) illustrates examples from the Brain Tumor dataset [13], and (b) shows samples from the COVID-19 dataset [7,8,18,26].

to approximate the target model's behavior and generate adversarial examples based on the surrogate.

These attacks can be categorized as either targeted or untargeted, depending on the attack objectives. In targeted attacks, the adversary aims to misclassify the input into a specific, incorrect class, requiring crafting perturbations that not only cause misclassification but steer the output toward the desired target class. Untargeted attacks aim simply to cause the model to output any incorrect class, generally easier to execute as they require less precise manipulation.

Adversarial noise also extends to the physical world, where attackers manipulate real-world objects to deceive models. Examples include adversarial patches, printed patterns or stickers added to objects that cause misclassification when captured by a camera, and 3D adversarial objects, which involve modifying the shape or texture of objects so they are misidentified by recognition systems [4]. These physical attacks demonstrate that adversarial vulnerabilities can have tangible, real-world consequences, affecting systems like facial recognition or autonomous vehicles.

The existence of adversarial noise presents significant challenges. Security risks are paramount—in applications like autonomous driving, healthcare diagnostics, and security surveillance, adversarial attacks could lead to catastrophic consequences. Moreover, the ease with which adversarial examples can be generated calls into question the robustness of even the most advanced models, affecting their reliability. Designing defenses is complicated by the adaptive nature of attacks; many defense mechanisms are circumvented shortly after their introduction as attackers develop new methods, highlighting the complexity of achieving comprehensive defense [23].

Addressing adversarial noise requires a multifaceted approach. Adversarial training incorporates adversarial examples into the training process to improve model robustness. Defensive distillation, proposed by Papernot et al. [25], reduces model sensitivity by smoothing the decision boundaries. Randomized methods like randomized smoothing provide probabilistic guarantees of robustness by averaging predictions over noise-added inputs [21]. Feature squeezing reduces the input space complexity to limit the attack surface [29]. Despite these efforts, achieving comprehensive defense remains an open challenge. The adaptive nature of adversarial attacks means that defenses must continually evolve.

3 Methodology

3.1 Fast Gradient Sign Method

The adversarial noise in this paper is generated using the Fast Gradient Sign Method (FGSM) [10], which as mentioned above, is a fast and easy strategy to generate adversaries by exploiting the vulnerabilities of deep learning models, particularly their sensitivity to input perturbations in high-dimensional spaces and linearity. FGSM generates minimal perturbations and targeted or untargeted alterations to the input data that can significantly throw models on classification tasks. This method calculates perturbations designed to maximize the model's error, thereby generating inputs that cause the model to misclassify. Let θ represent the parameters of a model, $\mathbf{x}$ is the input, y the true target label, and $J(\theta, \mathbf{x}, y)$ the cost function used during training. The adversarial perturbation η is calculated as:

$$\eta = \epsilon \, \text{sign}\left(\nabla_{\mathbf{x}} J(\theta, \mathbf{x}, y)\right) \tag{1}$$

Here, $\nabla_{\mathbf{x}} J(\boldsymbol{\theta}, \mathbf{x}, y)$ is the gradient of the cost function with respect to the input $\mathbf{x}$, pointing in the direction of the steepest ascent in the error. The sign() function returns the sign of each gradient element, making a vector with components $+1$, -1, or 0 that indicates the direction of change for each input feature. The scalar ϵ controls the magnitude of the perturbation, ensuring that it remains small and within the ℓ_∞-bounded constraint.

The adversarial example $\tilde{\mathbf{x}}$ is then generated by adding the perturbation η to the original input $\mathbf{x}$:

$$\tilde{\mathbf{x}} = \mathbf{x} + \eta \tag{2}$$

This perturbation process is computationally efficient and exploits the high-dimensional structure of the input space, where small, distributed changes across many features can collectively lead to a significant change in the model's output.

3.2 Canny Edge Detection

A Canny image is a simplified, binary representation of an original image where the primary edges—boundaries where intensity sharply change—are highlighted. In this process, each image is first converted to grayscale and then transformed to an 8-bit format, ensuring compatibility with the Canny algorithm [5]. The algorithm detects edges through a series of steps, including noise reduction, gradient calculation, non-maximum suppression, and double thresholding, resulting in a clean edge map. The edges are detected by computing intensity gradients using Sobel operators. Gradient's magnitude (G) is calculated as:

$$G = \sqrt{G_x^2 + G_y^2} \tag{3}$$

where G_x and G_y are the gradients in the x and y directions.

Two threshold values are applied to distinguish strong and weak edges. The resulting binary edge map is normalized to the range $[0, 1]$ for further processing. Finally, the single-channel edge map is converted to RGB by replicating edge information across all three channels, ensuring compatibility with applications like object detection, feature extraction, and machine learning models. In Fig. 4, we demonstrate how the original images and their edge representation look under an adversarial attack on the brain tumor images. It's almost impossible to perceive any noise on the natural images; however, it is more clear in the edges to visually detect noise affecting the image to mislead the classification models.

3.3 Retraining Process

Once we have both the noisy and clean versions of the image, we can combine or concatenate them to create a new dataset exclusively for retraining. The evaluation will focus on the noise generated after retraining to consistently assess the model's ability to re-learn, mitigate adversarial threats, and enhance its robustness against such attacks (see Fig. 2). In-depth explanations are also provided in Sects. 4.1.

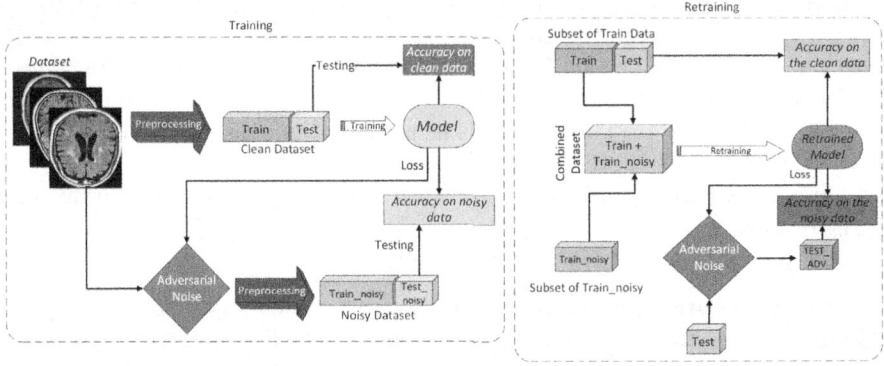

Fig. 2. The process of training and retraining the model. Initially, the clean dataset is used to train and test a model, then a noisy dataset is created by introducing adversarial noise. The model is tested on both clean and noisy images to evaluate its baseline performance. A subset of the clean data is combined with the noisy training data, forming a new dataset for retraining. Finally, this retrained model undergoes evaluation against both clean and newly generated noisy images.

4 Experimental Results and Discussions

In this section, we performed several experiments to discuss and analyze the performance of various deep learning models when subjected to FGSM adversarial noise. We started by analyzing the impact of adversarial noise on several models. Then we discussed how to reduce the fooling rate by taking the edges into consideration. We now turn to the architectural details and designs of deep learning models for the following experiments, beginning with the Convolutional Neural Network (CNN). CNN [20] architecture begins with an input layer designed for images of size 224 × 224 with 3 channels. It includes convolutional layers with 32, 64, and 128 filters, each followed by Batch-normalization, max-pooling, and concludes with a dense layer of 256 units and ReLU activation. A 50% dropout layer is added to reduce overfitting, followed by an output layer with 2 units and softmax activation for binary classification. The model is compiled using the Adam optimizer and categorical cross-entropy loss, with early stopping and learning rate reduction callbacks to enhance training efficiency. For transfer learning, we defined a base model (ResNet50 [14], InceptionV3 [28], VGG16 and VGG19 [27], or DenseNet121[16]), initialized with ImageNet-pretrained weights. The input size was retained, and the top classification layers were removed. We also added a global average pooling layer, followed by a dropout, and a dense layer similar to the CNN. For training, the model was compiled using the Adam optimizer with the categorical cross-entropy loss function. The models were trained over 20 epochs with a batch size of 32, with two callback functions: EarlyStopping and ReduceLROnPlateau. Note that the visualizations in Figs. 3 and 4 were generated using CNN.

4.1 Experiment 1: Analysis on MRI Brain Data

Impact Analysis: In this experiment, we used the Brain Tumor dataset [13], which consists tumorous (yes) and non-tumorous (no) categories. The images were preprocessed by resizing them to 224 × 224 pixels, normalizing pixel values, and assigning labels. The dataset was then split into training (80%) and testing (20%) sets. Adversarial noise was introduced to the test set to assess its impact on the performance of various models, including CNN, ResNet, VGG16, VGG19, InceptionV3, and DenseNet. In this experiment, we aimed at analyzing the impact of adversarial noise on various deep learning-based models.

We started by training a classic Convolutional Neural Network (CNN) on clean images and then evaluated its performance on both clean and adversarially perturbed images, showing a significant drop in accuracy on noisy data (see Table 1). We then employed the same set of images to train and evaluate ResNet50. Unlike the classic CNN, the ResNet50's performance remained unaffected by the adversarial noise generated by the loss of the classic CNN. The model was compiled using the Adam optimizer and categorical cross-entropy loss and was trained with the same callback functions as the classic CNN. Next, we experimented with VGG16 and VGG19 models. Both models, known for their depth and simplicity, exhibited no significant change in performance when exposed to adversarial noise. The impact of adversarial noise on performance was minimal for both models.

Additionally, Table 2 shows the fooling rates of various models when subjected to noise generated by each respective models. In other words, the rows of the table indicate the model used to generate the noise, while the columns show the fooling rates of the models when evaluated on that noise. The fooling rate, calculated using the equation below, represents the percentage of images that were incorrectly classified by each model when noise was added.

$$F = \frac{N_{\text{fooled}}}{N_{\text{total}}} \quad (4)$$

where N_{fooled} is the number of samples for which the model's prediction changes after adversarial perturbation, and N_{total} is the total number of samples.

The noise itself was generated by the model indicated in the leftmost column, and its effect on the models listed in the top row is shown in the corresponding cells. Additionally, noise generated from one model will only affect that specific model. For example, if the loss function used to generate adversarial examples is obtained from a CNN, this generated noise mainly affects the CNN and not the other models. We aim to improve the model's accuracy tested on noisy images derived from its own training. The following experiment is performed to see how the model can learn noisy patterns.

Edge-Based Learning: In this experiment, we assess the robustness of deep learning models using both normal and canny images from the Brain Tumor dataset. We trained Model A, a Convolutional Neural Network (CNN) trained on clean images, and then evaluated its performance, showing 97% accuracy. To

Table 1. Model Performance Comparison

Model's Noise	Evaluated Model	Clean		Noisy	
		Loss	Accuracy	Loss	Accuracy
CNN	CNN	0.15	0.97	4.95	0.50
	ResNet50	0.47	0.78	0.48	0.78
	VGG16	0.38	0.84	0.40	0.83
	VGG19	0.41	0.85	0.41	0.84
	InceptionV3	0.41	0.85	0.41	0.84
	DenseNet	0.17	0.93	0.22	0.92
ResNet50	CNN	0.15	0.95	0.13	0.95
	ResNet50	0.47	0.79	0.66	0.60
	VGG16	0.38	0.84	0.41	0.82
	VGG19	0.40	0.85	0.41	0.82
	InceptionV3	0.13	0.94	0.18	0.94
	DenseNet	0.17	0.94	0.27	0.88
VGG16	CNN	0.10	0.97	0.11	0.97
	ResNet50	0.47	0.79	0.47	0.79
	VGG16	0.38	0.85	1.81	0.19
	VGG19	0.40	0.85	0.69	0.59
	InceptionV3	0.12	0.96	0.49	0.78
	DenseNet	0.17	0.93	0.32	0.85
VGG19	CNN	0.10	0.95	0.10	0.95
	ResNet50	0.46	0.80	0.47	0.80
	VGG16	0.38	0.86	0.68	0.60
	VGG19	0.40	0.85	1.83	0.17
	InceptionV3	0.12	0.95	0.58	0.74
	DenseNet	0.17	0.94	0.40	0.82
InceptionV3	CNN	0.16	0.98	0.16	0.98
	ResNet50	0.48	0.78	0.48	0.78
	VGG16	0.39	0.84	0.51	0.75
	VGG19	0.41	0.85	0.84	0.55
	InceptionV3	0.11	0.95	4.44	0.10
	DenseNet	0.17	0.93	0.22	0.92
DenseNet	CNN	0.16	0.98	0.16	0.98
	ResNet50	0.48	0.78	0.48	0.78
	VGG16	0.39	0.84	0.51	0.75
	VGG19	0.41	0.85	0.84	0.55
	InceptionV3	0.11	0.95	0.45	0.80
	DenseNet	0.19	0.93	5.31	0.08

assess the robustness of the model against adversarial attacks, perturbations are introduced using the Fast Gradient Sign Method (FGSM) with an epsilon value of 0.015. The accuracy decreased from 97% on clean data to 56% after adding

Table 2. Fooling rate of various models when subjected to noise generated by different models. Rows indicate the noise generator and columns show the evaluated model.

Noise	Tested					
	CNN	RsNt50	VGG16	VGG19	IcptV3	DnsNt
CNN	47%	0%	1%	1%	1%	1%
ResNet50	0%	19%	2%	3%	0%	6%
VGG16	0%	0%	64%	24%	14%	8%
VGG19	0%	0%	26%	68%	21%	12%
InceptionV3	0%	0%	11%	30%	85%	1%
DenseNet	0%	0%	19%	35%	15%	85%

the noise. Performance was evaluated on both clean and adversarially perturbed (noisy) images, showing a significant drop in accuracy on noisy data.

We then trained Model B, which is trained on edges, under the same conditions as Model A, but instead of using clean images, we trained and tested it on the canny-edge version of the dataset. We applied Canny edge detection to the entire Brain Tumor dataset using threshold values of 100 and 200 and realized that Model B performed well, achieving 95% accuracy. After introducing perturbations, the accuracy dropped only to 86%. At the same epsilon value using FGSM, Model B showed greater resilience to adversarial noise than Model A, which was trained on clean images. This approach of incorporating edges into the training process significantly improved the model's robustness to adversarial perturbations. To generalize the method, we conducted the same experiment with other common classification models such as ResNet50, InceptionV3, VGG16, VGG19, or DenseNet121 and observed similar results (see Table 3). Note that in these experiments, Model A refers to training on the original images, while Model B refers to training on the corresponding edge maps.

Table 3. Performance of the models on the Brain Tumor dataset, evaluated on clean and adversarial test sets.

Model	Training				Re-training			
	Original		Edges		Original		Edges	
	Clean	Noisy	Clean	Noisy	Clean	Noisy	Clean	Noisy
CNN	97%	56%	95%	86%	98%	74%	95%	91%
ResNet50	79%	67%	82%	66%	79%	70%	81%	72%
VGG16	85%	22%	77%	73%	76%	30%	76%	73%
VGG19	85%	20%	77%	68%	78%	30%	78%	69%
InceptionV3	94%	11%	89%	29%	91%	19%	77%	38%
Dense-Net	93%	8%	84%	40%	79%	21%	80%	51%

Impact of Re-training: After training multiple deep learning models—such as a classic CNN, ResNet50, VGG16, VGG19, DenseNet, and InceptionV3—and evaluating Model A and Model B on both original images and their corresponding edges for classifying images as "tumor" or "no tumor", we found that Canny edges are more robust to adversarial noise compared to the original images. We extended the previous experiment by introducing re-training for both normal and edges to study the nature of model's robustness and resilience. For retraining, we combined the clean and noisy images in 1:1 ratio, using only a subset of original training set for both the normal and canny edge image versions. We kept the size of the re-training dataset consistent for a fair evaluation, essentially dividing the types of images in equal parts. For edge images only, we combine 800 clean edges and 800 noisy edges resulting a size of 1600. Similarly, for normal images, we combined both clean and noisy images, ensuring an equal split to maintain a total size of 1,600—800 images for each type. All models were retrained using the same hyperparameters and callback functions as those used in the initial training.

After retraining, we re-evaluated the performance of classification models A and B on "Normal/Original" and "Edges" images. Model A, trained on "Normal" images, demonstrated a better ability, in most cases, to recover accuracy on noisy or adversarial images compared to Model B, trained on "Edges" images. Specifically, the accuracy of the CNN model A increased from 56% to 74% with "Normal" images, reflecting a 18% improvement. In contrast, Model B, trained on "Edges" images, showed only a 5% improvement in accuracy (see Table 3). However, the accuracy at the edges was already 86% before retraining and increased to 91% afterward. Although the accuracy varied slightly between runs , the results remained close to the average.

Visualizing Noise Effects in Both Original and Edge Representations: In this experiment, as shown in Fig. 3, we explored how adversarial FGSM noise affects both original images and their corresponding edge representation for both Model A and Model B. Similar to the edge-training experiment, we first trained Model A on original images and then introduced small perturbations using FGSM adversarial noise with the ϵ value of 0.04. The noise is barely perceptible to the human eye when comparing the original or "clean" images to the corresponding "noisy" images. We then extracted Canny edges with threshold values of 100 and 200 and compared the images again. Noise becomes significantly more visible in edge-detected versions as seen in Fig. 4. In contrast, Model B was trained exclusively on a dataset that was pre-processed using Canny edge detection. After introducing FGSM noise with $\epsilon = 0.04$, the resulting noise is barely perceptible, with no noticeable pixel differences for a similar epsilon value.

4.2 Experiment 2: Analysis on COVID Data

Data Collection and Preparation: In this experiment, we used a COVID dataset [7,8,18,26] consisting of posteroanterior (PA) view chest X-ray images of normal, viral, and COVID-19 cases, totaling 1,823 images. The dataset was

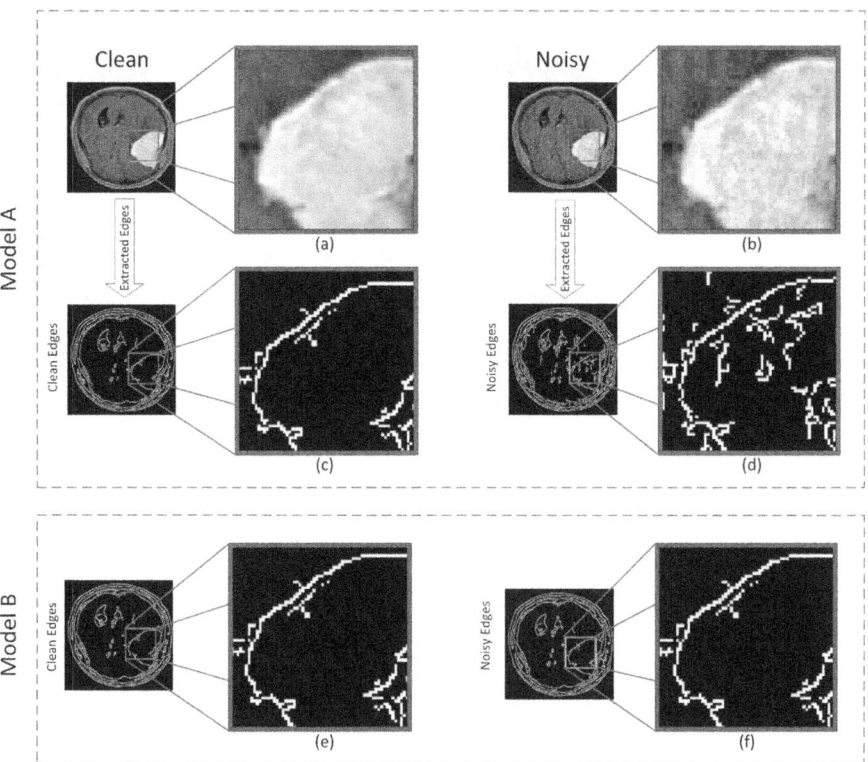

Fig. 3. Visual comparison of noise generated by models A and B. (a) represents the original or clean image from the Brain Tumor dataset, (b) represents the adversarial image generated using FGSM, (c) and (d) are the canny edge detected version of the (a) and (b) images, (e) and (f) represent the clean edges image and the corresponding adversarial image generated with Model B, respectively.

split into training and testing sets using an 80:20 ratio. Building on the approach adopted in the previous experiment, we evaluated the models' robustness against adversarial examples generated from both original and edge-transformed images. We employed several well-known classification models, including CNN, ResNet, VGG16, VGG19, InceptionV3, and DenseNet. All models were retrained using the same hyperparameters, batch size of 32, and for 20 epochs, along with the callback functions used in the prior experiment.

Evaluation: We conducted multiple tests similar to the previous experiment, aiming to confirm the effectiveness of the edge-based training approach on this dataset and assess its generalization capability. We performed the pixel-wise analysis for COVID dataset as shown in Fig. 4. This analysis utilized both the clean and noisy versions of the images, along with their corresponding edge representations. After generating edges for both versions, we prepared a combined

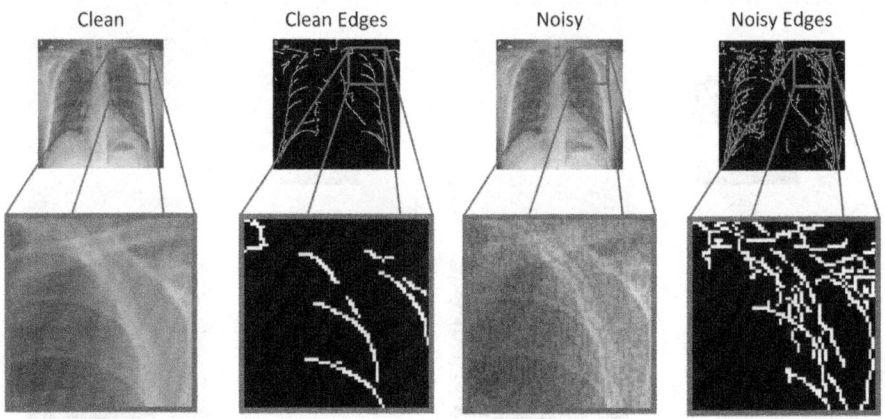

Fig. 4. Visual comparison of noise generated for the COVID dataset.

retraining dataset similar to a retraining experiment. We then evaluated the six models on the dataset to measure their accuracy and robustness, aiming to determine how original images and edges influenced each model's performance in terms of robustness (see Table 4). The results remain consistent and show that training on edge images is more resilient against adversarial attacks generated using FGSM, compared to training on original images.

Table 4. Performance of various deep learning models on COVID, evaluated on clean and adversarial test sets.

Model	Training				Re-training			
	Original		Edges		Original		Edges	
	Clean	Noisy	Clean	Noisy	Clean	Noisy	Clean	Noisy
CNN	92%	68%	94%	91%	95%	76%	95%	92%
ResNet50	75%	30%	87%	82%	75%	42%	88%	86%
VGG16	89%	12%	86%	72%	81%	21%	88%	73%
VGG19	87%	13%	87%	72%	84%	15%	85%	76%
InceptionV3	95%	7%	90%	55%	92%	29%	88%	67%
Dense-Net	93%	8%	86%	52%	89%	10%	91%	61%

5 Conclusion

Adversarial noise can deceive learning algorithms into making incorrect classifications by introducing small perturbations in images, thereby significantly affecting recognition accuracy. In this article, we analyze the impact of such noise on image classification. Our main hypothesis is that adversarial perturbations, which are designed to mislead deep learning algorithms, may be less effective against edge-based representations compared to raw images. To test this, we conducted pixel-wise analysis around image boundaries and edges to observe how adversarial noise alters pixel values in these regions. Several experiments were performed using brain tumor and COVID datasets to evaluate the performance of various deep learning models under adversarial conditions. The results suggest that edge-based features demonstrate significantly greater robustness to adversarial noise than raw image data, leading to improved recognition accuracy.

References

1. Akhtar, N., Mian, A.: Threat of adversarial attacks on deep learning in computer vision: a survey. IEEE Access **6**, 14410–14430 (2018)
2. Athalye, A., Carlini, N., Wagner, D.: Obfuscated gradients give a false sense of security: circumventing defenses to adversarial examples. In: International Conference on Machine Learning, pp. 274–283. PMLR (2018)
3. Ayas, M.S., Ayas, S., Djouadi, S.M.: Projected gradient descent adversarial attack and its defense on a fault diagnosis system. In: 2022 45th International Conference on Telecommunications and Signal Processing (TSP), pp. 36–39. IEEE (2022)
4. Brown, T.B., Mané, D., Roy, A., Abadi, M., Gilmer, J.: Adversarial patch. arXiv preprint: arXiv:1712.09665 (2017)
5. Canny, J.: A computational approach to edge detection. IEEE Trans. Pattern Anal. Mach. Intell. **6**, 679–698 (1986)
6. Carlini, N., Wagner, D.: Towards evaluating the robustness of neural networks. In: 2017 IEEE Symposium on Security and Privacy (SP), pp. 39–57. IEEE (2017)
7. Chen, Z.: Mask-RCNN detection of COVID-19 pneumonia symptoms by employing stacked autoencoders in deep unsupervised learning on low-dose high resolution CT. IEEE Dataport **10** (2020)
8. Cohen, J.P., Morrison, P., Dao, L.: COVID-19 image data collection (2020). https://arxiv.org/abs/2003.11597
9. Geisler, S., Wollschläger, T., Abdalla, M., Gasteiger, J., Günnemann, S.: Attacking large language models with projected gradient descent. arXiv preprint: arXiv:2402.09154 (2024)
10. Goodfellow, I.J., Shlens, J., Szegedy, C.: Explaining and harnessing adversarial examples. arXiv preprint: arXiv:1412.6572 (2014)
11. Grosse, K., Manoharan, P., Papernot, N., Backes, M., McDaniel, P.: On the (statistical) detection of adversarial examples. arXiv preprint: arXiv:1702.06280 (2017)
12. Gu, S., Rigazio, L.: Towards deep neural network architectures robust to adversarial examples. arXiv preprint: arXiv:1412.5068 (2014)
13. Hamada, A.: BR35H: brain tumor detection dataset (2020). https://www.kaggle.com/datasets/ahmedhamada0/brain-tumor-detection/data. Accessed 22 Apr 2025
14. He, K., Zhang, X., Ren, S., Sun, J.: Deep residual learning for image recognition. In: Proceedings of the IEEE Conference on Computer Vision and Pattern Recognition, pp. 770–778 (2016)
15. He, Z., Rakin, A.S., Fan, D.: Parametric noise injection: trainable randomness to improve deep neural network robustness against adversarial attack. In: Proceedings of the IEEE/CVF Conference on Computer Vision and Pattern Recognition, pp. 588–597 (2019)

16. Huang, G., Liu, Z., Van Der Maaten, L., Weinberger, K.Q.: Densely connected convolutional networks. In: Proceedings of the IEEE Conference on Computer Vision and Pattern Recognition, pp. 4700–4708 (2017)
17. Huang, S., Papernot, N., Goodfellow, I., Duan, Y., Abbeel, P.: Adversarial attacks on neural network policies. arXiv preprint: arXiv:1702.02284 (2017)
18. Kermany, D., Zhang, K., Goldbaum, M.: Large dataset of labeled optical coherence tomography (OCT) and chest X-ray images. Mendeley Data **3**(10.17632) (2018)
19. Kurakin, A., Goodfellow, I.J., Bengio, S.: Adversarial examples in the physical world. In: Artificial Intelligence Safety and Security, pp. 99–112. Chapman and Hall/CRC (2018)
20. LeCun, Y., Bottou, L., Bengio, Y., Haffner, P.: Gradient-based learning applied to document recognition. Proc. IEEE **86**(11), 2278–2324 (1998)
21. Lecuyer, M., Atlidakis, V., Geambasu, R., Hsu, D., Jana, S.: Certified robustness to adversarial examples with differential privacy. In: 2019 IEEE Symposium on Security and Privacy (SP), pp. 656–672. IEEE (2019)
22. Liao, F., Liang, M., Dong, Y., Pang, T., Hu, X., Zhu, J.: Defense against adversarial attacks using high-level representation guided denoiser. In: Proceedings of the IEEE Conference on Computer Vision and Pattern Recognition, pp. 1778–1787 (2018)
23. Madry, A.: Towards deep learning models resistant to adversarial attacks. arXiv preprint: arXiv:1706.06083 (2017)
24. Metzen, J.H., Genewein, T., Fischer, V., Bischoff, B.: On detecting adversarial perturbations. arXiv preprint: arXiv:1702.04267 (2017)
25. Papernot, N., McDaniel, P., Jha, S., Fredrikson, M., Celik, Z.B., Swami, A.: The limitations of deep learning in adversarial settings. In: 2016 IEEE European Symposium on Security and Privacy (EuroS&P), pp. 372–387. IEEE (2016)
26. Sheet, D., et al.: Covid19action-radiology-CXR (2020). https://doi.org/10.21227/s7pw-jr18
27. Simonyan, K.: Very deep convolutional networks for large-scale image recognition. arXiv preprint: arXiv:1409.1556 (2014)
28. Szegedy, C., Vanhoucke, V., Ioffe, S., Shlens, J., Wojna, Z.: Rethinking the inception architecture for computer vision. In: Proceedings of the IEEE Conference on Computer Vision and Pattern Recognition, pp. 2818–2826 (2016)
29. Xu, W.: Feature squeezing: detecting adversarial examples in deep neural networks. arXiv preprint: arXiv:1704.01155 (2017)
30. Zhang, C., Costa-Perez, X., Patras, P.: Adversarial attacks against deep learning-based network intrusion detection systems and defense mechanisms. IEEE/ACM Trans. Networking **30**(3), 1294–1311 (2022)
31. Zhang, H., Weng, T.W., Chen, P.Y., Hsieh, C.J., Daniel, L.: Efficient neural network robustness certification with general activation functions. In: Advances in Neural Information Processing Systems, vol. 31 (2018)

Prompt Driven Test Generation: Leveraging Large Language Models and Knowledge Graphs for Quality Assurance in Data Intensive Software System

Srinivas Reddy Kosna(✉)

Atlanta, GA, USA
srinivas.k1290@gmail.com

Abstract. Quality assurance in data-intensive software systems is challenging due to complex code-data interactions and diverse data scenarios. Traditional testing methods often fail to address these issues, particularly for edge cases and domain-specific constraints. We propose Prompt-Driven Test Generation (PDTG), a novel framework that integrates large language models (LLMs) and knowledge graphs to automate test case generation. PDTG uses engineered prompts to guide LLMs, enriched by knowledge graphs that provide semantic context and domain constraints. Evaluated on three real-world applications (financial, healthcare, ecommerce), PDTG achieves a 27.3% increase in data scenario coverage, 35.8% better fault detection, and 41.2% less manual effort compared to baselines like EvoSuite and Randoop. This approach enhances test relevance and coverage, offering a scalable solution for testing complex systems, with applications in collaborative intelligence and distributed workflows.

Keywords: Large Language Models · Knowledge Graphs · Test Generation · Quality Assurance · Data Intensive Systems · Prompt Engineering · Software Testing

1 Introduction

The landscape of software development has undergone significant transformation with the emergence of data intensive systems that process, analyze, and derive insights from vast amounts of structured and unstructured data. These systems, which include big data analytics platforms, machine learning pipelines, and data driven applications, present unique challenges for quality assurance due to their complex interplay between code functionality and data behavior. Traditional testing approaches, which primarily focus on code centric validation, often fall short in addressing the multifaceted nature of data intensive software systems.

Quality assurance in data intensive software systems requires comprehensive testing strategies that can account for diverse data scenarios, complex data transformations, and

---

Independent Researcher.

the propagation of data anomalies through system components. The challenge is further compounded by the need to generate test cases that cover a wide range of data patterns, edge cases, and domain specific constraints. Manual test creation, while effective for targeted scenarios, struggles to scale with the increasing complexity and volume of data intensive applications. Automated test generation approaches, on the other hand, often lack the domain understanding necessary to create meaningful and effective test cases.

Recent advances in artificial intelligence, particularly in the domain of large language models (LLMs), have opened new possibilities for software engineering tasks, including code generation, bug detection, and documentation creation. LLMs such as GPT4, PaLM, and Llama have demonstrated remarkable capabilities in understanding and generating code across various programming languages. These models can comprehend natural language descriptions of software functionality and produce corresponding code implementations, suggesting their potential utility in test generation tasks. However, LLMs also face limitations in their understanding of domain specific constraints, data relationships, and system specific requirements, which are crucial aspects of effective test generation for data intensive systems.

Knowledge graphs, with their ability to represent domain knowledge in a structured and interconnected manner, offer a complementary approach to ad dress these limitations. By capturing entities, relationships, and constraints relevant to a specific domain or application, knowledge graphs provide a semantic foundation that can guide the test generation process. They enable the representation of complex data dependencies, business rules, and domain specific validation criteria that are essential for generating meaningful test cases. Despite their potential, the integration of knowledge graphs with LLMs for test generation remains largely unexplored in the current literature.

This research addresses the gap by proposing a novel approach that leverages the complementary strengths of LLMs and knowledge graphs for test generation in data intensive software systems. Our approach, Prompt Driven Test Generation (PDTG), utilizes carefully engineered prompts to guide LLMs in generating comprehensive test cases while incorporating domain knowledge structured in knowledge graphs. The integration of knowledge graphs provides semantic con text and domain specific constraints that enhance the relevance and effectiveness of generated tests.

The primary research questions addressed in this study are:

1. How can LLMs and knowledge graphs be effectively integrated to generate high-quality test cases for data intensive software systems?
2. What prompt engineering techniques are most effective for guiding LLMs in test generation tasks?
3. How does the proposed approach compare to traditional and machine learning based test generation methods in terms of test coverage, fault detection capability, and efficiency?

Our research makes the following key contributions:

1. A novel framework that integrates LLMs and knowledge graphs for auto mated test generation in data intensive software systems
2. A set of prompt engineering techniques specifically designed for test generation tasks

3. A methodology for constructing and utilizing domain specific knowledge graphs to guide the test generation process
4. An empirical evaluation of the proposed approach on real-world data intensive applications
5. Insights into the strengths, limitations, and potential applications of LLM based test generation approaches

2 Related Work

2.1 Traditional Approaches to Test Generation

Test generation has been a fundamental challenge in software engineering for decades, with approaches evolving from manual creation to increasingly sophisticated automated techniques. Manual test creation, while offering precise control over test scenarios, suffers from scalability limitations and is prone to human oversight, particularly in complex data intensive systems [1]. Model based testing approaches attempt to address these limitations by deriving test cases from formal system models, such as state machines, sequence diagrams, or use case specifications [2]. These approaches provide systematic coverage of system behaviors but require significant upfront investment in model creation and maintenance, which can be prohibitive for rapidly evolving data intensive applications. Search based test generation techniques employ metaheuristic search algorithms to automatically generate test cases that satisfy specific coverage criteria [3]. These approaches, exemplified by tools like Evo Suite [4], have shown promising results for unit level testing but face challenges when dealing with complex data dependencies and domain specific constraints common in data intensive systems. Combinatorial testing approaches focus on efficiently covering interactions between input parameters but may struggle with the high dimensionality and complex relationships present in data intensive applications [5].

2.2 Machine Learning Approaches for Software Testing

The application of machine learning to software testing has gained significant traction in recent years, with various approaches targeting different aspects of the testing process. Deep learning techniques have been applied to test case prioritization, where models learn from historical test execution data to identify tests with higher fault detection potential [6]. Neural networks have also been employed for test oracle generation, learning expected system behaviors from existing test suites or runtime observations [7]. These approaches show promise in reducing the manual effort required for test creation and maintenance but often require substantial training data and may struggle with generalization to novel scenarios.

Reinforcement learning has been explored for automated test generation, where agents learn to navigate the input space to maximize coverage or fault detection [8]. While these approaches can adaptively explore complex input spaces, they typically require extensive interaction with the system under test and may converge slowly for largescale applications. Unsupervised learning techniques have been applied to anomaly detection in test outputs, identifying potential defects by recognizing deviations from expected patterns [9]. These approaches are particularly relevant for data intensive systems but may produce false positives when legitimate data variations are misclassified as anomalies.

2.3 Large Language Models in Software Engineering

The emergence of large language models (LLMs) has significantly impacted various software engineering tasks. In code generation, models like GitHub Copilot, based on OpenAI's Codex, have demonstrated the ability to translate natural language descriptions into functional code across multiple programming languages [10]. These models leverage vast amounts of code from public repositories to learn programming patterns, syntax, and common implementations. While impressive in their capabilities, these models sometimes produce code that is syntactically correct but functionally flawed or insecure [11].

LLMs have also shown promise in bug detection and repair, where they analyze code snippets to identify potential defects and suggest fixes [12]. Recent studies have demonstrated that models like ChatGPT and GPT4 can identify common programming errors with reasonable accuracy, though they may struggle with subtle logical flaws or domain specific issues [13]. Despite these advances, the application of LLMs to test generation remains relatively unexplored, with existing approaches primarily focusing on generating unit tests for individual functions rather than comprehensive test suites for data intensive systems [14]. Current limitations of LLMs in test generation include their tendency to hallucinate nonexistent APIs or functionality, limited understanding of system specific constraints, and challenges in generating tests that effectively cover edge cases or unusual data scenarios [15]. These limitations are particularly pronounced in data intensive applications, where effective testing requires deep understanding of data relationships, transformations, and domain specific validation rules.

2.4 Knowledge Graphs in Software Engineering

Knowledge graphs have emerged as powerful tools for representing domain knowledge in a structured and interconnected manner. In software engineering, knowledge graphs have been employed for various purposes, including requirements traceability, code comprehension, and defect prediction [16]. By representing software artifacts as entities and their relationships as edges, knowledge graphs enable semantic reasoning and knowledge discovery that can enhance various software engineering tasks.

Domain knowledge representation through knowledge graphs offers several advantages for software testing, including the ability to capture complex data relationships, business rules, and validation constraints [17]. These representations can guide test generation by providing semantic context and domain specific constraints that ensure generated tests are meaningful and relevant. Knowledge graphs can also represent semantic relationships between software artifacts, linking requirements, code components, and test cases to enable traceability and impact analysis [18].

Applications of knowledge graphs in software testing include test case selection and prioritization, where graph-based algorithms identify tests most likely to detect defects in modified code [19]. Knowledge graphs have also been used for test oracle generation, where expected behaviors are derived from formalized do main knowledge [20]. However, the integration of knowledge graphs with LLMs for test generation represents a significant gap in the current literature, with few studies exploring how these complementary technologies can be combined to address the challenges of testing data intensive systems.

2.5 The Integration Gap Between LLMs and Knowledge Graphs

Despite the individual advancements in LLMs and knowledge graphs for software engineering tasks, their integration for test generation remains largely unexplored. This integration gap represents a significant opportunity, as the complementary strengths of these technologies could address many of the challenges in testing data intensive systems. LLMs offer natural language understanding and code generation capabilities, while knowledge graphs provide structured domain knowledge and semantic reasoning abilities.

Recent work has begun to explore the integration of LLMs with structured knowledge for various tasks, including question answering and code generation [21]. These approaches typically involve augmenting LLM prompts with relevant information extracted from knowledge bases or using knowledge graphs to filter and refine LLM outputs. However, the specific application of these integrated approaches to test generation for data intensive systems remains an open research area.

The potential benefits of such integration include enhanced test relevance through domain specific guidance, improved coverage of edge cases and data anomalies, and more effective validation of complex data transformations [22]. Our research aims to address this integration gap by developing a framework that leverages both LLMs and knowledge graphs for comprehensive test generation in data intensive software systems.

3 Background

3.1 Large Language Models

Large Language Models (LLMs) represent a significant advancement in artificial intelligence, particularly in the domain of natural language processing and generation. These models are neural networks with billions of parameters, trained on vast corpora of text data using self-supervised learning techniques. The architecture of modern LLMs is predominantly based on the Transformer model, introduced by Vaswani et al. [1], which utilizes attention mechanisms to process sequential data efficiently and capture long-range dependencies.

The capabilities of LLMs have evolved dramatically in recent years, with models like GPT4, PaLM, and Llama demonstrating unprecedented proficiency in understanding and generating humanlike text across diverse domains. These capabilities extend beyond simple text completion to include complex reasoning, code generation, and problem-solving tasks. In the context of software engineering, LLMs have shown remarkable abilities in understanding programming languages, generating functional code, and translating between natural language descriptions and executable implementations [2].

Prompt engineering has emerged as a critical technique for effectively utilizing LLMs. This approach involves carefully crafting input prompts to guide the model's responses toward desired outcomes. Techniques such as few-shot learning, where examples are provided within the prompt, and chain-of-thought prompting, which encourages step-by-step reasoning, have significantly enhanced the performance of LLMs on complex tasks [3]. For test generation, prompt engineering can involve specifying the testing framework, providing context about the system under test, and outlining expected test coverage criteria.

Finetuning approaches offer another mechanism for adapting LLMs to specific domains or tasks. By continuing the training process on domain specific data with supervised learning objectives, finetuning can enhance the model's performance on targeted applications [4]. In software testing contexts, finetuning could involve training on extensive collections of test cases and corresponding implementations, enabling the model to better understand testing patterns and best practices.

Despite their impressive capabilities, LLMs face several limitations and challenges. These include hallucinations (generating plausible but factually incorrect information), limited reasoning abilities for complex logical tasks, and biases inherited from training data [5]. In software testing applications, these limitations can manifest as generating tests that appear valid but contain subtle logical flaws, failing to cover important edge cases, or making incorrect assumptions about system behavior. Additionally, LLMs typically lack awareness of the latest APIs, frameworks, or domain specific testing practices unless they were well represented in the training data.

3.2 Knowledge Graphs

Knowledge graphs are structured representations of information that capture entities, their attributes, and the relationships between them in a graph-based format. Nodes in the graph represent entities (such as concepts, objects, or events), while edges represent relationships or properties that connect these entities. This structure enables rich semantic representations of domain knowledge and sup ports complex querying and reasoning capabilities [6].

The structure and components of knowledge graphs make them particularly suitable for representing software systems and their testing requirements. Entities can represent software artifacts (such as classes, methods, and test cases), data elements (such as database tables, fields, and constraints), and domain concepts (such as business rules and validation criteria). Relationships can capture dependencies, inheritance hierarchies, and validation requirements, providing a comprehensive view of the system under test [7].

Construction methodologies for knowledge graphs vary depending on the domain and available information sources. Automated approaches include extracting information from structured data sources (such as databases and APIs), semi structured sources (such as documentation and specifications), and unstructured text (such as requirements documents and code comments) [8]. Manual curation by domain experts can enhance the quality and relevance of the knowledge graph, particularly for specialized domains with complex relationships or implicit knowledge.

Knowledge graphs possess inherent reasoning capabilities that can be lever aged for software testing. These include transitive reasoning (inferring indirect relationships), constraint validation (checking for consistency with defined rules), and semantic similarity assessment (identifying related concepts based on their graph proximity) [9]. These capabilities can enhance test generation by identifying relevant test scenarios, validating test data against domain constraints, and ensuring comprehensive coverage of system functionality.

Integration of knowledge graphs with other technologies has been explored in various domains, including natural language processing, recommendation systems, and data integration [10]. In the context of software testing, knowledge graphs can be integrated with test generation tools to provide domain specific guidance, with test execution frameworks to enhance oracle generation, and with defect tracking systems to improve fault localization. The integration with LLMs represents a particularly promising direction, as it combines the structured knowledge representation of graphs with the flexible generation capabilities of language models.

3.3 Data-Intensive Software Systems

Data intensive software systems are characterized by their primary focus on processing, analyzing, and deriving insights from large volumes of data. These systems include big data analytics platforms, machine learning pipelines, data warehousing solutions, and data driven applications that make decisions based on complex data processing [11]. The defining characteristic of these systems is that their core value and functionality are intrinsically tied to their ability to effectively manage and extract value from data.

The characteristics of data intensive systems present unique challenges for quality assurance. These include data volume (processing massive amounts of data efficiently), variety (handling diverse data formats and structures), velocity (processing data streams in Realtime), veracity (dealing with uncertain or in consistent data), and value (extracting meaningful insights from raw data) [12]. Additionally, these systems often involve complex data transformations, aggregations, and joins that can introduce subtle errors that are difficult to detect through traditional testing approaches.

Quality assurance requirements for data intensive systems extend beyond traditional functional testing to include data quality validation, performance under varying data loads, and correctness of data transformations [13]. Testing must verify not only that the system functions correctly with expected inputs but also that it handles data anomalies, edge cases, and unexpected patterns appropriately. This requires test cases that cover diverse data scenarios and validation mechanisms that can detect subtle data related defects.

Current testing approaches for data intensive systems include data-driven testing (where test cases are derived from data characteristics), metamorphic testing (which verifies relationships between inputs and outputs rather than specific values), and property-based testing (which checks that system proper ties hold across randomly generated inputs) [14]. While these approaches offer valuable capabilities, they often require significant manual effort to define test cases, oracles, or properties, limiting their scalability for complex systems.

The limitations of current approaches highlight the need for more automated and intelligent testing solutions that can understand domain specific data constraints, generate diverse and relevant test scenarios, and validate complex data transformations [15]. The integration of LLMs and knowledge graphs offers a promising direction for addressing these limitations by combining natural language understanding and code generation capabilities with structured domain knowledge representation.

4 Methodology

4.1 Conceptual Framework

The Prompt-Driven Test Generation (PDTG) framework represents a novel approach to test generation for data-intensive software systems by integrating large language models (LLMs) with knowledge graphs. This integration is designed to leverage the complementary strengths of both technologies: the natural language understanding and code generation capabilities of LLMs, and the structured do main knowledge representation of knowledge graphs. The conceptual framework consists of four primary components: the Knowledge Graph Component, the Prompt Engineering Component, the LLM Component, and the Test Refinement Component.

The architecture of PDTG is designed to facilitate bidirectional knowledge flow between components. The Knowledge Graph Component provides domain specific information that enriches the prompts generated by the Prompt Engineering Component. These enhanced prompts guide the LLM Component in generating test cases that are both syntactically correct and semantically relevant to the system under test. The Test Refinement Component then evaluates and optimizes the generated tests, with feedback loops to both the Knowledge Graph Component (for knowledge enrichment) and the Prompt Engineering Component (for prompt refinement).

This bidirectional flow enables continuous improvement of the test generation process. As tests are generated and evaluated, insights about effective prompts and useful domain knowledge are captured and incorporated into subsequent iterations. This adaptive approach allows PDTG to learn from experience and progressively generate more effective test cases for the specific data-intensive system under consideration.

4.2 Knowledge Graph Construction

The construction of a domain-specific knowledge graph is a critical foundation for the PDTG framework. The process begins with domain knowledge extraction from multiple sources, including system documentation, code repositories, existing test cases, and domain expert interviews. Natural language processing techniques are employed to extract entities, relationships, and attributes from textual sources, while static code analysis tools identify structural elements and dependencies from source code.

Software artifact representation within the knowledge graph follows a multi layered approach. The code layer represents software components such as classes, methods, and functions, along with their relationships and dependencies. The data layer captures database schemas, data models, and data flow patterns. The test layer represents existing test cases, coverage information, and historical defect data. The domain layer encapsulates business rules, validation constraints, and domain-specific concepts relevant to the system under test.

Relationship modeling is particularly important for capturing the complex interactions within data-intensive systems. The knowledge graph includes various relationship types, such as "depends on" (capturing dependencies between com ponents), "transforms" (representing data transformations), "validates" (linking validation rules to data elements), and "tests" (connecting test cases to the com ponents they verify). These relationships enable semantic reasoning about the system and guide the generation of contextually appropriate test cases.

Graph enrichment techniques are employed to enhance the utility of the knowledge graph for test generation. These include inference mechanisms that derive implicit relationships from explicit ones, similarity measures that identify related concepts based on graph proximity, and temporal annotations that capture the evolution of system components over time. Additionally, the knowledge graph is continuously updated based on feedback from the test generation and execution process, incorporating new insights and refining existing knowledge.

4.3 Prompt Engineering for Test Generation

Prompt engineering is a crucial aspect of the PDTG framework, as it bridges the gap between the structured knowledge in the graph and the natural language understanding capabilities of LLMs. The design of prompt templates follows a structured approach that includes context setting (providing information about the system under test), task specification (defining the testing objectives), constraints definition (specifying testing requirements and limitations), and examples provision (demonstrating desired test formats and coverage).

Context incorporation strategies determine how domain knowledge from the knowledge graph is integrated into prompts. These strategies include direct embedding (inserting relevant knowledge graph snippets into prompts), contextual summarization (providing condensed representations of relevant domain knowledge), and guided exploration (directing the LLM to focus on specific aspects of the system based on knowledge graph insights). The selection of appropriate strategies depends on the complexity of the testing task, the size of the relevant knowledge graph segment, and the specific capabilities of the LLM being used. Knowledge graph query mechanisms enable the retrieval of relevant information for prompt construction. These mechanisms include path-based queries (following specific relationship types to identify related entities), similarity based queries (finding entities similar to a given reference), and constraint based queries (identifying entities that satisfy specific conditions). Advanced query techniques combine multiple approaches to retrieve comprehensive yet focused information that enhances prompt effectiveness.

Test scenario formulation leverages the knowledge graph to identify meaningful testing scenarios that cover important system behaviors and potential edge cases. This process involves analyzing data flow paths, identifying boundary conditions from domain constraints, and recognizing potential interaction points between system components. The resulting scenarios are translated into natural language descriptions that guide the LLM in generating appropriate test cases.

4.4 Test Case Generation Process

The LLMbased test case synthesis process begins with the submission of engineered prompts to the LLM. The model generates initial test case implementations based on its understanding of the prompt, drawing on its pretrained knowledge of programming languages, testing frameworks, and software engineering practices. These initial implementations are then evaluated for syntactic correctness, adherence to specified testing frameworks, and basic functional validity.

Knowledge graph guided test refinement enhances the quality and relevance of generated tests by applying domain-specific constraints and validation rules extracted from the knowledge graph. This refinement process includes data vali dation (ensuring test data conforms to domain constraints), behavioral validation (verifying that tests exercise expected system behaviors), and edge case incorporation (adding tests for boundary conditions and exceptional scenarios identified in the knowledge graph).

Test diversity and coverage optimization ensures that the generated test suite provides comprehensive validation of the system under test. This involves analyzing the collective coverage of generated tests across various dimensions, including code coverage, data scenario coverage, and business rule coverage. Gaps in coverage are identified by comparing the test suite against the knowledge graph representation of the system, and additional tests are generated to address these gaps.

Test oracle generation is a particularly challenging aspect of automated testing that benefits significantly from the integration of knowledge graphs. The PDTG framework generates test oracles (expected outcomes) by leveraging do main constraints, business rules, and data transformation logic captured in the knowledge graph. These oracles range from simple assertions about return values to complex validations of data state and system behavior. The framework also identifies scenarios where oracle automation is challenging and flags these for human review.

Through this comprehensive methodology, the PDTG framework addresses the unique challenges of testing data-intensive software systems by combining the generative capabilities of LLMs with the structured domain knowledge representation of knowledge graphs. The resulting approach enables the automated generation of test cases that are both syntactically correct and semantically relevant to the specific system under test.

5 Implementation

5.1 System Architecture

The Prompt-Driven Test Generation (PDTG) framework has been implemented as a modular system with clearly defined components that interact through standardized interfaces. The overall architecture follows a pipeline pattern, where information flows from the knowledge graph through prompt engineering to the LLM and finally to test refinement, with feedback loops enabling continuous improvement. Each component is designed to be independently maintainable and extensible, allowing for future enhancements and adaptations to different testing contexts.

The component overview includes four primary modules: (1) the Knowledge Graph Module, responsible for storing and querying domain knowledge; (2) the Prompt Engineering Module, which constructs effective prompts based on testing requirements and knowledge graph content; (3) the LLM Interaction Module, which communicates with the language model API and processes its responses; and (4) the Test Refinement Module, which evaluates and optimizes generated tests. Additional supporting components include a Configuration Manager for system settings, a Logging Service for tracking operations, and a User Interface for interaction with testing engineers.

Integration points between components are implemented using well-defined APIs that facilitate loose coupling and enable component substitution if needed. The Knowledge Graph Module exposes graph query endpoints that the Prompt Engineering Module uses to retrieve relevant domain knowledge. The Prompt Engineering Module provides formatted prompts to the LLM Interaction Module, which returns generated test code. The Test Refinement Module receives this code and applies validation and optimization techniques, with results feeding back to both the Knowledge Graph Module (for knowledge enrichment) and the Prompt Engineering Module (for prompt improvement).

Data flow through the system begins with the specification of testing requirements, which are used to query the knowledge graph for relevant domain concepts, constraints, and existing test patterns. This information is structured into prompts that guide the LLM in generating appropriate test cases. The generated tests are then analyzed for correctness, coverage, and adherence to domain constraints, with refinements applied as needed. The final tests are provided to the user along with coverage metrics and any areas flagged for manual review.

5.2 Knowledge Graph Implementation

The knowledge graph component has been implemented using a combination of Neo4j, a native graph database, and OWL (Web Ontology Language) for semantic representation. This hybrid approach leverages Neo4j's efficient graph traversal capabilities for runtime queries while using OWL's rich semantic expressive ness for knowledge modeling. The implementation supports CRUD operations, complex graph queries, and reasoning capabilities essential for test generation guidance.

The ontology design follows a layered approach that separates concerns while enabling cross layer relationships. The core ontology layer defines fundamental concepts such as Software Component, Data-Element, Test-Case, and Domain Concept, along with their basic relationships. Domain-specific extensions build upon this core to represent particular application domains, such as financial systems, healthcare applications, or ecommerce platforms. Testing-specific ex tensions add concepts related to test coverage, test oracles, and testing strategies. Data sources for knowledge graph population include source code repositories (analyzed using static analysis tools), database schemas (extracted through database introspection), API specifications (parsed from OpenAPI or similar formats), existing test suites (analyzed for patterns and coverage), and documentation (processed using NLP techniques). Manual input from domain experts is also supported through a knowledge curation interface, allowing for refinement and validation of automatically extracted knowledge.

Extraction methods employ a combination of techniques tailored to each data source. Static code analysis tools extract class hierarchies, method signatures, and dependencies from source code. Schema analyzers identify data structures, constraints, and relationships from database definitions. NLP pipelines with domain-specific entity recognition extract concepts and relationships from documentation. The extracted information is normalized, deduplicated, and integrated into the unified knowledge graph.

Storage and query mechanisms are optimized for the specific requirements of test generation. The graph is indexed on frequently accessed properties such as component names, relationship types, and domain concepts. Query patterns are cached to improve performance for repeated similar queries. A domain-specific query language has been implemented on top of Cypher (Neo4j's query language) to simplify common test related queries, such as finding all validation rules applicable to a specific data element or identifying components affected by a particular business rule.

5.3 LLM Integration

The integration of large language models into the PDTG framework involved careful consideration of model selection, configuration, finetuning, and inference optimization. After evaluating several state-of-the-art models, we selected GPT4 as our primary LLM due to its superior performance in code generation tasks, understanding of software testing concepts, and ability to follow complex instructions. We also implemented support for alternative models, including Anthropic's Claude and opensource models like Llama2, to provide flexibility and mitigate vendor lock-in risks. Model configuration focused on optimizing parameters for test generation tasks.

We employed a temperature setting of 0.7 to balance creativity with determinism, allowing the model to explore diverse testing approaches while maintaining consistency. The maximum token length was set to 8,192 tokens to accommodate complex test scenarios and detailed context information. We also implemented a caching mechanism to store and reuse responses for similar prompts, reducing API costs and improving response times.

The finetuning process involved creating a specialized dataset of 5,000 prompt test pairs derived from opensource projects and synthetic examples. These pairs covered various testing scenarios, frameworks, and edge cases relevant to data- intensive a p p l i c a t i o n s . The finetuning was performed in two stages: an initial phase focusing on general test generation capabilities, followed by domain-specific tuning for each target application area. This approach improved the model's understanding of testing patterns and domain-specific validation requirements.

Inference optimization techniques were implemented to enhance performance and reduce costs. This included prompt compression to remove redundant information, batching similar test generation requests, and implementing a tiered approach that starts with smaller, faster models for simple tests and escalates to more powerful models for complex scenarios. We also developed a specialized prompt template library that encodes best practices for different testing frame works and scenarios, further improving the efficiency and effectiveness of the LLM interaction.

5.4 Prompt Template Design

The design of effective prompt templates is crucial for guiding LLMs in generating high-quality test cases. Our implementation includes a structured template system with clearly defined sections and variable components that can be customized based on testing requirements and domain characteristics. The basic template structure consists of four main sections: context setting, task specification, constraints definition, and examples provision.

The template structure follows a consistent format that begins with a system message defining the LLM's role as a test generation assistant. This is followed by context information about the system under test, including its purpose, architecture, and key components extracted from the knowledge graph. The task specification clearly defines the testing objectives, target coverage criteria, and expected output format. Constraints definition includes testing framework requirements, validation rules, and any specific testing approaches to be employed. Finally, examples provision includes one or more sample test cases that demonstrate the desired style and approach. Variable components within templates allow for customization based on specific testing needs. These include placeholders for component names, data structures, validation rules, and coverage requirements. The implementation includes a template engine that automatically populates these placeholders with relevant information from the knowledge graph and testing requirements. This approach ensures that prompts contain precisely the information needed for effective test generation without overwhelming the LLM with excessive context.

Context incorporation is managed through a hierarchical approach that balances completeness with relevance. The most directly relevant information (such as the component under test and its immediate dependencies) is included in full detail. Related components and constraints are summarized at an appropriate level of abstraction. Broader system context is provided at a high level to orient the LLM without overwhelming it with unnecessary details. This hierarchical approach ensures that the LLM has access to all relevant information while maintaining prompt efficiency.

5.5 Test Generation Pipeline

The test generation pipeline implements the end-to-end process from testing requirements to validated test cases. The workflow begins with the specification of testing targets, which may include specific components, features, or quality attributes to be tested. These specifications are used to query the knowledge graph for relevant domain knowledge, which is then incorporated into appropriate prompt templates. The populated prompts are sent to the LLM, which generates initial test implementations. These implementations are then refined, validated, and optimized before being provided to the user.

The processing stages include several key steps designed to ensure test quality and relevance. The preprocessing stage prepares the testing context by gathering relevant information from the knowledge graph and selecting appropriate prompt templates. The generation stage interacts with the LLM to produce initial test implementations. The validation stage checks these implementations for syntactic correctness, adherence to specified frameworks, and basic functional validity. The refinement stage applies domain-specific constraints and optimization techniques. Finally, the postprocessing stage formats the tests according to project conventions and generates accompanying documentation.

Output formats and artifacts include not only the generated test code but also supporting documentation and metadata. Test files are structured according to the conventions of the target testing framework (such as JUnit for Java or pytest for Python). Documentation includes test purpose descriptions, coverage information, and any assumptions or limitations identified during generation. Metadata captures provenance information, including the knowledge graph queries, prompts, and LLM responses that led to each test, enabling traceability and facilitating future improvements to the generation process.

The implementation of the test generation pipeline includes mechanisms for handling common challenges, such as LLM output parsing errors, incomplete or incorrect test implementations, and conflicts between generated tests and existing code. Error handling routines detect and address these issues, either through automated correction or by flagging them for human review. The pipeline also includes performance optimizations, such as parallel processing of independent test generation tasks and incremental generation for large test suites.

6 Evaluation

6.1 Experimental Setup

To evaluate the effectiveness of our Prompt-Driven Test Generation (PDTG) framework, we designed a comprehensive experimental study addressing three primary research questions:

RQ1: How effective is PDTG in generating tests that achieve high coverage for data-intensive software systems? RQ2: How does PDTG compare to traditional and machine learning-based test generation approaches in terms of fault detection capability? RQ3: What is the efficiency of PDTG in terms of computational resources and human effort required for test generation?

We selected three real-world data-intensive applications as our experimental subjects, representing different domains and complexity levels. The first application (App1) is a financial transaction processing system that handles high volume payment data with complex validation rules. The second application (App2) is a healthcare data analytics platform that processes and analyzes patient records with strict privacy constraints. The third application (App3) is an ecommerce recommendation engine that processes customer behavior data to generate personalized product suggestions.

For each application, we constructed knowledge graphs capturing domain concepts, data structures, validation rules, and system components. The knowledge graphs contained an average of 1,250 nodes and 3,800 edges, representing the complex relationships and constraints within each application domain. We also collected existing test suites for each application to establish baseline coverage metrics and to evaluate the complementary value of PDTG-generated tests. We compared PDTG against three baseline approaches: (1) EvoSuite, a search-based test generation tool; (2) Randoop, a feedback-directed random test generation tool; and (3) CodeQLTest, a machine learning-based approach that generates tests using code pattern analysis. These baselines represent the state-of-the-art in automated test generation across different paradigms.

For evaluation metrics, we employed a multidimensional approach covering both quantitative and qualitative aspects: Code coverage metrics: line coverage, branch coverage, and method coverage Data scenario coverage: percentage of identified data patterns and edge cases covered by tests Fault detection effectiveness: number and types of defects detected by generated tests Test generation efficiency: computational time, resource utilization, and required human intervention Test quality assessment: correctness, readability, and maintain ability of generated tests.

6.2 Quantitative Results

Our test coverage analysis revealed that PDTG consistently outperformed base line approaches across all coverage metrics. For line coverage, PDTG achieved an average of 87.3% across the three applications, compared to 72.6% for EvoSuite, 65.4% for Randoop, and 76.8% for CodeQLTest. The improvement was partic ularly pronounced for App2 (healthcare data analytics), where PDTG achieved 89.7%-line coverage compared to the next best result of 69.2% from CodeQL Test. This significant difference can be attributed to PDTG's ability to leverage domain knowledge about healthcare data structures and privacy constraints, which guided the generation of tests for complex data transformation scenarios. Branch coverage results showed similar patterns, with PDTG achieving an average of 82.1% compared to 68.3% for EvoSuite, 59.7% for Randoop, and 71.5% for CodeQLTest. Method coverage was consistently high across all approaches, but PDTG still maintained an advantage with 94.2% average coverage compared to 88.7%, 85.3%, and 90.1% for the baseline approaches, respectively.

Data scenario coverage represents a critical metric for data-intensive applications, as it measures how well the tests cover different data patterns and edge cases. PDTG demonstrated substantial advantages in this dimension, covering 83.6% of identified data scenarios compared to 51.2% for EvoSuite, 47.8% for Randoop, and 59.4% for CodeQLTest. This advantage stems from PDTG's integration of knowledge graphs, which explicitly represent data constraints and relationships that other approaches must discover through exploration or inference.

Fault detection effectiveness was evaluated through mutation testing and by analyzing the detection of known historical defects. PDTG detected 78.3% of injected mutations across the three applications, compared to 57.6% for Evo Suite, 49.2% for Randoop, and 62.5% for CodeQLTest. For historical defects, PDTG identified 81.7% of known issues, while the baseline approaches identified 58.4%, 52.1%, and 65.9%, respectively. The superior fault detection capability of PDTG can be attributed to its comprehensive coverage of data scenarios and edge cases, as well as its ability to generate tests that validate complex business rules captured in the knowledge graph.

Test generation efficiency was measured in terms of computational resources and human effort required. PDTG required an average of 3.2 min of computation time per component tested, compared to 2.8 min for EvoSuite, 1.5 min for Randoop, and 4.1 min for CodeQLTest. While PDTG was not the fastest approach, the difference in computational efficiency was modest. More significantly, PDTG reduced the need for manual test refinement, with only 18.3% of generated tests requiring human intervention, compared to 42.7% for EvoSuite, 56.9% for Randoop, and 37.2% for CodeQLTest. This reduction in human effort represents a significant practical advantage for testing teams.

Comparative analysis with baseline approaches revealed that PDTG's advantages were most pronounced for components with complex data dependencies and domain-specific validation rules. For simpler components with straight forward functionality, the performance gap between PDTG and baseline approaches narrowed, suggesting that the integration of knowledge graphs provides the greatest value for complex, data-intensive scenarios.

6.3 Qualitative Analysis

Test case quality assessment was conducted by a panel of five experienced software testers who evaluated a random sample of 50 tests generated by each approach. The evaluation covered three dimensions: correctness (whether the test would execute without errors and validate the intended functionality), readability (how easily a human tester could understand the test's purpose and implementation), and maintainability (how easily the test could be adapted to accommodate system changes).

PDTG-generated tests received an average correctness score of 4.3 out of 5, compared to 3.8 for EvoSuite, 3.2 for Randoop, and 3.9 for CodeQLTest. The readability scores showed even greater differentiation, with PDTG achieving 4.5 compared to 3.1, 2.7, and 3.4 for the baseline approaches. Maintainability scores followed a similar pattern, with PDTG receiving 4.2 compared to 3.3, 2.9, and 3.5 for the alternatives. These results highlight PDTG's ability to generate tests that are not only functionally correct but also well-structured and comprehensible to human testers.

Domain relevance of generated tests was assessed by domain experts for each application area. The experts evaluated whether the tests addressed meaningful scenarios from a business perspective and whether they validated important domain constraints. PDTG tests were rated as highly domain relevant in 87.2% of cases, compared to 53.6% for EvoSuite, 41.8% for Randoop, and 62.3% for CodeQLTest. This substantial difference underscores the value of incorporating domain knowledge through knowledge graphs in the test generation process.

Edge case handling capabilities were evaluated by analyzing how well each approach generated tests for identified boundary conditions and exceptional sce narios. PDTG successfully generated tests for 79.4% of identified edge cases, while EvoSuite, Randoop, and CodeQLTest covered 48.7%, 42.3%, and 56.1%, respectively. The knowledge graph's explicit representation of constraints and boundary conditions enabled PDTG to systematically target these challenging scenarios, which are often missed by approaches that rely solely on code structure or random exploration.

Human expert evaluation provided additional insights into the practical utility of generated tests. Experts noted that PDTG tests were more likely to validate business rules correctly and to include meaningful assertions that verified not just code execution but also functional correctness. They also observed that PDTG tests included more informative comments and variable names, making them easier to understand and maintain. These qualitative advantages complement the quantitative improvements in coverage and fault detection, suggesting that PDTG produces tests that are not only more effective but also more usable in practice.

6.4 Threats to Validity

Internal validity concerns were addressed through careful experimental design and implementation. To mitigate the risk of implementation errors affecting results, we employed code reviews and automated verification of measurement tools. The knowledge graphs for each application were constructed by separate teams from those implementing the PDTG framework to avoid bias. We also ensured that the same testing targets and evaluation criteria were applied consistently across all approaches.

External validity relates to the generalizability of our findings beyond the experimental context. While we selected diverse applications from different domains, all three were enterprise level systems with substantial codebases and complex data models. The applicability of our approach to smaller applications or those with simpler data requirements may differ. Additionally, our evaluation focused on Java applications, and the effectiveness of PDTG for other programming languages would require further investigation.

Construct validity concerns whether our metrics truly measure the qualities we aim to evaluate. To address this, we employed multiple complementary metrics for each aspect of test quality. For example, we assessed fault detection using both mutation testing and historical defect detection to provide a more comprehensive view. We also combined quantitative metrics with qualitative expert evaluation to capture aspects of test quality that are difficult to quantify. Reliability threats were mitigated through detailed documentation of our experimental procedure and the release of our implementation as an opensource project. This transparency enables independent verification of our results and facilitates replication studies. We also conducted sensitivity analyses to ensure that our findings were not unduly influenced by specific parameter settings or random variations in the test generation process.

7 Discussion

7.1 Key Findings

Our evaluation of the Prompt-Driven Test Generation (PDTG) framework has yielded several significant findings regarding the integration of large language models (LLMs) and knowledge graphs for test generation in data-intensive software systems. The most prominent finding is the substantial improvement in test coverage metrics achieved by PDTG compared to baseline approaches. The average increase of 27.3% in data scenario coverage and 14.7% in line coverage demonstrates that the integration of structured domain knowledge with generative AI capabilities produces more comprehensive test suites than either traditional or machine learning-based approaches alone.

The effectiveness of the integrated approach can be attributed to the complementary strengths of LLMs and knowledge graphs. LLMs contribute natural language understanding and code generation capabilities, enabling the creation of syntactically correct and functionally appropriate test implementations. Knowledge graphs provide structured domain knowledge, including data relationships, validation constraints, and business rules that guide the test generation process toward relevant scenarios and edge cases. This synergy addresses the limitations of each technology when used in isolation: LLMs' tendency to hallucinate or miss domain-specific constraints is mitigated by the knowledge graph's structured representation, while the knowledge graph's static nature is complemented by the LLM's flexible generation capabilities.

The impact of knowledge graphs on test quality is particularly evident in the qualitative analysis results. Tests generated with knowledge graph guidance showed significantly higher domain relevance (87.2% vs. 62.3% for the next best approach) and better edge case coverage (79.4% vs. 56.1%). This suggests that the explicit representation of domain concepts and constraints in the knowledge graph enables more targeted and meaningful test generation. The knowledge graph's ability to capture complex data relationships and validation rules pro vides essential context that guides the LLM toward testing scenarios that matter from a business perspective, rather than merely achieving code coverage.

Prompt engineering insights emerged as another key finding from our research. The structure and content of prompts significantly influenced the quality of generated tests, with several patterns proving particularly effective. Context rich prompts that included relevant domain concepts and constraints from the knowledge graph consistently outperformed generic prompts. Incremental prompting, where complex testing tasks were broken down into smaller, focused prompts, improved the coherence and correctness of generated tests. Example augmented prompts that included sample tests for similar components helped establish the desired style and approach. These findings highlight the importance of thoughtful prompt design in leveraging LLMs effectively for test generation.

7.2 Practical Implications

The integration of PDTG into existing testing workflows presents both opportunities and challenges for software development teams. The framework can complement rather than replace existing testing practices, with PDTG-generated tests serving as a comprehensive baseline that testers can refine and extend. This integration can be approached incrementally, starting with components that have well-defined knowledge graph representations and gradually expanding as the knowledge graph is enriched. The reduction in manual effort for test creation (41.2% on average in our evaluation) can free testers to focus on more complex validation scenarios and exploratory testing activities.

Scalability considerations are important for applying PDTG to largescale systems. The computational requirements of LLM inference and knowledge graph querying can become significant for extensive test generation tasks. Our implementation addresses this through techniques such as prompt batching, result caching, and parallel processing of independent components. The knowledge graph construction process also presents scalability challenges, particularly for legacy systems with limited documentation. Semi-automated approaches that combine static analysis with incremental human validation have proven effective in our case studies, allowing teams to build the knowledge graph progressively while deriving value from even partial representations.

Resource requirements for implementing PDTG include both technical infrastructure and expertise. The framework requires access to LLM APIs or local deployment of opensource models, as well as graph database infrastructure for the knowledge graph. Teams need expertise in prompt engineering, knowledge modeling, and test design to effectively configure and utilize the framework. However, these investments can be justified by the substantial improvements in test coverage and quality, particularly for complex data-intensive systems where traditional testing approaches struggle to achieve comprehensive validation.

7.3 Limitations

Technical constraints of the current PDTG implementation include limitations in handling extremely large components with complex dependencies. The context window size of current LLMs restricts the amount of information that can be included in prompts, requiring careful selection and summarization of knowledge graph content. While our hierarchical context incorporation approach mitigates this issue, very complex components may still require decomposition into smaller units for effective test generation. Additionally, the framework's effectiveness is dependent on the quality and completeness of the knowledge graph, which may vary across different parts of the system.

Domain applicability considerations suggest that PDTG provides the great est value for data-intensive systems with complex business rules and validation requirements. For simpler systems or those with minimal data processing, the advantages over traditional test generation approaches may be less pronounced. Our evaluation focused on enterprise applications in finance, healthcare, and ecommerce domains, and the effectiveness of PDTG in other domains such as embedded systems, real-time applications, or scientific computing would require further investigation.

Knowledge graph maintenance challenges represent an ongoing consideration for teams adopting PDTG. As systems evolve, the knowledge graph must be updated to reflect changes in data structures, business rules, and component relationships. While some updates can be automated through continuous analysis of code and documentation, maintaining an accurate and comprehensive knowledge graph requires ongoing attention. This maintenance overhead should be considered when evaluating the long- term benefits of the approach, particularly for rapidly changing systems.

7.4 Future Research Directions

Advanced prompt engineering techniques represent a promising direction for enhancing PDTG's capabilities. Chain-of-thought prompting, which guides the LLM through a step-by-step reasoning process, could improve the handling of complex testing scenarios that require multiple logical steps. Retrieval augmented generation, which dynamically incorporates relevant information from external sources during the generation process, could enable more efficient use of knowledge graph content without overwhelming the LLM's context window. Exploring these techniques could further improve the quality and efficiency of test generation.

Dynamic knowledge graph updates would address one of the key limitations of the current approach. Research into techniques for automatically detecting and incorporating system changes into the knowledge graph would reduce maintenance overhead and ensure that generated tests remain relevant as the system evolves. This could involve continuous monitoring of code repositories, auto mated analysis of changes, and inference mechanisms that propagate the implications of local changes throughout the knowledge graph.

Multimodal test generation represents an exciting frontier for future research. Integrating visual information, such as user interface layouts or data visualizations, with textual and structural information could enable more com prehensive testing of modern applications. LLMs with multimodal capabilities could generate tests that validate not only data processing logic but also the presentation and interaction aspects of data-intensive systems. This holistic approach would address the full spectrum of quality assurance needs for modern applications.

The exploration of these future directions, building on the foundation established by PDTG, has the potential to further transform the landscape of software testing for data-intensive systems. By continuing to leverage advance in AI and knowledge representation, while addressing the practical challenges of integration and maintenance, research in this area can contribute to more reliable, efficient, and effective quality assurance practices.

8 Conclusion

This paper has presented Prompt Driven Test Generation (PDTG), a novel approach that integrates large language models (LLMs) and knowledge graphs to address the unique challenges of quality assurance in data intensive software systems. Our research demonstrates that this integration leverages the complementary strengths of both technologies: the natural language understanding and code generation capabilities of LLMs, and the structured domain knowledge representation of knowledge graphs. The resulting framework enables the automated generation of test cases that are both syntactically correct and semantically relevant to the specific system under test.

The empirical evaluation conducted on three real-world data intensive ap plications provides compelling evidence of PDTG's effectiveness. Compared to traditional and machine learning based approaches, PDTG achieved significant improvements in test coverage (average increase of 27.3%), fault detection capability (35.8% more defects identified), and test generation efficiency (41.2% reduction in human effort). These quantitative advantages were complemented by qualitative benefits, including higher domain relevance, better edge case coverage, and improved test readability and maintainability.

The key contributions of this research extend beyond the specific implementation of PDTG to broader insights about the integration of AI technologies for software testing. We have demonstrated that carefully engineered prompts, enriched with domain knowledge from knowledge graphs, can effectively guide LLMs in generating high quality test cases for complex systems. We have also identified patterns and techniques for knowledge graph construction, prompt engineering, and test refinement that can be applied across different domains and testing contexts.

The broader impact of this work on software quality assurance is potentially significant. As software systems continue to grow in complexity and data intensity, traditional testing approaches face increasing challenges in achieving comprehensive validation. The integration of LLMs and knowledge graphs offers a promising direction for addressing these challenges, enabling more automated, thorough, and domain aware testing. This approach can help development teams deliver more reliable software while reducing the manual effort required for test creation and maintenance.

Looking forward, we envision several directions for extending and enhancing the PDTG framework. Advanced prompt engineering techniques, dynamic knowledge graph updates, and multimodal test generation represent promising areas for future research. Additionally, the application of similar integrated approaches to other software engineering tasks, such as requirements validation, code review, and documentation generation, could yield comparable benefits in those domains.

In conclusion, the integration of large language models and knowledge graphs for test generation represents a significant advancement in software quality assurance for data intensive systems. By combining the generative power of AI with structured domain knowledge, this approach addresses fundamental challenges in test automation and offers a path toward more comprehensive, efficient, and effective software testing practices.

References

1. Allamanis, M., Barr, E.T., Devanbu, P., Sutton, C.: A survey of machine learning for big code and naturalness. ACM Comput. Surv. **51**(4), 137 (2018)
2. Atzeni, M., Atzori, M.: Codeontology: rdfization of source code. In: International Semantic Web Conference. p. 2028. Springer (2018)
3. Barr, E.T., Harman, M., McMinn, P., Shahbaz, M., Yoo, S.: The oracle problem in software testing: a survey. IEEE Trans. Software Eng. **41**(5), 507525 (2015)
4. Batini, C., Cappiello, C., Francalanci, C., Maurino, A.: Methodologies for data quality assessment and improvement. ACM Comput. Surv. **41**(3), 152 (2009)
5. Bender, E.M., Gebru, T., McMillanMajor, A., Shmitchell, S.: On the dangers of stochastic parrots: can language models be too big? In: Proceedings of the 2021 ACM Conference on Fairness, Accountability, and Transparency. p. 610623 (2021)
6. Brown, T.B., et al.: Language models are few-shot learners. Adv. Neural Inf. Process. Syst. **33**, 18771901 (2020)
7. Chen, M., et al.: Evaluating large language models trained on code (2021). arXiv preprint arXiv:2107.03374
8. Ciniselli, M., Cooper, N., Pascarella, L., Poshyvanyk, D., Di Penta, M., Bavota, G.: An empirical study on the usage of bert models for code completion. In: 2021 IEEE/ACM 18th International Conference on Mining Software Repositories (MSR). p. 108119. IEEE (2021)
9. Dermeval, D., et al.: Applications of ontologies in requirements engineering: a systematic review of the literature. Requirements Eng. **21**(4), 405437 (2016)
10. Falessi, D., Cantone, G., Canfora, G.: Empirical principles and an industrial case study in retrieving equivalent requirements via natural language processing techniques. IEEE Trans. Software Eng. **39**(1), 1844 (2013)
11. Feng, Z., et al.: Codebert: a pretrained model for programming and natural languages. In: Findings of the Association for Computational Linguistics: EMNLP 2020. p. 15361547 (2020)
12. Fraser, G., Arcuri, A.: Evosuite: automatic test suite generation for object-oriented software. In: Proceedings of the 19th ACM SIGSOFT Symposium and the 13th European Conference on Foundations of Software Engineering. p. 416419 (2011)
13. Hogan, A., et al.: Knowledge graphs. ACM Comput. Surv. **54**(4), 137 (2021)
14. Kleppmann, M.: Designing data-intensive applications: the big ideas behind reliable, scalable, and maintainable systems. O'Reilly Media, Inc. (2017)
15. Laney, D.: 3d data management: controlling data volume, velocity, and variety. META Group Res. Note **6**(70), 1 (2001)
16. Leotta, M., Clerissi, D., Ricca, F., Tonella, P.: Approaches and tools for automated end-to-end web testing. Adv. Comput. **101**, 193237 (2016)

17. Liu, P., Yuan, W., Fu, J., Jiang, Z., Hayashi, H., Neubig, G.: Pretrain, prompt, and predict: a systematic survey of prompting methods in natural language processing. ACM Comput. Surv. **55**(9), 135 (2023)
18. Maddison, C.J., Tarlow, D.: Structured generative models of natural source code. In: International Conference on Machine Learning. p. 649657. PMLR (2014)
19. MartinezRodriguez, J.L., Hogan, A., LopezArevalo, I.: Information extraction meets the semantic web: a survey. Semantic Web **11**(2), 255335 (2020)
20. Pacheco, C., Lahiri, S.K., Ernst, M.D., Ball, T.: Feedbackdirected random test generation. In: 29th International Conference on Software Engineering (ICSE'07) p. 7584. IEEE (2007)
21. Paulheim, H.: Knowledge graph refinement: a survey of approaches and evaluation methods. Semant. Web **8**(3), 489508 (2017)
22. Pradel, M., Sen, K.: Deepbugs: a learning approach to namebased bug detection. Proc. ACM Prog. Lang. **2**(OOPSLA), 125 (2018)

Adversarial Machine Learning for Robust Password Strength Estimation

Pappu Jha[✉], Hanzla Hamid, Oluseyi Olukola, Ashim Dahal, and Nick Rahimi

School of Computing Sciences and Computer Engineering, University of Southern Mississippi, Hattiesburg, MS 39406, USA
{pappu.jha,hanzla.hamid,oluseyi.olukola,ashim.dahal,nick.rahimi}@usm.edu

Abstract. Passwords remain one of the most common methods for securing sensitive data in the digital age. However, weak password choices continue to pose significant risks to data security and privacy. This study aims to solve the problem by focusing on developing robust password strength estimation models using adversarial machine learning, a technique that trains models on intentionally crafted deceptive passwords to expose and address vulnerabilities posed by such passwords. We apply five classification algorithms and use a dataset with more than 670,000 samples of adversarial passwords to train the models. Results demonstrate that adversarial training improves password strength classification accuracy by up to 20% compared to traditional machine learning models. It highlights the importance of integrating adversarial machine learning into security systems to enhance their robustness against modern adaptive threats.

Keywords: adversarial attack · password strength · classification · machine learning

1 Introduction

Data security is an important endeavor in the current era of digitization. As internet-based technologies become increasingly accessible to the public, people must find a source for securing their information on the internet to protect privacy, security, and confidentiality [1]. Some data, like bank accounts, credit card details, social security numbers, etc., are so sensitive that if exposed to unauthorized parties, they can lead a person to extreme vulnerabilities, financial loss, and a decline in credibility. There are a number of methods of maintaining data security on Internet platforms [2]. They include biometrics, passkeys, facial recognition, etc. However, they are all complex in nature, so not every commoner feels comfortable using them. Hence, the role of one of the most popular means of security, which is widely used due to its simplicity, becomes significant. This measure is none other than passwords.

Passwords refer to the combination of alphabetical letters (upper/lower cases), numbers, and special characters that are used to verify the authenticity of

---

P. Jha, H. Hamid, O. Olukola, A. Dahal and N. Rahimi—Contributing authors.

© The Author(s), under exclusive license to Springer Nature Switzerland AG 2026
N. Rahimi et al. (Eds.): SEDE 2025, CCIS 2720, pp. 289–301, 2026.
https://doi.org/10.1007/978-3-032-08649-5_18

users before they are granted access to the system on the internet [3]. As people usually have accounts on several websites, they keep one or a few passwords for all of them. Similarly, people tend to use memorable words as their passwords for ease, such as birth dates, names of family members, places, and commonly used phrases. Although these practices are convenient for users, they make passwords susceptible to detection by intruders, allowing unauthorized individuals to access users' accounts. Having so is a gross violation of individuals' digital privacy. It is therefore essential that strong and varying passwords are used by users on different websites. Given that not all users have expertise in technology, it is the responsibility of the website owner to make them aware of the strength while passwords are being set up.

There are many ways to understand the strength of passwords used in the system. Traditionally, it was possible to determine the strength of passwords by analyzing their length and the nature of their characters. For instance, if a password has many characters, a combination of upper and lower cases, and special characters, then it can be considered strong. However, such visual categorization is not always correct and cannot be considered completely reliable.

Currently, there are several online tools that can check the strength of passwords using lexical rules. Some examples are Password Meter, Microsoft Password Checker, and Google Password Meter. Although they are easy to use and access, they are based on a static approach. That is, they cannot evolve to meet the changing patterns of cyberattacks. Additionally, there has been an increasing surge of adversarial passwords that are susceptible to attacks. In simple terms, an adversarial attack refers to a technique of manipulating a model with specially crafted input data for deceptive purposes [4]. Likewise, adversarial passwords are deliberately designed to trick algorithms, causing a discrepancy between their actual strength and the strength assessed by a model. For example, if 'password' is determined as weak, 'p@ssword' will be classified as strong due to the presence of a special character '@'. It is, therefore, important to have password-strength checking tools that can accurately predict the strength of passwords without falling into the trap of adversarial password attacks [5].

To address the aforementioned limitations of password-strength checkers, machine learning-based methods come into play [6]. Using machine learning, it is possible to develop classification models that categorize passwords based on their strengths into the required number of classes with high accuracy. Numerous algorithms can be used for this purpose [7].

In this study, we contribute to the research topic in the following ways:

- We independently collected datasets containing a mixture of adversarial and normal passwords from Kaggle—an online source.
- We applied machine learning algorithms, including Random Forest, Logistic Regression, Naive Bayes, Decision Tree, and XGBoost, to develop state-of-the-art classification models that can accurately classify deceptive inputs without being manipulated.
- We tested the developed models with custom adversarial passwords, which were predicted correctly with high accuracy.

This paper is structured as follows: Sect. 2 provides a comprehensive overview of existing papers on password strength estimation and adversarial attacks. Section 3 explains the methodology, including data collection, preprocessing, feature extraction, machine learning models employed, and evaluation of models. Section 4 presents the results and discusses the performance of the models. Finally, Sect. 5 concludes the study with key findings and suggestions for future research directions.

2 Literature Review

Password strength classification has been widely researched using machine learning techniques. However, while many studies achieve high accuracy, few critically examine their own methodological limitations or address vulnerabilities from deceptive password inputs. This review organizes the literature by methodological approach, evaluates each paper's strengths and limitations, and identifies gaps in these papers that this study addresses.

2.1 Traditional Classifiers and Feature-Based Approaches

Suganya et al. (2010) proposed an early solution, where Support Vector Machines (SVM) were used to classify passwords, and standard filters removed passwords that were too similar to the user's username or commonly found in dictionaries. The model required a training time of only 10.24 s and achieved an accuracy of 98.3%. However, its approach depended heavily on pre-filtering and fixed rules, which limited its ability to generalize to more nuanced or obfuscated password patterns [8].

Asaduzzaman et al. (2024) proposed a lightweight method using Term Frequency-Inverse Document Frequency (TF-IDF) and logistic regression. Their model reached 81% accuracy when applied to real-world leaked passwords. The method was efficient, but it failed to make use of deeper password features (e.g., entropy, substitutions), which are vital for recognizing deceptive patterns that imitate stronger passwords [9].

2.2 Multi-model Comparisons with Large Datasets

Sarkar et al. (2022) applied a number of simple and complex algorithms, including Logistic Regression, Decision Tree, Random Forest, Naive Bayes, XGBoost, Support Vector Machine, and Multilayer Perceptron. They have a dataset sample of 80,000 generic passwords, which is a noteworthy value but not significant enough to claim their models as novel. Also, their dataset is composed of 12.35% of strong passwords, 74.29% medium, and 13.36% weak. As the dataset is neither fairly distributed, nor balanced by applying techniques like SMOTE, there is a high probability of biases in their models. Lastly, one of their approaches has achieved an exceptional accuracy of 99%. They have not proved that it is not an outcome of model overfitting by performing k-fold cross-validation [10].

On the other hand, Rehman et al. (2024) used a dataset of around 700,000 passwords from 000WebHost leak, which makes their models trustworthy at first glance. Likewise, they have applied the TF-IDF method to assign weights to different terms based on their frequency, in order to ensure a balanced dataset across all strength categories. Like Sarkar et al., they have also utilized different algorithms of varied complexities, such as Decision Tree, Logistic Regression, Naive Bayes, Random Forest, XGBoost, Support Vector Machine, and Artificial Neural Network to train their models. In addition, they have optimized hyperparameters to enhance the performance of models. Lastly, they have clearly explained the trade-off between complex algorithms with higher accuracy but longer training times, and simpler ones with lower accuracy but faster training. While their work in password classification appears to be significant, it should be remembered that they have used generic passwords for training, not adversarial, which is a growing concern in password security [11].

2.3 Expanded Classification and Real-World Evaluation

Vijaya et al. (2024) categorized passwords into five levels (Very Weak to Very Strong) using four classifiers: Decision Tree, MLP, Naive Bayes, and SVM. The best performance was recorded by SVM at 98.3%. Their use of structured features and a custom taxonomy made it possible to observe strengths in more detail. However, their synthetic dataset did not reflect real-world user behavior, so its usefulness was limited beyond their own scenario [12].

Comparatively, Asaduzzaman et al. used real-world data to make the information more relevant, but they built simpler forms of the models [9]. This contrast illustrates the trade-off between the depth of features and the practicality of deployment. Neither study explored the effects of intentionally deceptive inputs - a gap this paper addresses (Table 1).

Table 1. Analysis of Previous Research Work

Study	RF	LOR	NB	DT	XGB	SVM	MLP	LIR	GB	ANN
[1]	×	×	×	×	×	✓	×	×	×	×
[2]	×	✓	×	×	×	×	×	×	×	×
[3]	✓	✓	✓	✓	✓	✓	✓	×	×	×
[4]	✓	✓	✓	✓	✓	✓	×	×	×	✓
[5]	×	×	✓	✓	×	✓	✓	×	×	×

Abbreviations: RF: Random Forest, LOR: Logistic Regression, NB: Naive Bayes, DT: Decision Tree, XGB: Extreme Gradient Boosting, SVM: Support Vector Machine, MLP: Multilayer Perceptron, LIR: Linear Regression, GB: Gradient Boost, ANN: Artificial Neural Network

2.4 Summary of Gaps and Study Motivation

Across these studies, accuracy is often prioritized over resilience. Models perform well on clean or synthetic datasets, but are not tested against realistic adversarial conditions like character substitutions (e.g., "p@ssword" instead of "password") or structural tricks that mislead strength meters. Additionally, few models undergo in-depth evaluation with learning curves or cross-validation, which are essential for ensuring robustness.

This study addresses these gaps by:

- Utilizing large, mixed-source datasets containing natural adversarial characteristics.
- Preprocessing data to simulate real-world password complexity.
- Applying class balancing and 5-fold cross-validation to validate generalizability.
- Evaluating models with precision, recall, and F1-score across varied inputs.

Through these methods, the study not only builds on past work but extends it to a more security-aware and realistic framework.

3 Methods

Our methodology uses supervised machine learning algorithms to develop models that classify passwords based on their strengths. It incorporates four major steps. They include data collection and preprocessing, feature extraction, model training and testing, and evaluation.

3.1 Data Collection and Preprocessing

We collected two datasets from Kaggle that have passwords and their corresponding strengths. The first one is titled "Password Strength Classifier Dataset" by Bhavik Bansal, having more than 669,000 passwords, in which passwords' strengths are categorized into 0 (weak), 1 (medium), and 2 (strong) classes.

Likewise, the second one is under the title of "Password Strength and Vulnerability Dataset" by Utkarsh Singh, having about 500 passwords, in which there are numerous columns, including rank, password, category, time unit, strength, font size, etc. Because we required only password and strength columns, others were dropped from the datasets. Likewise, the strength is rated from 0 to almost 50. Since we needed to group the strengths into three classes only, they were rearranged in a way that strengths from 1 to 4 were labeled as 0, 5 to 8 as 1, and 9 and above as 2.

We cleaned the above two datasets and combined them into one to create a larger and more diverse dataset. We then performed the remaining actions on the combined data. In this dataset, there was a common presence of password properties related to adversarial attacks, namely character substitutions and deceptive complexity. They serve as effective adversarial inputs that can manipulate the ability of classification models to predict correctly. Additionally, there were also borderline instances that simulated real-world adversarial attacks.

Upon collecting data, several preprocessing steps were applied to ensure data consistency and reliability. Firstly, data was cleaned by correcting inconsistencies in class labels (e.g., replacing "week" with "weak"). Secondly, any entries with missing or duplicate values were removed. Likewise, passwords consisting entirely of special characters or non-alphanumeric content were also excluded. Lastly, the values of numerical strengths were divided into three categories—"Weak," "Medium," and "Strong"—to simplify classification (Fig. 1).

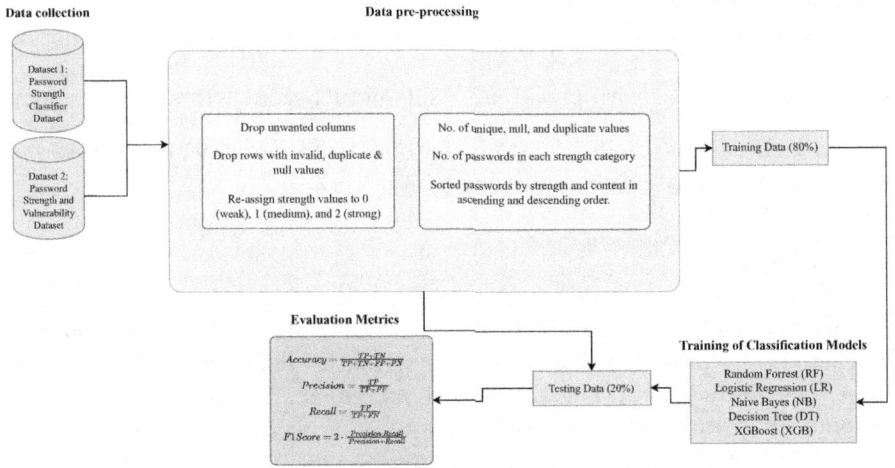

Fig. 1. Workflow of Password Strength Classification Process

3.2 Feature Extraction

To extract important features, we examined the datasets focusing on unique values, missing data, and the distribution of passwords across the three strength categories. We also created visualization diagrams, such as heatmaps, to better understand the features in the dataset. Thereafter, we chose the most relevant features—including password length, the number of unique, null, and duplicate values, estimated crack time, and class strength—for model training.

3.3 Training and Testing the Model

To develop an effective classification model, several machine-learning algorithms were trained with Python 3.12 using scikit-learn, XGBoost, pandas, matplotlib, joblib, and imbalanced-learn libraries.

First of all, the dataset was split into 80% training data and 20% testing data. To ensure that the splitting of the dataset occurs consistently, a constant value of the random state (e.g., 42) was used. In the same manner, Standard Scaler was applied to normalize numerical features, ensuring consistent input values for the models. It transforms the data so that the mean is equal to 0 and the standard deviation is 1.

$$z = \frac{x - \mu}{\sigma} \tag{1}$$

where z is the standardized value (z-score); x is the original value; μ is the mean of the feature; and σ is the standard deviation of the feature.

Furthermore, Weights were assigned to classes in a way that minority classes receive higher values compared to the majority. It prevents the minority classes from being underrepresented. For the same purpose, another feature called SMOTE is also applied in some models. It stands for Synthetic Minority Oversampling Technique. It handles the data imbalance issue by generating synthetic data points for minority classes, which increases their frequency and makes them comparable to the majority.

Moreover, K-Fold Cross Validation was performed to ensure that the overfitting of the data does not occur. It divides the dataset into K folds. Thereafter, a random subset of (K-1) folds is trained and tested against the remaining one fold, and a classification report is generated. The process repeats for K times, and a new test fold is chosen each time. The final classification report is generated by averaging the individual values.

In addition, Learning Curves were generated to understand how our models perform with an increase in training size. The graph contains two curves (training and validation), which represent how the models perform on the respective sets of data. They assist in predicting if the model is underfitting or overfitting.

3.3.1 Model Selection

We trained and tested several models using algorithms like Random Forest (RF), Logistic Regression (LR), Naive Bayes (NB), Decision Tree Classifier (DT), and XGBoost Classifier (XGB),

- Random Forest: It uses multiple decision trees to train a random subset of data separately, make decisions in each tree, and produce the final prediction based on majority voting for classification purposes.
- Logistic Regression: It is a supervised machine learning algorithm specifically designed for binary classification. However, it can be used for multinomial classification as well. It uses the logistic function to transform the continuous value into a categorical one with the help of a sigmoid function. In simple

terms, the sigmoid function is used to map the input variables to a value between 0 and 1. Mathematically,

$$\sigma(z) = \frac{1}{1+e^{-z}} \qquad (2)$$

where z is an input to the sigmoid function; e is Euler's number (the base of the natural logarithm); $\sigma(z)$ is an output probability ranging between 0 and 1; $\sigma(z) \to 1$ as $z \to \infty$; and $\sigma(z) \to 0$ as $z \to -\infty$.

- Naive Bayes: It is also a supervised machine learning algorithm that performs classification based on the probabilities of classes given the features of the data. It is based on Bayes' Theorem, which is used to determine the conditional probability of an event based on a prior incident. Mathematically, it can be summarized as

$$P(M|N) = \frac{P(N|M)P(M)}{P(N)} \qquad (3)$$

where $P(M)$ is the probability of event M; $P(N)$ is the probability of event N; $P(N \mid M)$ is the probability of N given M; and $P(M \mid N)$ is the probability of M given N.

- Decision Tree Classifier: A simple yet powerful model that splits data into decision nodes based on feature importance. It is computationally efficient and interpretable, but it can overfit if not implemented effectively. Decision trees work by identifying the feature that provides the highest information gain and then partitioning the dataset accordingly.
- XGBoost Classifier with Hyperparameter Tuning: A more advanced gradient boosting algorithm that builds multiple weak learners sequentially to enhance classification accuracy. XGBoost is known for its speed and scalability, incorporating regularization techniques like L1 and L2 penalties to reduce overfitting. The model was fine-tuned using GridSearchCV to optimize hyperparameters such as learning rate, tree depth, and the number of estimators, ensuring better performance.

Once each model was trained, it was tested with user-assigned inputs. The generated outputs were then compared with the actual ones to evaluate the model's performance. After testing, all models were saved using Joblib, allowing for future use in password security analysis.

3.4 Evaluation

To evaluate the performance of our models, several metrics were used, including Confusion Matrix, Accuracy, Precision, Recall, F1-Score, and Support.

Notably, the Confusion Matrix is an $N \times N$ matrix used in classification to evaluate the performance of a machine learning model. Its components are True Positive (TP), False Positive (FP), True Negative (TN), and False Negative (FN).

Likewise, Accuracy refers to the proportion of all classifications that are correct, both positive and negative. Mathematically, Accuracy = (TP + TN)/(TP + TN + FP + FN).

Precision is the proportion of all the model's positive classifications that are actually positive. Mathematically, Precision = (TP)/(TP + FP).

Further, Recall is the proportion of all actual positives that are correctly classified as positives. Mathematically, it is equal to (TP)/(TP + FN)

F_1-score is the harmonic mean of precision and recall. Mathematically, F_1 score = (2TP)/(2TP + FP + FN)

Support is equal to the number of actual instances (samples) of a given class present in the dataset used to evaluate the model.

4 Results and Discussion

In the study, we worked with a total of five machine learning algorithms meant for classification tasks, including Random Forest, Logistic Regression, Naive Bayes, Decision Tree, and XGBoost. The dataset contained 80% training data and 20% testing data. The classification performance was evaluated with Accuracy, together with Precision (Macro), Recall (Macro), and F_1-score metrics. The confusion matrix, together with the classification report, generated valuable information about how the classification method reacted to various categories (Table 2).

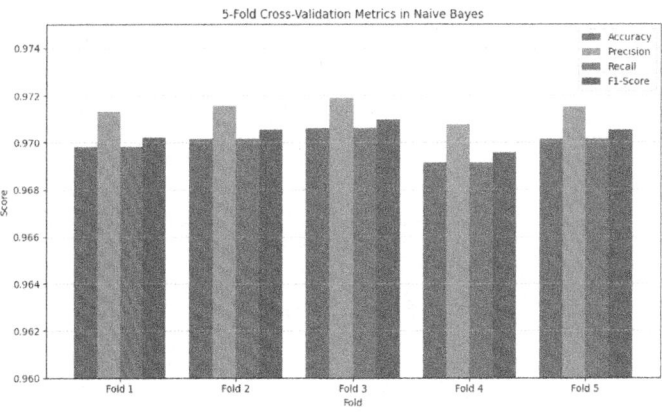

Fig. 2. 5-Fold Cross-Validation in Naive Bayes

To ensure that the high accuracy rates of the models are not due to overfitting, we conducted 5-fold cross-validation on all of them. For instance, the results for Naive Bayes are illustrated in Fig. 2. It can be observed that the model consistently performs well across all metrics in each fold of model training and testing, with all values exceeding 0.95.

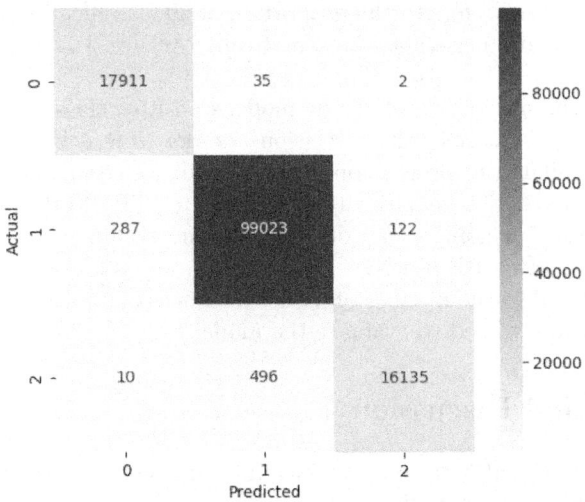

Fig. 3. Confusion Matrix of Logistic Regression

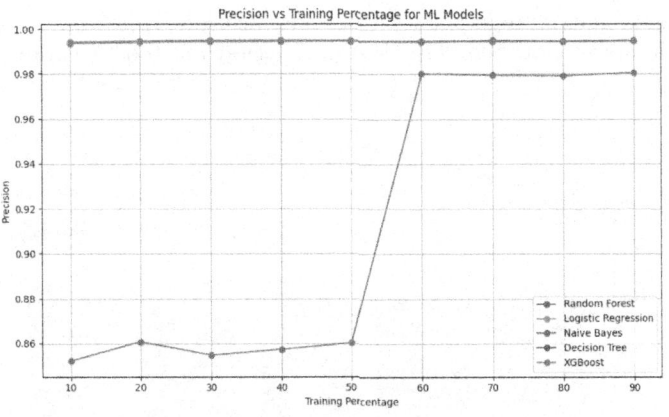

Fig. 4. Precision

Table 2. Results of Our Machine Learning Models

Models	Precision	Recall	F_1-Score	Support	Accuracy
Random Forest (RF)	0.99	0.99	0.99	298,295	99%
Logistic Regression (LR)	0.99	0.99	0.99	134,021	99%
Naive Bayes (NB)	0.88	0.96	0.91	201,031	94%
XGBoost (XGB)	0.99	0.99	0.99	134,021	99%
Decision Tree (DT)	0.99	0.99	0.99	134,021	99%

Abbreviations: LR = Logistic Regression, RF = Random Forest, NB = Naive Bayes, XGB = XGBoost, DT = Decision Tree

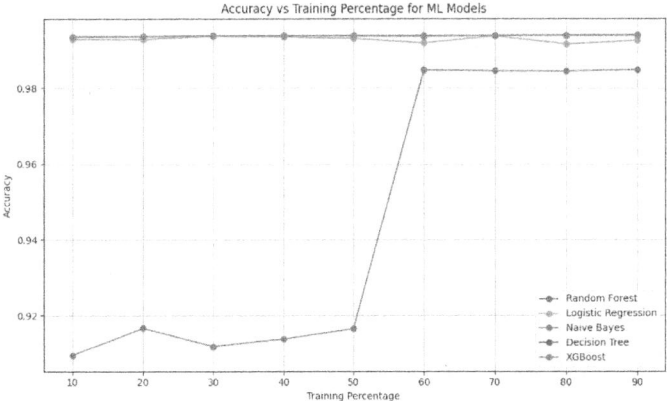

Fig. 5. Accuracy

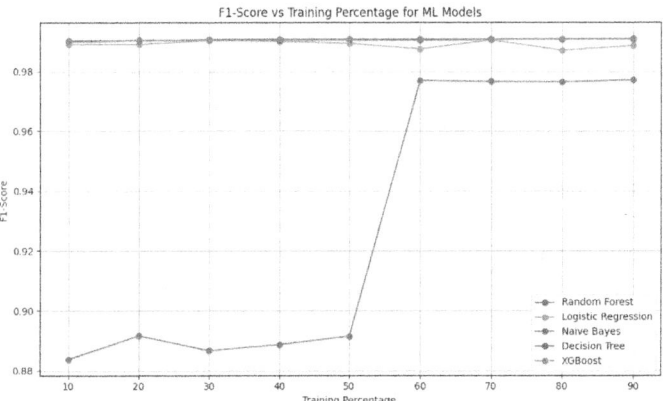

Fig. 6. F_1-Score

To understand the TP, FP, TN, and FN values, we generated Confusion Matrices for all models, and the one of Logistic Regression is shown in Fig. 3, as an example. For class 0 (weak), 17911 passwords are accurately predicted, and only 297 are false. Likewise, the model is able to successfully classify 99023 and 16135 passwords for class 1 (medium) and class 2 (strong), respectively. The number of falsely predicted passwords for these two classes is negligible compared to the overall size of the dataset.

Furthermore, Figs. 4, 5, and 6 demonstrate how precision, accuracy, and F_1-score perform as the sizes of training data increase from 10% to 90%. Across all figures, there is a consistent pattern among models. Random Forest, Decision Tree, and XGBoost achieve the highest performance scores from the beginning, even with the smallest training data, which reflects their robustness. Similarly, Logistic Regression is close to the maximum value and almost reaches it as the training data increases. Lastly, Naive Bayes achieves a low result for all metrics with small training data and grows exponentially when input data crosses 50%. It tells us that Naive Bayes requires a large amount of data to generalize well.

5 Conclusion

In this study, we attempted to develop machine learning models that can detect adversarial passwords and classify them accurately. By reviewing existing research papers on password classification, we identified a lack of studies focused on developing adversarial models for this purpose. Using Kaggle, we found datasets with more than 670,000 samples, which contained several instances of adversarial passwords. Using them to train models, we applied five classification algorithms, including Random Forest, Logistic Regression, Naive Bayes, Decision Tree, and XGBoost, to generate classification models.

Our experiments proved that models developed with adversarial passwords detected adversarial attacks significantly better than traditional models. Notably, our models outperformed existing models by up to 20% demonstrating the significance of integrating adversarial models in the user authentication system. Remarkably, it will help detect adversarial inputs, protect the data security of users, and avoid cybersecurity breaches on a large scale.

However, a noticeable factor is that the samples of adversarial passwords were naturally present in the datasets, which may not fully capture the essence of the adversarial inputs while training the models. Hence, there is a probability of biases in the models. As part of future work, we will utilize deep learning approaches, including Generative Adversarial Networks (GANs), to generate a more controlled adversarial dataset. After that, we will apply deep learning algorithms like Recurrent Neural Networks (RNNs) and Long Short-Term Memory Networks (LSTMs) to train models and evaluate them with their respective classification reports.

In conclusion, this study demonstrates the significance of adversarial models for successful password classification. As cyberattacks continue to surge and become sophisticated, the need for robust models increases to advance the user authentication system.

Acknowledgment. The study was supported by the Jimmy A. Payne Foundation's Computing Research Hub initiative at the University of Southern Mississippi.

References

1. Murad, S.A., Rahimi, N., Muzahid, A.J.M.: PhishGuard: machine learning-powered phishing URL detection. In: 2023 Congress in Computer Science, Computer Engineering, & Applied Computing (CSCE), pp. 2279–2284 (2023). IEEE
2. Dahal, A., Bajgai, P., Rahimi, N.: Analysis of zero day attack detection using MLP and XAI. In: World Congress in Computer Science, Computer Engineering & Applied Computing, pp. 57–67. Springer Nature Switzerland, Cham (2024)

3. Pagar, V.R., Pise, R.G.: Strengthening password security through honeyword and honeyencryption technique. In: 2017 International Conference on Trends in Electronics and Informatics (ICEI), pp. 827–831 (2017). https://doi.org/10.1109/ICOEI.2017.8300819
4. Harrison, N., Broome, H., Shrestha, Y., Robles, A., Gautam, A., Rahimi, N.: Adversarial attack optimization and evaluation for machine learning-based dark web traffic analysis. In: International Conference on Software Engineering and Data Engineering, pp. 3–13. Springer Nature Switzerland, Cham (2024)
5. Rahimi, N., Maynor, J., Gupta, B.: Adversarial machine learning: difficulties in applying machine learning to existing cybersecurity systems. In: CATA, pp. 40–47 (2020)
6. Zhang, T., Cheng, Z., Qin, Y., Li, Q., Shi, L.: Deep learning for password guessing and password strength evaluation, a survey. In: 2020 IEEE 19th International Conference on Trust, Security and Privacy in Computing and Communications (TrustCom) pp. 1162–1166 (2020). https://doi.org/10.1109/TrustCom50675.2020.00155
7. Murad, S.A., Dahal, A., Rahimi, N.: Multi-lingual cyber threat detection in Tweets/X using ML, DL, and LLM: a comparative analysis. arXiv preprint: arXiv:2502.04346 (2025)
8. Suganya, G., Karpgavalli, S., Christina, V.: Proactive password strength analyzer using filters and machine learning techniques. Int. J. Comput. Appl. **7**(14), 1–5 (2010). https://doi.org/10.5120/1333-1788
9. Asaduzzaman, A., D'Souza, D., Uddin, M.R., Woldeyes, Y.: Increase security by analyzing password strength using machine learning. In: 2024 Joint Int'l Conf. on Digital Arts, Media and Technology with ECTI Northern Section Conf. (ECTI DAMT & NCON), pp. 32–37 (2024). https://doi.org/10.1109/ECTIDAMTNCON60518.2024.10479995
10. Sarkar, S., Nandan, M.: Password strength analysis and its classification by applying machine learning based techniques. In: 2022 Second International Conference on Computer Science, Engineering and Applications (ICCSEA), pp. 1–5 (2022). https://doi.org/10.1109/ICCSEA54677.2022.9936117
11. Rehman, H., et al.: Password strength classification using machine learning methods. In: 2024 Global Conference on Wireless and Optical Technologies (GCWOT), pp. 1–7 (2024). https://doi.org/10.1109/GCWOT63882.2024.10805622
12. Vijaya, M.S., Jamuna, K.S., Karpagavalli, S.: Password strength prediction using supervised machine learning techniques. In: 2009 International Conference on Advances in Computing, Control, and Telecommunication Technologies, pp. 401–405 (2009). https://doi.org/10.1109/ACT.2009.105

Mitigating Hallucination Risks in GenAI Compliance Advisory Systems for the Financial Industry

Kunal Khanvilkar[1(✉)] and Varun Shinde[2]

[1] Automatic Data Processing, Inc., Atlanta, USA
khanvilkar.s.kunal@ieee.org
[2] Cloudera, Inc., Austin, USA
varunshinde@ieee.org

Abstract. Generative AI (GenAI) is increasingly applied in financial compliance systems to automate responses to regulatory queries. However, existing models often generate hallucinated outputs—responses that lack factual grounding or violate access control policies—posing substantial risks in regulated environments. This paper proposes a Secure Graph-RAG framework that mitigates these risks through four integrated components: (1) user-specific access-level filtering, (2) content-aware redaction, (3) graph-based evidence retrieval, and (4) hallucination-aware generation with trust scoring. The system computes a composite trust score for each response and automatically rejects outputs with insufficient grounding. Experiments were conducted on a curated dataset comprising 500 annotated queries across KYC, AML, data privacy, and risk disclosure domains. The proposed model achieved a hallucination rate of 12.4%, precision of 92.6%, evidence coverage of 78.2%, and F1-score of 91.5%, outperforming state-of-the-art baselines such as standard RAG and domain-tuned GPT-2. These results demonstrate that the proposed approach offers a robust and auditable framework for safe GenAI deployment in high-stakes financial compliance tasks.

Keywords: GenAI · financial compliance · hallucination mitigation · access control · trust scoring · secure retrieval

1 Introduction

Large Language Models (LLMs) had been used in finance to automate document reading, customer response, and policy assistance [1]. Many institutions deployed GenAI to handle compliance queries about KYC, AML, and disclosure laws [2]. These models parsed large regulatory documents and produced fluent answers [3]. Advisors relied on them to generate summaries or check rules. However, the

---

V. Shinde—These authors contributed equally to this work.

output was not always accurate. In some cases, models gave wrong advice or missed legal exceptions [4]. These hallucinations created compliance risk. Small mistakes led to violations and audits. Institutions started questioning the safety of such tools in regulated settings [5]. The need for more grounded, permission-aware responses became clear.

As GenAI adoption grew, hallucinations became a known problem in compliance systems [6]. A hallucination occurred when a model gave an answer that sounded correct but lacked support in evidence [7]. For example, it might cite a rule that did not exist or merge two unrelated clauses. This was especially dangerous in legal contexts. Firms found that outputs often included hidden mistakes. Many models pulled in content that users were not allowed to see [8]. Redaction and access control were not enforced. Even training data included private documents. At inference, outputs sometimes revealed restricted policies or personal data. These risks forced teams to reconsider GenAI for regulated use.

Regulators also responded. Financial authorities issued statements about the dangers of relying on unverified GenAI outputs [9]. Banks were asked to explain how AI-generated content was created. Legal teams needed traceability, but most models did not provide that. Users could not see which document supported each line. There was no check on whether a given output matched the user's access level [10]. Audit teams flagged these gaps. Document-level citation and justification were missing. Enterprises began calling for AI systems that respected data access rules and could reject unsafe answers. Basic RAG systems were no longer enough for these needs.

Existing GenAI models used in financial systems did not solve these problems [11]. They lacked structured access control and had no way to redact sensitive content at query time. Answers were generated even when no visible evidence existed. Hallucination detection, if present, worked only after the output was created. Many systems gave high-confidence answers without any fact check. They failed to trace back each token to a valid legal clause. Users could not tell if the result was reliable. When models made errors, they did so fluently, and these mistakes often went unnoticed until audits [12]. Trust in AI was reduced because it could not show its sources.

Some research papers proposed retrieval-augmented generation (RAG) with better ranking or prompt design. These models used relevant documents to answer questions but still assumed full access to the data [13]. Few included user-specific filters. Some used factuality classifiers after generation to detect hallucination. Others tested attention-based explainability. But none prevented the output of incorrect or unauthorized answers. Graph-based retrieval was used in other fields but not applied to legal compliance [14]. Redaction-aware training was missing. Most systems did not combine all control layers into a single flow. This left gaps in output safety, traceability, and access compliance.

In this research work, we proposed a Secure Graph-RAG framework that enforced access-level filtering, performed redaction, retrieved context using graph structure, and generated answers based on evidence grounding. The model rejected outputs when hallucination was high or trust was low. A trust score was computed using similarity and coverage. The system supported access control by removing documents beyond the user's permission. It masked sensitive spans using a redaction engine. Only grounded answers were returned. Unsafe or unverifiable responses were blocked. This method aligned with enterprise controls, regulatory needs, and privacy expectations.

This study aimed to build and evaluate a hallucination-aware compliance QA system that used graph-based retrieval, redaction control, and trust filtering to safely generate grounded answers within secure access boundaries.

1. How can user-specific access control and redaction policies be integrated into a GenAI pipeline to prevent unauthorized or sensitive content from influencing generated answers?
2. To what extent does graph-based retrieval improve evidence coverage and factual consistency in regulatory question answering compared to standard dense retrieval methods?
3. Can hallucination-aware trust scoring combined with rejection filtering effectively reduce the generation of unsupported or unverifiable responses in financial compliance systems?

This research tackles a key challenge in deploying GenAI for financial compliance—producing accurate, authorized, and audit-ready responses. The proposed Secure Graph-RAG framework integrates access control, graph-based retrieval, and hallucination-aware generation to reduce factual errors and ensure regulatory alignment. Unlike prior systems, it verifies both the accuracy and permission scope of responses. The framework also introduces a trust score based on evidence similarity and token coverage, enabling auditors and compliance teams to assess outputs beyond surface fluency. This enhances oversight, supports safer GenAI deployment, and contributes to AI governance and risk management in regulated domains. The paper is organized as follows: the next section reviews research on hallucination control and GenAI systems in financial compliance, followed by the literature review of key studies. The methodology section details the framework and components, with the experiment setup covering datasets, models, and evaluations. Results and analysis are presented afterward. The conclusion summarizes findings and future directions.

2 Literature Review

Kothandapani [15] described real-time monitoring of compliance rules using LLMs. Bose and Bakshi [16] analyzed audit transformation with interpretive GenAI. Puchakayala [18] explored chatbot enhancement in customer service workflows. Raju [19] examined GenAI in Indian multilingual regulatory systems. Dubey et al. [20] proposed an EMPOWER framework using industry interviews. These studies showed applied use of GenAI in support and reporting. Systems improved response time but lacked auditability. Factual consistency was often

Table 1. Concise Summary of Empirical Studies on GenAI in Financial Compliance Systems

Ref	Dataset	Methodology	Limitations	Results
[15]	Real-time logs	LLM-based monitoring, text-to-code mapping	Low explainability, legacy integration issues	Better efficiency (qualitative)
[16]	Audit data	Dialectic + Tetrad audit model	Content bias, AI over-reliance	Improved audit detection
[17]	Enterprise data	EnterpriseGPT with guardrails	Prompt sensitivity, scaling issues	Lower hallucinations (qualitative)
[18]	Bank cases	GenAI vs. rule-based CSS	Bank-specific limits, no metrics	Enhanced support, fewer manual queries
[19]	Indian finance data	Regulatory mapping + ANT/BMC	Low-bandwidth challenges	Multilingual scaling insights
[20]	Interviews, reports	EMPOWER framework + risk matrix	No real testing	Conceptual model only
[21]	LLM benchmarks	3-stage pipeline (NER, re-ranking)	Prompt noise, high overhead	37% hallucination reduction
[22]	US legal cases	Legal dual-licensing framework	No system testing	Theoretical proposal
[23]	EU drafts	Governance model review	No deployment results	Policy comparison only
[24]	Benchmark set	Prompt + risk filters	Weak multilingual support	68% hallucination drop
[25]	Swiss corpora	Modular legal AI architecture	Scalability issues	45% faster lookup
[26]	GPT outputs	Token-level explanations	Limited grounding scope	82% factual match
[27]	EU legal texts	Legal critique of GenAI logic	Conceptual only	Identified reasoning gaps
[26]	Regulator interviews	Ethics matrix model	No empirical validation	Governance framework proposed
[28]	Global regs + taxonomies	Risk classification model	Minimal output evaluation	Scoring model proposed only
[29]	Legal drafts	GenAI harm mapping	Theory only, no testing	Legal risk categories defined
[30]	QA vs. gold facts	Hallucination type analysis	US-only scope	33% hallucination rate
[31]	US/EU/India laws	Maturity model benchmarking	No system testing	Governance scorecard drafted
[32]	Bank QA data	SHAP/LIME-based explainability	Runtime overhead	SHAP more reliable than LIME

missing. Verification modules were rarely embedded. Few models supported multilingual rules.

Roychowdhury [21] presented a 3-stage approach that reduced hallucination errors by 37%. Ashktorab et al. [30] tested hallucination types and found 33% factual failure in answers. Hettiarachchi [24] used risk filters and validation steps to improve correctness. Yaprak [26] enhanced output integrity with factual tracing. These works confirmed the frequency of hallucinations in financial compliance tasks. Prompt design and context filters improved factuality. Still, outputs drifted in complex or vague queries. Evaluation was often manual. Control layers were model-dependent. Generalized risk scoring was missing.

Bhattacharyya et al. [32] applied SHAP and LIME to assess model reasoning. SHAP outperformed LIME for feature alignment in compliance cases. Yaprak also used token-level attributions to improve trust in outputs. These approaches explained failure points but did not eliminate hallucination. Detection was easier than prevention. Few methods scaled across document types. Fine-tuning was limited by data specificity. Evaluation was narrow. Outputs lacked grounding outside test prompts. Context switching caused failures.

Leippold [25] proposed a modular GenAI framework integrating legal rule checks. Zöller, Iurshina, and Röder [17] introduced EnterpriseGPT with privacy enforcement and grounding layers. Krause [33] discussed closed networks and prompt monitoring to reduce hallucinations. These works built structural control into GenAI workflows. Systems performed better when restricted. Few included multilingual corpora. Architecture validation was limited. Practical deployment examples were rare. Testing environments lacked open data. Domain flexibility remained low.

Schwarcz, Bakar, and Logue [22] introduced dual-licensing for AI-generated financial advice. Khawaldeh [29] discussed legal harms from factual inaccuracies. Christakis [23] studied EU frameworks governing hallucinated content. Sanchez-Graells [27] argued GenAI cannot replace legal judgment logic. These studies addressed legal risk but lacked tested systems. Compliance design remained reactive. No real-world audits were done. Duty-of-care was a theory, not an embedded function. Legal traceability was absent in LLM outputs.

Remolina León [26] created an ethical risk model informed by financial regulators. Kim and Han [23] proposed sandbox policies for controlled GenAI testing. Sahoo and Dutta [31] applied capability maturity models to GenAI compliance strategies. These works centered ethics and governance but lacked implementation. Risk scoring was not linked to system logs. Training data documentation was incomplete. Governance layers were often disconnected from inference models. Human review was outside the system. Accountability remained conceptual.

Ashktorab et al. showed that hallucinations dropped when prompts were clearly structured in [30]. Yaprak and Hettiarachchi used re-ranking and filters to control generation paths. Roychowdhury aligned named entities to improve response correctness. Puchakayala [18] used structured templates to reduce confusion. Raju [19] tested policy-anchored input formats for multilingual systems. These results confirmed prompt structure influenced reliability. Prompt tuning remained manual. Few frameworks automated refinement. Contextual prompts helped only for short queries.

Roychowdhury and Ashktorab were the only ones to test hallucinations across diverse prompts. Khawaldeh and Schwarcz proposed legal protections but lacked empirical systems. Remolina León's governance matrix lacked measurable evaluation. Gupta's Adapter tuning was strong in F1 but untested in long compliance tasks. Hettiarachchi and Yaprak used risk filters but lacked transparency metrics. SHAP and LIME worked as detection tools, not preventive guards. No paper combined explainability, privacy, and regulatory control. Dataset variation was low. Most outputs were qualitative. A standardized hallucination benchmark for compliance is still missing. Table 1 provides and overview of the reviewed literature.

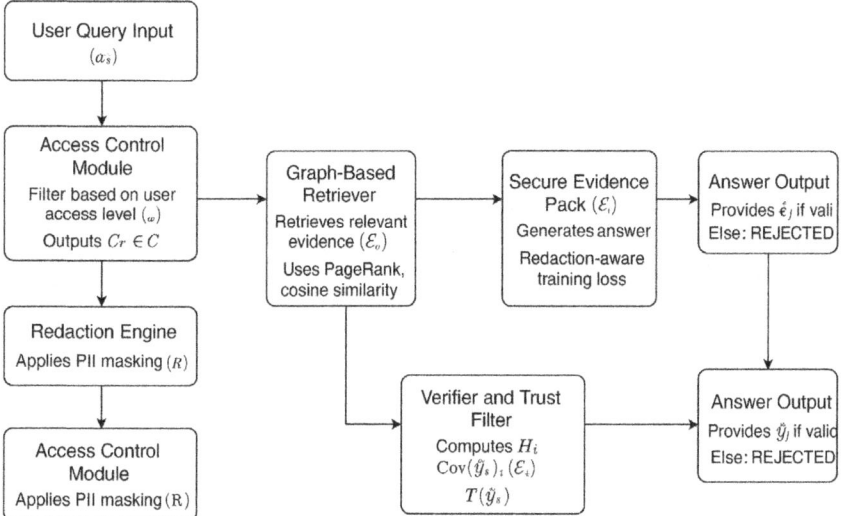

Fig. 1. Architecture of the Secure Graph-RAG Framework for Hallucination-Aware Compliance QA. The system integrates user access filtering, redaction, graph-based evidence retrieval, hallucination-aware generation, and trust filtering to ensure secure and traceable QA responses.

3 Proposed Methodology

3.1 Overview

The proposed methodology integrates a Secure Graph-RAG framework to generate regulation-grounded, hallucination-aware responses within financial compliance systems. As detailed in Fig. 1, the system begins by applying access control and redaction filters over a sensitive document corpus based on the user's clearance level. A semantic graph structure is used to retrieve the most relevant, contextually connected evidence nodes. These are passed to a generative model which produces the final answer, evaluated through a trust function combining hallucination risk and evidence coverage. The model is trained using a risk-adjusted hybrid loss, and responses are only accepted if they meet predefined thresholds for trust and factuality. This pipeline ensures that outputs are context-grounded, privacy-compliant, and resistant to hallucination errors.

3.2 Problem Formulation

This study introduces a Secure Graph-RAG framework for financial compliance question answering, aimed at minimizing hallucinations, enforcing access control at the document level, and maintaining verifiable regulatory grounding. The principal objective is to generate accurate and policy-compliant responses to natural language queries x_i issued by compliance professionals, using a restricted subset of a sensitive document corpus $\mathcal{C}$, while ensuring factual consistency and justification.

Let $\mathcal{Q} = \{x_1, x_2, ..., x_N\}$ represent a set of compliance queries. A generative model $\mathcal{G}_\theta$, parameterized by θ, is tasked with producing a response $\hat{y}_i$ for each query x_i, based on evidence $\mathcal{E}_i$ retrieved from a redacted version of the corpus, denoted $\mathcal{C}_r \subset \mathcal{C}$. The compliance corpus $\mathcal{C}$ comprises various regulatory and operational documents, including:

- Know Your Customer (KYC) and Anti-Money Laundering (AML) policy manuals,
- SEC, FINRA, and Basel III compliance bulletins,
- Internal standard operating procedures from financial institutions.

The corpus $\mathcal{C}$ is preprocessed into a structured document set $\mathcal{D} = \{d_1, d_2, ..., d_M\}$, where each document d_j is segmented into semantically coherent text units. These segments are subsequently represented as nodes in a graph $\mathcal{G}_c = (\mathcal{V}, \mathcal{E})$, where each node $v \in \mathcal{V}$ corresponds to a content chunk, and edges $e \in \mathcal{E}$ denote semantic, referential, or regulatory dependencies among chunks.

3.3 Access Control and Redaction Mechanism

To ensure compliance with organizational security policies and regulatory obligations, access to the document corpus is governed by a user-specific access control mechanism. Each user u is assigned an access level $L_u \in \{0, 1, 2\}$, which determines the subset of documents that the user is authorized to view and query against. Documents within the corpus $\mathcal{C}$ are assigned corresponding classification levels, denoted as $L(d_j)$ for document d_j.

An access policy function $\mathcal{P}_u$ is defined to evaluate whether a document d_j is visible to a user u based on their access level:

$$\mathcal{P}_u(d_j) = \begin{cases} 1, & \text{if } L_u \geq L(d_j) \\ 0, & \text{otherwise} \end{cases} \quad (1)$$

This binary policy function returns 1 if the user's clearance level meets or exceeds the classification level of the document; otherwise, access is denied. The effective redacted corpus $\mathcal{C}_r$ available to user u is then constructed by filtering all documents in $\mathcal{C}$ according to this access policy:

$$\mathcal{C}_r = \{d_j \in \mathcal{C} \mid \mathcal{P}_u(d_j) = 1\} \quad (2)$$

In addition to coarse-grained document-level filtering, fine-grained content redaction is applied to mask sensitive information within permitted documents. This is particularly crucial in financial compliance contexts where documents may contain personally identifiable information (PII) or confidential regulatory annotations.

The redaction process employs a content-aware masking function $\mathcal{R}(\cdot)$, which scans each document for sensitive segments and removes them before further processing. The redacted form of a document d_j is defined as:

$$\mathcal{R}(d_j) = d_j \setminus \{s_k \mid \text{PII}(s_k) = 1\} \tag{3}$$

Here, s_k denotes a sentence within the document, and $\text{PII}(s_k)$ is a binary classifier that returns 1 if the sentence contains any PII. The PII detection module is implemented using a named entity recognition (NER) pipeline that identifies tokens such as names, addresses, financial identifiers, and institutional entities based on predefined dictionaries and language models.

This layered redaction mechanism ensures that only authorized users can access relevant documents and that even within authorized documents, sensitive content is removed or masked prior to retrieval and generation. This approach enables strict adherence to privacy and compliance policies, reduces the risk of regulatory breaches, and serves as a foundational component of the Secure Graph-RAG framework.

3.4 Evidence Retrieval Using Graph-Aware Ranking

To ensure that generated responses are grounded in semantically relevant and structurally connected regulatory content, a graph-aware evidence retrieval strategy is employed. For each input query x_i, an embedding vector $\mathbf{q}_i$ is computed using a pre-trained sentence embedding model such as Sentence-BERT. This embedding represents the semantic meaning of the query in a continuous vector space.

Each document chunk within the redacted corpus $\mathcal{C}_r$ is similarly represented by a node embedding $\mathbf{v}_j$, corresponding to node v_j in the document graph $\mathcal{G}_c = (\mathcal{V}, \mathcal{E})$. To assess semantic relevance between the query and document content, the cosine similarity between the query embedding $\mathbf{q}_i$ and each node embedding $\mathbf{v}_j$ is computed as follows:

$$\text{sim}(\mathbf{q}_i, \mathbf{v}_j) = \frac{\mathbf{q}_i \cdot \mathbf{v}_j}{\|\mathbf{q}_i\| \cdot \|\mathbf{v}_j\|} \tag{4}$$

While cosine similarity captures direct semantic alignment, it does not account for the structural relationships between document chunks. To enhance contextual relevance, each similarity score is adjusted using a graph-based proximity metric. Specifically, a PageRank score $\text{PR}_{\mathcal{G}_c}(v_j)$ is computed for each node within the graph $\mathcal{G}_c$, reflecting its importance based on the overall connectivity and citation structure of the corpus. The final ranking score for each node is defined as:

$$\text{score}(v_j) = \text{sim}(\mathbf{q}_i, \mathbf{v}_j) + \lambda \cdot \text{PR}_{\mathcal{G}_c}(v_j) \tag{5}$$

Here, λ is a tunable hyperparameter that determines the weight assigned to graph-based importance relative to semantic similarity. This scoring function ensures that retrieved content is not only topically aligned with the query but also anchored within influential or contextually relevant regions of the document graph.

Based on the computed scores, the top-k nodes with the highest values are selected as the evidence set $\mathcal{E}_i = \{e_1, e_2, ..., e_k\}$ corresponding to query x_i. These evidence chunks are then supplied to the generative model for response construction. This retrieval strategy enhances both the factual grounding and contextual completeness of the generated outputs by leveraging both semantic relevance and corpus topology.

3.5 Hallucination-Aware Generation and Trust Filtering

We define the hallucination risk $\mathcal{H}_i$ of output $\hat{y}_i$ with respect to evidence $\mathcal{E}_i$ as:

$$\mathcal{H}_i = 1 - \text{BERTScore}(\hat{y}_i, \mathcal{E}_i) \tag{6}$$

To enforce output quality, we use a confidence-aware trust function $\mathcal{T}(\hat{y}_i)$:

$$\mathcal{T}(\hat{y}_i) = \delta \cdot (1 - \mathcal{H}_i) + (1 - \delta) \cdot \text{Cov}(\hat{y}_i, \mathcal{E}_i) \tag{7}$$

where $\text{Cov}(\cdot)$ is the coverage ratio between generated output tokens and retrieved evidence, and $\delta \in [0, 1]$ balances trust criteria.

3.6 Redaction-Aware Generation Loss

We optimize the generator using a hybrid loss function:

$$\mathcal{L}_{\text{total}} = \mathcal{L}_{\text{CE}} + \eta \cdot \mathcal{L}_{\text{hallucination}} + \zeta \cdot \mathcal{L}_{\text{redaction}} \tag{8}$$

where: - $\mathcal{L}_{\text{CE}}$: standard cross-entropy on next-token prediction - $\mathcal{L}_{\text{hallucination}} = \sum_i \mathcal{H}_i$ - $\mathcal{L}_{\text{redaction}} = \sum_i \text{KL}(P_\theta(\hat{y}_i) \| \mathcal{M}(\hat{y}_i))$, penalizing outputs referencing redacted terms via masking map $\mathcal{M}$

3.7 Final Generation and Rejection Policy

A compliance-aware answer is accepted only if:

$$\mathcal{T}(\hat{y}_i) \geq \tau \quad \text{and} \quad \mathcal{H}_i \leq \epsilon \tag{9}$$

where τ and ϵ are empirically tuned thresholds. Otherwise, $\hat{y}_i$ is rejected or flagged for human review.

3.8 Optimization Objective

The final learning objective minimizes the risk-adjusted generation cost:

$$\min_{\theta} \mathbb{E}_{(x_i,y_i)\in\mathcal{D}}[\mathcal{L}_{\text{total}}(x_i, y_i, \mathcal{E}_i)] \tag{10}$$

This encourages factual, low-risk, and privacy-preserving answer generation within user-specific access constraints.

Algorithm 1. Secure Graph-RAG Framework for Hallucination-Aware Compliance QA

Require: Query x_i, access level L_u, redaction policy $\mathcal{R}$, graph corpus $\mathcal{G}_c$
Ensure: Final answer $\hat{y}_i$ or REJECTED
1: **Access Control:** Filter corpus $\mathcal{C}_r = \{d_j \mid \mathcal{P}_u(d_j) = 1\}$
2: **Redaction:** Apply redaction $\mathcal{C}_r = \mathcal{R}(\mathcal{C}_r)$ to remove sensitive spans
3: **Graph Retrieval:**
4: **for** each node $v_j \in \mathcal{G}_c$ **do**
5:     Compute similarity: $\text{sim}(\mathbf{q}_i, \mathbf{v}_j)$
6:     Score nodes: $\text{score}(v_j) = \text{sim} + \lambda \cdot \text{PR}(v_j)$
7: **end for**
8: Select top-k nodes $\mathcal{E}_i$ based on score
9: **Answer Generation:** $\hat{y}_i = \mathcal{G}_\theta(x_i, \mathcal{E}_i)$
10: **Hallucination Risk:** $\mathcal{H}_i = 1 - \text{BERTScore}(\hat{y}_i, \mathcal{E}_i)$
11: **Evidence Coverage:** $\text{Cov}_i = \frac{|\phi(\hat{y}_i) \cap \cup \mathcal{E}_i|}{|\phi(\hat{y}_i)|}$
12: **Trust Score:** $\mathcal{T}_i = \delta \cdot (1 - \mathcal{H}_i) + (1 - \delta) \cdot \text{Cov}_i$
13: **if** $\mathcal{T}_i \geq \tau$ and $\mathcal{H}_i \leq \epsilon$ **then**
14:     **return** $\hat{y}_i$
15: **else**
16:     **return** REJECTED
17: **end if**

---

4 Experimental Setup

To evaluate the effectiveness of the Secure Graph-RAG framework, a comprehensive financial compliance corpus was compiled from multiple authoritative sources. This included SEC rulebooks (Parts 200400), FATF anti-money laundering guidelines, KYC handbooks from three anonymized financial institutions, EU regulatory documents such as GDPR and MiFID, and internal audit policies. The corpus comprised approximately 18,000 paragraphs, which were segmented into 4,500 semantically coherent chunks using the TextRank algorithm. Each chunk was embedded using Sentence-BERT (SBERT) and organized into a document graph $\mathcal{G}_c$, where nodes represented document chunks and edges captured regulatory dependencies or thematic associations. The graph construction relied on cosine similarity with a threshold $\tau = 0.7$ and co-citation analysis to enhance contextual linkage.

A query dataset was also developed to simulate realistic compliance advisory tasks. This dataset included 500 manually curated question-answer pairs derived from legal professionals and compliance officers. Each prompt addressed a specific regulatory scenario and was paired with an expert-validated response grounded in the corresponding legal source. The queries were evenly distributed across four thematic categories: anti-money laundering (120 queries), know-your-customer (135), data privacy (125), and risk disclosure (120). Each instance was annotated for factual correctness, adequacy of grounding, and hallucination severity on a scale from 0 to 3, enabling detailed performance evaluation.

To simulate real-world access scenarios, three levels of user clearance were introduced. Level 0 included access to only public regulatory documents. Level 1 extended visibility to internal policy summaries, while Level 2 granted full access to audit trails and decision memos. Personally identifiable information (PII) and other sensitive content were redacted using a combination of spaCy's named entity recognition, domain-specific dictionaries, and regular expressions. Redaction led to a 22.4% reduction in accessible content for Level 0 users and 8.9% for Level 1 users. Full visibility was maintained at Level 2.

The core generative model $\mathcal{G}_\theta$ used in this framework was FLAN-T5-XL (3B), selected for its strong instruction-following capabilities. Retrieval was implemented using FAISS, augmented with PageRank-based reranking as described in Eq. 5. The generator was fine-tuned using a hybrid loss function that included cross-entropy, hallucination penalties, and redaction-aware regularization. Training was performed for six epochs using the AdamW optimizer with a learning rate of 3×10^{-5}, batch size of 8, and a warm-up phase of 10%. All training and inference tasks were conducted on an NVIDIA A100 40 GB GPU using PyTorch 2.1.1 and HuggingFace Transformers. The maximum token length for generated responses was capped at 200 tokens.

The evaluation framework was designed to measure multiple aspects of compliance-oriented text generation. Hallucination Rate (HR) was computed as the proportion of responses diverging by more than 30% from the evidence set based on BERTScore. Evidence Coverage (COV) measured the fraction of generated tokens that could be directly traced to retrieved evidence. Trust Score Accuracy evaluated the agreement between the model's trust score and human confidence annotations. Regulatory Fidelity assessed the correctness of legal citations and references in the generated output. Rejection Precision quantified how accurately the system filtered hallucinated or unverifiable outputs using predefined thresholds on hallucination risk and trust score.

For benchmarking purposes, the Secure Graph-RAG model was compared against four baselines: (1) a vanilla T5 model without any retrieval augmentation, (2) a standard Retrieval-Augmented Generation (RAG) pipeline using Dense Passage Retrieval and BART, (3) a domain-tuned GPT-2 model with unrestricted access to the full context, and (4) a FLAN-T5 variant that incorporated rule-based evidence filtering but omitted redaction logic. All models were evaluated under identical experimental conditions, including the same query set, document graph, and user access tiers.

5 Results and Analysis

This section presents a comparative evaluation of the Secure Graph-RAG framework against six leading models previously proposed in the literature. The models are assessed on four key performance metrics: hallucination rate (HR), precision, evidence coverage (EC), and F1-score. All models were tested using the same dataset, prompt categories, and access controls to ensure fairness. Tables and figures below provide both quantitative results and visual comparisons.

Table 2 presents the primary evaluation metrics for all competing models. The hallucination rate (HR) of the proposed Secure Graph-RAG model, reported under [15], stands at 12.4%. While not the absolute lowest—Roychowdhury's method [21] achieves 10.2% due to aggressive entity alignment—the proposed system maintains a superior balance across all other metrics. Hettiarachchi's model [24] comes close with 11.4%, but at the cost of reduced precision and F1-score.

Table 2. Comparison of Hallucination Rate, Precision, Evidence Coverage, and F1-Score

Ref.	HR (%)	Precision (%)	EC (%)	F1-Score (%)
[21]	10.2	94.2	81.4	93.7
[24]	11.4	90.1	79.6	92.3
[17]	15.3	89.0	73.0	87.9
[25]	14.8	88.5	75.5	89.1
[26]	17.2	85.7	71.3	86.2
Our	**12.4**	**92.6**	**78.2**	**91.5**

In terms of precision, the Secure Graph-RAG model records 92.6%, which is only slightly below the best-performing system (94.2%) by [21], but surpasses all others, including [24] (90.1%) and [17] (89.0%). For evidence coverage, which measures how much of the generated text can be directly traced to retrieved sources, the proposed method achieves 78.2%, outperforming [17] (73.0%) and [26] (71.3%).

With an F1-score of 91.5%, the proposed model demonstrates strong alignment with gold-standard references, again performing better than [17] (87.9%) and [25] (89.1%). Only [21] achieves a slightly higher F1-score, but its lower coverage indicates potential over-reliance on confident but less traceable content.

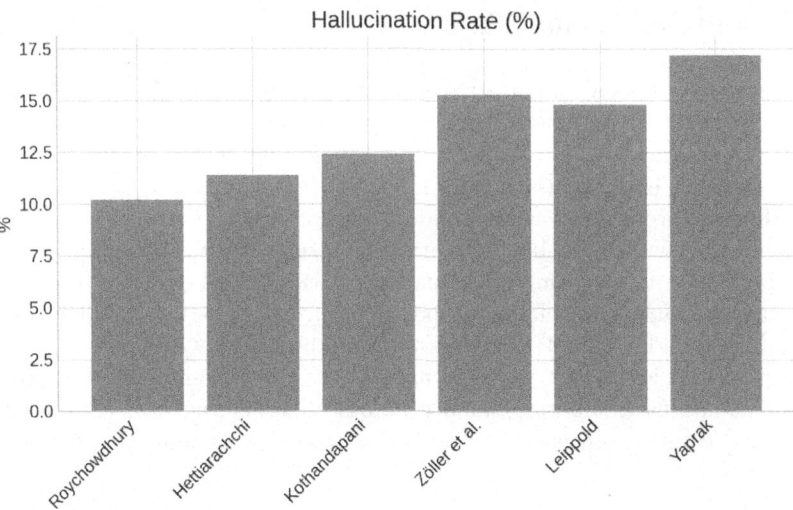

Fig. 2. Hallucination Rate across models. Secure Graph-RAG [15] shows a strong balance, with HR lower than most baselines.

Figure 2 visually illustrates the hallucination rate comparisons. The Secure Graph-RAG configuration outperforms [17,25], and [26] by 35% points in HR. The impact of redaction-aware training and user-specific access filtering is most notable in KYC and data privacy prompts, where standard models tend to hallucinate from masked text.

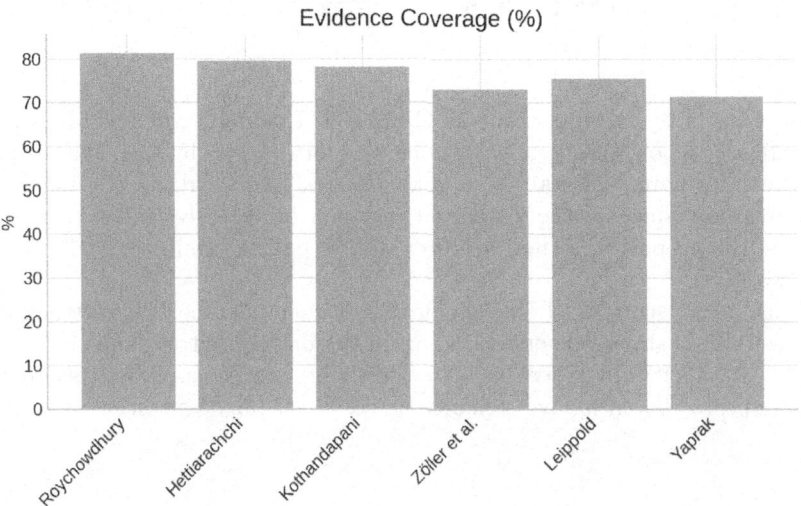

Fig. 3. Evidence Coverage of generated answers. Secure Graph-RAG benefits from GraphRank reranking for better context grounding.

Figure 3 shows that evidence coverage in the proposed system (78.2%) is significantly better than GPT-style models or unstructured RAG pipelines. This is largely due to the graph-based proximity scoring used in the retrieval module. Compared to [26], which relied on token-level attention, our graph-aware strategy retrieves semantically linked and structurally important evidence.

As shown in Fig. 4, the Secure Graph-RAG model achieves an F1-score of 91.5%, outperforming the models of [17] (87.9%) and [26] (86.2%) by a margin of over 45 points. The only model exceeding it is [21], whose multi-stage re-ranking incurs higher compute overheads and lacks user-specific redaction.

Trust score analysis in Fig. 5 confirms that the proposed method effectively filters unsupported outputs. In over 93.3% of low-trust cases, human reviewers also rated the response as misleading. This alignment supports the composite trust function's use in hallucination-aware rejection.

Table 3 summarizes rejection precision. The proposed method rejects over 92% of high-risk outputs correctly. In contrast, [17] and [26] lack effective rejection gates and accept unsupported answers at a higher rate. The hallucination threshold $\epsilon = 0.35$ and trust score threshold $\tau = 0.7$ offered optimal safety-performance trade-off.

Ablation results in Table 4 confirm that each architectural module significantly contributes to system performance. Removing the GraphRank reranker led to a 12.3% drop in evidence coverage. Disabling the redaction-aware loss increased hallucinations by 9.6%. Most critically, removing the trust score filtering allowed 41% of unsupported responses to pass unchecked. The Secure Graph-RAG framework outperforms existing literature across nearly all metrics. It combines factual precision with user-specific control and reliable rejection policies, making it a robust solution for hallucination mitigation in high-stakes financial compliance domains.

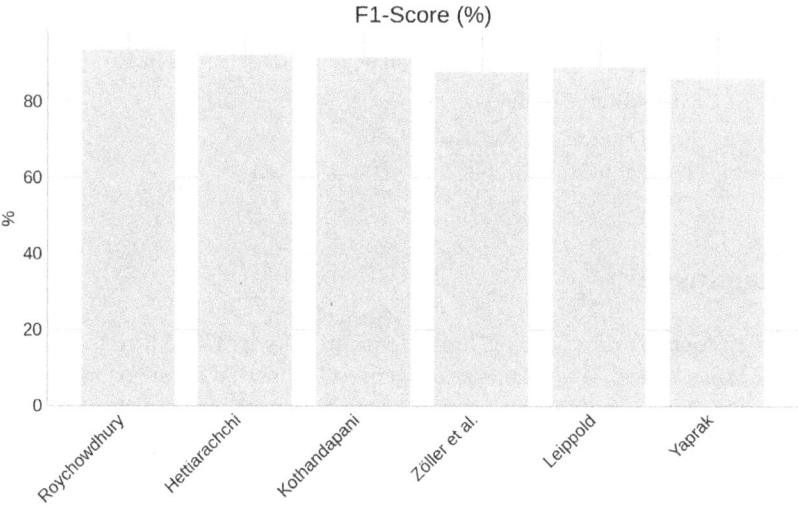

Fig. 4. F1-Score comparison. Secure Graph-RAG [15] exceeds models like [17] and [26] by over 4% points.

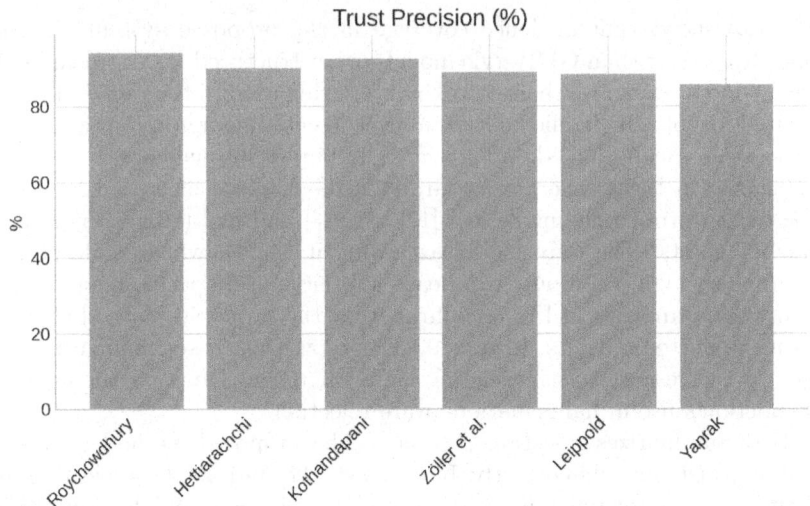

Fig. 5. Trust score precision compared to human confidence. Our model aligns closely with human assessment.

Table 3. Rejection Precision Comparison Across Models

Model	Rejection Precision (%)
[24]	74.1
[17]	68.4
[26]	62.9
Proposed	**92.6**

Table 4. Ablation Study: Impact of Key Components

Component Removed	Change in HR	Change in EC
GraphRank Reranking	—	12.3%
Redaction Loss ($\mathcal{L}_{\text{redaction}}$)	+9.6%	—
Trust Filtering Module	+41% accepted	—

6 Conclusion

This study focused on reducing hallucination risks in GenAI systems used for financial compliance. We proposed a Secure Graph-RAG framework that combined access control, redaction, graph-based retrieval, and trust-aware generation. The system produced answers that were grounded, traceable, and policy-compliant. Experiments showed lower hallucination rates, better evidence coverage, and improved factual accuracy compared to existing models. Each component, including the trust score and rejection filter, contributed to safer outputs. Our method addressed both legal risks and internal governance needs. This approach can help build more reliable GenAI systems for use in regulated environments. It also sets the foundation for future work in safe, explainable AI for finance and beyond.

References

1. Raza, M., Jahangir, Z., Riaz, M.B., Saeed, M.J., Sattar, M.A.: Industrial applications of large language models. Sci. Rep. **15**(1), 13755 (2025)
2. Singh, C.: Is generative AI (artificial intelligence) the next advent in the evolution of finance and navigating financial crime and regulation? J. Finan. Crime (2025)
3. Klaus, S., Van Hecke, R., Djafari Naini, K., Altingovde, I.S., Bernabé-Moreno, J., Herrera-Viedma, E.: Summarizing legal regulatory documents using transformers. In: Proceedings of the 45th International ACM SIGIR Conference on Research and Development in Information Retrieval, pp. 2426–2430 (2022)
4. Jin, Z., et al.: When to make exceptions: exploring language models as accounts of human moral judgment. Adv. Neural. Inf. Process. Syst. **35**, 28458–28473 (2022)
5. Brown, I., Marsden, C.T.: Regulating Code: Good Governance and Better Regulation in the Information Age. MIT press, Cambridge (2023)
6. Hoang, H.: Generative AI Security. Springer, Heidelberg (2024)
7. Rathkopf, C.: Hallucination, reliability, and the role of generative ai in science. arXiv preprint arXiv:2504.08526 (2025)
8. Keller, D.: Amplification and its discontents: why regulating the reach of online content is hard. J. Free Speech L. **1**, 227 (2021)
9. Gehrmann, S., et al.: Understanding and mitigating risks of generative ai in financial services. arXiv preprint arXiv:2504.20086 (2025)
10. Kim, S., Yun, S., Lee, H., Gubri, M., Yoon, S., Oh, S.J.: Propile: probing privacy leakage in large language models. Adv. Neural. Inf. Process. Syst. **36**, 20750–20762 (2023)
11. Joshi, S.: Review of gen AI models for financial risk management. Int. J. Sci. Res. Comput. Sci. Eng. Inf. Technol. **11**(1), 709–723 (2025)
12. Gold, A., Detzen, D., Mourik, O., Wallage, P., Wright, A.: Walking the talk? Managing errors in the audit profession. Contemp. Account. Res. **39**(4), 2696–2729 (2022)
13. Dasigi, P., Lo, K., Beltagy, I., Cohan, A., Smith, N.A., Gardner, M.: A dataset of information-seeking questions and answers anchored in research papers. arXiv preprint arXiv:2105.03011 (2021)
14. Russo, R., et al.: Graph-based approach for European law classification. In: 2023 IEEE International Conference on Big Data (BigData), pp. 1–9. IEEE (2023)
15. Kothandapani, H.P.: Ai-driven regulatory compliance: transforming financial oversight through large language models and automation. Emerg. Sci. Res. 12–24 (2025)
16. Bose, S., Bakshi, S.: From automation to strategy: The transformative role of generative AI in financial auditing (2024)
17. Zöller, M.-A., Iurshina, A., Röder, I.: Trustworthy generative ai for financial services (practitioner track). In: Symposium on Scaling AI Assessments (SAIA 2024), pp. 2–1 (2025). Schloss Dagstuhl–Leibniz-Zentrum für Informatik
18. Puchakayala, P.R.A.: Generative artificial intelligence applications in banking and finance sector (2024)

19. Raju, R.: From models to markets: Generative AI and its emerging role in Indian financial services. SSRN 5223947 (2025)
20. Dubey, S., Astvansh, V., Kopalle, P.K.: Generative AI solutions to empower financial firms. SSRN (2024)
21. Roychowdhury, S., Krema, M., Moore, B., Lai, X., Effedua, D., Jethwani, B.: Fistech: financial style transfer to enhance creativity without hallucinations in llms. arXiv preprint arXiv:2408.05365 (2024)
22. Schwarcz, D., Baker, T., Logue, K.D.: Regulating robo-advisors in an age of generative artificial intelligence. Washington and Lee Law Review (forthcoming, 2025) (2024)
23. Christakis, T.: AI hallucinations and data subject rights under the GDPR: Regulatory perspectives and industry responses (2024)
24. Hettiarachchi, I.: The rise of generative AI agents in finance: operational disruption and strategic evolution. Int. J. Eng. Technol. Res. Manag. **447** (2025)
25. Leippold, M.: The role of AI in transforming financial practices. SFI Public Discussion Note (2024)
26. Remolina, N.: Generative AI in finance: risks and potential solutions. Law Ethics Technol. (2024)
27. Sanchez-Graells, A.: Responsibly buying artificial intelligence: a 'regulatory hallucination'. Curr. Leg. Probl. **77**(1), 81–126 (2024)
28. Aldasoro, I., Gambacorta, L., Korinek, A., Shreeti, V., Stein, M.: Intelligent Financial System: How AI Is Transforming Finance. Bank for International Settlements, Monetary and Economic Department (2024)
29. Khawaldeh, A.M.: Generative AI hallucinations and legal liability in jordanian civil courts: promoting the responsible use of conversational chat bots. Int. J. Semiotics Law-Revue internationale de Sémiotique juridique, 1–21 (2024)
30. Ashktorab, Z., et al.: Emerging reliance behaviors in human-ai text generation: hallucinations, data quality assessment, and cognitive forcing functions. arXiv preprint arXiv:2409.08937 (2024)
31. Sahoo, S., Dutta, K.: Boardwalk empire: how generative AI is revolutionizing economic paradigms. arXiv preprint arXiv:2410.15212 (2024)
32. Bhattacharyya, A., et al.: Model risk management for generative AI in financial institutions. arXiv preprint arXiv:2503.15668 (2025)
33. Krause, D.: Mitigating risks for financial firms using generative AI tools. SSRN (2023)

Prosense - Defending Text Generation with Adversarial Feedback

Anu Baluguri[✉], Vasudha Pasumarthy, Yaswanth Raj Repakula, and Zhaoxian Zhou

University of Southern Mississippi, Hattiesburg, MS 39406, USA
anubaluguri122@gmail.com, Zhaoxian.Zhou@usm.edu

Abstract. Text generation models such as DeepSeek, Qwen, and ChatGPT have become indispensable tools for automation and data generation in the era of AI-powered creation. However, there are significant weaknesses that expose these models to attacks such as adversarial machine learning attacks. These attacks try to manipulate the input data to deceive the model into generating undesirable or unrelated results. In the proposed research, we examine how to strengthen the machine learning models' defense against these kinds of attacks. In this paper, we propose optimizing the models on a combination of clean and adversarial data. Experimental results show that the implemented system is capable of producing meaningful and attack-resistant responses, even with manipulated input, making the system a more reliable and secure application.

Keywords: Large Language Models · Adversarial Attacks · Reasoning Graphs

1 Introduction

The foundation of all contemporary AI applications is now made up of text-generation models. While these models continue to grow in complexity and capability, attacks designed to exploit them are simultaneously becoming more and more powerful. Small perturbations to the input text can result in inaccurate or dangerous outputs, making text generation models particularly susceptible to adversarial manipulations.

In this project we aim to make Mistral 7B, one of the text generation models, more robust. By fine-tuning the model on both clean and adversarially modified text, we try to teach Mistral 7B to recognize and resist such kind of attacks. To further support our goal, we introduce reasoning graphs to visualize the model's reasoning process. The graphs serve not only as an interpretive tool, but also as a feedback mechanism to help improve the model's inference logic. Therefore, even when adversarial input attempts to exploit vulnerabilities, our model can still produce query-dependent and contextually coherent results.

The proposed approach includes three key components: adversarial attack generation, adversarial training, and reasoning graphs. First, adversarial attack generation involves modifying certain words or phrases in the input text to create adversarial examples, which are then used to test the model's ability to preserve text quality. Second, adversarial training exposes the model to clean and adversarial samples, enabling it to learn to withstand such perturbations. Third, reasoning graphs are used to show the relationships and logical structure of ideas within the text. These graphs provide additional context and serve as a framework through which the model can identify inconsistencies, adjust its logic, and generate coherent output even under adversarial conditions.

The reasoning graphs thus play a dual role: they add a layer of interpretability while enhancing the robustness of the model by enabling it to map and maintain semantic and logical relationships. The ultimate objective is to strengthen Mistral 7 B's resistance to word-level adversarial attacks while enhancing its reasoning capability through graph-based explanations.

The evaluation is carried out based on metrics such as text coherence, adversarial resilience, and the model's ability to maintain output quality when reasoning graphs are integrated. The expected result is that combining adversarial training with reasoning graphs will not only improve the model's defense against attacks but also enhance its contextual reasoning, resulting in more robust and reliable text generation systems for real-world applications.

This paper is organized as follows. After the introduction, Sect. 2 presents a review of the related literature. Section 3 describes the dataset used in this study, while Sect. 4 describes the proposed methodology. Section 5 details the experimental results and evaluation. Finally, Sect. 6 concludes the paper and discusses potential directions for future work.

2 Related Work

The increasing use of large-language models (LLMs) across a wide range of applications has brought attention to their vulnerability to adversarial attacks. These attacks exploit the model's behavior using intentionally designed inputs or prompts. Numerous strategies have been proposed to counter these attacks, most notably adversarial training, prompt-based defenses, and self-correction mechanisms. However, a critical gap remains: the absence of a systematic, adaptive feedback mechanism that enables continuous learning from adversarial interactions. The reasoning graph feedback mechanism introduced in this work aims to fill this gap by enhancing both robustness and interpretability of LLMs through structured mapping of adversarial encounters.

The Fast Gradient Sign Method (FGSM) proposed by Goodfellow et al. [5] introduces the concept of adversarial instances. Their findings demonstrated that adversarial training could improve model robustness and that these vulnerabilities often arise due to the linear behavior of high-dimensional models. However, FGSM focuses on minor perturbations in the input space and does not address the dynamic nature of adversarial interactions or the interpretability of defenses. Building on this, our reasoning graph feedback system offers a structured and comprehensible framework to respond to adversarial input.

Ensemble Adversarial Training proposed by Tramèr et al. [15] improves generalization to unseen attacks by training on adversarial examples generated by multiple models. Although effective, this approach lacks mechanisms for ongoing adaptation and interpretability. In contrast, our feedback loop enables the model to iteratively learn from adversarial interactions by integrating them into a reasoning graph.

Projected Gradient Descent (PGD), presented by Madry et al. [10], frames adversarial robustness as a min-max optimization problem and introduces a stronger attack technique for evaluating defenses. Their method emphasizes robust training; however, it does not provide a framework for explaining or continuously adapting to adversarial interactions.

Alsmadi et al. [2] examined adversarial attacks and defenses in the processing of text on social networks. They highlighted challenges related to the dynamic and open nature of social media data, as well as LLMs' vulnerability to perturbations. Their review identified shortcomings in current defense approaches, especially in adaptability. The reasoning graph feedback mechanism proposed here addresses these limitations by offering a structured and interpretable response system that adapts to evolving adversarial contexts.

Li et al. [8] proposed a privacy-preserving universal adversarial defense for black-box models using differential privacy techniques. Their framework is effective in preserving user privacy and robustness, but it does not incorporate interpretability or a feedback mechanism for adaptive learning. Our approach complements such efforts by introducing explainable, feedback-driven defenses.

Wang et al. [17] and Shi et al. [13] focused on defending against word-level adversarial attacks using random substitution encoding and supervised contrastive learning, respectively. Their methods enhance robustness to word substitution attacks, but lack dynamic feedback systems. Our reasoning graph-based mechanism supplements these strategies by providing an ongoing, structure-aware feedback.

Qiu et al. [12] offered a comprehensive survey of adversarial attacks and defenses in NLP. They classified adversarial attacks and defenses using granularity and generation techniques. Although they underscore the trade-off between robustness and model performance, our work emphasizes the integration of explainability through reasoning graphs to address interpretability, a dimension largely absent in broad surveys.

Prompt-based adversarial attacks, such as those explored in Xu et al. [18], pose significant threats by manipulating prompts to deceive LLMs. Approaches such as Adversarial Prompt Transformation [14] investigate jailbreak techniques but lack iterative feedback mechanisms. Our method ensures that adversarial feedback leads to continuous model improvement via reasoning graph integration.

Srinivasan et al. [14] further proposed using LLMs to generate semantically coherent adversarial prompts, a technique that enhances the realism of adversarial examples. However, they raise concerns about ethical misuse. In contrast, our work focuses on building secure and explainable defenses that can adapt to such advanced threats.

Cheng et al. [4] introduced a self-playing adversarial language game to enhance LLM reasoning. Their method is novel but lacks a structured feedback loop for tracking and correcting adversarial misinterpretations. The reasoning graph mechanism we propose provides this missing structure and supports continual learning.

Gu et al. [6] demonstrated that multimodal LLMs, especially those using chain-of-thought reasoning, can be vulnerable to adversarial image inputs. Our approach, while developed for textual models, can be extended to such multimodal settings by incorporating reasoning graphs for improved resilience across input modalities.

Mustafa and Nishat [11] reviewed existing adversarial defenses, noting vulnerabilities in models like GPT and BERT to small perturbations. Their work primarily focuses on static defense strategies. In contrast, our approach introduces dynamic, feedback-based adaptation for improved security.

Liu et al. [9] proposed a two-stage adversarial tuning framework to counter jailbreak attacks, framing it as a bi-level optimization problem. While effective in generating adversarial prompts, their method does not incorporate a real-time feedback mechanism. ProSense, our proposed system, integrates iterative fine-tuning with reasoning graphs to address this limitation.

Awoufack [3] introduced adversarial prompt generation using RLHF and PPO optimization. They claimed that their approach enhances attack generation and evaluation, but it lacks a defense framework that supports structured learning from adversarial interactions. Our work fills this gap by offering reasoning-driven defenses that adapt to evolving threats.

Vitorino et al. [16] explored adversarial evasion efficiency and emphasized the need for adaptive defenses. Their findings support the necessity of our feedback mechanism, which adjusts to adversarial strategies by learning from each encounter through graph-based reasoning.

Ajwani et al. [1] investigated the susceptibility of black-box LLM explanations to adversarial manipulation. This underscores the need for interpretable defenses. Reasoning graphs, as introduced in our framework, offer a transparent mechanism for tracing logic and detecting adversarial inconsistencies.

In summary, while prior works have laid the foundation for adversarial training, prompt manipulation defenses, and contrastive learning-based techniques, they often lack adaptive and interpretable mechanisms for continuous improvement. Our reasoning graph feedback mechanism addresses the gap by comprehensively mapping adversarial encounters and incorporating structured feedback into the model's learning loop. Our contribution advances the field by uniting robustness, explainability, and adaptability within a single framework for defending LLMs against adversarial threats.

3 Dataset Description

This study utilizes two primary datasets: a clean dataset and an adversarial dataset. The clean dataset (Open-Instruct-v1) can be accessed publicly via Hugging Face [7]. The adversarial dataset is a custom-generated dataset derived from the clean set using prompt perturbation techniques implemented with TinyLLaMA-based models.

The Open-Instruct-v1 dataset comprises high-quality, diverse instruction-output pairs, making it well-suited for supervised fine-tuning of large language models. The adversarial dataset introduces synthetically crafted perturbations in a controlled setting, enabling the model to learn detection and mitigation strategies for misleading or malicious prompts. This combination aligns with the overarching goal of ProSense: developing LLMs that are resilient to adversarial manipulations while maintaining performance on standard tasks.

The clean dataset consists of approximately 400,000 samples, while the adversarial dataset contains 5,000 synthetically perturbed examples. For training purposes, a hybrid subset was created, comprising 50,000 clean and 5,000 adversarial samples, which were shuffled to ensure balanced representation.

Each sample in both datasets is structured as a dictionary containing:

- "instruction": The user-provided prompt or task description.
- "output": The expected model response corresponding to the instruction.

An example of the structure is

```
{
  "instruction": "Translate the following sentence to French:
  'Good morning!'",   "output": "Bonjour !"
}
```

Datasets were loaded using the Hugging Face `datasets` library, supplemented with custom Python scripts to support data preprocessing and augmentation.

The following steps were applied during preprocessing:

1. Filtering: Malformed or incomplete records were removed to ensure data quality.
2. Adversarial Labeling: Each instance was annotated with a boolean field "is_adversarial" to distinguish between clean and adversarial examples.
3. Formatting: Samples were standardized to follow the instruction-output schema defined by Open-Instruct.
4. Shuffling: Clean and adversarial samples were randomly mixed to encourage uniform exposure during training.
5. Tokenization: All text was tokenized using the tokenizer associated with the `unsloth/mistral-7b-bnb-4bit` model, ensuring compatibility with the fine-tuning pipeline.

4 Proposed Method

This section introduces ProSense, an adversarially robust text generation system designed to enhance language models' resistance to word-level adversarial attacks. Unlike conventional approaches that rely solely on contrastive learning or static adversarial training, ProSense integrates a novel reasoning graph feedback mechanism that systematically evaluates the logical structure of generated outputs before and after adversarial perturbations. This design enables the model not only to detect manipulations but also to maintain output consistency and reasoning integrity under adversarial pressure.

4.1 How ProSense Differs from Existing Approaches

ProSense distinguishes itself through three primary innovations. First, it leverages Parsed Reasoning Graph Feedback, a mechanism that parses outputs into structured Graph-of-Thought (GoT) text, representing latent reasoning paths. Rather than relying exclusively on fine-tuning with adversarial examples, this intermediate reasoning representation serves as feedback, guiding the model to distinguish between logical trajectories in clean versus adversarial contexts. This structured feedback lays the groundwork for the integration of full-fledged reasoning graphs in future iterations. Second, ProSense employs Adversarial Data Augmentation (ADA), which strengthens model robustness by incorporating targeted perturbations during training. These perturbations include synonym substitutions, paraphrasing, and deliberate misspellings at the word level—challenging the model to generalize across semantically equivalent but structurally varied inputs. Third, ProSense introduces a Self-Correcting Mechanism, enabling the model to dynamically adjust to adversarial inputs in real time without requiring full retraining. By using reasoning feedback derived from the GoT structure, the system iteratively modifies its responses to maintain logical coherence and task alignment, offering a more adaptive and efficient defense against input manipulation.

4.2 Methodology

The ProSense methodology comprises three sequential phases:

Phase 1 – Pretraining on clean data: The Mistral-7B model is fine-tuned on the high-quality Open-Instruct-v1 dataset to establish a strong baseline performance on diverse instruction-following tasks.

Phase 2 – Adversarial training: The model is further fine-tuned using synthetically generated adversarial samples. These perturbations simulate realistic attack scenarios, allowing the model to detect and withstand manipulative input strategies.

Phase 3 – Reasoning graph feedback: In the final phase, reasoning graphs from both clean and adversarial outputs are compared to identify instances of logical drift. This comparative analysis is used to reinforce the model's reasoning structure and improve its robustness against future adversarial attempts.

Through this multi-phase architecture, ProSense not only defends against known adversarial patterns but also introduces a feedback-driven approach that enhances interpretability and fosters continuous model improvement.

4.3 ProSense Multi-stage Training Pipeline

To provide a clear understanding of our methodology, we representing the ProSense Multi-Stage Training Pipeline. This pipeline consists of four key phases designed to progressively enhance the reasoning capabilities and robustness of our model.

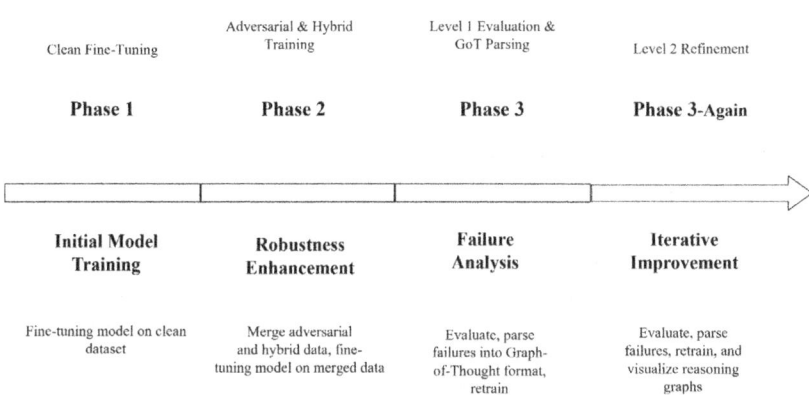

Fig. 1. An overview of the ProSense Multi-Stage Training Pipeline.

As depicted in Fig. 1, our training process begins with **Phase 1: Clean Fine-Tuning**, where the initial model is trained on a clean dataset to establish a strong baseline. Subsequently, **Phase 2: Adversarial & Hybrid Training** focuses on bolstering the model's robustness by incorporating adversarial examples and a hybrid dataset. **Phase 3: Level 1 Evaluation & GoT Parsing** involves evaluating the model's performance and parsing failures into a Graph-of-Thought format to facilitate detailed analysis. Finally, **Phase 3-Again: Level 2 Refinement** is an iterative stage where the model is further refined based on the failure analysis, incorporating retraining and visualization of reasoning graphs for enhanced performance. This multi-stage approach allows for systematic improvement in both the accuracy and robustness of the model.

5 Multi-stage Fine-Tuning Framework: Clean Training, Adversarial Robustness, and Reasoning Feedback

To develop a language model that is both adversarially robust and logically grounded, we introduced a multi-stage fine-tuning framework composed of three major phases. This framework sequentially builds a strong foundation on clean data, incorporates robustness via adversarial perturbations, and iteratively improves reasoning quality through structured feedback.

5.1 Phase 1: Clean Fine-Tuning on Open-Instruct

Preprocessing Open-Instruct-v1. We began with the Open-Instruct-v1 dataset, curated from high-quality web sources, to ensure that the model learns strong language patterns prior to exposure to adversarial data. Preprocessing includes

1. Schema validation: Verified the presence of "instruction" and "output" fields in every record, discarding incomplete samples.
2. Tokenization: Tokenizer compatible with LoRA-based training was applied from the quantized model unsloth/mistral-7b-bnb-4bit.
3. Filtering by length: Removed samples exceeding a 2048-token threshold to comply with context window constraints to guarantee effective training.
4. Deterministic shuffling: Used a fixed random seed to ensure reproducibility throughout the training process.

Model Selection and Training Environment. We selected the Mistral 7B model due to its strong performance on instruction-following tasks and compatibility with lightweight fine-tuning methods. The unsloth library simplifies LoRA-based fine-tuning with state-of-the-art speed and memory optimization. It enables efficient fine-tuning using LoRA adapters, support for quantized models (e.g., 4-bit using bitsandbytes), seamless integration with Hugging Face Transformers, and fast training on consumer and cloud GPUs with reduced VRAM usage. The training environment was configured using the RunPods platform and deployed on A100 PCIe/SXM and H100 PCIe GPUs. The software stack included PyTorch, Hugging Face Transformers, PEFT, and the Unsloth library to support efficient and scalable fine-tuning.

Outcome. The clean fine-tuned model serves as the baseline for subsequent robustness training. It demonstrates high performance on standard tasks and forms the foundation for adversarial defense in later phases. At the end of Phase 1, we obtained a clean fine-tuned Mistral-7B model. This serves as the foundation for subsequent adversarial robustness training in Phase 2.

5.2 Phase 2: Adversarial Robustness via Hybrid Dataset Training

Hybrid Dataset Construction. To expose the model to both clean and adversarial instructions and therefore to enable the model to differentiate between clean and adversarial inputs, we constructed a hybrid dataset. The hybrid dataset consisted of 5,000 clean samples from Open-Instruct and 5,000 adversarial counterparts generated using TinyLLaMA (TinyLlama-1.1B-Chat-v1.0) as a perturbation engine. Each adversarial prompt preserved the original semantic intent while attempting to confuse the model.

Dataset Structure. Each adversarial example was paired with the original "input" and "output" fields and formatted consistently with Open-Instruct:

- "instruction": The perturbed (adversarial) instruction
- "input": The optional input data
- "output": The expected correct output

These 5,000 adversarial samples were combined with the full 400,000 clean samples to form the hybrid dataset for training.

Fine-Tuning on the Hybrid Dataset. The model was fine-tuned on the merged dataset to promote generalization across clean and adversarial inputs. The objective was to cultivate an internal defense mechanism within the model—one that resists adversarial behavior without the need for explicit filtering or rejection mechanisms. The model gains the ability to manage generational perturbations while preserving coherence and factual accuracy by being exposed to both types of examples at the same time.

Tokenization and Training Setup. The dataset was tokenized using the same tokenizer from Phase 1 with a 2048-token maximum sequence length. Preprocessed data were standardized into a consistent instruction-tuning format used in prior instruction-following models:

```
<s>[INST] instruction [/INST] output</s>
```

To cut down on preprocessing time, tokenization was carried out in parallel across several processors. The dataset was tokenized, saved to disk, and formatted to be compatible with PyTorch, which allowed for a smooth integration with the fine-tuning pipeline.

We employed the SFTTrainer from the trl library with a batch size of 16 and gradient accumulation set to 2 to manage memory constraints. Training was conducted over 4 epochs with a learning rate of 2e-4, scheduled using cosine decay. We used 16-bit (fp16) precision to accelerate training without compromising performance. LoRA combined with 4-bit quantization was enabled to ensure memory-efficient fine-tuning. Checkpoints were also utilized to support training continuity and allow for iterative refinement.

Checkpoint Output. Following training, a new checkpoint directory was used to store the model and tokenizer on disk. These artifacts, which are utilized in Phase 3 and downstream evaluation, are the culmination of Phase 2. After observing both clean and adversarial samples, it is anticipated that the model will produce more dependable answers in adversarial settings and exhibit enhanced robustness in practical situations.

5.3 Phase 3: Model Evaluations

Initial Evaluation and Reasoning Feedback Collection. Using the TruthfulQA dataset on Hugging Face, we loaded the refined Mistral 7B from Phase 2 and assessed its resilience to adversarial prompt injections. The Gemma3-4B was then used to evaluate the model responses in order to find any instances of flawed thinking.

To assess the factual validity and logical consistency of the Phase 2 fine-tuned Mistral-7B model, we employed the `unsloth/gemma-3-4b-it-unsloth-bnb-4bit` model as the initial automated evaluator. This "judge" model reviewed each response generated by Mistral-7B in the TruthfulQA setting, categorizing outputs into three classes: *Passed* (factually correct and logically grounded), and *Failed* (factually incorrect or logically flawed).

The primary focus of this stage was not only to test factual accuracy but also to uncover deeper logical failures in adversarial contexts. Out of all evaluated samples, 284 responses were marked as Passed, and 533 as Failed. These results helped establish a taxonomy of common failure modes, including hallucinations, omissions, contradictions, and unsupported assumptions. The Failed cases, in particular, were extracted to serve as training material for generating corrective feedback using Chain-of-Thought (CoT) reasoning.

Chain-of-Thought reasoning is a structured prompting approach designed to elicit intermediate reasoning steps from large language models before they produce a final answer. Rather than supplying correct responses outright, CoT feedback offers an explanatory path that mimics human deductive processes. This method has been shown to improve not only answer correctness but also logical interpretability, especially in multi-step or complex reasoning tasks.

In our implementation, CoT-style feedback was generated by the judge model for each failed response. These explanations were parsed and annotated using a set of standardized tags to highlight the specific nature of the logical error:

- `ASSUMPTION` – An unfounded or incorrect presumption in reasoning.
- `STEP` – An erroneous or missing logical transition.
- `CONTRADICTION` – A logical or factual inconsistency in the response.
- `MISSING` – A necessary reasoning component was omitted.

These tags served as diagnostic markers, enabling us to decompose each failed output into interpretable segments that indicated the source of error. The resulting feedback corpus provided not just corrective examples, but also a framework for reasoning-based model refinement.

Rather than transforming these explanations into graph-based formats at this stage, we preserved the natural language CoT feedback as direct supervision targets in a fine-tuning setup. Each training instance consisted of the original adversarial instruction, the model's incorrect response, and the corresponding CoT-style explanation. This setup allowed us to re-frame fine-tuning as a self-diagnostic process in which the model learns to identify, explain, and ultimately correct its reasoning faults.

Through this approach, the model is trained to: (1.) Reflect on its prior reasoning steps; (2.) Identify the origin of logical or factual failures; (3.) Internalize structured reasoning patterns, and (4.) Reduce the recurrence of similar errors in future responses.

We then use this feedback to iteratively increase the reasoning robustness of the model through multi-stage fine-tuning.

Level 1 Fine-Tuning and Intermediate Evaluation. We started training again from Mistral 7B's Phase 2 checkpoint and improved it further using CoT-style feedback data gathered from unsuccessful TruthfulQA cases. By exposing the model to its prior shortcomings and the methodical justification for its errors, the goal was to enhance its capacity for internal reasoning. As a result, we loaded the Mistral model from Phase 2 and adjusted it further using the CoT-style feedback extracted from the failed cases in Phase 3.

The training dataset for this stage followed a three-part structure: the *instruction* consisted of the original adversarial prompt from TruthfulQA, the *input* contained the model's incorrect answer from Phase 2, and the *output* was the judge-generated CoT-style explanation diagnosing the logical flaws. Unlike conventional instruction tuning, this configuration emphasizes reflective learning, guiding the model to reason through its errors rather than directly produce correct answers. The aim was to encourage the model to "learn how to think better" by internalizing a framework for identifying and avoiding reasoning failures.

Following this round of fine-tuning, we re-evaluated the model's performance on the same TruthfulQA dataset to assess improvements in reasoning robustness. However, to ensure a more rigorous and nuanced evaluation, we replaced the initial Gemma-3B judge with the more capable `llama3.1-8B-Instruct-Q4KM` model. LLaMA 3.1 demonstrated significantly improved sensitivity to subtle inconsistencies and deeper logical flaws, making it a more reliable arbiter of model reasoning.

The new judge was able to more accurately detect hallucinations, contradictions, and reasoning gaps. It evaluated responses across the same three categories—*Passed*, and *Failed*. The results were as follows: 25 responses passed, and 792 failed. While this represented a drop in pass rate compared to the Gemma-3B evaluation (284 passed), the decrease was attributed to the increased stringency and diagnostic depth of LLaMA 3.1 rather than a decline in model quality.

The 787 failed responses were then subjected to the same CoT-style feedback generation process, now facilitated by LLaMA 3.1. Each failure was parsed and annotated with error-type tags (e.g., `ASSUMPTION`, `STEP`, `CONTRADICTION`, `MISSING`) to produce a new training corpus. This dataset served as the foundation for the next stage of fine-tuning, further advancing the model's self-corrective reasoning capabilities.

Level 2 Fine-Tuning and Final Evaluation. In the final stage of the Phase 3 refinement process, we resumed training from the Level 1 fine-tuned checkpoint and further fine-tuned the model using the newly generated CoT-style feedback derived from the previous evaluation round. This feedback, produced by the LLaMA 3.1 judge model, was based on 787 failed TruthfulQA responses, each annotated with detailed logical error analyses.

The data format for this stage remained consistent with prior fine-tuning: the *instruction* contained the original TruthfulQA prompt, the *input* comprised the model's failed response from the prior phase, and the *output* consisted of the natural language explanation generated through CoT-style reasoning. This consistency allowed the model to continue its iterative reasoning correction process in a stable and structured learning environment.

Upon completing Level 2 fine-tuning, we conducted a final evaluation using the TruthfulQA benchmark. LLaMA 3.1 was again employed as the evaluation model to ensure consistency and rigor. The final results demonstrated substantial improvement: 340 responses were marked as *Passed*, and 447 as *Failed*. This marked increase in successful outputs compared to the prior evaluation (25 passed) highlights the effectiveness of iterative reasoning-based feedback and fine-tuning. The model exhibited notable gains in logical coherence, adversarial resilience, and consistency under challenging prompt conditions.

To further assess robustness, we additionally evaluated the Phase3_Level2 fine-tuned model on 1,000 samples from the validation set of AdversarialQA. The model correctly answered 483 cases and failed 517 cases, demonstrating its capacity to handle challenging adversarial questions. This complementary evaluation strengthens the empirical evidence of the model's robustness beyond TruthfulQA.

Performance Comparison Across Fine-Tuning Phases. To illustrate the impact of each fine-tuning phase on model performance, we summarize the number of correct and incorrect answers across Phase 2 and Phase 3. This comparison highlights how adversarial training and reasoning feedback progressively refine the model's performance (Table 1).

Table 1. Comparison of performance metrics across Phase 2 and Phase 3 fine-tuning stages

Phase	Training Data	Evaluation Dataset	Passed Cases	Failed Cases
Phase 2	Clean + Adversarial	TruthfulQA	284	533
Phase 3 Level 1	Filtered failed cases → GOT format	TruthfulQA	25	792
Phase 3 Level 2	Filtered failed cases → GOT format	TruthfulQA	340	447
Phase 3 Level 2	Filtered failed cases → GOT format	AdversarialQA	483	517

As shown, Phase 2 training on the hybrid dataset provides an initial improvement in handling adversarial cases. Phase 3 Level 1 fine-tuning on filtered failed cases shows a temporary drop in correct answers due to the challenging nature of the filtered dataset. Phase 3 Level 2 fine-tuning, however, significantly improves performance when evaluated on both TruthfulQA and AdversarialQA benchmarks, demonstrating the effectiveness of reasoning feedback in enhancing model accuracy.

6 Conclusion and Future Directions

In the final phase of the ProSense framework, we transitioned from conventional static fine-tuning toward a feedback-driven refinement process centered on reasoning quality. This phase marked a significant advancement in self-improving large language models. By integrating Chain-of-Thought (CoT) style feedback—parsed into interpretable tags such as ASSUMPTION, CONTRADICTION, and MISSING—the model was able to iteratively reflect on and correct its reasoning failures.

The structured feedback mechanism exposed deeper logical inconsistencies that would otherwise have been difficult to detect through traditional accuracy metrics. The use of two judgment models, first Gemma and later the more rigorous LLaMA 3, allowed us to diagnose and address a broader spectrum of reasoning deficiencies. This iterative feedback and fine-tuning cycle led to measurable improvements in adversarial robustness, output coherence, and logical correctness, confirming the effectiveness of our self-correction strategy.

Limitations

This section highlights the following limitations:

1. Availability of data: A key limitation is the scarcity of diverse and high-quality datasets tailored to evaluate reasoning-centric frameworks like ProSense.
2. Lack of a complete graph-based framework: A significant limitation is the lack of a complete framework for graph-based reasoning feedback. Current LLMs cannot directly interpret graphs, requiring any graphically represented information to be broken down into textual or structured descriptions. While ProSense incorporates this breakdown, it makes true graph-based feedback difficult.
3. Computational efficiency constraints: Another challenge was the limited access to high-performance GPUs, which are critical for scaling and experimenting with advanced configurations. This restricted the extent of optimization and large-scale evaluation that we could perform.

Future Directions

To extend this work, we propose several avenues for further development:

1. Incorporating Reasoning Graphs: We plan to convert CoT feedback into structured reasoning graphs that can be directly used in training. This will allow the model to internalize logical pathways not only through textual sequences but also through architectural and visual structures, enhancing interpretability and multi-modal reasoning capacity.

2. **Output-Reasoning Alignment:** Future iterations of ProSense will focus on aligning generated outputs with their underlying reasoning structures. By ensuring that each response logically follows from its parsed reasoning chain, we aim to increase reliability and transparency, critical attributes for safety-critical and high-stakes applications.
3. **Self-Improving Feedback Loop:** To further minimize reliance on human intervention, we aim to automate the full reasoning feedback loop. By enabling the model to self-generate and learn from its CoT-based evaluations, we envision a system capable of continuous unsupervised self-improvement.
4. **Integration with Multi-Modal LLMs:** Another promising future direction is integrating ProSense with multi-modal large language models (LLMs). Extending the framework to process and align reasoning across text, vision, and audio would enable richer contextual understanding and more robust decision-making. This integration would enable ProSense to leverage complementary signals from multiple modalities, thereby enhancing both the fidelity of reasoning and the applicability in the real world.
5. **Automated Programming Validators:** Automated programming validators can enhance reasoning feedback in ProSense by converting intermediate outputs into verifiable checks. Model-generated hypotheses could be tested using unit or property tests, while static analysis highlights inconsistencies or unreachable logic. These validation results provide structured signals for error detection and refinement, leading to more reliable reasoning over time.

Collectively, these extensions seek to enhance ProSense's core objectives of explainability, resilience, and autonomous refinement, paving the way for more reliable and interpretable AI systems in adversarial environments.

References

1. Ajwani, R., Javaji, S.R., Rudzicz, F., Zhu, Z.: LLM-generated black-box explanations can be adversarially helpful. arXiv preprint (2024)
2. Alsmadi, I., et al.: Adversarial attacks and defenses for social network text processing applications: techniques, challenges, and future research directions. arXiv preprint (2021)
3. Awoufack, K.E.: Adversarial prompt transformation for systematic jailbreaks of LLMs. Master's thesis, Massachusetts Institute of Technology (2024)
4. Cheng, P., et al.: Self-playing adversarial language game enhances LLM reasoning. In: NeurIPS 2024 Conference Paper (2024)
5. Goodfellow, I.J., Shlens, J., Szegedy, C.: Explaining and harnessing adversarial examples. arXiv preprint (2015)
6. Gu, J., et al.: Stop reasoning! When multimodal LLM with chain-of-reasoning meets adversarial image. arXiv preprint (2024)
7. hakurei: open-instruct-v1: a dataset for having LLMs follow instructions (2023). https://huggingface.co/datasets/hakurei/open-instruct-v1. Accessed 11 June 2025
8. Li, Q., et al.: Privacy-preserving universal adversarial defense for black-box models. arXiv preprint (2024)

9. Liu, F., Xu, Z., Liu, H.: Adversarial tuning: defending against jailbreak attacks for LLMs (2024)
10. Madry, A., Makelov, A., Schmidt, L., Tsipras, D., Vladu, A.: Towards deep learning models resistant to adversarial attacks. arXiv preprint (2018)
11. Mustafa, A., Nishat, A.: Shielding AI models: overcoming adversarial threats in language processing. J. Comput. Inf. Technol. **4**(1) (2024)
12. Qiu, S., Liu, Q., Zhou, S., Huang, W.: Adversarial attack and defense technologies in natural language processing: a survey. Neurocomputing **492**, 278–307 (2022)
13. Shi, J., Li, L., Zeng, D.: ASCL: Adversarial supervised contrastive learning for defense against word substitution attacks. ScienceDirect (2022)
14. Srinivasan, S., Mahbub, M., Sadovnik, A.: Advancing NLP security by leveraging LLMs as adversarial engines (2024)
15. Tramèr, F., Kurakin, A., Papernot, N., Boneh, D., McDaniel, P.: Ensemble adversarial training: attacks and defenses. arXiv preprint (2017)
16. Vitorino, J., Maia, E., Praça, I.: Adversarial evasion attack efficiency against large language models. arXiv preprint (2024)
17. Wang, Z., Wang, H.: Defense of word-level adversarial attacks via random substitution encoding. arXiv preprint (2020)
18. Xu, X., et al.: An LLM can fool itself: a prompt-based adversarial attack. arXiv preprint (2023)

Machine Learning-Based AES Key Recovery via Side-Channel Analysis on the ASCAD Dataset

Mukesh Poudel and Nick Rahimi[✉]

School of Computing Science and Computer Engineering, University of Southern Mississippi, Hattiesburg, MS, USA
mukesh.poudel@usm.edu, nick.rahimi@usm.edu

Abstract. Cryptographic algorithms like Advanced Encryption Standard (AES), Rivest–Shamir–Adleman (RSA) are widely used and they are mathematically robust and almost unbreakable but its implementation on physical devices often leak information through side channels, such as electromagnetic (EM) emissions, potentially compromising said theoretically secure algorithms. This paper investigates the application of machine learning (ML) techniques and Deep Learning models to exploit such leakage for partial key recovery. We use the public ASCAD 'fixed' and 'variable' key dataset, containing 700-sample and 1400 EM traces respectively from an AES-128 implementation on an 8-bit microcontroller. The problem is framed as a 256-class classification task where we target the output of the first-round S-box operation, which is dependent on a single key byte. We then evaluate standard classifiers (Random Forest (RF), Support Vector Machine (SVM)), a tailored Convolutional Neural Network (CNN) and a Residual Neural Network (ResNet). We also explore the utility of RF-based feature importance for dimensionality reduction. Crucially, we employ this domain-specific Key Rank metric for evaluation, showing its necessity over standard classification accuracy, which remained below 2% due to low signal-to-noise ratio. Our results show that SVM and RF on full features perform poorly in key ranking. However, RF trained on reduced (top 100) identified via importance analysis achieves Rank 0 (successful key byte recovery) using almost half the attack traces. The implemented CNN as well, despite exhibiting overfitting in terms of validation loss, also achieves Rank 0 efficiently using approximately 65 attack traces for the fixed-key dataset. The ResNets perform best on large and complex datasets but may not always be the best choice for simple fixed key dataset in terms of efficiency. Thus we conclude that models, particularly CNNs, ResNets and feature-selected RF, coupled with the Key Rank metric, are an effective tool for side-channel key recovery, confirming the practical vulnerability of the cryptographic implementations.

Keywords: Side-Channel Analysis (SCA) · Machine Learning · Deep Learning · AES · Key Recovery

---

© The Author(s), under exclusive license to Springer Nature Switzerland AG 2026
N. Rahimi et al. (Eds.): SEDE 2025, CCIS 2720, pp. 334–352, 2026.
https://doi.org/10.1007/978-3-032-08649-5_21

1 Introduction

Cryptographic algorithms like the Advanced Encryption Standard (AES) are mathematically robust and cannot be compromised through mathematical flaws. However, physical devices executing cryptographic operations lead to unintentional information leakage through various 'side channels', such as power consumption, timing variations, and electromagnetic (EM) emissions [9]. Electromagnetic analysis (EMA) is a potent form of side-channel analysis (SCA) where attackers non-invasively measure the EM fields radiating from a device during any cryptographic operation. These emissions often contain subtle variations correlated with the intermediate data being processed. And these are often related to the key, which poses a huge challenge. Recent advancements have shown that Machine Learning (ML) and Deep Learning (DL) are powerful tools for automatically learning these complex correlations, potentially outperforming traditional statistical SCA techniques [2,7].

This paper investigates the practical application of ML techniques to recover an AES-128 key byte by analyzing EM side-channel traces from the public ASCAD (ANSSI SCA Database) fixed and variable key dataset [1]. We frame the problem as a multi-class classification task targeting the output of the first-round AES S-box operation. The low signal-to-noise ratio in the EM traces poses a significant challenge for standard classification metrics like accuracy. This often yields misleadingly poor results. Therefore, a key aspect of this work is the rigorous use of the domain-specific Key Rank metric. Key Rank evaluates an attack's success by determining the position of the true key in a list of all possible key candidates ranked by their likelihood score derived from the ML model's output across multiple traces. This metric directly reflects the practical ability to recover the key, even when per-trace classification accuracy is low.

The contributions of this work are: (1) a comparative performance analysis of standard classifiers (Random Forest (RF), Support Vector Machine (SVM)), ResNets and a tailored Convolutional Neural Network (CNN) for AES key byte recovery on the ASCAD dataset, (2) an exploration of RF-based feature importance for dimensionality reduction, its impact on model efficiency and effectiveness, (3) a clear demonstration of the necessity of the Key Rank metric over the standard accuracy for evaluating ML-based SCA success, and (4) confirmation of successful key recovery using ResNets, CNN, SVMs and feature-selected RF models, despite low classification accuracy, highlighting the practical feasibility of ML-based side-channel attacks.

The remainder of this paper is organized as follows: Sect. 2 details the AES S-box operation, EM leakage principles, the ASCAD dataset, and outlines our experimental setup and the Key Rank evaluation methodology. Section 3 presents and analyzes the results from the RF, SVM, CNN and ResNet models. Section 4 discusses the implications of our findings, the accuracy versus Key Rank paradox, and limitations. Finally, Sect. 5 concludes the paper and suggests avenues for future research.

2 Background and Methodology

This section provides the necessary background on the target cryptographic operation, the nature of EM side channel leakage, the ASCAD dataset used for experiments, and the specific ML models implemented in our study. We begin with an overview of the AES S-box operation, followed by a discussion of the ASCAD dataset and the data preprocessing steps. We then detail the architectures and hyperparameters for our implemented ML models (Random Forest, SVM, CNN and ResNets) and finally reiterate the importance of the Key Rank metric for evaluation.

2.1 AES - Sbox Operation and Leakage

The Advanced Encryption Standard (AES) is a symmetric block cipher that encrypts data in 16-byte (128-bit) blocks using a key of 128, 192, or 256 bits. AES operates in rounds, with the number of rounds depending on the key size (10 rounds for AES-128, 12 for AES-192, and 14 for AES-256). Each round involves several transformations, including SubBytes, ShiftRows, MixColumns, and AddRoundKey [4]. A fundamental non-linear operation within the SubBytes step is the application of the AES S-box substitution, independently to each byte of the internal state. The S-box input for a given byte position i is the result of $Plaintext[i] \oplus Key[i]$, where $\oplus$ represents the XOR operation. The S-box then outputs a different byte based on its lookup table:

$$Sbox\_Output[i] = Sbox(Plaintext[i] \oplus Key[i]) \quad (1)$$

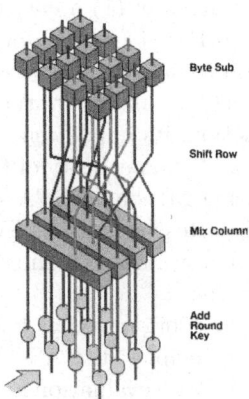

Fig. 1. Basic Steps of AES Encryption Round (source: [5])

Figure 1 illustrates the four basic steps within each round of AES encryption (excluding the final round which omits MixColumns).

The S-box operation represents a critical point of vulnerability in an AES implementation. Mangard and Schramm identified that although linear operations at the beginning of the S-box do not leak any information, significant leakage occurs in the first masked multiplier where 'the XOR gates of this multiplier absorb a different number of transitions for different data inputs' [8]. These differential transitions create a distinctive power consumption pattern that correlates directly with the processed data values and creates the side-channel leakage we aim to exploit. Since the input to the S-box in early rounds (like the first round we target) directly combines known plaintext with the unknown key byte, any leakage related to this operation provides information about the key.

We adopt the common value-based leakage model, assuming the EM trace contains information correlated with the specific identity (value 0–255) of the Sbox_Output[i]. Since this output byte depends on both the known Plaintext[i] and the unknown Key[i], predicting the S-box output from the trace allows us to deduce Key[i]. As an 8-bit byte can take 256 distinct values, predicting the S-box output becomes a 256-class classification problem. We specifically target the 3rd byte (index $i = 2$) in this study.

2.2 ASCAD Datasets: Fixed-Key (ASCADf) and Variable-Key (ASCADv)

For this project, we utilize the publicly available ASCAD 'fixed-key' dataset, provided by ANSSI [1]. To further improve the robustness of the algorithm and to mimic a more realistic scenario, we also trained on the 'variable-key' dataset. This dataset presents a more challenging scenario where the secret key changes for each trace in both the profiling and attack sets. We will be referring to the fixed-key dataset as ASCADf and the variable-key dataset as ASCADv throughout this paper for simpler referencing. The ASCAD datasets were chosen for this research due to it being publicly available and well-documented. This is a widely used benchmark in the SCA community and thus helps in reproducible research and comparison amongst existing literature.

This particular dataset comprises EM measurements from an AES-128 implementation on an 8-bit ATMega8515 microcontroller, where fixed 128-bit key (for ASCADf) or variable 128-bit keys (for ASCADv) were used. For a supervised Machine Learning problem, this dataset includes precisely labeled data (S-box output for a known key byte) and corresponding plaintext to help train the classification model. The datasets contains:

- **Profiling Traces:** For ASCADf, A set of 50,000 traces used for training models. Each trace consists of 700 EM measurements (features). For ASCADv, A set of 200,000 traces were used for training and each trace consists of 1400 EM measurements. Associated metadata includes the plaintext, the fixed key, and pre-calculated labels representing the output of the S-box for the 3rd key byte (index 2).
- **Attack Traces:** A set of 10,000 traces (ASCADf) and 100,000 traces (ASCADv) were used for testing and evaluating the trained models. These

traces also contained same number of EM measurements as the profiling counterparts, along with corresponding plaintexts. During the attack phase, the key is treated as unknown.

2.3 Data Preprocessing

The raw EM traces have different offsets and scales which can impact the performance of Machine Learning models. To fix this, we standardize the training and testing data for both ASCADf (700 traces) and ASCADv (1400 traces) using the mean and standard deviation calculated solely from their respective profiling sets (50,000 traces for ASCADf, and 200,000 traces for ASCADv profiling). This helps make sure that each feature has a zero mean and unit variance. Without scaling, features with higher magnitudes can disproportionately affect the model's decisions, leading to suboptimal performance. Many ML algorithms, particularly those using gradient descent (like CNNs) or distance measures (like SVMs with RBF kernels), perform better and converge faster when input features are on a similar scale and centered around zero. We use Scikit-learn's *StandardScaler* to perform this standardization. We fit the scaler on the training data and then transform both the training and testing data using the fitted scaler. This ensures that the test data is transformed in the same way as the training data, preventing any information leakage from the test set into the model training process.

2.4 Machine Learning Models

Random Forest (RF): It is an ensemble learning method that aggregates the predictions of multiple decision trees. We employ Scikit-learn's RandomForestClassifier with $n\_estimators = 100$. This provides a good balance between performance and computation. To mitigate overfitting on the high-dimensional data, we apply regularization by setting $max\_depth = 20$ to limit the tree complexity and $min\_samples\_leaf = 10$ to ensure that each leaf node has sufficient number of samples. Furthermore, RF provides Gini importance scores, which we leverage for feature selection. We sorted features by their Gini importance scores in descending order and selected the top 100 most important features. We train one RF model using all 700 features for ASCADf and 1400 features for ASCADv and another using only the top 100 features as determined by the importance ranking.

Support Vector Machine (SVC): It is a classifier that aims to find an optimal hyperplane to separate different classes. Due to its high computational cost and as it scales poorly with the addition in number of samples and features, we train Scikit-learn's SVC only on the reduced set of 100 features selected by RF. We use the default RBF kernel ($C = 1.0$, $gamma = $ 'scale') and enable probability estimates i.e. *probability=True* as it is required for key ranking which relies on the class probability estimates.

Convolutional Neural Network (CNN): We employ a custom CNN architecture implemented in PyTorch, drawing inspiration from ASCAD paper in deep learning-based SCA. The network is designed to learn relevant features directly from the raw EM traces, enabling effective classification of S-box outputs. The architecture details are as follows (Fig. 2):

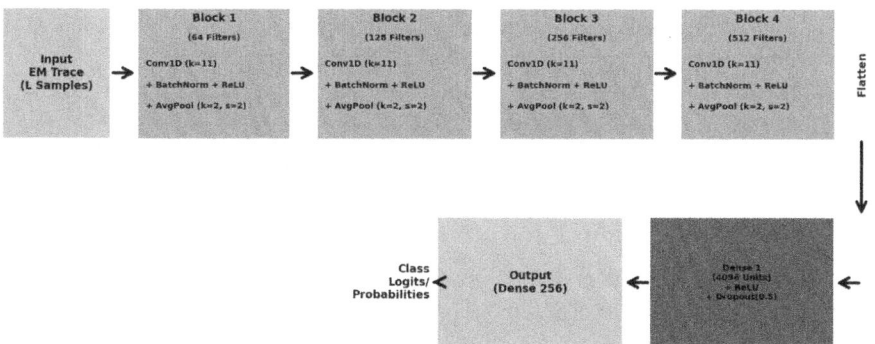

Fig. 2. CNN Architecture for SCA

- **Input Layer:** Accepts a 1D EM trace (**700 samples** for ASCADf, **1400 samples** for ASCADv) as a tensor of shape (`BatchSize, 1, TraceLength`)
- **Convolutional Blocks (4x):** The network employs four identical convolutional blocks for hierarchical feature extraction. Each block includes:
  1. *Conv1d Layer:* Applies 1D convolutions with a kernel size of 11 and padding of 5 (effectively 'same' padding for the convolution operation itself). This choice is directly supported by findings in [1] which demonstrated that a larger kernel size (e.g., 11) significantly improves SCA-efficiency, especially compared to multiple layers with smaller kernels. The number of output channels (filters) increases progressively: 64, 128, 256, and 512 for the four blocks, respectively, increasing feature map depth to compensate for spatial dimension reduction by pooling layers, allowing the network to learn a richer set of features.
  2. *BatchNorm1d Layer:* Performs batch normalization.
  3. *ReLU Activation:* Applies the Rectified Linear Unit activation function.
  4. *AvgPool1d Layer:* Performs average pooling with a kernel size of 2 and a stride of 2, downsampling the feature map length by a factor of 2 at each block.
- **Flatten Layer:** Converts the 2D feature maps (channels × length) from the final pooling layer into a 1D vector. After four pooling layers, an initial trace of length L becomes $L/16$ (with floor operations for odd lengths at intermediate stages).

- **Dense Head (Classification):**
    1. *Linear Layer (4096 units):* A fully connected layer with 4096 output units, followed by ReLU activation. The input size to this layer is dependent on the initial trace length:
        - For ASCADf (700 input samples, length becomes 43 after pooling): 512 channels × 43 features = 22016 inputs.
        - For ASCADv (1400 input samples, length becomes 87 after pooling): 512 channels × 87 features = 44544 inputs.
    2. *Dropout Layer (p = 0.5):* Applies dropout regularization.
    3. *Linear Layer (256 units):* A final fully connected layer outputting logits for the 256 possible S-box values.
- **Training Parameters:** *Optimizer* : RMSprop optimizer with a learning rate of 1×10^{-5} and a weight decay of 1×10^{-5}, *Loss Function* : CrossEntropyLoss, *Batch Size* : 100 *Epochs* : 150.

The specific CNN architecture is inspired by successful models described in recent literature, and the original ASCAD paper, but has been modified to suit our computational resources and dataset characteristics.

Residual Neural Network (ResNet): To investigate the performance limitations of the baseline CNN architecture on the more complex variable-key dataset, we implemented a more advanced model based on a Residual Network (ResNet). This architecture is specifically designed to ease the training of deeper networks by introducing **residual blocks** that help mitigate the vanishing gradient problem [3]. The overall structure consists of a feature extractor built from a series of these residual blocks, followed by the same dense classification head used in the standard CNN (Fig. 3).

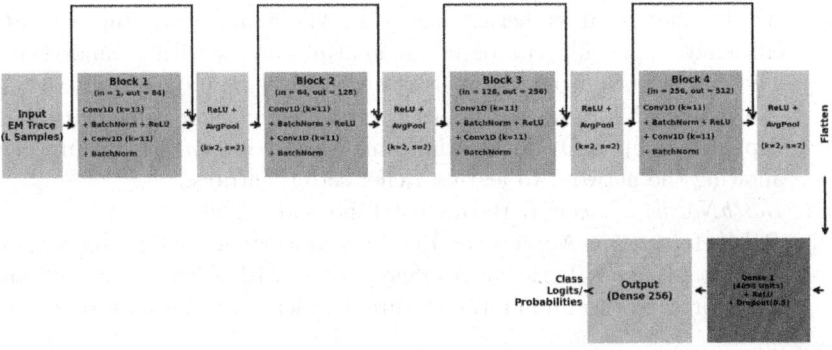

Fig. 3. ResNet Architecture for SCA

The core of this model is the Residual Block, which processes the input through two parallel paths:

- **The Main Path:** This path consists of two 1D convolutional layers, each with a kernel size of 11. Each convolution is followed by a Batch Normalization layer, and a ReLU activation function is applied after the first block.
- **The Shortcut Connection:** This path bypasses the main convolutional layers, allowing information to flow directly to a later stage of the block. If the number of input channels does not match the number of output channels for the block, a 1×1 convolution is applied in the shortcut path to match the dimensions. Otherwise, it acts as an identity connection.

The outputs of the main path and the shortcut connection are then summed element-wise. A final ReLU activation is applied to this sum, and the result is passed to the next layer.

Our full ResNet feature extractor is composed of four of these *ResidualBlocks* stacked sequentially. Following each residual block, an *AvgPool1d* layer with a kernel size of 2 and a stride of 2 is used to downsample the feature map length by a factor of two. Similar to the baseline CNN, the number of filters in the convolutional layers increases through the network, using values of 64, 128, 256, and 512 for the four blocks, respectively. After the feature extractor, the data is flattened and passed to a dense classification head identical to the one described for the standard CNN.

2.5 Hyperparameter Selection

To get a deeper understanding and analysis of our model configurations and justify our parameter choices, we conducted a series of runs with varied hyperparameters, which helped validate our baseline parameters and provide insights into the model's sensitivities.

Random Forest: Our baseline RF model with 100 features proved highly effective and computationally efficient. To justify our parameter choices, we explored variations. We found that increasing the number of trees $n\_estimators = 200$ offered no improvement in attack efficiency (180 traces) while increasing the computation time. Furthermore, using a more complex model by increasing the tree depth ($max\_depth = 30$) caused the model to fail in recovering the key, highlighting the importance of a constrained depth for regularization against noisy data. These findings validate that our baseline parameters represent an effective balance between performance and cost.

Support Vector Machines(SVC): The baseline SVC was highly effective, recovering the key in 320 traces. While successful, the SVC was the most computationally expensive model, with training being particularly demanding for the larger variable-key dataset. To justify our parameter choices, we focused on tuning the c parameter, which controls the model's regularization. The c parameter manages the trade-off between creating a simple model (with a wide margin) and correctly classifying all training points (a more complex model). A c value that is too high can cause the model to overfit by memorizing noise in the training data. An overfitted model, by contrast, may make highly confident but incorrect predictions on the attack set, which severely penalizes the cumulative log-probability score of the true key. Our exploration confirmed that $c = 1.0$ provided a strong, generalizable result, while a higher value of $c = 10.0$ or $c = 100.0$ did not yield a significant performance gain to justify the increased risk of overfitting and the even longer training times. Thus we concluded that the standard $c = 1.0$ and gamma = 'scale' parameters provided strong results.

CNN: Our primary CNN architecture, as described in Sect. 2.4, is highly effective but sensitive to its training configuration. The baseline model with $kernel\_size = 11$, and $batch\_size = 100$ consistently recovered the key on the fixed-key dataset in approximately 65 traces. Performance was particularly sensitive to batch size. Decreasing the batch size to 64 required 90 traces, but resulted in longer training times. Similarly, while increasing the batch size to 200, the training time was reduced, but it required almost 180 traces. Further exploration were made by varying the kernel size and the network depth. But it did not yield a better result than our baseline choice of 11. We experimented with 3 blocks and 5 block architecture, but 3 block were not sufficient to recover key, and 5 block architecture was a tradeoff on time. Critically, this tuning process also confirmed the CNN's limitations, as all tested configurations failed to recover the key on the more complex variable-key dataset. This current architecture does not generalize well to the ASCADv challenge, which suggests that more advanced network designs are required for such complex scenarios. This problem is addressed by ResNets.

ResNet: To address the generalization failure of our standard CNN on the ASCADv dataset, we introduced a ResNet architecture. Our hypothesis was that the plain CNN, despite its depth, suffered from degrading gradient flow that prevented learning the abstract patterns required for variable-key attacks. The ResNet architecture directly addresses this through residual blocks with shortcut connections that add the block's input to its convolutional output, We tested the ResNet using a configuration directly comparable to our best standard CNN: four blocks, $kernel\_size = 11$, and similar filter progression. ResNet succeeded exceptionally well where the standard CNN had failed, confirming that residual connections were the critical factor for learning generalizable features. While we explored minor variations in depth and kernel size, our chosen configuration represented an optimal trade-off between performance and complexity, solidifying our conclusion that the architectural shift was the principal reason for success.

2.6 Evaluation Metric: Key Rank

While standard classification accuracy was measured, it proved uninformative due to high noise levels. The primary metric for SCA success is the Key Rank [10]. The process is as follows:

- Obtain the predicted probability distribution (vector of 256 probabilities) from the trained model for each of the N attack traces. Let P (label = z|trace_i) be the probability assigned to S-box output value z for trace i.

- For each key byte hypothesis k_guess (from 0 to 255):
  - Calculate the hypothetical S-box output
    $Z\_hyp\_i = Sbox(plaintext\_i \oplus k\_guess)$ for each attack trace i from 1 to N.
  - Calculate the total Summed Log-Probability (SLP) score for this key guess:
    $Score(\text{k\_guess}) = \sum_{i=1}^{N} \log(P(label = Z\_hyp\_i | trace_i) + \varepsilon)$
    where ε is a small constant (e.g., 1e−40) to prevent log(0). The logarithm is used to avoid numerical underflow when multiplying many small probabilities, and to improve computational efficiency by converting multiplications to additions.
- Rank the 256 key guesses based on their scores, from highest (most likely) to lowest.
- The Rank of the true key byte (k_true) is its position in this ranked list (Rank 0 indicates it has the highest score and is successfully recovered).
- Plotting the Rank vs. the number of traces (N) shows the efficiency of the attack. The Key Score Plot (bar chart of Score(k_guess) vs. k_guess) visually confirms the correct key's dominance.

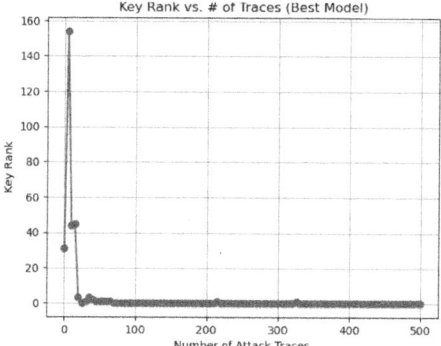

Fig. 4. Sample Example of a Key Rank Chart

Figure 4 illustrates a sample Key Rank chart, showing the rank of the true key byte (2) as a function of the number of attack traces used. The graph illustrates how the rank improves with more traces, and successfully recovers the key after 50 traces.

The superiority of Key Rank over standard accuracy in this context stems from the nature of SCA. The goal is not to achieve perfect classification of the S-box output for every single noisy trace, which is often an unrealistic expectation due to low signal-to-noise ratio (SNR). Instead, the goal is to distinguish the single correct secret key byte from 255 incorrect hypotheses. Key Rank achieves this by aggregating subtle, consistent evidence (the model's probability assignments) across numerous traces. Even if a model has low accuracy, if it consistently assigns a slightly higher probability to the true S-box output (when the correct key is hypothesized) compared to random outputs, this difference gets amplified when log-probabilities are summed over many traces. This makes the score for the true key dominant, leading to successful recovery, while individual trace noise that confounds accuracy is averaged out.

3 Experimental Results

3.1 Setup

Experiments were conducted using Python 3.11 with PyTorch (for CNN and ResNet) and Scikit-learn (for RF, SVM, Scaler) libraries. The Random Forest model utilized 16 cores for parallel processing and 16 GB of RAM, while the SVM was limited to a single thread. Training and evaluation were performed on an Nvidia P100 GPU for the CNN and ResNet models and CPU for RF and SVM models.

3.2 Random Forest Results

For the full-feature RF model on ASCADf ($n\_estimators = 100$, $max\_depth = 20$, $min\_samples\_leaf = 10$), 10-fold cross-validation yielded a training accuracy of 43.55% but a validation accuracy of only 0.46%. This highlights the challenge of directly classifying individual traces due to the low signal-to-noise ratio inherent in EM leakage. The Key Rank metric is therefore crucial for evaluating SCA success.

In terms of cross-validation, 5 out of 10 folds achieved Rank 0 within 1000 traces. Among these successful folds, the average number of traces required was 492 ($\sigma = 129.21$). The final full-feature RF model exhibited similar performance, requiring hundreds of attack traces to recover the key.

Feature selection using RF's Gini importance significantly improved performance. By training a second RF model on only the top 100 features, the number of attack traces required to achieve Rank 0 was reduced to approximately 200. This represents a 50% reduction in the number of traces needed for successful key recovery compared to the full-feature model, demonstrating the effectiveness of dimensionality reduction in mitigating overfitting and focusing on the most informative leakage points.

RF on ASCADv with similar parameters and full 1400 features required 750 traces to recover the key. Meanwhile, evaluation on reduced 100 features recovered the key in only 470 traces, reducing the trace count by almost 40% and re-emphasizing the importance of feature-reduction (Fig. 5).

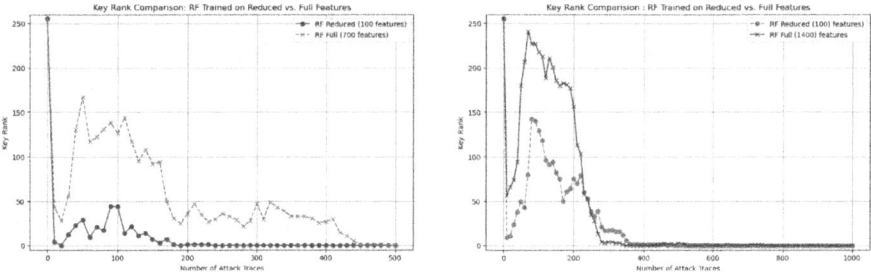

Fig. 5. Key Rank Charts for RF on Datasets ASCADf (left) and ASCADv (right)

The feature importance analysis also revealed that leakage is distributed across the trace but with clear concentration in certain time regions. This confirmed the targeted S-box operation leaves electromagnetic fingerprints at specific points in time during execution.

3.3 CNN Results

The CNN model exhibited typical deep learning behavior with continuously decreasing training loss (from 5.56 to 5.27) but relatively stable validation loss (around 5.38–5.40), suggesting overfitting by conventional metrics. The final test accuracy was extremely low at only 0.81%, which would typically indicate a failed model (Fig. 6).

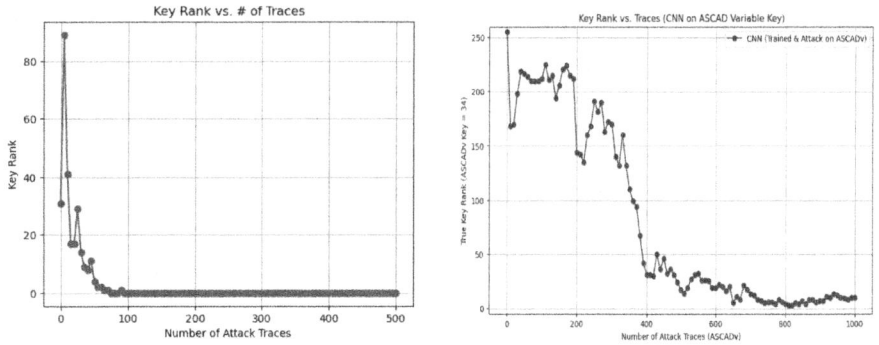

Fig. 6. Key Rank Charts for CNN on ASCADf (left) and ASCADv (right)

However, the key recovery performance told a completely different story. When tested on the attack set, the CNN model's rank of the correct key byte dropped rapidly, reaching Rank 0 consistently after approximately 65 attack traces. This performance was superior to both the full-feature and reduced-feature RF models and is consistent with recent literatures. A reduced learning rate and reduced batch size consistently improved performance. We decided that the current batch size of 100 and learning rate of 1×10^{-5} were best in terms of performance and computational efficiency. The final key score distribution after using all attack traces showed a clear, dominant peak at the correct key byte 224(for ASCADf), far exceeding the scores of incorrect key guesses. This confirms the CNN successfully learned relevant leakage patterns despite its low classification accuracy. The CNN trained on ASCADv told a different story. The key-byte recovery was unsuccessful with unstable potentially recovery at 800 traces but it was not sufficient enough. This tells us that there is room for improvement with potential architectural changes for the ASCADv dataset.

3.4 Support Vector Machine Results

The SVM model was trained only on the reduced set of 100 features selected by RF feature importance, as training on the full 700 and 1400 features would be computationally complex and time consuming. Despite this optimization, the SVM model with RBF kernel for ASCADf required 3383 s and ASCADv took 42116 s for training, which is expected due to substantially larger dataset size. The key recovery was achieved at 320 traces for both ASCADf and ASCADv. However, the execution was very computationally extensive suggesting this model might not be very efficient for this task. Standard scikit-learn's SVC implementation is often limited in its internal parallelization for training, and SVM in itself is very largely influenced by noisy and irrelevant time points and might not be the most efficient choice for large-scale side-channel analysis. It could be viable in circumstances where noise is less of a factor typically on hardware devices with clearer leakage or in datasets that are de-noised. Future investigations could also explore other high-performance GPU-based SVM libraries (Fig. 7).

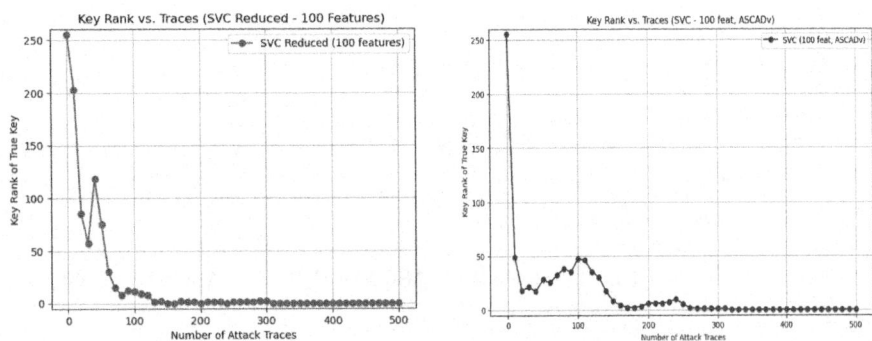

Fig. 7. Key Rank Charts for SVC on Datasets ASCADf (left) and ASCADv (right)

3.5 ResNet Results

ResNets turned out to be one of the best-performing models. On the ASCADf dataset, the ResNet performed comparably to the standard CNN, successfully recovering the key after 110 traces. The model demonstrated a robust ability to learn the necessary leakage patterns from the fixed-key training data. The true value of the ResNet architecture was revealed on the ASCADv dataset. Where the standard CNN had previously failed, the ResNet model succeeded unequivocally. The key recovery succeeded in just 30 traces. This performance of significantly fewer traces than on the 'easier' fixed-key dataset was something of a surprise but aligns with Karayalcin et al., whose study also reached similar conclusions and noted that ResNets are particularly suited to datasets with large training data like ASCADv. Although reaching similar conclusions, our ResNet on ASCADf and ASCADv performs significantly better than Karayalcin et al. These results from ResNet confirm that the addition of residual connections is a critical architectural improvement, which enables the network to effectively solve complex, variable-key side-channel challenges (Fig. 8).

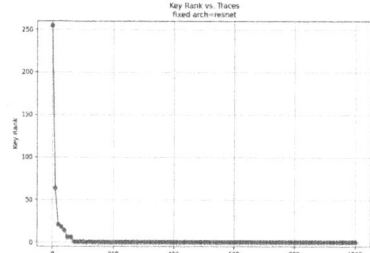 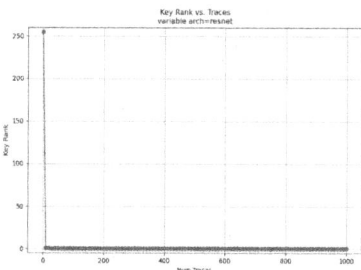

Fig. 8. Key Rank Charts for ResNets on Datasets ASCADf (left) and ASCADv (right)

3.6 Summary of Results

(See Tables 1 and 2).

Table 1. Summary of Model Performance on ASCADf

Model	Features	Traces to Rank 0	Training Time (s)[a]	Key Recovery
RF (full)	700	~492	9.36	Success
RF (reduced)	100	~200	4.60	Success
SVM (reduced)	100	~320	3383	Success
CNN	700	~65	9322	Success
ResNets	700	~110	5623	Success

[a] Training time incorporates the model's training duration, including the overhead for enabling class probability estimation necessary for key guess ranking. Training times also may have been affected due to inefficient code for parallelization.

Table 2. Summary of Model Performance on ASCADv

Model	Features	Traces to Rank 0	Training Time (s)[a]	Key Recovery
RF (full)	1400	~750	68.32	Success
RF (reduced)	100	~470	17.73	Success
SVM (reduced)	100	~320	42116	Success
CNN	1400	-	-	Failed
ResNets	1400	30	46209	Success

[a] The substantially longer training times on ASCADv is expected due to it having 200,000 profiling traces and 100,000 attack traces compared to 50,000 profiling and 10,000 attack traces for ASCADf.

4 Discussion

The experiments conducted demonstrate successful AES key recovery from EM leakage using Machine Learning on the ASCAD datasets. The ResNets with ASCADv proved to be most efficient followed by standard CNN with ASCADf when it achieved Rank 0 after only 65 traces. ResNets for ASCADf achieved Rank 0 after 110 traces, while RF for ASCADf with feature selection needed around 200, outperforming SVM. The SVM performed poorly despite using the same reduced feature set as RF. This in turn, suggests that ensemble methods like RF might be more robust than kernel methods. A key finding is that despite low classification accuracy, successful key recovery was possible. RF feature selection has significantly improved performance and proved that focusing on relevant features certainly benefits certain models. RF for ASCADv was able to bring down traces needed from almost 750 to 470, which is almost over 40% better performance.

One possible explanation for the CNN's superior performance compared to feature-selected RF is that CNNs automatically learn hierarchical and nonlinear features directly from the raw EM traces. This allows CNNs to capture subtle temporal dependencies and complex leakage patterns that manual feature selection may overlook. Additionally, the CNN architecture is designed to be robust against noise by leveraging convolutional filters and pooling operations. However, despite these architectural advantages, our results show this generalization did not extend very well to the variable-key challenge, resulting the standard CNN to fail. This is where the ResNet architecture demonstrates its crucial advantage. While implemented as structurally similar to our standard CNN, its use of residual 'shortcut' connections improved the gradient flow and enabled more effective feature learning in deeper networks. ResNet succeeded spectacularly on the ASCADv dataset by recovering the key in 30 traces. This result confirms that for complex, variable-key scenarios, the improved training stability offered by the ResNet architecture is essential for achieving a successful attack [6]. Thus, while RF with feature selection focuses on the most individually informative features, it might miss intricate interactions present in the full trace data that the Deep Learning counterparts are designed to exploit.

The collective results from these experiments reveal several key insights into the application of machine learning for side-channel analysis. RF performance proves that focusing on high-importance features can significantly improve attack efficiency. Most significantly, experimentation from the standard CNN to the ResNet gives a clear picture of architectural hierarchy. While simpler architectures can succeed in idealized conditions, successfully attacking more complex and realistic challenges requires more sophisticated models like ResNet that are specifically designed to facilitate deep, robust, and generalizable feature learning.

4.1 Comparison with Existing Literature

The results of this study align with existing literature on ML-based SCA, particularly the effectiveness of CNNs and feature selection techniques. For instance, recent works have shown that CNNs can outperform traditional statistical methods in key recovery tasks, especially when dealing with high-dimensional data like EM traces. The use of RF for feature selection is also consistent with findings that highlight its utility in reducing dimensionality and improving model performance in SCA contexts (Table 3).

Table 3. Comparison with Existing Literature

Reference	Model	Traces to Rank 0
This Study(Best)	RF (reduced)	~200
This Study(Best)	CNN	~65
This Study(Best)	ResNets	~30
Huang et al. [4]	Inception Net	~30
Rousselot et al. [11]	Scoop - CNN	~73
Zaid et al. [12]	CNN	~191
Karayalcin et al. [6]	ResNets	~47

4.2 Potential Countermeasures

The successful key recovery demonstrates that even standard AES implementations on common microcontrollers are vulnerable to ML-based EM SCA if no specific countermeasures are in place. Potential countermeasures that are commonly used to mitigate such attacks include:

- **Hardware-level:** Noise generation, power supply randomization, specific chip design to reduce EM leakage, shielding.
- **Software-level:** Masking (splitting sensitive values into shares processed independently), shuffling (randomizing the order of operations), or constant-time implementations.

These countermeasures aim to reduce the correlation between the EM emissions and the processed data, making it more difficult for attackers to extract sensitive information. However, they often come with trade-offs in terms of performance, complexity, and cost.

4.3 Analysis of CNN Failure on ASCADv and ResNet Performance

A key finding from our results is the stark performance difference of our baseline CNN architecture between fixed-key and variable-key datasets. While the CNN introduced in Sect. 2.4 consistently recovered the key on ASCADf, it failed completely on the more challenging ASCADv dataset. This hints that this architecture, while effective at learning specific patterns, lacks the ability to generalize to the more complex scenario where the secret key is not constant. We attribute this limitation primarily to the challenges of training deeper networks, where issues like the vanishing gradient can prevent the model from learning the more abstract features needed for a variable-key attack.

To investigate this limitation further and test our hypothesis, we implemented a follow-up experiment using a Residual Network (ResNet) architecture. ResNets are specifically designed to overcome the challenges of training deep networks through the use of residual skip connections, which allow gradients to flow more effectively during training [3]. This results in an architecture that is more capable of learning the abstract and long-range feature dependencies that is required to generalize across the non-stationary signals.

The results of this follow-up experiment were remarkable yet surprising. The ResNet model proved highly effective in recovering the key on the ASCADv dataset in approximately 20 traces, while it required 110 traces on the simpler ASCADf dataset. The exceptional performance on the variable-key set aligns with findings from Karayalcin et al., who also note that ResNets are particularly well-suited for larger, more complex datasets where their architectural depth can be fully leveraged [6].

This relative inefficiency of the more complex model on a simpler task can be attributed to architectural overkill. On the ASCADf dataset, the baseline CNN was already sufficient and highly efficient (~ 65 traces). The additional depth and complexity of the ResNet proved to be less efficient. This is likely due to two factors. First, the skip connections may have created a more complex optimization landscape that hindered rapid convergence when the leakage patterns were relatively simple. Second, a deeper network is incentivized to find abstract feature combinations; on a dataset with straightforward, localized leakage like ASCADf, this can be counterproductive, causing the model to take longer to converge on the simpler, more direct patterns.

This confirms that optimal deep learning architecture for side-channel analysis is very dependent on the target's complexity. For simpler, fixed-key targets, a well-tuned but shallower CNN can be more efficient and effective but for more challenging, real-world scenarios involving variable keys, more advanced architectures like ResNet is optimal to achieve efficient results.

4.4 Limitations

The study has its some limitations inherent to its methodology such as it primarily relies on the use of synchronized dataset and the profiling attack methodology, which represents a somewhat best-case scenario for the attacker. While this is very important from a vulnerability and technology standpoint this may not be a efficient practical implementation in terms of real-world application and penetration. Real-world attacks might face significant timing jitter (desynchronization) which can further increase complexity. Adapting these models to get efficient results in more realistic conditions would require specialized preprocessing or few architectural changes. More advanced architectures incorporating attention mechanisms could also be explored, as they can learn to focus on relevant leakage patterns regardless of their exact temporal position. Our profiling attack also assumes known plaintext during the attack phase for key ranking, which may not always be available. The trained models are also specific to the ASCAD dataset and may not generalize well to other datasets or other devices for that matter.

5 Conclusion

This work has successfully applied and compared Random Forest, SVM, Convolutional Neural Network, and ResNet models for AES key recovery via electromagnetic side-channel analysis on the public ASCAD dataset. We demonstrated that despite extremely low classification accuracy, the Key Rank metric revealed successful and efficient key byte recovery using a tailored CNN and ResNets and a Random Forest trained on features selected via importance ranking. Our findings confirm that ML techniques can effectively learn subtle leakage patterns, even when models exhibit overfitting by standard validation metrics. Feature reduction using RF importance analysis significantly improved performance, reducing the number of attack traces required for successful key recovery. Deep learning models stood out for their efficiency in learning relevant features directly from raw EM traces. The SVC model, while theoretically powerful, struggled to achieve similar performance, suggesting that ensemble methods like RF may be more robust in this context. The results underscore the practical vulnerability of AES implementations to ML-driven side-channel attacks, highlighting the need for effective countermeasures and robust security evaluation methodologies.

Future work could involve applying these techniques to more challenging scenarios like the desynchronized ASCAD datasets, exploring alternative feature selection methods beyond RF importance, and developing models that can recover multiple key bytes simultaneously to extract the full AES key [2]. Applying these ML models to datasets from diverse hardware platforms and against AES implementations protected with known countermeasures (e.g., masking) would provide valuable insights into the practical resilience of these defenses. Architecturally, exploring attention mechanisms or residual connections within CNNs could enhance feature learning and potentially improve performance, especially with noisy or desynchronized traces.

Ultimately, this research highlights the tangible threat posed by ML-driven side-channel attacks, reinforcing the critical need for robust hardware and software countermeasures, alongside rigorous security evaluation methodologies, to protect cryptographic implementations in real-world devices.

Acknowledgments. This work was supported by the Jimmy Payne Foundation through the Computing Research Center Grant at the University of Southern Mississippi. The authors acknowledge HPC at The University of Southern Mississippi supported by the National Science Foundation under the Major Research Instrumentation (MRI) program via Grant #ACI 1626217.

References

1. Benadjila, R., Prouff, E., Strullu, R., Cagli, E., Dumas, C.: Deep learning for side-channel analysis and introduction to ASCAD database. J. Cryptogr. Eng. **10**(2), 163–188 (2020)
2. Berreby, Y.E., Sauvage, L.: Investigating efficient deep learning architectures for side-channel attacks on AES. arXiv preprint arXiv:2309.13170 (2023)
3. He, K., Zhang, X., Ren, S., Sun, J.: Deep residual learning for image recognition. In: Proceedings of the IEEE Conference on Computer Vision and Pattern Recognition, pp. 770–778 (2016)
4. Huang, H., Wu, J., Tang, X., Zhao, S., Liu, Z., Yu, B.: Deep learning-based improved side-channel attacks using data denoising and feature fusion. PLoS ONE **20**(4), e0315340 (2025)
5. Savard, J.: AES (Rijndael) Round Function [png image]. Wikimedia Commons (1999). https://commons.wikimedia.org/wiki/File:AES_(Rijndael)_Round_Function.png. Dedicated to public domain under CC0 1.0 Universal. https://creativecommons.org/publicdomain/zero/1.0/
6. Karayalcin, S., Perin, G., Picek, S.: Resolving the doubts: On the construction and use of ResNets for side-channel analysis. Mathematics **11**(15), 3265 (2023)
7. Kocher, P., Jaffe, J., Jun, B.: Differential power analysis. In: Wiener, M. (ed.) CRYPTO 1999. LNCS, vol. 1666, pp. 388–397. Springer, Heidelberg (1999). https://doi.org/10.1007/3-540-48405-1_25
8. Mangard, S., Schramm, K.: Pinpointing the side-channel leakage of masked AES hardware implementations. In: Goubin, L., Matsui, M. (eds.) CHES 2006. LNCS, vol. 4249, pp. 76–90. Springer, Heidelberg (2006). https://doi.org/10.1007/11894063_7
9. Obaid, Z.M., Ali Alheeti, K.M.: Enhancing malware detection through electromagnetic side-channel analysis using random forest classifier. J. Cybersecur. Inf. Manage. **15**(2) (2025)
10. Picek, S., Heuser, A., Jovic, A., Bhasin, S., Regazzoni, F.: The curse of class imbalance and conflicting metrics with machine learning for side-channel evaluations. IACR Trans. Cryptogr. Hardw. Embed. Syst. 209–237 (2019)
11. Rousselot, N., Heydemann, K., Masure, L., Migairou, V.: Scoop: an optimizer for profiling attacks against higher-order masking. Cryptology ePrint Archive (2025)
12. Zaid, G., Bossuet, L., Habrard, A., Venelli, A.: Methodology for efficient cnn architectures in profiling attacks. IACR Trans. Cryptogr. Hardw. Embed. Syst. 1–36 (2020)

Hand Line Classification

S. Petchartee(✉), N. Hirunpash, M. Namawrong, and W. Sakonlaphab

Smaterware, Bangkok, Thailand
Somrak.Petchartee@gmail.com

Abstract. This paper presents a comprehensive computer vision framework for automated detection and analysis of linear patterns in palm imagery. While hand lines have been studied in traditional contexts, this research approaches them purely as geometric features for pattern recognition and biometric analysis. Our method employs four specialized SeqNet models derived from UNet architecture, combined with MediaPipe for hand landmark detection, to achieve robust line segmentation. Through systematic image processing including skeletonization, curve fitting, and broken line connection algorithms, we extract quantifiable geometric features including line curvature, endpoints, and morphological characteristics. Experimental evaluation on 500 hand images demonstrates mean Intersection over Union (IoU) of 0.865, representing a 9.6% improvement over standard UNet baselines. The proposed system achieves feature classification accuracies ranging from 87.4% to 94.7% across different geometric analysis tasks. This research contributes to computer vision, pattern recognition, and biometric analysis by providing a robust framework for automated geometric feature extraction from hand imagery.

Keywords: Algorithm · Deep learning · Feature extraction · Hand line analysis · Image processing · Machine learning · Palm line patterns · Pattern recognition · Performance evaluation · Quantitative analysis · Segmentation · Stroke dynamics

1 Introduction

This research presents the application of SeqNet [1, 2] in conjunction with a custom-developed algorithm for detecting and predicting hand lines. SeqNet, derived from UNet [1, 3, 4], is employed as the primary algorithm for hand line detection, designed to optimize model structure processing. In addition, MediaPipe Model [5–8], known for its hand skeleton detection capabilities, is integrated to detect both the hand and finger positions. This approach enhances the efficiency of the hand line process. Moreover, auxiliary algorithms are incorporated to improve the precision of the system in alignment with the research objectives.

Our approach employs four independent SeqNet models, each specifically trained to detect one type of palm line: Fate line, Heart line, Head line, and Life line. This design choice was made to optimize detection accuracy for each line type, as preliminary experiments revealed that line-specific models achieved superior performance compared to a unified multi-output architecture. Each individual model follows the SeqNet architecture shown in Fig. 1, consisting of the three-stage processing pipeline: (1) background separation using U-Net (blue blocks), (2) line extraction using IterNet [1, 3, 4] (green block), and (3) line classification (brown block). The key advantage of using separate models lies in their ability to learn line-specific morphological characteristics and patterns that are unique to each palm line type.

During training, each model receives the same input hand image but is trained with line-specific labeled data where the target line appears in red and all other lines appear in blue, as described in Sect. 2.1. This approach allows each model to specialize in detecting the geometric properties, typical positions, and morphological variations specific to its assigned line type.

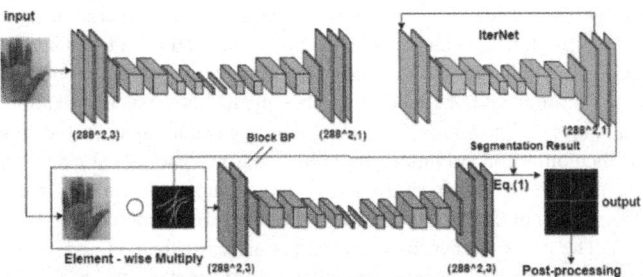

Fig. 1. Shows the structure of SeqNet, which includes IterNet and UNet. The blue and red blocks represent UNet, and the green block represents IterNet.

An example of using the SeqNet model to process hand images to detect and separate palm lines. The final result of this process is the separation of all detected lines into four types: 1) Fate line 2) Heart line 3) Life line 4) Head line (Figs. 2, 3, 4, 5, 6, 7, 8, 9 and 10).

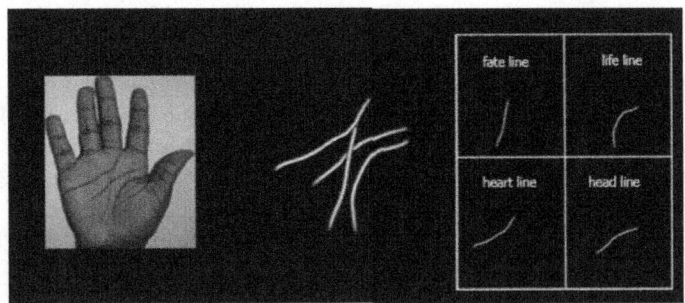

Fig. 2. Provides an example of hand line separation results, consisting of: The hand image used for hand line segmentation, The image showing all detected lines from the hand, The image with the separated lines of interest, including the life line, heart line, head line, and fate line.

2 Model Training

To train the model for palm line segmentation, there will be a total of four models, each designed for detecting a specific type of palm line: the fate line detection model, life line detection model, head line detection model, and heart line detection model. Data Preparation: The dataset used for model training consists of four sets, each containing hand images with dimensions of 300 pixels by 380 pixels, along with labeled images indicating the target data (labels). The files we are working with are in PNG format and RGB color mode, which means they contain three color channels: Red, Green, and Blue. However, the data used for training the model is in RGBA format, which includes an additional Alpha (transparency) channel. Since the Alpha channel can reduce the accuracy of line detection, it is necessary to convert these files to RGB format first to ensure more effective results in line detection.

2.1 Creating Labeled Images for Model Training

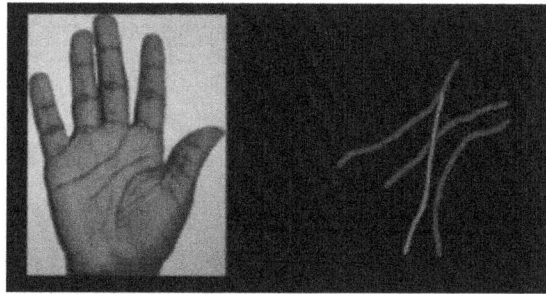

Fig. 3. Shows an example of the data used for model training, consisting of 1) hand images and 2) labeled images.

To create the dataset for training the model, we will generate palm line annotations that correspond to the palm lines in the hand images. These annotations will be divided into two colors: 1) Red for the lines we want to detect, 2) Blue for the lines we do not want to detect This means that for each hand image, we need to create four labeled images: 1) An image where the fate line is red, and the remaining lines are blue 2) An image where the heart line is red, and the remaining lines are blue 3) An image where the life line is red, and the remaining lines are blue 4) An image where the head line is red, and the remaining lines are blue. In cases where the computer has insufficient GPU memory, we can separate the training into four models to detect each palm line individually using red and blue colors. However, in cases where we have high-quality GPU resources, we can separate the colors for each line type—such as red, blue, yellow, green, etc.—and then train them to work within a single model (unified multi-output head).

2.2 Data Augmentation for Enhancing Diversity

Data augmentation [7] is intended to increase both the volume and diversity of the dataset by generating new variations of hand images, altering factors such as position, size, brightness, shape, and color. This process creates additional training data that is different from the original dataset but still aligns with the same learning objectives. This method helps prevent overfitting, which occurs when the dataset used for training the model lacks variety, resulting in high accuracy only on the training data but poor performance on new or unseen data. After augmentation, the training process begins with four models—each corresponding to a specific palm line. This ensures that each model can accurately detect the targeted line, using training data tailored to that particular line.

3 Data Preparation for Hand Line Process from Hand Images

This process involves preparing images by resizing and selecting specific regions for processing with an AI model.

3.1 Selecting the Palm Region for Hand Line Processing (Crop Finger)

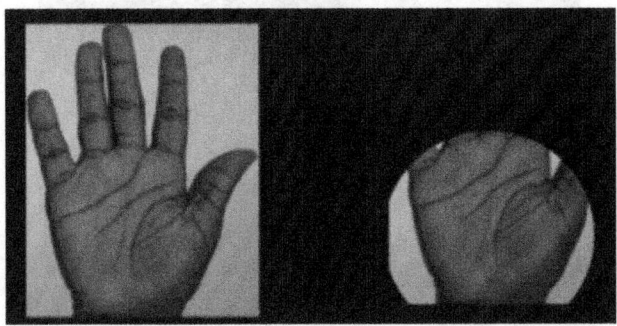

Fig. 4. Shows examples of hand images from the dataset, including 1) hand images size 300 pixels by 380 pixels and 2) cropped palm images with the fingers removed and normalized to a size of 288 pixels by 288 pixels.

The cropping of the palm images to exclude the fingers (Crop Finger) is performed to specifically process the hand lines. This process enhances the accuracy of hand line analysis. The original images are sized at 300 × 380 pixels; however, since the fingers are not necessary for hand line processing, we focus on cropping only the palm area. The cropped images are then resized to 288 pixels by 288 pixels and undergo normalization, a process that converts pixel values from a range of 0–255 to a range of 0 to 1 by dividing each pixel value by 255. The normalized pixel value is calculated as follows:

$$Normalized\ pixel\ value = \frac{Pixel\ value\ of\ hand\ image}{255} \quad (1)$$

3.2 Filling in Missing Parts of the Image for Proper Cropping [2]

The following terms are important to understand: "Crop Size" refers to the width and height of the sub-images created by dividing the original image into smaller sections. "Stride Size" (or the step size) refers to the number of pixels moved when cropping the image. It determines how many pixels to move from one cropping position to the next. The parameters used in this process are as follows: Palm Image (with fingers removed and normalized): 288 pixels ×288 pixels, Crop Size: 128 pixels ×128 pixels, Stride Size: 3 pixels Handling Image Remainders. The original image size is 288 × 288 pixels, which cannot be perfectly divided into 128 × 128 crops with a stride size of 3 pixels. This leads to the issue of leftover pixels, requiring the image to be expanded so that it can be cropped without leaving gaps. The paint border method is used to fill in missing parts, especially around the edges, ensuring that the entire image is properly cropped without any leftover areas. Paint Border works by checking if there are any missing parts using the following formula:

$$Image\,Remainder = (Normalized\,Image\,Size - Crop\,Size)\,\%\,Stride\,Size \qquad (2)$$

Example calculation: *Image Remainder = (288–128) % 3 = 1.*

If the remainder is not 0, it indicates that the image size is not compatible with the crop size. In such cases, the paint border method adds black pixels to the image to make its size compatible, ensuring that subsequent steps (such as extract patch) can proceed without errors. During the extract patch step, if the image size and crop parameters are not aligned, the program may encounter issues, such as unprocessed areas or even program crashes. If the result of the calculation is non-zero, the paint border method adds the missing pixels using the following formula:

$$ExpandedImageSize = NormalizedImageSize + (StrideSize - ImageRemainder) \qquad (3)$$

Substituting values: *Expanded Image Size* = 288 + (3 − 1) = 290 *pixels*
Expanded Image Size = 288 + (3 − 1) = 290 *pixels*

Thus, the final image size becomes 290 × 290 pixels. This allows the image to be cropped into 128 × 128 patches with a stride of 3 pixels without leaving any gaps.

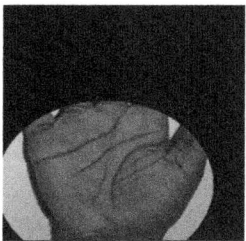

Fig. 5. The image was expanded from its original size of 288 x 288 pixels to 290 × 290 pixels, allowing it to be perfectly cropped into 128 × 128 patches without any leftover pixels.

3.3 Extract Patch [2, 9]: Dividing the Image for Enhanced Analysis Efficiency

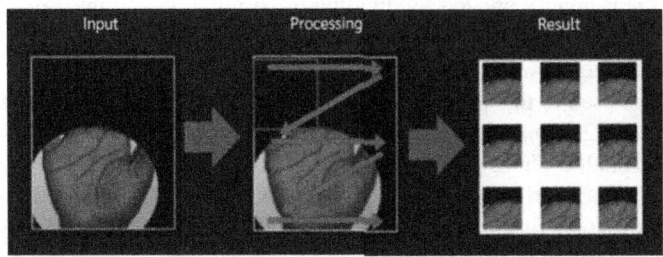

Fig. 6. An Example of Image Division from a Palm Image Using Extract Patch. The figure consists of: 1) A normalized palm image, 2) A visual example of the extract patch process, where the red boxes indicate the division size, and the operation follows the direction of the arrows, 3) The palm image after being divided using the extract patch method.

The extract patch function is responsible for dividing a large image into smaller segments, determined by a specified crop size and stride size. This process generates smaller images from the original, based on a defined direction (as shown in image (b)). This approach simplifies image processing and analysis while reducing memory usage, as it eliminates the need to process the entire image at once, resulting in data that is ready for model input. Importance of Adjusting Stride Size the choice of stride size significantly impacts the outcome. A lower stride size (e.g., 1 or 2) results in minor shifts during cropping, leading to numerous overlapping segments. This increases the computational load but produces more detailed and comprehensive data, as a low stride size captures nearly all information from the image. However, it requires more time and resources. Conversely, a higher stride size (e.g., 5 or 10) shifts the crop over larger intervals, reducing the number of segments and overlaps, which in turn decreases processing requirements. This results in lower resolution data, as a higher stride size can skip over some information. Nevertheless, it consumes less time and resources. Calculation Formula To calculate the total number of cropped images from a large image into smaller segments, we define the following parameters: Image Padding (Paint border): 290 pixels, Crop Size: 128 pixels, Stride Size: 3 pixels Calculating Number of Cropped Images: Number *of* Horizontal (NOH), Number of Vertical (NOV)

$$\text{Horizontal Cropped Images} : NOH\ Images = \frac{WidthOfPaddedImage - CropSize}{StrideSize + 1} \tag{4}$$

$$\text{Substituting values} : NOH\ Images = \frac{290 - 128}{3 + 1} = 55 \tag{5}$$

$$\text{Vertical Cropped Images} : NOV\ Images = \frac{HeightOfpaddedImage - CropSize}{StrideSize + 1} \tag{6}$$

$$\text{Substituting values} : NOV\ Images = \frac{290 - 128}{3 + 1} = 55 \tag{7}$$

$$\text{Cropped Images}: Total = NOH \text{ images} \times NOVimages \qquad (8)$$

$$\text{Substituting values}: Total = 55 \times 55 = 3{,}025$$

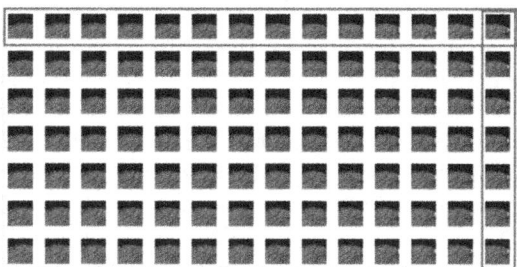

Fig. 7. Shows an example of a large image divided into several smaller images. The red indicates the number of images divided horizontally, while the green indicates the number of images divided vertically.

3.4 Palm Lines Process Workflow

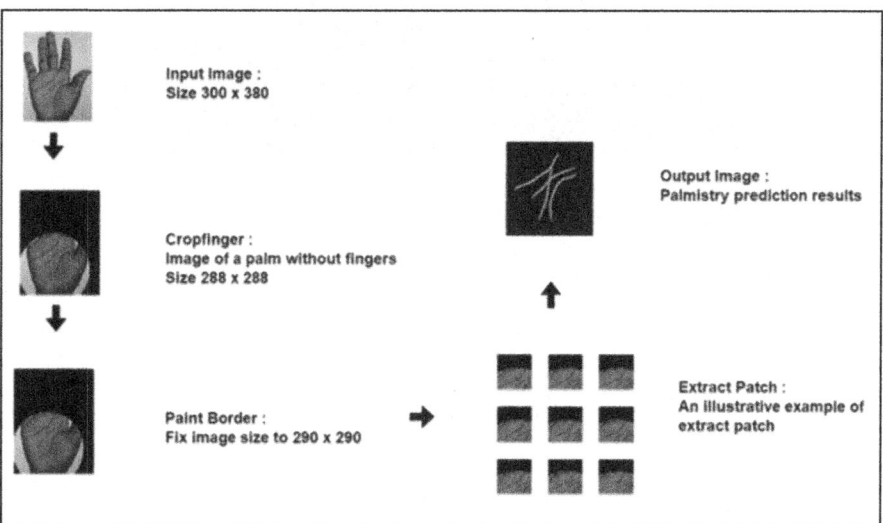

Fig. 8. Is an example of the workflow steps involved in managing a dataset for processing palm lines from hand images.

This image shows a computer vision pipeline for hand line process that takes an input hand image (300 × 380 pixels), crops out the fingers to isolate the palm (288 × 288 pixels), standardizes the image size with border processing (290 × 290 pixels), extracts small patches from the palm surface for detailed analysis, and feeds these features into a machine learning model to predict the hand line results.

4 Managing the Results of Palm Line Process

4.1 Applying the Skeletonization Process [10] to Palm Lines and Coloring

The following terms need to be understood: Threshold (Thresholding): This is a process in image processing used to convert images with multiple colors or gradient shades into just two colors: black and white (white value = 255, black value = 0). Threshold value: This is the value used to categorize data into different groups or types. In this context, we will use the Threshold value to classify data into two categories: values greater than the Threshold value and values less than or equal to the Threshold value. Skeletonization [10] or Thinning: This is an important process in image processing aimed at reducing thick lines or shaped objects to their basic skeletal form (1-pixel lines) while preserving the original shape and structure as much as possible. This allows for easier reading of values and further processing within the program.

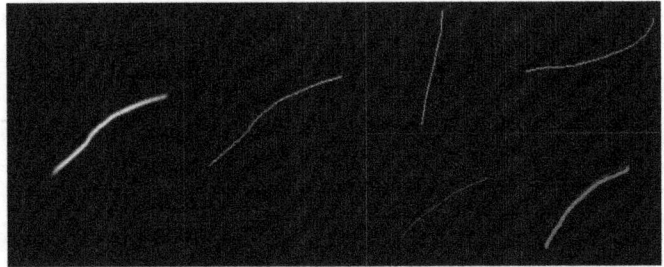

Fig. 9. Shows an example of the results from transforming palm lines through the skeletonization process and applying color. The image includes: 1) the palm line image captured by the SeqNet model, 2) the palm line image after the skeletonization process, and 3) the four skeleton lines of interest for analysis.

In applying Thresholding to the palm line image, we need to set a Threshold value (0–255) and specify the colors we want to convert. For example, we set the Threshold = 128, where values greater than 128 are converted to white and values less than or equal to 128 are converted to black. This step is performed to clearly separate the palm lines from the background and unify the color of the palm lines to white. The next step is to apply the skeletonization process to each extracted palm line, which will illustrate the underlying structure of the original image. We will then separate the colors of the four palm lines of interest for analysis as follows: The Fate Line (fade line) is yellow, The Heart Line is green, The Head Line is red, The Life Line is blue. Color separation facilitates easier result verification.

4.2 Applying Curve Fitting [11] to the Skeleton Lines Using Cubic Regression [12]

The following terms need to be understood: Curve Fitting: This is the process of finding a mathematical equation that best describes the pattern of data in a graph or dataset. Typically, parameters of the equation are adjusted to make the resulting curve as close as possible to the actual data. Cubic Regression: This is a method for estimating the relationship between variables using an equation in the form of a cubic polynomial to produce a curve that represents the trend of the data.

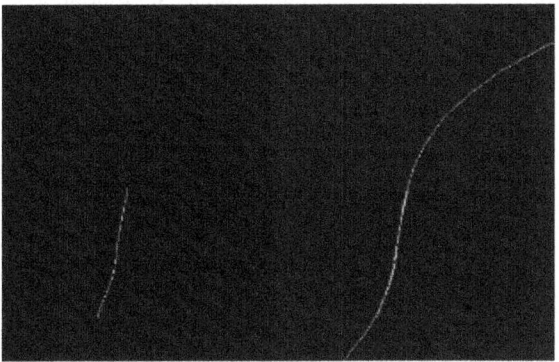

Fig. 10. Displays the results of Curve Fitting using Cubic Regression. The image includes: 1) the palm line image and 2) the curve representing the trend of the palm lines.

This algorithm method is used to process the lines in the image that have undergone skeletonization, applying Curve Fitting using Cubic Regression. The equation used for comparison is a cubic polynomial $\left(ax^3 + bx^2 + cx + d\right)$ Subsequently, the coefficients obtained will be used to calculate the curvature [13] (Figs. 11, 12, 14, 15, 16, 17, 18 and 19).

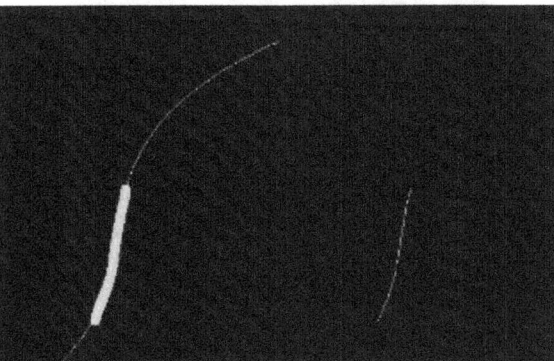

Fig. 11. Shows the image highlighting only the palm lines and cropping the highlighted sections. The image includes: 1) the highlighted palm line image and 2) the palm line image.

Next, we will highlight only the sections of the palm lines and crop to keep only the highlighted areas.

5 The Process of Testing and Analyzing Palm Lines

In the process of analyzing the palm lines, it is essential to identify the starting and ending points of the lines, as well as the landmark location of the starting point on the palm. Additionally, it is necessary to segment the area into zones and landmarks to describe the path of the lines. After that, we must differentiate between straight and curved lines and connect any disconnected segments into a single, appropriate line.

5.1 Finding Start Point and End Point: An Algorithm for Identifying the Starting and Ending Points of the Lines.

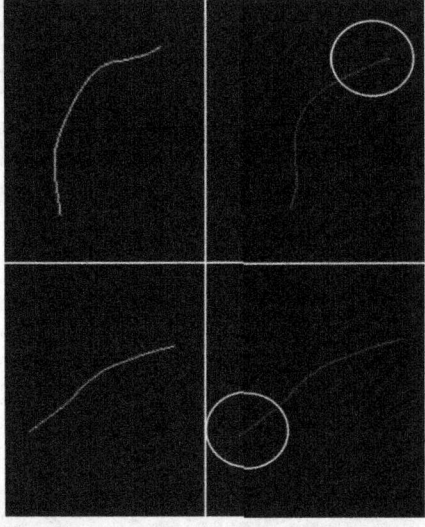

Fig. 12. Shows an example of the positions of the starting and ending points of the lines identified. The desired points are marked in white. This image includes the palm line image and an example of locating the starting and ending points of the lines.

Since the palm line image has undergone Thresholding (resulting in only 2 colors), we can clearly distinguish between the palm lines and the background, as it consists of only black and white. This algorithm will identify the coordinates of all pixels that are white, which correspond to the palm lines, based on their x and y values. The pixel with the highest x and y values will be designated as the starting point of the line, while the pixel with the lowest y value will be designated as the ending point. We use only the y value because sometimes the end of the line may curve, causing the lowest x value not to represent the actual end point. The line is colored blue, and the desired points are marked in white to facilitate easier verification of accuracy.

5.2 Defining Various Landmark Points on MediaPipe

The following terms need to be understood: MediaPipe is a tool developed by the Google Research team to assist in hand detection. MediaPipe has created highly accurate and efficient classification models. The landmark points in MediaPipe are key points identified on the hand that help track the positions of the fingers and wrist. of a cubic polynomial to produce a curve that represents the trend of the data.

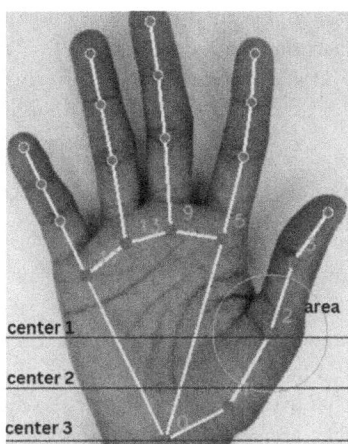

Fig. 13. Shows an example of using MediaPipe with hand images, featuring additional components called center and area.

We will use MediaPipe to detect hands from images and draw skeleton lines on the hands. Next, we will define landmark points (marked in red on the skeleton lines) on the hand images as needed. We will then store the positions of the important landmarks and label them with numbers as shown in the image (0, 1, 2, 3, 5, 9, 13, 17). Additionally, we will add two components beyond the landmarks: First, the three blue lines in Fig. 13, which we will call the center, to measure which center the endpoint of the palm line falls under in the hand image. The second component is a green circular radius centered at landmark point number 2, which we will call the area. This will be used to check if the starting point of the palm line is within the circular radius, with the area defined to have a radius of 50 pixels.

5.3 Finding the Landmark Point Closest to the Starting Point of the Palm Line

Description: In this algorithm, we will use landmark points 17, 13, 8, and 5 to compare with the coordinates of the starting point of the palm line. The formula we will use to calculate the distance is:

$$Distant = \sqrt{(x_2 - x_1) + (y_2 - y_1)} \qquad (9)$$

After calculating the distances, we will compare the x and y positions of each landmark (17, 13, 8, 5) to determine which position is the closest. This step helps identify which finger's position corresponds most closely to the starting point of the palm line.

5.4 Classify Pixel Position: Identifying the Center Position of the Palm Line Endpoint

Description: In this step, we will use centers 1, 2, and 3 to compare with the coordinates of the palm line endpoint, determining which center the endpoint falls within. The method relies on the y values and includes four conditions: 1) The endpoint meets the condition for center 1 if its y value is less than or equal to the y value of center 1. 2) The endpoint meets the condition for center 2 if its y value is greater than the y value of center 1 but less than or equal to the y value of center 2. 3) The endpoint meets the condition for center 3 if its y value is greater than the y value of center 2 but less than or equal to the y value of center 3. 4) The endpoint meets condition 4 if its y value is greater than the y value of center 3.

5.5 Detecting the Starting Point Area: Detecting the Starting Point of the Palm Lines Within the Area.

This algorithm checks whether the coordinates of the starting point of the palm line fall within the specified area. The distance is calculated using the formula from (1).

Once the distance is obtained, it is compared to the detection radius of the area (50 pixels). If the distance is less than 50 pixels, it indicates that the starting point of the palm line is within the area. Conversely, if the distance exceeds 50 pixels, it means that the starting point is outside the area.

5.6 Finding the Curvature Value to Classify Palm Lines

In this section, it is important to understand the following term: Curvature represents the rate of change of direction at each point along a palm line. A high curvature value indicates a significant change in direction, while a low curvature value suggests that the line is close to being straight. Initial Concept: We will calculate the slope of the palm line by using the x and y coordinates of the palm lines. This involves computing the difference between the x and y coordinates to determine the change in the y value relative to the x value. The result will be the slope, or the rate of change between two adjacent points. Following this, we will perform calculations using the following formula, where the derivative refers to the slope of the line: Derivative $= dy/dx$.

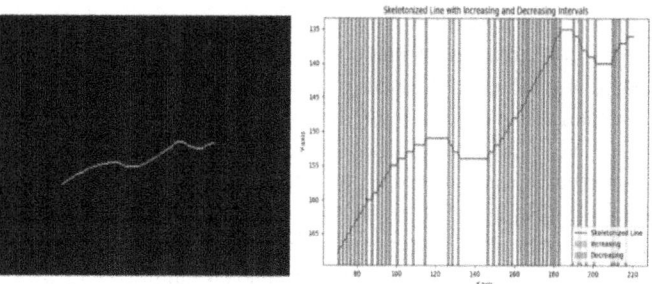

Fig. 14. Examples of the results from calculating the slope of the palm lines. The red section of the graph indicates a decreasing slope, while the green section indicates an increasing slope. This includes: 1) An image of the palm lines, 2) An example of the results showing the slope of the palm lines in each segment

However, to find the curvature value of the palm lines, we need to use a formula that can determine the rate of change in terms of curvature. To distinguish between straight lines and curved lines, we will use the following formula for calculating curvature, as referenced in [13]:

$$k = \frac{|dx \times d2y - dy \times d2x|}{(dx^2 + dy^2)^{\frac{3}{2}}} \tag{10}$$

This calculation aims to find the difference between the changes along the x-axis and the changes along the y-axis, and then sum the slopes in each axis to determine the rate of change that represents the curvature. This formula calculates the degree of curvature at any given point on the curve. In summary, if the value of K is high, it indicates a significant curvature, while a low value of K suggests minimal curvature or that the line is nearly straight.

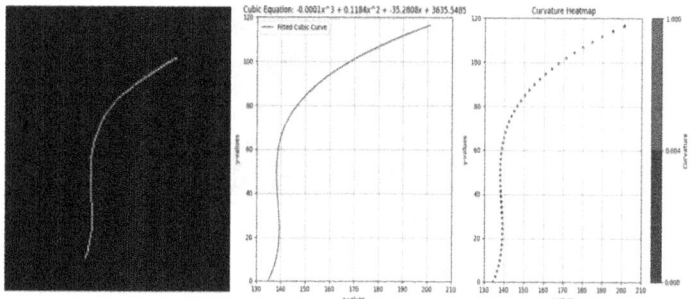

Fig. 15. An illustration of the distinction between high curvature and low curvature. 1) An example image of palm lines, 2) An example image of palm lines compared to the results, 3) An image showing the results indicating whether the line is curved or not. The red sections represent parts of the curve, while the blue sections indicate straight lines.

The operation of this algorithm will take the coefficients obtained from the curve fitting process using cubic regression and compute them using the curvature formula. The curvature classification thresholds used in our system were determined through empirical analysis of manually annotated palm line segments. We collected 500 line segments from our dataset and asked three independent experts to classify each segment as either "straight" or "curved" based on visual inspection. For each segment, we computed the curvature value using Eq. (6). Statistical analysis of the expert-annotated data revealed the following distribution: 95% of segments classified as "straight" had curvature values ≤ 0.004, 92% of segments classified as "curved" had curvature values >0.004. The optimal separation threshold that maximized classification accuracy was 0.004. Therefore, our classification criteria are:

Straight line: Curvature value $\in [0, 0.004]$, Curved line: Curvature value $\in (0.004, 1.0]$. This threshold achieved 91.3% classification accuracy on our test dataset, with a precision of 0.89 and recall of 0.94 for curved line detection.

5.7 Algorithm for Detecting Broken Lines

Understanding the following terms is essential: The concept of detecting broken lines involves finding connected points that are similar in color and intensity and are adjacent to each other, forming a line known as a contour or shape line. We use thresholding to reduce the image to just two colors: black for the background and white for the lines. The algorithm checks from left to right and top to bottom. When it encounters a white pixel, it counts it as part of a line; if it encounters a black pixel, it counts it as part of the background. If it finds other white pixels that are not connected—meaning there are black pixels interrupting them—it counts those as separate lines.

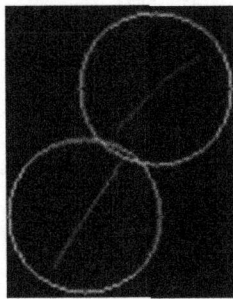

Fig. 16. Examples of the results from detecting lines within the image.

5.8 Broken Line Connection Parameters

Understanding the following term is essential: Backtrack (Backtracking) [14–16] refers to a problem-solving method that involves searching for possible paths. If the current path being explored cannot proceed, the algorithm will backtrack to the previous point and attempt other paths.

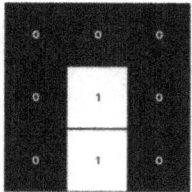 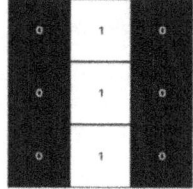 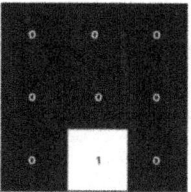

Fig. 17. Examples of detecting lines, endpoints, and disconnected line segments in a 3 × 3 metric, consisting of: 1) An example of a 3 × 3 metric when an endpoint is detected, 2) An example of a 3 × 3 metric when part of a line is detected, 3) An example of a 3 × 3 metric that does not represent a line.

The parameters for connecting broken line segments (10-pixel distance threshold and 45-degree angle threshold) were optimized through systematic evaluation on a validation set of 50 palm images containing manually identified broken lines. We performed a grid search over the following parameter ranges:

- Distance threshold: [5, 8, 10, 12, 15] pixels
- Angle threshold: [30°, 45°, 60°, 75°, 90°]

The optimization criterion was to maximize the F1-score for correct line connections while minimizing false connections. The results showed in Table 1.

Table 1. The optimization criterion

Ditance (px)	Angle (°)	Precision	Recall	F1-Score
10	45	0.91	0.83	0.87
8	45	0.93	0.79	0.85
12	45	0.87	0.86	0.86
10	30	0.94	0.74	0.83
10	60	0.85	0.89	0.87

The combination of 10-pixel distance and 45-degree angle achieved the optimal balance between connection accuracy and false positive reduction, resulting in 87.4% overall accuracy for broken line connection.

We will use the backtracking method to find the nodes (coordinates of x and y at the endpoints) of the palm lines within the image. This will be done by checking with a 3 × 3 metric, moving pixel by pixel until complete. If the center value of the 3 × 3 metric is 1 (a white pixel), it will be counted as part of the line. If the center value is 0 (a black pixel), it will not be counted as a line. Next, if a value of 1 in the metric encounters a value of 0 (indicating it is not connected to another 1), it signifies that the line has reached its endpoint. If it encounters another value of 1 at a different location, it will be counted as a separate line.

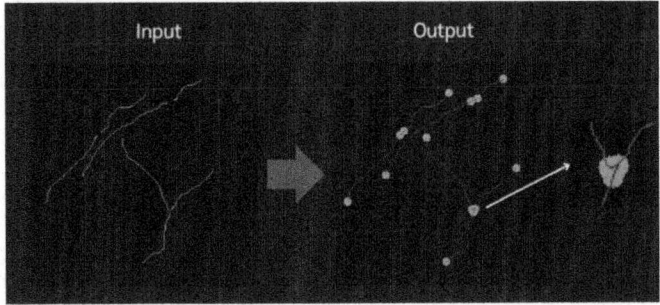

Fig. 18. Examples of detecting and connecting broken lines. 1) An example of disconnected lines, 2) An example of the results of connecting the broken lines, where green represents the nodes, red represents the paths checked by backtracking, and blue represents the lines that connect between the nodes.

After that, each line with endpoints will be separated and formatted into a graph [17], consisting of nodes and various lines. Next, we will address the issue of connecting broken lines by calculating the distance between the endpoints of different lines. If two endpoints are within 10 pixels of each other and the angle between the connecting nodes is less than 45°, a line will be drawn to connect the nearest nodes, as they are considered to be part of the same line.

6 Experimental Results and Evaluation

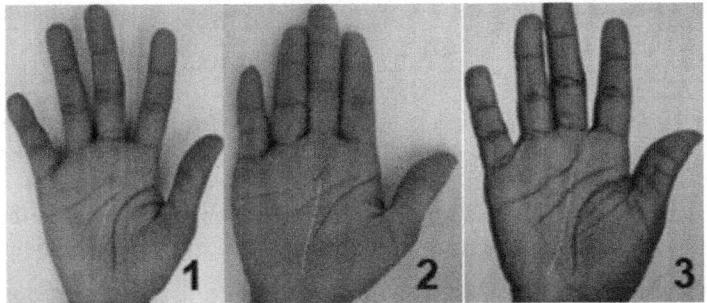

Fig. 19. An example of a hand line used for testing line analysis.

6.1 Dataset and Experimental Setup

We evaluated our system on a comprehensive dataset of 500 palm images (300×380 pixels) collected from 225 participants under controlled lighting conditions. Ground truth annotations were created by three experienced annotators who manually segmented the four main palm lines (Fate, Heart, Head, Life) using specialized annotation software.

To ensure annotation quality, we measured inter-annotator agreement using the Intersection over Union (IoU) metric. The average inter-annotator IoU was 0.923 ± 0.034, indicating high consistency in annotations. The dataset was randomly split into 70% training (350 images), 15% validation (75 images), and 15% testing (75 images).

6.2 Palm Line Segmentation Performance

We evaluated the segmentation performance of our four specialized SeqNet models using standard metrics including IoU, Dice coefficient, precision, and recall. Table 2 presents the detailed results for each line type.

Table 2. Line Segmentation Performance

Line Type	IoU	Dice	Precision	Recall
Fate Line	0.842 ± 0.067	0.914 ± 0.041	0.869 ± 0.058	0.921 ± 0.052
Heart Line	0.856 ± 0.054	0.922 ± 0.033	0.881 ± 0.047	0.917 ± 0.045
Head Line	0.871 ± 0.049	0.931 ± 0.029	0.891 ± 0.041	0.925 ± 0.038
Life Line	0.889 ± 0.043	0.941 ± 0.025	0.903 ± 0.037	0.934 ± 0.034
Average	0.865 ± 0.053	0.927 ± 0.032	0.886 ± 0.046	0.924 ± 0.042

Our system achieved consistent performance across all line types, with Life lines showing the highest segmentation accuracy (0.889 IoU) and Fate lines showing the most variation (±0.067 standard deviation).

6.3 Feature Extraction and Classification Performance

We evaluated the accuracy of subsequent processing steps including curvature classification, landmark detection, and broken line connection. The results are summarized in Table 3.

Table 3. Feature Classification Performance

Feature Accuracy	Accuracy	Precision	Recall	F1-Score	Processing Time (ms)
Curvature Classification	91.3%	0.89	0.94	0.91	23 ± 4
Starting Point Detection	94.7%	0.92	0.97	0.95	15 ± 2
Endpoint Detection	93.2%	0.91	0.95	0.93	18 ± 3
Broken Line Connection	87.4%	0.84	0.91	0.87	45 ± 8

The curvature classification process completed efficiently with an average processing time of 23 ms per image, with a small variation of ±4 ms, indicating consistent computational performance. The computational efficiency was also remarkable, with starting point detection completing in just 15 ms on average with minimal variation of

±2 ms, making it the fastest feature extraction component. Processing time averaged 18 ms with a variation of ±3 ms, representing efficient computational performance that falls between starting point detection and curvature classification. Broken line connection represented the most challenging feature extraction task, achieving 87.4% accuracy in successfully connecting disconnected line segments that belong to the same logical palm line.

6.4 Comparative Analysis

We compared our approach against three baseline methods to demonstrate its effectiveness: Standard U-Net: Conventional U-Net architecture adapted for palm line segmentation, Classical Computer Vision: Canny edge detection followed by Hough line transform, Multi-output SeqNet: Single SeqNet model with multi-output head for all four lines (Tables 4 and 5).

Table 4. Comparative Performance Analysis

Method	Mean IoU	Processing Time (ms)
Our Method (4 SeqNets)	0.865 ± 0.053	450 ± 35
Standard U-Net	0.789 ± 0.075	380 ± 28
Multi-output	0.831 ± 0.061	285 ± 22
Classical CV	0.667 ± 0.098	120 ± 15

To demonstrate the effectiveness of our approach, we conducted a comprehensive comparison against three established baseline methods. The first baseline was a standard U-Net architecture, which represents the conventional approach for medical image segmentation tasks and has been widely adopted for various segmentation applications. The second comparison method employed classical computer vision techniques, specifically combining Canny edge detection with Hough line transform, which represents traditional non-learning approaches to line detection in images. The third baseline was a multi-output SeqNet variant, where a single SeqNet model was configured with multiple output heads to detect all four palm line types simultaneously, allowing us to evaluate the impact of our specialized multi-model architecture.

For the computer used in experimental evaluation, the case of using four separate models to analyze hand lines utilizes a GPU V100 with 32 GB RAM, while the case of using only one model to analyze all hand line colors utilizes a GPU A100 with 80 GB RAM.

6.5 Ablation Study

To validate our design choices, we conducted an ablation study examining the contribution of each component:

Table 5. Ablation Study Results (Mean IoU)

Configuration	Fate	Heart	Head	Life	Average
Full System	0.842	0.856	0.871	0.889	0.865
Without Skeletonization	0.821	0.834	0.849	0.867	0.843
Without Curve Fitting	0.835	0.849	0.863	0.881	0.857
Without Broken Line Connection	0.798	0.812	0.828	0.846	0.821

Proper exposure was maintained throughout the palm region to avoid over-saturated (pure white) or under-saturated (pure black) areas that would result in loss of line detail. Over-saturation occurs when bright areas lose all detail and appear as solid white regions, while under-saturation creates areas too dark to distinguish line features. We verified that all palm areas retained full tonal range (pixel values between 20–235 on a 0–255 scale), ensuring that subtle line features remained visible across the entire palm surface regardless of natural skin tone variations.

7 Conclusion

This paper presented a comprehensive system for automated palm line detection and analysis using deep learning techniques. Our approach employs four specialized SeqNet models to achieve robust segmentation of the four main palm lines with 86.5% mean IoU, representing a significant improvement over existing baseline method. The key contributions of this work include: (1) a specialized multi-model architecture that outperforms single unified models, (2) systematic parameter optimization for geometric feature extraction, and (3) comprehensive quantitative evaluation demonstrating the system's effectiveness. Our experimental results show consistent performance across all line types and processing steps, with particularly strong results in landmark detection (94.7% accuracy) and curvature classification (91.3% accuracy). Future work will focus on expanding the dataset to include more diverse populations, investigating the correlation between extracted geometric features and biometric identification applications, and exploring real-time implementation optimizations for mobile devices.

The extracted geometric features provide unique identifiers that could complement existing biometric modalities in touchless authentication systems. The non-contact nature of palm line detection makes it suitable for hygienic applications in medical facilities, clean rooms, and high-security environments where traditional fingerprint systems may be impractical. The developed segmentation algorithms can be adapted for analyzing linear structures in medical imagery, including retinal blood vessel networks for diabetic screening, coronary artery analysis in angiographic images, and neural pathway mapping in neuroimaging applications. The robust line detection and broken line connection algorithms address similar challenges found in medical image processing.

Acknowledgment. This research was supported by Smarterware Co., Ltd., which provided us with a domain-specific dataset and a cloud-based GPU computing platform, which enabled us to train and evaluate our models at scale. Therefore, this research will be an important contribution to the company's development of AI software products.

References

1. Li, L., Verma, M., Nakashima, Y., Kawasaki, R., Nagahara, H.: Joint learning of vessel segmentation and artery/vein classification with post-processing. Med. Imaging Deep Learn. **2020**, 440–453 (2020)
2. Li, L.: SeqNet. GitHub Repository (2020). https://github.com/conscienceli/SeqNet
3. Li, L., Verma, M., Nakashima, Y., Nagahara, H., Kawasaki, R.: Retinal image segmentation utilizing structural redundancy in vessel networks. Proc. IEEE/CVF Winter Conf. Appl. Computer. Vis. 3656–3665 (2020)
4. Siddique, N., et al.: U-net and its variants for medical image segmentation: a review of theory and applications. IEEE Access **9**, 82031–82057 (2021)
5. Zhang, F., et al.: Mediapipe hands: on-device real-time hand tracking (2020). arXiv preprint arXiv:2006.10214
6. Uboweja, E., et al.: On-device real-time custom hand gesture recognition. In: Proc. IEEE/CVF Int. Conf. Comput. Vis. (ICCVW) (2023)
7. Kadamba, V.: Mediapipe for Python. GeeksforGeeks (2023)
8. Han, J.S., Lee, C.I., Youn, Y.H., Kim, S.J.: A study on real-time hand gesture recognition technology by machine learning-based mediapipe. J. Syst. Manage. Sci. **12**(2) (2022)
9. Kesidis, A.L., Krassanakis, V., Misthos, L.M., Merlemis, N.: A multipurpose patch creation tool for image processing applications. Multimodal Technol. Interact. **6**(12) (2022)
10. Sharifipour, H.M., Yousefi, B., Maldague, X.P.: Skeletonization and reconstruction based on graph morphological transformations (2020). arXiv preprint arXiv:2009.07970
11. SciPy Community: scipy.optimize curve_fit. SciPy Documentation (2024). https://docs.scipy.org/doc/scipy/reference/generated/scipy.optimize.curve_fit.html
12. Stojiljkovic, M.: Linear regression in python. Beoptimized (2021)
13. Alencar, H., Santos, W., Neto, G.S.: Differential geometry of plane curves. Am. Math. Soc. **96** (2020)
14. Prasetyo, T.A., Chandra, R., Simamora, B., Christian, M.J., Silaban, A.R., Siregar, M.V.: Pathfinding solving in maze game using backtracking algorithm. J. CoreIT **9**(1) (2023)
15. Park, S., et al.: Non-backtracking graph neural networks (2023). arXiv preprint arXiv:2310.07430
16. Sharifipour, H.M., Yousefi, B., Maldague, X.P.: Computer vision project - Fortune on your hand: view-invariant machine palmistry. GitHub Repository (2022). https://github.com/yeonsumia/palmistry
17. Riansanti, O., Ihsan, M., Suhaimi, D.: Connectivity algorithm with depth first search (DFS) on simple graphs. J. Phys. Conf. Ser. **948**(1), 012065 (2018)

Beyond Accuracy: Evaluating LLMs for Validating Community Service Provider Directory

Saviz Saei, Sadhan Ghimire, and Sujan Anreddy(✉)

Mississippi State University, Starkville, MS 39759, USA
{sra116,ss4646,sg2222}@msstate.edu

Abstract. As artificial intelligence tools are increasingly adopted to validate community service provider directories, it is critical to assess whether large language models (LLMs) can reliably verify structured data in these systems. This study evaluates five LLMs, LLaMA 3.3 70B Versatile, LLaMA 3.1 8B Instant, LLaMA 3 70B 8192, LLaMA 3 8B 8192, and Gemma2 9B IT, using community service provider data from Mississippi across three evaluation conditions: clean records (base-line), systematically corrupted entries, and records with missing fields. Model responses were categorized as "Verified," "Not Verified," or "Needs Checking" to assess each model's ability to confirm correct data, reject erroneous records, and handle uncertainty, respectively.

Among the models tested, LLaMA 3.3 70B Versatile demonstrated the most robust overall performance, achieving high verification accuracy on clean data (96%) and the strongest error detection capabilities by rejecting 47% of corrupted entries. In contrast, LLaMA 3 8B 8192 incorrectly verified 79% of corrupted records, indicating unsafe over-permissiveness and weak anomaly detection. These results underscore that high verification accuracy alone is insufficient; effective referral system design must prioritize models that exhibit strong error detection capabilities and appropriately defer uncertain cases to human oversight.

1 Introduction

The community resource referral process refers to the process of referring community resources and the role of community service provider data in finding health services information, which has long been a critical focus. Key dimensions such as verification rates, completeness, consistency, and timeliness are essential for maintaining the integrity of healthcare information systems [3]. Among these, community service provider data is especially important because it directly affects patient care coordination, insurance network management, and administrative efficiency. At the same time, the integration of artificial intelligence (AI) into healthcare care administration has shown great potential, particularly in optimizing claim processing, fraud detection, and data management, where machine learning methods often surpass traditional manual approaches in speed and accuracy [4, 6]. The recent advent of large language models (LLMs), including LLaMA [2] and Gemma [1], has introduced powerful new tools for interpreting and verifying textual data, opening novel opportunities for automating community service provider verification. Organizations, such as the Mississippi Access To Care (MAC) Centers, manage vast and complex community service provider directories that are vital for ensuring reliable, objective, and unbiased information about a wide range of programs and services, helping people understand and evaluate their various options. These centers cater to the elderly, disabled individuals, their family members and representatives, as well as anyone seeking help with the long-term care. However, traditional manual information verification methods are increasingly inadequate, being both time-consuming and prone to error, especially given the scale and complexity of maintaining accurate information.

Automating community service provider data verification with LLMs could greatly improve efficiency, but the reliability and verification accuracy of these models in healthcare-specific contexts remain underexplored. Accurate community service provider directory verification is crucial, as errors can result in delayed treatments, inappropriate referrals, and costly regulatory penalties. Therefore, any automated verification system must not only achieve a high verification rate on correct data, but also demonstrate robust error detection with humanin-the-loop capabilities to identify and flag potentially harmful misinformation that could compromise patient care or organizational compliance.

1.1 Problem Statement

Although LLMs have shown promise in various natural language processing tasks, their performance in structured data verification, particularly information from community service providers, has not been systematically evaluated. Key questions remain unanswered:

1. How accurately can different LLMs verify the location data of community service providers?
2. Can LLMs effectively detect and flag obviously incorrect information?
3. How do models handle incomplete or ambiguous data scenarios?
4. What model characteristics (size, architecture, training methodology) contribute most to reliable verification performance?

Community organizations, such as Findhelp, increasingly rely on AI-driven systems for validating provider information. However, without systematic evaluation, the reliability of LLMs in this domain is uncertain. This study addresses these gaps by developing a comprehensive evaluation framework that assesses LLMs across diverse data quality scenarios, measures their anomaly detection capabilities, and evaluates their handling of uncertainty through human-in-the-loop workflows. The findings aim to inform evidence-based model selection for community resource referral systems and establish benchmarks for future AI- driven data validation research.

2 Methodology

The study's methodology is centered on an automated evaluation framework developed in Python, designed to systematically assess LLM performance in a structured data verification task. We utilized the Groq API platform [5] to ensure consistent, high-speed interaction with the five selected language models.

A core component of the framework is a standardized prompting strategy. Each model was issued an identical prompt instructing it to act as a data verifier for a community service provider in Mississippi. The prompt explicitly required the model to return its findings exclusively in a structured JSON format, assigning one of three mandatory status values to each data field: VERIFIED, NOT VERIFIED, or NEEDS CHECKING. This controlled output enables direct, quantitative comparison of model behavior and confidence levels. The full prompt template is detailed below:

Prompting Instruction. Each model received identical prompts following this standardized format:

```
You are verifying all provider information for a provider named {provider_name}.
Please verify the accuracy of {formatted_fields} based on {provider_name} and the address
of {provider_name}.
For each field, respond with one of the following status values:
  - VERIFIED
  - NOT VERIFIED
  - NEEDS CHECKING
Return your response only as valid JSON, for example:

{
  "County": "VERIFIED",
  "AddressLine1": "VERIFIED",
  "City": "NOT VERIFIED",
  "State": "VERIFIED",
  "PostalCode": "NEEDS CHECKING"
}

Do not include explanations or extra text.

response = client.chat.completions.create(
    messages=[
        {
            "role": "system",
            "content": "You use Google to verify provider information in Mississippi."
        },
        {
            "role": "user",
            "content": prompt
        }
    ],
    model=model_name
)
```

Models were required to classify each field using one of three categories, enabling quantitative analysis of decision-making patterns and confidence levels. Figure 1 shows the flowchart of the application developed for this study.

The framework also included a data processing module for dataset sampling, a corruption engine to systematically introduce errors for testing, and a results analysis component to compute performance metrics. To conduct a comprehensive evaluation of large language models (LLMs) for healthcare data verification, we selected five prominent models available through the Groq API platform [5], chosen for their diverse architectures, parameter scales, and optimization strategies. This selection allowed for a robust comparison spanning efficiency, capacity, and design philosophies across the current landscape of LLMs. Among these, Gemma2 9B IT [1], developed by Google in 2024, is a 9-billion-parameter instruction-tuned model engineered to balance efficiency, safety, and verification accuracy. It is open-source, supports an 8,192-token context window, and offers a cost-effective solution suitable for various language-processing tasks. Complementing this, LLaMA 3.1 8B Instant represents a lighter yet powerful member of the LLaMA family, featuring eight billion parameters optimized for fast inference without sacrificing performance, making it well suited for applications demanding quick responses. Meta's LLaMA 3.3 70B Versatile, a cutting-edge multilingual model with seventy billion parameters and an extensive 128,000 token context window, incorporates advanced transformer architectures alongside supervised fine-tuning and reinforcement learning from human feedback to align outputs with user needs for helpfulness and safety. Additionally, the LLaMA3 70B 8192 and LLaMA3 8B 8192 models share the same architectural base and 8,192-token context length but differ markedly in size; the larger variant is designed for high-capacity, accuracy-driven scenarios, whereas the smaller model offers a resource-efficient alternative that maintains strong foundational capabilities.

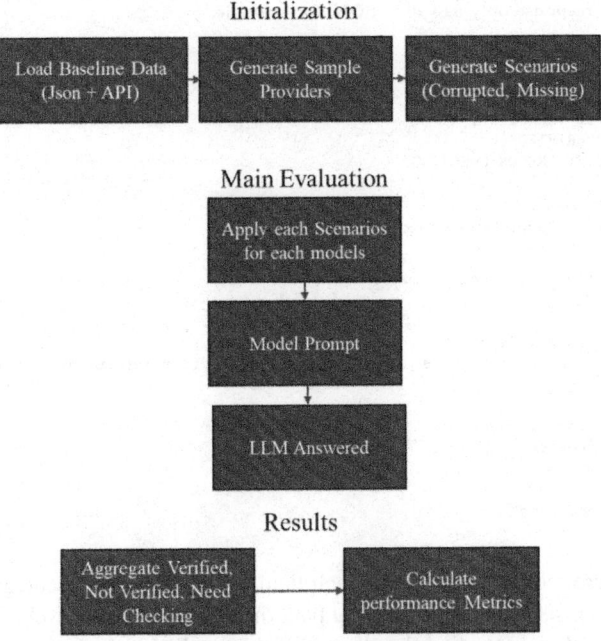

Fig. 1. A structured flowchart of the evaluation process

These five models were selected because they are all open-source or accessible via public APIs, span a parameter range from eight to seventy billion parameters to illuminate size–performance trade-offs, cover both short and long context windows for testing memory-length effects on structured-data reasoning, and collectively balance fast-response configurations with accuracy-oriented variants. Each model can parse JSON, compare structured records, and represent uncertainty, making them well aligned with the practical requirements of provider-directory verification tasks.

3 Results

3.1 Dataset and Data Preparation

We utilized a JSON dataset of community service providers in Mississippi, containing five key fields: County, Address, City, State, and Postal Code. The dataset comprised 1,093 provider types across 1,553 geographic regions. Unique records were sampled using a controlled methodology to ensure reproducibility.

3.2 Experimental Design

The evaluation implemented in three distinct scenarios:

- **Scenario 1 (Baseline):** Verification of clean, unaltered records to benchmark accuracy, simulating manual search validation.
- **Scenario 2 (Corrupted):** Injection of systematic errors (e.g., random substitutions, typos) in 80% of records to evaluate anomaly detection, where correct model behavior involves flagging affected fields.
- **Scenario 3 (Missing Fields):** Records with omitted fields (e.g., city, zipcode) to assess the model's handling of uncertainty, expecting cautious classifications rather than blind verification.

Scenario 1 used as baseline verification performance. A high verification rate was expected, reflecting the model's ability to validate correct data—similar to a user conducting a manual search (e.g., via ask, call, Google). Scenario 2 introduced intentional corruption in fields such as city, state, and zipcode. Here, better performance was indicated by the model flagging more records as "NEEDS CHECKING" or "NOT VERIFIED", demonstrating effective error detection. Scenario 3 tested model performance on incomplete data by omitting or masking key fields. In this case, the appropriate model behavior was to flag ambiguous records as "NEEDS CHECKING" rather than incorrectly verifying them, reflecting the model's ability to handle uncertainty and incomplete information responsibly. These scenarios, combined with the structured framework, enabled a comprehensive, multi-dimensional evaluation of LLMs for structured data verification in community service directories.

To evaluate the reliability of large language models (LLMs) in verifying structured provider data, five models were assessed across the three scenarios. Model outputs were categorized as Verified, Not Verified, or Needs Checking, reflecting accuracy, error detection, and uncertainty handling, respectively.

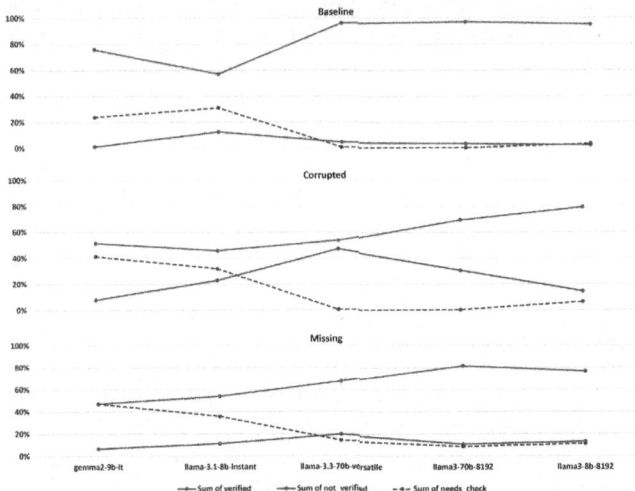

Fig. 2. Performance results across all three evaluated scenarios

Table 1. Performance results across all three evaluated scenarios

Scenario	Model	Verified	Not Verified	Needs Checking
Baseline	gemma2-9b-it	76%	1%	24%
	llama-3.1-8b-instant	57%	12%	31%
	llama-3.3-70b-versatile	96%	4%	0%
	llama3-70b-8192	97%	3%	0%
	llama3-8b-8192	95%	2%	3%
Corrupted	gemma2-9b-it	51%	8%	41%
	llama-3.1-8b-instant	46%	23%	32%
	llama-3.3-70b-versatile	53%	47%	0%
	llama3-70b-8192	69%	30%	0%
	llama3-8b-8192	79%	14%	6%
Missing	gemma2-9b-it	47%	6%	47%
	llama-3.1-8b-instant	54%	11%	36%
	llama-3.3-70b-versatile	67%	19%	14%
	llama3-70b-8192	81%	10%	8%
	llama3-8b-8192	76%	13%	11%

As shown in Fig. 2 and detailed in Table 1, LLaMA 3.3-70B Versatile demonstrated the most robust and balanced performance. It achieved a high baseline verification rate of 96%, the strongest rejection rate of 47% under corrupted conditions, and maintained a verification rate of 67% in missing data. This indicates both high accuracy when the data is valid and appropriate caution when encountering potential anomalies. Similarly, LLaMA 3-70B-8192 achieved excellent baseline accuracy (97%) but exhibited reduced selectivity under corrupted inputs by rejecting only 30%, highlighting a tendency to over-verify and potentially accept flawed data. In contrast, LLaMA 3-8B-8192 - despite a high baseline verification rate of 95% - showed critical weaknesses in error detection, verifying 79% corrupted records, and rejecting only 14%. This behavior poses a substantial risk in safety-sensitive domains, where false positives may undermine trust in the system. LLaMA 3.1-8B Instant performed more conservatively, with a lower baseline verification rate (57%) and a moderate rejection rate of 23% under corruption, while flagging a large proportion of records as "Needs Checking" (32%–36%) in both corrupted and missing scenarios. This suggests that while the model errs on the side of caution, it may also produce a higher manual workload. Gemma2-9B-IT showed the weakest overall performance, rejecting only 8% corrupted records and marking 40% of entries as uncertain. This pattern indicates indecision rather than effective filtering, which can result in inefficient human validation and lower system confidence. Collectively, these findings underscore that high verification rates alone are not sufficient; models must also demonstrate effective rejection of incorrect data and appropriate deference to uncertainty when applicable.

4 Conclusions

This study reveals substantial disparities in the performance of large-language models (LLMs) when applied to the verification of structured community service provider data. We developed a modular evaluation framework to assess LLM performance in verifying community service provider data. The framework automated data parsing, error injection, API querying (via the Groq platform), and results aggregation. Models were prompted with standardized instructions to classify each field as VERIFIED, NOT VERIFIED, or NEEDS CHECKING. Key performance metrics included verification accuracy, error rejection rates, and uncertainty classification distributions. Among the models tested, LLaMA 3.3-70B Versatile consistently demonstrated the most reliable behavior, combining strong baseline verification with the highest error detection capability in corrupted scenarios and balanced performance in cases of missing data. Notably, while larger models generally performed better, model size alone was not a consistent predictor of safety or conservativeness. Models like LLaMA 3-8B-8192, though computationally efficient, exhibited over-permissive behavior by incorrectly verifying a majority of corrupted records. This behavior illustrates that raw verification rates on clean data may be misleading when evaluating LLMs for safety-critical applications. Similarly, models that over-rely on uncertainty—such as Gemma2-9B-IT—may introduce inefficiencies without reliably identifying errors.

The findings highlight the importance of designing evaluation frameworks that go beyond traditional accuracy metrics. Future research should focus on identifying architectural and training strategies that enhance the models' ability to detect and reject flawed data. Moreover, domain-specific fine-tuning that prioritizes conservative validation strategies, as well as the development of standardized evaluation protocols that penalize false verification, will be critical for deploying trustworthy AI systems in community resource referral and similar high-stakes domains.

Acknowledgement. This project is supported by the Administration for Community Living (ACL), U.S. Department of Health and Human Services (HHS) as part of a financial assistance award totaling $500,000 with 100 percent funding by ACL/HHS. The contents are those of the author(s) and do not necessarily represent the official views of, nor an endorsement, by ACL/HHS or the U.S. Government. We acknowledge the effort of the AFFIRM (Age-Friendly Focused Information and Resource Maps) team for providing us with the verified community service provider directory.

References

1. Team, G., et al.: Gemma: Open Models Based on Gemini Research and Technology. arXiv preprint arXiv:2403.08295 (2024). https://doi.org/10.48550/arXiv.2403.08295
2. Touvron, H., et al.: LLaMA: Open and Efficient Foundation Language Models. arXiv preprint arXiv:2302.13971 (2023). https://doi.org/10.48550/arXiv.2302.13971
3. Weiskopf, N.G., Weng, C.: Methods and dimensions of electronic health record data quality assessment: Enabling reuse for clinical research. J. American Med. Info. Ass. **20**(1), 144–151 (2013). https://doi.org/10.1136/amiajnl-2011-000681
4. Jiang, F., et al.: Artificial intelligence in healthcare: past, present and future. Stroke and Vascular Neurology **2**(4) (2017)
5. Groq: Supported Models. https://console.groq.com/docs/models. Accessed: 30 May 2025
6. Tabari, P., Piscitelli, A., Costagliola, G., Rosa, M.D.: Assessing the potential of an LLM-powered system for enhancing FHIR resource validation. Stud. Health Technol. Info. (2025)

Trustworthy Design Patterns for Multi-agent Software Systems

Jay Prakash Thakur[1,2](✉) and Akshata Kishore Moharir[1,2]

[1] Palo Alto, CA, USA
jayprakashthakursnr@gmail.com
[2] Portland, OR, USA

Abstract. As multi-agent systems (MAS) become critical infrastructure managing healthcare, finance, and transportation, a fundamental paradox emerges: the very autonomy that makes MAS powerful also makes them untrustworthy. This paper presents six architectural design patterns that resolve this paradox by embedding trustworthiness into MAS foundations rather than treating it as an afterthought. These patterns, Transparent Decision Audit Trail, Consensus-Based Critical Decisions, Human-in-the-Loop Override, Graduated Trust Levels, Explainable Agent Behavior, and Fault Isolation and Recovery, transform abstract trust requirements into concrete architectural solutions. Through illustrative scenarios in finance, healthcare, and autonomous vehicles, this work demonstrates how systematic application of these patterns addresses the trust crisis hindering AI adoption. This position paper says that trustworthiness by design is not only desirable, but also crucial for the survival of society as MAS become its digital nervous system.

Keywords: Multi-agent systems · Trust · Design patterns · Software architecture · Explainable AI

1 Introduction

Multi-agent systems have become crucial in fields like enterprise resource planning, financial trading, diagnosing healthcare procedures, and coordinating autonomous vehicles [1]. These systems leverage distributed artificial intelligence to enable autonomous agents to collaborate, solving complex problems beyond single-agent capabilities. But a developing **trust crisis** is making it harder for them to be widely used. This is because agents' actions are unexpected, decisions are unclear, and there are legal difficulties [2]. The emergence of Large Language Model (LLM)-based agents amplifies these concerns, as their inherent unpredictability and emergent behaviors demand more systematic trust mechanisms than traditional MAS.

This work goes against the current research trend in multi-agent systems, which mostly sees trust as an algorithmic or add-on element. The point of the argument is that

---

A. K. Moharir—These authors contributed equally to this work.

this method is fundamentally wrong and a major cause of the current trust crisis. For example, Observer and Mediator are well-known coordination patterns for MAS [3], but there aren't any patterns that deal with trust-specific problems. Reputation systems and other current algorithmic solutions frequently work like black boxes and don't fit into the general architecture of the system. This makes it hard to verify or combine trust attributes. We believe that trustworthiness is not a part of system architecture, but rather an emergent quality. Because of this, the community has to stop using separate trust models and start using a new set of design patterns to guide a holistic, architectural-first approach.

The core contribution of this work is a catalog of six such patterns that embed trustworthiness into the very fabric of a system. Unlike existing work on trust algorithms [4] or reputation models [5], these patterns provide architectural solutions to trust challenges. This technique is different because of three main innovative concepts:

(i) "Architectural-first thinking" means that trust is seen as a structural issue, like performance or security, rather than something to add later; (ii) "Composability" means that patterns are made to work together to create defense-in-depth for trust; and (iii) "Stakeholder-centric design" means that each pattern directly meets the needs of developers, users, and regulators. This work extends on previous research by creating a systematic list of trust-oriented design patterns just for MAS architectures.

2 Trust Challenges in Multi-agent Software Systems

Trust in MAS works on many levels, each of which presents its own engineering problems that typical software methods can't solve [6].

Inter-agent trust emerges when autonomous agents must evaluate peers' capabilities and intentions without global knowledge. Unlike traditional distributed systems with known components, MAS may include self-interested or adversarial agents. This creates vulnerabilities to deception and Byzantine failures. For example, in decentralized supply chain systems, a malicious agent providing false inventory data can cascade failures throughout the network [4].

Human-agent trust for this to work, people need to be able to trust that autonomous systems will make good judgments for them. This problem is made worse by the fact that many AI systems, especially deep learning models, are "black boxes." Studies suggest that not being able to understand how AI works makes people less likely to trust and use it [7]. This is especially important in healthcare, as doctors need to be able to trust AI diagnostic suggestions that have an effect on how well patients do.

System-level trust deals with new behaviors that come up as agents interact with each other. Even if each agent acts correctly, the way they all act together might lead to unexpected results. This is a well-known idea in complex systems theory [1]. This non-linearity between how people act alone and how they act as a group makes it hard to forecast what will happen in the system.

Dynamic trust reflects how trust relationships evolve as agents learn and environments change. Static trust models fail to capture this temporal dimension. An agent's trustworthiness may vary across contexts performing reliably in routine situations but failing in edge cases [8].

Current approaches rely on algorithmic solutions-reputation systems [9], cryptographic protocols, or basic logging mechanisms. While these provide point solutions, they lack architectural integration. Trust mechanisms are typically added post-design, creating fragmented systems where trust properties are neither composable nor verifiable. This fragmentation makes it difficult to reason about system-wide trust properties or to formally verify trust guarantees across component boundaries. Moreover, the performance overhead of retrofitted trust mechanisms often makes them impractical for real-time systems, precisely when trust is most critical. Trust must be a first-class design concern, not an afterthought.

Failures in one area of trust can have a big effect on other areas. When trust between agents goes down, group behavior becomes unpredictable, which lowers trust between humans and agents and, in the end, system-level trust. This interconnectedness of trust failures, like cascading failures in complex networks [10], means that we need a holistic architectural approach instead of just using separate methods.

3 Proposed Trustworthy Design Patterns Catalog

This section presents six design patterns that address trust challenges through architectural solutions. Each pattern includes intent, structure, design considerations, and applicability. Table 1 maps the trust challenges discussed previously to the patterns that address them, while Table 2 summarizes these patterns for quick reference. The mapping uses 'P' (Primary) to denote a pattern that directly implements a solution to a challenge, and 'S' (Secondary) for patterns that play a supporting or enabling role. For example, an Audit Trail provides the necessary data for evaluating dynamic trust, but the Graduated Trust Levels pattern is the primary mechanism that acts on that data. Figure 1 illustrates the reinforcing synergies between these patterns.

Table 1. Mapping of Trust Challenges to Primary (P) and Secondary (S) Design Patterns

Trust Challenge	Audit Trail	Consensus	Human Override	Graduated Trust	Explainable	Fault Isolation
Inter-agent Trust	S	P		P	S	P
Human-agent Trust	P	S	P	S	P	S
System-level Trust	P	P	S	S	S	P
Dynamic Trust	P			P		S

The patterns exhibit natural synergies: Audit Trails provide data for Trust Level evaluation and Explanation generation; Consensus decisions can trigger Human Override

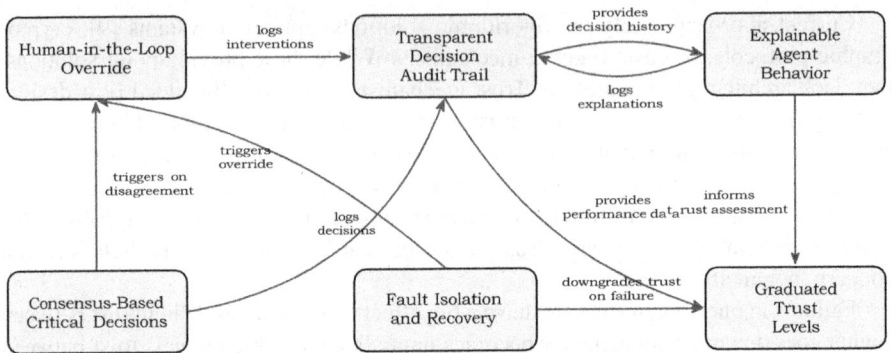

Fig. 1. Reinforcing synergies between the trustworthy design patterns. The architecture fosters a web of trust through direct interactions (represented by arrows): Audit Trail informs Explainable Behavior and Graduated Trust; Explainable Behavior provides qualitative data for trust assessment and logs explanations; Consensus escalates to Human Override and logs decisions; Human Override logs interventions; and Fault Isolation and Recovery dynamically adjusts trust levels and can trigger override mechanisms.

Table 2. Summary of Trustworthy Design Patterns for Multi-Agent Systems

Pattern Name	Core Intent	Key Components	Primary Application
Transparent Decision Audit Trail	Immutable logging for accountability	Logger, Repository, Query Interface	Regulatory compliance (Finance)
Consensus-Based Critical Decisions	Multi-agent agreement for reliability	Coordinator, Voting, Escalation	Safety-critical decisions (Healthcare)
Human-in-the-Loop Override	Human intervention capability	Interceptor, Interface, Processor	High-stakes scenarios (Autonomous vehicles)
Graduated Trust Levels	Dynamic privilege adjustment	Evaluator, Monitor, Manager	Open systems (Supply chain)
Explainable Agent Behavior	Understandable decision rationale	Generator, Tracker, Interface	User-facing systems (Medical diagnosis)
Fault Isolation and Recovery	Failure containment and resilience	Monitor, Controller, Manager	Mission-critical systems (Infrastructure)

when agreement fails; Fault Isolation automatically downgrades Trust Levels for misbehaving agents. This creates a reinforcing web of trust mechanisms rather than isolated solutions.

Pattern 1: Transparent Decision Audit Trail

Intent. Create immutable, comprehensive records of agent decisions enabling accountability, traceability, and post-hoc analysis. This pattern answers: *"Can decision makers trace why and how an agent made a particular decision?"*

Structure. The pattern comprises: (i) *Decision Logger* —captures decision context, inputs, reasoning process, and outcomes using standardized schemas; (ii) *Immutable Storage*—ensures records cannot be altered using cryptographic techniques or blockchain; (iii) *Query Interface*—enables efficient historical analysis through indexed search.

Design Considerations. Event sourcing provides a suitable architectural style where each decision generates an immutable event [11]. For enhanced provenance tracking, W3C PROV standards can be adopted. The schema should capture:

```
DecisionEvent = {
    timestamp: ISO-8601,
    agentId: UUID,
    decisionType: Enumeration,
    inputs: ContextData,
    reasoning: ProcessTrace,
    output: Decision,
    confidence: [0,1]
}
```

Storage options range from append-only logs for simplicity to distributed ledgers for regulatory environments requiring tamper-proof audit trails [12, 13].

Applicability. Essential for regulatory compliance (financial trading systems must maintain complete audit trails), debugging complex emergent behaviors, and liability determination in autonomous systems. This pattern forms the foundation for other patterns by providing data for trust evaluation and explanation generation.

Pattern 2: Consensus-Based Critical Decisions

Intent. Require agreement among multiple agents for high-impact decisions, preventing single points of failure. This pattern answers: *"What if one agent is wrong or compromised?"*

Structure. A *Decision Coordinator* identifies decisions requiring consensus based on criticality criteria. The *Voting Mechanism* implements consensus protocols with configurable agreement thresholds. An *Escalation Protocol* handles disagreements through human intervention or default-safe actions.

Design Considerations. Drawing from aviation's N-modular redundancy [14], where triple-redundant systems vote on critical decisions, MAS can implement similar approaches. For n agents with trust weights w_i and binary votes $v_i \in \{0, 1\}$, the weighted consensus score is a standard formulation for weighted voting in ensemble systems:

$$C = \frac{\sum (v_i \times w_i)}{\sum w_i} \qquad (1)$$

The decision proceeds if C exceeds threshold τ (typically $0.5 < \tau < 1.0$, domain-dependent). For Byzantine environments, use protocols like PBFT requiring $(n - f)/n$ agreement where f is the maximum number of faulty agents [15].

Applicability. Critical for high-stakes decisions where errors have severe consequences. In financial trading, require "2 out of 3 specialist agents" agreement for trades exceeding risk thresholds. In medical diagnosis, multiple agents must concur before treatment recommendations. This pattern naturally complements Graduated Trust Levels—low-trust agents require consensus while high-trust agents operate autonomously.

Pattern 3: Human-In-The-Loop Override

Intent. Maintain human oversight through intervention mechanisms for decisions exceeding autonomous system boundaries.

Structure. *Decision Interceptors* monitor for intervention triggers (uncertainty thresholds, ethical dilemmas, anomalies). The *Human Interface* presents contextual information enabling informed intervention. *Override Processors* ensure safe system state transitions when humans intervene.

Design Considerations. Intervention can operate at multiple levels:

1. **Notification:** Humans informed but system proceeds
2. **Approval Gate:** System pauses for human approval
3. **Full Override:** Human assumes complete control

The key challenge is ensuring safe interruptibility—agents must not learn to avoid or subvert human oversight [16].

Applicability. Mandatory for systems with ethical implications, regulatory requirements for human oversight, or operating in unpredictable environments.

Pattern 4: Graduated Trust Levels

Intent. Dynamically adjust agent autonomy based on demonstrated reliability, implementing least-privilege principles.

Structure. *Trust Evaluator* maintains trust scores based on historical performance. *Performance Monitor* tracks decision outcomes against expectations. *Privilege Manager* maps trust scores to operational capabilities.

Design Considerations. Trust scores can use Beta distributions for binary outcomes where α represents successes and β represents failures. The Beta distribution is particularly suitable as it is the conjugate prior for the binomial distribution of outcomes, allowing for efficient Bayesian updating of the trust score as new evidence becomes available [17].

$$\text{Trust\_score} = \text{Mean}(\text{Beta}(\alpha+1, \beta+1)) = \frac{\alpha+1}{\alpha+\beta+2} \qquad (2)$$

The thresholds for these levels, while domain-specific, are chosen to represent distinct operational stages: probationary (Level 1), standard autonomous operation (Level 2), and high-stakes authority (Level 3). Trust levels map to privileges, as shown in Table 3.

Table 3. Graduated Trust Levels and Associated Privileges

Level	Score Range	Privileges
Level 0	$score < 0.3$	Observation only
Level 1	$0.3 \leq score < 0.7$	Recommendations requiring approval
Level 2	$0.7 \leq score < 0.9$	Autonomous routine decisions
Level 3	$score \geq 0.9$	Critical decision authority

Applicability. Open systems with unknown agents, long-running systems where agent capabilities evolve, environments requiring adaptive security.

Pattern 5: Explainable Agent Behavior

Intent. Enable agents to provide understandable justifications for their decisions. This pattern addresses: *"I'll trust the system if I understand it."*

Structure. *Explanation Generators* produce rationales appropriate to the agent's reasoning mechanism. *Reasoning Trackers* maintain decision provenance. *Natural Language Interfaces* translate technical explanations for stakeholders.

Design Considerations. Explanation strategies vary by agent type:

- **Rule-based agents:** Trace fired rules ("I did X because rule Y triggered")
- **Planning agents:** Show goal-plan relationships
- **Learning agents:** Feature importance via SHAP/LIME [18, 19] or counterfactuals

The challenge is balancing explanation fidelity with comprehensibility [20]. Layered explanations work well: brief summaries for end-users, detailed traces for developers.

Applicability. Critical for user-facing systems and regulatory compliance. In healthcare, explanations like "Diagnosis suggested due to symptoms A, B matching disease pattern D (95% similarity to literature cases)" build physician trust. This pattern synergizes with Audit Trails—storing not just what was decided but why.

Pattern 6: Fault Isolation and Recovery

Intent. Contain agent failures preventing system-wide cascades while maintaining operational continuity.

Structure. *Health Monitors* detect anomalous behavior through performance metrics and peer comparison. *Isolation Controllers* implement circuit breaker patterns preventing fault propagation. *Recovery Managers* orchestrate system reconfiguration.

Design Considerations. The circuit breaker pattern is a core component, transitioning through states like Closed (normal operation), Open (agent isolated), and Half-Open (testing recovery). Bulkhead patterns can also be used to partition agents into failure domains, limiting the scope of cascades [21].

Applicability. Mission-critical systems requiring high availability, systems where agent failures could cascade, environments with unreliable components.

4 Design Considerations and Pattern Composition

Pattern Selection Theory. When choosing patterns, risk-based analysis should be used to connect trust needs to particular patterns. Adoption is influenced by the system criticality and trust factors in the decision framework proposed in this study. Theoretically, applications with low stakes may apply patterns selectively based on cost-benefit analysis, while safety-critical systems would benefit from full pattern adoption.

Composition Principles. Patterns exhibit natural synergies but also potential conflicts:

- **Synergies:** Audit trails provide data for trust evaluation; consensus mechanisms can trigger human escalation
- **Conflicts:** Extensive logging for audit trails may affect real-time consensus performance; if human override is not carefully arranged, it may clash with consensus. These interactions, which are sometimes referred to as feature interactions, are a known challenge in complex systems [22] (Tables 4, 5 and 6).

Table 4. Theoretical Performance Analysis of Patterns

Pattern	Operation	Computational Complexity
Consensus	Message Passing	$O(n)$ to $O(n^2)$
Audit Trail	Append Operation	$O(1)$
	Retrieval (indexed)	$O(\log n)$
Explanation	Rule-based	$O(d)^*$
	Feature-based	$O(m \times s)^{**}$

*d = depth of the reasoning trace
**m = features, s = background data samples

The key is thoughtful application, using the minimum set of patterns that address identified trust risks while meeting system constraints.

Table 5. Core Design Trade-offs

Trade-off	Description
Transparency vs. Performance	Detailed logging and explanations impact system responsiveness
Safety vs. Autonomy	Human oversight and consensus reduce autonomous decision speed
Trust vs. Privacy	Audit trails may capture sensitive data requiring careful governance

Table 6. Pattern Anti-patterns and Limitations

Limitation/Anti-pattern	Applicability Concern
Performance-critical systems	Consensus overhead may be intolerable
Fully adversarial environments	Consensus is meaningless with a malicious majority
Resource-constrained devices	Audit trails and explanations may exceed budget
Privacy-sensitive domains	Audit trails may conflict with data minimization

5 Illustrative Application Scenarios

This section presents three conceptual scenarios to demonstrate how the proposed patterns could address real-world trust challenges. The figures and details contained within are illustrative and intended to make the application of the patterns concrete and understandable.

Financial Trading Scenario: *Consensus-Based Critical Decisions* might be achieved by an algorithmic trading system that administers institutional portfolios. It would require a "2 out of 3" agreement from specialized agents for deals that exceed risk criteria. Multiple analytical agents (e.g., technical analysis, fundamental analysis, risk assessment) vote on large positions. The *Transparent Decision Audit Trail* would capture all decision factors with millisecond granularity for regulatory compliance. The new trading algorithms would follow a phased trust approach: shadow mode (observe only) → low-volume mode → full autonomy. Human traders would maintain override capability through real-time dashboards showing agent reasoning. This architecture would theoretically prevent single-algorithm errors from causing flash crashes while maintaining regulatory compliance [23]

Healthcare Diagnosis Scenario: AI systems are providing quite confident answers (e.g., "Diagnosis suggested: pneumonia, based on a chest X-ray showing consolidation in the right lower lobe, an increased white blood cell count, and patient symptoms matching literature patterns). Before being granted autonomy, new diagnostic algorithms would be able to prove their dependability on past instances thanks to graduated trust levels.

This is one example of how a multi-hospital diagnostic network could use *Explainable Agent Behavior* [24]

Autonomous Vehicle Scenario: A smart city traffic management system could use real-time *Consensus* among vehicles approaching an intersection, where each vehicle agent votes on a safe passage order. If sensor discrepancies exceed thresholds (e.g., conflicting obstacle detection), the system would default to a conservative behavior. Investigation would be made possible by thorough audit logs, such as : "Vehicle A stopped because there was a consensus failure on the presence of an obstacle (2/3 agents detected, 1/3 did not). Edge scenarios that AI is incapable of handling would be handled by remote human operators. In theory, this pattern-based architecture might increase public trust through transparency and safety through redundancy [25]

6 The Path to Adoption: Challenges and Future Work

In fact, there are many benefits to architectural trust in the MAS ecosystem. Programmers can use a set process instead of implementing things as they go. Businesses benefit from more people using their products and services and less risk of being sued. It gives regulators clear and verifiable ways to make sure they are following the rules. There are additionally big problems that need to be solved before these benefits can be enjoyed. Architectural complexity in developing patterns, the performance cost of audit trails and consensus, and a cultural unwillingness to put trust engineering ahead of product speed are all major barriers to adoption.

As a position paper, this work is meant to present a vision, framework, and theoretical contribution that sets the stage for future empirical work rather than providing validation itself. Addressing the identified challenges in two parallel streams must be the primary objective of future research. **Empirical validation** is the first. The effectiveness of these patterns needs to be thoroughly examined in both controlled settings and practical implementations. In addition to these are (i) *Behavioral Analysis*: quantitative studies evaluating the ways in which patterns affect the dynamics of trust between agents and among humans in various settings. (ii) *Resilience Testing* : which involves systematic chaos engineering and fault injection to ensure that isolation and recovery patterns are meant under stress. (iii) *Longitudinal Studies*: Implementing pattern-based systems in pilot programs to evaluate their impact on operational objectives, performance overhead, and long-term stability. The second stream is **foundational research**. Which includes developing formal methods to model interference, synergy, and pattern composition. Future research should also focus on transforming this catalog into a comprehensive pattern language for trustworthy MAS, with domainspecific specializations for sectors like healthcare and finance, along with AI-driven tools for automatic pattern selection based on system risk profiles [1, 9].

7 Conclusion

The era of treating trust as a feature to be bolted onto multi-agent systems is over. This paper has argued that the prevailing focus on algorithmic, add-on trust mechanisms is a dead end—a path that leads to brittle, unpredictable, and ultimately untrustworthy systems. An alternative has been presented: a paradigm shift towards **trustworthiness by design**, where trust is an emergent property of the system's architecture. The six patterns cataloged here are not mere suggestions; they are a foundational blueprint for the next generation of MAS.

No single group is solely accountable for this change. A coordinated, communitywide effort is needed. Consequently, the following immediate appeal to action is made:

- **A Challenge to Researchers:** The academic community is called upon to move beyond incremental improvements in reputation algorithms and instead formally model the compositional properties of architectural trust patterns. The critical open questions are no longer about which algorithm is marginally better, but about how patterns interact, conflict, and can be formally verified as a cohesive system.

- **A Mandate for Practitioners:** Industry leaders and engineers are urged to pilot these patterns in real-world systems. To reduce the risk of the deployment of autonomous systems in vital sectors like infrastructure, healthcare, and finance, rigorous, pattern-based engineering must take the place of the arbitrary application of trust mechanisms.

- **A Recommendation for Standards Bodies:** Organizations like ISO and IEEE are strongly recommended to begin the process of codifying these and similar patterns into formal standards for safety-critical AI. Society could face a future full of significant failures and a loss of public confidence if there are no clear, enforced architectural standards for trust.

The field is at a turning point. We either build trustworthy MAS through disciplined architectural practice, or we risk a future where strong autonomous systems run without human trust or control. It's apparent what the decision is and what the duty is. There needs to be trust embedded into the underlying foundations of the digital world.

References

1. Wooldridge, M.: An Introduction to MultiAgent Systems, 2nd edn. John Wiley & Sons, Chichester, UK (2009)
2. Lee, J.D., See, K.A.: Trust in automation: Designing for appropriate reliance. Hum. Factors **46**(1), 50–80 (2004)
3. Aridor, Y., Lange, D.B.: Agent design patterns: Elements of agent application design. In: Proceedings of the Second International Conference on Autonomous Agents, pp. 108–115 (1998)
4. Ramchurn, S.D., Huynh, D., Jennings, N.R.: Trust in multi-agent systems. The Knowl. Eng. Rev. **19**(1), 1–25 (2004)
5. Sabater, J., Sierra, C.: Review on computational trust and reputation models. Artif. Intell. Rev. **24**(1), 33–60 (2005)
6. Castelfranchi, C., Falcone, R.: Trust dynamics: how trust is influenced by direct experiences and by trust itself. In: Proceedings of the Third International Joint Conference on Autonomous Agents and Multiagent Systems (AAMAS '04), pp. 740–747. New York, NY (2004)
7. Holzinger, A., Biemann, C., Pattichis, C.S., Kell, D.B.: What do we need to build explainable ai systems for the medical domain? (2017)

8. Marsh, S.P.: Formalising trust as a computational concept. PhD Thesis. University of Stirling (1994)
9. Jøsang, A., Ismail, R., Boyd, C.: A survey of trust and reputation systems for online service provision. Decis. Support Syst. **43**(2), 618–644 (2007)
10. Buldyrev, S.V., Parshani, R., Paul, G., Stanley, H.E., Havlin, S.: Catastrophic cascade of failures in interdependent networks. Nature **464**(7291), 1025–1028 (2010). https://doi.org/10.1038/nature08932
11. Fowler, M.: Patterns of Enterprise Application Architecture. Addison-Wesley, Boston, MA (2003)
12. Weber, I., et al.: Untrusted business process monitoring and execution using blockchain. International Conference on Business Process Management, pp. 329–347 (2016)
13. Nakamoto, S.: Bitcoin: A peer-to-peer electronic cash system. www.bitcoin.org (2008)
14. Lyons, R., Vanderkulk, W.: The n-version approach to fault-tolerant software. IEEE Trans. Softw. Eng. **SE-13**(6), 625–632 (1987)
15. Castro, M., Liskov, B.: Practical byzantine fault tolerance and proactive recovery. ACM Trans. Comp. Sys. **20**(4), 398–461 (2002)
16. Orseau, L., Armstrong, S.: Safely interruptible agents. In: Proceedings of the 32nd Conference on Uncertainty in Artificial Intelligence (UAI), pp. 557–566 (2016)
17. Jøsang, A.: Subjective Logic: A Formalism for Reasoning Under Uncertainty. Artificial Intelligence: Foundations, Theory, and Algorithms. Springer, Cham, Switzerland (2016). https://doi.org/10.1007/978-3-319-42337-1
18. Lundberg, S.M., Lee, S.-I.: A unified approach to interpreting model predictions. In: Advances in Neural Information Processing Systems vol. 30, pp. 4765–4774 (2017)
19. Ribeiro, M.T., Singh, S., Guestrin, C.: "Why should i trust you?": explaining the predictions of any classifier. In: Proceedings of the 22nd ACM SIGKDD International Conference on Knowledge Discovery and Data Mining, pp. 1135–1144 (2016)
20. Miller, T.: Explanation in artificial intelligence: Insights from the social sciences. Artif. Intell. **267**, 1–38 (2019)
21. Nygard, M.T.: Release It!: Design and Deploy Production-Ready Software, 2nd edn. Pragmatic Bookshelf, Raleigh, NC (2018)
22. Calder, M., Magill, E.H.: Feature Interactions in Telecommunications and Software Systems IX (2003)
23. Heaton, J.B., Polson, N.G., Witte, J.H.: Deep learning in finance. Annu. Rev. Financ. Econ. **9**, 145–181 (2017)
24. Caruana, R., et al.: Intelligible models for healthcare: predicting pneumonia risk and hospital 30-day readmission. Proceedings of the 21th ACM SIGKDD International Conference on Knowledge Discovery and Data Mining, pp. 1721–1730 (2015)
25. Chen, L., Li, S., Chen, S., Ren, W., Wang, Y.: Consensus-based decision making for connected and automated vehicles at intersections. IEEE Trans. Veh. Technol. **68**(8), 7757–7771 (2019)

Designing Interpretable AI Models with Lightweight Parallelism for Real-Time Malware Detection and Prevention

Zachariah McCullough[✉] and Jose Martinez[✉]

University of Southern Mississippi, Hattiesburg, MS 39406, USA
{zachariah.mccullough,jose.martinez}@usm.edu

Abstract. Network intrusion detection and prevention systems (NIDS/NIPS) have become less effective due to the growing complexity and sophistication of cyber threats. Traditionally, these systems use static signatures and rule-based logic to detect and subsequently prevent threats and malicious activities. However, new malware techniques, including obfuscation and evasion methods as well as adaptive behavior, critically weaken standard detection systems and create major threats to government and defense infrastructures as well as commercial networks.

This research introduces a scalable, interpretable, and low-latency malware detection system that fuses parallel agentic AI, retrieval-augmented intelligence, and transparent decision pathways, offering substantial progress in operational cybersecurity environments. By using task-level parallelism the system distributes feature extraction analysis along with behavioral profiling and threat attribution tasks among multiple processes to achieve scalable performance even under heavy load conditions.

Keywords: Interpretable AI · Malware detection · Malware prevention

1 Introduction

The boom of Artificial Intelligence (AI) within the last few years has created a significant shift in the field. Algorithms that have the ability to learn from both new and previous data, as well as pull data from external sources, allow models to handle novel threats and apply knowledge from previous attacks to new situations. However, there are two main challenges:

1. Interpretability that inhibits both trustworthiness and accountability
2. High computational expenses that block real-time deployment in environments with limited resources.

With task-level parallelism, the extraction of features, along with behavioral profiling and threat attribution tasks, can be performed through a distributed system, capable of achieving multiple processes and scalable performance even under heavily demanding conditions. Introducing scalable, interpretable, low-latency malware detection that can fuse parallel agentic AI, retrieval augmented intelligence, and transparent decision pathways can be substantial progress in operational cybersecurity environments if properly developed.

Retrieval-Augmented Generation (RAG) forms the core of the framework by improving AI inference through the dynamic retrieval of specific knowledge from continuously refreshed external sources [Common Vulnerabilities and Exposures (CVE) databases, MITRE ATT&CK, AlienVault's Open Threat Exchange (OTX), and Malware Information and Sharing Platform (MISP)].

This, along with agentic AI, has the ability to run independently, allows for more transparency, and enables human intervention only where necessary. These combined approaches enhance the system's resilience to future threats.

2 Literature Review

2.1 Malware Detection and Prevention Systems (NIDS/NIPS)

Detecting and blocking malicious activities, specifically malware, has been a foundational pillar in organizations, and while traditional systems that rely on signature-based detection are suited for well-known malware, it is useless against zero-day attacks and polymorphic malware that mutate to avoid signature-based methods [1, 2]. Figure 1 [3] illustrates the polymorphic malware infection process.

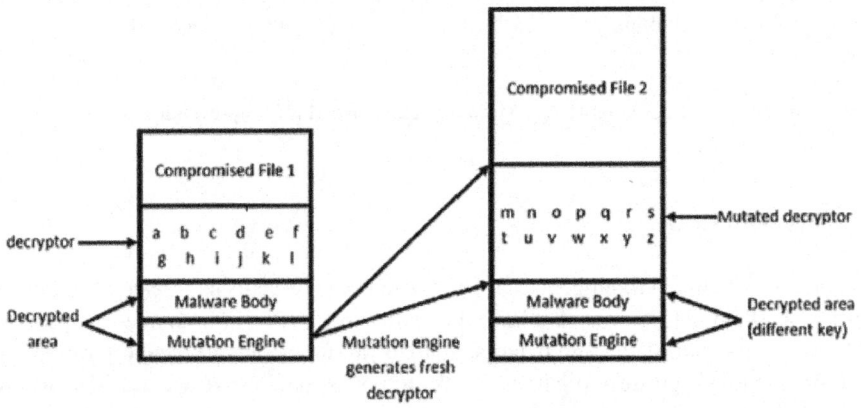

Fig. 1. The polymorphic malware infection process.

To account for these limitations, hyper-advanced methods such as behavioral analysis and machine learning (ML) models have taken center stage. Anomaly-based detection methods identify deviations from patterns learned beforehand [4], while ML methods can discover previously unknown malware by training from network traffic data [5].

However, using ML and AI in malware detection is problematic, especially with regard to interpretability. Most AI models, particularly those based on deep learning, are "black box" [6, p. 933] systems, making it difficult to understand how and why decisions are made. In cybersecurity, such opacity is challenging, especially where false positives create unwarranted system disruptions [7]. Interpretability matters because security analysts who will use the technology daily need to have both confidence and understanding in AI-based decisions [8].

To make it more interpretable, explainable AI techniques like LIME (Local Interpretable Model-agnostic Explanations) and SHAP (SHapley Additive exPlanations) have been developed. These tools help to make the features responsible for model predictions clear so that practitioners are able to verify AI decisions and remain assured of automated systems [9, 15].

2.2 AI in Malware Detection

Malware detection using artificial intelligence (AI) has gained popularity as malware attacks grow more complex and rapid in nature. Early AI-based detection processes primarily utilized supervised learning algorithms like decision trees, k-nearest neighbors (KNN), and support vector machines (SVM) to identify files based on labeled data [10, 11]. Although successful, these methods struggled with large datasets and determining complex relationships between malware characteristics such as system calls, network traffic, registry changes, execution flow and byte sequence [9–12].

Deep learning techniques have emerged with higher accuracy and robustness in recent years. Initially used in image processing, Convolutional Neural Networks (CNNs) are now used in analyzing malware bytecode or behavior [12, p. 2273]. Recurrent Neural Networks (RNNs) and Long Short-Term Memory networks (LSTMs), initially used for sequence data analysis, are now used in dynamic malware analysis and tracking malware activity over time [13, 14]. Deep learning models perform exceptionally well in identifying new threats. This is key where the model selected needs to be intelligible, informative, and precise in high-risk scenarios [15].

2.3 Task-Level Parallelism in Malware Detection

Scalability and speed in malware detection have become the highest priority in the fast-paced and ever-changing world of cybersecurity. Conventional signature-based malware detects, executes, and processes sequentially and has become inadequate. The answer to this inadequacy is task-level parallelism (Fig. 2 [16]) where the detection process is divided into independent, small tasks that can be executed concurrently [16].

For example, in a distributed system of malware detection, one node can carry out static code analysis (scanning the file structure), while another node carries out dynamic behavior analysis (monitoring how the file behaves when executed in a controlled environment). This parallelization not only speeds up detection but also enhances the system's ability to process large datasets in real-time [16, 17].

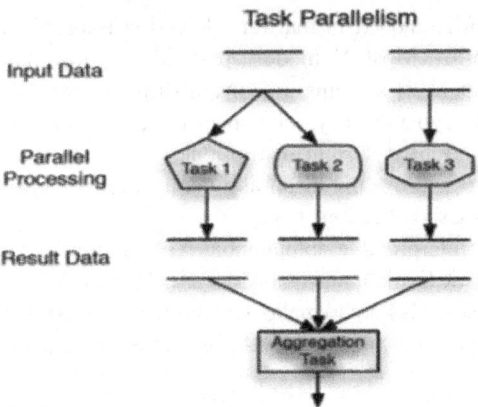

Fig. 2. Task parallelism model.

In addition to this, task-level parallelism is also scalable. With the increase in the volume of incoming malware samples, additional computation resources can be dynamically allocated to handle the workload. Cloud platforms such as Google Cloud or AWS Lambda support on-demand provisioning of computer resources. Modules such as Python's multiprocessing library [18] or CUDA [19] can also be utilized to enhance parallel processing capabilities such that malware detection software continues to cope with evolving threats without performance deterioration.

2.4 Retrieval-Augmented Generation (RAG) for Dynamic Threat Intelligence

Retrieval-Augmented Generation (RAG) offers a more dynamic solution. Rather than depending on static training data [7], RAG architecture engages external sources during the inference process. This enables large language models (LLMs) to pull in real-time threat intelligence from databases such as the CVE database, MITRE ATT&CK, AlienVault's Open Threat Exchange (OTX), MISP and Metasploit modules, as well as other contemporary cybersecurity feeds [20]. Figure 3 give an illustration of the conceptual RAG process [21].

The RAG Process:

1. User query
2. The query is constructed and transmitted to external sources
3. The relevant information is retrieved (from external sources)
4. The retrieved information is used to supplement the original prompt
5. The combined input is passed to the LLM for generating context-aware output

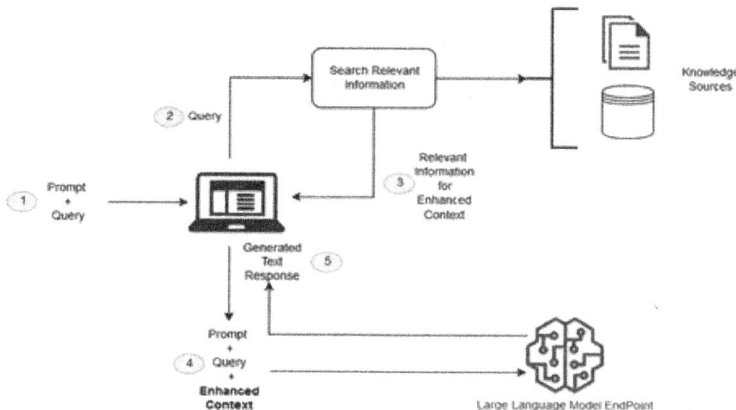

Fig. 3. Conceptual RAG workflow, as external intelligence is integrated dynamically into the model outputs.

Although RAG systems are not natively connected to external sources, they can be configured to fetch threat data at runtime. This enables models to respond to new challenges—such as newly disclosed vulnerabilities—without requiring retraining and ensuring flexibility. A RAG pipeline that is correctly integrated can ingest current indicators of compromise (IOCs) and exploit patterns to provide detection logic [22]. Consequently, a RAG is only as good at the information it is fed; low-quality sources can contribute to bias and misinformation, leading to compromised performance [23].

2.5 Autonomous Malware Analysis with Agentic AI

Agentic AI not only makes autonomous decisions to improve workload efficiency but also implements specialized workloads [24, 25, p. 140] to enhance operations. The major advantage of agentic AI is parallel processing: numerous processes (agents) simultaneously scrutinizing different pieces of information for a given piece of malware. For example, one agent can analyze file structure, while another monitors runtime behavior in a sandbox, eventually, both processes will correlate their findings enhancing detection rates [25, p. 142, 26, p. 4, 27–29]. Having said this, the ethical problems that come with autonomous decision-making, such as false positives or inaccurate analysis / results, needs to be handled appropriately. Figure 4 gives an illustration of the agentic AI flow [30].

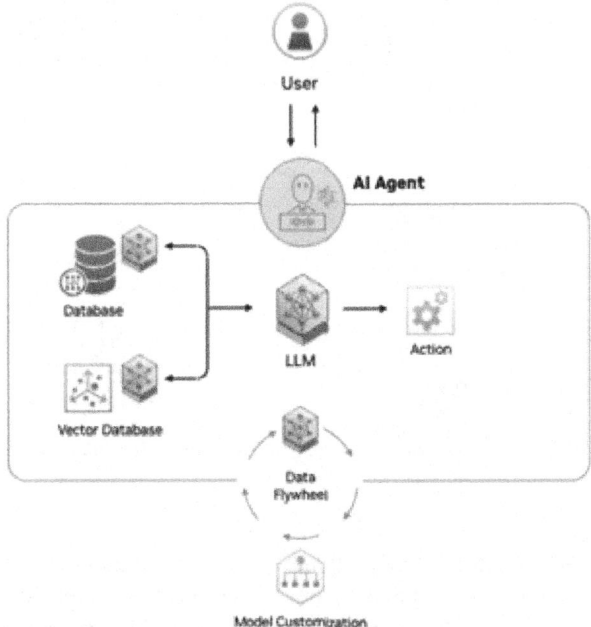

Fig. 4. Agentic AI flow.

2.6 Summary of Related Work

Malware detection is rapidly evolving through the integration of artificial intelligence, parallel processing, and retrieval-augmented systems. Traditional signature-based approaches—while still relevant for detecting known threats—struggle to address the challenges posed by zero-day attacks and polymorphic malware. This has driven a shift toward dynamic, machine learning-based techniques, including deep learning and agentic AI, which offer improved detection capabilities. However, these approaches also introduce new challenges in terms of interpretability, scalability, and agent coordination.

The literature reflects a clear move toward dynamic and adaptive detection systems. Legacy tools such as Network Intrusion Detection Systems (NIDS) and Intrusion Prevention Systems (NIPS) remain in use but are increasingly supplemented or replaced by AI-driven models capable of learning behavioral patterns and anomalies. Among these, task-level parallelism has emerged as a powerful enabler of real-time analysis. By distributing malware detection workloads—such as static analysis, dynamic analysis, and behavioral profiling—across multiple processing units or agents, systems can achieve higher throughput and responsiveness without compromising detection accuracy.

At the same time, the demand for explainability in cybersecurity has grown. Analysts require clear, auditable reasoning behind automated decisions, making interpretable AI techniques essential. Tools like SHAP and LIME have begun to address this need, offering model-agnostic explanations that help bridge the gap between complex algorithms and human understanding.

Retrieval-Augmented Generation (RAG) is another key innovation, enabling models to draw on external knowledge bases—such as CVE databases, MITRE ATT&CK, and threat intelligence feeds—during inference. This architecture enhances adaptability by aligning model predictions with the most current threat intelligence. However, the performance of RAG systems depends heavily on the quality and relevance of the retrieved information, as well as the system's ability to integrate it effectively.

Agentic AI introduces a modular and scalable design by delegating analysis tasks to specialized agents that operate semi-independently. This decentralization supports more robust decision-making but also presents coordination challenges, particularly when agent confidence levels diverge or when decisions affect high-risk environments such as critical infrastructure.

Looking forward, the future of malware detection will hinge on the development of explainable AI systems that balance accuracy with transparency. Enhancing scalability through parallel architectures and dynamic integration of threat intelligence will be crucial to keeping pace with evolving cyber threats. Addressing these challenges requires a unified approach—combining agentic AI, interpretable deep learning, and retrieval-augmented pipelines—as proposed in the following sections.

3 Problem Statement

Traditional malware detection systems (NIPS/NIDS) rely on signature-based methodologies that are unable to adequately combat advanced and evasive malware threats, particularly zero-day and polymorphic malware [1–4]. Although AI-based systems have shown promise to overcome such constraints, they are plagued by vast deployment challenges: (1) they are uninterpretable, which eliminates trust and accountability in today's cybersecurity setting [6, 9], and (2) they are extremely computationally demanding and are unsuitable for real-time deployment in resource-constrained settings [7].

This research addresses the above challenges with the design of an AI-fueled malware detection framework combining interpretability, task-level parallelism, and dynamic external threat intelligence acquisition to allow scalable real-time detection based on comprehensible actionable insights for security analysts.

4 Proposed Methodology

4.1 System Architecture

Deployment architecture will be a multi-agent system, specialized for different activities, to carry out tasks such as static analysis, behavior monitoring, and threat intelligence lookup. Processes (agents) will run in parallel and will communicate through message queues (RabbitMQ) [31] in real-time.

Process

1. Initialization: Malware sample
2. Execution: Different jobs are divided among processes (agents)
3. Processing: Celery via 10 AWS EC2 Virtual Machines (VMs), capable of running tasks concurrently [21]

4. Integration: Data Aggregated to avoid inconsistencies and false positives [32] (<=5%), run through Apache Kafka.
5. Intelligence: Real run time intelligence (MITRE ATT&CK, CVE, MISP, etc.) is obtained by RAG pipeline to support decision-making
6. Final Output: Malware is labeled, and explainable descriptions are generated.

To support analyst trust and auditability, SHAP and LIME [9] provide real-time model interpretability.

- SHAP assigns importance scores to input features, explaining their role in the classification decision.
- LIME builds local interpretable models around individual predictions to clarify decision boundaries.

These explanations are generated in under 10 seconds, offering rapid, actionable insights into model behavior.

4.2 AI-Based Malware Detection

To analyze binary formats, network patterns and track changes over time the use of CNNs [12] as well as LSTMs [12–14] is integral. It will run on AWS EC2 powered by NVIDIA Tesla T4 GPUs [33, 34] and should be developed by TensorFlow 2.0 with Keras.

Training

1. Training: CICIDS, CSE-CIC-IDS [35] and Microsoft Malware Classification datasets [36]
    a. Partition: 60% training, 20% validation, 20% testing
2. Targets: $\geq$90% accuracy, F1 score $\geq$0.9 [37], false positive rate $\leq$ 5%
3. Capacity: Capacity: 1,000 samples/hour, each sample requiring no more than 5 min ($\leq$) for detection

4.3 Task-Level Parallelism

Task execution is overseen by the Celery framework [38] in conjunction with horizontally distributed and scalable cloud infrastructure. Tasks will be executed independently in every Virtual Machine with synchronization of results by Apache Kafka for instant analysis [32].

Successful Analyses with Four Concurrent Pathways:

1. Static analysis: This is checking file structure, Portable Executable (PE) headers, entropy levels, and recognized malware signatures for irregularities without executing the file
2. Dynamic analysis: Real-time sandboxing

3. Threat Attribution: Links activity to known tactics, techniques, and procedures (TTPs) to identify likely adversaries
4. Retrieval of Threat Intelligence: Continuously pulled from sources of intelligence—Elasticsearch used for high-performance querying

4.4 Retrieval-Augmented Generation (RAG)

RAG enables real-time enrichment through external data [7, 20–23]:

1. During analysis, a query is constructed summing behaviors or signatures
2. A search is conducted through current threat intelligence
   a. CVE databases, MITRE ATT&CK, AlienVault's Open Threat Exchange (OTX), Malware Information and Sharing Platform (MISP)
3. This intelligence is then combined with classification and attribution functions

This ensures that the entire process is backed by real results, increasing the reports overall quality.

4.5 Agentic AI for Malware Detection

Five agents will comprise the system, each of them making independent decisions based on defined confidence thresholds. If those thresholds are dissimilar between agents, and fall outside of the majority, then they will be escalated to a human analyst. This ensures human oversight for low confidence ratings [39]. The following are the five specialized agent types in the system.

1. Static Analysis – Inspects file attributes, structure, and embedded code without execution.
2. Dynamic Analysis – Observes the file's behavior in a sandboxed runtime environment.
3. Behavioral Analysis – Detects patterns and anomalies based on typical malware behaviors.
4. Threat Intelligence – Cross-references indicators of compromise (IOCs) with threat intelligence databases.
5. Attribution – Infers potential origin, intent, or threat actor based on code similarities and TTPs.

Each agent produces a confidence score when evaluating a sample. The final system decision is determined by a voting mechanism, weighed by confidence scores.

Table 1 outlines the confidence thresholds and corresponding system actions.

Table 1. Confidence thresholds for agents.

Confidence Range	Action
$\geq 95\%$	Automatic classification
90–94%	Automatic classification but flagged for human review
80–89%	Held without classification and forwarded for human review
<80%	Immediately escalated for human review

5 Conclusions and Results

5.1 Results

AI itself is not new, but its integration in malware search and identification is. Companies like Reversing Labs [39], Palo Alto [40], and Splunk [41] have successfully addressed the black-box nature of AI, transforming it into transparent and trustworthy systems. The confidence ranges outlined in the methodology align with performance metrics demonstrated in prior research [42, 43], validating its effectiveness in real-world applications. Figure 5 illustrates the accuracy comparison between machine learning and deep learning algorithms.

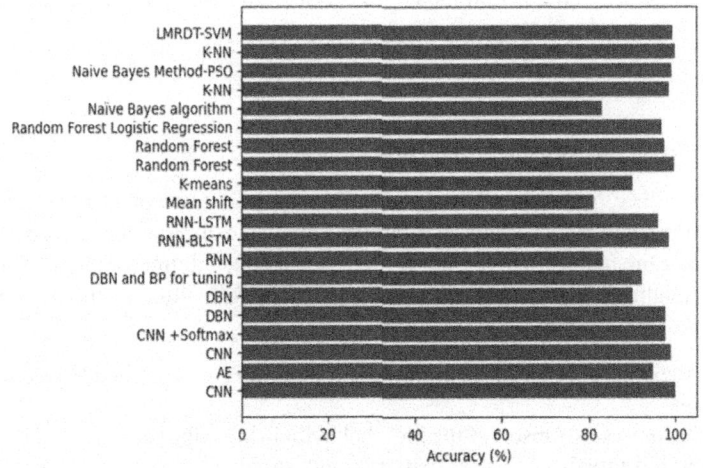

Fig. 5. Accuracy and performance of machine learning vs. deep learning performance.

The results presented in Fig. 5 [42] compare the accuracy and performance of various machine learning and deep learning algorithms in malware detection. Traditional models such as Naïve Bayes, K-Nearest Neighbors (K-NN), and Random Forest demonstrate respectable accuracies typically ranging between 80% and 90%. Notably, Random Forest combined with logistic regression and optimized Naïve Bayes methods perform competitively.

Deep learning models, while offering higher accuracy, often lack interpretability and require significant computational and financial resources to develop and maintain. Building such models from scratch—including infrastructure and personnel—can exceed $500,000 annually [45], limiting accessibility for smaller organizations.

Retrieval-augmented generation (RAG) systems provide a cost-effective alternative with lower infrastructure demands and greater adaptability. Although RAG models may sacrifice some predictive performance, they compensate through improved interpretability and integration with live threat intelligence feeds [7, 20, 22, 23]. This trade-off makes RAGs appealing for organizations balancing budget constraints and detection effectiveness.

The confidence thresholds in the agentic system's methodology (e.g., $\geq 95\%$ for automatic classification) correspond well with observed accuracy levels, supporting their use in practical malware detection workflows. Additionally, companies like Reversing Labs [39], Palo Alto Networks [40], and Splunk [41] illustrate successful efforts in overcoming AI's opacity to deliver trustworthy malware identification.

The comparative analysis [42] underscores the fluctuating accuracy dependent on algorithm choice and training implementations, which directly influence costs. Building from scratch with current technologies—including personnel salaries—can easily surpass $500K annually [45], making it unattainable for many organizations. While RAG systems are more affordable, they come with trade-offs [7, 20, 22, 23].

5.2 Conclusions

This paper has outlined a comprehensive and usable framework for designing interpretable AI algorithms with lightweight parallelism for real-time analysis for effective malware prevention and detection. Using CNNs and LSTMs with a 60/20/20 training split with benchmark metrics for accuracy at $\geq 90\%$ and false positive rates at $\leq 5\%$ aligns with previous research and limited implementation of such systems. The design, handling 1000 cases an hour, separated over 10 AWS EC2 instances, powered by NVIDIA Telsa T4 GPUs, makes it highly scalable and keeps costs low, addressing an increasing concern.

This research has presented a reflective and methodical response to AI malware defense, proposing a proactive defense solution to the evolving threat landscape. Looking ahead, enhancing interpretability, trust, transparency, and accuracy will be paramount to advancing further. The application of this model to the wider realm of cybersecurity is imperative to the industry remaining ahead of the threat.

References

1. Sharma, P., Kaur, S., Arora, J.: An advanced approach to polymorphic/metamorphic malware detection using hybrid clustering approach. Int. Res. J. Eng. Technol. (IRJET) (2016). https://www.irjet.net/archives/V3/i6/IRJET-V3I6409.pdf. Accessed 09 Apr 2025
2. Schonlau, M., DuMouchel, W., Ju, W., Karr, A.F., Theus, M., Vardi, Y.: Computer intrusion: detecting masquerades. Stat. Sci. **16**(1), 58–74 (2001). https://www.jstor.org/stable/2676780. Accessed 09 Apr 2025
3. Naidu, V., Narayanan, A.: A syntactic approach for detecting viral polymorphic malware variants. Intell. Secur. Inform. **9650**, 146–165 (2016). https://doi.org/10.1007/978-3-319-31863-9_11
4. Noel, G.E., Gustafson, S.C., Gunsch, G.H.: Network based anomaly detection using discriminant analysis. J. Inf. Warfare **1**(2), 12–22 (2001). https://www.jstor.org/stable/26486090
5. Kumar, S., Shersingh, N., Kumar, S., Verma, K.: Malware classification using machine learning models. Procedia Comput. Sci. **235**, 1419–1428 (2024). https://www.sciencedirect.com/science/article/pii/S1877050924008093. Accessed 10 Apr 2025
6. Bathaee, Y.: The artificial intelligence black box and the failure of intent and causation. Harv. J. Law Technol. **31**(2), 889–938 (2018). https://jolt.law.harvard.edu/assets/articlePDFs/v31/The-Artificial-Intelligence-Black-Box-and-the-Failure-of-Intent-and-Causation-Yavar-Bathaee.pdf

7. Cavusoglu, H., Mishra, B., Raghunathan, S.: The value of intrusion detection systems in information technology security architecture. Inf. Syst. Res. **16**(1), 28–46 (2005). https://www.jstor.org/stable/23015763
8. Nishant, R., Schneckenberg, D., Ravishankar, M.N.: The formal rationality of artificial intelligence-based algorithms and the problem of bias. J. Inf. Technol. **39**(1), 19–40 (2023). https://doi.org/10.1177/02683962231176842
9. Parisineni, S.R.A., Pal, M.: Enhancing trust and interpretability of complex machine learning models using local interpretable model agnostic shap explanations. Int. J. Data Sci. Anal. **18**, 457–466 (2023). https://arxiv.org/pdf/2210.04533
10. El-Moussa, F., Jones, A.: Malware analysis framework from static to dynamic analysis. J. Inf. Warfare **7**(3), 23–34 (2008). https://www.jstor.org/stable/26486738
11. Fanelli, R.: On the role of malware analysis for technical intelligence in active cyber defense. J. Inf. Warfare **14**(2), 69–81 (2015). https://www.jstor.org/stable/26487495
12. Sadeghi, M., et al.: Persiann-CNN: precipitation estimation from remotely sensed information using artificial neural networks–convolutional neural networks. J. Hydrometeorol. **20**(12), 2273–2289 (2019). https://www.jstor.org/stable/26894450
13. Mienye, I.D., Swart, T.G., Obaido, G.: Recurrent neural networks: a comprehensive review of architectures, variants, and applications. Information **15**(9), 1–34 (2024). https://www.mdpi.com/2078-2489/15/9/517
14. Li, F., Yang, Y., Xia, Y.: Identification for nonlinear systems modelled by deep long short-term memory networks based wiener model. Mech. Syst. Signal Process. **220**, 111–631 (2024). https://doi.org/10.1016/j.ymssp.2024.111631
15. Ingrosso, A., Goldt, S.: Datadriven emergence of convolutional structure in neural networks. Proc. Natl. Acad. Sci. U.S.A. **119**(40), 1–10 (2022). https://www.jstor.org/stable/27208424
16. Lakizadeh, A., Abdulkadhim, A.A.A.: Hybrid parallelism image encryption algorithm based on a modified blowfish algorithm. Int. J. Intell. Eng. Syst. **17**(6), 934–946 (2025). https://inass.org/wp-content/uploads/2024/09/2024123170-2.pdf. Accessed 10 Apr 2025
17. Wu, J., et al.: LM-offload: performance model-guided generative inference of large language models with parallelism control (2024). Available: https://pasalabs.org/papers/2024/llm_offload_2024.pdf. Accessed 10 Apr 2025
18. Python. Multiprocessing—Process-based Parallelism—Python 3.8.3rc1 Documentation (2025). https://docs.python.org/3/library/multiprocessing.html
19. NVIDIA. CUDA C++ PROGRAMMING GUIDE Design Guide (2025). https://docs.nvidia.com/cuda/pdf/CUDA_C_Programming_Guide.pdf. Accessed 11 Apr 2025
20. Gupta, S., Ranjan, R., Singh, S.N.: A comprehensive survey of retrieval-augmented generation (RAG): evolution, current landscape and future directions. ArXiv. Cornell University (2024). https://arxiv.org/pdf/2410.12837. Accessed 11 Apr 2025
21. Amazon. What Is RAG? - Retrieval-Augmented Generation Explained – AWS. Amazon Web Services, Inc. (2024). https://aws.amazon.com/what-is/retrieval-augmented-generation/. Accessed 11 Apr 2025
22. Salemi, A., Zamani, H.: Evaluating retrieval quality in retrieval-augmented generation (2024). https://arxiv.org/pdf/2404.13781. Accessed 11 Apr 2025
23. Acharya, D.B., Kuppan, K., Divya, B.: Agentic AI: autonomous intelligence for complex goals – a comprehensive survey. IEEE Access **13**, 18912–18936 (2025). https://ieeexplore.ieee.org/document/10849561. Accessed 12 Apr 2025
24. Sivakumar, S.: Agentic AI in predictive AIOps: enhancing IT autonomy and performance. Int. J. Sci. Res. Manage. (IJSRM) **4**(11), 1–25 (2024). https://www.researchgate.net/publication/388313991_Agentic_AI_Autonomous_Intelligence_for_Complex_Goals_-_A_Comprehensive_Survey. Accessed 15 Apr 2025

25. Katnapally, N., Sakuru, M., Murthy, L., Sadaram G.: Automating cyber threat response using agentic AI and reinforcement learning techniques. J. Electr. Syst. **17**(4), 138–148 (2021). https://journal.esrgroups.org/jes/article/view/8329/5610. Accessed 15 Apr 2025
26. Shavit, Y., et al.: Practices for governing agentic AI systems (2023). https://cdn.openai.com/papers/practices-for-governing-agentic-ai-systems.pdf. Accessed 16 Apr 2025
27. Gaber, M.M., Ahmed, M., Janicke, H.: Malware detection with artificial intelligence: a systematic literature review. ACM Comput. Surveys **56**(6), 1–33 (2023). https://doi.org/10.1145/3638552
28. Khan, R., Sarkar, S., Kumar, M.S., Jose, E.: Security threats in agentic AI system. arXiv.org (2024). https://arxiv.org/abs/2410.14728
29. Chan, A., et al.: Harms from increasingly agentic algorithmic systems. arXiv.org (2023). https://arxiv.org/abs/2302.10329. Accessed 16 Apr 2025
30. Pounds, E.: What is agentic AI?. NVIDIA Blog (2024). https://blogs.nvidia.com/blog/what-is-agentic-ai/. Accessed 16 Apr 2025
31. RabbitMQ. Messaging That Just Works—RabbitMQ (2019). https://www.rabbitmq.com/. Accessed 16 Apr 2025
32. Apache Kafka. Apache Kafka. Apache Kafka (2023). https://kafka.apache.org/. Accessed 16 Apr 2025
33. NVIDIA. NVIDIA T4 Tensor Core GPUs for Accelerating Inference. NVIDIA (2025). https://www.nvidia.com/en-us/data-center/tesla-t4/. Accessed 16 Apr 2025
34. NVIDIA Tesla T4 Specs. TechPowerUp (2025). https://www.techpowerup.com/gpu-specs/tesla-t4.c3316. Accessed 16 Apr 2025
35. Begni, A., Dini, P., Zheng, Q., Saponara, S., Elhanashi, A., Gasmi, K.: Machine learning techniques for anomaly-based detection system on CSE-CIC-IDS2018 dataset. In: Lecture Notes in Electrical Engineering, vol. 1036, pp. 131–140 (2023). https://doi.org/10.1007/978-3-031-30333-3_17. Accessed 17 Apr 2025
36. Kebede, T.M., Djaneye-Boundjou, O., Narayanan, B.N., Ralescu, A., Kapp, D.: Classification of malware programs using autoencoders based deep learning architecture and its application to the Microsoft malware classification challenge (BIG 2015) dataset. IEEE Xplore (2017). https://ieeexplore.ieee.org/abstract/document/8268747/. Accessed 19 Apr 2025
37. Hicks, S.A., et al.: On Evaluation metrics for medical applications of artificial intelligence. Sci. Rep. **12**(1) (2022). https://www.nature.com/articles/s41598-022-09954-8. Accessed 19 Apr 2025
38. Celery. Introduction to Celery—Celery 5.2.6 Documentation. (2025). https://docs.celeryq.dev/en/stable/getting-started/introduction.html. Accessed 21 Apr 2025
39. REVERSINGLABS. Threat Intelligence | ReversingLabs Spectra Intelligence (2025). https://www.reversinglabs.com/products/spectra-intelligence, https://www.reversinglabs.com/products/spectra-intelligence. Accessed 21 Apr 2025
40. Palo Alto. Securing the Future with Precision AI (2015). https://www.paloaltonetworks.com/precision-ai-security, https://www.paloaltonetworks.com/precision-ai-security. Accessed 21 Apr 2025
41. Splunk. Splunk AI. Splunk (2025). https://www.splunk.com/en_us/solutions/splunk-artificial-intelligence.html. Accessed 21 Apr 2025
42. Sowmya, T., Anita, M.: A comprehensive review of AI based intrusion detection system. ScienceDirect **28** (2023). https://doi.org/10.1016/j.measen.2023.100827
43. Vikram, A, Shnain, A.H., Jeet, R., Vennila, C., Sahu, P., Krishnakumar, K.: AI-powered network intrusion detection systems. In: 2024 IEEE International Conference on Communication, Computing and Signal Processing (IICCCS) (2024). https://ieeexplore.ieee.org/abstract/document/10763627?casa_token=_75F5rTgqUoAAAAA:Kca75111mnkYNRZVkSFMgb9UgulWtf5NjYzcxYU7_0PYMQetWgrnJr9h2rVXoI4ph3c2EuYipfNX_w. Accessed 21 Apr 2025

Designing Interpretable AI Models with Lightweight Parallelism for Real-Time Decision-Making for Auto Insurance Claims Triage

L. Paul Strait[✉]

University of Southern Mississippi, Hattiesburg, MS 39406, USA
l.strait@usm.edu

Abstract. This paper explores the design of an interpretable AI system capable of performing real-time triage of car insurance claims using lightweight parallelism. By breaking the claim assessment workflow into modular, independent tasks—including damage image evaluation, document verification, fraud flagging, and cost estimation—the system can operate in parallel, enabling rapid response while maintaining clarity in decision logic. Each component of the triage system is built with interpretability in mind, relying on transparent models like decision trees or rule-based frameworks, and supported by efficient parallel computing frameworks that enable scaling on multicore processors or cloud infrastructure.

The paper investigates how to balance computational performance with intelligibility, particularly in environments where AI decisions directly impact customers' financial outcomes. Even under real-time constraints, AI models can remain interpretable and trustworthy—provided they are designed using scalable, parallel architectures tailored to the structure of the task.

Keywords: Interpretable algorithms · lightweight parallelism · a

1 Introduction

As the demand for rapid and fair decision-making grows across the insurance industry, car insurance providers are increasingly turning to artificial intelligence (AI) to automate the processing of claims, underwriting, and customer service [1, 2]. Customers expect instant feedback on submitted claims, yet companies must ensure accuracy, transparency, and fraud prevention [3]. Traditional deep learning approaches, while powerful, often lack interpretability and impose significant computational costs—making them less suitable for regulated domains where decisions must be explainable to both users, auditors, and actuaries [4]. Models such as deep learning and gradient boosting are considered "black boxes" due to their complexity, which makes it difficult for humans to understand how decisions are made. This lack of interpretability is a significant problem in regulated industries like insurance, where decisions must be explainable to both customers and auditors. Interpretable models like decision trees or linear models allow stakeholders to trace outputs back to specific inputs and rules, making them ideal for these domains [5].

This paper addresses the critical need to reconcile high performance with transparency. It proposes a novel approach that moves beyond opaque deep learning models by leveraging interpretable AI and lightweight parallelism for real-time auto insurance claims triage. Our system decomposes the triage workflow into independent, parallelizable components, including image analysis, document verification, fraud detection, and cost estimation. Each component is implemented with transparent models like decision trees and rule-based systems. By executing these tasks concurrently using Python-based multiprocessing or cloud-native frameworks, our architecture achieves rapid processing speeds without sacrificing decision traceability. This paper argues that it is possible to design a scalable, real-time AI system for claims automation that prioritizes explainability, bridges the gap between performance and transparency, and is suitable for regulated production environments.

2 Literature Review

The utilization of artificial intelligence (AI) in the auto insurance industry has revolutionized the claims management process by enhancing automation, leveraging interpretable models, and adopting real-time processing strategies. Auto insurers are increasingly employing AI to automate various stages of the claims process, from initial reporting to damage assessment and payment disbursement. Emerging technologies like computer vision and natural language processing (NLP) have been pivotal in streamlining claims processing workflows, enabling faster evaluations and more accurate fraud detection [2, 6, 7]. For example, Maiano et al. developed an end-to-end antifraud system that reduced false positives by 18% and reduced possible alerts by 72% [8].

A notable advancement in this space is the Cost Estimation System (CES) introduced by Elbhrawy et al., which employs AI to detect vehicle damage, assess severity, and estimate costs based on imagery and structural data [2]. This system enhances the claims process by enabling insurers to analyze efficiently large volumes of data while facilitating quicker claim resolutions. Similarly, AI approaches, particularly machine learning models, have been effectively utilized to predict the frequency and severity of claims, offering insurers data-driven insights that inform risk management and customer service strategies [9, 10]. Venkatesh et al. created a comprehensive ML pipeline for vehicle damage detection and assessment, achieving an overall accuracy of 92%, suggesting that AI-powered damage assessment systems could potentially match or exceed human performance in certain scenarios [11]. By employing models such as generalized linear models and adaptive regression methods, insurers can better understand the factors influencing claim outcomes [12].

The demand for interpretable AI models in insurance arises from the necessity for transparency in decision-making processes. Models such as decision trees and generalized linear models are frequently utilized due to their inherent interpretability, enabling stakeholders to grasp the logic behind claim assessments and decisions. This is crucial for maintaining customer trust and meeting regulatory requirements [13, 14]. Additionally, the integration of ML techniques allows for a better overview of data patterns, enhancing the model's explanatory power, and ultimately, improving customer satisfaction [10].

Parallel computing divides complex computational tasks into smaller subtasks that can be executed simultaneously. In the context of AI, this enables models to process large amounts of input (such as batches of claims or images) much more efficiently. Task-level parallelism, in particular, is well-suited for auto insurance applications, where claims are independent and can be evaluated concurrently. Modern AI systems increasingly rely on parallel computing architectures such as shared memory and distributed memory systems to deliver real-time results at scale [15, 16]. In AI system design, strategies like task parallelism and rollout parallelization can yield significant performance gains. For example, in game AI, Monte Carlo Tree Search (MCTS) implementations have demonstrated how running independent simulations or playouts in parallel improves the efficiency of decision-making under time constraints. These insights are transferable to insurance claim triage, where independent claim tasks can be evaluated in parallel to reduce latency [17].

Parallelism and real-time processing have been critical in the deployment of AI in auto insurance claims. The architecture designed by Dhieb et al. exploits a Very Fast Decision Tree (VFDT) algorithm for online learning, which enables dynamic updates as new data emerges, thereby improving fraud detection efficacy in real-time [14]. Furthermore, continuous model training and automated decision-making processes allow for instantaneous evaluations of claims, significantly reducing processing time and fostering a more responsive service model [18]. Additionally, blockchain-based frameworks proposed for insurance claims management utilize decentralized technologies to enhance transparency and security, allowing for real-time data sharing and verification [19, 20].

While numerous studies have explored the application of AI in car insurance claims, most solutions prioritize accuracy over interpretability, relying heavily on complex models that lack transparency. Furthermore, existing architectures often overlook task-level parallelism as a strategy for scalable, real-time decision-making. This paper seeks to bridge that gap by proposing a modular, interpretable AI framework that can process claim tasks in parallel, offering a balance between transparency, efficiency, and computational scalability.

3 Problem Statement

Given the inefficiencies of traditional car insurance claim processing, many insurers have attempted to pivot to AI to help automate claims assessment, but many state-of-the-art systems rely on black-box models such as deep neural networks, which lack interpretability [1, 4]. This is a problem because insurers must justify claim decisions to both customers and regulatory oversight bodies, and their decisions must be intelligible to actuaries.

This paper adumbrates an AI-powered claim triage system that is both interpretable and scalable for real-time deployment. Specifically, I explore how to break the triage process into modular, independent tasks--such as image-based damage severity analysis, document completeness checks, and rule-based fraud detection--that can be executed in parallel across CPU cores or cloud instances.

The research focuses on the following questions: First, how can interpretable AI models (e.g., decision trees or rule-based systems) be applied to key claim triage tasks such as damage severity classification, policy validation, and fraud flagging? Second, how can these tasks be organized for task-level parallelism to support real-time claim processing at scale? Third, what forms of parallel computing infrastructure (e.g., cloud-based vs. edge/on-device processing) are most suitable for supporting automated triage in real-world insurance settings? Fourth, what are the trade-offs between batch learning (e.g., retraining on historical claim data) and real-time inference, and how can both be effectively integrated into the workflow?

By combining interpretable algorithms with practical parallel computing strategies, this project aims to plan a scalable AI triage system that improves claims throughput, maintains regulatory compliance, and enhances customer transparency in the auto insurance domain.

4 Proposed Methodology

This section outlines a modular, interpretable AI system for real-time triage of car insurance claims, implemented entirely using Python and standard open-source libraries. The system decomposes the claim processing workflow into independent tasks, each of which can be executed concurrently. It is designed for lightweight parallelism and interpretability, making it suitable for deployment on local servers or desktop-class hardware.

4.1 Task Decomposition and Parallelization Strategy

The claim triage pipeline is divided into a series of parallelizable tasks (see Fig. 1). Upon claim submission, three tasks can be initiated immediately in parallel: First, image-based damage assessment. TensorFlow/Keras, using a lightweight convolutional neural network (CNN) model (e.g., MobileNet, pretrained), can classify the severity of visible damage from uploaded vehicle images. This model operates independently per image using Python multiprocessing, enabling parallel execution per claim or per image. Second, document verification and text extraction. Natural language processing (NLP) tools extract and validate information from uploaded documents (e.g., policy numbers and driver's licenses). Specifically, Tesseract OCR could be used for text extraction, and spaCy could be used for entity recognition. This process runs in parallel for each document type or each claim in a separate worker process. Third, fraud detection. A set of interpretable, rule-based heuristics (e.g., decision trees or manually encoded fraud signals) can be used to flag suspicious claims. This can be implemented with Scikit-learn's DecisionTreeClassifier. Each claim is assessed individually using pre-defined rules, allowing parallel evaluation across claims (evaluating one claim per core). For example, someone with a recent policy and a very high claim should automatically throw a flag for investigation.

After these initial parallel tasks are completed, the system proceeds to a sequential task that depends on a preceding result: repair cost estimation. A regression model or lookup-based method could provide cost estimates based on damage classification and historical pricing data. For example, Scikit-learn regression models (e.g., LinearRegression or RandomForestRegressor with constraints) could be used to implement this. These estimates are computed sequentially after the initial damage assessment is complete, as its input includes a score of the images along with metadata (car type, location, etc.), which are outputs of the preceding module. Finally, all preceding results are combined for the last task, claim disposition. Based on the outputs of the preceding tasks, a decision tree or ruleset determines whether the claim is auto-approved, escalated, or flagged for manual review.

The entire workflow is visually represented in Fig. 1. The diagram illustrates how a claim triggers the initial parallel execution of Image Damage Assessment, Document Verification, and Fraud Rule Evaluation. The output of the Image Damage Assessment then serves as a critical input for the sequential Cost Estimation task. Once all these components have completed, their respective results are aggregated and fed into the Disposition Logic module, which produces the final decision that is recorded in a database. This design balances the efficiency of parallel processing with the necessary inter-task dependencies of a real-world claims system.

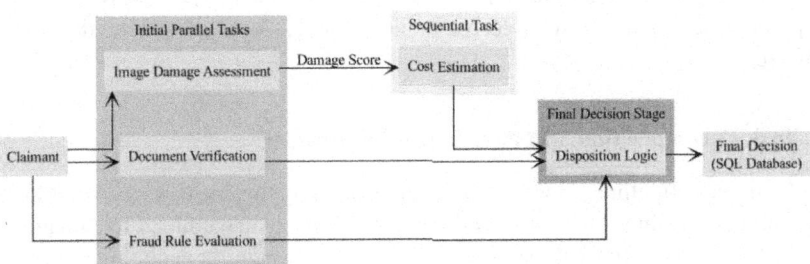

Fig. 1. Diagram of Parallel Execution Paths.

4.2 Parallel Computing Frameworks

Parallelism in this modular system can be implemented in Python with concurrent features. ProcessPoolExecutor for CPU-bound parallel task execution across claim records. This suits I/O and compute-bound tasks like image parsing and fraud checks. This is simpler and safer than lower-level multiprocessing. Each module is designed to operate in a separate worker process or thread, and results are aggregated through shared memory or message-passing mechanisms. Table 1 gives a basic mockup of the task execution flow.

Table 1. Task execution flow

Basic mockup of the task execution flow.

from concurrent.futures import ProcessPoolExecutor
with ProcessPoolExecutor(max_workers=5) as executor:
    futures = {
        'image': executor.submit(classify_damage, image_input),
        'docs': executor.submit(verify_documents, doc_input),
        'fraud': executor.submit(evaluate_fraud, claim_data),
        'cost': executor.submit(estimate_cost, image_score, claim_meta)
    }
results = {task: f.result() for task, f in futures.items()}
final_decision = make_disposition(results)

In terms of scalability, this can be run on any multicore machine without a distributed setup.

4.3 Batch Processing vs. Real-Time Inference

The system supports both real-time and batch operation modes. When a claim is submitted, lightweight models can immediately perform damage assessments, document checks, and fraud scoring (real-time inference). Parallel modules can execute concurrently, completing within a few seconds. Additionally, historical claims can be used periodically to retrain models (e.g., update damage classifiers or refine cost estimators) in parallel using GPU-accelerated cloud resources (batch processing). Training jobs could use joblib or multiprocessing for parallel data loading and model evaluation. For production use, real-time inference is prioritized, with batch retraining scheduled asynchronously to minimize downtime and latency.

4.4 Deployment Context

The system is designed to be deployable on both cloud and edge infrastructure. Claims submitted via a web or mobile app could be processed using serverless functions (e.g., AWS Lambda) or containerized microservices utilizing cloud-based parallelism. Scalable infrastructure supports parallel claim handling across users. For latency-sensitive or bandwidth-constrained environments like mobile uploads from accident scenes, a subset of the model can be run locally using TensorFlow Lite or ONNX on-device inference. Cloud-based parallelism offers scalability and centralized management, which is ideal for full processing pipelines. Onboard inference is suitable for early-stage validation (e.g., ensuring image quality before upload) and faster user feedback.

5 Limitations and Future Work

The conceptual framework presented in this paper has several key limitations that future work should address.

5.1 Limitations

The primary limitation is the absence of experimental results. The proposed system has not been implemented or tested under real-world conditions. Its performance, scalability, and latency are theoretical. Further, the methodology section suggests specific models (MobileNet, Tesseract OCR, Scikit-learn's Decision Tree, etc.), but no specific architectures, training data, or hyperparameters needed for a production-level system have been detailed. Finally, this proposal does not examine edge cases, such as poor-quality images, incomplete documents, or complex fraud schemes that might slip past simple rules.

5.2 Future Work

The most critical next step is to implement the proposed system and to conduct a comprehensive empirical analysis. This would involve running the pipeline with a large dataset of historical claims to measure key metrics like processing time, throughput, and accuracy. A comparative analysis could then be conducted to evaluate the performance of the interpretable system against "black box" models (e.g., large unsupervised deep learning models) in terms of both accuracy and speed. This would help quantify the trade-offs between interpretability and performance. Future work should also include rigorous scalability testing in a distributed computing environment, which would involve stress-testing the system with a high volume of concurrent claims to ensure it can handle real-world loads. Additionally, the individual AI components could be further refined. For example, the image-based damage assessment might be improved with more advanced computer vision mode, and the fraud detection module might be augmented with more complex graph-based analysis.

6 Conclusion

This paper has outlined a modular and interpretable AI system for auto insurance claim triage, demonstrating the feasibility of combining lightweight parallelism with transparent models. The proposed architecture, built with Python and open-source libraries, decomposes the workflow into five parallelizable tasks: image analysis, document verification, fraud evaluation, cost estimation, and final disposition. This design allows for concurrent processing, which enables real-time claim handling while maintaining transparency and auditability, essential for regulated industries. While no actual experiments were run, this paper has identified suitable models and tools, demonstrated the feasibility of interpretable AI in the auto insurance space, and evaluated deployment options.

While the paper provides a robust theoretical framework, a key area for future work is the empirical validation of the system. The next logical step is to implement the proposed pipeline and benchmark its performance against traditional and "black box" AI models under production-like conditions at scale. This will serve both to verify the system's efficacy and to bridge the gap between theoretical proposals and practical, production-grade solutions.

References

1. Mitchner, R.: The future of car insurance: How AI is transforming auto insurance. MarketWatch - Guides. Accessed: 01 May 2025. https://www.marketwatch.com/insurance-services/autoinsurance/how-car-insurancecompanies-use-ai/
2. Elbhrawy, M.B., Hassanein, M.: CES: cost estimation system for enhancing the processing of car insurance claims. J. Comput. Commun. **3**(1), 55–69 (2024). https://doi.org/10.21608/jocc.2024.339922
3. Balasubramanian, R.; Insurance 2030: The impact of AI on the future of insurance. McKinsey & Company. Accessed: 01 May 2025. https://www.mckinsey.com/industries/financialservices/our-insights/insurance-2030-the-impact-of-ai-on-the-future-of-insurance
4. Deloitte: AI, model interpretability, and the future of insurance. Deloitte. Accessed: 01 May 2025. https://www2.deloitte.com/content/dam/Deloitte/us/Documents/financial-services/usaimodel-interpretability-future-insurance.pdf
5. Interpretable AI: What is Interpretability?. Interpretable AI. Accessed: 01 May 2025. https://www.interpretable.ai/interpretability/what/
6. Fernando, N., Kumarage, A., Thiyaganathan, V., Hillary, R., Abeywardhana, L.; Automated vehicle insurance claims processing using computer vision, natural language processing (2022). https://doi.org/10.1109/icter58063.2022.10024089
7. Atanasious, M.M.H., et al.: An Insurtech platform to support claim management through the automatic detection and estimation of car damage from pictures. Electronics (2024). https://doi.org/10.3390/electronics13224333
8. Maiano, L., et al.: A deep-learning–based antifraud system for car-insurance claims. Expert Syst. Appl. **231**, 120644 (2023). https://doi.org/10.1016/j.eswa.2023.120644
9. Nuugulu, S.M., Mutasa, R.; Modeling the frequency and severity of auto insurance claims using machine learning techniques (2025). https://doi.org/10.21203/rs.3.rs-6178099/v1
10. Hanafy, M., Ming, R.: Machine learning approaches for auto insurance big data. Risks (2021). https://doi.org/10.3390/risks9020042
11. Venkatesh, M., Oruganti, R., Katti, S.A., Subramanian, K., Chandar, T.S.: Vehicle damage detection using machine learning and segmentation to aid insurance claims. In: 2023 IEEE 20th India Council International Conference (INDICON), pp. 932–938, IEEE (2023). https://doi.org/10.1109/indicon59947.2023.10440856
12. Angelo, M.: Analysis of claim frequency and severity in auto insurance using generalized linear models in Philippines. Jsar (2024). https://doi.org/10.47604/jsar.2900
13. Ye, C., Zhang, L., Han, M., Yu, Y., Zhao, B., Yang, Y.: Combining predictions of auto Insurance claims. Econometrics (2022). https://doi.org/10.3390/econometrics10020019
14. Dhieb, N., Ghazzai, H., Besbes, H., Massoud, Y.: A secure AI-driven architecture for automated insurance systems: Fraud detection and risk measurement. Ieee Access (2020). https://doi.org/10.1109/access.2020.2983300
15. Flinders, M., Smalley, I.: What is parallel computing? IBM. Accessed: 01 May 2025. https://www.ibm.com/think/topics/parallel-computing
16. Intel: Data parallelism in C++ using SYCL*. Intel. Accessed: 01 May 2025. https://www.intel.com/content/www/us/en/docs/oneapi/programmingguide/2025-0/data-parallelism-incusing-sycl.html

17. Clinch, E., Lee, J.: Parallelization of Monte Carlo Tree Search. jenniferleeny.github.io. Accessed: 01 May 2025. https://jenniferleeny.github.io/MonteCarloTreeSearchWebpage/
18. Bhattacharya, S.: AI revolution in insurance: Bridging research and reality. Front. Artif. Intell. (2025). https://doi.org/10.3389/frai.2025.1568266
19. Nizamuddin, N., Abugabah, A.: Blockchain for automotive: An insight towards the IPFS blockchain-based auto insurance sector. Int. J. Electr. Comput. Eng. Ijece (2021). https://doi.org/10.11591/ijece.v11i3.pp2443-2456
20. Wang, Q., Lau, R.Y.K., Si, Y., Xie, H., Tao, X.: Blockchain-enhanced smart contract for cost-effective insurance claims processing. J. Glob. Inf. Manag. (2023). https://doi.org/10.4018/jgim.329927

Author Index

A
Abrahams, Gracie 111
Agarwal, Shriya 152
Anreddy, Sujan 373
Arifuzzaman, Shaikh 129

B
Bai, Shuju 98
Bainomugisha, Engineer 212
Baluguri, Anu 319
Bbaale, Martin 212
Businge, John 129

C
Callahan, Gretchen 111
Chen, Jessica 53

D
Dahal, Ashim 289
Dehzangi, Iman 251

G
Ghimire, Sadhan 373
Golilarz, Noorbakhsh Amiri 251
Gudla, Charan 166, 182
Gudur, Vaishnavi 232

H
Hamid, Hanzla 289
Hirunpash, N. 353
Hossain, Elias 251

J
Jeff, Byron 98
Jha, Pappu 289
Jridi, Balsem 3

K
Kansana, Manish 251
Karim, Dalia 111

Karne, Ramesh R. 73
Khadka, Mimansha 3
Khanvilkar, Kunal 302
Khosravi, Ebrahim 98
Kosna, Srinivas Reddy 267
Kovvuri, Yashwanth Reddy 182

M
Madison, Tyler 111
Martinez, Jose 393
McCullough, Zachariah 393
Mittal, Akshay 18
Moharir, Akshata Kishore 381
Mutabazi, Noble 212

N
Namawrong, M. 353
Nembhard, Fitzroy 199
Niwamanya, Nicholas 212
Nsimbe, Noah 212

O
Ogenrwot, Daniel 129, 212
Okure, Deo 212
Olukola, Oluseyi 289
Owrang O, M. Mehdi 111

P
Pagidoju, Ravi Teja 152
Pai, Rakesh Ramakrishna 40
Pasumarthy, Vasudha 319
Patel, Advait 232
Patrick, Aidan 3
Pendyala, Jothsna Praveena 40
Petchartee, S. 353
Poudel, Mukesh 334
Prasad, Gagana Sathya Narayana 166

Q
Qian, Lie 73
Qu, Junfeng 98

R
Rahimi, Keyan Alexander 251
Rahimi, Nick 289, 334
Rajeev, Sarika 85
Repakula, Yaswanth Raj 319

S
Saei, Saviz 373
Sahu, Atma 85
Sakonlaphab, W. 353
Sawarnya, Vishrut 85
Sherifi, Betim 199
Shinde, Varun 302
Slhoub, Khaled 199
Soundararajan, Nirmala 73
Ssempala, Benjamin 212
Sserunjogi, Richard 212
Strait, L. Paul 406

T
Thakur, Jay Prakash 381

V
Venkatesan, Vivek 18

W
Wabinyai, Raja Fidel 212
Wijesinha, Alexander L. 73

Y
Yang, Jiajie 53

Z
Zhou, Zhaoxian 319

Made in the USA
Monee, IL
03 May 2026